Chapter Reviews and Working Papers
With Peachtree and Spreadsheet Guides

GLENCOE
Accounting
Real-World Applications & Connections

First-Year Course
Fourth Edition

Chapter Reviews and Working Papers
With Peachtree and Spreadsheet Guides

GLENCOE
Accounting
Real-World Applications & Connections

First-Year Course
Fourth Edition

Donald J. Guerrieri
Norwin Senior High School
North Huntingdon, Pennsylvania

F. Barry Haber
Fayetteville State University
Fayetteville, North Carolina

William B. Hoyt
Wilton High School
Wilton, Connecticut

Robert E. Turner
Northeast Louisiana University
Monroe, Louisiana

New York, New York   Columbus, Ohio   Woodland Hills, California   Peoria, Illinois

Glencoe/McGraw-Hill

A Division of The **McGraw·Hill** *Companies*

Send inquiries to:

Glencoe/McGraw-Hill
21600 Oxnard Street Suite 500
Woodland Hills, CA 91367

ISBN 0-02-643970-0 (Student Edition)
ISBN 0-02-643971-9 (Teacher's Annotated Edition)

Printed in the United States of America.

4 5 6 7 8 9   079   01 00

CONTENTS

CHAPTER 1   You and the World of Accounting

Study Plan

Check Your Understanding

Section 1
Read Section 1 on pages 6–12 and complete the following exercises on page 13.
- ❏ Thinking Critically
- ❏ Computing in the Business World
- ❏ Problem 1-1   *Studying Yourself*
- ❏ Problem 1-2   *Gathering Career Resources*

Section 2
Read Section 2 on pages 14–16 and complete the following exercises on page 17.
- ❏ Thinking Critically
- ❏ Communicating Accounting
- ❏ Problem 1-3   *Checking Out Accounting Careers*
- ❏ Problem 1-4   *Matching Interests and Careers*
- ❏ Problem 1-5   *Researching Public Accounting Firms*
- ❏ Problem 1-6   *Researching Accounting Firms in Your City*

Summary
Review the Chapter 1 Summary on page 19 in your textbook.
- ❏ Key Concepts

Review and Activities
Complete the following questions and exercises on pages 20–21 in your textbook.
- ❏ Using Key Terms
- ❏ Understanding Accounting Concepts and Procedures
- ❏ Case Study
- ❏ Internet Connection
- ❏ Workplace Skills

Problems
Complete the following end-of-chapter problems for Chapter 1 in your textbook.
- ❏ Problem 1-7   *Researching Careers in Your Library*
- ❏ Problem 1-8   *Researching Careers in Your Local Newspaper*
- ❏ Problem 1-9   *Assessing Your Skills and Interests*
- ❏ Problem 1-10   *Working with Others*
- ❏ Problem 1-11   *Summarizing Personal Traits*
- ❏ Problem 1-12   *Gathering Career Information*
- ❏ Problem 1-13   *Exploring Careers in Accounting*

Challenge Problem
- ❏ Problem 1-14   *Exploring Global Careers*

Chapter Reviews and Working Papers
Complete the following exercises for Chapter 1 in your Chapter Reviews and Working Papers.
- ❏ Chapter Review
- ❏ Self-Test

CHAPTER **1** REVIEW   You and the World of Accounting

Part 1   Accounting Vocabulary (11 points)

Total Points	17
Student's Score	

Directions: *Using terms from the following list, complete the sentences below. Write the letter of the term you have chosen in the space provided. The first statement has been completed for you.*

A. accountant	**D.** for-profit businesses	**G.** not-for-profit organizations	**I.** personality
B. accounting clerk	**E.** lifestyle	**H.** personal interest tests	**J.** public accounting
C. certified public accountant	**F.** networking		**K.** skills
			L. values

_____L_____ **0.** _____ are the principles you live by and the beliefs that are important to you.

_____ **1.** _____ is a set of unique qualities that makes us different from all other people.

_____ **2.** Your _____ is the way you use your time, energy, and resources.

_____ **3.** _____ is a way to find out about particular careers by asking people in the career to share information and advice.

_____ **4.** A(n) _____ handles a broad range of responsibilities, including making business decisions, and preparing and interpreting financial reports.

_____ **5.** _____ help you identify the things you like to do.

_____ **6.** _____ operate to earn money for their owners.

_____ **7.** _____ operate for reasons other than to make money, like protecting and preserving the environment.

_____ **8.** A(n) _____ usually performs one or two accounting tasks.

_____ **9.** A(n) _____ firm provides accounting services to clients on a fee basis.

_____ **10.** To become a(n) _____, you must pass a national test and meet specified experience and education standards.

_____ **11.** _____ are activities you do well.

Part 2   Careers in Accounting (6 points)

Directions: *Read each of the following statements to determine whether the statement is true or false. Write your answer in the space provided. The first statement is completed for you.*

_____F_____ **0.** An accountant only tracks the expenses of a business to make sure the business stays within a budget.

_____ **1.** There are many opportunities to work with not-for-profit organizations as an accountant.

_____ **2.** Accounting involves only adding and subtracting numbers.

_____ **3.** Laptop computers and modems connect accountants to their work as they travel to other cities and countries.

_____ **4.** A Certified Public Accountant, or CPA, must pass a national test, but no specific experience is necessary to become certified.

_____ **5.** Consultants who work for public accounting firms help their clients make decisions and analyze business opportunities.

_____ **6.** Large companies, such as General Motors, do not need accountants to assist in running the business.

Working Papers *for Section Problems*

Problem 1-1   Studying Yourself

List at least five personal interests or skills.

_____

_____

_____

_____

_____

Identify one or more careers that match the interests and skills you listed above.

_____

_____

_____

_____

Choose one of the above careers and write a description of how your skills and interests fit into this career.

_____

_____

_____

_____

_____

_____

_____

_____

_____

_____

_____

_____

Problem 1-2 Gathering Career Resources

Personal Career Profile Form	
Name: **Date:**	**Career:**
Your Values	Career Values
Your Interests	Career Duties and Responsibilities
Your Personality	Personality Type Needed
Skills and Aptitudes	Skills and Aptitudes Required
Education/Training Acceptable	Education/Training Required

Problem 1-2   (continued)

Personal Career Profile Form	
Name: **Date:** **Career:**	
Your Values	Career Values
Your Interests	Career Duties and Responsibilities
Your Personality	Personality Type Needed
Skills and Aptitudes	Skills and Aptitudes Required
Education/Training Acceptable	Education/Training Required

Problem 1-2   (concluded)

Personal Career Profile Form	
Name: **Date:**	**Career:**
Your Values	Career Values
Your Interests	Career Duties and Responsibilities
Your Personality	Personality Type Needed
Skills and Aptitudes	Skills and Aptitudes Required
Education/Training Acceptable	Education/Training Required

Problem 1-3 Checking Out Accounting Careers

Career	Formal Training Needed	Work Experience Needed

Which of the careers listed above do you prefer? _____

Why does this career appeal to you?

_____

_____

_____

_____

_____

Problem 1-4   Matching Interests and Careers

List the personal interests and skills of the accountants described in the text.

_____

_____

_____

_____

List three types of businesses (or actual companies) for which you might like to work.

_____

_____

_____

How would you learn about accounting career opportunities in the above companies?

_____

_____

_____

_____

_____

_____

Aside from pursuing needed training and education, what else would you do to prepare to work in that career?

_____

_____

_____

_____

_____

Problem 1-5   Researching Public Accounting Firms

Company's name: Web site:	Services provided:
Company's name: Web site:	Services provided:
Company's name: Web site:	Services provided:
Company's name: Web site:	Services provided:
Company's name: Web site:	Services provided:

Problem 1-6   Researching Accounting Firms in Your City

List the public accounting firms in your area.

_____

_____

_____

Do any of the Big Five have offices near you?

_____

_____

Do you recognize the names of the smaller, regional firms?

_____

_____

Working Papers *for End-of-Chapter Problems*

Problem 1-7   Researching Careers in Your Library

_____

_____

_____

_____

Problem 1-8   Researching Careers in Your Local Newspaper

Job Title	Skills Required	Education Required

Problem 1-9   Assessing Your Skills and Interests

What are your aptitudes and abilities?

_____

_____

_____

What are your interests?

_____

_____

_____

What are your values?

_____

_____

_____

Do you like working with people?

_____

_____

_____

Do you like working with data?

_____

_____

_____

Do you like working with numbers?

_____

_____

_____

Using your answers above, list three careers that might match your skills
and interests.

_____

_____

_____

Problem 1-10   Working with Others

Situation	Skills Needed	How can you get those skills?
Training new hires in the accounting department		
Discuss project cost overruns with a department manager		
Present operating results to senior managers		

Problem 1-11   Summarizing Personal Traits

1. _____ _____ _____
2. _____ _____ _____
3. _____ _____ _____
4. _____ _____ _____
5. _____ _____ _____
6. _____ _____ _____
7. _____ _____ _____
8. _____ _____ _____
9. _____ _____ _____
10. _____ _____ _____

Which five characteristics were mentioned most often?

_____

_____

_____

_____

Do these descriptions match your self-perception? Why or why not?

_____

_____

_____

_____

Problem 1-12 Gathering Career Information

_____

_____

_____

_____

_____

_____

_____

_____

_____

_____

_____

_____

_____

_____

_____

_____

_____

_____

_____

_____

_____

_____

_____

_____

_____

_____

_____

_____

_____

Problem 1-13   Exploring Careers in Accounting

Problem 1-14   Exploring Global Careers

CHAPTER 1   You and the World of Accounting

Self-Test

Part A   True or False

Directions: *Circle the letter* T *in the Answer column if the statement is true; circle the letter* F *if the statement is false.*

Answer

T   F   **1.** You are more likely to enjoy a career that uses your individual interests, skills, and traits.

T   F   **2.** Values are activities you do well.

T   F   **3.** Assessing your interests, skills, and personality traits will help you to determine a career path.

T   F   **4.** Your personality is what makes you the same as other people.

T   F   **5.** Your lifestyle is the way you use your time, energy, and resources.

T   F   **6.** Networking is not a good way to find out about a particular career you are interested in.

T   F   **7.** When planning a career, it is not important to consider the education and training needed for that career.

T   F   **8.** The Internet and professional organizations are good sources for career information.

T   F   **9.** A majority of businesses in the United States are for-profit businesses.

T   F   **10.** Not-for-profit businesses operate for reasons other than to earn a profit, such as to protect the environment.

Part B   Matching

Directions: *Determine whether each business listed below is a for-profit or not-for-profit business. Write the letter corresponding to your choice in the blank next to the item.*

A. for-profit	**B.** not-for-profit

Answer

_____ **1.** General Motors

_____ **2.** United Way

_____ **3.** Virgin Atlantic Airlines

_____ **4.** Columbia Pictures

_____ **5.** World Wildlife Fund

_____ **6.** Polygram Records

_____ **7.** Barnes & Noble

_____ **8.** Greenpeace

_____ **9.** Boeing

_____ **10.** Coca-Cola

_____ **11.** American Cancer Society

CHAPTER  2   The World of Business and Accounting

Study Plan

Check Your Understanding

Section 1

Read Section 1 on pages 26–30 and complete the following exercises on page 31.
- ❏ Thinking Critically
- ❏ Communicating Accounting
- ❏ Problem 2-1   *Assess Your Entrepreneurship Potential*

Section 2

Read Section 2 on pages 32–34 and complete the following exercises on page 35.
- ❏ Thinking Critically
- ❏ Computing in the Business World
- ❏ Problem 2-2   *Using Financial Information*
- ❏ Problem 2-3   *Identifying Accounting Assumptions*

Summary

Review the Chapter 2 Summary on page 37 in your textbook.
- ❏ Key Concepts

Review and Activities

Complete the following questions and exercises on pages 38–39 in your textbook.
- ❏ Using Key Terms
- ❏ Understanding Accounting Concepts and Procedures
- ❏ Case Study
- ❏ Internet Connection
- ❏ Workplace Skills

Problems

Complete the following end-of-chapter problems for Chapter 2 in your textbook.
- ❏ Problem 2-4   *Identifying Types of Businesses*
- ❏ Problem 2-5   *Understanding Accounting Assumptions*
- ❏ Problem 2-6   *Understanding Business Operations*
- ❏ Problem 2-7   *Categorizing Forms of Business Organizations*

Challenge Problem
- ❏ Problem 2-8   *Working as an Entrepreneur*

Chapter Reviews and Working Papers

Complete the following exercises for Chapter 2 in your Chapter Reviews and Working Papers.
- ❏ Chapter Review
- ❏ Self-Test

CHAPTER 2 REVIEW — The World of Business and Accounting

Part 1 Accounting Vocabulary (16 points)

Total Points	36
Student's Score	

Directions: *Using terms from the following list, complete the sentences below. Write the letter of the term you have chosen in the space provided. The first sentence has been completed for you.*

A. accounting system	**F.** financial accounting	**K.** managerial accounting	**N.** partnership
B. business entity	**G.** accounting period	**L.** manufacturing	**O.** profit
C. capital	**H.** GAAP	business	**P.** service business
D. corporation	**I.** going concern	**M.** merchandising	**Q.** sole proprietorship
E. entrepreneur	**J.** loss	business	

___Q___ **0.** A(n)_____ has one owner.

_____ **1.** The time period covered by an accounting report is called _____.

_____ **2.** A(n) _____ has at least two owners.

_____ **3.** Money invested in a business by an owner is called _____.

_____ **4.** The amount of money earned over and above the amount spent to keep a business operating is called _____.

_____ **5.** Businesses that spend more than they receive operate at a _____.

_____ **6.** A(n) _____ is concerned with the process of recording and reporting financial information.

_____ **7.** A(n) _____ is willing to take the risks of running a business.

_____ **8.** Accounting for external users of accounting information is called _____.

_____ **9.** Generally Accepted Accounting Principles refers to _____.

_____ **10.** Accounting for internal users of accounting information is called _____.

_____ **11.** A(n) _____ exists independently of its owner's personal holdings.

_____ **12.** A business expected to operate in the future is called a(n) _____.

_____ **13.** A business that buys finished products and then sells them is called a(n) _____.

_____ **14.** A business that transforms raw material into products is called a(n) _____.

_____ **15.** A business organization that is recognized by law to have a life of its own is called a(n) _____.

_____ **16.** A business organized to operate by providing professional services for a fee is called a(n) _____.

Part 2 Forms of Business Organizations (10 points)

Directions: *Using the three forms of business organizations listed, complete the sentences below. Write the letter of the term you have chosen in the space provided.*

S. Sole Proprietorship	**P.** Partnership	**C.** Corporation

___S___ **0.** Owned by a single individual

_____ **1.** Often formed when the need for capital is greater than one person can invest

_____ **2.** Must have a charter to operate as an organization

_____ **3.** Usually enter into a written legal agreement before operating the business

_____ **4.** Owners share in the risks and the profits

_____ **5.** Advantages related to its freedom of operations and simplicity

_____ **6.** A form of business organization used by large accounting firms

_____ **7.** Recognized by law to have a life of its own

_____ **8.** Shares of stock represent an individual's investment and percentage of ownership

_____ **9.** May have to follow more regulations and pay higher taxes

_____ **10.** Success or failure of the business depends heavily on the efforts of the owner

Part 3   Entrepreneurship (5 points)

Directions: *Read each of the following statements to determine whether the statement is true or false. Write your answer in the space provided. Use a T for true and an F for false. The first statement is completed for you.*

   T   **0.** Each person in a business organization has a different role.

         1. Entrepreneurs seek opportunities that other people do not seem to care about.

         2. To be an entrepreneur you do not need to worry about good writing or verbal skills.

         3. Entrepreneurs do not get to choose the people they work with.

         4. To be an entrepreneur you have to work long hours and be a self-starter.

         5. A business plan is a key to entrepreneurial success.

Part 4   Financial and Managerial Accounting (5 points)

Directions: *Read each of the following statements to determine whether the statement is true or false. Write your answer in the space provided. Use a T for true and an F for false. The first statement is completed for you.*

   F   **0.** Managerial accounting focuses on reports based on GAAP.

         1. Financial accounting prepares reports for people directly involved in day-to-day operations.

         2. Managerial accounting is often referred to as accounting for internal users of information.

         3. People with an indirect interest in a business would use reports based on GAAP.

         4. Financial accounting is for people thinking of investing money in a business.

         5. Management accounting helps determine whether business results match the business plan.

Working Papers *for Section Problems*

Problem 2-1   Assess Your Entrepreneurship Potential

	Most Like Me			Least Like Me	
Persistent	5	4	3	2	1
Creative	5	4	3	2	1
Responsible	5	4	3	2	1
Inquisitive	5	4	3	2	1
Goal-oriented	5	4	3	2	1
Independent	5	4	3	2	1
Demanding	5	4	3	2	1
Self-confident	5	4	3	2	1
Risk-taking	5	4	3	2	1
Restless	5	4	3	2	1

Problem 2-2   Using Financial Information

Problem 2-3   Identifying Accounting Assumptions

_____

_____

_____

_____

_____

_____

_____

_____

_____

_____

_____

_____

Working Papers *for End-of-Chapter Problems*

Problem 2-4   Identifying Types of Businesses

1. _____	5. _____	9. _____
2. _____	6. _____	10. _____
3. _____	7. _____	11. _____
4. _____	8. _____	12. _____

Problem 2-5   Understanding Accounting Assumptions

1. _____	3. _____	5. _____
2. _____	4. _____	6. _____

Problem 2-6   Understanding Business Operations

1. _____

2. profit on bread sales: _____

   space for calculations:

3. _____

   _____

Problem 2-7 Categorizing Forms of Business Organizations

1. _____
2. _____
3. _____
4. _____
5. _____

6. _____
7. _____
8. _____
9. _____
10. _____

Problem 2-8 Working as an Entrepreneur

	Advantage	Disadvantage
1. Risking the loss of your savings	_____	_____
2. Deciding what you and everyone else needs to do each day	_____	_____
3. Lacking steady wages and employee benefits	_____	_____
4. Choosing when and where to work	_____	_____
5. Keeping the financial benefits of your hard work	_____	_____
6. Choosing the people you want to work with	_____	_____
7. Paying all the expenses of a new business	_____	_____

_____
_____
_____
_____
_____
_____
_____
_____
_____
_____
_____
_____
_____
_____

CHAPTER  The World of Business and Accounting

Self-Test

Part A   True or False

Directions: *Circle the letter* T *in the Answer column if the statement is true; circle the letter* F *if the statement is false.*

Answer

T	F	**1.** The United States' economy is referred to as a private enterprise system.
T	F	**2.** Financial accounting is often referred to as accounting for internal users.
T	F	**3.** The period of time covered by an accounting report is the fiscal period.
T	F	**4.** Manufacturers make products and sell them while service businesses buy products and sell them.
T	F	**5.** Only through profits can businesses continue to operate.
T	F	**6.** Entrepreneurs are people willing to take risks.
T	F	**7.** Going into business for yourself has few drawbacks.
T	F	**8.** A sole proprietorship is the most difficult business to start.
T	F	**9.** GAAP stands for Generally Accepted Accounting Procedures.
T	F	**10.** Accountants assume that a business will operate forever.

Part B   Matching

Directions: *Using the business types listed below, write the letter of the term you have chosen in the space provided.*

A. Sole Proprietorship	**B.** Partnership	**C.** Corporation

Answer

       1. The business has one owner

       2. Easy to start

       3. Easy to transfer ownership

       4. Must share profits

       5. Owner has all the risks

       6. Complex to organize

       7. Owner has total control

       8. Pays higher taxes

       9. Hard to raise money

       10. Losses limited to investment

       11. Limited expertise

CHAPTER 3   Business Transactions and the Accounting Equation

Study Plan

Check Your Understanding

Section 1   *Read Section 1 on pages 46–48 and complete the exercises on page 49.*
- ❏ Thinking Critically
- ❏ Computing in the Business World
- ❏ Problem 3-1   *Balancing the Accounting Equation*

Section 2   *Read Section 2 on pages 50–55 and complete the exercises on page 56.*
- ❏ Thinking Critically
- ❏ Communicating Accounting
- ❏ Problem 3-2   *Determining the Effects of Transactions on the Accounting Equation*

Section 3   *Read Section 3 on pages 57–59 and complete the exercises on page 60.*
- ❏ Thinking Critically
- ❏ Analyzing Accounting
- ❏ Problem 3-3   *Determining the Effects of Transactions on the Accounting Equation*

Summary   *Review the Chapter 3 Summary on page 61 in your textbook.*
- ❏ Key Concepts

Review and Activities   *Complete the following questions and exercises on pages 62–63.*
- ❏ Using Key Terms
- ❏ Understanding Accounting Concepts and Procedures
- ❏ Case Study
- ❏ Internet Connection
- ❏ Workplace Skills

Computerized Accounting   *Read the Computerized Accounting information on page 64 in your textbook.*
- ❏ *Exploring Electronic Spreadsheets*

Problems   *Complete the following end-of-chapter problems for Chapter 3.*
- ❏ Problem 3-4   *Classifying Accounts*
- ❏ Problem 3-5   *Completing the Accounting Equation*
- ❏ Problem 3-6   *Classifying Accounts Within the Accounting Equation*
- ❏ Problem 3-7   *Determining Increases and Decreases in Accounts*
- ❏ Problem 3-8   *Determining the Effects of Transactions on the Accounting Equation*
- ❏ Problem 3-9   *Determining the Effects of Business Transactions on the Accounting Equation*
- ❏ Problem 3-10   *Describing Business Transactions*

Challenge Problem
- ❏ Problem 3-11   *Completing the Accounting Equation*

Chapter Reviews and Working Papers   *Complete the following exercises for Chapter 3 in your Chapter Reviews and Working Papers.*
- ❏ Chapter Review
- ❏ Self-Test

CHAPTER 3 REVIEW — Business Transactions and the Accounting Equation

Part 1 Accounting Vocabulary (15 points)

Directions: *Using terms from the following list, complete the sentences below. Write the letter of the term you have chosen in the space provided.*

Total Points **39**
Student's Score

A. account	**E.** asset	**I.** equity	**M.** owner's equity
B. accounting equation	**F.** business transaction	**J.** expenses	**N.** property
C. accounts payable	**G.** capital	**K.** liabilities	**O.** revenue
D. accounts receivable	**H.** creditor	**L.** on account	**P.** withdrawal

___B___   **0.** The _____ is Assets = Liabilities + Owner's Equity.

_____   **1.** A(n) _____ is an economic event that causes a change in assets, liabilities, or owner's equity.

_____   **2.** The owner's claims to the total assets of the business are called _____.

_____   **3.** A(n) _____ is any property or item of value owned by a business.

_____   **4.** _____ are the creditor's claims to the assets of the business.

_____   **5.** _____ is anything of value that is owned or controlled.

_____   **6.** The increases or decreases in a specific item caused by business transactions are recorded in a(n) _____.

_____   **7.** Buying _____ is the same as buying on credit.

_____   **8.** _____ is income earned from the sale of goods and services.

_____   **9.** The costs of goods and services used to operate a business are _____.

_____   **10.** _____ is the total amount of money to be received in the future for goods and services sold on credit.

_____   **11.** A person or business that sells property on credit, or any person or business to which money is owed, is called a(n) _____.

_____   **12.** The total financial claims to the assets of a business are known as _____.

_____   **13.** The amount of money owed to the creditors of a business is _____.

_____   **14.** _____ refers to the dollar amount of the owner's equity in the business.

_____   **15.** When the owner takes cash or other assets from the business for personal use, a _____ occurs.

Part 2 Property and Financial Claims (4 points)

Directions: *Read each of the following statements to determine whether the statement is true or false. Write your answer in the space provided.*

___F___   **0.** When you buy property on account, you acquire all of its property rights.

_____   **1.** One of the purposes of accounting is to provide financial information about property and the rights of a business to that property.

_____   **2.** A person who has control over but does not own an item of property has a legal right to that item.

_____   **3.** Both businesses and individuals may own and control property.

_____   **4.** The creditor's financial claim minus the owner's financial claim to an item of property always equals the total cost of the property.

Part 3   Analyzing Business Transactions (10 points)

Directions: *Listed below are the account names that are used by In-a-Minute Messenger Service for recording and reporting the financial information from business transactions.*

1. Cash in Bank	**4.** Delivery Equipment	**7.** B. McCann, Capital
2. Accounts Receivable	**5.** Office Equipment	**8.** B. McCann, Withdrawals
3. Office Supplies	**6.** Accounts Payable	

Analyze each of the following transactions to determine the accounts affected. Then enter the numbers of the accounts affected by each transaction in the space at the left. Remember that at least two accounts will be affected by each transaction. The first transaction has been completed as an example.

Accounts Affected

  1,7   **0.** The owner invested cash in the business.
_____ **1.** Paid for the monthly rent by check.
_____ **2.** The owner transferred a new bicycle to the business for deliveries.
_____ **3.** Received cash for delivering messages.
_____ **4.** Purchased office equipment on account.
_____ **5.** Delivered messages for a client on account.
_____ **6.** Sold to a friend a bicycle helmet owned by the business on account.
_____ **7.** Issued a check to a creditor in partial payment of amount owed.
_____ **8.** Purchased office supplies on account.
_____ **9.** Withdrew cash for personal use.
_____ **10.** Wrote a check for the monthly telephone bill.

Part 4   Effects of Business Transactions on the Accounting Equation
(10 points)

Directions: *The business transactions completed by Carolyn Corley, Attorney at Law, appear below. Each business transaction will cause an increase (+), decrease (−), or no change (0) in the classification of accounts in the accounting equation. Analyze each transaction to determine how it affects the accounting equation (increase, decrease, no change). Then, in the space at the left, use +, −, or 0 to indicate the effect of each transaction on each part of the accounting equation.*

Assets = Liabilities + Owner's Equity

+	0	+	
			0. The owner transferred a typewriter to the business.
			1. Bought office furniture on account.
			2. The owner invested cash in the business.
			3. Paid the monthly utility bill by check.
			4. Purchased office supplies for cash.
			5. Prepared a lease for a client on account.
			6. Withdrew cash from the business for personal use.
			7. Bought a computer for cash.
			8. Received cash for completing legal services.
			9. Wrote a check to a creditor for an amount owed on account.
			10. Wrote a check for the monthly rent.

Working Papers *for Section Problems*

Problem 3-1   Balancing the Accounting Equation

	Assets	=	Liabilities	+	Owner's Equity
1	$ 17,000	=	$ 7,000	+	
2		=	$ 6,000	+	$ 20,000
3	$ 10,000	=		+	$ 7,000
4		=	$ 9,000	+	$ 17,000
5	$ 8,000	=	$ 2,000	+	
6	$ 20,000	=	$ 7,000	+	
7		=	$ 12,000	+	$ 4,000
8	$ 30,000	=		+	$ 22,000
9	$ 22,000	=	$ 1,000	+	
10	$ 25,000	=	$ 5,000	+	
11		=	$ 10,000	+	$ 25,000
12	$ 7,500	=		+	$ 3,000

Problem 3-2   Determining the Effects of Transactions on the Accounting Equation

Trans.	Assets				= Liabilities	+	Owner's Equity
	Cash in Bank	+ Accounts Receivable	+ Computer Equipment	+ Office Furniture	= Accounts Payable	+	Jan Swift, Capital
1							
2							
3							
4							
5							
6							
Bal.							

Problem 3-3   Determining the Effects of Transactions on the Accounting Equation

| Trans. | Assets | | | | | | | = | Liabilities | + | Owner's Equity |
	Cash in Bank	+	Accounts Receivable	+	Computer Equipment	+	Office Furniture	=	Accounts Payable	+	Jan Swift, Capital
Bal.	24,000		700		4,000		5,000		3,000		30,700
1											
2											
3											
4											
5											
Bal.											

Computerized Accounting Using Spreadsheets

Learning to Use a Spreadsheet Program

Introduction

Accountants use several tools to help them evaluate and present various financial information. One tool that has proven to be invaluable to accountants is the **electronic spreadsheet**. An electronic spreadsheet is simply a computerized version of the paper work sheet with which you are probably already familiar. The advantage of using an electronic spreadsheet is that changes and corrections can be made to the spreadsheet very quickly.

Before you begin using spreadsheet software, there are some terms with which you should become familiar:

Column: a vertical area of varying width that is labeled with a letter.

Row: a horizontal area that is labeled with a number.

Cell: the intersection of a column and a row. The intersection is referenced by the column and row. For example, cell C12 is the point at which column C and row 12 intersect.

Cell pointer: a rectangular block that highlights the current cell. When you want to enter data in a cell, first use the mouse or arrow keys to move the cell pointer to that position.

Template: a spreadsheet that contains formulas, labels, and formatting codes; the template can be used simply by entering information in the appropriate cells.

Work sheet: a spreadsheet document. The cells where you enter labels, amounts, and formulas are collectively referred to as a work sheet.

Opening a Spreadsheet Problem Using Glencoe Accounting:
Electronic Learning Center

Step 1 Turn on your computer.
Step 2 Open the Glencoe Accounting: Electronic Learning Center software.
Step 3 From the Program Menu, click the **Peachtree Accounting Software and Spreadsheet Applications** icon.
Step 4 Log onto the Accounting Management System by typing in your user name and password.
Step 5 Under the Chapter Problems tab, select the chapter and problem you want to work on. Click **OK.**
Step 6 Your spreadsheet application will launch and the template will load.
Step 7 Complete the spreadsheet problem according to the instructions in the problem's *Spreadsheet Guide.*

Continuing a Session

- If you've been directed to save your work to a network, select the problem from the Chapter Problems list. The system will automatically retrieve your files from the previous session.
- If you've been directed to save your work to a floppy disk, and you want to continue to work on the problem you've saved, be sure the correct floppy is in the drive before selecting the problem from the Chapter Problems list. If the Management System doesn't find a file on the floppy corresponding to the problem you've selected, it assumes you want to start the problem with a fresh template, in which case you may lose any work you previously completed.

Entering Data into a Spreadsheet

- **Navigation.** As you work with a template, you will be required to enter text and numbers into various cells to complete a problem. When instructed to "enter" information, use the mouse or the arrow keys to move the cell pointer to the specified cell, key the data (text or numbers), and then press the **ENTER** key.
- **Types of Data.** There are two kinds of data that you will enter—numbers and labels. When you type *425* the software knows that you are entering a number. Numeric data begins with a digit (0–9) or a symbol (+ – (. @ $ # or any currency symbol). All other symbols signify a label.
- **Cell Protection.** Depending on the spreadsheet program you are using, many of the cells are "protected" to prevent you from accidentally erasing information. If you attempt to enter a number or label in a protected cell, the spreadsheet program displays a message indicating the cell is locked or protected.
- **Errors.** If you make a mistake while keying the information and you have not yet pressed **ENTER**, simply use the **BACKSPACE** key to erase the incorrect data and rekey the entry. When the entry is correct, press **ENTER** to accept the data. If you notice an error after you press **ENTER**, simply re-enter the data.
- **Overflows.** Sometimes, the data you enter may be too wide to fit into one cell. When you press **ENTER**, the data "overflows" from the current cell into the next cell. As long as data has not been entered in the adjoining cell, the entire cell contents appear on the work sheet.
- **Placeholders.** Placeholders appear in each template to identify where to enter your name and the date. Simply move to the cell with *(name)* and type your name. Then, move to the cell with *(date)* and type the date.

Saving a Spreadsheet

After you complete a problem, or if you need to save your work before you finish an activity, use the **Save** option from the *File* menu. When closing the problem, you will be asked to save your work to the network or to floppy disks. It is good practice to always move your cursor to cell A1 before saving your spreadsheet. This will ensure that your spreadsheet opens in the first cell when your reopen it. For many spreadsheet applications, a shortcut for moving to cell A1 is by holding down the **CTRL** key and pressing the **HOME** key. Check your software's Help file for its specific shortcut commands.

Printing a Spreadsheet

Use your software's Print command to print your completed spreadsheet. Access your software's Help file for detailed printing instructions.

Sometimes a spreadsheet will be too wide to fit vertically on an 8½" x 11" piece of paper. If your spreadsheet is too wide to fit on an 8½-inch wide piece of paper, you can change your print settings to print the worksheet *landscape*. Landscape means that the worksheet will be printed broadside on the page. Some spreadsheet applications also allow you to choose a "print to page" option. This function will reduce the width and/or depth of the worksheet to fit on one page.

Ending a Session

After working with the software, you should exit the program. Remove the template disk from the drive (if necessary) and turn off the computer.

Problem 3-9   Determining the Effects of Business Transactions on the Accounting Equation

Completing the Spreadsheet

Step 1   Read the instructions for Problem 3-9 in your textbook.

Step 2   Open the Glencoe Accounting: Electronic Learning Center software.

Step 3   From the Program Menu, click on the **Peachtree Accounting Software and Spreadsheet Applications** icon.

Step 4   Log onto the Management System by typing your user name and password.

Step 5   Under the Chapter Problems tab, select the template: PRO3-9a.xls. The template should look like the one shown below.

```
PROBLEM 3-9
DETERMINING THE EFFECTS OF BUSINESS
TRANSACTIONS ON THE ACCOUNTING EQUATION

(name)
(date)
```

		ASSETS			LIABILITIES	OWNER'S EQUITY
Transaction	Cash in Bank	Accounts Receivable	Hiking Equipment	Rafting Equipment	Office Equipment =	Accounts Payable +	Juanita Ortega, Capital
1							
2							
3							
4							
5							
6							
7							
8							
9							
10							
BALANCE	$0	$0	$0	$0	$0	$0	$0

```
TOTAL ASSETS                           $0

TOTAL LIABILITIES                      $0
TOTAL OWNER'S EQUITY                   $0
TOTAL LIABILITIES + OWNER'S EQUITY     $0
```

Step 6   Key your name in the cell containing the *(name)* placeholder. After you key your name and press **ENTER,** the *(name)* placeholder will be replaced by the information you just keyed.

Step 7   Key today's date in the cell containing the *(date)* placeholder. After you key the date and press **ENTER,** the *(date)* placeholder will be replaced by the information you just keyed. When you work with any of the other spreadsheet templates, your name and date should always be keyed in the cells containing the *(name)* and *(date)* placeholders.

TIP: Options you select in the Regional Settings of Control Panel determine the default format for the current date and time and the characters recognized as date and time separators—for example, the slash (/) and colon (:) on United States-based systems. Be careful not to enter an equal sign before entering a date with slashes, as your spreadsheet application may view the date as a formula and the slashes as division symbols.

Step 8 In the first transaction, Ms. Ortega opened a checking account for the business. Cash in Bank is increasing, and Juanita Ortega, Capital, is increasing. To record this transaction in the spreadsheet template, move the cell pointer to cell B12 and enter **60000**.

TIP: To enter data into the cell, you must first key the data and then press **ENTER**. Do _not_ enter a dollar sign or a comma when you enter the data—the spreadsheet template will automatically format the data when it is entered.

TIP: Depending on the spreadsheet program you are using, the spreadsheet templates may be formatted to protect you from accidentally erasing information in selected cells. For example, the column headings in the spreadsheet for Problem 3-9 are protected. If you attempt to key a number or label in a protected cell, the spreadsheet program displays a message indicating that the cell is locked or protected. Simply move to the correct cell and re-enter the information.

Step 9 Next, move the cell pointer to cell J12. Enter **60000** in cell J12 to record the increase in Juanita Ortega, Capital. Again, do _not_ include a dollar sign or a comma as part of the cell entry—the spreadsheet template will automatically format the data when it is entered. Move the cell pointer to cell J23. Notice that the spreadsheet automatically calculates the balance in each account as you enter the data.

Step 10 To check your work, look at rows 26 through 30 in column D. Total assets equal $60,000. Total liabilities plus owner's equity also equal $60,000. The accounting equation is in balance.

Spreadsheet Guide

Step 11   Analyze the remaining transactions in Problem 3-9 and enter the appropriate data into the spreadsheet template.

TIP: To decrease an account balance, precede the amount entered by a minus sign. For example, to decrease Cash in Bank by $3,000, enter **−3000** in the Cash in Bank column.

Check the totals at the bottom of the spreadsheet after each transaction has been entered. Remember, total assets should always equal total liabilities plus owner's equity. If the accounting equation becomes out of balance, check your work to find the error.

Step 12   Save the spreadsheet using the **Save** option from the *File* menu. You should accept the default location for the save as this is handled by the management system.

TIP: It is good practice to always move your cursor to cell A1 before saving your spreadsheet. This will ensure that your spreadsheet opens in the first cell when you reopen it. For many spreadsheet applications, a shortcut for moving to cell A1 is by holding down the **CTRL** key and pressing the **HOME** key. Check your software's Help file for its specific shortcut commands.

Step 13   Print the completed spreadsheet.

TIP: If your spreadsheet is too wide to fit on an 8.5-inch wide piece of paper, you can change your print settings to print the worksheet *landscape.* Landscape means that the worksheet will be printed broadside on the page. Some spreadsheet applications also allow you to choose a "print to page" option. This function will reduce the width and/or depth of the worksheet to fit on one page.

Step 14   Exit the spreadsheet program.
Step 15   In the Close Options box, select the location where you would like to save your work.
Step 16   Answer the Analyze question from your textbook for this problem.

What-If Analysis

TIP: Always save your work before performing What-If Analysis. It is not necessary to save your work after performing What-If Analysis unless your teacher instructs you to do so. If you are required to save your work after performing What-If Analysis, be sure to rename the spreadsheet to avoid saving over your original work.

If Ms. Ortega withdrew an additional $1,500 from the business for personal use, what would the balance in the Juanita Ortega, Capital account be?

_____

Working Papers *for End-of-Chapter Problems*

Problem 3-4   Classifying Accounts

1. _____   5. _____   9. _____

2. _____   6. _____   10. _____

3. _____   7. _____

4. _____   8. _____

Problem 3-5   Completing the Accounting Equation

Assets		=	Liabilities		+	Owner's Equity	
Cash in Bank	$ 4,500		Accts. Pay.			Mike Murray, Capital	$9,250
Accts. Rec.	1,350						
Office Equipment	5,000						

Analyze:

Assets _____ = Liabilities _____ + Owner's Equity _____

Problem 3-6   Classifying Accounts Within the Accounting Equation

Account Title   **Balance**

(1) _____   _____

   _____   _____

   _____   _____

   _____   _____

   _____   _____

                          Total   _____

(2) _____   _____

   _____   _____

(3) _____   _____

Analyze:

Assets _____ = Liabilities _____ + Owner's Equity _____

Problem 3-7   Determining Increases and Decreases in Accounts

Transaction	Accounts Affected	Classification	Amount of Increase (+) or Decrease (-)
1	Cash in Bank	Asset	+ $ 25,000
	Regina Delgado, Capital	Owner's Equity	+ $ 25,000
2			
3			
4			
5			
6			
7			
8			

Analyze: _____

_____

Problem 3-8   Determining the Effects of Transactions on the Accounting Equation

Transaction	Assets				=	Liabilities	+	Owner's Equity
	Cash in Bank	Accounts Receivable	Office Equipment	Grooming Equipment	=	Accounts Payable	+	Abe Shultz, Capital
1	+$10,000							+$10,000
Balance					=		+	
2								
Balance					=		+	
3								
Balance					=		+	
4								
Balance					=		+	
5								
Balance					=		+	
6								
Balance					=		+	
7								
Balance					=		+	

Analyze: _____

_____

Problem 3-9   Determining the Effects of Business Transactions on the Accounting Equation

Transaction	Assets					=	Liabilities	+	Owner's Equity
	Cash in Bank	Accounts Receivable	Hiking Equipment	Rafting Equipment	Office Equipment	=	Accounts Payable	+	Juanita Ortega, Capital
1									
Balance						=		+	
2									
Balance						=		+	
3									
Balance						=		+	
4									
Balance						=		+	
5									
Balance						=		+	
6									
Balance						=		+	
7									
Balance						=		+	
8									
Balance						=		+	
9									
Balance						=		+	
10									
Balance						=		+	

Analyze: _____

_____

Problem 3-10   Describing Business Transactions

1. *The owner invested $30,000 in the business.* _____

2. _____

3. _____

4. _____

5. _____

_____

6. _____

7. _____

_____

8. _____

9. _____

10. _____

Analyze: _____

_____

Problem 3-11   Completing the Accounting Equation

	Assets					=	Liabilities	+	Owner's Equity
	Cash in Bank	+	Accounts Receivable	+	Business Equipment	=	Accounts Payable	+	Richard Tang, Capital
1		+	$ 2,000	+	$ 1,000	=	$ 500	+	$ 7,500
2	$ 3,000	+	$ 9,000	+		=	$ 2,000	+	$ 16,000
3	$ 8,000	+	$ 1,000	+	$ 10,000	=		+	$ 15,000
4	$ 4,000	+		+	$ 4,000	=	$ 1,000	+	$ 17,000
5	$ 9,000	+	$ 7,000	+	$ 6,000	=	$ 5,000	+	
6	$ 10,000	+	$ 14,000	+		=	$ 6,000	+	$ 32,000
7	$ 6,000	+	$ 4,000	+	$ 10,000	=		+	$ 15,000
8		+	$ 5,000	+	$ 9,000	=	$ 1,000	+	

Analyze: _____

_____

CHAPTER 3 — Business Transactions and the Accounting Equation

Self-Test

Part A   True or False

Directions: *Circle the letter* T *in the Answer column if the statement is true; circle the letter* F *if the statement is false.*

Answer

T   F   **1.** The accounting equation should remain in balance after each transaction.

T   F   **2.** A business transaction affects at least two accounts.

T   F   **3.** "Assets + Liabilities = Owner's Equity" is another way to express the accounting equation.

T   F   **4.** The increases and decreases caused by business transactions are recorded in specific accounts.

T   F   **5.** The private enterprise system is based on the right to own property.

T   F   **6.** The owner's personal financial transactions are part of the business's records.

T   F   **7.** The total financial claims to the assets of a business are referred to as equity.

T   F   **8.** The owner's claims to the assets of a business are liabilities.

T   F   **9.** When a business transaction occurs, the financial position of the business changes.

T   F   **10.** A creditor has a financial claim to the assets of a business.

T   F   **11.** An account is a record of only the increases in the balance of a specific item such as cash or equipment.

T   F   **12.** The total financial claims do not have to equal the total cost of the property.

Part B   Multiple Choice

Directions: *Only one of the choices given with each of the following state-ments is correct. Write the letter of the correct answer in the Answer column.*

Answer

_____   **1.** If the creditor's financial claim to property totals $1,000 and the owner's financial claim to property totals $11,000, the property value is
- (A) $10,000.
- (B) $11,000.
- (C) $12,000.
- (D) $1,000.

_____   **2.** The account Accounts Receivable is an example of a(n)
- (A) asset.
- (B) liability.
- (C) owner's equity.
- (D) none of the above.

_____   **3.** All of the following account names are asset names, except
- (A) Office Furniture.
- (B) Accounts Payable.
- (C) Cash in Bank.
- (D) Equipment.

_____   **4.** If a business has assets of $5,600 and liabilities of $900, the owner's equity is
- (A) $6,500.
- (B) $900.
- (C) $4,700.
- (D) $5,600.

_____   **5.** A business transaction that involves a purchase on account is considered to be a(n)
- (A) cash transaction.
- (B) credit transaction.
- (C) investment by the owner.
- (D) expense transaction.

_____   **6.** If a business purchases a calculator on account, the accounts affected by this transaction are.
- (A) Cash in Bank and Accounts Payable.
- (B) Office Equipment and Accounts Receivable.
- (C) Office Equipment and Cash in Bank.
- (D) Office Equipment and Accounts Payable.

_____   **7.** Each of the following is a business expense, except pay-ment for
- (A) advertising.
- (B) monthly rent.
- (C) utility bills.
- (D) equipment.

_____   **8.** The purchase of a desk on account will increase Office Furniture and will also increase
- (A) Cash in Bank.
- (B) Accounts Payable.
- (C) Accounts Receivable.
- (D) Jon McIvey, Capital.

CHAPTER 4

Transactions That Affect Assets, Liabilities, and Owner's Equity

Study Plan

Check Your Understanding

Section 1	*Read Section 1 on pages 72–76 and complete the following exercises on page 77.* ❏ Thinking Critically ❏ Computing in the Business World ❏ Problem 4-1 *Applying the Rules of Debit and Credit*
Section 2	*Read Section 2 on pages 78–82 and complete the following exercises on page 83.* ❏ Thinking Critically ❏ Communicating Accounting ❏ Problem 4-2 *Identifying Increases and Decreases in Accounts*
Summary	*Review the Chapter 4 Summary on page 85 in your textbook.* ❏ Key Concepts
Review and Activities	*Complete the following questions and exercises on pages 86–87 in your textbook.* ❏ Using Key Terms ❏ Understanding Accounting Concepts and Procedures ❏ Case Study ❏ Conducting an Audit with Alex ❏ Internet Connection ❏ Workplace Skills
Computerized Accounting	*Read the Computerized Accounting information on page 88 in your textbook.* ❏ *Making the Transition from a Manual to a Computerized System* ❏ *A Quick Overview of Peachtree Accounting*
Problems	*Complete the following end-of-chapter problems for Chapter 4 in your textbook.* ❏ Problem 4-3 *Identifying Accounts Affected by Transactions* ❏ Problem 4-4 *Using T Accounts to Analyze Transactions* ❏ Problem 4-5 *Analyzing Transactions into Debit and Credit Parts* ❏ Problem 4-6 *Analyzing Transactions into Debit and Credit Parts*
Challenge Problem	❏ Problem 4-7 *Analyzing Transactions Recorded in T Accounts*
Chapter Reviews and Working Papers	*Complete the following exercises for Chapter 4 in your Chapter Reviews and Working Papers.* ❏ Chapter Review ❏ Self-Test

CHAPTER 4 REVIEW — Transactions That Affect Assets, Liabilities, and Owner's Equity

Part 1 Accounting Vocabulary (7 points)

Total Points 82
Student's Score

Directions: *Using terms from the following list, complete the sentences below. Write the letter of the term you have chosen in the space provided.*

A. accounting equation	**C.** credit	**E.** double-entry accounting	**G.** ledger
B. balance side	**D.** debit	**F.** T account	**H.** chart of accounts

_____F_____ **0.** A _____ is a tool used by accountants to analyze business transactions.

_____ **1.** The _____ of an account is the same side used to increase the account.

_____ **2.** The left side of the T account is the _____ side.

_____ **3.** Assets = Liabilities + Owner's Equity is the _____.

_____ **4.** The _____ side is the right side of the T account.

_____ **5.** _____ is the financial recordkeeping system in which each business transaction affects at least two accounts.

_____ **6.** A _____ is a list of all the accounts a business uses.

_____ **7.** Accounts are grouped together in a _____.

Part 2 The Rules of Debit and Credit (15 points)

Directions: *Read each of the following statements to determine whether the statement is true or false. Write your answer in the space provided.*

_____T_____ **0.** Each account has a specific side that is its normal balance side.

_____ **1.** Every business transaction affects at least two accounts that are on different sides of the basic accounting equation.

_____ **2.** For every debit entry made in one account, a credit entry must be made in another account.

_____ **3.** The T account is an inefficient method for analyzing many business transactions.

_____ **4.** Double-entry accounting is the recordkeeping system in which each business transaction affects at least one account.

_____ **5.** "Debit" means to increase an account balance.

_____ **6.** The normal balance side of an account is the same side that is used to record increases to the account.

_____ **7.** Liability and capital accounts are increased on the debit side.

_____ **8.** Debits and credits are used to record increases and decreases in each account affected by a business transaction.

_____ **9.** Asset accounts are increased on the credit side.

_____ **10.** A credit is an amount entered on the right side of the T account.

_____ **11.** If the accounting equation is not in balance after a transaction has been recorded, one reason may be that the debit or credit part of the transaction was not recorded.

_____ **12.** When analyzing business transactions, you should ask yourself which accounts are affected.

_____ **13.** A credit to an asset account will decrease the account, while a credit to a liability account will increase that account.

_____ **14.** The normal balance side of an owner's capital account is the debit side.

_____ **15.** If one asset account is debited for $75 and a different asset account is credited for $75, the total assets will increase by $75.

Part 3   Analyzing Asset, Liability, and Capital Accounts (20 points)

Directions: *For each T account below, indicate the debit and credit sides, the increase and decrease sides, and the normal balance side. The first account has been completed as an example.*

Store Equipment		Accounts Payable	Cash in Bank
Debit	*Credit*		
Increase	*Decrease*		
Balance			

Accounts Receivable	Abe Dunn, Capital

Part 4   Analyzing Business Transactions (40 points)

Directions: *Analyze the following transactions by answering the questions in the table below. Use the account names that follow. The first transaction has been completed as an example.*

Cash in Bank	Office Equipment	Accounts Payable
Accounts Receivable	Office Supplies	J. Adams, Capital

0. The business bought office supplies from Central Supply for $850 cash.
1. The business sold a used laser printer on account for $1,500.
2. Ms. Adams invested $75,000 of her personal savings in the business.
3. The business purchased word processing equipment for $9,500 on account from Northern Office Equipment Company.
4. The business paid $3,500 on account to Northern Office Equipment Company.
5. Ms. Adams transferred an office file cabinet of her own valued at $375 to the business.

Trans. No.	Which accounts are affected?	What is the classification of each account?	Is each account increased or decreased?	Which account is debited and for what amount?	Which account is credited and for what amount?
0	*Office Supplies*	*Asset*	*Increased*	*$ 850*	
	Cash in Bank	*Asset*	*Decreased*		*$ 850*
1					
2					
3					
4					
5					

Working Papers *for Section Problems*

Problem 4-1　Applying the Rules of Debit and Credit

Account Title	Account Classification	Increase Side	Decrease Side	Normal Balance
Cash in Bank	*Asset*	*Debit*	*Credit*	*Debit*

Problem 4-2　Identifying Increases and Decreases in Accounts

1. a. _____

　b. _____

2. a. _____

　b. _____

3. a. _____

　b. _____

Computerized Accounting Using Spreadsheets

Problem 4-6   Analyzing Transactions into Debit and Credit Parts

Completing the Spreadsheet

Step 1 Read the instructions for Problem 4-6 in your textbook.

Step 2 Open the Glencoe Accounting: Electronic Learning Center software.

Step 3 From the Program Menu, click on the **Peachtree Accounting Software and Spreadsheet Applications** icon.

Step 4 Log onto the Management System by typing your user name and password.

Step 5 Under the Chapter Problems tab, select the template: PR04-6a.xls. The template should look like the one shown below.

```
PROBLEM 4-6
ANALYZING TRANSACTIONS INTO
DEBIT AND CREDIT PARTS

(name)
(date)

                                    Accounts Receivable -
          Cash in Bank                  Mary Johnson                Office Equipment
  _____      _____      _____
  |            |           |    |            |           |    |            |           |
  |            |           |    |            |           |    |            |           |
  |            |           |    |            |           |    |            |           |
  |            |           |    |            |           |    |            |           |
  |_____0|_____|    |_____0|_____|    |_____0|_____|

       Computer Equipment            Hiking Equipment             Rafting Equipment
  _____      _____      _____
  |            |           |    |            |           |    |            |           |
  |            |           |    |            |           |    |            |           |
  |            |           |    |            |           |    |            |           |
  |            |           |    |            |           |    |            |           |
  |_____0|_____|    |_____0|_____|    |_____0|_____|

     Accounts Payable -           Accounts Payable -            Juanita Ortega,
       Peak Equipment              Premier Processors              Capital
  _____      _____      _____
  |            |           |    |            |           |    |            |           |
  |            |           |    |            |           |    |            |           |
  |            |           |    |            |           |    |            |           |
  |            |           |    |            |           |    |            |           |
  |_____0|_____|    |_____0|_____|    |_____0|_____|

SUM OF DEBIT BALANCES                    $0
SUM OF CREDIT BALANCES                   $0
```

Step 6 Key your name and today's date in the cells containing the *(name)* and *(date)* placeholders.

Step 7 In the first transaction, Juanita Ortega transferred an additional $53,250 from her personal account to the business. Two accounts are affected by this transaction: Cash in Bank and Juanita Ortega, Capital. To record this transaction, move to cell A10, the first cell on the debit side of the Cash in Bank T account, and enter **53250**.

Spreadsheet Guide

TIP: To enter data into a cell, you must first key the data and then press **ENTER.** Do *not* enter a comma when you enter the data.

Step 8   Next, move to cell H30, the first cell on the credit side of the Juanita Ortega, Capital T account. Enter **53250** in cell H30 to record the credit to Juanita Ortega, Capital. Move the cell pointer to cell H35. Notice that the spreadsheet automatically calculates the balance in each T account.

Step 9   To check your work, look at cells D39 and D40. The sum of debit balances equals $53,250. The sum of credit balances also equals $53,250.

Step 10   Analyze the remaining transactions in Problem 4-6 and enter the appropriate data into the spreadsheet template.

Check the totals at the bottom of the spreadsheet after each transaction has been entered. Remember, the sum of debit balances should always equal the sum of credit balances. If the debit and credit balances become out of balance, check your work to find the errors.

Step 11   Save the spreadsheet using the **Save** option from the *File* menu. You should accept the default location for the save as this is handled by the management system.

Step 12   Print the completed spreadsheet.

Step 13   Exit the spreadsheet program.

Step 14   In the Close Options box, select the location where you would like to save your work.

Step 15   Answer the Analyze question from your textbook for this problem.

What-If Analysis

TIP: Always save your work before performing What-If Analysis. It is not necessary to save your work after performing What-If Analysis unless your teacher instructs you to do so. If you are required to save your work after performing What-If Analysis, be sure to rename the spreadsheet to avoid saving over your original work.

If Juanita Ortega purchased a computer for $1,500 cash, what would the balance in the Cash in Bank account be?

Working Papers *for End-of-Chapter Problems*

Problem 4-3   Identifying Accounts Affected by Transactions

1. _____

_____

2. _____

_____

3. _____

_____

4. _____

_____

Analyze: _____

_____

Problem 4-4   Using T Accounts to Analyze Transactions

Analyze: _____

_____

_____

Problem 4-5   Analyzing Transactions into Debit and Credit Parts

Analyze: _____

_____

_____

Problem 4-6 Analyzing Transactions into Debit and Credit Parts

Sum of debit balances = _____ . Sum of credit balances = _____ .

Analyze: _____

Problem 4-7   Analyzing Transactions Recorded in T Accounts

Trans. No.	Account Debited	Increase (I) or Decrease (D)	Account Credited	Increase (I) or Decrease (D)	Description
1	*Cash in Bank*	*I*	*Richard Tang, Capital*	*I*	*Richard Tang invested $15,000 in the business.*
2					
3					
4					
5					
6					
7					
8					
9					
10					

Analyze: _____

_____

_____

CHAPTER 4   Transactions That Affect Assets, Liabilities, and Owner's Equity

Self-Test

Part A   True or False

Directions: *Circle the letter* T *in the Answer column if the statement is true; circle the letter* F *if the statement is false.*

Answer

T	F	**1.**	The normal balance side for an asset account is the debit side.
T	F	**2.**	"Debit" means the increase side of an account.
T	F	**3.**	A credit to a liability account decreases the account balance.
T	F	**4.**	Assets are increased on the debit side.
T	F	**5.**	Capital is increased on the credit side.
T	F	**6.**	Liabilities are decreased on the credit side.
T	F	**7.**	The basic accounting equation may be expressed as $A - L = OE$
T	F	**8.**	The right side of a T account is always the debit side.
T	F	**9.**	For every debit there must be an equal credit.
T	F	**10.**	A debit to one asset account and a credit to another asset account will result in the basic accounting equation being out of balance.
T	F	**11.**	The left side of a T account is always the credit side.
T	F	**12.**	Credit means to decrease a liability.

Part B   Identify the Normal Balance

Directions: *For each T account below, indicate with an (N) the normal balance side. The first account has been completed as an example.*

Computer Equipment		Accounts Payable		Cash in Bank	
Debit	Credit	Debit	Credit	Debit	Credit
(N)					

Accounts Receivable		Abe Dunn, Capital		Office Equipment	
Debit	Credit	Debit	Credit	Debit	Credit

Part C   Complete the T Account

Directions: *Analyze the transactions below and enter them in the T accounts provided.*

1. Ms. Adams invested $12,000 cash in the business.
2. Bought office equipment for cash, $1,000.
3. Bought a computer on account, $3,000.

Cash in Bank	Office Equipment	Computer Equipment

Accounts Payable	J. Adams, Capital

CHAPTER 5   Transactions That Affect Revenue, Expenses, and Withdrawals

Study Plan

Check Your Understanding

Section 1	*Read Section 1 on pages 96–102 and complete the following exercises on page 103.*
	❏ Thinking Critically
	❏ Communicating Accounting
	❏ Problem 5-1 *Applying the Rules of Debit and Credit*
Section 2	*Read Section 2 on pages 104–108 and complete the following exercises on page 109.*
	❏ Thinking Critically
	❏ Analyzing Accounting
	❏ Problem 5-2 *Identifying Accounts Affected by Transactions*
Summary	*Review the Chapter 5 Summary on page 111 in your textbook.*
	❏ Key Concepts
Review and Activities	*Complete the following questions and exercises on pages 112–113 in your textbook.*
	❏ Using Key Terms
	❏ Understanding Accounting Concepts and Procedures
	❏ Case Study
	❏ Conducting an Audit with Alex
	❏ Internet Connection
	❏ Workplace Skills
Computerized Accounting	*Read the Computerized Accounting information on page 114 in your textbook.*
	❏ *Making the Transition from a Manual to a Computerized System*
	❏ *Setting Up General Ledger Accounts in Peachtree*
Problems	*Complete the following end-of-chapter problems for Chapter 5 in your textbook.*
	❏ Problem 5-3 *Identifying Increases and Decreases in Accounts*
	❏ Problem 5-4 *Using T Accounts to Analyze Transactions*
	❏ Problem 5-5 *Analyzing Transactions into Debit and Credit Parts*
	❏ Problem 5-6 *Analyzing Transactions into Debit and Credit Parts*
	❏ Problem 5-7 *Analyzing Transactions*
Challenge Problem	❏ Problem 5-8 *Completing the Accounting Equation*
Chapter Reviews and Working Papers	*Complete the following exercises for Chapter 5 in your Chapter Reviews and Working Papers.*
	❏ Chapter Review
	❏ Self-Test

CHAPTER 5 REVIEW — Transactions That Affect Revenue, Expenses, and Withdrawals

Part 1   Accounting Vocabulary (6 points)

Total Points	62
Student's Score	

Directions: *Using terms from the following list, complete the sentences below. Write the letter of the term you have chosen in the space provided.*

A. capital	**D.** revenue accounts	**F.** temporary capital accounts
B. expense accounts	**E.** revenue recognition principle	**G.** withdrawal
C. permanent accounts		

_____G_____   **0.** An amount of money taken out of the business by the owner is a _____.

_____   **1.** _____ record business income only.

_____   **2.** _____ are used to record information for only one accounting period.

_____   **3.** The _____ account shows the amount of the owner's investment, or equity, in a business.

_____   **4.** Accounts that are used to record information continuously from one accounting period to the next are called _____.

_____   **5.** _____ are used to record the costs and services used by a business.

_____   **6.** Recognizing and recording revenue on the date it is earned even if cash has not been received on that date is known as the _____.

Part 2   Effects of a Transaction on an Account (24 points)

Directions: *For each of the business transactions below, indicate whether the left or right side of the account is affected and whether the account balance is increased or decreased.*

	Left	Right	Increase	Decrease
0. A credit of $850 to Accounts Payable	_____	✓	✓	_____
1. A debit of $400 to B. Barns, Withdrawals	_____	_____	_____	_____
2. A debit of $200 to Advertising Expense	_____	_____	_____	_____
3. A credit of $300 to Cash in Bank	_____	_____	_____	_____
4. A credit of $450 to Fees	_____	_____	_____	_____
5. A debit of $650 to Rent Expense	_____	_____	_____	_____
6. A credit to B. Barns, Capital of $1,500	_____	_____	_____	_____
7. A credit to Accounts Receivable of $925	_____	_____	_____	_____
8. A debit to Office Supplies of $40	_____	_____	_____	_____
9. A debit of $3,000 to B. Barns, Capital	_____	_____	_____	_____
10. A debit of $150 to Accounts Payable	_____	_____	_____	_____
11. A debit to Accounts Receivable of $2,000	_____	_____	_____	_____
12. A debit to Cash in Bank of $750	_____	_____	_____	_____

Part 3   Analyzing Transactions Using T Accounts (20 points)

Directions: *Use T accounts to analyze each of the transactions below. Use the following account names.*

Cash in Bank	Martha Russo, Withdrawals	Advertising Expense
Accounts Receivable—Tim Ochi	Service Fees	Telephone Expense

0. Provided typing services and billed Tim Ochi $400 for the work.

Accounts Receivable—Tim Ochi

400	

Service Fees

	400

1. Paid $45 cash for an advertisement in the newspaper.

2. Martha Russo withdrew $250 cash for personal use.

3. Provided word processing services for $975 cash.

4. Paid the telephone bill with a check for $90.

5. Received $400 on account from Tim Ochi.

Part 4   Testing for the Equality of Debits and Credits (12 points)

Directions: *The balance of each account is indicated directly after the account name. Indicate the normal balance side of each account by placing the dollar amount in the appropriate debit or credit column. Add each column. The total debit balance should equal the total credit balance.*

Account	Balance	Debits	Credits
Cash in Bank	$3,725	$ 3,725	$
Accounts Receivable	800		
Office Supplies	200		
Office Equipment	8,500		
Accounts Payable	3,000		
G. Steiner, Capital	5,905		
G. Steiner, Withdrawals	625		
Fees	6,550		
Advertising Expense	650		
Rent Expense	725		
Utilities Expense	230		
Totals		$	$

Working Papers *for Section Problems*

Problem 5-1   Applying the Rules of Debit and Credit

Account Title	Account Classification	Increase Side	Decrease Side	Normal Balance
Cash in Bank	*Asset*	*Debit*	*Credit*	*Debit*

Problem 5-2   Identifying Accounts Affected by Transactions

1. _____
2. _____
3. _____
4. _____

Computerized Accounting Using Peachtree

Software Objectives

When you have completed this chapter, you will be able to use Peachtree to:

1. Change the company name.
2. Set the system date.
3. Print a Chart of Accounts report.
4. Enter a new general ledger account.
5. Record a beginning balance for a general ledger account.
6. Explain the purpose of the account type settings.

Problem 5-3   Identifying Increases and Decreases in Accounts

Follow the instructions provided below to print a Chart of Accounts report for Wilderness Rentals. Although the instructions in your textbook direct you to analyze the transactions, you will not use Peachtree to complete this analysis. In the next chapter, however, you will use the Wilderness Rentals general ledger accounts to enter transactions.

INSTRUCTIONS

Beginning a Session

Step 1   Open the Glencoe Accounting: Electronic Learning Center software and click on the **Peachtree Accounting Software and Spreadsheet Applications** icon.

Step 2   Log onto the system by entering your user name and password.

Step 3   From the scrolling list of chapter problems, select the problem set: Wilderness Rentals (Prob. 5-3).

Step 4   Rename the company by adding your initials, e.g., Wilderness (Prob. 5-3: XXX).

- Choose **Company Information** from the **Maintain** menu.
- Review the information in the Maintain Company Information window. (See Figure 5-3A.)
- Click in the *Company Name* field.
- Change the company name by adding your initials as shown in the figure.
- Click [✓ Ok] to record the new company name.

> **DO YOU HAVE A QUESTION**
>
> **Q.** *Are there any differences between a manual system and computerized system when you set up a chart of accounts?*
>
> **A.** When you set up a chart of accounts using Peachtree, you must enter an account number and a title for each general ledger account just like you would in a manual system. Using a computerized system such as Peachtree, however, you must categorize each account by assigning an account type (e.g., asset, liability, equity, income, expense, etc.).

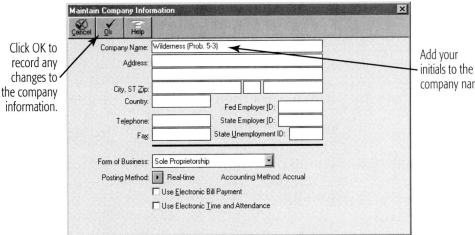

Figure 5-3A *Maintain Company Information Window*

Peachtree Guide

Step 5   Set the system date to January 31, 2004.

- Click the ***Options*** menu and choose **Change System Date**.
- Type **1/31/04**.
- Click **OK** to record the new system date.

Preparing a Report

Step 6   Print a Chart of Accounts report.

To print a Chart of Accounts report:

- Choose **General Ledger** from the ***Reports*** menu to display the Select a Report window. (See Figure 5-3B.)

Notes

You must set the accounting date each time you begin working with Peachtree.

TIP: You can double-click a report title to go directly to that report, skipping the options window.

- Select Chart of Accounts in the report list.
- Click [Screen] and then click **OK** to display the Chart of Accounts report.
- Review the report as shown in Figure 5-3C and then click [Print] to print the report.
- Click [Close] to close the report window.

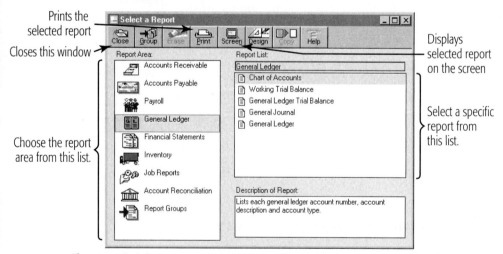

Figure 5-3B *Select a Report Window with the General Ledger Reports*

Indicates if an account is active

Account description (or name)

Account ID (or number)

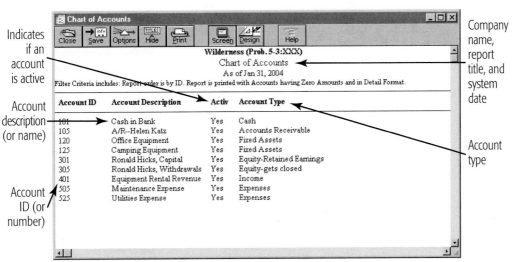

Company name, report title, and system date

Account type

Figure 5-3C *Chart of Accounts Report*

Step 7 Review the information shown on the report.

As you can see, the Chart of Accounts report shows the general ledger account numbers and account titles for Wilderness Rentals. The report also includes two other columns—*Active* and *Account Type*.

The *Active* column includes information that identifies whether or not an account is active. You can post transactions to an active account, but not to an inactive account. The account type identifies the account category (e.g., Cash, Accounts Receivable, Fixed Assets, Equity—Retained Earnings, Equity—gets closed, Income, and Expenses). Peachtree uses this information to group accounts for financial reports and to determine which accounts are permanent and which are temporary when it closes an accounting period.

Ending the Session

When you finish the problem or if you must stop at the end of a class period, follow the instructions given here to end the session.

Step 8 Click the **Close Problem** button in the Glencoe Smart Guide window and select the appropriate save option as directed by your teacher.

Continuing a Problem from a Previous Session

- If you were previously directed to save your work on the network, select the problem from the scrolling menu and click **OK.** The system will retrieve your files from your last session.
- If you were previously directed to save your work on a floppy disk, insert the floppy, select the corresponding problem from the scrolling menu and click **OK.** The system will retrieve your files from the floppy disk.

Mastering Peachtree

What account types are used by the Peachtree software? On a separate sheet of paper, list these account types.

TIP: Search the help information to learn about the account types.

Chapter 5 ■ 63

Peachtree Guide

Problem 5-4   Using T Accounts to Analyze Transactions

Follow the instructions provided below to print a Chart of Accounts report for Hot Suds Car Wash. You will use the general ledger accounts to enter transactions in the next chapter.

INSTRUCTIONS

Beginning a Session

Step 1   Open the Glencoe Accounting: Electronic Learning Center software and click on the **Peachtree Accounting Software and Spreadsheet Applications** icon.

Step 2   Log onto the system by entering your user name and password.

Step 3   From the scrolling list of chapter problems, select the problem set: Hot Suds Car Wash (Prob. 5-4).

Step 4   Rename the company by adding your initials, e.g., Hot Suds (Prob. 5-4: XXX).

Step 5   Set the system date to January 31, 2004.

Preparing a Report

Step 6   Print a Chart of Accounts report.

TIP: You can use the General Ledger Navigation Aid at the bottom of the Peachtree main window to access the General Ledger Reports including the Chart of Accounts.

Step 7   Review the information shown on the report.

Ending the Session

Step 8   Click the **Close Problem** button in the Glencoe Smart Guide window and select the appropriate save option as directed by your teacher.

DO YOU HAVE A QUESTION

Q. *What is the purpose of the "Filter Criteria includes: ..." section at the top of the Chart of Accounts report?*

A. Almost every report you print with Peachtree includes the report criteria at the top of the report. This information identifies which filters (or options) are set for the report. For example, you could choose to print a Chart of Account with only the general ledger accounts that have a balance. Or, you could choose to print only the asset accounts. The information at the top of the report reflects any special options you may have set. On some reports, the filter criteria may run past the edge of the page. The content of the report is not affected when this occurs.

Notes

Refer to the instructions in Problem 5-3 if you need help installing a problem set, changing the company name, or setting the system date.

Problem 5-5   Analyzing Transactions into Debit and Credit Parts

Follow the instructions provided below to add new general ledger accounts for Kits & Pups Grooming. You will also learn how to enter the beginning balance for an account.

INSTRUCTIONS

Beginning a Session

Step 1   Open the Glencoe Accounting: Electronic Learning Center software and click on the **Peachtree Accounting Software and Spreadsheet Applications** icon.

Step 2   Log onto the system by entering your user name and password.

Step 3   From the scrolling list of chapter problems, select the problem set: Kits & Pups Grooming (Prob. 5-5).

Step 4   Rename the company and set the system date to January 31, 2004.

Completing the Accounting Problem

Step 5   Add the **Advertising Expense** general ledger account.

To add a new account:

- Choose **Chart of Accounts** from the *Maintain* menu.
- Click 🔍 in the Maintain Chart of Accounts window to view those accounts already recorded for the company.
- Type **501** in the *Account ID* field and press **TAB** to move to the next field.

As you type an account number, Peachtree displays a list of the general ledger accounts and highlights the first account that matches what you have entered. This feature is helpful if you are entering an account number for an account you want to change. **Note:** This feature may be disabled if your teacher changed the Peachtree preferences.

TIP: Press **TAB** to move to the next field in a data entry window and press **SHIFT+TAB** to move to the previous field.

- Type **Advertising Expense** in the *Description* field.
- Click the *Account Type* pop-up field and select **Expenses** since this account is an expense.
- Review the information you just entered. (See Figure 5-5A.)

You do not have to complete any of the other fields shown in the Maintain Chart of Accounts window. The account activity appears in this window as a company uses the software to record its transactions. You can also enter budget amounts, as you will learn in a later chapter.

- Click 🔲 or press **ALT+S** to record the new account.
- Click 🔲 to clear the data entry fields in preparation to enter a new account.

DO YOU HAVE A QUESTION

Q. *When you add a new account or enter a transaction using the Peachtree software, is it necessary to manually save your work?*

A. Some applications, such as a word processor or a spreadsheet program, require that you choose to save your work by choosing the **Save** command or by clicking the **Save** button on a toolbar. Peachtree does not require you to manually choose to save your work. It automatically updates the company files for you. However, you must always be sure to properly exit Peachtree to avoid losing any data.

Notes

Refer to the instructions in Problem 5-3 if you need help installing a problem set, changing the company name, or setting the system date.

Peachtree Guide

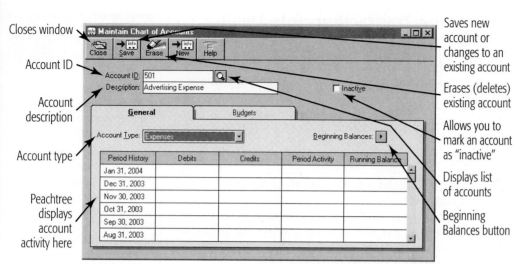

Closes window

Account ID

Account description

Account type

Peachtree displays account activity here

Saves new account or changes to an existing account

Erases (deletes) existing account

Allows you to mark an account as "inactive"

Displays list of accounts

Beginning Balances button

Figure 5-5A *Maintain Chart of Accounts Window (Advertising Expense)*

Step 6 Enter the remaining expense accounts shown below for Kits & Pups Grooming.

Account No.	Description	Account Type
505	Equipment Repair Expense	Expenses
510	Maintenance Expense	Expenses
520	Rent Expense	Expenses
530	Utilities Expense	Expenses

Note: To edit an account description or account type, enter the account number and then change the account information.

Click to save the changes. If you enter the wrong account number, enter or select the account. Then, click

[Erase] to remove it from the chart of accounts.

Step 7 Enter the beginning balances for **Cash in Bank** ($15,000) and **Abe Shultz** ($15,000).

To enter beginning balances:

- Click the **Beginning Balances** button in the Maintain Chart of Accounts window.
- Choose **From 1/1/04 through 1/31/04** from the Select Period window and click **OK**.
- Type **15000.00** in the *Cash in Bank* field. Be sure to enter the decimal point.
- Tab to the *Abe Shultz, Capital* field and enter **15000.00**.
- Review the entry. (See Figure 5-5B.)
- Click [Ok] to record the beginning balances.

Step 8 Click [Close] to close the Maintain Chart of Accounts window.

Notes

*If you do not click the **New** button, Peachtree does not clear the description field for the next new account. However, you can type over the account number and account description to enter a new account.*

Peachtree Guide

Records beginning balances →

Accounting period for beginning balances →

Describes the concept of the basic accounting equation →

← Cash account beginning balance

← Capital account beginning balance

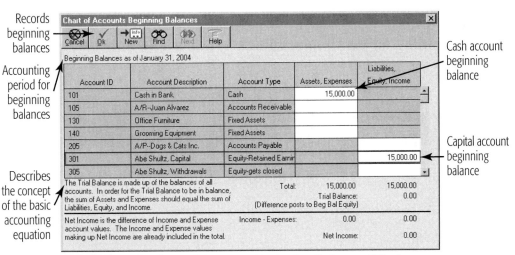

Figure 5-5B *Chart of Accounts Beginning Balances Window*

Preparing a Report

Step 9   Print a Chart of Accounts report.

Step 10 Review the information shown on the report.

Step 11 If you notice an error, use the **Chart of Accounts** option in the **Maintain** menu to edit/delete a general ledger account.

Ending the Session

Step 12 Click the **Close Problem** button in the Glencoe Smart Guide window and select the appropriate save option.

Problem 5-6   Analyzing Transactions into Debit and Credit Parts

Follow the instructions provided below to add new general ledger accounts for Outback Guide Service. You will enter transactions in the next chapter.

INSTRUCTIONS

Beginning a Session

Step 1 Open the Glencoe Accounting: Electronic Learning Center software and click on the **Peachtree Accounting Software and Spreadsheet Applications** icon.

Step 2 Log onto the system by entering your user name and password.

Step 3 From the scrolling list of chapter problems, select the problem set: Outback Guide Service (Prob. 5-6).

Step 4 Rename the company and set the system date to January 31, 2004.

Completing the Accounting Problem

Step 5 Enter the capital, income, and expense accounts.

Account No.	Description	Account Type
301	Juanita Ortega, Capital	Equity—Retained Earnings
302	Juanita Ortega, Withdrawals	Equity—gets closed
401	Guide Service Revenue	Income
505	Maintenance Expense	Expenses
515	Rent Expense	Expenses
525	Utilities Expense	Expenses

Notes

Refer to the instructions in Problem 5-3 if you need help installing a problem set, changing the company name, or setting the system date.

Notes

The withdrawal account is a temporary capital account and gets closed at the end of each accounting period.

TIP: Review the instructions for the previous problem if you need help entering a new account.

Step 6   Click to close the Maintain Chart of Accounts window.

Preparing a Report

Step 7   Print a Chart of Accounts report.

Step 8   Proof your work and make any corrections, as needed.

Ending the Session

Step 9   Click the **Close Problem** button in the Glencoe Smart Guide window and select a save option.

Problem 5-7   Analyzing Transactions

Follow the instructions provided below to add new general ledger accounts for Showbiz Video. You will enter transactions into the accounts in the next chapter.

INSTRUCTIONS

Beginning a Session

Step 1   Open the Glencoe Accounting: Electronic Learning Center software and click on the **Peachtree Accounting Software and Spreadsheet Applications** icon.

Step 2   Log onto the system by entering your user name and password.

Step 3   From the scrolling list of chapter problems, select the problem set: Showbiz Video (Prob. 5-7).

Step 4   Rename the company and set the system date to January 31, 2004.

Completing the Accounting Problem

Step 5   Review all of the accounts listed in your textbook for Showbiz Video.

Step 6   Determine the account type for each account.

Step 7   Enter all of the new accounts.

TIP: You must abbreviate some account names to fit in the *Description* field. For example, use *A/R* instead of *Accounts Receivable*.

Preparing a Report

Step 8   Print a Chart of Accounts report.

Step 9   Proof your work and make any corrections, as needed.

Ending the Session

Step 10   Click the **Close Problem** button in the Glencoe Smart Guide window and select a save option.

Mastering Peachtree

Peachtree allows you to enter a budget amount for each general ledger account. On a separate sheet of paper, describe why a company would record budget figures.

Computerized Accounting Using Spreadsheets

Problem 5-8   Completing the Accounting Equation

Completing the Spreadsheet

Step 1 Read the instructions for Problem 5-8 in your textbook. This problem involves determining the missing amounts for the accounting equations given.

Step 2 Open the Glencoe Accounting: Electronic Learning Center software.

Step 3 From the Program Menu, click on the **Peachtree Accounting Software and Spreadsheet Applications** icon.

Step 4 Log onto the Management System by typing your user name and password.

Step 5 Under the Chapter Problems tab, select the template: PR05-8a.xls. The template should look like the one shown below.

```
PROBLEM 5-8
COMPLETING THE ACCOUNTING EQUATION

(name)
(date)

                                       Owner's
        Assets   =  Liabilities  +  Equity  -  Withdrawals  +  Revenue  -  Expenses
   1    $64,400        $8,200       $56,300        $500        $10,000       $9,600
   2
   3
   4
   5
   6
   7
   8
   9

Total Assets                                                                $64,400

Total Liabilities + Owner's Equity - Withdrawals + Revenue - Expenses       $64,400
```

Step 6 Key your name and today's date in the cells containing the *(name)* and *(date)* placeholders.

Step 7 The first equation is completed for you. Notice that Assets ($64,400) equal Liabilities ($8,200) + Owner's Equity ($56,300) – Withdrawals ($500) + Revenue ($10,000) – Expenses ($9,600).

Step 8 To complete the second equation, enter the amounts given in your textbook for Assets, Liabilities, Owner's Equity, Withdrawals, and Revenue in the appropriate cells. To calculate the amount for Expenses, add Liabilities ($525) + Owner's Equity ($18,800) – Withdrawals ($1,200) + Revenue ($12,100) to get a total of $30,225. Subtract Assets ($22,150) from this amount to get $8,075, the missing amount for Expenses. Enter **8075** in cell L12.

TIP: Remember, do *not* enter a dollar sign or a comma when you enter the data—the spreadsheet template will automatically format the data when it is entered.

Chapter 5 ■ 69

Step 9 To check your work, look at cells L23 and L25. Total Assets should equal Total Liabilities + Owner's Equity – Withdrawals + Revenue – Expenses.

Step 10 Complete the remaining equations in Problem 5-8 by entering the appropriate data from your text into the spreadsheet template and calculating the missing amounts.

Check the totals at the bottom of the spreadsheet after the amounts have been entered to make sure they are in balance. If the totals do not balance, check your work to find the error.

Step 11 Save the spreadsheet using the **Save** option from the *File* menu. You should accept the default location for the save as this is handled by the management system.

Step 12 Print the completed spreadsheet.

Step 13 Exit the spreadsheet program.

Step 14 In the Close Options box, select the location where you would like to save your work.

Step 15 Answer the Analyze question from your textbook for this problem.

What-If Analysis

TIP: Always save your work before performing What-If Analysis. It is not necessary to save your work after performing What-If Analysis unless your teacher instructs you to do so. If you are required to save your work after performing What-If Analysis, be sure to rename the spreadsheet to avoid saving over your original work.

If Liabilities are $50,000, Owner's Equity is $39,250, Withdrawals are $1,176, Revenue is $15,802, and Expenses are $11,660, what are Assets?

TIP: Use row 11 of the spreadsheet template to answer this question. Enter the amounts for Liabilities, Owner's Equity, Withdrawals, Revenue, and Expenses. Note that the amount for Assets is automatically computed for you! This is because cell B11 contains a *formula* that automatically calculates the missing amount. Formulas are very useful in spreadsheets, saving time and improving accuracy.

Working Papers *for End-of-Chapter Problems*

Problem 5-3   Identifying Increases and Decreases in Accounts

1. a. _____

_____

b. _____

_____

2. a. _____

_____

b. _____

_____

3. a. _____

_____

b. _____

_____

Analyze: _____

Problem 5-4   Using T Accounts to Analyze Transactions

1.

2.

3.

4.

Analyze: _____

Problem 5-5   Analyzing Transactions into Debit and Credit Parts

Problem 5-5   (concluded)

Analyze: _____

Problem 5-6   Analyzing Transactions into Debit and Credit Parts
(1), (2), (3)

Problem 5-6 (concluded)

```
          |
          |
          |
          |
          |
          |
```

(4)

Account Name	Debit Balances	Credit Balances
_____	$ _____	$ _____
_____	_____	_____
_____	_____	_____
_____	_____	_____
_____	_____	_____
_____	_____	_____
_____	_____	_____
_____	_____	_____
_____	_____	_____
Totals	$ _____	$ _____

Analyze: _____

_____

Problem 5-7 Analyzing Transactions

```
          |                    |                    |
          |                    |                    |
          |                    |                    |
          |                    |                    |
          |                    |                    |
          |                    |                    |
```

Problem 5-7   (continued)

Problem 5-7   (concluded)

(4)

Account Name	Debit Balances	Credit Balances
_____	$ _____	$ _____
_____	_____	_____
_____	_____	_____
_____	_____	_____
_____	_____	_____
_____	_____	_____
_____	_____	_____
_____	_____	_____
_____	_____	_____
_____	_____	_____
_____	_____	_____
_____	_____	_____
Totals	$ _____	$ _____

Analyze: _____

Problem 5-8   Completing the Accounting Equation

	Assets	=	Liabilities	+	Owner's Equity	–	Withdrawals	+	Revenue	–	Expenses
1.	$64,400		$ 8,200		$56,300		$ 500		$10,000		$ 9,600
2.	22,150		525		18,800		1,200		12,100		_____
3.	17,500		75		21,650		_____		4,115		3,250
4.	49,450		_____		47,840		1,500		20,300		17,610
5.	21,900		1,150		20,005		950		_____		16,570
6.	72,640		2,790		_____		10,750		67,908		39,749
7.	_____		1,988		41,194		6,196		52,210		42,597
8.	_____		3,840		61,774		_____		40,163		21,637

(Expenses plus withdrawals equal $27,749.)

	Assets	=	Liabilities	+	Owner's Equity	–	Withdrawals	+	Revenue	–	Expenses
9.	64,070		_____		49,102		4,875		53,166		_____

(Total owner's equity after adding revenue and subtracting expenses and withdrawals is $50,643.)

Analyze: _____

_____

CHAPTER 5 — Transactions That Affect Revenue, Expenses, and Withdrawals

Self-Test

Part A   True or False

Directions: *Circle the letter* T *in the Answer column if the statement is true; circle the letter* F *if the statement is false.*

Answer

T   F   **1.** The normal balance side for a revenue account is the debit side.

T   F   **2.** "Credit" means the increase side of an account.

T   F   **3.** A credit to an expense account decreases the account balance.

T   F   **4.** Withdrawals are increased on the debit side.

T   F   **5.** Revenue is increased on the credit side.

T   F   **6.** Expenses are decreased on the credit side.

T   F   **7.** The basic accounting equation may be expressed as $A = L + OE$.

T   F   **8.** The left side of a T account is always the debit side.

T   F   **9.** You may have two debits and one credit as long as the amounts are equal.

T   F   **10.** A debit to an expense account and a credit to a capital account will result in the basic accounting equation being out of balance.

T   F   **11.** Capital is always increased by credits.

T   F   **12.** Debits decrease the withdrawals account.

Part B   Identify the Normal Balance

Directions: *For each T account below, indicate with an (N) the normal balance side. The first account has been completed as an example.*

Cash in Bank		Accounts Payable		Jones, Capital	
Debit	Credit	Debit	Credit	Debit	Credit
(N)					

Rent Expense		Fees Revenue		Jones, Withdrawals	
Debit	Credit	Debit	Credit	Debit	Credit

Part C   Complete the T Account

Directions: *Analyze the transactions below and enter them in the T accounts provided.*

1. Ms. Adams invested $12,000 cash in the business.
2. Bought office equipment for cash, $1,000.
3. Bought a computer on account, $3,000.

Cash in Bank		Office Equipment		Computer Equipment	

Accounts Payable		Adams, Capital	

CHAPTER  Recording Transactions in a General Journal

Study Plan

Check Your Understanding

Section 1	*Read Section 1 on pages 122–124 and complete the following exercises on page 125.*
	❏ Thinking Critically
	❏ Communicating Accounting
	❏ Problem 6-1 *Analyzing a Source Document*
Section 2	*Read Section 2 on pages 126–139 and complete the following exercises on page 140.*
	❏ Thinking Critically
	❏ Computing in the Business World
	❏ Problem 6-2 *Recording Business Transactions*
	❏ Problem 6-3 *Analyzing Transactions*
Summary	*Review the Chapter 6 Summary on page 141 in your textbook.*
	❏ Key Concepts
Review and Activities	*Complete the following questions and exercises on pages 142–143 in your textbook.*
	❏ Using Key Terms
	❏ Understanding Accounting Concepts and Procedures
	❏ Case Study
	❏ Conducting an Audit with Alex
	❏ Internet Connection
	❏ Workplace Skills
Computerized Accounting	*Read the Computerized Accounting information on page 144 in your textbook.*
	❏ *Making the Transition from a Manual to a Computerized System*
	❏ *Entering Transactions in Peachtree*
Problems	*Complete the following end-of-chapter problems for Chapter 6 in your textbook.*
	❏ Problem 6-4 *Recording General Journal Transactions*
	❏ Problem 6-5 *Recording General Journal Transactions*
	❏ Problem 6-6 *Recording General Journal Transactions*
	❏ Problem 6-7 *Recording General Journal Transactions*
Challenge Problem	❏ Problem 6-8 *Recording General Journal Transactions*
Chapter Reviews and Working Papers	*Complete the following exercises for Chapter 6 in your Chapter Reviews and Working Papers.*
	❏ Chapter Review
	❏ Self-Test

CHAPTER **6** REVIEW — Recording Transactions in a General Journal

Part 1   Accounting Vocabulary (12 points)

Directions: *Using terms from the following list, complete the sentences below. Write the letter of the term you have chosen in the space provided.*

A. accounting cycle	**D.** general journal	**H.** manual accounting system
B. check stub	**E.** invoice	**I.** memorandum
C. computerized accounting system	**F.** journal	**J.** receipt
	G. journalizing	**K.** source document

_____C_____ **0.** A system in which information is recorded by entering it into a computer is called a(n) _____.

_____ **1.** The source document for recording a cash payment transaction is a(n) _____.

_____ **2.** The business document prepared when cash is received is a(n) _____.

_____ **3.** A business paper that verifies that a transaction actually occurred is a(n) _____.

_____ **4.** A(n) _____ is the source document that shows the date of a business transaction, the items purchased, the quantity of each item, and the cost of each item.

_____ **5.** A sequence of business activities completed throughout a fiscal period to keep accounting records in an orderly fashion is the _____.

_____ **6.** A chronological record of business transactions is a(n) _____.

_____ **7.** Recording business information by hand is done in a(n) _____.

_____ **8.** The process of recording business transactions in a journal is called _____.

_____ **9.** A brief message written to describe a transaction that takes place within a business is a(n) _____.

_____ **10.** An all-purpose journal in which all transactions of a business may be recorded is the _____.

Part 2   The Accounting Cycle (8 points)

Directions: *Shown below are the nine steps in the accounting cycle. Rearrange these activities in the order in which they would be completed by a business in its accounting period.*

_____3_____ **0.** Record the debit and credit parts of each business transaction in a journal.

_____ **1.** Prepare a work sheet to summarize the financial information for the accounting period.

_____ **2.** Record and post the closing entries.

_____ **3.** Post each journal entry to the ledger accounts.

_____ **4.** Collect source documents and verify the financial information.

_____ **5.** Analyze business transactions into their debit and credit parts.

_____ **6.** Prepare a trial balance.

_____ **7.** Prepare a post-closing trial balance.

_____ **8.** Prepare the financial statements.

Part 3   The General Journal (5 points)

Directions: *The following list contains the steps for journalizing business transactions. In the general journal on the next page, show where each step is recorded by writing the identifying letter.*

A. The amount of the credit	**D.** The amount of the debit
B. Source document reference or an explanation	**E.** The date of the transaction
C. The name of the account credited	**F.** The name of the account debited

Total Points 85 · Student's Score

GENERAL JOURNAL   PAGE _____

	DATE	DESCRIPTION	POST. REF.	DEBIT	CREDIT	
1						1
2						2
3						3

Part 4   Analyzing the Effects of Transactions on Accounts (60 points)

Directions: *Sally Silva, who owns and operates Sally's Salon, uses the following accounts.*

Cash in Bank	Accts. Pay.—A Touch of Class	Fees
Accts. Rec.—Donna Deluca	Accts. Pay.—Town News	Advertising Expense
Beauty Supplies	Sally Silva, Capital	Rent Expense
Shop Equipment	Sally Silva, Withdrawals	Utilities Expense

Use the form below to analyze each of the following transactions. For each debit and credit, write the account name, its classification (A, L, OE, R, or E), and whether the account is increased (+) or decreased (–).

0. Sally Silva purchased $100 in beauty supplies for cash, Check 201.
1. Received $50 for services rendered, Receipt 15.
2. Bought a $75 ad on account from Town News, Invoice 601.
3. As a personal favor, sold $20 in beauty supplies on account to Donna Deluca, Invoice 10.
4. Wrote Check 202 for $500 to pay the monthly rent.
5. Sally Silva transferred shop equipment valued at $350 into the business, Memorandum 20.
6. Received a check for $20 from Donna Deluca in payment of her account, Receipt 16.
7. Issued Check 203 for $75 to Town News to apply on account.
8. Purchased $150 in beauty supplies on account from A Touch of Class, Invoice 405.
9. Sally Silva withdrew $125 cash for personal use, Check 204.
10. Issued Check 205 to pay the $85 electric bill.

Trans. No.	Account Name Debited	Classification	+ or –	Account Name Credited	Classification	+ or –
0	*Beauty Supplies*	*A*	+	*Cash in Bank*	*A*	–
1						
2						
3						
4						
5						
6						
7						
8						
9						
10						

Working Papers *for Section Problems*

Problem 6-1   Analyzing a Source Document

1. _____
2. _____
3. _____
4. _____
5. _____
6. _____
7. _____

Problem 6-2   Recording Business Transactions

Step 1 _____
Step 2 _____
Step 3 _____
Step 4 _____
Step 5 _____
Step 6 _____

Problem 6-3   Analyzing Transactions

Trans.	Account	Account Classification	Account Increase	Account Decrease	General Journal Debit	General Journal Credit
1	Passenger Van	Asset	✓		✓	
	Cash in Bank	Asset		✓		✓

Computerized Accounting Using Peachtree

Software Objectives

When you have completed this chapter, you will be able to use Peachtree to:

1. Record and post a general journal entry.
2. Print a General Journal report.
3. Edit a general journal entry.
4. Print a General Ledger report.
5. Continue a problem from a previous session.

Problem 6-4   Recording General Journal Transactions

Review the accounts and the transactions listed in your textbook for Wilderness Rentals. You will record these transactions using the **General Journal Entry** option in the **Tasks** menu.

INSTRUCTIONS

Beginning a Session

Step 1 Open the Glencoe Accounting: Electronic Learning Center software and click on the **Peachtree Accounting Software and Spreadsheet Applications** icon.

Step 2 Log onto the system by entering your user name and password.

Step 3 From the scrolling list of chapter problems, select the problem set: Wilderness Rentals (Prob. 6-4).

Step 4 If you haven't already done so, follow these steps to rename the company by adding your initials, e.g., Wilderness (Prob. 6-4: XXX).

- Choose **Company Information** from the **Maintain** menu.
- Review the information in the Maintain Company Information window. (See Figure 6-4A.)
- Click in the *Company Name* field.
- Add your initials to the company name.
- Click ✓ Ok to record the new company name.

> ## DO YOU HAVE A QUESTION
>
> **Q.** *Are the steps to enter a general journal transaction using Peachtree similar to the steps that you follow for a manual system?*
>
> **A.** The steps you follow to manually record a general journal entry are very similar to those steps required to record a general journal entry using Peachtree. For both systems, you must enter a transaction date, source document reference, account numbers, and debit/credit amounts. The Peachtree data entry form even looks like a manual journal.

> ## Notes
>
> *Using the **Company Information** option, you can also enter/change a company's address, telephone numbers, tax ID numbers, business form (sole proprietorship, corporation, or partnership), and posting method (real-time or batch).*

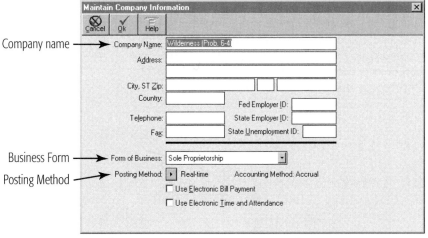

Company name ⟶ Company Name: Wilderness (Prob. 6-4)

Business Form ⟶ Form of Business: Sole Proprietorship

Posting Method ⟶ Posting Method: ▶ Real-time   Accounting Method: Accrual

Figure 6-4A *Maintain Company Information Window*

Step 5 Set the system date to January 31, 2004.

- Click the *Options* menu and choose **Change System Date**.
- Type **1/31/04**.
- Click **OK** to record the new system date.

Completing the Accounting Problem

The instructions in this section explain how to enter and post general journal transactions using the Peachtree software.

Step 6 Review the transactions for Wilderness Rentals shown in your textbook.

Step 7 Enter the transaction for January 1.

> *January 1, Wrote Check 310 for the part-time secretary's salary, $270.*

To enter the general journal transaction:

- Choose **General Journal Entry** from the *Tasks* menu to display the General Journal Entry window.
- Type **1/1/04** and press the **TAB** key to record the transaction date in the *Date* field.

  Make sure that Peachtree shows 2004 for the year. If not, close the window without recording the transaction and change the system date as outlined in the *Beginning a Session* instructions.

TIP: You can save time by entering just the day in a date field. Peachtree will automatically show the full date (e.g., Jan. 1, 2004).

- Type **Check 310** in the *Reference* field and then press **TAB** to move to the next field.
- Enter **520** in the first *Account No.* field and press **TAB** to record the account number for **Salaries Expense**.

  As you type an account number, Peachtree displays a list of the general ledger accounts and highlights the first account that matches what you have entered. This feature is helpful if you do not know an account number. For example, what if you did not know the **Salaries Expense** account number? You do know, however, that this account is an expense account and that expense accounts begin with the digit **5**. When you type a **5**, Peachtree highlights the first account that begins this digit. From this point, you can scroll through the list to locate the account you need. **Note:** This feature may be disabled if your teacher changed the Peachtree preferences.

- Type **Part-time secretary's salary** for the description.

  Every time you type or enter information in a field, you must press **TAB** or **ENTER** to record the information. You can also use these keys to move from field to field. Press **SHIFT+TAB** to move backwards.

Notes

Changing the system date in Peachtree does not affect the clock settings for your computer.

- Type **270.00** in the *Debit* field to record the debit to **Salaries Expense**.

TIP: Unless your teacher changed the default Peachtree settings, you must include the decimal point when you enter an amount. If you type 270 without the period, the program will automatically format the amount to $2.70.

- Press **TAB** to move to the *Account No.* field on the next line.
- Click 🔍 to display a Lookup list that shows the general ledger account numbers.
- Use the arrow keys or the mouse to highlight **101 Cash in Bank**.

  Click [Ok] or press **ENTER** to select this account.

- Type **Part-time secretary's salary** for the description for this part of the transaction, too.
- Move to the *Credit* field and enter **270.00**.
- Verify that the *Out of Balance* amount shows 0.00. If it does not, check the transaction amounts.
- Proof the information you just recorded. Check the account numbers, descriptions, and amounts. If you notice a mistake, move to that field and make the correction. Compare the information on your screen to the completed transaction shown in Figure 6-4B.

Notes

You do not have to enter information in the Job *field. It is used to link a transaction to a specific job or project.*

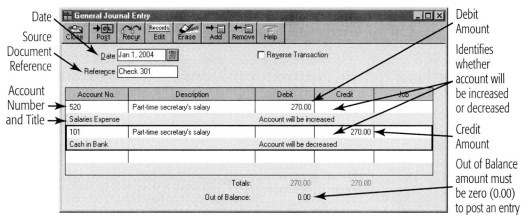

Figure 6-4B *Completed General Journal Entry (January 1, Check 301)*

- Click [Post] to post the transaction.

   When you post a general journal transaction, the Peachtree software automatically updates the general ledger accounts.

Step 8 Enter the remaining transactions for the month.

> **IMPORTANT:** If you realize that you made a mistake after you have posted an entry, make a note to correct the entry after you record all of the transactions. Instructions to edit a general journal entry are provided in the next section.

> For each transaction:

> —Enter the date. Use the year 2004.
> —Enter the source document reference.
> —Enter the number of the account debited.
> —Enter a description.
> —Enter the amount of the debit.
> —Enter the number of the account credited.
> —Enter a description.
> —Enter the amount of the credit.
> —Verify that the *Out of Balance* total is 0.00.
> —Proof your work.
> —Post the entry.

Step 9 Click [Close] to close the General Journal Entry window.

Preparing a Report and Proofing Your Work

After you enter the transactions, the next step is to print a report and proof your work. This section explains how to print a General Journal report. You will also learn how to edit a general journal entry.

Step 10 Print a General Journal report.

> *To print a General Journal report:*

> • Choose **General Ledger** from the **Reports** menu to display the Select a Report window. (See Figure 6-4C.)

TIP: As an alternative, you can click the [General Ledger] navigation aid and then choose the General Journal report to go directly to the report.

> • Select General Journal in the report list.

> • Click [Screen] and then click **OK** to display the General Journal report.

> • Review the report as shown in Figure 6-5D and then click [Print] to print the report.

> • Click [Close] to close the report window.

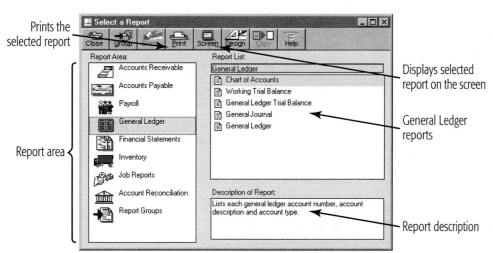

Figure 6-4C *Select a Report Window with the General Ledger Reports*

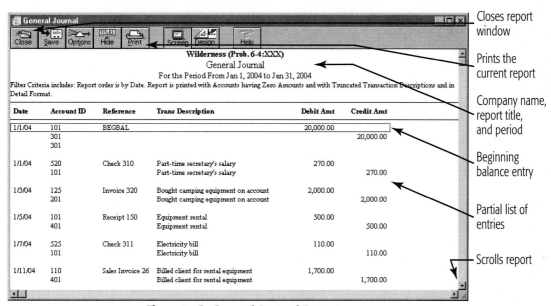

Figure 6-4D *General Journal Report*

Step 11 Proof the information shown on the report.

Find the beginning balance (BEGBAL) entry for $20,000 on the General Journal report. This entry was included as part of the problem set file for Wilderness Rentals to record the owner's initial investment. As you complete other problems using the Peachtree software, you may notice other entries with a BEGBAL reference. These entries are used to establish the beginning balances for various general ledger accounts, but will not affect your work.

Step 12 If there are any corrections needed, follow these instructions to edit/delete a transaction.

- Choose **General Journal Entry** from the *Tasks* menu to display the General Journal Entry window.

- Click the Records Edit button to display a list of the general journal entries.

(See Figure 6-4E.)

- Select the transaction that you want to edit/delete and click the **OK** button.
- To edit a transaction, simply make the necessary changes to the date, reference, account numbers, descriptions, and/or amounts. Post the transaction to record the change.
- To delete a transaction, click 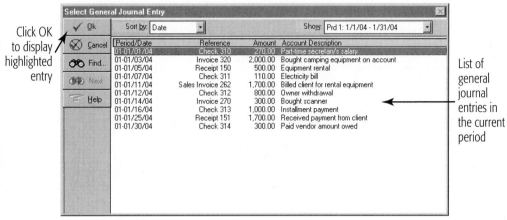 and then confirm that you want to remove the transaction.
- Select another entry to edit or close the General Journal window if you are finished making changes.

Click OK to display highlighted entry

List of general journal entries in the current period

Figure 6-4E *Select General Journal Entry Window*

Step 13 Print a revised General Journal report if you changed or deleted any of the transactions.

Analyzing Your Work

To answer the **Analyze** question, print a General Ledger report.

Step 14 Choose **General Ledger** from the *Reports* menu to display the Select a Report window.

Step 15 Double-click the General Ledger report title to display the report.

Step 16 Locate the **Cash in Bank** account on the General Ledger report. What is the sum of the credits to this account during January?

Ending the Session

Step 17 Click the **Close Problem** button in the Glencoe Smart Guide window and select a save option as directed by your teacher.

Continuing a Problem from a Previous Session

- If you were previously directed to save your work on the network, select the problem from the scrolling menu and click **OK.** The system will retrieve your files from your last session.
- If you were previously directed to save your work on a floppy disk, insert the floppy, select the corresponding problem from the scrolling menu and click **OK.** The system will retrieve your files from the floppy disk.

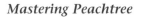

Mastering Peachtree

On a separate sheet of paper, answer the following questions:
How do you enter a beginning balance for a general ledger account? Why would a company need to enter beginning balances?

TIP: Search the help information to learn how to enter beginning balances.

Problem 6-5 Recording General Journal Transactions

Review the accounts and the transactions listed in your textbook for Hot Suds Car Wash. Use the **General Journal Entry** option to record the transactions for the month of January.

INSTRUCTIONS

Beginning a Session

Notes

Refer to Problem 6-4 if you need instructions to begin a session.

Step 1 Open the Glencoe Accounting: Electronic Learning Center software and click on the **Peachtree Accounting Software and Spreadsheet Applications** icon.

Step 2 Log onto the system by entering your user name and password.

Step 3 From the scrolling list of chapter problems, select the problem set: Hot Suds Car Wash (Prob. 6-5).

Step 4 Rename the company by adding your initials, e.g., Hot Suds (Prob. 6-5: XXX).

Step 5 Set the system date to January 31, 2004.

Completing the Accounting Problem

Step 6 Review the transactions shown in your textbook for Hot Suds Car Wash.

Step 7 Record all of the transactions using the **General Journal Entry** option.

TIP: Remember to proof each general journal entry before you post it. Check the account numbers, descriptions, and amounts.

Step 8 Close the General Journal Entry window after you finish recording the transactions.

Preparing a Report and Proofing Your Work

Step 9 Print a General Journal report.

Step 10 Proof your work. Make any corrections as needed and print a revised report, if necessary.

TIP: While viewing a General Journal report, you can double-click on an entry to display it in the General Journal Entry window. You can edit the transaction and then close the window to see an updated report.

Analyzing Your Work

Step 11 Print a General Ledger report.

Step 12 Sum the asset account balances to answer the Analyze question.

Checking Your Work and Ending the Session

Step 13 Click the **Close Problem** button in the Glencoe Smart Guide window.

Step 14 If your teacher has asked you to check your solution, select *Check my answer to this problem.* Review, print, and close the report.

Step 15 Click the **Close Problem** button. In the Close Options box, select the save option as directed by your teacher. Click **OK.**

Mastering Peachtree

On a separate sheet of paper, answer the following questions:
Why does the General Journal Entry form include a *Job* field? How might a company use the information recorded in this field?

Problem 6-6   Recording General Journal Transactions

Review the accounts and the transactions listed in your textbook for Kits & Pups Grooming. Follow the instructions provided to record the transactions for the month of January.

INSTRUCTIONS

Beginning a Session

Step 1 Begin the session and select the problem set for Kits & Pups Grooming (Prob. 6-6).

Step 2 Rename the company and set the system date to January 31, 2004.

> **Notes**
> *Refer to Problem 6-4 if you need instructions to begin a session.*

Completing the Accounting Problem

Step 3 Record all of the transactions.

TIP: Check the Out of Balance and Totals amounts for each entry before you post it.

Step 4 Print a General Journal report.

Step 5 Proof your work. Make any corrections as needed and print a revised report.

Step 6 Answer the Analyze question shown in your textbook.

Ending the Session

Step 7 Click the **Close Problem** button in the Glencoe Smart Guide window and select a save option.

Problem 6-7   Recording General Journal Transactions

Review the accounts and the transactions listed in your textbook for Outback Guide Service. Follow the instructions provided to record the transactions for the month of January.

INSTRUCTIONS

Beginning a Session

Step 1   Begin the session and select the problem set for Outback Guide Service (Prob. 6-7).

Step 2   Rename the company and set the system date to January 31, 2004.

Completing the Accounting Problem

Step 3   Record all of the transactions.

The General Journal Entry window can accommodate multi-part transactions such as the January 1 transaction, which includes five parts—four debits and one credit. (See Figure 6-7A.)

What should you do if you accidentally omit a part of a multi-part entry? First, select the line just below where you want to insert the omitted part of the entry. Next, click to insert a blank line in the entry and then enter the missing part.

If you type a line in an entry twice, highlight the occurrence you want to delete and click [Remove]. Peachtree removes the line from the entry.

TIP: As a shortcut, press **ALT+S** to post a transaction.

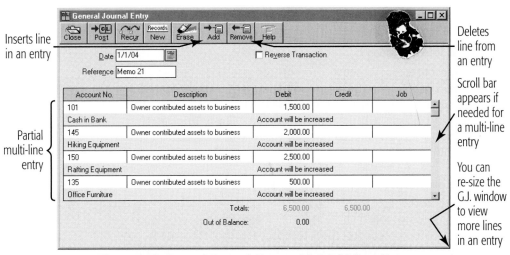

Figure 6-7A *General Journal Entry with Multi-Part Entry*

Step 4   Print a General Journal report.

Step 5   Proof your work. Make any corrections as needed and print a revised report.

If you need to end the session before you finish this problem, refer to the instructions given in Problem 6-4. Steps are also provided to continue a problem at the beginning of the next session.

Step 6   Answer the Analyze question.

Checking Your Work and Ending the Session

Step 7   Click the **Close Problem** button in the Glencoe Smart Guide window.

Step 8   If your teacher has asked you to check your solution, select *Check my answer to this problem*. Review, print, and close the report.

Step 9   Click the **Close Problem** button. From the Close Options box, select the Save Option as directed by your teacher. Click **OK.**

Problem 6-8   Recording General Journal Transactions

Review the accounts and the transactions listed in your textbook for Showbiz Video. Follow the instructions provided to record the transactions for the month of January.

INSTRUCTIONS

Beginning a Session

Step 1   Begin the session and select the problem set for Showbiz Video (Prob. 6-8).

Step 2   Rename the company and set the system date to January 31, 2004.

Completing the Accounting Problem

Step 3   Record all of the transactions.

Step 4   Print a General Journal report.

Step 5   Proof your work. Make any corrections as needed and print a revised report.

Step 6   Answer the Analyze question.

Ending the Session

Step 7   Click the **Close Problem** button and select a save option.

FAQs

How do you correct a general journal entry?

You can edit/delete a general journal entry at any time unless you have closed the current period. To make a change, choose the **General Journal Entry** option. Click the **Edit Records** button and select the entry you want to update. Make the changes and post the corrected transaction. Peachtree automatically applies the corrections. To delete an entry, click the **Erase** button when the transaction is displayed in the General Journal Entry window.

Is there a way to turn off the automatic drop-down lists and the automatic field completion features?

As you type in an account field, Peachtree will show the accounts in a drop-down list and will automatically attempt to complete the field for you. Choose **Global** from the **Options** menu and then change Smart Data Entry options to enable/disable these features.

Working Papers *for End-of-Chapter Problems*

Problem 6-4   Recording General Journal Transactions

GENERAL JOURNAL   PAGE _____

	DATE	DESCRIPTION	POST. REF.	DEBIT	CREDIT	
1						1
2						2
3						3
4						4
5						5
6						6
7						7
8						8
9						9
10						10
11						11
12						12
13						13
14						14
15						15
16						16
17						17
18						18
19						19
20						20
21						21
22						22
23						23
24						24
25						25
26						26
27						27
28						28
29						29
30						30
31						31
32						32
33						33

Analyze: _____

Problem 6-5   Recording General Journal Transactions

GENERAL JOURNAL   PAGE _____

	DATE	DESCRIPTION	POST. REF.	DEBIT	CREDIT	
1						1
2						2
3						3
4						4
5						5
6						6
7						7
8						8
9						9
10						10
11						11
12						12
13						13
14						14
15						15
16						16
17						17
18						18
19						19
20						20
21						21
22						22
23						23
24						24
25						25
26						26
27						27
28						28
29						29
30						30
31						31
32						32
33						33
34						34
35						35
36						36
37						37

Analyze: _____

Problem 6-6   Recording General Journal Transactions

GENERAL JOURNAL   PAGE _____

	DATE	DESCRIPTION	POST. REF.	DEBIT	CREDIT	
1						1
2						2
3						3
4						4
5						5
6						6
7						7
8						8
9						9
10						10
11						11
12						12
13						13
14						14
15						15
16						16
17						17
18						18
19						19
20						20
21						21
22						22
23						23
24						24
25						25
26						26
27						27
28						28
29						29
30						30
31						31
32						32
33						33
34						34
35						35
36						36
37						37

Analyze: _____

Problem 6-7 Recording General Journal Transactions

GENERAL JOURNAL   PAGE _____

	DATE	DESCRIPTION	POST. REF.	DEBIT	CREDIT	
1						1
2						2
3						3
4						4
5						5
6						6
7						7
8						8
9						9
10						10
11						11
12						12
13						13
14						14
15						15
16						16
17						17
18						18
19						19
20						20
21						21
22						22
23						23
24						24
25						25
26						26
27						27
28						28
29						29
30						30
31						31
32						32
33						33
34						34
35						35
36						36
37						37
38						38
39						39

Problem 6-7   (concluded)

Analyze: _____

Problem 6-8   Source Documents

Instructions: *Use the following source documents to record the transactions for this business.*

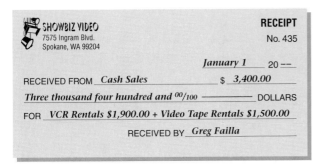

SHOWBIZ VIDEO	RECEIPT
7575 Ingram Blvd.	No. 435
Spokane, WA 99204	

January 1   20 – –

RECEIVED FROM *Cash Sales* $ *3,400.00*

Three thousand four hundred and 00/100 ———— DOLLARS

FOR *VCR Rentals $1,900.00 + Video Tape Rentals $1,500.00*

RECEIVED BY *Greg Failla*

NEW MEDIA SUPPLIERS   **INVOICE NO. NM101**
14308 San Mateo Blvd.
Los Angeles, CA 90016   DATE: *Jan. 7, 20– –*
ORDER NO.:
TO   *Showbiz Video*   SHIPPED BY: *UPS*
     7575 Ingram Blvd.   TERMS: *Balance payable*
     Spokane, WA 99204   *in 30 days*

QTY.	ITEM	UNIT PRICE	TOTAL
8	VCRs -- model ALG45	$ 80.00	$ 640.00
4	13" TV/VCR -- model LX44	100.00	400.00
6	Camcorders -- model GR77	260.00	1,560.00
			$2,600.00
	Less down payment	–	600.00
			$2,000.00

$ *325.00*	No. 1250

Date *January 3*   20 – –
To *Washington Repairs & Service*
For *Equipment repairs*

	Dollars	Cents
Balance brought forward	11,310	00
Add deposits *6/1*	3,400	00
Total	14,710	00
Less this check	325	00
Balance carried forward	14,385	00

SHOWBIZ VIDEO	INVOICE NO. 1650
7575 Ingram Blvd.	
Spokane, WA 99204	DATE: *Jan. 10, 20– –*

ORDER NO.:
    Spring Branch School District   SHIPPED BY: *Katie's Kouriers*
TO   *2023 Sampson Drive*   TERMS: *Payable in 30 days*
    Spokane, WA 99204

QTY.	ITEM	UNIT PRICE	TOTAL
18	*Video rental -- History & Government series*	$100.00	$1,800.00

Palace Films   **INVOICE NO. PF32**
606 Lei Min Street
San Francisco, CA 94133   DATE: *Jan. 5, 20– –*
ORDER NO.:
    Showbiz Video   SHIPPED BY: *Freight Systems*
TO   *7575 Ingram Blvd.*   TERMS: *Payable in 30 days*
    Spokane, WA 99204

QTY.	ITEM	UNIT PRICE	TOTAL
40	Videos X117–X205	$ 8.50	$340.00
4	Videos VV27–VW29	15.00	60.00
			$400.00

$ *750.00*	No. 1252

Date *January 12*   20 – –
To *Computer Horizons*
For *On account*

	Dollars	Cents
Balance brought forward	13,785	00
Add deposits		
Total	13,785	00
Less this check	750	00
Balance carried forward	13,035	00

$ *600.00*	No. 1251

Date *January 7*   20 – –
To *New Media Suppliers*
For *Down payment on account*

	Dollars	Cents
Balance brought forward	14,385	00
Add deposits		
Total	14,385	00
Less this check	600	00
Balance carried forward	13,785	00

SHOWBIZ VIDEO	RECEIPT
7575 Ingram Blvd.	No. 436
Spokane, WA 99204	

January 15   20 – –

RECEIVED FROM *Cash Sales* $ *5,600.00*

Five thousand six hundred and 00/100 ———— DOLLARS

FOR *VCR Rentals $4,400.00 + Video Tape Rentals $1,200.00*

RECEIVED BY *Greg Failla*

Problem 6-8   (continued)

$ 100.00		No. 1253
Date January 18		20 --
To Clear Vue Window Cleaners		
For Maintenance		

	Dollars	Cents
Balance brought forward	13,035	00
Add deposits 1/15	5,600	00
Total	18,635	00
Less this check	100	00
Balance carried forward	18,535	00

$ 1,000.00		No. 1254
Date January 25		20 --
To New Media Suppliers		
For On account		

	Dollars	Cents
Balance brought forward	18,535	00
Add deposits		
Total	18,535	00
Less this check	1,000	00
Balance carried forward	17,535	00

Problem 6-8   Recording General Journal Transactions

GENERAL JOURNAL   PAGE _____

DATE	DESCRIPTION	POST. REF.	DEBIT	CREDIT	
					1
					2
					3
					4
					5
					6
					7
					8
					9
					10
					11
					12
					13
					14
					15
					16
					17
					18
					19
					20
					21
					22
					23
					24
					25
					26
					27
					28
					29
					30
					31
					32
					33
					34

Analyze: _____

_____

Notes

CHAPTER 6   Recording Transactions in a General Journal

Self-Test

Part A   True or False

Directions: *Circle the letter* T *in the Answer column if the statement is true; circle the letter* F *if the statement is false.*

Answer

T   F   **1.** A fiscal year is an accounting period that begins on January 1 and ends on December 31.

T   F   **2.** When recording a business transaction, the amount is always entered first because it is the most important part of the journal entry.

T   F   **3.** A source document is a business paper that proves a transaction occurred.

T   F   **4.** A journal is sometimes called a "book" of original entry because it is the only place in which the details of the transaction are recorded.

T   F   **5.** A check was written on April 15. It is being recorded today, April 17. The date used for recording the transaction is April 17.

T   F   **6.** The analysis of a business transaction into its debit and credit parts is required for both manual and computerized accounting systems.

T   F   **7.** The different kinds of source documents a business uses depends on the nature of the transaction.

T   F   **8.** If an error is discovered before posting occurs, simply draw a line through the incorrect item and write the correct item above it.

T   F   **9.** The debit part of a business transaction should be indented one-half inch from the left edge of the paper.

T   F   **10.** The accounting cycle is a series of activities a business completes over a period of time.

Part B   Multiple Choice

Directions: *Choose the letter of the correct answer and write it in the space provided.*

Answer

_____   **1.** Most businesses use an accounting period of:
                    (A) one month
                    (B) three months
                    (C) six months
                    (D) twelve months

_____   **2.** A form listing specific information about a business transaction that involves the buying and selling of goods is a:
                    (A) check
                    (B) invoice
                    (C) memorandum
                    (D) receipt

_____   **3.** Which of the following is a calendar year accounting period?
                    (A) Jan. 1–Dec. 31
                    (B) Feb. 1–Jan. 31
                    (C) July 1–June 30
                    (D) April 15–March 31

_____   **4.** Which source document is used within the business?
                    (A) check
                    (B) invoice
                    (C) memorandum
                    (D) receipt

_____   **5.** Which of the following is entered with each transaction?
                    (A) date
                    (B) debit account title and amount
                    (C) credit account title and amount
                    (D) source document or explanation
                    (E) all of the above

CHAPTER 7   Posting Journal Entries to General Ledger Accounts

Study Plan

Check Your Understanding

Section 1	*Read Section 1 on pages 152–155 and complete the following exercises on page 156.*
	❏ Thinking Critically
	❏ Communicating Accounting
	❏ Problem 7-1 *Opening Ledger Accounts*
Section 2	*Read Section 2 on pages 157–163 and complete the following exercises on page 164.*
	❏ Thinking Critically
	❏ Analyzing Accounting
	❏ Problem 7-2 *Posting from the General Journal to the Ledger*
Section 3	*Read Section 3 on pages 166–169 and complete the following exercises on page 170.*
	❏ Thinking Critically
	❏ Computing in the Business World
	❏ Problem 7-3 *Analyzing a Source Document*
	❏ Problem 7-4 *Recording and Posting a Correcting Entry*

Summary	*Review the Chapter 7 Summary on page 171 in your textbook.*
	❏ Key Concepts
Review and Activities	*Complete the following questions and exercises on pages 172–173 in your textbook.*
	❏ Using Key Terms
	❏ Understanding Accounting Concepts and Procedures
	❏ Case Study
	❏ Conducting an Audit with Alex
	❏ Internet Connection
	❏ Workplace Skills
Computerized Accounting	*Read the Computerized Accounting information on page 174 in your textbook.*
	❏ *Making the Transition from a Manual to a Computerized System*
	❏ *Posting to the General Ledger in Peachtree*
Problems	*Complete the following end-of-chapter problems for Chapter 7 in your textbook.*
	❏ Problem 7-5 *Posting General Journal Transactions*
	❏ Problem 7-6 *Preparing a Trial Balance*
	❏ Problem 7-7 *Journalizing and Posting Business Transactions*
	❏ Problem 7-8 *Journalizing and Posting Business Transactions*
Challenge Problem	❏ Problem 7-9 *Recording and Posting Correcting Entries*
Chapter Reviews and Working Papers	*Complete the following exercises for Chapter 7 in your Chapter Reviews and Working Papers.*
	❏ Chapter Review
	❏ Self-Test

CHAPTER 7 REVIEW — Posting Journal Entries to General Ledger Accounts

Part 1   Accounting Vocabulary (7 points)

Total Points	57
Student's Score	

Directions: *Using terms from the following list, complete the sentences below. Write the letter of the term you have chosen in the space provided.*

A. correcting entry	C. ledger account form	E. proving the ledger	G. transposition error
B. ledger	D. posting	F. slide	H. trial balance

_____A_____ **0.** A _____ must be made when an error in a journal entry is discovered after posting.

_____ **1.** Adding all the debit balances and all the credit balances of accounts in the ledger to determine whether the two totals are equal is called _____.

_____ **2.** A _____ results when two numbers are accidentally reversed.

_____ **3.** The process of transferring the information in a journal entry to an individual account is called _____.

_____ **4.** A _____ is the accounting stationery used to record financial information about specific accounts.

_____ **5.** A _____ is a proof of the equality of total debits and total credits.

_____ **6.** When an amount such as $90 is written as $900, a _____ error has occurred.

_____ **7.** A _____ is a book or file that contains the pages or cards for the accounts used by a business.

Part 2   The Posting Process (12 points)

Directions: *Read each of the following statements to determine whether the statement is true or false. Write your answer in the space provided.*

____True____ **0.** Posting to the ledger is the fourth step in the accounting cycle.

_____ **1.** The accounts of a business are kept in a special book called a ledger.

_____ **2.** You can easily see the increases and decreases taking place in the accounts of a business by looking at the general journal entries.

_____ **3.** Errors discovered after posting has occurred should be corrected by drawing a line through the incorrect item and writing the correction directly above.

_____ **4.** An account may be opened by writing the account title and account number on the account form.

_____ **5.** All businesses do their posting daily.

_____ **6.** A trial balance is prepared before posting.

_____ **7.** To avoid forgetting a step in the posting process, always post from right to left.

_____ **8.** The first step in posting is to write the date of the journal entry in the Date column of the account debited.

_____ **9.** A dash across the debit balance column shows that an asset account has a zero balance.

_____ **10.** Every journal entry requires a posting to at least three ledger accounts.

_____ **11.** The purpose of a trial balance is to prove the equality of the ledger.

_____ **12.** If the trial balance is not in agreement, an error has been made in either journalizing or posting.

Part 3 Determining Account Balances (24 points)

Directions: 1. *Open the ledger account by writing the account title and account number, 105.*
2. *Record the account balance of $450 as of June 1 of the current year.*
3. *Assume the following transactions have been recorded on page 1 of the general journal. The transactions that follow affect the account, Accounts Receivable—Amy Anderson. Post these transactions to the account of Amy Anderson.*

Date Transaction

June 2 Received $200 from Amy Anderson on account.
5 Completed services for Amy Anderson and billed her $70.
21 Received a check for $320 from Amy Anderson to apply to her account.
29 Sent Invoice 417 to Amy Anderson for services completed, $90.

GENERAL LEDGER

ACCOUNT _____ ACCOUNT NO. _____

DATE	DESCRIPTION	POST. REF.	DEBIT	CREDIT	BALANCE DEBIT	BALANCE CREDIT

Part 4 Correcting Errors (14 points)

Directions: *Several errors are described below. Use the form below. For each error:*
1. *Determine whether the error will affect the totals of the trial balance.*
2. *Indicate whether the error requires a correcting entry.*
The first item has been completed for you as an example.

Errors:

0. A $50 debit was not posted to the Office Supplies account.
1. A $200 purchase of store equipment was journalized and posted to Store Supplies.
2. A $30 job completed for Sarah James was recorded and posted to James Scott's account.
3. A $500 check received as payment for services was journalized and posted to the capital account.
4. A $69 debit to the withdrawals account was posted as $96.
5. A $100 debit to Cash in Bank was posted as $10.
6. After posting a $75 credit to a creditor's account, the account balance was incorrectly calculated.
7. A $25 debit to the Store Supplies account was posted as a credit.

Error	Does Error Affect Trial Balance?	Correcting Entry Required?	Error	Does Error Affect Trial Balance?	Correcting Entry Required?
0	Yes	No	4		
1			5		
2			6		
3			7		

Working Papers _for Section Problems_

Problem 7-1   Opening Ledger Accounts

GENERAL LEDGER

ACCOUNT _____ ACCOUNT NO. _____

DATE	DESCRIPTION	POST. REF.	DEBIT	CREDIT	BALANCE	
					DEBIT	CREDIT

ACCOUNT _____ ACCOUNT NO. _____

DATE	DESCRIPTION	POST. REF.	DEBIT	CREDIT	BALANCE	
					DEBIT	CREDIT

ACCOUNT _____ ACCOUNT NO. _____

DATE	DESCRIPTION	POST. REF.	DEBIT	CREDIT	BALANCE	
					DEBIT	CREDIT

ACCOUNT _____ ACCOUNT NO. _____

DATE	DESCRIPTION	POST. REF.	DEBIT	CREDIT	BALANCE	
					DEBIT	CREDIT

ACCOUNT _____ ACCOUNT NO. _____

DATE	DESCRIPTION	POST. REF.	DEBIT	CREDIT	BALANCE	
					DEBIT	CREDIT

Problem 7-2   Posting from the General Journal to the Ledger

GENERAL JOURNAL   PAGE ___1___

	DATE		DESCRIPTION	POST. REF.	DEBIT	CREDIT	
1	20--						1
2	May	1	Cash in Bank		1000000		2
3			David Serlo, Capital			1000000	3
4			Memorandum 101				4
5							5
6							6
7							7

GENERAL LEDGER (PARTIAL)

ACCOUNT ___Cash in Bank___   ACCOUNT NO. ___101___

DATE	DESCRIPTION	POST. REF.	DEBIT	CREDIT	BALANCE DEBIT	BALANCE CREDIT

ACCOUNT ___David Serlo, Capital___   ACCOUNT NO. ___301___

DATE	DESCRIPTION	POST. REF.	DEBIT	CREDIT	BALANCE DEBIT	BALANCE CREDIT

Problem 7-3   Analyzing a Source Document

FUNTIME
AMUSEMENT ARCADE   **MEMORANDUM 47**

TO: *Accounting Clerk*
FROM: *Dan Vonderhaar*
DATE: *May 20, 20--*
SUBJECT: *Correction of error*

On May 10, we purchased an office copier for $1,500. I noticed in the general journal that the entry was recorded and posted to the Computer Equipment account. Please record the necessary entry to correct this error.

GENERAL JOURNAL   PAGE ___6___

	DATE	DESCRIPTION	POST. REF.	DEBIT	CREDIT	
1	20--					1
2	May 10	Computer Equipment	120	150000		2
3		Cash in Bank	101		150000	3
4		Check 8099				4
5						5
6						6
7						7
8						8
9						9

GENERAL LEDGER (PARTIAL)

ACCOUNT __Office Equipment__   ACCOUNT NO. __115__

DATE	DESCRIPTION	POST. REF.	DEBIT	CREDIT	BALANCE DEBIT	BALANCE CREDIT
20--						
May 1	Balance	✓			70000	

ACCOUNT __Computer Equipment__   ACCOUNT NO. __120__

DATE	DESCRIPTION	POST. REF.	DEBIT	CREDIT	BALANCE DEBIT	BALANCE CREDIT
20--						
May 1	Balance	✓			300000	
10		G6	150000		450000	

Name _____ **Date** _____ **Class** _____

Problem 7-4   Recording and Posting a Correcting Entry

GENERAL JOURNAL   PAGE ___5___

	DATE		DESCRIPTION	POST. REF.	DEBIT	CREDIT	
1	20--						1
2	July	3	Rent Expense	530	30000		2
3			Cash in Bank	101		30000	3
4			Check 1903				4
5							5
6							6
7							7
8							8
9							9

GENERAL LEDGER (PARTIAL)

ACCOUNT _Advertising Expense_   ACCOUNT NO. ___502___

DATE		DESCRIPTION	POST. REF.	DEBIT	CREDIT	BALANCE DEBIT	BALANCE CREDIT
20--							
July	1	Balance	✓			260000	

ACCOUNT _Rent Expense_   ACCOUNT NO. ___530___

DATE		DESCRIPTION	POST. REF.	DEBIT	CREDIT	BALANCE DEBIT	BALANCE CREDIT
20--							
July	1	Balance	✓			1500000	
	3		G5	30000		1530000	

Conducting an Audit with Alex

Palmer's Flying School								
Trial Balance								
Cash in Bank	4	7 0 0	00					
Accounts Receivable	1	6 0 0	00					
Airplanes	90	0 0 0	00					
Accounts Payable					2	6 8 0	00	
Frank Palmer, Capital					68	6 5 0	00	
Frank Palmer, Withdrawals	3	0 0 0	00					
Flying Fees					40	0 0 0	00	
Advertising Expense		1 5 0	00					
Fuel and Oil Expense	5	6 0 0	00					
Repairs Expense	6	2 0 0	00					
Totals								

Computerized Accounting Using Peachtree

Software Objectives

When you have completed this chapter, you will be able to use Peachtree to:

1. Print a General Ledger report.
2. Print a General Ledger Trial Balance report.
3. Make corrections to General Journal entries.

Problem 7-5   Posting General Journal Transactions

INSTRUCTIONS

Beginning a Session

Step 1   Select the problem set: Wilderness Rentals (Prob. 7-5).
Step 2   Rename the company and set the system date to March 31, 2004.

Preparing a Report

Step 3   Print a General Ledger report.
Step 4   Review the information shown on the report.

A partial General Ledger report is shown in Figure 7-5A. As you can see, the General Ledger report is very similar to a General Ledger report you have learned how to prepare manually. One difference, however, is that Peachtree does not show a running balance after each posting. For each line item, Peachtree shows the transaction reference (e.g., Memo 21) and the journal (e.g., GENJ) from which the entry was posted. Unlike a manual General Ledger report, the Peachtree report includes the current period change (debits/credits) for each account.

> ### DO YOU HAVE A QUESTION
>
> **Q.** *Do you have to post general journal transactions to the general ledger?*
>
> **A.** No. Peachtree automatically updates the general ledger accounts every time you record (post) a general journal entry. A separate step to post the transactions is not required.

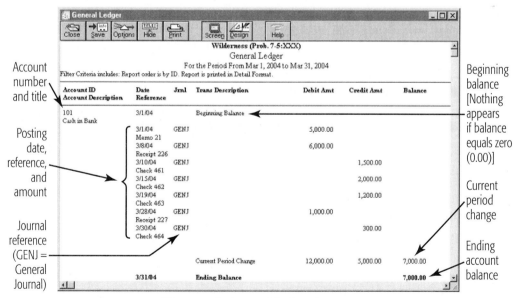

Figure 7-5A *General Ledger Report*

Step 5   Use the General Ledger report to answer the Analyze question shown in your textbook.

> ### Notes
>
> *Credit balances appear as negative amounts on a General Ledger report.*

Ending the Session

When you finish the problem or if you must stop at the end of a class period, follow the instructions given here to end the session.

Step 6 Click the **Close Problem** button in the Glencoe Smart Guide window.

Continuing a Problem from a Previous Session

If you want to continue working on a problem that you did not complete in a previous session, follow step 1 on the previous page. If you saved your work to the network, the management system will retrieve your files from that session. If you saved your work to a floppy, insert the floppy. Your files will be retrieved from the floppy disk.

Mastering Peachtree

How do you print a General Ledger report with summary information only? Record your answer on a separate sheet of paper.

TIP: Explore the help system. Search for information on how to change the options for a General Ledger report.

Problem 7-6   Preparing a Trial Balance

INSTRUCTIONS

Beginning a Session
Step 1 Select the problem set: Hot Suds Car Wash (Prob. 7-6).
Step 2 Rename the company and set the system date to March 31, 2004.

Preparing a Report
Step 3 Print a General Ledger Trial Balance report.
Step 4 Review the information shown on the report.
Step 5 Answer the Analyze question.

Ending the Session
Step 6 Click the **Close Problem** button in the Glencoe Smart Guide window.

Problem 7-7   Journalizing and Posting Business Transactions

INSTRUCTIONS

Beginning a Session
Step 1 Select the problem set: Kits & Pups Grooming (Prob. 7-7).
Step 2 Rename the company and set the system date to March 31, 2004.

Completing the Accounting Problem
Step 3 Record all of the March transactions using the **General Journal Entry** task option.
Step 4 Print a General Journal report and proof your work.

Step 5   Print a General Ledger report summarized by transaction.

Sometimes, you may not need all of the information on a standard (default) report. Summary reports show the critical information, but leave out some of the detailed parts.

To print a summary General Ledger report:

- Choose **General Ledger** from the **Reports** menu.
- Select General Ledger report.
- Click .
- Choose **Summary by Transaction** from the Report Format pop-up menu.
- Click **OK** to print the summary report.

 TIP: While viewing a report, you can click to change the report options.

Notes

Remember that Peachtree may sometimes truncate certain fields on a report depending on the space available.

Step 6   Print a General Ledger Trial Balance report.
Step 7   Answer the Analyze question.

Checking Your Work and Ending the Session

Step 8   Click the **Close Problem** button in the Glencoe Smart Guide window.
Step 9   If your teacher has asked you to check your solution, select *Check my answer to this problem.* Click **OK** and review, print, and close the report on your screen.
Step 10 Click the **Close Problem** button. In the Close Options box, select the save option as directed by your teacher. Click **OK.**

Mastering Peachtree

Answer the following question on a separate sheet of paper:
How do you print a General Ledger report for only one account?

Problem 7-8   Journalizing and Posting Business Transactions

INSTRUCTIONS

Beginning a Session

Step 1   Select the problem set: Outback Guide Service (Prob. 7-8).
Step 2   Rename the company and set the system date to March 31, 2004.

Completing the Accounting Problem

Step 3   Record the March transactions using the **General Journal Entry** task option.
Step 4   Print a General Journal report and proof your work.

 TIP: While viewing a General Journal report, you can double-click on a transaction to display the General Journal Entry window where you can edit that transaction. Posting the correction automatically updates the General Journal report.

Peachtree Guide

Step 5 Print a General Ledger report summarized by transaction.
Step 6 Print a General Ledger Trial Balance.
Step 7 Answer the Analyze question.

Ending the Session

Step 8 Click the **Close Problem** button in the Glencoe Smart Guide window and select a save option.

Mastering Peachtree

Can you customize a report, such as the General Journal report, to make more space for selected fields? Explain your answer on a separate sheet of paper. Also, print a General Journal report so that the information in the *Reference* column is not truncated.

Problem 7-9   Recording and Posting Correcting Entries

INSTRUCTIONS

Beginning a Session

Step 1 Select the problem set: Showbiz Video (Prob. 7-9).
Step 2 Rename the company and set the system date to March 31, 2004.

Completing the Accounting Problem

Step 3 Review the auditor's memo shown in your textbook.
Step 4 Correct the general journal transactions based on the auditor's comments.

Use the **General Journal Entry** option in the *Tasks* menu to display the General Journal Entry window. Click [Records Edit] to display a list of the general journal entries. Select an entry to edit, make your changes, and then post the corrected entry.

IMPORTANT: The posting errors (March 7 and March 19) do not apply when you complete this problem with Peachtree. These errors noted in the auditor's memo deal with errors in the posting process to the general ledger. Since Peachtree automatically posts entries, these errors are not applicable.

Step 5 Print a General Journal report and proof your work.
Step 6 Print a General Ledger report.
Step 7 Answer the Analyze question.

Checking Your Work and Ending the Session

Step 8 Click the **Close Problem** button in the Glencoe Smart Guide window.
Step 9 If your teacher has asked you to check your solution, select *Check my answer to this problem*. Review, print, and close the report on your screen.
Step 10 Click the **Close Problem** button. Select the save option as directed by your teacher. Click **OK**.

Mastering Peachtree

Does Peachtree include any features that let you keep track of daily tasks—pay a vendor, place an ad in the local newspaper, or contact a client? On a separate sheet of paper, explain your answer.

> **Notes**
>
> *If you change the default settings for a report, such as the General Ledger report, Peachtree may not allow you to double-click an entry to edit it.*

DO YOU HAVE A QUESTION

Q. *What is the best method to make a correction to a general journal entry?*

A. In a manual system, you were taught how to make a correcting entry to correct a general journal entry error. Using Peachtree, you can make a correcting entry or you can edit an entry to correct it. Although changing an entry is often easier and faster than making a new entry, you will not have an audit trail that shows any corrections you may have made. Unless your teacher instructs you to make correcting entries, follow the instructions in this workbook to edit an entry if you identify a mistake.

Working Papers *for End-of-Chapter Problems*

Problem 7-5 Posting General Journal Transactions

GENERAL JOURNAL   PAGE ___*1*___

	DATE		DESCRIPTION	POST. REF.	DEBIT	CREDIT	
1	20--						1
2	Mar.	1	Cash in Bank		500000		2
3			Ronald Hicks, Capital			500000	3
4			Memorandum 21				4
5		3	Office Equipment		300000		5
6			Accts. Pay.—Digital Tech Computers			300000	6
7			Invoice 500				7
8		4	Camping Equipment		250000		8
9			Accts. Pay.—Adventure Equip.			250000	9
10			Invoice 318				10
11		6	Office Equipment		10000		11
12			Ronald Hicks, Capital			10000	12
13			Memorandum 22				13
14		8	Cash in Bank		600000		14
15			Equipment Rental Revenue			600000	15
16			Receipt 226				16
17		10	Accts. Pay.—Digital Tech Computers		150000		17
18			Cash in Bank			150000	18
19			Check 461				19
20		12	Accts. Rec.—Helen Katz		100000		20
21			Equipment Rental Revenue			100000	21
22			Sales Invoice 354				22
23		15	Ronald Hicks, Withdrawals		200000		23
24			Cash in Bank			200000	24
25			Check 462				25
26		19	Accts. Pay.—Adventure Equip.		120000		26
27			Cash in Bank			120000	27
28			Check 463				28
29		28	Cash in Bank		100000		29
30			Accts. Rec.—Helen Katz			100000	30
31			Receipt 227				31
32		29	Accts. Rec.—Polk and Co.		240000		32
33			Equipment Rental Revenue			240000	33
34			Sales Invoice 355				34
35		30	Advertising Expense		30000		35
36			Cash in Bank			30000	36
37			Check 464				37

Problem 7-5 (continued)

GENERAL LEDGER

ACCOUNT __*Cash in Bank*_____ ACCOUNT NO. ___101___

DATE	DESCRIPTION	POST. REF.	DEBIT	CREDIT	BALANCE	
					DEBIT	CREDIT

ACCOUNT __*Accounts Receivable—Helen Katz*_____ ACCOUNT NO. ___105___

DATE	DESCRIPTION	POST. REF.	DEBIT	CREDIT	BALANCE	
					DEBIT	CREDIT

ACCOUNT __*Accounts Receivable—Polk and Co.*_____ ACCOUNT NO. ___110___

DATE	DESCRIPTION	POST. REF.	DEBIT	CREDIT	BALANCE	
					DEBIT	CREDIT

ACCOUNT __*Office Equipment*_____ ACCOUNT NO. ___120___

DATE	DESCRIPTION	POST. REF.	DEBIT	CREDIT	BALANCE	
					DEBIT	CREDIT

ACCOUNT __*Camping Equipment*_____ ACCOUNT NO. ___125___

DATE	DESCRIPTION	POST. REF.	DEBIT	CREDIT	BALANCE	
					DEBIT	CREDIT

Problem 7-5   (concluded)

ACCOUNT __*Accounts Payable—Adventure Equipment Inc.*__   ACCOUNT NO. __*201*__

DATE	DESCRIPTION	POST. REF.	DEBIT	CREDIT	BALANCE DEBIT	BALANCE CREDIT

ACCOUNT __*Accounts Payable—Digital Tech Computers*__   ACCOUNT NO. __*203*__

DATE	DESCRIPTION	POST. REF.	DEBIT	CREDIT	BALANCE DEBIT	BALANCE CREDIT

ACCOUNT __*Ronald Hicks, Capital*__   ACCOUNT NO. __*301*__

DATE	DESCRIPTION	POST. REF.	DEBIT	CREDIT	BALANCE DEBIT	BALANCE CREDIT

ACCOUNT __*Ronald Hicks, Withdrawals*__   ACCOUNT NO. __*305*__

DATE	DESCRIPTION	POST. REF.	DEBIT	CREDIT	BALANCE DEBIT	BALANCE CREDIT

ACCOUNT __*Equipment Rental Revenue*__   ACCOUNT NO. __*401*__

DATE	DESCRIPTION	POST. REF.	DEBIT	CREDIT	BALANCE DEBIT	BALANCE CREDIT

ACCOUNT __*Advertising Expense*__   ACCOUNT NO. __*501*__

DATE	DESCRIPTION	POST. REF.	DEBIT	CREDIT	BALANCE DEBIT	BALANCE CREDIT

Analyze: _____

Problem 7-6   Preparing a Trial Balance

GENERAL LEDGER

ACCOUNT ___Cash in Bank_____ ACCOUNT NO. ___101___

DATE		DESCRIPTION	POST. REF.	DEBIT	CREDIT	BALANCE DEBIT	BALANCE CREDIT
20--							
Mar.	1	Balance	✓			1500000	
	15		G1	400000		1900000	
	31		G2		200000	1700000	

ACCOUNT ___Accounts Receivable—Valley Auto_____ ACCOUNT NO. ___110___

DATE		DESCRIPTION	POST. REF.	DEBIT	CREDIT	BALANCE DEBIT	BALANCE CREDIT
20--							
Mar.	1	Balance	✓			200000	
	12		G1		100000	100000	

ACCOUNT ___Detergent Supplies_____ ACCOUNT NO. ___120___

DATE		DESCRIPTION	POST. REF.	DEBIT	CREDIT	BALANCE DEBIT	BALANCE CREDIT
20--							
Mar.	1	Balance	✓			150000	
	17		G1	50000		200000	

ACCOUNT ___Car Wash Equipment_____ ACCOUNT NO. ___135___

DATE		DESCRIPTION	POST. REF.	DEBIT	CREDIT	BALANCE DEBIT	BALANCE CREDIT
20--							
Mar.	1	Balance	✓			2000000	

ACCOUNT ___Accounts Payable—Allen Vacuum Systems___ ACCOUNT NO. ___201___

DATE		DESCRIPTION	POST. REF.	DEBIT	CREDIT	BALANCE DEBIT	BALANCE CREDIT
20--							
Mar.	1	Balance	✓				100000
	31		G2	50000			50000

ACCOUNT ___Regina Delgado, Capital_____ ACCOUNT NO. ___301___

DATE		DESCRIPTION	POST. REF.	DEBIT	CREDIT	BALANCE DEBIT	BALANCE CREDIT
20--							
Mar.	1	Balance	✓				4000000

Problem 7-6 (continued)

ACCOUNT _Regina Delgado, Withdrawals_ ACCOUNT NO. _305_

DATE		DESCRIPTION	POST. REF.	DEBIT	CREDIT	BALANCE DEBIT	BALANCE CREDIT
20--							
Mar.	1	Balance	✓			200000	
	31		G2	200000		400000	

ACCOUNT _Income Summary_ ACCOUNT NO. _310_

DATE	DESCRIPTION	POST. REF.	DEBIT	CREDIT	BALANCE DEBIT	BALANCE CREDIT

ACCOUNT _Wash Revenue_ ACCOUNT NO. _401_

DATE		DESCRIPTION	POST. REF.	DEBIT	CREDIT	BALANCE DEBIT	BALANCE CREDIT
20--							
Mar.	1	Balance	✓				400000
	31		G2		350000		750000

ACCOUNT _Wax Revenue_ ACCOUNT NO. _405_

DATE		DESCRIPTION	POST. REF.	DEBIT	CREDIT	BALANCE DEBIT	BALANCE CREDIT
20--							
Mar.	1	Balance	✓				50000
	31		G2		80000		130000

ACCOUNT _Interior Detailing Revenue_ ACCOUNT NO. _410_

DATE		DESCRIPTION	POST. REF.	DEBIT	CREDIT	BALANCE DEBIT	BALANCE CREDIT
20--							
Mar.	1	Balance	✓				100000
	31		G2		20000		120000

ACCOUNT _Utilities Expense_ ACCOUNT NO. _530_

DATE		DESCRIPTION	POST. REF.	DEBIT	CREDIT	BALANCE DEBIT	BALANCE CREDIT
20--							
Mar.	1	Balance	✓			600000	
	15		G1	50000		650000	

Problem 7-6 (concluded)

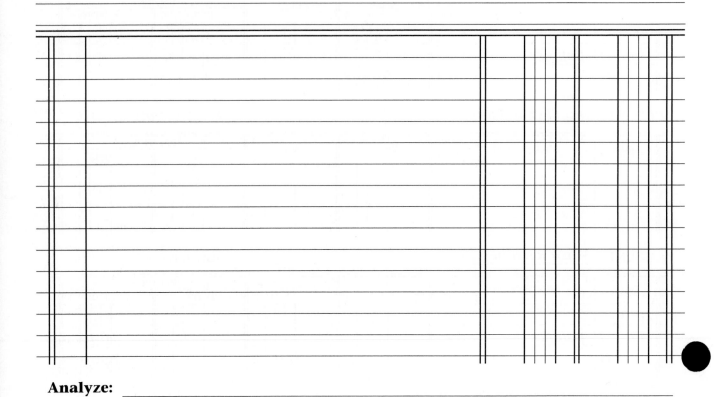

Analyze: _____

Problem 7-7   Journalizing and Posting Business Transactions
(1), (3)

GENERAL LEDGER

ACCOUNT _____ ACCOUNT NO. _____

DATE	DESCRIPTION	POST. REF.	DEBIT	CREDIT	BALANCE DEBIT	BALANCE CREDIT

ACCOUNT _____ ACCOUNT NO. _____

DATE	DESCRIPTION	POST. REF.	DEBIT	CREDIT	BALANCE DEBIT	BALANCE CREDIT

ACCOUNT _____ ACCOUNT NO. _____

DATE	DESCRIPTION	POST. REF.	DEBIT	CREDIT	BALANCE DEBIT	BALANCE CREDIT

ACCOUNT _____ ACCOUNT NO. _____

DATE	DESCRIPTION	POST. REF.	DEBIT	CREDIT	BALANCE DEBIT	BALANCE CREDIT

ACCOUNT _____ ACCOUNT NO. _____

DATE	DESCRIPTION	POST. REF.	DEBIT	CREDIT	BALANCE DEBIT	BALANCE CREDIT

Problem 7-7 (continued)

ACCOUNT _____ ACCOUNT NO. _____

DATE	DESCRIPTION	POST. REF.	DEBIT	CREDIT	BALANCE	
					DEBIT	CREDIT

ACCOUNT _____ ACCOUNT NO. _____

DATE	DESCRIPTION	POST. REF.	DEBIT	CREDIT	BALANCE	
					DEBIT	CREDIT

ACCOUNT _____ ACCOUNT NO. _____

DATE	DESCRIPTION	POST. REF.	DEBIT	CREDIT	BALANCE	
					DEBIT	CREDIT

ACCOUNT _____ ACCOUNT NO. _____

DATE	DESCRIPTION	POST. REF.	DEBIT	CREDIT	BALANCE	
					DEBIT	CREDIT

ACCOUNT _____ ACCOUNT NO. _____

DATE	DESCRIPTION	POST. REF.	DEBIT	CREDIT	BALANCE	
					DEBIT	CREDIT

ACCOUNT _____ ACCOUNT NO. _____

DATE	DESCRIPTION	POST. REF.	DEBIT	CREDIT	BALANCE	
					DEBIT	CREDIT

Problem 7-7 (continued)

(2)

GENERAL JOURNAL   PAGE _____

	DATE	DESCRIPTION	POST. REF.	DEBIT	CREDIT	
1						1
2						2
3						3
4						4
5						5
6						6
7						7
8						8
9						9
10						10
11						11
12						12
13						13
14						14
15						15
16						16
17						17
18						18
19						19
20						20
21						21
22						22
23						23
24						24
25						25
26						26
27						27
28						28
29						29
30						30
31						31
32						32
33						33
34						34
35						35
36						36

Problem 7-7   (concluded)

(4)

Analyze: _____

_____

Problem 7-8   Source Documents

Instructions: *Use the following source documents to record the transactions for*
this problem.

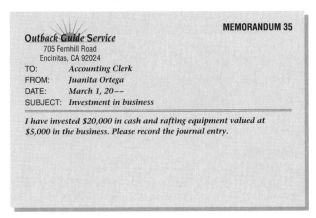

MEMORANDUM 35

Outback Guide Service
705 Fernhill Road
Encinitas, CA 92024

TO: Accounting Clerk
FROM: *Juanita Ortega*
DATE: *March 1, 20––*
SUBJECT: *Investment in business*

I have invested $20,000 in cash and rafting equipment valued at
$5,000 in the business. Please record the journal entry.

RECEIPT
No. 311

Outback Guide Service
705 Fernhill Road
Encinitas, CA 92024

March 2   20 ––

RECEIVED FROM *Chad Schmidt* $ *80.00*

Eighty and ⁰⁰/₁₀₀ ———————————— DOLLARS

FOR *Guide Service*

RECEIVED BY *Juanita Ortega*

PEAK EQUIPMENT INC.
402 Industry Blvd.
San Diego, CA 92122

INVOICE NO. 101

DATE: *March 3, 20––*
ORDER NO.:
SHIPPED BY: *Speedy Delivery*
TERMS: *Payable in 30 days*

TO   *Outback Guide Service*
     705 Fernhill Road
     Encinitas, CA 92024

QTY.	ITEM	UNIT PRICE	TOTAL
3	Daypacks -- DP41714-0	$100.00	$300.00
2	Backpacks -- BP43714-1	150.00	300.00
			$600.00

RECEIPT
No. 312

Outback Guide Service
705 Fernhill Road
Encinitas, CA 92024

March 3   20 ––

RECEIVED FROM *Jason & Brittany Kelley* $ *135.00*

One hundred thirty-five and ⁰⁰/₁₀₀ ———————— DOLLARS

FOR *Guide Service*

RECEIVED BY *Juanita Ortega*

RECEIPT
No. 313

Outback Guide Service
705 Fernhill Road
Encinitas, CA 92024

March 5   20 ––

RECEIVED FROM *Clancey McMichael* $ *80.00*

Eighty and ⁰⁰/₁₀₀ ———————————— DOLLARS

FOR *Guide Service*

RECEIVED BY *Juanita Ortega*

Premier Processors
5775 Lemon Grove Drive
San Diego, CA 92107

INVOICE NO. 616

DATE: *March 5, 20––*
ORDER NO.:
SHIPPED BY: *Pick up*
TERMS: *Payable in 60 days*

TO   *Outback Guide Service*
     705 Fernhill Road
     Encinitas, CA 92024

QTY.	ITEM	UNIT PRICE	TOTAL
1	Computer system -- IEF407	$2,800.00	$2,800.00

RECEIPT
No. 314

Outback Guide Service
705 Fernhill Road
Encinitas, CA 92024

March 5   20 ––

RECEIVED FROM *Louise Wicker & Dudley Hartel* $ *135.00*

One hundred thirty-five and ⁰⁰/₁₀₀ ———————— DOLLARS

FOR *Guide Service*

RECEIVED BY *Juanita Ortega*

RECEIPT
No. 310

Outback Guide Service
705 Fernhill Road
Encinitas, CA 92024

March 2   20 ––

RECEIVED FROM *Cathy & Jonathon Smith* $ *135.00*

One hundred thirty-five and ⁰⁰/₁₀₀ ———————— DOLLARS

FOR *Guide Service*

RECEIVED BY *Juanita Ortega*

Problem 7-8 (continued)

Outback Guide Service
705 Fernhill Road
Encinitas, CA 92024

RECEIPT
No. 315

March 7   20 --

RECEIVED FROM _Greg & Ann Ingram_ $ _135.00_

One hundred thirty-five and 00/100 ——————— DOLLARS

FOR _Guide Service_

RECEIVED BY _Juanita Ortega_

$ _1,400.00_   No. 654
Date _March 18_   20 --
To _Premier Processors_
For _On account_

	Dollars	Cents
Balance brought forward	19,500	00
Add deposits		
Total	19,500	00
Less this check	1,400	00
Balance carried forward	18,100	00

$ _400.00_   No. 652
Date _March 9_   20 --
To _Daily Courier_
For _Ad_

		Dollars	Cents
Balance brought forward		0	00
Add deposits	2/1	20,000	00
	2/7	700	00
Total		20,700	00
Less this check		400	00
Balance carried forward		20,300	00

Outback Guide Service
705 Fernhill Road
Encinitas, CA 92024

RECEIPT
No. 316

March 22   20 --

RECEIVED FROM _Podaski Systems Inc._ $ _900.00_

Nine hundred and 00/100 ——————— DOLLARS

FOR _Payment on account_

RECEIVED BY _Juanita Ortega_

Outback Guide Service
705 Fernhill Road, Encinitas, CA 92024

INVOICE NO. 352
DATE: _March 12, 20--_
ORDER NO.:
SHIPPED BY:
TERMS: _Payment due upon receipt_

TO   _Podaski Systems Inc._
    115 Beach Blvd.
    San Diego, CA 92103

DATE	SERVICE	AMOUNT
3/10/--	_Group rafting trip_	$900.00

$ _500.00_   No. 655
Date _March 27_   20 --
To _Live TV_
For _Ad_

		Dollars	Cents
Balance brought forward		18,100	00
Add deposits	2/22	900	00
Total		19,000	00
Less this check		500	00
Balance carried forward		18,500	00

$ _600.00_   No. 656
Date _March 28_   20 --
To _Peak Equipment Inc._
For _On account_

	Dollars	Cents
Balance brought forward	18,500	00
Add deposits		
Total	18,500	00
Less this check	600	00
Balance carried forward	17,900	00

$ _800.00_   No. 653
Date _March 15_   20 --
To _Cash_
For _Personal use_

	Dollars	Cents
Balance brought forward	20,300	00
Add deposits		
Total		
Less this check	800	00
Balance carried forward	19,500	00

Problem 7-8   Journalizing and Posting Business Transactions
(1), (3)

GENERAL LEDGER

ACCOUNT _____   ACCOUNT NO. _____

DATE	DESCRIPTION	POST. REF.	DEBIT	CREDIT	BALANCE DEBIT	CREDIT

ACCOUNT _____   ACCOUNT NO. _____

DATE	DESCRIPTION	POST. REF.	DEBIT	CREDIT	BALANCE DEBIT	CREDIT

ACCOUNT _____   ACCOUNT NO. _____

DATE	DESCRIPTION	POST. REF.	DEBIT	CREDIT	BALANCE DEBIT	CREDIT

ACCOUNT _____   ACCOUNT NO. _____

DATE	DESCRIPTION	POST. REF.	DEBIT	CREDIT	BALANCE DEBIT	CREDIT

ACCOUNT _____   ACCOUNT NO. _____

DATE	DESCRIPTION	POST. REF.	DEBIT	CREDIT	BALANCE DEBIT	CREDIT

Problem 7-8 (continued)

ACCOUNT _____ ACCOUNT NO. _____

DATE	DESCRIPTION	POST. REF.	DEBIT	CREDIT	BALANCE	
					DEBIT	CREDIT

ACCOUNT _____ ACCOUNT NO. _____

DATE	DESCRIPTION	POST. REF.	DEBIT	CREDIT	BALANCE	
					DEBIT	CREDIT

ACCOUNT _____ ACCOUNT NO. _____

DATE	DESCRIPTION	POST. REF.	DEBIT	CREDIT	BALANCE	
					DEBIT	CREDIT

ACCOUNT _____ ACCOUNT NO. _____

DATE	DESCRIPTION	POST. REF.	DEBIT	CREDIT	BALANCE	
					DEBIT	CREDIT

ACCOUNT _____ ACCOUNT NO. _____

DATE	DESCRIPTION	POST. REF.	DEBIT	CREDIT	BALANCE	
					DEBIT	CREDIT

ACCOUNT _____ ACCOUNT NO. _____

DATE	DESCRIPTION	POST. REF.	DEBIT	CREDIT	BALANCE	
					DEBIT	CREDIT

Problem 7-8 (continued)

(2)

GENERAL JOURNAL   PAGE _____

	DATE		DESCRIPTION	POST. REF.	DEBIT	CREDIT	
1							1
2							2
3							3
4							4
5							5
6							6
7							7
8							8
9							9
10							10
11							11
12							12
13							13
14							14
15							15
16							16
17							17
18							18
19							19
20							20
21							21
22							22
23							23
24							24
25							25
26							26
27							27
28							28
29							29
30							30
31							31
32							32
33							33
34							34
35							35
36							36

Problem 7-8 (concluded)

(4)

Analyze: _____

_____

Problem 7-9   Recording and Posting Correcting Entries

GENERAL JOURNAL   PAGE ___*21*___

	DATE		DESCRIPTION	POST. REF.	DEBIT	CREDIT	
1	20--						1
2	Mar.	3	Office Furniture	135	125 00		2
3			Cash in Bank	101		125 00	3
4			Check 1401				4
5		5	Cash in Bank	101	400 00		5
6			Accts. Rec.—James Coletti	110		400 00	6
7			Receipt 602				7
8		7	Accts. Pay.—Broad Street Office Supply	201	200 00		8
9			Cash in Bank	101		200 00	9
10			Check 1402				10
11		9	Office Furniture	135	500 00		11
12			Cash in Bank	101		500 00	12
13			Check 1403				13
14		13	Greg Failla, Capital	301	1200 00		14
15			Cash in Bank	101		1200 00	15
16			Check 1404				16
17		17	Cash in Bank	101	2000 00		17
18			Greg Failla, Capital	301		2000 00	18
19			Receipt 603				19
20		19	Cash in Bank	101	75 00		20
21			Accts. Rec.—Shannon Flannery	113		75 00	21
22			Receipt 604				22
23		20	Cash in Bank	101	100 00		23
24			Accts. Rec.—James Coletti	110		100 00	24
25			Receipt 605				25
26		24	Utilities Expense	530	75 00		26
27			Cash in Bank	101		75 00	27
28			Check 1405				28
29		27	Cash in Bank	101	3000 00		29
30			Greg Failla, Withdrawals	305		3000 00	30
31			Memorandum 40				31
32		29	Cash in Bank	101	1000 00		32
33			VCR Rental Revenue	405		1000 00	33
34			Receipt 606				34
35							35
36							36

Problem 7-9 (continued)

GENERAL LEDGER

ACCOUNT ___Cash in Bank_____ ACCOUNT NO. ___101___

DATE		DESCRIPTION	POST. REF.	DEBIT	CREDIT	BALANCE	
						DEBIT	CREDIT
20--							
Mar.	1	Balance	✓			9 855 00	
	3		G21		1 250 0	9 730 00	
	5		G21	4 000 00		10 130 00	
	7		G21		2 000 0	9 930 00	
	9		G21		5 000 0	9 430 00	
	13		G21		1 200 0 0	8 230 00	
	17		G21	2 000 00		10 230 00	
	19		G21	75 00		10 305 00	
	20		G21	100 00		10 405 00	
	24		G21		75 0 0	10 330 00	
	27		G21	3 000 00		13 330 00	
	29		G21	1 000 00		14 330 00	

ACCOUNT ___Accounts Receivable—Shannon Flannery___ ACCOUNT NO. ___113___

DATE		DESCRIPTION	POST. REF.	DEBIT	CREDIT	BALANCE	
						DEBIT	CREDIT
20--							
Mar.	1	Balance	✓			300 00	
	19		G21		57 00	243 00	

ACCOUNT ___Office Supplies_____ ACCOUNT NO. ___120___

DATE		DESCRIPTION	POST. REF.	DEBIT	CREDIT	BALANCE	
						DEBIT	CREDIT
20--							
Mar.	1	Balance	✓			120 00	

ACCOUNT ___Office Furniture_____ ACCOUNT NO. ___135___

DATE		DESCRIPTION	POST. REF.	DEBIT	CREDIT	BALANCE	
						DEBIT	CREDIT
20--							
Mar.	1	Balance	✓			1 500 00	
	3		G21	125 00		1 625 00	
	9		G21	500 00		2 125 00	

Problem 7-9   (continued)

ACCOUNT __Accounts Payable—Broad Street Office Supply__   ACCOUNT NO. __201__

DATE		DESCRIPTION	POST. REF.	DEBIT	CREDIT	BALANCE DEBIT	BALANCE CREDIT
20--							
Mar.	1	Balance	✓				2 20000

ACCOUNT __Greg Failla, Capital__   ACCOUNT NO. __301__

DATE		DESCRIPTION	POST. REF.	DEBIT	CREDIT	BALANCE DEBIT	BALANCE CREDIT
20--							
Mar.	1	Balance	✓				13 00000
	13		G21	1 20000			11 80000
	17		G21		2 00000		13 80000

ACCOUNT __Greg Failla, Withdrawals__   ACCOUNT NO. __305__

DATE		DESCRIPTION	POST. REF.	DEBIT	CREDIT	BALANCE DEBIT	BALANCE CREDIT
20--							
Mar.	27		G21		3 00000	3 00000	

ACCOUNT __Video Rental Revenue__   ACCOUNT NO. __401__

DATE	DESCRIPTION	POST. REF.	DEBIT	CREDIT	BALANCE DEBIT	BALANCE CREDIT

ACCOUNT __VCR Rental Revenue__   ACCOUNT NO. __405__

DATE		DESCRIPTION	POST. REF.	DEBIT	CREDIT	BALANCE DEBIT	BALANCE CREDIT
20--							
Mar.	29		G21		1 00000		1 00000

Problem 7-9 (concluded)

GENERAL JOURNAL

PAGE _____

	DATE	DESCRIPTION	POST. REF.	DEBIT	CREDIT	
1						1
2						2
3						3
4						4
5						5
6						6
7						7
8						8
9						9
10						10
11						11
12						12
13						13
14						14
15						15
16						16
17						17
18						18
19						19
20						20
21						21
22						22
23						23
24						24
25						25
26						26
27						27
28						28
29						29
30						30
31						31
32						32
33						33
34						34

Analyze: _____

_____

CHAPTER 7   Posting Journal Entries to General Ledger Accounts

Self-Test

Part A   True or False

Directions: *Read each of the following statements to determine whether the statement is true or false. Write your answer in the space provided.*

Answer

_____ 1. The accounts in a business are kept in a book called a ledger.

_____ 2. Posting is the process of transferring information from the journal to the ledger accounts.

_____ 3. Every posting requires the year, month, and day to be entered in the Date column of the ledger account for every transaction.

_____ 4. Every journal entry requires a posting to at least two accounts.

_____ 5. If a transaction is journalized on the 6th, but not posted until the 8th, the date of the posting should be the 8th.

_____ 6. If an account has a zero balance, it is not necessary to list it on the trial balance.

_____ 7. A ledger is sometimes called a book of "final" entry.

_____ 8. Ideally, all businesses should post on a daily basis; however, businesses having few transactions may post only once a week.

_____ 9. An example of a transposition error is writing the number 45 when you should have written 54.

_____ 10. If you discover an error before posting, a correcting entry is required.

Part B Multiple Choice

Directions: *Choose the letter of the correct answer and write it in the space provided.*

Answer

_____ 1. The first step in the posting process is to:
(A) post the amount.
(B) enter the page number in the Posting Reference column of the ledger account.
(C) enter the date in the Date column of the ledger account.
(D) compute the new balance.

_____ 2. If the total debits and total credits of the trial balance do not agree, the first step in locating the error is to:
(A) re-add the debit and credit columns.
(B) find the amount you are out of balance.
(C) make certain you copied the amount correctly from the ledger account to the trial balance.
(D) divide the amount you are out of balance by 2.

_____ 3. All of the following about a trial balance are true *except:*
(A) it includes all general ledger accounts.
(B) it includes only the permanent accounts.
(C) it is completed after posting.
(D) it proves the ledger.

_____ 4. Transposition errors are evenly divisible by the number:
(A) 2
(B) 3
(C) 4
(D) 9

_____ 5. Which of the following steps in the accounting cycle is in the correct order?
(A) Post to the ledger, prepare a trial balance, journalize, analyze each transaction, and collect source documents.
(B) Analyze each transaction, journalize, collect source documents, prepare a trial balance, and post.
(C) Collect and verify source documents, analyze each transaction, journalize each transaction, post to the ledger, and prepare a trial balance.
(D) Collect and verify source documents, analyze each transaction, prepare a trial balance, journalize each transaction, and post to the ledger.

MINI PRACTICE SET 1

Canyon.com Web Sites

CHART OF ACCOUNTS

ASSETS
101   Cash in Bank
105   Accounts Receivable—Andrew Hospital
110   Accounts Receivable—Indiana Trucking
115   Accounts Receivable—Sunshine Products
130   Office Supplies
135   Office Equipment
140   Office Furniture
145   Web Server

LIABILITIES
205   Accounts Payable—Computer Specialists Inc.
210   Accounts Payable—Office Systems
215   Accounts Payable—Service Plus Software Inc.

OWNER'S EQUITY
301   Jack Hines, Capital
305   Jack Hines, Withdrawals

REVENUE
401   Web Service Fees

EXPENSES
505   Membership Expense
506   Telecommunications Expense
507   Rent Expense
508   Utilities Expense

Mini Practice Set 1   Source Documents

Instructions: *Use the following source documents to record the transactions for this practice set.*

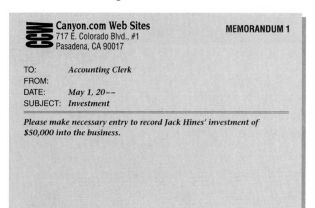

Canyon.com Web Sites
717 E. Colorado Blvd., #1
Pasadena, CA 90017

MEMORANDUM 1

TO: *Accounting Clerk*
FROM:
DATE: *May 1, 20--*
SUBJECT: *Investment*

Please make necessary entry to record Jack Hines' investment of $50,000 into the business.

COMPUTER SPECIALISTS INC.
1231 Reseda Blvd., #2A
Reseda, CA 91124

INVOICE NO. WS4658421

DATE: *May 3, 20--*
ORDER NO.:
SHIPPED BY:
TERMS:

TO   *Canyon.com Web Sites*
717 E. Colorado Blvd., #1
Pasadena, CA 90017

QTY.	ITEM	UNIT PRICE	TOTAL
1	Web server	$35,000.00	$35,000.00

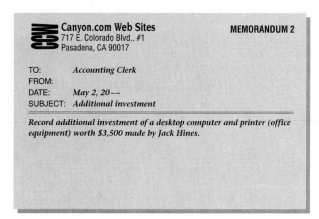

Canyon.com Web Sites
717 E. Colorado Blvd., #1
Pasadena, CA 90017

MEMORANDUM 2

TO: *Accounting Clerk*
FROM:
DATE: *May 2, 20--*
SUBJECT: *Additional investment*

Record additional investment of a desktop computer and printer (office equipment) worth $3,500 made by Jack Hines.

Canyon.com Web Sites
717 E. Colorado Blvd., #1
Pasadena, CA 90017

RECEIPT

No. 101

May 9   20 --

RECEIVED FROM *James Market* $ *1,000.00*

One thousand and ⁰⁰/₁₀₀   DOLLARS

FOR   *Web site services*

RECEIVED BY *Jack Hines*

Canyon.com Web Sites
717 E. Colorado Blvd., #1
Pasadena, CA 90017

101

90-7177
3222

DATE *May 2*   20 --

PAY TO THE
ORDER OF   *Office Mart* $ *125.00*

One hundred twenty-five and ⁰⁰/₁₀₀   DOLLARS

1st *First Bank*

MEMO *Office supplies*   *Jack Hines*

⑆3222⑆1779⑈ 0710613 ⑈101

Canyon.com Web Sites
717 E. Colorado Blvd., #1
Pasadena, CA 90017

INVOICE NO. 101

DATE: *May 11, 20--*
ORDER NO.:
SHIPPED BY:
TERMS:

TO   *Andrew Hospital*
1314 Sherman Way
Van Nuys, CA 91331

QTY.	ITEM	UNIT PRICE	TOTAL
N/A	Web site design services	$3,000.00	$3,000.00

Office Systems
9177 California Blvd.
Pasadena, CA 91210

INVOICE NO. 457

DATE: *May 3, 20--*
ORDER NO.:
SHIPPED BY:
TERMS:

TO   *Canyon.com Web Sites*
717 E. Colorado Blvd., #1
Pasadena, CA 90017

QTY.	ITEM	UNIT PRICE	TOTAL
3	Tables	$300.00	$ 900.00
4	Swivel Chairs	250.00	1,000.00
1	Fax Machine	800.00	800.00
			$2,700.00

Service Plus Software Inc.
616 Cordova Street, #7
Glendale, CA 90121

INVOICE NO. 876

DATE: *May 12, 20--*
ORDER NO.:
SHIPPED BY:
TERMS:

TO   *Canyon.com Web Sites*
717 E. Colorado Blvd., #1
Pasadena, CA 90017

QTY.	ITEM	UNIT PRICE	TOTAL
N/A	Software for Web server	$10,000.00	$10,000.00

Mini Practice Set 1   (continued)

Canyon.com Web Sites   102
717 E. Colorado Blvd., #1
Pasadena, CA 90017   90-7177 / 3222

DATE _May 14_ 20 --

PAY TO THE ORDER OF _DWP_ $ _118.00_

One hundred eighteen and 00/100 ————— DOLLARS

1st _First Bank_

MEMO _Electric bill_   _Jack Hines_

⑆322271779⑆ 0710613 ⑈102

Canyon.com Web Sites   103
717 E. Colorado Blvd., #1
Pasadena, CA 90017   90-7177 / 3222

DATE _May 15_ 20 --

PAY TO THE ORDER OF _Jack Hines_ $ _2,500.00_

Two thousand five hundred and 00/100 ————— DOLLARS

1st _First Bank_

MEMO _Personal withdrawal_   _Jack Hines_

⑆322271779⑆ 0710613 ⑈103

Canyon.com Web Sites   INVOICE NO. 102
717 E. Colorado Blvd., #1
Pasadena, CA 90017

DATE: _May 17, 20--_
ORDER NO.:
SHIPPED BY:
TERMS:

TO   _Sunshine Products_
1213 Oceanview Street
Santa Monica, CA 90171

QTY.	ITEM	UNIT PRICE	TOTAL
N/A	Web site design	$5,000.00	$5,000.00

Canyon.com Web Sites   104
717 E. Colorado Blvd., #1
Pasadena, CA 90017   90-7177 / 3222

DATE _May 18_ 20 --

PAY TO THE ORDER OF _Office Mart_ $ _275.00_

Two hundred seventy-five and 00/100 ————— DOLLARS

1st _First Bank_

MEMO _Filing cabinet_   _Jack Hines_

⑆322271779⑆ 0710613 ⑈104

Canyon.com Web Sites   RECEIPT
717 E. Colorado Blvd., #1
Pasadena, CA 90017   No. 102

May 19 20 --

RECEIVED FROM _Intercom Inc._ $ _4,000.00_

Four thousand and 00/100 ————— DOLLARS

FOR _Web site maintenance for one year_

RECEIVED BY _Jack Hines_

Canyon.com Web Sites   INVOICE NO. 103
717 E. Colorado Blvd., #1
Pasadena, CA 90017

DATE: _May 20, 20--_
ORDER NO.:
SHIPPED BY:
TERMS:

TO   _Indiana Trucking_
28111 Soledad Canyon
Newhall, CA 90011

QTY.	ITEM	UNIT PRICE	TOTAL
N/A	Design services	$2,000.00	$2,000.00

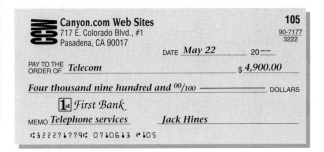

Canyon.com Web Sites   RECEIPT
717 E. Colorado Blvd., #1
Pasadena, CA 90017   No. 103

May 21 20 --

RECEIVED FROM _Sunshine Products_ $ _2,500.00_

Two thousand five hundred and 00/100 ————— DOLLARS

FOR _Payment on account_

RECEIVED BY _Jack Hines_

Canyon.com Web Sites   105
717 E. Colorado Blvd., #1
Pasadena, CA 90017   90-7177 / 3222

DATE _May 22_ 20 --

PAY TO THE ORDER OF _Telecom_ $ _4,900.00_

Four thousand nine hundred and 00/100 ————— DOLLARS

1st _First Bank_

MEMO _Telephone services_   _Jack Hines_

⑆322271779⑆ 0710613 ⑈105

Mini Practice Set (continued)

Canyon.com Web Sites 106
717 E. Colorado Blvd., #1
Pasadena, CA 90017 90-7177
3222
DATE *May 22* 20—
PAY TO THE ORDER OF *Service Plus Software Inc.* $ *3,333.00*
Three thousand three hundred thirty-three and 00/100 — DOLLARS
1st *First Bank*
MEMO *On account* *Jack Hines*
⑆322271779⑆ 0710613 ⑈106

Canyon.com Web Sites 109
717 E. Colorado Blvd., #1
Pasadena, CA 90017 90-7177
3222
DATE *May 30* 20—
PAY TO THE ORDER OF *Property Management* $ *750.00*
Seven hundred fifty and 00/100 DOLLARS
1st *First Bank*
MEMO *Rent* *Jack Hines*
⑆322271779⑆ 0710613 ⑈109

Canyon.com Web Sites 107
717 E. Colorado Blvd., #1
Pasadena, CA 90017 90-7177
3222
DATE *May 25* 20—
PAY TO THE ORDER OF *Office Systems* $ *2,000.00*
Two thousand and 00/100 DOLLARS
1st *First Bank*
MEMO *On account* *Jack Hines*
⑆322271779⑆ 0710613 ⑈107

Canyon.com Web Sites 110
717 E. Colorado Blvd., #1
Pasadena, CA 90017 90-7177
3222
DATE *May 30* 20—
PAY TO THE ORDER OF *Jack Hines* $ *2,500.00*
Two thousand five hundred and 00/100 DOLLARS
1st *First Bank*
MEMO *Personal withdrawal* *Jack Hines*
⑆322271779⑆ 0710613 ⑈110

Canyon.com Web Sites RECEIPT
717 E. Colorado Blvd., #1 No. 104
Pasadena, CA 90017
May 26 20—
RECEIVED FROM *Job Info. Services* $ *1,000.00*
One thousand and 00/100 DOLLARS
FOR *2 months of Web site services*
RECEIVED BY *Jack Hines*

Canyon.com Web Sites 111
717 E. Colorado Blvd., #1
Pasadena, CA 90017 90-7177
3222
DATE *May 30* 20—
PAY TO THE ORDER OF *Computer Specialists Inc.* $ *25,000.00*
Twenty-five thousand and 00/100 DOLLARS
1st *First Bank*
MEMO *On account* *Jack Hines*
⑆322271779⑆ 0710613 ⑈111

Canyon.com Web Sites 108
717 E. Colorado Blvd., #1
Pasadena, CA 90017 90-7177
3222
DATE *May 27* 20—
PAY TO THE ORDER OF *All Inclusive Group* $ *7,000.00*
Seven thousand and 00/100 DOLLARS
1st *First Bank*
MEMO *Membership dues* *Jack Hines*
⑆322271779⑆ 0710613 ⑈108

Computerized Accounting Using Peachtree

Mini Practice Set 1

INSTRUCTIONS

Beginning a Session

Step 1 Open the Glencoe Accounting: Electronic Learning Center software.

Step 2 From the Program Menu, click on the **Peachtree Accounting Software and Spreadsheet Applications** icon.

Step 3 Log onto the Management System by typing your user name and password.

Step 4 Under the Chapter Problems tab, select the problem set: Canyon.com Web Sites (MP-1).

Step 5 Rename the company by adding your initials, e.g., Canyon (MP-1: XXX).

Step 6 Set the system date to May 31, 2004.

Completing the Accounting Problem

Step 7 Review the transactions shown in your textbook for Canyon.com Web Sites.

Step 8 Record all of the transactions using the **General Journal Entry** option.

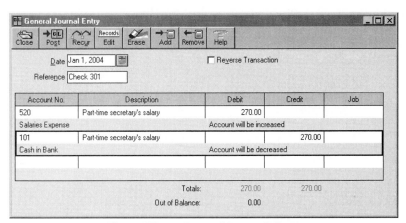

Figure MP1-1 *General Journal Entry*

TIP: Proof each general journal entry before you post it. Check the account numbers, descriptions, and amounts.

Preparing Reports and Proofing Your Work

Step 9 Print a General Journal report.

Step 10 Proof your work. Make any corrections as needed and print a revised report, if necessary.

TIP: While viewing a General Journal report, you can double-click on an entry to display it in the General Journal Entry window. You can edit the transaction and then close the window to see an updated report.

Step 11 Print a General Ledger report.
Step 12 Print a Trial Balance.

Analyzing Your Work

Step 13 Answer the Analyze question.
Step 14 Complete the Audit Test.

Checking Your Work and Ending the Session

Step 15 Click the **Close Problem** button in the Glencoe Smart Guide window.
Step 16 If your teacher has asked you to check your solution, select *Check my answer to this problem*. Review, print, and close the report.
Step 17 Click the **Close Problem** button. Select the close option as directed by your teacher. Click **OK.**

Notes

Use the reports you prepared to answer the Analyze question and to complete the Audit Test.

Continuing from a Previous Session

If you want to continue from a previous session, follow steps 1–4 on the previous page. If you saved your work to the network, the management system will retrieve your files. If you saved your work to a floppy disk, insert the disk. The system will then retrieve your files from the floppy disk.

FAQs

Does Peachtree produce an audit trail if you edit a general journal entry?

No. Peachtree does not create an audit trail when you edit a general journal entry. If you want to keep track of any corrections, you should make separate correcting entries.

Why doesn't Peachtree allow you to access the General Journal Entry window directly from a customized General Journal report?

When you display the standard (default) General Journal report, you can double-click an entry to access the General Journal Entry window where you can edit the selected transaction. If you change the standard report format (e.g., print a summary report), Peachtree may not allow you to edit transactions in this manner.

Mini Practice Set 1 (continued)

GENERAL JOURNAL   PAGE _____

	DATE	DESCRIPTION	POST. REF.	DEBIT	CREDIT	
1						1
2						2
3						3
4						4
5						5
6						6
7						7
8						8
9						9
10						10
11						11
12						12
13						13
14						14
15						15
16						16
17						17
18						18
19						19
20						20
21						21
22						22
23						23
24						24
25						25
26						26
27						27
28						28
29						29
30						30
31						31
32						32
33						33
34						34
35						35
36						36
37						37
38						38
39						39

Mini Practice Set 1 (continued)

GENERAL JOURNAL

PAGE _____

	DATE		DESCRIPTION	POST. REF.	DEBIT	CREDIT	
1							1
2							2
3							3
4							4
5							5
6							6
7							7
8							8
9							9
10							10
11							11
12							12
13							13
14							14
15							15
16							16
17							17
18							18
19							19
20							20
21							21
22							22
23							23
24							24
25							25
26							26
27							27
28							28
29							29
30							30
31							31
32							32
33							33
34							34
35							35
36							36
37							37
38							38
39							39

Mini Practice Set 1 (continued)

GENERAL LEDGER

ACCOUNT _____ ACCOUNT NO. _____

DATE	DESCRIPTION	POST. REF.	DEBIT	CREDIT	BALANCE DEBIT	CREDIT

ACCOUNT _____ ACCOUNT NO. _____

DATE	DESCRIPTION	POST. REF.	DEBIT	CREDIT	BALANCE DEBIT	CREDIT

ACCOUNT _____ ACCOUNT NO. _____

DATE	DESCRIPTION	POST. REF.	DEBIT	CREDIT	BALANCE DEBIT	CREDIT

ACCOUNT _____ ACCOUNT NO. _____

DATE	DESCRIPTION	POST. REF.	DEBIT	CREDIT	BALANCE DEBIT	CREDIT

Mini Practice Set 1 (continued)

ACCOUNT _____ ACCOUNT NO. _____

DATE	DESCRIPTION	POST. REF.	DEBIT	CREDIT	BALANCE	
					DEBIT	CREDIT

ACCOUNT _____ ACCOUNT NO. _____

DATE	DESCRIPTION	POST. REF.	DEBIT	CREDIT	BALANCE	
					DEBIT	CREDIT

ACCOUNT _____ ACCOUNT NO. _____

DATE	DESCRIPTION	POST. REF.	DEBIT	CREDIT	BALANCE	
					DEBIT	CREDIT

ACCOUNT _____ ACCOUNT NO. _____

DATE	DESCRIPTION	POST. REF.	DEBIT	CREDIT	BALANCE	
					DEBIT	CREDIT

ACCOUNT _____ ACCOUNT NO. _____

DATE	DESCRIPTION	POST. REF.	DEBIT	CREDIT	BALANCE	
					DEBIT	CREDIT

ACCOUNT _____ ACCOUNT NO. _____

DATE	DESCRIPTION	POST. REF.	DEBIT	CREDIT	BALANCE	
					DEBIT	CREDIT

Mini Practice Set 1   (continued)

ACCOUNT _____ ACCOUNT NO. _____

DATE	DESCRIPTION	POST. REF.	DEBIT	CREDIT	BALANCE	
					DEBIT	CREDIT

ACCOUNT _____ ACCOUNT NO. _____

DATE	DESCRIPTION	POST. REF.	DEBIT	CREDIT	BALANCE	
					DEBIT	CREDIT

ACCOUNT _____ ACCOUNT NO. _____

DATE	DESCRIPTION	POST. REF.	DEBIT	CREDIT	BALANCE	
					DEBIT	CREDIT

ACCOUNT _____ ACCOUNT NO. _____

DATE	DESCRIPTION	POST. REF.	DEBIT	CREDIT	BALANCE	
					DEBIT	CREDIT

Mini Practice Set 1   (continued)

ACCOUNT _____ ACCOUNT NO. _____

DATE	DESCRIPTION	POST. REF.	DEBIT	CREDIT	BALANCE	
					DEBIT	CREDIT

ACCOUNT _____ ACCOUNT NO. _____

DATE	DESCRIPTION	POST. REF.	DEBIT	CREDIT	BALANCE	
					DEBIT	CREDIT

ACCOUNT _____ ACCOUNT NO. _____

DATE	DESCRIPTION	POST. REF.	DEBIT	CREDIT	BALANCE	
					DEBIT	CREDIT

ACCOUNT _____ ACCOUNT NO. _____

DATE	DESCRIPTION	POST. REF.	DEBIT	CREDIT	BALANCE	
					DEBIT	CREDIT

● Mini Practice Set 1 (continued)

Mini Practice Set 1 (concluded)

Analyze: _____

_____

_____

_____

_____

_____

_____

_____

_____

_____

_____

MINI PRACTICE SET **1**

Canyon.com Web Sites

Audit Test

Directions: *Use your completed solutions to answer the following questions. Write the answer in the space to the left of each question.*

_____ **1.** In the entry to record the May 1 transaction, which account was debited?

_____ **2.** Were assets increased, decreased, or unaffected by the May 3 transaction?

_____ **3.** What type of account is Web Server?

_____ **4.** Which account was credited in the May 9, 17, and 26 transactions?

_____ **5.** What account was credited for the purchase of the Web server on May 7?

_____ **6.** What was the source document for the May 17 transaction?

_____ **7.** How does the May 20 transaction affect the owner's capital account?

_____ **8.** Was Accounts Receivable—Sunshine Products increased or decreased by the transaction on May 21?

_____ **9.** What was the balance of Cash in Bank on May 27?

_____ **10.** What were the account numbers entered in the posting Reference column of the general journal for the May 25 transaction?

_____ **11.** Which account was debited to record the issue of Check 110?

_____ **12.** What is the ending balance of the Utilities Expense account?

_____ **13.** Has the amount owed to Office Systems been paid off?

_____ **14.** How many transactions recorded during May affected the Cash in Bank account?

_____ 15. What was the total cost of the office equipment purchased during the month?

_____ 16. How many checks were written by the business during May?

_____ 17. What was the total amount credited to Web Services Fees during May?

_____ 18. What was the total amount debited to Cash in Bank for May?

_____ 19. At the end of the month, did the Jack Hines, Withdrawals account have a debit or credit balance?

_____ 20. On May 30, what was the total amount owed to Canyon.com Web Sites for services performed for clients?

_____ 21. What was the date of the trial balance?

_____ 22. What was the amount of the debit and credit totals on the trial balance?

_____ 23. How many accounts are listed in the trial balance for Canyon.com Web Sites?

_____ 24. How many accounts on the trial balance have debit balances?

_____ 25. Which account on the trial balance has the largest balance?

CHAPTER  8   The Six-Column Work Sheet

Study Plan

Check Your Understanding

Section 1	*Read Section 1 on pages 182–185 and complete the following exercises on page 186.*

    ❑ Thinking Critically
    ❑ Communicating Accounting
    ❑ Problem 8-1   *Entering Account Balances on the Work Sheet*
    ❑ Problem 8-2   *Analyzing a Source Document*

Section 2	*Read Section 2 on pages 187–193 and complete the following exercises on page 194.*

    ❑ Thinking Critically
    ❑ Computing in the Business World
    ❑ Problem 8-3   *Extending Amounts Across the Work Sheet*

Summary	*Review the Chapter 8 Summary on page 195 in your textbook.*

    ❑ Key Concepts

Review and Activities	*Complete the following questions and exercises on pages 196–197 in your textbook.*

    ❑ Using Key Terms
    ❑ Understanding Accounting Concepts and Procedures
    ❑ Case Study
    ❑ Conducting an Audit with Alex
    ❑ Internet Connection
    ❑ Workplace Skills

Computerized Accounting	*Read the Computerized Accounting information on page 198 in your textbook.*

    ❑ *Making the Transition from a Manual to a Computerized System*
    ❑ *Preparing a Trial Balance in Peachtree*

Problems	*Complete the following end-of-chapter problems for Chapter 8 in your textbook.*

    ❑ Problem 8-4   *Preparing a Six-Column Work Sheet*
    ❑ Problem 8-5   *Preparing a Six-Column Work Sheet*
    ❑ Problem 8-6   *Preparing a Six-Column Work Sheet*
    ❑ Problem 8-7   *Preparing a Six-Column Work Sheet*

Challenge Problem	❑ Problem 8-8 *Completing the Work Sheet*

Chapter Reviews and Working Papers	*Complete the following exercises for Chapter 8 in your Chapter Reviews and Working Papers.*

    ❑ Chapter Review
    ❑ Self-Test

CHAPTER 8 REVIEW   The Six-Column Work Sheet

Part 1   Accounting Vocabulary (12 points)

Total Points	42
Student's Score	

Directions: *Using terms from the following list, complete the sentences below. Write the letter of the term you have chosen in the space provided.*

A. Balance Sheet section	**E.** extending	**H.** matching principle	**K.** ruling
B. capital	**F.** heading	**I.** net income	**L.** Trial Balance section
C. credit	**G.** Income Statement	**J.** net loss	**M.** work sheet
D. debit	section		

_____D_____   **0.** A net income is entered in the _____ column of the Income Statement section.

_____   **1.** Drawing a line under a column of amounts is known as _____.

_____   **2.** The _____ explains the who, what, and when of the work sheet.

_____   **3.** A net income or loss will increase or decrease the _____ account.

_____   **4.** The _____ of the work sheet includes all the general ledger accounts.

_____   **5.** According to the _____, expenses are matched against revenue for the same period.

_____   **6.** When the Income Statement debit column total is greater than the Income Statement credit column total, a(n) _____ occurs.

_____   **7.** The _____ of the work sheet includes only the temporary general ledger accounts.

_____   **8.** A net income is entered in the _____ column of the Balance Sheet section.

_____   **9.** The _____ of the work sheet includes all permanent general ledger accounts.

_____   **10.** The amount left after expenses for the period have been subtracted from revenue for the period is _____.

_____   **11.** Transferring balances from the Trial Balance section is called _____ the balances.

_____   **12.** A working paper used to collect information from the ledger accounts is a(n) _____.

Part 2   Account Balances (7 points)

Directions: *For each of the following account titles, indicate whether the account will have a normal debit or credit balance on the Trial Balance section of the work sheet. Place an "X" in the appropriate column.*

Account Title	Debit Balance	Credit Balance
Cash in Bank	X	_____
Utilities Expense	_____	_____
Joseph Kwiatek, Capital	_____	_____
Accounts Payable—Lynn Austin	_____	_____
Accounts Receivable—Richard Adzima	_____	_____
Office Equipment	_____	_____
Commissions Revenue	_____	_____
Joseph Kwiatek, Withdrawals	_____	_____

Part 3   The Capital Account (6 points)

Directions: *In the space provided, enter "I" or "D" to indicate whether each of the following accounts or items increases or decreases the capital account.*

I	Net income
_____	Net loss
_____	Kate Wagner, Withdrawals
_____	Rent Expense
_____	Utilities Expense
_____	Owner's investment
_____	Admissions Revenue

Part 4   Extension of Account Balances on the Work Sheet (8 points)

Directions: *For each of the following Trial Balance accounts, indicate the section of the work sheet to which each account balance will be extended. Place an "X" in the appropriate column.*

Account Title	Income Statement Section	Balance Sheet Section
Cash in Bank	_____	_X_
Accounts Payable—Kathleen Rowe	_____	_____
Advertising Expense	_____	_____
Sales Revenue	_____	_____
Angel Torres, Capital	_____	_____
Angel Torres, Withdrawals	_____	_____
Accounts Receivable—James Yun	_____	_____
Office Equipment	_____	_____
Delivery Expense	_____	_____

Part 5   Completing the Work Sheet (9 points)

Directions: *Read each of the following statements to determine whether the statement is true or false. Write your answer in the space provided.*

True   **0.** The work sheet is used to pull together all the information needed to prepare the financial statements and complete the end-of-period activities.

_____ **1.** A single rule under a column of amounts means that the amounts are to be added or subtracted.

_____ **2.** The work sheet is prepared in pen because it is a formal document.

_____ **3.** The work sheet has four sections: the heading, the Trial Balance section, the Income Statement section, and the Balance Sheet section.

_____ **4.** The maximum period covered by the accounting cycle is one month.

_____ **5.** A double rule across both amount columns of the Trial Balance section means that no more entries will be made.

_____ **6.** If the debit column of the Income Statement section of the work sheet is greater than the credit column of the Income Statement section, there is a net income for the period.

_____ **7.** Amounts from the Trial Balance section are first extended to the Balance Sheet section.

_____ **8.** Account titles are listed on the work sheet in the same order as they appear in the general ledger.

_____ **9.** A ledger account having a zero balance is not listed on the Trial Balance section of the work sheet.

Working Papers *for Section Problems*

Problem 8-1   Entering Account Balances on the Work Sheet

Account Name	Classification	Trial Balance Debit	Trial Balance Credit
Store Equipment	Asset	X	
Rent Expense			
Service Fees Revenue			
Accounts Payable—Rubino Supply			
Scott Lee, Capital			
Advertising Expense			
Accounts Receivable—John Langer			
Scott Lee, Withdrawals			
Maintenance Expense			
Office Supplies			

Problem 8-2   Analyzing a Source Document

1. Which company shipped the supplies? _____

2. Which company ordered the supplies? _____

3. On what date were the supplies received? _____

4. What does one box of file folders cost? _____

5. How many ring binders were ordered? _____

6. What is the invoice number? _____

Problem 8-3   Extending Amounts Across the Work Sheet

Account Name	Income Statement Debit	Income Statement Credit	Balance Sheet Debit	Balance Sheet Credit
Store Equipment			X	
Rent Expense				
Service Fees Revenue				
Accounts Payable—Rubino Supply				
Scott Lee, Capital				
Advertising Expense				
Accounts Receivable—John Langer				
Scott Lee, Withdrawals				
Maintenance Expense				
Office Supplies				

Computerized Accounting Using Peachtree

Software Objectives

When you have completed this chapter, you will be able to use Peachtree to:

1. Print a General Ledger Trial Balance report.
2. Verify the information on a General Ledger Trial Balance.

Problem 8-5   Preparing a Six-Column Work Sheet

INSTRUCTIONS

Beginning a Session

> **Step 1**   Select the problem set: Hot Suds Car Wash (Prob. 8-5).
> **Step 2**   Rename the company and set the system date to May 31, 2004.

Preparing a Report

> **Step 3**   Print a General Ledger Trial Balance report.

 TIP: You can access the Trial Balance report using the General Ledger navigation aid.

> **Step 4**   Review the General Ledger Trial Balance report. Verify that the debit/credit column totals are the same. The total debits/credits should be $49,862.

Ending the Session

> **Step 5**   Click the **Close Problem** button in the Glencoe Smart Guide window.

Mastering Peachtree

Use the report design/layout options to widen the *Account Description* column on the General Ledger Trial Balance report. Print a revised report.

Problem 8-6   Preparing a Six-Column Work Sheet

INSTRUCTIONS

Beginning a Session

> **Step 1**   Select the problem set: Kits & Pups Grooming (Prob. 8-6).
> **Step 2**   Rename the company and set the system date to May 31, 2004.

Preparing a Report

> **Step 3**   Print a General Ledger Trial Balance report.

 TIP: Choose **General Ledger** from the *Reports* menu to print a General Ledger Trial Balance.

Ending the Session

> **Step 4**   Click the **Close Problem** button in the Glencoe Smart Guide window.

DO YOU HAVE A QUESTION

Q. *Why doesn't Peachtree include a six-column work sheet report?*

A. The six-column work sheet is a convenient way to manually prepare the income statement and balance sheet. When you use accounting software, such as Peachtree, the program automatically generates these financial statements. A six-column work sheet is not needed to prepare these reports.

Notes

Some of the longer account titles may be truncated (or cut off) on the General Ledger Trial Balance to fit in the space available.

Problem 8-7   Preparing a Six-Column Work Sheet

INSTRUCTIONS

Beginning a Session

Step 1   Select the problem set: Outback Guide Service (Prob. 8-7).

Step 2   Rename the company and set the system date to May 31, 2004.

Preparing a Report

Step 3   Print a General Ledger Trial Balance report.

Ending the Session

Step 4   Click the **Close Problem** button in the Glencoe Smart Guide window.

FAQs

Does Peachtree include an option to print a six-column work sheet?

No. Peachtree does not provide an option to print a work sheet. The program allows you to print an Income Statement and a Balance Sheet. To print an Income Statement or a Balance Sheet, choose the **Financial Statements** option from the *Tasks* menu.

Computerized Accounting Using Spreadsheets

Problem 8-4   Preparing a Six-Column Work Sheet

Completing the Spreadsheet

Step 1   Read the instructions for Problem 8-4 in your textbook. This problem involves preparing a six-column work sheet for Wilderness Rentals.

Step 2   Open the Glencoe Accounting: Electronic Learning Center software.

Step 3   From the Program Menu, click on the **Peachtree Accounting Software and Spreadsheet Applications** icon.

Step 4   Log onto the Management System by typing your user name and password.

Step 5   Under the Chapter Problems tab, select the template: PRO8-4a.xls. The template should look like the one shown below.

```
PROBLEM 8-4
PREPARING A SIX-COLUMN WORK SHEET

(name)
(date)


WILDERNESS RENTALS
WORK SHEET
FOR THE MONTH ENDED MAY 31, 20—
```

ACCOUNT NUMBER	ACCOUNT NAME	TRIAL BALANCE DEBIT	TRIAL BALANCE CREDIT	INCOME STATEMENT DEBIT	INCOME STATEMENT CREDIT	BALANCE SHEET DEBIT	BALANCE SHEET CREDIT
101	Cash in Bank					0.00	
105	Accounts Receivable – Helen Katz					0.00	
110	Accounts Receivable – Polk and Co.					0.00	
115	Office Supplies					0.00	
120	Office Equipment					0.00	
125	Camping Equipment					0.00	
201	Accounts Payable – Adventure Equip. Inc.						0.00
203	Accounts Payable – Digital Tech Computers						0.00
205	Accounts Payable – Greg Mollaro						0.00
301	Ronald Hicks, Capital						0.00
305	Ronald Hicks, Withdrawals					0.00	
310	Income Summary	----	----	----	----		
401	Equipment Rental Revenue				0.00		
501	Advertising Expense			0.00			
505	Maintenance Expense			0.00			
515	Rent Expense			0.00			
525	Utilities Expense			0.00			
		0.00	0.00	0.00	0.00	0.00	0.00
	Net Income			0.00			0.00
				0.00	0.00	0.00	0.00

Step 6   Key your name and today's date in the cells containing the *(name)* and *(date)* placeholders.

Step 7   The first account, Cash in Bank, has a month-end debit balance of $5,814. Move the cell pointer to cell C14 and enter the account balance into the Trial Balance section of the spreadsheet template: **5814**.

TIP: It is not necessary to include a comma or the decimal point and two zeroes as part of the amount. The spreadsheet will automatically format the data when it is entered.

Step 8   Enter the remaining balances into the Trial Balance section of the spreadsheet template. When you have entered all of the balances, move the cell pointer into the Income Statement and Balance Sheet sections of the spreadsheet template. Notice that the amounts for the Income Statement and Balance Sheet are automatically entered. As you enter the data into the Trial Balance section of the spreadsheet template, the program automatically calculates the remaining sections of the work sheet for you. The program also calculates the column totals and the net income for Wilderness Rentals.

Step 9   Save the spreadsheet using the **Save** option from the *File* menu. You should accept the default location of the save as this is handled by the management system.

Step 10   Print the completed spreadsheet.

TIP: If your spreadsheet is too wide to fit on an 8.5-inch wide piece of paper, you can change your print settings to print the worksheet *landscape*. Landscape means that the worksheet will be printed broadside on the page. Some spreadsheet applications also allow you to choose a "print to page" option. This function will reduce the width and/or depth of the worksheet to fit on one page.

Step 11   Exit the spreadsheet program.

Step 12   In the Close Options box, select the location where you would like to save your work.

Step 13   Answer the Analyze question from your textbook for this problem.

What-If Analysis

TIP: Always save your work before performing What-If Analysis. It is not necessary to save your work after performing What-If Analysis unless your teacher instructs you to do so. If you are required to save your work after performing What-If Analysis, be sure to rename the spreadsheet to avoid saving over your original work.

If Cash in Bank were $4,314 and Rent Expense were $5,000, what would Wilderness Rentals' net income (or net loss) be?

Problem 8-8   Completing the Work Sheet

Completing the Spreadsheet

Step 1 Read the instructions for Problem 8-8 in your textbook. This problem involves completing a six-column work sheet for Job Connect.

Step 2 Open the Glencoe Accounting: Electronic Learning Center software.

Step 3 From the Program Menu, click on the **Peachtree Accounting Software and Spreadsheet Applications** icon.

Step 4 Log onto the Management System by typing your user name and password.

Step 5 Under the Chapter Problems tab, select the template: PR08-8a.xls. The template should look like the one shown below.

```
PROBLEM 8-8
COMPLETING THE WORK SHEET

(name)
(date)


JOB CONNECT
WORK SHEET
FOR THE MONTH ENDED MAY 31, 20—
```

ACCOUNT NUMBER	ACCOUNT NAME	TRIAL BALANCE DEBIT	CREDIT	INCOME STATEMENT DEBIT	CREDIT	BALANCE SHEET DEBIT	CREDIT
101	Cash in Bank	18,972.00				18,972.00	
105	Accounts Receivable – CompuRite Systems	765.00				765.00	
110	Accounts Receivable – Marquez Manufacturing	AMOUNT				908.00	
113	Accounts Receivable – Roaring Rivers Water Park	1,268.00				AMOUNT	
115	Accounts Receivable – Melanie Spencer	AMOUNT				86.00	
120	Training Class Supplies	AMOUNT				413.00	
125	Office Supplies	3,061.00				AMOUNT	
130	Office Equipment	4,719.00				AMOUNT	
135	Office Furniture	AMOUNT				19,960.00	
140	Computer Equipment	9,382.00				AMOUNT	
201	Accounts Payable – Micro Solutions, Inc.		AMOUNT				3,019.00
205	Accounts Payable – Vega Internet Services		AMOUNT				8,397.00
207	Accounts Payable – Wildwood Furniture		AMOUNT				5,284.00
301	Richard Tang, Capital		AMOUNT				41,500.00
302	Richard Tang, Withdrawals	1,500.00				AMOUNT	
303	Income Summary	– – – –	– – – –	– – – –	– – – –		
401	Placement Fees Revenue		3,385.00		AMOUNT		
405	Technology Classes Revenue		7,600.00		7,600.00		
501	Advertising Expense	2,174.00		2,174.00			
505	Maintenance Expense	AMOUNT		1,385.00			
510	Miscellaneous Expense	AMOUNT		206.00			
520	Rent Expense	4,100.00		AMOUNT			
530	Utilities Expense	286.00		286.00			
		46,227.00	10,985.00	4,051.00	7,600.00	41,104.00	58,200.00
	Net Income			3,549.00			3,549.00
				7,600.00	7,600.00	41,104.00	61,749.00

Step 6 Key your name and today's date in the cells containing the *(name)* and *(date)* placeholders.

Step 7 The work sheet for Job Connect is given in the spreadsheet template. However, several amounts are missing from various columns. Calculate the missing amounts and enter them in the cells containing the AMOUNT placeholders. For example, the first amount missing is the Trial Balance debit amount for Accounts Receivable—Marquez Manufacturing. By looking in the Balance Sheet debit column, you can see this amount is $908.00. Enter **908** in cell C16. Remember, it is not necessary to enter a dollar sign or the decimal point and ending zeroes.

Step 8 Enter the remaining missing amounts into the work sheet. Notice that the template recalculates the column totals and the net income for Job Connect as you enter the missing amounts.

Step 9 Save the spreadsheet using the **Save** option from the *File* menu. You should accept the default location of the save as this is handled by the management system.

Step 10 Print the completed spreadsheet.

TIP: If your spreadsheet is too wide to fit on an 8.5-inch wide piece of paper, you can change your print settings to print the worksheet *landscape.* Landscape means that the worksheet will be printed broadside on the page. Some spreadsheet applications also allow you to choose a "print to page" option. This function will reduce the width and/or depth of the worksheet to fit on one page.

Step 11 Exit the spreadsheet program.

Step 12 In the Close Options box, select the location where you would like to save your work.

Step 13 Answer the Analyze question from your textbook for this problem.

Working Papers for End-of-Chapter Problems

Problem 8-4   Preparing a Six-Column Work Sheet

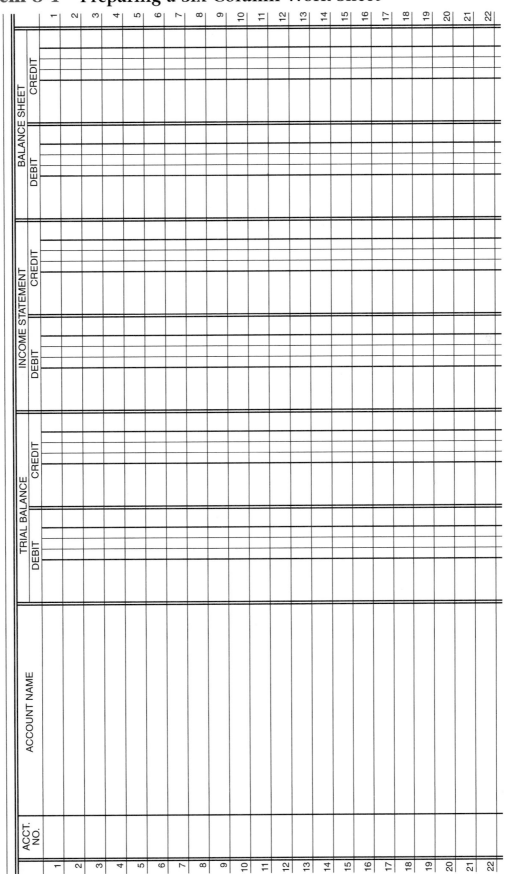

Analyze:

Problem 8-5 Preparing a Six-Column Work Sheet

ACCT. NO.	ACCOUNT NAME	TRIAL BALANCE		INCOME STATEMENT		BALANCE SHEET	
		DEBIT	CREDIT	DEBIT	CREDIT	DEBIT	CREDIT
1							
2							
3							
4							
5							
6							
7							
8							
9							
10							
11							
12							
13							
14							
15							
16							
17							
18							
19							
20							
21							
22							
23							
24							

Analyze:

Problem 8-6 Preparing a Six-Column Work Sheet

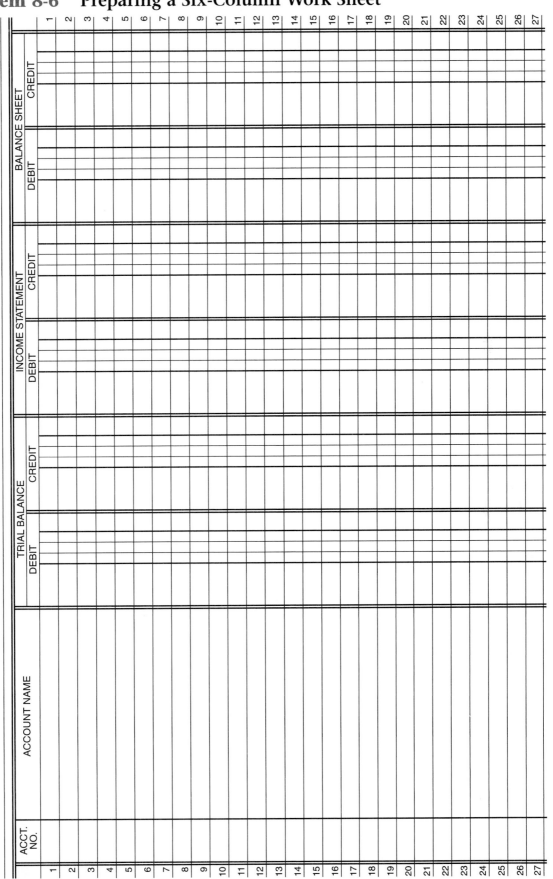

ACCT. NO.	ACCOUNT NAME	TRIAL BALANCE DEBIT	TRIAL BALANCE CREDIT	INCOME STATEMENT DEBIT	INCOME STATEMENT CREDIT	BALANCE SHEET DEBIT	BALANCE SHEET CREDIT

Analyze:

Problem 8-7 Preparing a Six-Column Work Sheet

ACCT. NO.	ACCOUNT NAME	TRIAL BALANCE DEBIT	TRIAL BALANCE CREDIT	INCOME STATEMENT DEBIT	INCOME STATEMENT CREDIT	BALANCE SHEET DEBIT	BALANCE SHEET CREDIT	
								1
								2
								3
								4
								5
								6
								7
								8
								9
								10
								11
								12
								13
								14
								15
								16
								17
								18
								19
								20
								21

Analyze:

Problem 8-8   Completing the Work Sheet

Job Connect
Work Sheet
For the Month Ended May 31, 20--

	ACCT. NO.	ACCOUNT NAME	TRIAL BALANCE DEBIT	TRIAL BALANCE CREDIT	INCOME STATEMENT DEBIT	INCOME STATEMENT CREDIT	BALANCE SHEET DEBIT	BALANCE SHEET CREDIT
1	101	Cash in Bank	1897200				1897200	
2	105	Accts. Rec.—CompuRite Systems	76500				76500	
3	110	Accts. Rec.—Marquez Manuf.	90800				90800	
4	113	Accts. Rec.—Roaring Rivers	126800					
5	115	Accts. Rec.—Melanie Spencer	8600				8600	
6	120	Training Class Supplies	41300				41300	
7	125	Office Supplies	306100					
8	130	Office Equipment	471900					
9	135	Office Furniture	1996000					
10	140	Computer Equipment	938200					
11	201	Accts. Pay.—Micro Solutions Inc.		301900				301900
12	205	Accts. Pay.—Vega Internet Svcs.		839700				
13	207	Accts. Pay.—Wildwood Furniture		528400				528400
14	301	Richard Tang, Capital		4150000				4150000
15	302	Richard Tang, Withdrawals	150000					
16	303	Income Summary						
17	401	Placement Fees Revenue		338500				
18	405	Technology Classes Revenue		760000				
19	501	Advertising Expense	217400		217400			
20	505	Maintenance Expense	138500		138500			
21	510	Miscellaneous Expense	20600		20600			
22	520	Rent Expense	410000					
23	530	Utilities Expense	28600		28600			
24			6918500	6918500				
25		Net Income						
26								
27								

Analyze:

CHAPTER 8   The Six-Column Work Sheet

Self-Test

Part A   True or False

Directions: *Circle the letter* T *in the Answer column if the statement is true; circle the letter* F *if the statement is false.*

Answer

T   F   **1.** A work sheet always covers a period of one month.

T   F   **2.** A net loss decreases the balance in the owner's equity account.

T   F   **3.** A net income for the period is the amount left after the expenses for the period have been subtracted from revenue.

T   F   **4.** Account names are listed on the work sheet in alphabetical order.

T   F   **5.** A net loss for the period is entered in the debit column of the Balance Sheet section.

T   F   **6.** Amounts from the Trial Balance section are extended first to the Income Statement section.

T   F   **7.** Total expenses for the period are reflected in the totals of the credit column of the Income Statement section and the credit column of the Balance Sheet section.

T   F   **8.** All liability accounts are listed in the credit column of the Income Statement section.

T   F   **9.** The Trial Balance section will have entries for all accounts in the general ledger including those with zero balances.

T   F   **10.** All asset accounts are extended to the Balance Sheet section.

Part B   Fill in the Missing Term

Directions: *In the Answer column, write the letter of the word or phrase that best completes the sentence. Some answers may be used more than once.*

A. Balance Sheet section	**E.** extending	**I.** net income
B. capital	**F.** heading	**J.** net loss
C. credit	**G.** Income Statement section	**K.** trial balance
D. debit	**H.** matching principle	**L.** work sheet

Answer

_____   **1.** The first two columns of the work sheet are used to enter the _____.

_____   **2.** The permanent general ledger accounts are extended to the _____ of the work sheet.

_____   **3.** A(n) _____ results when revenue is larger than expenses.

_____   **4.** A net loss is entered in the _____ column of the Income Statement section.

_____   **5.** If the total of the credit column of the Income Statement section is less than the debit column, there is a _____ for the period.

_____   **6.** The amount of net income for the period is added to the total of the credit column of the Balance Sheet section because it increases the balance in the _____ account.

_____   **7.** The _____ of the work sheet answers the questions "who," "what," and "when."

_____   **8.** A paper used to collect information from the general ledger accounts is a(n) _____.

_____   **9.** _____ is transferring balances from the Trial Balance section of the work sheet to either the Balance Sheet section or the Income Statement section.

_____   **10.** The _____ allows a business to match revenue against expenses as a means of measuring profit for the period.

CHAPTER 9   Financial Statements for a Sole Proprietorship

Study Plan

Check Your Understanding

Section 1	*Read Section 1 on pages 204–208 and complete the questions and problems on page 209.*
	❏ Thinking Critically
	❏ Communicating Accounting
	❏ Problem 9-1 *Analyzing a Source Document*
Section 2	*Read Section 2 on pages 210–213 and complete the questions and problems on page 214.*
	❏ Thinking Critically
	❏ Analyzing Accounting
	❏ Problem 9-2 *Determining Ending Capital Balances*
Section 3	*Read Section 3 on pages 216–221 and complete the questions and problems on page 222.*
	❏ Thinking Critically
	❏ Communicating Accounting
	❏ Problem 9-3 *Calculating Return on Sales*
Summary	*Review the Chapter 9 Summary on page 223 in your textbook.*
	❏ Key Concepts
Review and Activities	*Complete the following questions and exercises on pages 224–225 in your textbook.*
	❏ Using Key Terms
	❏ Understanding Accounting Concepts and Procedures
	❏ Case Study
	❏ Conducting an Audit with Alex
	❏ Internet Connection
	❏ Workplace Skills
Computerized Accounting	*Read the Computerized Accounting information on page 226 in your textbook.*
	❏ *Making the Transition from a Manual to a Computerized System*
	❏ *Preparing Financial Statements in Peachtree*
Problems	*Complete the following end-of-chapter problems for Chapter 9 in your textbook.*
	❏ Problem 9-4 *Preparing an Income Statement*
	❏ Problem 9-5 *Preparing a Statement of Changes in Owner's Equity*
	❏ Problem 9-6 *Preparing Financial Statements*
	❏ Problem 9-7 *Preparing Financial Statements*
Challenge Problem	❏ Problem 9-8 *Preparing a Statement of Changes in Owner's Equity*
Chapter Reviews and Working Papers	*Complete the following exercises for Chapter 9 in your Chapter Reviews and Working Papers.*
	❏ Chapter Review
	❏ Self-Test

CHAPTER 9 REVIEW   Financial Statements for a Sole Proprietorship

Part 1   Accounting Vocabulary (24 points)

Total Points	66
Student's Score	

Directions: *Using terms from the following list, complete the sentences below. Write the letter of the term you have chosen in the space provided.*

A. balance sheet	**F.** income statement	**H.** liquidity ratio	**L.** return on sales
B. current assets	**G.** Income Statement	**I.** net income	**M.** statement of changes
C. current liabilities	section of the	**J.** profitability ratios	in owner's equity
D. current ratio	work sheet	**K.** report form	**N.** work sheet
E. financial statements			

   _G_   **0.** The source of information for completing the income statement is the _____.

         1. The financial statement that reports the net income or net loss for the fiscal period it covers is the _____.

         2. The classifications of balance sheet accounts are shown one under the other in the _____.

         3. Reports prepared to summarize the changes resulting from business transactions that have occurred during a fiscal period are called _____.

         4. A financial statement that is prepared to summarize the effects on the capital account of the various business transactions that occurred during the fiscal period is called a(n) _____.

         5. _____ occurs when total revenue is greater than total expenses.

         6. The net income or net loss amount shown on the income statement must agree with the amount shown on the _____.

         7. A financial statement that is a report of the final balances in all asset, liability, and owner's equity accounts at the end of the fiscal period is the _____.

         8. The _____ is the relationship between current assets and current liabilities.

         9. The _____ ratio is used to examine the portion of each sales dollar that represents profit.

         10. A _____ is a measure of a business's ability to pay its current debts as they become due and to provide for unexpected needs of cash.

         11. _____ are the debts of the business that must be paid within the next accounting period.

         12. _____ are assets used up or converted to cash during the normal operating cycle of the business.

         13. _____ are used to evaluate the earnings performance of the business during the accounting period.

Part 2   Determining Account Balances (17 points)

Directions: *The beginning capital balance for several different businesses appears in the first column below. The other columns list the withdrawals, investments, total revenue, total expenses, and ending capital balances for each business. Fill in the blank spaces by adding or subtracting across each line.*

	Capital Oct. 1	Withdrawals	Owner's Investment	Total Revenue	Total Expenses	Capital Oct. 31
0	$28,394	$500	$ 2,000	$7,394	*$4,203*	$33,085
1	$36,495	$300	$ 0	$4,395	$3,127	
2	$84,393	$600	$ 1,000	$5,584		$86,410
3	$52,815	$700		$8,721	$5,906	$55,780
4		$400	$ 0	$6,849	$6,127	$13,943
5	$19,302	$600	$ 0		$3,833	$18,229
6	$31,304		$ 1,000	$9,494	$8,048	$33,250

Part 3   Analyzing Information on Financial Statements (9 points)

Directions: *Read each of the following statements to determine whether the statement is true or false. Write your answer in the space provided.*

True	**0.** The statement of changes in owner's equity is prepared before the balance sheet.
_____	**1.** The balance sheet is prepared from the information in the Balance Sheet section of the work sheet and from the statement of changes in owner's equity.
_____	**2.** A net loss and withdrawals both cause an increase in the capital account.
_____	**3.** The balance sheet represents the basic accounting equation.
_____	**4.** The wording of the date line in the heading on the income statement is important.
_____	**5.** The balance sheet contains only the permanent general ledger accounts.
_____	**6.** The statement of changes in owner's equity is completed as a supporting document for the income statement.
_____	**7.** The sections listed on the income statement are the heading, the revenue for the period, the capital for the period, and the net income or loss for the period.
_____	**8.** The primary financial statements prepared for a sole proprietorship are the income statement and the statement of changes in owner's equity.
_____	**9.** The statement of changes in owner's equity shows the changes in the Cash in Bank account from the beginning of the fiscal period through the end of the period.

Part 4   Reporting Information on Financial Statements (16 points)

Directions: *Each of the following types of information appears on one or more of the financial statements. Indicate the appropriate financial statements by placing an "X" in the appropriate space.*

Financial Information	Income Statement	Statement of Changes in Owner's Equity	Balance Sheet
0. Cash in Bank	_____	_____	X
1. Total Expenses	_____	_____	_____
2. Ending Capital	_____	_____	_____
3. Accounts Payable—Beacon Co.	_____	_____	_____
4. Rent Expense	_____	_____	_____
5. Total Liabilities	_____	_____	_____
6. Commissions Revenue	_____	_____	_____
7. Investment by owner	_____	_____	_____
8. Total Assets	_____	_____	_____
9. Beginning Capital	_____	_____	_____
10. Withdrawals by owner	_____	_____	_____
11. Net Loss	_____	_____	_____
12. Computer Equipment	_____	_____	_____
13. Net Income	_____	_____	_____
14. Service Fees	_____	_____	_____
15. Accounts Receivable	_____	_____	_____
16. Total Liabilities and Owner's Equity	_____	_____	_____

Working Papers *for Section Problems*

Problem 9-1 Analyzing a Source Document

1. _____
2. _____
3. _____
4. _____
5. _____
6. _____
7. _____

Problem 9-2 Determining Ending Capital Balances

	Beginning Capital	Investments	Revenue	Expenses	Withdrawals	Ending Capital
1	$60,000	$ 500	$ 5,100	$2,400	$ 700	
2	$24,075	$ 0	$13,880	$7,240	$ 800	
3	$28,800	$ 1,000	$ 6,450	$6,780	$ 0	
4	$ 0	$10,500	$ 5,320	$4,990	$ 200	
5	$ 6,415	$ 0	$ 4,520	$3,175	$ 700	
6	$20,870	$ 1,300	$13,980	$9,440	$1,700	

Problem 9-3 Calculating Return on Sales

Return on sales _____ %

Space for calculations:

Computerized Accounting Using Peachtree

Software Objectives

When you have completed this chapter, you will be able to use Peachtree to:

1. Print a Trial Balance report.
2. Print an Income Statement.
3. Print a Balance Sheet.

Problem 9-4   **Preparing an Income Statement**
Problem 9-5   **Preparing a Statement of Changes in Owner's Equity**

INSTRUCTIONS

Beginning a Session

> **Step 1**   Select the problem set: Wilderness Rentals (Prob. 9-4).
> **Step 2**   Rename the company and set the system date to September 30, 2004.

Preparing Reports

> **Step 3**   Print a General Ledger Trial Balance report.
> **Step 4**   Print an Income Statement.

> *To print an Income Statement:*
>
> - Choose **Financial Statements** from the **Reports** Menu.
> - Select **Income Statement (Monthly)** shown at the bottom of the report list. (See Figure 9-5A.)
> - Click 🖥️ Screen .
> - Click **OK** to accept the report options.
> - Review the report.
> - Click 🖨️ Print to print the report.

DO YOU HAVE A QUESTION❓

Q. *Does the Peachtree software include an option to print a Statement of Changes in Owner's Equity?*

A. No. Peachtree does not provide the capability to print the Statement of Changes in Owner's Equity report. The balance sheet, however, shows the beginning capital balance, withdrawals, net income (loss), and the ending capital balance.

❋**Notes**

    Peachtree lets you create customized financial statement reports. A customized report appears in the Report List with a special icon. (See Figure 9-5A.)

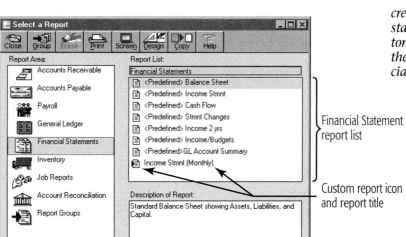

Figure 9-5A   *Select a Report Window (Financial Statements)*

Step 5   Print the Balance Sheet.
Step 6   Answer the Analyze questions shown in your textbook.

TIP: Use the calculator accessory available on your computer to calculate the return on sales and the current ratio.

Ending the Session

Step 7   Click the **Close Problem** button in the Glencoe Smart Guide window.

Problem 9-6   Preparing Financial Statements

INSTRUCTIONS

Beginning a Session

Step 1   Select the problem set: Hot Suds Car Wash (Prob. 9-6).
Step 2   Rename the company and set the system date to September 30, 2004.

Preparing Reports

Step 3   Print a General Ledger Trial Balance report.
Step 4   Print the quarterly Income Statement report, not the predefined report.
Step 5   Print the predefined (standard) Balance Sheet.
Step 6   Answer the Analyze question shown in your textbook.

Ending the Session

Step 7   Click the **Close Problem** button in the Glencoe Smart Guide window.

Mastering Peachtree

Customize the predefined balance sheet to summarize the financial information. Change the layout of the report to combine all assets into one section. Also, combine the liabilities into one section. Print your results.

DO YOU HAVE A QUESTION

Q. *Can you use the pre-defined income statement instead of the customized report?*

A. Yes. You can use the pre-defined income statement. The only difference, however, is that the predefined report includes year-to-date figures. For the problems in this chapter, the current month and year-to-date figures are the same.

Notes

Peachtree does not offer a Statement of Changes in Owner's Equity report.

Problem 9-7   Preparing Financial Statements

INSTRUCTIONS

Beginning a Session

Step 1   Select the problem set: Kits & Pups Grooming (Prob. 9-7).
Step 2   Rename the company and set the system date to September 30, 2004.

Preparing Reports

Step 3   Print a General Ledger Trial Balance report.
Step 4   Print an Income Statement.
Step 5   Print a Balance Sheet.
Step 6   Manually prepare a Statement of Changes in Owner's Equity.
Step 7   Answer the Analyze question shown in your textbook.

Ending the Session

Step 8   Click the **Close Problem** button in the Glencoe Smart Guide window.

Computerized Accounting Using Spreadsheets

Problem 9-8   Preparing a Statement of Changes in Owner's Equity

Completing the Spreadsheet

Step 1   Read the instructions for Problem 9-8 in your textbook. This problem involves preparing a statement of changes in owner's equity.

Step 2   Open the Glencoe Accounting: Electronic Learning Center software.

Step 3   From the Program Menu, click on the **Peachtree Accounting Software and Spreadsheet Applications** icon.

Step 4   Log onto the Management System by typing your user name and password.

Step 5   Under the Chapter Problems tab, select the template: PR09-8a.xls. The template should look like the one shown below.

```
PROBLEM 9-8
PREPARING A STATEMENT OF CHANGES IN OWNER'S EQUITY


(name)
(date)


                             OUTBACK GUIDE SERVICE
                     STATEMENT OF CHANGES IN OWNER'S EQUITY
                       FOR THE MONTH ENDED SEPTEMBER 30, 20--
Beginning Capital, September 1, 20--                                   0.00
Add: Investments by owner                          AMOUNT
     Net Income                                    AMOUNT
Total Increase in Capital                                              0.00
Subtotal                                                              0.00
Less: Withdrawals by owner                                         AMOUNT
Ending Capital, September 30, 20--                                 AMOUNT
```

Step 6   Key your name and today's date in the cells containing the *(name)* and *(date)* placeholders.

Step 7   Enter the investments by owner, net income, withdrawals by owner, and ending capital in the cells containing the AMOUNT placeholders. Remember, it is not necessary to add the decimal point and ending zeroes. The beginning capital and the total increase in capital will be automatically computed. When you have finished entering the amounts, ask your teacher to check your work.

Step 8   Save the spreadsheet using the **Save** option from the *File* menu. You should accept the default location of the save as this is handled by the management system.

Step 9   Print the completed spreadsheet.

Step 10 Exit the spreadsheet program.

Step 11 In the Close Options box, select the location where you would like to save your work.

Step 12 Answer the Analyze question from your textbook for this problem.

What-If Analysis

TIP: Remember, always save your work before performing What-If Analysis. Be sure to rename the spreadsheet if you save your work after performing What-If Analysis.

If the owner withdrew $3,200 during the period, what would beginning capital be?

_____

Working Papers *for End-of-Chapter Problems*
Problem 9-4   Preparing an Income Statement

Wilderness Rentals
Work Sheet
For the Month Ended September 30, 20--

ACCT. NO.	ACCOUNT NAME	TRIAL BALANCE Debit	TRIAL BALANCE Credit	INCOME STATEMENT Debit	INCOME STATEMENT Credit	BALANCE SHEET Debit	BALANCE SHEET Credit
101	Cash in Bank	551000				551000	
105	Accts. Rec.—Helen Katz	92900				92900	
110	Accts. Rec.—Polk and Co.	46700				46700	
115	Office Supplies	97400				97400	
120	Office Equipment	451900				451900	
125	Camping Equipment	630000				630000	
201	Accts. Pay.—Adventure Equip.		231600				231600
203	Accts. Pay.—Digital Tech		110900				110900
205	Accts. Pay.—Greg Mollaro		90200				90200
301	Ronald Hicks, Capital		1326000				1326000
305	Ronald Hicks, Withdrawals	70000				70000	
310	Income Summary						
401	Equipment Rental Revenue		1062900		1062900		
501	Advertising Expense	211300		211300			
505	Maintenance Expense	120000		120000			
515	Rent Expense	350000		350000			
525	Utilities Expense	200400		200400			
		2821600	2821600	881700	1062900	1939900	1758700
	Net Income			181200			181200
				1062900	1062900	1939900	1939900

Problem 9-4 (concluded)

Analyze: _____

Problem 9-5 Preparing a Statement of Changes in Owner's Equity

Problem 9-5   (concluded)

Analyze:

Problem 9-6   Preparing Financial Statements

(1)

Hot Suds Car Wash

Work Sheet

For the Month Ended September 30, 20--

	ACCT. NO.	ACCOUNT NAME	TRIAL BALANCE DEBIT	TRIAL BALANCE CREDIT	INCOME STATEMENT DEBIT	INCOME STATEMENT CREDIT	BALANCE SHEET DEBIT	BALANCE SHEET CREDIT	
1	101	Cash in Bank	845700						1
2	105	Accts. Rec.—Linda Brown	58400						2
3	110	Accts. Rec.—Valley Auto	61900						3
4	115	Detailing Supplies	81000						4
5	120	Detergent Supplies	46000						5
6	125	Office Equipment	1524000						6
7	130	Office Furniture	216000						7
8	135	Car Wash Equipment	752200						8
9	201	Accts. Pay.—Allen Vacuum		352800					9
10	204	Accts. Pay.—O'Brian's Office		121500					10
11	301	Regina Delgado, Capital		2384500					11
12	305	Regina Delgado, Withdrawals	150000						12
13	310	Income Summary							13
14	401	Wash Revenue		962300					14
15	405	Wax Revenue		801900					15
16	410	Interior Detailing Revenue		262800					16
17	501	Advertising Expense	196300						17
18	505	Equipment Rental Expense	413700						18
19	510	Maintenance Expense	118600						19
20	520	Rent Expense	350000						20
21	530	Utilities Expense	72000						21
22			4885800	4885800					22
23									23
24									24
25									25

Problem 9-6 (continued)

(2)

(3)

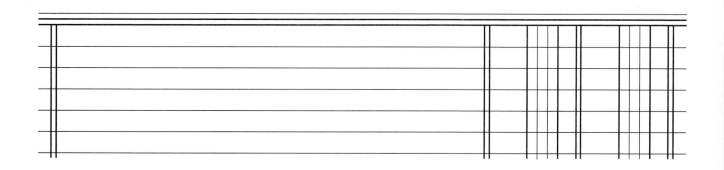

Problem 9-6 (concluded)

(4)

_____

_____

Analyze: _____

Problem 9-7   Preparing Financial Statements

(1)

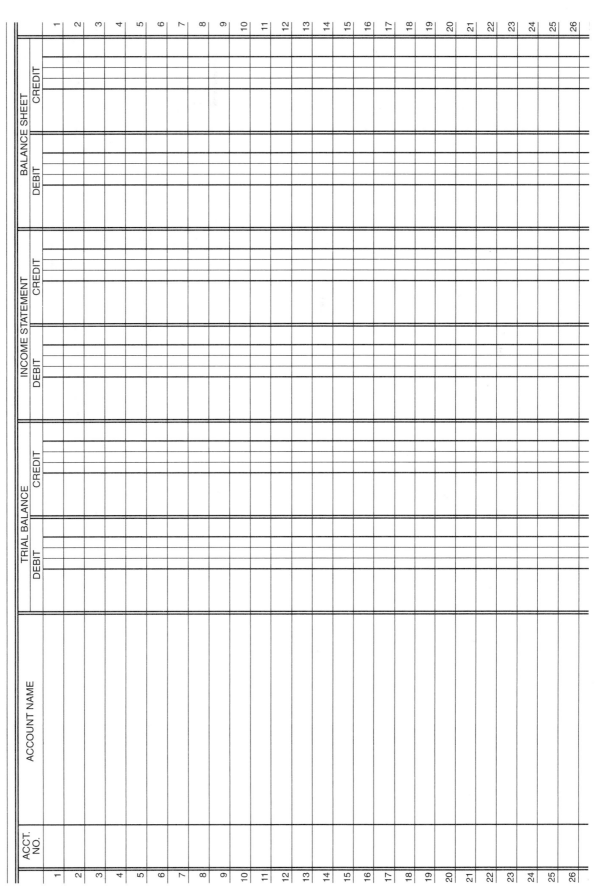

Problem 9-7   (continued)

(2)

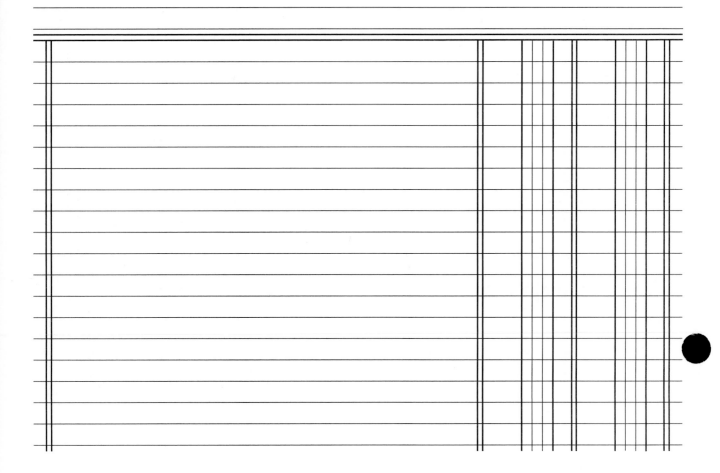

(3)

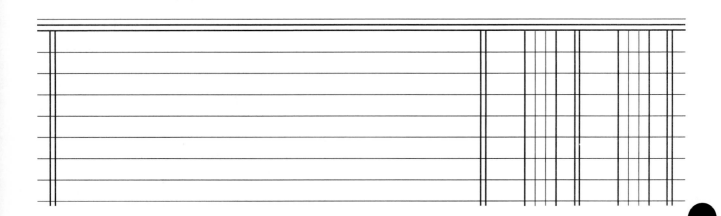

Problem 9-7 (concluded)

(4)

Analyze: _____

_____

Problem 9-8   Preparing a Statement of Changes in Owner's Equity

Analyze: _____

CHAPTER 9   Financial Statements for a Sole Proprietorship

Self-Test

Part A   True or False

Directions: *Circle the letter* T *in the Answer column if the statement is true; circle the letter* F *if the statement is false.*

Answer

T	F	**1.** The Trial Balance section of the work sheet provides the information used in preparing the income statement.
T	F	**2.** The changes in the Cash in Bank account are reported in the statement of changes in owner's equity.
T	F	**3.** The balance sheet reports the final balances of the permanent accounts at the end of the fiscal period.
T	F	**4.** The balance sheet is prepared before the statement of changes in owner's equity.
T	F	**5.** The income statement represents the basic accounting equation.
T	F	**6.** A net income will increase the owner's capital account.
T	F	**7.** The heading is the same on all three financial statements.
T	F	**8.** The statement of changes in owner's equity summarizes the effects on the capital account of the various business transactions that occurred during the period.
T	F	**9.** The primary financial statements prepared for a sole proprietorship are the income statement and the balance sheet.
T	F	**10.** The information on the statement of changes in owner's equity is used in preparing the income statement.

Part B Fill in the Missing Term

Directions: *In the Answer column, write the letter of the word or phrase that best completes the sentence. Some answers may be used more than once.*

A. balance sheet	**E.** Income Statement section of the work sheet	**H.** on a specific date
B. Balance Sheet section of the work sheet		**I.** report form
	F. heading	**J.** statement of changes in owner's equity
C. financial statements		
D. income statement	**G.** net income or net loss	**K.** work sheet

Answer

_____ 1. The _____ is completed as a support document for the balance sheet.

_____ 2. The balance sheet reports financial information _____.

_____ 3. The information needed to prepare the income statement comes from the _____.

_____ 4. _____ is reported on the income statement.

_____ 5. The amount of net income or net loss reported on the income statement must match the amount shown on the _____.

_____ 6. _____ summarize the changes resulting from business transactions that have occurred during a fiscal period.

_____ 7. A(n) _____ is the financial statement that reports the final balances in all asset, liability, and owner's equity accounts at the end of the fiscal period.

_____ 8. In the _____, the classification of balance sheet accounts are shown one under the other.

_____ 9. The _____ reports a business's net income or net loss over an entire fiscal period.

_____ 10. The source of information for completing the balance sheet comes from the work sheet and the _____.

_____ 11. The _____ of a financial statement answers the questions: Who?, What?, and When?

CHAPTER 10

Completing the Accounting Cycle for a Sole Proprietorship

Study Plan

Check Your Understanding

Section 1   *Read Section 1 on pages 232–241 and complete the following exercises on page 242.*
- ❏ Thinking Critically
- ❏ Communicating Accounting
- ❏ Problem 10-1   *Preparing Closing Entries*
- ❏ Problem 10-2   *Analyzing a Source Document*

Section 2   *Read Section 2 on pages 243–245 and complete the following exercises on page 246.*
- ❏ Thinking Critically
- ❏ Communicating Accounting
- ❏ Problem 10-3   *Determining Accounts Affected by Closing Entries*

Summary   *Review the Chapter 10 Summary on page 247 in your textbook.*
- ❏ Key Concepts

Review and Activities   *Complete the following questions and exercises on pages 248–249 in your textbook.*
- ❏ Using Key Terms
- ❏ Understanding Accounting Concepts and Procedures
- ❏ Case Study
- ❏ Conducting an Audit with Alex
- ❏ Internet Connection
- ❏ Workplace Skills

Computerized Accounting   *Read the Computerized Accounting information on page 250 in your textbook.*
- ❏ *Making the Transition from a Manual to a Computerized System*
- ❏ *Closing the Accounting Period in Peachtree*

Problems   *Complete the following end-of-chapter problems for Chapter 10 in your textbook.*
- ❏ Problem 10-4   *Preparing Closing Entries*
- ❏ Problem 10-5   *Preparing a Post-Closing Trial Balance*
- ❏ Problem 10-6   *Journalizing Closing Entries*
- ❏ Problem 10-7   *Posting Closing Entries and Preparing a Post-Closing Trial Balance*
- ❏ Problem 10-8   *Completing End-of-Period Activities*

Challenge Problem
- ❏ Problem 10-9   *Completing End-of-Period Activities*

Chapter Reviews and Working Papers   *Complete the following exercises for Chapter 10 in your Chapter Reviews and Working Papers.*
- ❏ Chapter Review
- ❏ Self-Test

CHAPTER 10 REVIEW — Completing the Accounting Cycle for a Sole Proprietorship

Part 1   Accounting Vocabulary (7 points)

Directions: *Using terms from the following list, complete the sentences below. Write the letter of the term you have chosen in the space provided.*

A. closing entries	**D.** Income Summary	**G.** temporary capital accounts
B. "Closing Entries"	**E.** permanent accounts	**H.** zero balances
C. compound entry	**F.** post-closing trial balance	

Total Points 34
Student's Score ____

___*B*___   **0.** _____ is written in the Description column of the general journal to explain the entries that close out the balances in the temporary capital accounts.

_____   **1.** A(n) _____ has two or more debits or credits in the general journal.

_____   **2.** The only accounts and balances listed on the post-closing trial balance are the _____ of the business.

_____   **3.** The _____ are used to record transactions involving revenue, expenses, and withdrawals.

_____   **4.** The general ledger account used to accumulate and summarize the revenue and expenses for the period is _____.

_____   **5.** The trial balance prepared after the closing entries have been posted is the _____.

_____   **6.** The temporary capital accounts are not listed on the post-closing trial balance because they have _____.

_____   **7.** Journal entries that close out the balances in the temporary capital accounts and transfer net income or net loss for the period to the capital account are called _____.

Part 2   Recording Closing Entries (9 points)

Directions: *Read each of the following statements to determine whether the statement is true or false. Write your answer in the space provided.*

___*False*___   **0.** The last step in the accounting cycle is to journalize and post closing entries.

_____   **1.** Before the closing entries are journalized and posted, there is only one account in the general ledger that shows the revenue and expenses for the fiscal period.

_____   **2.** When the revenue account is closed, Income Summary is credited.

_____   **3.** To close an expense account, debit it for the amount of its credit balance.

_____   **4.** Closing the withdrawals account into the capital account is the last closing entry to be made.

_____   **5.** Closing entries are made for all temporary capital accounts and all permanent accounts.

_____   **6.** To close a revenue account, credit it for the amount of its debit balance.

_____   **7.** The Income Summary account can be found on the income statement.

_____   **8.** A separate closing entry is needed for each expense account.

_____   **9.** The balances of the revenue and expense accounts apply to only one fiscal period.

Part 3   The Final Steps of the Accounting Cycle (10 points)

Directions: *For each of the following statements, select the answer that correctly completes the statement. Write your answer in the space provided.*

___*C*___   **0.** Closing entries are used to transfer the net income or net loss for the period to the
(A) revenue account.　　　(C) capital account.
(B) withdrawals account.　　(D) Cash in Bank account.

_____   **1.** Of the following accounts, a closing entry would be required for
(A) Accounts Receivable.　　(C) Cash in Bank.
(B) Rent Expense.　　　　　(D) Equipment.

_____   **2.** To close the withdrawals account, the amount of its balance is debited to the
(A) Income Summary account.　　(C) Cash in Bank account.
(B) withdrawals account.　　　　(D) capital account.

_____ **3.** Which of the following is **not** a true statement?
(A) The Income Summary account is used only at the end of the fiscal period.
(B) The Income Summary account is located in the owner's equity section of the general ledger.
(C) The Income Summary account does not have a normal balance.
(D) The Income Summary account is a permanent capital account.

_____ **4.** If a business had a net loss for the period, the journal entry to close out the balance of the Income Summary account into the capital account would be
(A) a debit to Income Summary, a credit to the capital account.
(B) a debit to the capital account, a credit to Income Summary.
(C) a debit to the revenue account, a credit to the capital account.
(D) a debit to the capital account, a credit to Cash in Bank.

_____ **5.** In the accounting cycle, the closing process represents the
(A) sixth step.   (C) eighth step.
(B) seventh step.   (D) ninth step.

_____ **6.** Which account would appear in the post-closing trial balance?
(A) Leah Moore, Capital.   (C) Rent Expense.
(B) Professional Fees.   (D) Leah Moore, Withdrawals.

_____ **7.** Temporary capital accounts start each fiscal period with
(A) credit balances.
(B) debit balances.
(C) zero balances.
(D) debit balances for expenses and credit balances for revenue.

_____ **8.** The first step in the closing procedure is to transfer the balance of the
(A) expense accounts into Income Summary.
(B) withdrawals account to the capital account.
(C) Income Summary account into the capital account.
(D) revenue account to Income Summary.

_____ **9.** The source of information for the closing entries is the
(A) work sheet.   (C) general ledger.
(B) income statement.   (D) balance sheet.

_____ **10.** In the closing process, the journal entry made to transfer the balance of the Income Summary account into the capital account is the
(A) first step.   (C) third step.
(B) second step.   (D) fourth step.

Part 4 Analyzing Closing Entries (8 points)

Directions: *Using the following list of account names, determine the account names to be debited and credited for the closing entries below.*

A. Della Lane, Capital	**C.** Income Summary	**E.** Rent Expense
B. Della Lane, Withdrawals	**D.** Membership Fees	**F.** Utilities Expense

Debit	**Credit**	
A	*B*	**0.** Close out the balance of the withdrawals account.
_____	_____	**1.** Close out the amount of a net loss for the period.
_____	_____	**2.** Close out the balance of the revenue account.
_____	_____	**3.** Close out the balances of the expense accounts.
_____	_____	**4.** Close out the amount of a net income for the period.

Working Papers *for Section Problems*

Problem 10-1   Preparing Closing Entries

GENERAL JOURNAL   PAGE ___*22*___

	DATE	DESCRIPTION	POST. REF.	DEBIT	CREDIT	
1						1
2						2
3						3
4						4
5						5
6						6
7						7
8						8
9						9

Problem 10-2   Analyzing a Source Document

(1), (3)

GENERAL JOURNAL   PAGE ___*18*___

	DATE	DESCRIPTION	POST. REF.	DEBIT	CREDIT	
1						1
2						2
3						3
4						4
5						5
6						6
7						7
8						8
9						9

(2), (4)

Cash in Bank   Income Summary   Utilities Expense

Problem 10-3   Determining Accounts Affected by Closing Entries

Account Name	Financial Statement	Is the account affected by a closing entry?	Does the account appear on the post-closing trial balance?
Accounts Payable—The Fitness Shop	*Balance Sheet*	*No*	*Yes*
Accounts Receivable—Linda Brown			
Advertising Expense			
Cash in Bank			
Exercise Class Revenue			
Exercise Equipment			
Income Summary			
Laundry Equipment			
Maintenance Expense			
Membership Fees			
Miscellaneous Expense			
Office Furniture			
Rent Expense			
Repair Tools			
Ted Chapman, Capital			
Ted Chapman, Withdrawals			
Utilities Expense			

Computerized Accounting Using Peachtree

Software Objectives

When you have completed this chapter, you will be able to use Peachtree to:

1. Close the current fiscal year.
2. Print a Post-Closing Trial Balance.

Problem 10-4   Preparing Closing Entries

INSTRUCTIONS

Beginning a Session

Step 1   Select the problem set: Wilderness Rentals (Prob. 10-4).

Step 2   Rename the company and set the system date to December 31, 2004.

Completing the Accounting Problem

Step 3   Perform the closing process.

To close the fiscal year:

- Choose **System** from the *Tasks* menu and then choose **Close Fiscal Year**.
- Click **Continue** when prompted to backup your work since you do not have to make a backup for this problem.
- Peachtree displays an alert to close the payroll year first if you are using the payroll features or 1099s. Since you are not using any of the features mentioned in the warning message, click **Yes** to continue.
- Click **No** when prompted to print the reports.

   If you haven't printed the final reports for the year, Peachtree lets you print the General Ledger report before you continue the closing process. You do not have to print these reports unless instructed otherwise.

- Click **OK** when Peachtree displays a warning message that identifies which account it will use for the closing process.

   When you setup a company, you must identify the capital account that Peachtree uses to close the temporary capital accounts (revenue and expenses). Peachtree refers to this account as the retained earnings account. As you can see, Peachtree will use account 301, the owner's capital account. If this were not the correct account, you could cancel the posting process.

- Click **OK** to complete the closing process when the Close Fiscal Year window appears. (See Figure 10-4A.)

   The Close Fiscal Year window shows the number of periods (12) in the next fiscal year, the current period (Jan. 1 to Jan. 31, 2005), and the calendar year. You can change only the current period, but you do not have to change it since the first period is correct. When you click **OK**, Peachtree creates the closing entries and then automatically switches to the next period.

DO YOU HAVE A QUESTION

Q. *Should you create a backup before closing the fiscal year?*

A. In a real-life situation, it is strongly recommended that you make a backup of your work. You should do this because you cannot access transactions from a closed period. Also, the company data files may be damaged if the closing process is interrupted. Taking a few moments to make a backup could save you many hours of work in the event that your data files are accidentally damaged.

For the chapter problems in your textbook, however, you do not have to make a backup disk unless specifically instructed. If a problem occurs, you can always restore the original problem set.

Notes

You do not have to manually enter the closing entries since the Peachtree software automatically performs the closing process.

Peachtree Guide

- Click **No** when prompted to purge data.

  You do not have to purge data for the problems in your text-book, but this step would be necessary if you were using Peachtree in a real-life company. Over a year, you may enter thousands of transactions. These transactions take up a considerable amount of space on a hard drive. Purging the transactions consolidates the transactions and deletes the detailed information, freeing space for the new transactions.

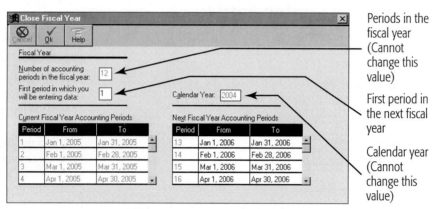

Figure 10-4A *Close Fiscal Year Window*

Step 4   Change the system date to January 1, 2005.

Step 5   Answer the Analyze question.

TIP: Display a General Ledger report or a Trial Balance to view an account balance after you perform the closing process.

Ending the Session

Step 6   Click the **Close Problem** button in the Glencoe Smart Guide window.

Mastering Peachtree

Review the online help information to learn how to make a backup disk. Backup your work to a floppy disk. Then, use the backup disk to restore the files for the company.

Problem 10-5   Preparing a Post-Closing Trial Balance

INSTRUCTIONS

Beginning a Session

Step 1   Select the problem set: Hot Suds Car Wash (Prob. 10-5).

Step 2   Rename the company and set the system date to January 1, 2005.

Preparing a Report

Step 3   Print a Post-Closing Trial Balance.

Step 4   Answer the Analyze question.

Ending the Session

Step 5   Click the **Close Problem** button in the Glencoe Smart Guide window.

> **DO YOU HAVE A QUESTION**
>
> **Q.** *How do you print a post-closing trial balance since Peachtree does not include this report?*
>
> **A.** Peachtree does not include a predefined report called Post-Closing Trial Balance, but the standard General Ledger Trial Balance provides the same information. The only difference is the title of the report which you can change using the report options.

Mastering Peachtree

Print a General Ledger Trial Balance, but change the report title to *Post-Closing Trial Balance*. Review the online help to learn how to change a report title.

Problem 10-6 Journalizing Closing Entries

INSTRUCTIONS

Beginning a Session

    Step 1   Select the problem set: Kits & Pups Grooming (Prob. 10-6).

    Step 2   Rename the company and set the system date to December 31, 2004.

Completing the Accounting Problem

    Step 3   Perform the closing process.

> **TIP:** Review the steps presented in Problem 10-4 if you need help closing the fiscal year.

    Step 4   Change the system date to January 1, 2005.

    Step 5   Answer the Analyze question.

Ending the Session

    Step 6   Click the **Close Problem** button in the Glencoe Smart Guide window.

Problem 10-7 Posting Closing Entries and Preparing a Post-Closing Trial Balance

INSTRUCTIONS

Beginning a Session

    Step 1   Select the problem set: Outback Guide Service (Prob. 10-7).

    Step 2   Rename the company and set the system date to December 31, 2004.

Completing the Accounting Problem

    Step 3   Perform the closing process.

> **TIP:** Review the steps presented in Problem 10-4 if you need help closing the fiscal year.

    Step 4   Change the system date to January 1, 2005.

    Step 5   Print a General Ledger Trial Balance.

    Step 6   Answer the Analyze question.

Ending the Session

    Step 7   Click the **Close Problem** button in the Glencoe Smart Guide window.

DO YOU HAVE A QUESTION

Q. *Can you undo the closing process?*

A. No. Once you close a fiscal year, you cannot undo the process and reset the company data files. For this reason, Peachtree strongly recommends that you backup your work. Before you close a fiscal year, you should proof the transactions, print summary reports, and print the financial statements for the current period.

DO YOU HAVE A QUESTION

Q. *Do you have to manually post the closing entries?*

A. No. When you choose to close the fiscal year, Peachtree generates the closing entries behind the scenes for you. The Peachtree software also automates the posting process just as it automatically posts the entries when you record a general journal transaction.

Notes

Choose to print the General Ledger Trial Balance whenever you need a Post-Closing Trial Balance.

Problem 10-8   Completing End-of-Period Activities

INSTRUCTIONS

Beginning a Session

  Step 1   Select the problem set: Showbiz Video (Prob. 10-8).

  Step 2   Rename the company and set the system date to December 31, 2004.

Completing the Accounting Problem

  Step 3   Print a General Ledger Trial Balance.

  Step 4   Print the financial statements.

  Step 5   Perform the closing process.

  Step 6   Change the system date to January 1, 2005.

  Step 7   Print a General Ledger Trial Balance.

  Step 8   Answer the Analyze question.

Ending the Session

  Step 9   Click the **Close Problem** button in the Glencoe Smart Guide window.

FAQs

What if you notice a mistake after you close the fiscal year?

You have two options if you notice a mistake after you close the fiscal year. If you made a backup before the closing, you can restore the company data, correct the error, and then close the fiscal year again. If you did not make a backup or you do not want to restore the company data, make a correcting entry in the new period.

Can you undo the closing process?

No. Once you close a fiscal year, you cannot undo the process and reset the company data files. For this reason, Peachtree strongly recommends that you backup your work. Before you close a fiscal year, you should proof the transactions, print summary reports, and print the financial statements for the current period.

How do you print a post-closing trial balance since Peachtree does not include this report?

Peachtree does not include a predefined report called Post-Closing Trial Balance, but the standard General Ledger Trial Balance provides the same information. The only difference is the title of the report which you can change using the report options.

Computerized Accounting Using Spreadsheets

Problem 10-9 Completing End-of-Period Activities

Completing the Spreadsheet

Step 1 Read the instructions for Problem 10-9 in your textbook. This problem involves preparing a six-column work sheet and the end-of-period financial statements for Job Connect.

Step 2 Open the Glencoe Accounting: Electronic Learning Center software.

Step 3 From the Program Menu, click on the **Peachtree Accounting Software and Spreadsheet Applications** icon.

Step 4 Log onto the Management System by typing your user name and password.

Step 5 Under the Chapter Problems tab, select the template: PR10-9a.xls. The template should look like the one shown below.

```
PROBLEM 10-9
COMPLETING END-OF-PERIOD ACTIVITIES


(name)
(date)


JOB CONNECT
WORK SHEET
FOR THE MONTH ENDED DECEMBER 31, 20--
```

ACCOUNT NUMBER	ACCOUNT NAME	TRIAL BALANCE DEBIT	CREDIT	INCOME STATEMENT DEBIT	CREDIT	BALANCE SHEET DEBIT	CREDIT
101	Cash in Bank					0.00	
105	Accounts Receivable – CompuRite Systems					0.00	
110	Accounts Receivable – Marquez Manufacturing					0.00	
113	Accounts Receivable – Roaring Rivers Water Park					0.00	
115	Accounts Receivable – M. Spencer					0.00	
130	Office Equipment					0.00	
135	Office Furniture					0.00	
140	Computer Equipment					0.00	
201	Accounts Payable – Micro Solutions Inc.						0.00
205	Accounts Payable – Vega Internet Services						0.00
207	Accounts Payable – Wildwood Furniture Sales						0.00
301	Richard Tang, Capital						0.00
302	Richard Tang, Withdrawals					0.00	
303	Income Summary	----	----	----	----		
401	Placement Fees Revenue				0.00		
405	Technology Classes Revenue				0.00		
501	Advertising Expense			0.00			
505	Maintenance Expense			0.00			
510	Miscellaneous Expense			0.00			
520	Rent Expense			0.00			
530	Utilities Expense			0.00			
		0.00	0.00	0.00	0.00	0.00	0.00
	Net Income			0.00			0.00
				0.00	0.00	0.00	0.00

Step 6 Key your name and today's date in the cells containing the *(name)* and *(date)* placeholders.

Step 7 The first account, Cash in Bank, has a month-end balance of $6,000. Move the cell pointer to cell C14 and enter the account balance into the Trial Balance debit column of the work sheet: **6000**.

Step 8   Enter the remaining balances into the Trial Balance section of the work sheet. When you have entered all of the balances, move the cell pointer into the Income Statement and Balance Sheet sections of the work sheet. Notice that the amounts for the Income Statement and Balance Sheet are automatically entered. As you enter the data into the Trial Balance section of the work sheet, the program automatically calculates the remaining sections of the work sheet for you. The program also calculates the column totals and the net income for Job Connect.

Step 9   Now scroll down below the work sheet and look at the income statement, statement of changes in owner's equity, and balance sheet for Job Connect. Notice the financial statements are already completed. This is because the spreadsheet template includes formulas that automatically pull information from the filled-in work sheet to complete the financial statements.

Step 10   Now scroll down below the balance sheet and complete the closing entries in the general journal. The account names and posting references are given for you.

Step 11   Scroll down below the closing entries and look at the post-closing trial balance. The amounts have been automatically calculated using formulas.

Step 12   Save the spreadsheet using the **Save** option from the *File* menu. You should accept the default location for the save as this is handled by the management system.

Step 13   Print the completed spreadsheet.

TIP: When printing a long spreadsheet with multiple parts, you may want to insert page breaks between the sections so that each one begins printing at the top of a new page. Page breaks have already been entered into this spreadsheet template. Check your program's Help file for instructions on how to enter page breaks.

Step 14   Exit the spreadsheet program.

Step 15   In the Close Options box, select the location where you would like to save your work.

Step 16   Answer the Analyze question from your textbook for this problem.

What-If Analysis

TIP: Remember, always save your work before performing What-If Analysis. Be sure to rename the spreadsheet if you save your work after performing What-If Analysis.

If Cash in Bank were $5,000 and Advertising Expense were $4,000, what would Job Connect's net income be? What would Job Connect's ending capital be?

_____

_____

Working Papers *for End-of-Chapter Problems*

Problem 10-4 Preparing Closing Entries

(1), (2), (3), (4)

GENERAL JOURNAL
PAGE ___39___

	DATE	DESCRIPTION	POST. REF.	DEBIT	CREDIT	
1						1
2						2
3						3
4						4
5						5
6						6
7						7
8						8
9						9
10						10
11						11
12						12
13						13

Analyze: _____

Problem 10-5 Preparing a Post-Closing Trial Balance

Analyze: _____

_____

Problem 10-6   Journalizing Closing Entries

GENERAL JOURNAL   PAGE _____

	DATE	DESCRIPTION	POST. REF.	DEBIT	CREDIT	
1						1
2						2
3						3
4						4
5						5
6						6
7						7
8						8
9						9
10						10
11						11
12						12
13						13
14						14
15						15
16						16

Analyze: _____

_____

Problem 10-7   Posting Closing Entries and
Preparing a Post-Closing Trial Balance

(1)

GENERAL LEDGER

ACCOUNT _Cash in Bank_ _____ ACCOUNT NO. ___101___

DATE		DESCRIPTION	POST. REF.	DEBIT	CREDIT	BALANCE DEBIT	BALANCE CREDIT
20--							
Dec.	31	Balance	✓			1200000	

ACCOUNT _Accounts Receivable—Mary Johnson_ _____ ACCOUNT NO. ___105___

DATE		DESCRIPTION	POST. REF.	DEBIT	CREDIT	BALANCE DEBIT	BALANCE CREDIT
20--							
Dec.	31	Balance	✓			60000	

ACCOUNT _Accounts Receivable—Feldman, Jones & Ritter_ ___ ACCOUNT NO. ___110___

DATE		DESCRIPTION	POST. REF.	DEBIT	CREDIT	BALANCE DEBIT	BALANCE CREDIT
20--							
Dec.	31	Balance	✓			100000	

ACCOUNT _Accounts Receivable—Podaski Systems Inc._ ___ ACCOUNT NO. ___115___

DATE		DESCRIPTION	POST. REF.	DEBIT	CREDIT	BALANCE DEBIT	BALANCE CREDIT
20--							
Dec.	31	Balance	✓			90000	

ACCOUNT _Office Equipment_ _____ ACCOUNT NO. ___130___

DATE		DESCRIPTION	POST. REF.	DEBIT	CREDIT	BALANCE DEBIT	BALANCE CREDIT
20--							
Dec.	31	Balance	✓			550000	

ACCOUNT _Office Furniture_ _____ ACCOUNT NO. ___135___

DATE		DESCRIPTION	POST. REF.	DEBIT	CREDIT	BALANCE DEBIT	BALANCE CREDIT
20--							
Dec.	31	Balance	✓			740000	

Problem 10-7   (continued)

ACCOUNT ___Computer Equipment_____ ACCOUNT NO. ___140___

DATE		DESCRIPTION	POST. REF.	DEBIT	CREDIT	BALANCE	
						DEBIT	CREDIT
20--							
Dec.	31	Balance	✓			710000	

ACCOUNT ___Hiking Equipment_____ ACCOUNT NO. ___145___

DATE		DESCRIPTION	POST. REF.	DEBIT	CREDIT	BALANCE	
						DEBIT	CREDIT
20--							
Dec.	31	Balance	✓			1500000	

ACCOUNT ___Rafting Equipment_____ ACCOUNT NO. ___150___

DATE		DESCRIPTION	POST. REF.	DEBIT	CREDIT	BALANCE	
						DEBIT	CREDIT
20--							
Dec.	31	Balance	✓			3000000	

ACCOUNT ___Accounts Payable—A-1 Adventure Warehouse___ ACCOUNT NO. ___201___

DATE		DESCRIPTION	POST. REF.	DEBIT	CREDIT	BALANCE	
						DEBIT	CREDIT
20--							
Dec.	31	Balance	✓				1200000

ACCOUNT ___Accounts Payable—Peak Equipment Inc.___ ACCOUNT NO. ___205___

DATE		DESCRIPTION	POST. REF.	DEBIT	CREDIT	BALANCE	
						DEBIT	CREDIT
20--							
Dec.	31	Balance	✓				900000

ACCOUNT ___Accounts Payable—Premier Processors___ ACCOUNT NO. ___207___

DATE		DESCRIPTION	POST. REF.	DEBIT	CREDIT	BALANCE	
						DEBIT	CREDIT
20--							
Dec.	31	Balance	✓				600000

Problem 10-7   (continued)

ACCOUNT _Juanita Ortega, Capital_ _____ ACCOUNT NO. ___301___

DATE	DESCRIPTION	POST. REF.	DEBIT	CREDIT	BALANCE DEBIT	BALANCE CREDIT
20-- Dec. 31	Balance	✓				50 20 00 00

ACCOUNT _Juanita Ortega, Withdrawals_ _____ ACCOUNT NO. ___302___

DATE	DESCRIPTION	POST. REF.	DEBIT	CREDIT	BALANCE DEBIT	BALANCE CREDIT
20-- Dec. 31	Balance	✓			40 00 00	

ACCOUNT _Income Summary_ _____ ACCOUNT NO. ___310___

DATE	DESCRIPTION	POST. REF.	DEBIT	CREDIT	BALANCE DEBIT	BALANCE CREDIT

ACCOUNT _Guide Service Revenue_ _____ ACCOUNT NO. ___401___

DATE	DESCRIPTION	POST. REF.	DEBIT	CREDIT	BALANCE DEBIT	BALANCE CREDIT
20-- Dec. 31	Balance	✓				16 30 00 00

ACCOUNT _Advertising Expense_ _____ ACCOUNT NO. ___501___

DATE	DESCRIPTION	POST. REF.	DEBIT	CREDIT	BALANCE DEBIT	BALANCE CREDIT
20-- Dec. 31	Balance	✓			30 00 00	

ACCOUNT _Maintenance Expense_ _____ ACCOUNT NO. ___505___

DATE	DESCRIPTION	POST. REF.	DEBIT	CREDIT	BALANCE DEBIT	BALANCE CREDIT
20-- Dec. 31	Balance	✓			11 00 00	

Problem 10-7   (concluded)

ACCOUNT _Rent Expense_   ACCOUNT NO. _515_

DATE		DESCRIPTION	POST. REF.	DEBIT	CREDIT	BALANCE	
						DEBIT	CREDIT
20--							
Dec.	31	Balance	✓			400000	

ACCOUNT _Utilities Expense_   ACCOUNT NO. _525_

DATE		DESCRIPTION	POST. REF.	DEBIT	CREDIT	BALANCE	
						DEBIT	CREDIT
20--							
Dec.	31	Balance	✓			190000	

(2)

Analyze: _____

Problem 10-8 Completing End-of-Period Activities

(1)

ACCT. NO.	ACCOUNT NAME	TRIAL BALANCE		INCOME STATEMENT		BALANCE SHEET	
		DEBIT	CREDIT	DEBIT	CREDIT	DEBIT	CREDIT
1							
2							
3							
4							
5							
6							
7							
8							
9							
10							
11							
12							
13							
14							
15							
16							
17							
18							
19							
20							
21							
22							
23							
24							
25							
26							
27							

Problem 10-8 (continued)

(2)

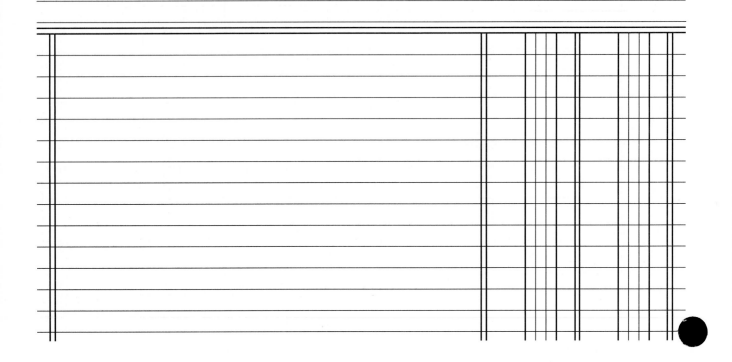

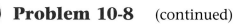

Problem 10-8 (continued)

_____

_____

(3)

GENERAL JOURNAL   PAGE _____

	DATE	DESCRIPTION	POST. REF.	DEBIT	CREDIT	
1						1
2						2
3						3
4						4
5						5
6						6
7						7
8						8
9						9
10						10
11						11

Problem 10-8   (continued)

GENERAL JOURNAL   PAGE _____

	DATE	DESCRIPTION	POST. REF.	DEBIT	CREDIT	
1						1
2						2
3						3
4						4
5						5

(4)

GENERAL LEDGER (PARTIAL)

ACCOUNT __Greg Failla, Capital__   ACCOUNT NO. __301__

DATE	DESCRIPTION	POST. REF.	DEBIT	CREDIT	BALANCE DEBIT	BALANCE CREDIT
20--						
Dec. 31	Balance	✓				33775 00

ACCOUNT __Greg Failla, Withdrawals__   ACCOUNT NO. __305__

DATE	DESCRIPTION	POST. REF.	DEBIT	CREDIT	BALANCE DEBIT	BALANCE CREDIT
20--						
Dec. 31	Balance	✓			4000 00	

ACCOUNT __Income Summary__   ACCOUNT NO. __310__

DATE	DESCRIPTION	POST. REF.	DEBIT	CREDIT	BALANCE DEBIT	BALANCE CREDIT
20--						

ACCOUNT __Video Rental Revenue__   ACCOUNT NO. __401__

DATE	DESCRIPTION	POST. REF.	DEBIT	CREDIT	BALANCE DEBIT	BALANCE CREDIT
20--						
Dec. 31	Balance	✓				9600 00

Problem 10-8 (continued)

ACCOUNT ___VCR Rental Revenue___   ACCOUNT NO. ___405___

DATE	DESCRIPTION	POST. REF.	DEBIT	CREDIT	BALANCE DEBIT	BALANCE CREDIT
20--						
Dec. 31	Balance	✓				350000

ACCOUNT ___Advertising Expense___   ACCOUNT NO. ___501___

DATE	DESCRIPTION	POST. REF.	DEBIT	CREDIT	BALANCE DEBIT	BALANCE CREDIT
20--						
Dec. 31	Balance	✓			160000	

ACCOUNT ___Equipment Repair Expense___   ACCOUNT NO. ___505___

DATE	DESCRIPTION	POST. REF.	DEBIT	CREDIT	BALANCE DEBIT	BALANCE CREDIT
20--						
Dec. 31	Balance	✓			120000	

ACCOUNT ___Maintenance Expense___   ACCOUNT NO. ___510___

DATE	DESCRIPTION	POST. REF.	DEBIT	CREDIT	BALANCE DEBIT	BALANCE CREDIT
20--						
Dec. 31	Balance	✓			40000	

ACCOUNT ___Rent Expense___   ACCOUNT NO. ___520___

DATE	DESCRIPTION	POST. REF.	DEBIT	CREDIT	BALANCE DEBIT	BALANCE CREDIT
20--						
Dec. 31	Balance	✓			100000	

ACCOUNT ___Utilities Expense___   ACCOUNT NO. ___530___

DATE	DESCRIPTION	POST. REF.	DEBIT	CREDIT	BALANCE DEBIT	BALANCE CREDIT
20--						
Dec. 31	Balance	✓			37500	

Problem 10-8 (concluded)

(5)

Analyze: _____

_____

Problem 10-9   Completing End-of-Period Activities

(1)

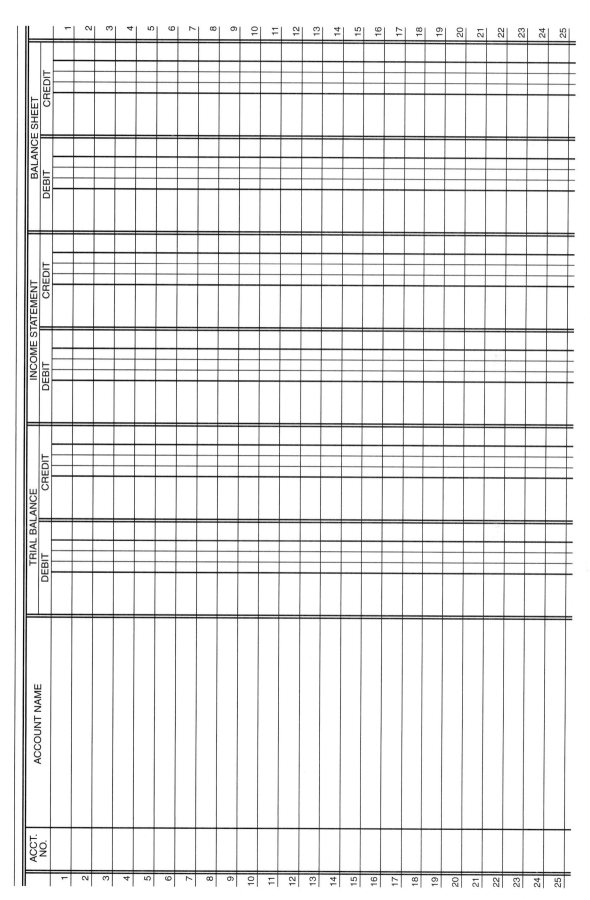

Problem 10-9 (continued)

(2)

Problem 10-9 (continued)

(3)

_____

_____

GENERAL JOURNAL

PAGE _____

	DATE	DESCRIPTION	POST. REF.	DEBIT	CREDIT	
1						1
2						2
3						3
4						4
5						5
6						6
7						7
8						8
9						9
10						10
11						11
12						12
13						13
14						14

Problem 10-9 (continued)

(4)

GENERAL LEDGER (PARTIAL)

ACCOUNT _Richard Tang, Capital_   ACCOUNT NO. __301__

DATE		DESCRIPTION	POST. REF.	DEBIT	CREDIT	BALANCE	
						DEBIT	CREDIT
20--							
Dec.	31	Balance	✓				2360000

ACCOUNT _Richard Tang, Withdrawals_   ACCOUNT NO. __302__

DATE		DESCRIPTION	POST. REF.	DEBIT	CREDIT	BALANCE	
						DEBIT	CREDIT
20--							
Dec.	31	Balance	✓			300000	

ACCOUNT _Income Summary_   ACCOUNT NO. __303__

DATE		DESCRIPTION	POST. REF.	DEBIT	CREDIT	BALANCE	
						DEBIT	CREDIT
20--							

ACCOUNT _Placement Fees Revenue_   ACCOUNT NO. __401__

DATE		DESCRIPTION	POST. REF.	DEBIT	CREDIT	BALANCE	
						DEBIT	CREDIT
20--							
Dec.	31	Balance	✓				690000

ACCOUNT _Technology Classes Revenue_   ACCOUNT NO. __405__

DATE		DESCRIPTION	POST. REF.	DEBIT	CREDIT	BALANCE	
						DEBIT	CREDIT
20--							
Dec.	31	Balance	✓				240000

Problem 10-9 (continued)

ACCOUNT __Advertising Expense__ ACCOUNT NO. __501__

DATE		DESCRIPTION	POST. REF.	DEBIT	CREDIT	BALANCE	
						DEBIT	CREDIT
20--							
Dec.	31	Balance	✓			3 00 00 0	

ACCOUNT __Maintenance Expense__ ACCOUNT NO. __505__

DATE		DESCRIPTION	POST. REF.	DEBIT	CREDIT	BALANCE	
						DEBIT	CREDIT
20--							
Dec.	31	Balance	✓			8 00 00	

ACCOUNT __Miscellaneous Expense__ ACCOUNT NO. __510__

DATE		DESCRIPTION	POST. REF.	DEBIT	CREDIT	BALANCE	
						DEBIT	CREDIT
20--							
Dec.	31	Balance	✓			8 00 00	

ACCOUNT __Rent Expense__ ACCOUNT NO. __520__

DATE		DESCRIPTION	POST. REF.	DEBIT	CREDIT	BALANCE	
						DEBIT	CREDIT
20--							
Dec.	31	Balance	✓			2 00 00 0	

ACCOUNT __Utilities Expense__ ACCOUNT NO. __530__

DATE		DESCRIPTION	POST. REF.	DEBIT	CREDIT	BALANCE	
						DEBIT	CREDIT
20--							
Dec.	31	Balance	✓			9 00 00	

Problem 10-9 (concluded)

(5)

Analyze: _____

_____

CHAPTER 10 Completing the Accounting Cycle for a Sole Proprietorship

Self-Test

Part A   True or False

Directions: *Circle the letter* T *in the Answer column if the statement is true; circle the letter* F *if the statement is false.*

Answer

T   F   **1.** Revenue and expense accounts must be closed out because their balances apply to only one fiscal period.

T   F   **2.** Closing entries transfer the net income or net loss to the withdrawals account.

T   F   **3.** To close a revenue account, debit it for the amount of its credit balance.

T   F   **4.** When expense accounts are closed, the Income Summary account is credited.

T   F   **5.** Before closing entries are journalized and posted, the Income Summary account in the general ledger has a normal credit balance.

T   F   **6.** The Income Summary account is a simple income statement in the ledger.

T   F   **7.** After the closing entries have been posted, the balance in the capital account reflects the net income or net loss and the withdrawals for the period.

T   F   **8.** The Income Summary account is located in the owner's equity section of the general ledger.

T   F   **9.** Closing the revenue account is the second closing entry.

T   F   **10.** If a business reports a net loss for the period, the journal entry to close the Income Summary account would be a debit to capital and a credit to Income Summary.

T   F   **11.** The last step in the accounting cycle is the preparation of the post-closing trial balance.

T   F   **12.** To close the withdrawals account, the amount of its balance is debited to the capital account and credited to the withdrawals account.

Part B   Multiple Choice

Directions: *Only one of the choices given with each of the following state-ments is correct. Write the letter of the correct answer in the Answer column.*

Answer

_____   **1.** Which of the following accounts does *not* require a closing entry?
(A) Fees.
(B) Income Summary.
(C) Maintenance Expense.
(D) Klaus Braun, Capital.

_____   **2.** Transferring the expense account balances to the Income Summary account is the
(A) first closing entry.
(B) second closing entry.
(C) third closing entry.
(D) fourth closing entry.

_____   **3.** Accounts that start each new fiscal period with zero balances are
(A) permanent.
(B) assets.
(C) liabilities.
(D) temporary.

_____   **4.** Which of the following is a true statement?
(A) The Income Summary account is located in the owner's equity section of the general ledger.
(B) The Income Summary account has a normal balance on the debit side.
(C) The Income Summary account is a permanent account.
(D) The Income Summary account is used throughout the accounting period.

_____   **5.** The balance of the revenue account is transferred to the
(A) debit side of the Cash in Bank account.
(B) credit side of the owner's capital account.
(C) credit side of the Income Summary account.
(D) debit side of the owner's withdrawals account.

_____   **6.** If a business has a net income for the period, the journal entry to close the balance of the Income Summary account is
(A) a debit to owner's capital, a credit to Income Summary.
(B) a debit to Fees, a credit to owner's capital.
(C) a debit to Income Summary, a credit to owner's capital.
(D) a debit to owner's capital, a credit to Fees.

CHAPTER *11*   Cash Control and Banking Activities

Study Plan

Check Your Understanding

Section 1	*Read Section 1 on pages 258–263 and complete the following exercises on page 264.*
	❑ Thinking Critically
	❑ Communicating Accounting
	❑ Problem 11-1 *Preparing a Deposit Slip and Writing Checks*
Section 2	*Read Section 2 on pages 265–272 and complete the following exercises on page 273.*
	❑ Thinking Critically
	❑ Computing in the Business World
	❑ Problem 11-2 *Analyzing a Source Document*
Summary	*Review the Chapter 11 Summary on page 275 in your textbook.*
	❑ Key Concepts
Review and Activities	*Complete the following questions and exercises on pages 276–277 in your textbook.*
	❑ Using Key Terms
	❑ Understanding Accounting Concepts and Procedures
	❑ Case Study
	❑ Conducting an Audit with Alex
	❑ Internet Connection
	❑ Workplace Skills
Computerized Accounting	*Read the Computerized Accounting information on page 278 in your textbook.*
	❑ *Making the Transition from a Manual to a Computerized System*
	❑ *Reconciling the Bank Statement in Peachtree*
Problems	*Complete the following end-of-chapter problems for Chapter 11 in your textbook.*
	❑ Problem 11-3 *Handling Deposits*
	❑ Problem 11-4 *Maintaining the Checkbook*
	❑ Problem 11-5 *Reconciling the Bank Statement*
	❑ Problem 11-6 *Reconciling the Bank Statement*
	❑ Problem 11-7 *Reconciling the Bank Statement*
Challenge Problem	❑ Problem 11-8 *Reconciling the Bank Statement Using the Account Form*
Chapter Reviews and Working Papers	*Complete the following exercises for Chapter 11 in your Chapter Reviews and Working Papers.*
	❑ Chapter Review
	❑ Self-Test

CHAPTER 11 REVIEW — Cash Control and Banking Activities

Part 1   Accounting Vocabulary (21 points)

Directions: *Using terms from the following list, complete the sentences below. Write the letter of the term you have chosen in the space provided.*

A. bank service charge	**G.** deposit slip	**M.** NSF check	**R.** restrictive endorsement
B. bank statement	**H.** drawee	**N.** outstanding checks	**S.** signature card
C. canceled checks	**I.** drawer	**O.** outstanding deposits	**T.** stop payment order
D. check	**J.** endorsement	**P.** payee	**U.** voiding a check
E. checking account	**K.** external controls	**Q.** reconciling the	**V.** electronic funds transfer
F. depositor	**L.** internal controls	bank statement	

_____*I*_____   **0.** The person who signs a check is the _____.

_____   **1.** The process of determining any differences between the balance shown on the bank statement and the checkbook balance is known as _____.

_____   **2.** Checks that are paid by the bank, deducted from the depositor's account, and returned with the bank statement are called _____.

_____   **3.** The bank on which a check is written is called the _____.

_____   **4.** The person or business to whom a check is written is the _____.

_____   **5.** A(n) _____ is a bank form on which the currency (bills and coins) and checks to be deposited are listed.

_____   **6.** A(n) _____ is an authorized signature that is written or stamped on the back of a check.

_____   **7.** A(n) _____ limits how a check may be handled and protects a check from being cashed by anyone except the payee.

_____   **8.** A written order from a depositor telling the bank to pay cash to a person or business is a(n) _____.

_____   **9.** A(n) _____ is a demand by the depositor that the bank not honor a certain check.

_____   **10.** A bank account that allows a bank customer to deposit cash and to write checks against the account balance is a(n) _____.

_____   **11.** Checks that have been written but not yet presented to the bank for payment are called _____.

_____   **12.** A fee charged to the depositor by the bank for maintaining bank records and for processing bank statement items is a(n) _____.

_____   **13.** Deposits that have been made and recorded in the checkbook but that do not appear on the bank statement are called _____.

_____   **14.** A person or business that has cash on deposit in a bank is a(n) _____.

_____   **15.** The card containing the signature(s) of the person(s) authorized to write checks on the bank account is called a(n) _____.

_____   **16.** Those steps the business takes to protect cash are called _____.

_____   **17.** A check returned by the bank because there are not enough funds in the drawer's checking account to cover the amount of the check is a(n) _____.

_____   **18.** Those controls on cash from outside the business are called _____.

_____   **19.** Writing the word "VOID" across the front of a check is known as _____.

_____   **20.** A(n) _____ is an itemized record of all the transactions occurring in a depositor's account over a given period, usually a month.

_____   **21.** _____ allows banks to transfer funds between accounts without the exchange of paper checks.

Part 2 Parts of a Check (8 points)

Directions: *Match the identifying labels of the following check to the descriptions below. Write the letter of your choice in the space provided.*

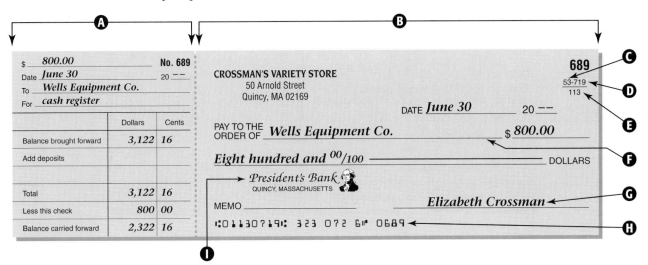

_____ H _____ **0.** MICR number
_____ **1.** The portion that is torn out of the checkbook
_____ **2.** The section completed first
_____ **3.** Code for the specific bank on which the check is written
_____ **4.** The payee
_____ **5.** Code for the Federal Reserve district in which the bank is located
_____ **6.** The drawer
_____ **7.** Code for the city or state in which the bank is located
_____ **8.** The drawee

Part 3 Protecting Cash (11 points)

Directions: *Read each of the following statements to determine whether the statement is true or false. Write your answer in the space provided.*

_____ False _____ **0.** Checks written in ink may be easily altered.
_____ **1.** Bank service charges should be recorded in the checkbook to keep the checkbook balance up to date.
_____ **2.** Verifying the accuracy of signatures on checks is an example of an internal control.
_____ **3.** The ending balance on the bank statement usually agrees with the balance in the checkbook.
_____ **4.** The EFTS enables banks to transfer funds from the account of one depositor to the account of another quickly and accurately without the immediate exchange of checks.
_____ **5.** The balance of Cash in Bank in the general ledger should agree with the checkbook balance after all transactions have been posted.
_____ **6.** Businesses should make daily deposits to protect the cash they receive.
_____ **7.** The check stub is the source document for journalizing the bank service charge.
_____ **8.** A check received by a business should be endorsed with a restrictive endorsement as soon as it is received.
_____ **9.** The check stub should be filled out after the check is written.
_____ **10.** The account debited for an NSF check is Accounts Payable.
_____ **11.** An endorsement on a check represents a promise to pay.

Working Papers *for Section Problems*

Problem 11-1   Preparing a Deposit Slip and Writing Checks

First Bank of the Cape HYANNIS, MA 02601		DOLLARS	CENTS
Date _____ **20** ____	CASH		
Checks and other items are received for deposit subject to the terms and conditions of this bank's collection agreement.	CHECKS (List Singly)		
	1		
Peabody CARDS AND GIFTS	2		
	3		
113 Old Cape Road	4		
Dennis, MA 02638	5		
	6		
	7		
	8		
⑆0111 0160 2⑈ 749 2454⑈	**TOTAL**		

BE SURE EACH ITEM IS ENDORSED

	No. 41
$ _____	
Date _____ 20 ___	
To _____	
For _____	

	Dollars	Cents
Balance brought forward	1,641	96
Add deposits		
Total		
Less this check		
Balance carried forward		

Peabody CARDS AND GIFTS   **41**
113 Old Cape Road
Dennis, MA 02638   51-160 / 111

DATE _____ 20 ____

PAY TO THE
ORDER OF _____ $ _____

_____ DOLLARS

First Bank of the Cape
HYANNIS, MA 02601

MEMO _____   _____

⑆0111 0160 2⑈ 749 2454⑈ 41

	No. 42
$ _____	
Date _____ 20 ___	
To _____	
For _____	

	Dollars	Cents
Balance brought forward		
Add deposits		
Total		
Less this check		
Balance carried forward		

Peabody CARDS AND GIFTS   **42**
113 Old Cape Road
Dennis, MA 02638   51-160 / 111

DATE _____ 20 ____

PAY TO THE
ORDER OF _____ $ _____

_____ DOLLARS

First Bank of the Cape
HYANNIS, MA 02601

MEMO _____   _____

⑆0111 0160 2⑈ 749 2454⑈ 42

Problem 11-2   Analyzing a Source Document

1. _____

2. _____

3. _____

Computerized Accounting Using Peachtree

Software Objectives

When you have completed this chapter, you will be able to use Peachtree to:

1. Record a payment.
2. Use the **Account Reconciliation** feature to reconcile a bank statement.
3. Adjust an account.
4. Print the Account Reconciliation reports.

Problem 11-4   Maintaining the Checkbook

INSTRUCTIONS

Beginning a Session

Step 1   Select the problem set: Hot Suds Car Wash (Prob. 11-4).

Step 2   Rename the company and set the system date to October 31, 2004.

Completing the Accounting Problem

Step 3   Record Check 504 issued on October 3.

> ***Issued Check 504 for $868.45 to Custom Construction for construction supplies.***

To record a payment:

- Choose **Payments** from the *Tasks* menu.
- Type **CC** (the account ID for Custom Construction) in the *Vendor ID* field.

  If you do not know the account code for a payee, click the button, highlight the vendor name, and click the **OK** button.

- Type **504** in the *Check Number* field.
- Type **10/3/04** in the *Date* field. Make sure that Peachtree shows 2004 for the year. If not, change the system date.

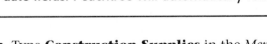
TIP: As a shortcut, you can just type the day of the month in most date fields. Peachtree will automatically format the date.

- Type **Construction Supplies** in the *Memo* field.
- Move to the *Description* field on the **Apply to Expenses** tab and type **Construction Supplies.**
- Skip the *GL Account* field since the default account code, **Maintenance Expense**, is correct.
- Type **868.45** in the *Amount* field to record the amount of the check.

  When you enter the amount, Peachtree automatically displays the amount in the upper portion of the entry window.

DO YOU HAVE A QUESTION

Q. *Do you have to use Peachtree to print checks?*

A. No. You do not have to use Peachtree to print checks, although Peachtree does offer this feature. If you prefer, you can manually write checks and then use Peachtree to record these payments.

Notes

    Lookup fields, such as the Vendor ID *field, are case-sensitive.*

• Proof the information you just recorded. Check all of the information you entered. If you notice a mistake, move to that field and make the correction. Compare the information on your screen to the completed transaction shown in Figure 11-4A.

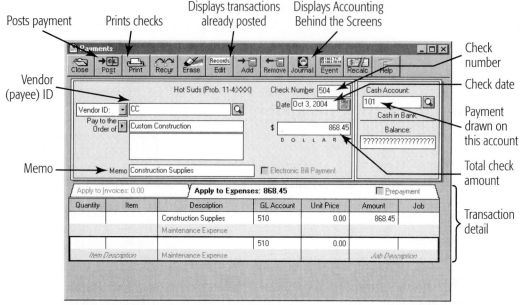

Figure 11-4A *Completed Payment Transaction (October 3, Check 504)*

• Click 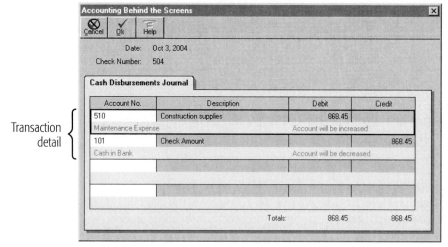 to display the Accounting Behind the Screens window. Use the information in this window to check your work again. (See Figure 11-4B.)

Figure 11-4B *Accounting Behind the Screens (Payment)*

The Accounting Behind the Screens window shows you the accounts and the debit/credit amounts that Peachtree will record for this transaction. For the payment, the window should show the following: **Maintenance Expense** ($868.45 DR) and **Cash in Bank** ($868.45 CR).

- Click to close the Accounting Behind the Screens window.
- Click to post the payment.

Although not required, you could use Peachtree to print real checks either on pre-printed checks or duplicate checks on blank paper. If you choose to print a real check, you would leave the check number blank and click . Select a check form (e.g., *AP Preprint 1 Stub*). Then, click the **Real** button to print the check. If you enter a check number, Peachtree prints *Duplicate* on the check. The software automatically posts the transaction and is ready for the next payment after the check is printed.

> **TIP:** If you notice an error after you post an entry, click Records Edit and choose the transaction you want to edit. Make the corrections and post the transaction again to record the changes.

Step 4   Record the remaining checks issued during the month: Checks 505–507.

For each of the payments, do not change the default GL Account. These default accounts have already been setup for you in the problem set. For example, whenever you choose to pay Union Utilities, Peachtree displays account **530 Utilities Expense**. You will learn more about payments in a later chapter.

Step 5   Record the deposits—October 3 ($601.35—Tape 303) and October 10 ($342.80—Tape 304).

Use the **General Journal Entry** option to enter the deposits. For both deposits, debit **101 Cash** and credit **401 Wash Revenue**.

Step 6   Print an Account Register report.

To print an Account Register report:

- Choose **Account Reconciliation** from the **Reports** menu.
- Make sure the *Account Reconciliation* report area is selected.
- Select **Account Register** in the report list and click .
- Click **OK** to accept the standard option settings.

> **Notes**
>
> *The Account Register report shows all of the account activity (withdrawals and deposits) for the current period.*

Step 7   Proof the information on the report. If you notice an error, select the appropriate task option (**Payments** or **General Journal Entry**) and choose to edit the incorrect entry. Print a revised Account Register report.

Step 8   Answer the Analyze question.

Ending the Session

Step 9   Click the **Close Problem** button in the Glencoe Smart Guide window.

Mastering Peachtree

On a separate sheet of paper, answer the following questions:
How would you purchase pre-printed checks if you wanted to use Peachtree to prepare real checks? What security features are available on Peachtree checks? Use the online help to learn how to order pre-printed checks.

Peachtree Guide *(side margin)*

Problem 11-5   Reconciling the Bank Statement

INSTRUCTIONS

Beginning a Session

    Step 1   Select the problem set: Kits & Pups Grooming (Prob. 11-5).

    Step 2   Rename the company and set the system date to October 31, 2004.

Completing the Accounting Problem

    Step 3   Reconcile the bank statement.

         The problem set includes all of the transaction data needed to perform the account reconciliation. Payments and deposits made throughout the month have already been recorded for you. Bank service charges and other fees have not been recorded.

         To reconcile the bank statement:

- Choose **Account Reconciliation** from the *Tasks* menu.
- Type **101** (the **Cash in Bank** account ID) in the *Account to Reconcile* field.

         You must identify the account you want to reconcile. Some companies may have more than one checking account. For example, a company may have one account for regular payments and another account for payroll.

- Change the statement date to **10/30/04**.
- Identify the checks that have cleared (those that would appear on the bank statement). Click the *Clear* box for all of the checks except Check 768 and Check 772 since these two are outstanding.
- Identify which deposits have cleared. If a deposit was made, but does not appear on the bank statement, do not check the *Clear* box.
- Type **1380.00** in the *Statement Ending Balance* field.
- Compare the Account Reconciliation window on your screen to the one shown in Figure 11-5A. Outstanding checks should total $835.00 and deposits in transit should be $405.00. The GL (System) Balance is the same as the checkbook balance.

         The unreconciled difference should show −$10.00 because you have yet to account for the bank service charge. When this amount is zero ($0.00), the account will be reconciled.

DO YOU HAVE A QUESTION

Q. *When you use the* **Account Reconciliation** *option and record an adjustment, do you have to make a separate entry to update the general ledger?*

A. No. Peachtree automatically creates a general journal entry behind the scenes when you enter an adjustment (e.g., bank service charge) using the **Account Reconciliation** option.

Notes

     Peachtree displays the checks and deposits in the Account Reconciliation window after you identify the account you want to reconcile.

Records account reconciliation data

Click here to mark check as cleared

Do not mark outstanding checks

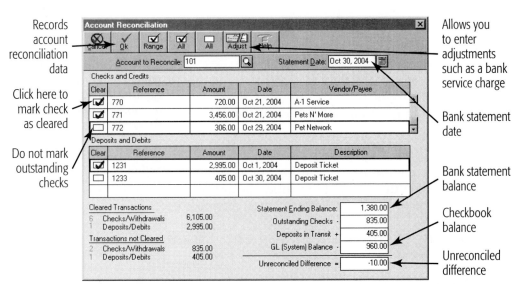

Allows you to enter adjustments such as a bank service charge

Bank statement date

Bank statement balance

Checkbook balance

Unreconciled difference

Figure 11-5A *Account Reconciliation Window (Checks/Deposits Marked)*

- Click [Adjust] to enter the bank service charge.
- Record the bank service charge as a withdrawal in the Additional Transactions window. Enter **10.00** for the amount, type **Bank Service Charge** for the description, and record **512** (Miscellaneous Expense) for the account. (See Figure 11-5B.) Click **OK** to record the additional transaction.

Record bank service charge here

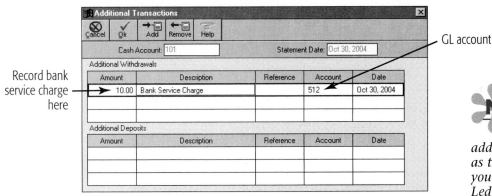

GL account

Figure 11-5B *Additional Transactions Window*

- Scroll the *Checks and Credits* list to display the first entry in the Account Reconciliation window. You should see the bank service charge you just entered.
- Click the *Clear* box next to the service charge to mark it as cleared.
- Verify that the unreconciled difference is zero ($0.00). Also, notice that the GL (System) Balance is $950.00. Peachtree automatically updated the **Cash in Bank** GL account to reflect the service charge. If these figures do not match your screen, verify which checks/deposits you marked as cleared. Also, check the bank statement amount and the bank service charge amount.
- Click [Ok] to complete the reconciliation process.

Notes

When you enter an additional charge such as the bank service charge, you must enter a General Ledger account number. Peachtree automatically generates a general journal entry for you behind the scenes.

Name Date Class

Step 4 Print the following Account Reconciliation reports: Account Register, Account Reconciliation, Deposits in Transit, and Outstanding Checks.
Step 5 Answer the Analyze question.

Ending the Session

Step 6 Click the **Close Problem** button in the Glencoe Smart Guide window.

Mastering Peachtree

Do you know how to change the layout of reports? Adjust the Account Reconciliation report layout to widen the date field to show the entire date (month, day, year). Print an updated Account Reconciliation report.

Notes

*If you make a mistake when you enter an additional (adjustment) transaction, you must close the Account Reconciliation window and then use **General Journal Entry** option to edit or delete the entry.*

Problem 11-7 Reconciling the Bank Statement

INSTRUCTIONS

Beginning a Session

Step 1 Select the problem set: Showbiz Video (Prob. 11-7).
Step 2 Rename the company and set the system date to October 31, 2004.

Completing the Accounting Problem

Step 3 Reconcile the bank statement.

TIP: Use the account reconciliation **Adjust** option to record a bank service charge. Apply the charge to the **Miscellaneous Expense** account.

Step 4 Print the following Account Reconciliation reports: Account Register, Account Reconciliation, Deposits in Transit, and Outstanding Checks.
Step 5 Answer the Analyze question.

Ending the Session

Step 6 Click the **Close Problem** button in the Glencoe Smart Guide window.

Notes

You do not have to make a separate general journal entry to record a bank service charge. Peachtree automatically creates this entry when you make an adjustment to reconcile an account.

Problem 11-8   Reconciling the Bank Statement Using the Account Form

INSTRUCTIONS

Beginning a Session

    Step 1   Select the problem set: Job Connect (Prob. 11-8).

    Step 2   Rename the company and set the system date to October 20, 2004.

Completing the Accounting Problem

    Step 3   Reconcile the bank statement.

               Note: The $200 check issued to Fontenot Inc. was issued to pay for maintenance and repairs.

 TIP: Apply any bank service fees and stop payment charges to the **Miscellaneous Expense** account.

    Step 4   Print the following Account Reconciliation reports: Account Register, Account Reconciliation, Deposits in Transit, and Outstanding Checks.

    Step 5   Answer the Analyze question.

Ending the Session

    Step 6   Click the **Close Problem** button in the Glencoe Smart Guide window.

Mastering Peachtree

Does Peachtree support electronic funds transfer? On a separate sheet of paper, describe how you could use these features in a real-life setting.

 TIP: Search for "electronic bill payment procedures" to learn about electronic funds transfer.

Peachtree Guide

FAQs

How do you edit/delete an additional (adjustment) transaction entered using the Account Reconciliation feature?

Once you enter an additional transaction when reconciling an account, Peachtree will not allow you to edit the transaction. You must close the Account Reconciliation window and then choose the **General Journal Entry** option. Click the **Edit Records** button and select the entry you want to change. Edit or delete the transaction and then choose the **Account Reconciliation** option to continue where you left off.

When you use the Account Reconciliation option and record an adjustment, do you have to make a separate entry to update the general ledger?

No. Peachtree automatically creates a general journal entry behind the scenes when you enter an adjustment (e.g., bank service charge) using the **Account Reconciliation** option.

Computerized Accounting Using Spreadsheets

Problem 11-6   Reconciling the Bank Statement

Completing the Spreadsheet

Step 1 Read the instructions for Problem 11-6 in your textbook. This problem involves reconciling a bank statement for Outback Guide Service.

Step 2 Open the Glencoe Accounting: Electronic Learning Center software.

Step 3 From the Program Menu, click on the **Peachtree Accounting Software and Spreadsheet Applications** icon.

Step 4 Log onto the Management System by typing your user name and password.

Step 5 Under the Chapter Problems tab, select the template: PR11-6a.xls. The template should look like the one shown below.

```
PROBLEM 11-6
RECONCILING THE BANK STATEMENT

(name)
(date)

OUTBACK GUIDE SERVICE
BANK RECONCILIATION
OCTOBER 30, 20--

Balance on bank statement                                          AMOUNT

Deposits in transit:
                        30-Oct                      AMOUNT
TOTAL DEPOSITS                                                       0.00

Outstanding checks:
               Check #872                           AMOUNT
               Check #881                           AMOUNT
               Check #883                           AMOUNT
               Check #887                           AMOUNT
TOTAL OUTSTANDING CHECKS                                            0.00
ADJUSTED BANK BALANCE                                               0.00

Balance in checkbook                                              AMOUNT

Additions:
       Interest earned                              AMOUNT
TOTAL ADDITIONS                                                     0.00

Deductions:
       Bank service charge                          AMOUNT
       NSF check                                    AMOUNT
TOTAL DEDUCTIONS                                                    0.00
ADJUSTED CHECKBOOK BALANCE                                          0.00
```

Step 6 Key your name and today's date in the cells containing the *(name)* and *(date)* placeholders.

Step 7 The balance shown on the bank statement is $2,272.36. Move the cell pointer to cell E12 and enter the bank statement balance: **2272.36**. (Remember, it is not necessary to include a comma as part of the entry.)

Step 8 A deposit was not reflected on the bank statement. Move the cell pointer to cell D15 and enter the amount of the deposit.

Step 9 Beginning in cell D19, enter the amounts for the outstanding checks. The spreadsheet template will automatically calculate the adjusted bank balance.

Step 10 Move the cell pointer to cell E26 and enter the checkbook balance.

Step 11 No interest was earned for the period, so there are no additions to the checkbook balance. Move the cell pointer to cell D29 and enter **0** as the amount of interest earned.

Step 12 Move the cell pointer to cell D33 and enter the amount of the bank service charge.

Step 13 Move the cell pointer to cell D34 and enter the amount of the NSF check. The spreadsheet template will automatically calculate the adjusted checkbook balance.

Step 14 The adjusted bank balance and adjusted checkbook balance should be equal. If they are not equal, find the error(s) and make the necessary corrections.

Step 15 Save the spreadsheet using the **Save** option from the *File* menu. You should accept the default location for the save as this is handled by the management system.

Step 16 Print the completed spreadsheet.

Step 17 Exit the spreadsheet program.

Step 18 In the Close Options box, select the location where you would like to save your work.

Step 19 Answer the Analyze question from your textbook for this problem.

Working Papers *for End-of-Chapter Problems*

Problem 11-3   Handling Deposits

(1)

(2)

		DOLLARS	CENTS
First National Bank LITTLE ROCK, AR	CASH		
	CHECKS (List Singly)		
Date _____ **20** ___	1		
Checks and other items are received for deposit subject to the terms and conditions of this bank's collection agreement.	2		
	3		
	4		
Wilderness Rentals	5		
Center Street	6		
Little Rock, AR 72219	7		
	8		
⑈0631 02948⑈ 7008 497⑈	**TOTAL**		

(BE SURE EACH ITEM IS ENDORSED)

(3)

$ _____ No. 651		
Date _____ 20 ___		
To _____		
For _____		

	Dollars	Cents
Balance brought forward	3,306	54
Add deposits		
Total		
Less this check		
Balance carried forward		

Wilderness Rentals
Center Street
Little Rock, AR 72219

651

63-294 / 631

DATE _____ 20 ___

PAY TO THE
ORDER OF _____ $ _____

_____ DOLLARS

First National Bank
LITTLE ROCK, AR

MEMO _____

⑈0631 02948⑈ 7008 497⑈ 651

Analyze: _____

_____

Problem 11-4   Maintaining the Checkbook

	Dollars	Cents
$ _____ No. 504		
Date _____ 20 ___		
To _____		
For _____		
Balance brought forward	3,486	29
Add deposits		
Total		
Less this check		
Balance carried forward		

Hot Suds Car Wash
248 Seventh Avenue
Colorado Springs, CO 80943

504
2-1116
710

DATE _____ 20 ___

PAY TO THE
ORDER OF _____ $ _____

_____ DOLLARS

★ American Bank
COLORADO SPRINGS, CO

MEMO _____

⑈071001116⑈ 323 0019⑈ 504

	Dollars	Cents
$ _____ No. 505		
Date _____ 20 ___		
To _____		
For _____		
Balance brought forward		
Add deposits		
Total		
Less this check		
Balance carried forward		

Hot Suds Car Wash
248 Seventh Avenue
Colorado Springs, CO 80943

505
2-1116
710

DATE _____ 20 ___

PAY TO THE
ORDER OF _____ $ _____

_____ DOLLARS

★ American Bank
COLORADO SPRINGS, CO

MEMO _____

⑈071001116⑈ 323 0019⑈ 505

	Dollars	Cents
$ _____ No. 506		
Date _____ 20 ___		
To _____		
For _____		
Balance brought forward		
Add deposits		
Total		
Less this check		
Balance carried forward		

Hot Suds Car Wash
248 Seventh Avenue
Colorado Springs, CO 80943

506
2-1116
710

DATE _____ 20 ___

PAY TO THE
ORDER OF _____ $ _____

_____ DOLLARS

★ American Bank
COLORADO SPRINGS, CO

MEMO _____

⑈071001116⑈ 323 0019⑈ 506

	Dollars	Cents
$ _____ No. 507		
Date _____ 20 ___		
To _____		
For _____		
Balance brought forward		
Add deposits		
Total		
Less this check		
Balance carried forward		

Hot Suds Car Wash
248 Seventh Avenue
Colorado Springs, CO 80943

507
2-1116
710

DATE _____ 20 ___

PAY TO THE
ORDER OF _____ $ _____

_____ DOLLARS

★ American Bank
COLORADO SPRINGS, CO

MEMO _____

⑈071001116⑈ 323 0019⑈ 507

Problem 11-4   (concluded)

Analyze: _____

Problem 11-5   Reconciling the Bank Statement
(1)

	No. 773
$ _____	
Date _____ 20 ___	
To _____	
For _____	

	Dollars	Cents
Balance brought forward	960	00
Add deposits		
Total		
Less this check		
Balance carried forward		

(2)

BANK RECONCILIATION FORM

PLEASE EXAMINE YOUR STATEMENT AT ONCE. ANY DISCREPANCY SHOULD BE REPORTED TO THE BANK IMMEDIATELY.

CHECKS OUTSTANDING		
Number	Amount	
TOTAL		

1. Record any transactions appearing on this statement but not listed in your checkbook.

2. List any checks still outstanding in the space provided to the right.

3. Enter the balance shown on this statement here.

4. Enter deposits recorded in your checkbook but not shown on this statement.

5. Total Lines 3 and 4 and enter here.

6. Enter total checks outstanding here.

7. Subtract Line 6 from Line 5. This adjusted bank balance should agree with your checkbook balance.

Problem 11-5 (concluded)

(3)

GENERAL JOURNAL   PAGE ___4___

	DATE	DESCRIPTION	POST. REF.	DEBIT	CREDIT	
1						1
2						2
3						3
4						4
5						5
6						6

(4)

GENERAL LEDGER (PARTIAL)

ACCOUNT *Cash in Bank*   ACCOUNT NO. ___101___

DATE		DESCRIPTION	POST. REF.	DEBIT	CREDIT	BALANCE DEBIT	BALANCE CREDIT
20--							
Oct.	1	Balance	✓			2 0 5 0 00	
	30		G3		4 0 5 00	9 6 0 00	

ACCOUNT *Miscellaneous Expense*   ACCOUNT NO. ___512___

DATE		DESCRIPTION	POST. REF.	DEBIT	CREDIT	BALANCE DEBIT	BALANCE CREDIT
20--							
Oct.	1	Balance	✓			4 9 5 00	
	17		G2	1 0 00		6 0 5 00	

Analyze: _____

_____

Problem 11-6   Reconciling the Bank Statement

(1)

	No. 888
$ _____	
Date _____ 20 ___	
To _____	
For _____	

	Dollars	Cents
Balance brought forward	*2,551*	*34*
Add deposits		
Total		
Less this check		
Balance carried forward		

(2)

BANK RECONCILIATION FORM

PLEASE EXAMINE YOUR STATEMENT AT ONCE. ANY DISCREPANCY SHOULD BE REPORTED TO THE BANK IMMEDIATELY.

CHECKS OUTSTANDING		
Number	Amount	
TOTAL		

1. Record any transactions appearing on this statement but not listed in your checkbook.

2. List any checks still outstanding in the space provided to the right.

3. Enter the balance shown on this statement here.

4. Enter deposits recorded in your checkbook but not shown on this statement.

5. Total Lines 3 and 4 and enter here.

6. Enter total checks outstanding here.

7. Subtract Line 6 from Line 5. This adjusted bank balance should agree with your checkbook balance.

Problem 11-6 (continued)

(3)

GENERAL JOURNAL   PAGE _____

	DATE	DESCRIPTION	POST. REF.	DEBIT	CREDIT	
1						1
2						2
3						3
4						4
5						5
6						6
7						7

(4)

GENERAL LEDGER (PARTIAL)

ACCOUNT __Cash in Bank__   ACCOUNT NO. __101__

DATE		DESCRIPTION	POST. REF.	DEBIT	CREDIT	BALANCE DEBIT	BALANCE CREDIT
20--							
Oct.	1	Balance	✓			308950	
	30		G6		6864	255134	

ACCOUNT __Accounts Receivable—Podaski Systems Inc.__   ACCOUNT NO. __115__

DATE		DESCRIPTION	POST. REF.	DEBIT	CREDIT	BALANCE DEBIT	BALANCE CREDIT
20--							
Oct.	1	Balance	✓			1950	
	10		G4	1800		6244	
	18		G5		6244	——	

ACCOUNT __Miscellaneous Expense__   ACCOUNT NO. __507__

DATE		DESCRIPTION	POST. REF.	DEBIT	CREDIT	BALANCE DEBIT	BALANCE CREDIT
20--							
Oct.	10		G4	2000		2000	
	25		G6	1000		5000	

Problem 11-6 (concluded)

Analyze: _____

Problem 11-7 Reconciling the Bank Statement

(1)

		No. 1772
$ _____		
Date _October 31_____		20 __
To _____		
For _____		

	Dollars	Cents
Balance brought forward	13,462	96
Add deposits		
Total		
Less this check		
Balance carried forward		

(2)

BANK RECONCILIATION FORM

PLEASE EXAMINE YOUR STATEMENT AT ONCE. ANY
DISCREPANCY SHOULD BE REPORTED TO THE BANK
IMMEDIATELY.

CHECKS OUTSTANDING		
Number	Amount	
TOTAL		

1. Record any transactions appearing on this statement but not
   listed in your checkbook.

2. List any checks still outstanding in the space provided to the right.

3. Enter the balance shown on this
   statement here.

4. Enter deposits recorded in your
   checkbook but not shown on this
   statement.

5. Total Lines 3 and 4 and enter here.

6. Enter total checks outstanding here.

7. Subtract Line 6 from Line 5. This
   adjusted bank balance should agree
   with your checkbook balance.

Problem 11-7 (concluded)

(3)

GENERAL JOURNAL   PAGE _____

	DATE	DESCRIPTION	POST. REF.	DEBIT	CREDIT	
1						1
2						2
3						3
4						4
5						5
6						6
7						7

(4)

GENERAL LEDGER (PARTIAL)

ACCOUNT __Cash in Bank__   ACCOUNT NO. ___101___

DATE		DESCRIPTION	POST. REF.	DEBIT	CREDIT	BALANCE DEBIT	BALANCE CREDIT
20--							
Oct.	30	Balance	✓			1346296	

ACCOUNT __Miscellaneous Expense__   ACCOUNT NO. ___512___

DATE		DESCRIPTION	POST. REF.	DEBIT	CREDIT	BALANCE DEBIT	BALANCE CREDIT
20--							
Oct.	30	Balance	✓			61047	

Analyze: _____

_____

Problem 11-8   Reconciling the Bank Statement Using the Account Form

SNB *Security National Bank*
3001 Porterfield Street, Durham, NC 27704

Job Connect
405 McLocklin Drive
Durham, NC 27713

FDIC

Account Number: 555113

Statement Date: 10/18/20--

Balance Last Statement	Deposits & Other Credits		Checks & Other Debits		Balance This Statement
	No.	Amount	No.	Amount	
452.46	1	288.66	4	396.54	344.58

Description	Checks & Other Debits	Deposits & Other Credits	Date	Balance
Balance Forward			09/15	452.46
Check	105.00		09/18	347.46
Check	59.71		09/22	287.75
Check	87.00		09/29	200.75
Check	45.41		09/29	155.34
Deposit		288.66	10/06	444.00
Returned Check	68.42		10/13	375.58
Service Charge	7.00		10/13	368.58
Service Charge	10.00		10/15	358.58
Service Charge	14.00		10/18	344.58

PLEASE EXAMINE YOUR STATEMENT CAREFULLY. DIRECT ALL INQUIRIES IMMEDIATELY.

Problem 11-8 (concluded)

Analyze: _____

_____

_____

CHAPTER **11** Cash Control and Banking Activities

Self-Test

Part A   Fill in the Missing Term

Directions: *In the Answer column, write the letter of the word or phrase that best completes the sentence.*

A. bank service charge	**E.** NSF check	**H.** reconciling the
B. bank statement	**F.** outstanding checks	bank statement
C. canceled checks	**G.** outstanding deposits	**I.** restrictive
D. internal controls		**J.** stop payment

Answer

_____ 1. An itemized record of all the transactions occurring in a depositor's account over a given period is a(n) _____.

_____ 2. A(n) _____ is a fee charged by the bank for maintaining bank records and for processing bank statement items for the depositor.

_____ 3. A(n) _____ is a check returned by the bank because there are not sufficient funds in the drawer's checking account to cover the amount of the check.

_____ 4. _____ are checks that are paid by the bank, deducted from the depositor's account, and returned with the bank statement.

_____ 5. _____ are checks that have been written but not yet presented to the bank for payment.

_____ 6. _____ are steps that a business takes to protect its cash and other assets.

_____ 7. A demand by the depositor that the bank not honor a certain specific check is a(n) _____.

_____ 8. _____ is the process of determining any differences between the balance shown on the bank statement and the checkbook balance.

_____ 9. _____ are deposits that have been made and recorded in the checkbook but that do not appear on the bank statement.

_____ 10. A type of endorsement that limits how a check may be handled to protect the check from being cashed by anyone except the payee is a(n) _____ endorsement.

Part B True or False

Directions: *Circle the letter* T *in the Answer column if the statement is true; circle the letter* F *if the statement is false.*

Answer

T	F	**1.**	A check should be written before the check stub is filled out.
T	F	**2.**	Cash is the most liquid asset of a business.
T	F	**3.**	The ending balance on the bank statement seldom agrees with the balance in the checkbook.
T	F	**4.**	Bank service charges should be recorded in the checkbook before reconciling the bank statement.
T	F	**5.**	An example of an internal control is the daily deposit of cash receipts in the bank.
T	F	**6.**	A stop payment order and voiding a check mean the same thing.
T	F	**7.**	Prompt reconciliation of the bank statement is a good way to guard against disorderly cash records or cash loss.
T	F	**8.**	Checks written in pencil are acceptable.
T	F	**9.**	When a business receives a check in payment for a product or service, it acquires the right to that check.
T	F	**10.**	Outstanding checks and voided checks are the most frequent causes for differences between the bank statement balance and the checkbook balance.

MINI PRACTICE SET

Fast Track Tutoring Service

CHART OF ACCOUNTS

ASSETS
101   Cash in Bank
105   Accounts Receivable—Sally Chaplin
110   Accounts Receivable—Carla DiSario
120   Accounts Receivable—George McGarty
130   Accounts Receivable—Joyce Torres
140   Office Supplies
145   Office Furniture
150   Office Equipment
155   Instructional Equipment

LIABILITIES
205   Accounts Payable—Custom Designs
210   Accounts Payable—Educational Software
215   Accounts Payable—T & N School Equip.

OWNER'S EQUITY
301   Jennifer Rachael, Capital
305   Jennifer Rachael, Withdrawals
310   Income Summary

REVENUE
401   Group Lessons Fees
405   Private Lessons Fees

EXPENSES
505   Maintenance Expense
510   Miscellaneous Expense
515   Rent Expense
525   Utilities Expense

Mini Practice Set 2 Source Documents

Instructions: *Use the following source documents to record the transactions for this practice set.*

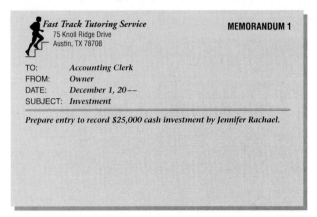

Fast Track Tutoring Service
75 Knoll Ridge Drive
Austin, TX 78708

MEMORANDUM 1

TO: Accounting Clerk
FROM: Owner
DATE: December 1, 20--
SUBJECT: Investment

Prepare entry to record $25,000 cash investment by Jennifer Rachael.

Fast Track Tutoring Service
75 Knoll Ridge Drive
Austin, TX 78708

RECEIPT
No. 1

December 5   20--

RECEIVED FROM   **Shirley Stevenson** $950.00

Nine hundred fifty and 00/100 —————— DOLLARS

FOR   **Private instruction**

RECEIVED BY   **Jennifer Rachael**

EDUCATIONAL SOFTWARE
913 Walnut St., #2
Coxville, TX 78701

INVOICE NO. 395

DATE: Dec. 6, 20--
ORDER NO.:
SHIPPED BY:
TERMS:

TO   **Fast Track Tutoring Service**
75 Knoll Ridge Drive
Austin, TX 78708

QTY.	ITEM	UNIT PRICE	TOTAL
	Software (Windows NT, Office 98, Goldmine)		$8494.00
			$8494.00

Fast Track Tutoring Service
75 Knoll Ridge Drive
Austin, TX 78708

101
71-627
3222

DATE *December 2*   20--

PAY TO THE ORDER OF   **Office Max** $525.00

Five hundred twenty-five and 00/100 —————— DOLLARS

🏛 Citibank

MEMO **cash register**   Jennifer Rachael

⑆3222 7⑆627⑆ 1123 4533⑆ 0101

Fast Track Tutoring Service
75 Knoll Ridge Drive
Austin, TX 78708

102
71-627
3222

DATE *December 2*   20--

PAY TO THE ORDER OF   **Office Depot** $73.00

Seventy-three and 00/100 —————— DOLLARS

🏛 Citibank

MEMO **office supplies**   Jennifer Rachael

⑆3222 7⑆627⑆ 1123 4533⑆ 0102

Fast Track Tutoring Service
75 Knoll Ridge Drive
Austin, TX 78708

INVOICE NO. 101

DATE: Dec. 8, 20--
ORDER NO.:
SHIPPED BY:
TERMS:

TO   **Carla DiSario**
99 Louise St.
Austin, TX 78708

QTY.	ITEM	UNIT PRICE	TOTAL
2	Group Classes	$18.00	$36.00

Fast Track Tutoring Service
75 Knoll Ridge Drive
Austin, TX 78708

103
71-627
3222

DATE *December 5*   20--

PAY TO THE ORDER OF   **Best Buy** $13,924.00

Thirteen thousand nine hundred twenty-four and 00/100 DOLLARS

🏛 Citibank

MEMO **computers**   Jennifer Rachael

⑆3222 7⑆627⑆ 1123 4533⑆ 0103

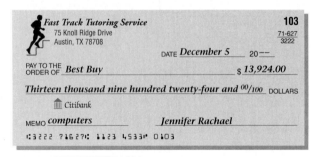

Fast Track Tutoring Service
75 Knoll Ridge Drive
Austin, TX 78708

104
71-627
3222

DATE *December 9*   20--

PAY TO THE ORDER OF   **Carlo Property Realty** $850.00

Eight hundred fifty and 00/100 —————— DOLLARS

🏛 Citibank

MEMO **rent**   Jennifer Rachael

⑆3222 7⑆627⑆ 1123 4533⑆ 0104

Mini Practice Set 2   (continued)

Fast Track Tutoring Service
75 Knoll Ridge Drive
Austin, TX 78708

INVOICE NO. 102

DATE: *Dec. 10, 20—*
ORDER NO.:
SHIPPED BY:
TERMS:

TO
George McGarty
31 Vale Street
Austin, TX 78705

QTY.	ITEM	UNIT PRICE	TOTAL
5	Special Group Classes	$55.00	$275.00

Fast Track Tutoring Service
75 Knoll Ridge Drive
Austin, TX 78708

105
71-627
3222

DATE *December 14* 20—

PAY TO THE ORDER OF *Educational Software* $ *200.00*

Two hundred and $^{00}/_{100}$ ———————— DOLLARS

Citibank

MEMO *software*   *Jennifer Rachael*

⑆3222 ⑈1627⑆ 1123 4533⑈ 0105

T&N School Equipment
111 Stratford Drive, #2A
Rollingwood, TX 77081

INVOICE NO. 5495

DATE: *Dec. 10, 20—*
ORDER NO.:
SHIPPED BY:
TERMS:

TO
Fast Track Tutoring Service
75 Knoll Ridge Drive
Austin, TX 78708

QTY.	ITEM	UNIT PRICE	TOTAL
	Microcomputer System		$2,735.00

Fast Track Tutoring Service
75 Knoll Ridge Drive
Austin, TX 78708

106
71-627
3222

DATE *December 15* 20—

PAY TO THE ORDER OF *Union Painting Service* $ *750.00*

Seven hundred fifty and $^{00}/_{100}$ ———————— DOLLARS

Citibank

MEMO *painting*   *Jennifer Rachael*

⑆3222 ⑈1627⑆ 1123 4533⑈ 0106

Fast Track Tutoring Service
75 Knoll Ridge Drive
Austin, TX 78708

107
71-627
3222

DATE *December 18* 20—

PAY TO THE ORDER OF *Jennifer Rachael* $ *500.00*

Five hundred and $^{00}/_{100}$ ———————— DOLLARS

Citibank

MEMO *personal withdrawal*   *Jennifer Rachael*

⑆3222 ⑈1627⑆ 1123 4533⑈ 0107

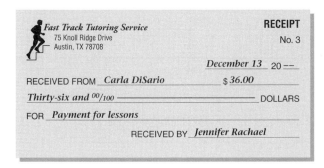

Fast Track Tutoring Service
75 Knoll Ridge Drive
Austin, TX 78708

RECEIPT
No. 2

December 11 20—

RECEIVED FROM *Cash customers* $ *695.00*

Six hundred ninety-five and $^{00}/_{100}$ ———— DOLLARS

FOR *20 private lessons between 3/1 and 3/10*

RECEIVED BY *Jennifer Rachael*

Fast Track Tutoring Service
75 Knoll Ridge Drive
Austin, TX 78708

108
71-627
3222

DATE *December 20* 20—

PAY TO THE ORDER OF *Edison Electric* $ *183.00*

One hundred eighty-three and $^{00}/_{100}$ ———————— DOLLARS

Citibank

MEMO *electricity bill*   *Jennifer Rachael*

⑆3222 ⑈1627⑆ 1123 4533⑈ 0108

Fast Track Tutoring Service
75 Knoll Ridge Drive
Austin, TX 78708

RECEIPT
No. 3

December 13 20—

RECEIVED FROM *Carla DiSario* $ *36.00*

Thirty-six and $^{00}/_{100}$ ———————— DOLLARS

FOR *Payment for lessons*

RECEIVED BY *Jennifer Rachael*

Fast Track Tutoring Service
75 Knoll Ridge Drive
Austin, TX 78708

109
71-627
3222

DATE *December 24* 20—

PAY TO THE ORDER OF *U.S. Postal Service* $ *45.00*

Forty-five and $^{00}/_{100}$ ———————— DOLLARS

Citibank

MEMO *stamps*   *Jennifer Rachael*

⑆3222 ⑈1627⑆ 1123 4533⑈ 0109

Notes

Computerized Accounting Using Peachtree

Mini Practice Set 2

INSTRUCTIONS

Beginning a Session

Step 1 Open the Glencoe Accounting: Electronic Learning Center software.

Step 2 From the Program Menu, click on the **Peachtree Accounting Software and Spreadsheet Applications** icon.

Step 3 Log onto the Management System by typing your user name and password.

Step 4 Under the Chapter Problems tab, select the problem set: Fast Track Tutoring Service (MP-2).

Step 5 Rename the company by adding your initials, e.g., Fast Track (MP-2: XXX).

Step 6 Set the system date to December 31, 2004.

Completing the Accounting Problem

Step 7 Analyze each business transaction shown in your textbook for Fast Track Tutoring Service.

Step 8 Record all of the transactions using the **General Journal Entry** option.

TIP: Proof each general journal entry before you post it. Check the account numbers, descriptions, and amounts.

Step 9 Use the **Account Reconciliation** option to reconcile the bank statement.

TIP: If you use the account reconciliation feature, Peachtree automatically inserts the general journal entry behind the scenes.

Preparing Reports and Proofing Your Work

Step 10 Print a General Journal report.

Step 11 Proof your work. Make any corrections as needed and print a revised report, if necessary.

TIP: While viewing a General Journal report, you can double-click on an entry to display it in the General Journal Entry window. You can edit the transaction and then close the window to see an updated report.

Step 12 Print the Account Register and Account Reconciliation reports.

Step 13 Print a General Ledger report.

Step 14 Print a Trial Balance.

Preparing Financial Statements

Step 15   Print an Income Statement.

Step 16   Print a Balance Sheet.

Checking Your Work

IMPORTANT: Save your work for the mini practice set before you perform the closing process.

Step 17   Click the **Save Pre-closing Balances** button in the Glencoe Smart Guide window.

> **Note:** When this button is clicked the *first time*, balances will be saved automatically. When this button is clicked subsequent times, a dialog box appears asking you if you want to overwrite previously saved pre-closing balances.

Close the Accounting Period

Step 18   Optional: Backup the company data files to a floppy disk. Choose the **Backup** command from the *File* menu. Specify **A:\MP2** for the destination and use the simple copy method. Label the disk accordingly.

Step 19   Close the fiscal year.

Step 20   Print a Post-Closing Trial Balance.

Analyzing Your Work

Step 21   Answer the Analyze question.

Step 22   Complete the Audit Test.

Ending the Session

Step 23   Click the **Close Problem** button in the Glencoe Smart Guide window.

Continuing from a Previous Session

- If you were previously directed to save your work on the network, select the problem from the scrolling menu and click **OK.** The system will retrieve your files from your last session.

- If you were previously directed to save your work on a floppy disk, insert the floppy, select the corresponding problem from the scrolling menu, and click **OK.** The system will retrieve your files from the floppy disk.

Notes

Use the custom income statement and the predefined balance sheet report when you print the financial statements.

Notes

Use the reports you prepared to answer the Analyze question and to complete the Audit Test.

Mini Practice Set 2

GENERAL JOURNAL   PAGE _____

	DATE		DESCRIPTION	POST. REF.	DEBIT	CREDIT	
1							1
2							2
3							3
4							4
5							5
6							6
7							7
8							8
9							9
10							10
11							11
12							12
13							13
14							14
15							15
16							16
17							17
18							18
19							19
20							20
21							21
22							22
23							23
24							24
25							25
26							26
27							27
28							28
29							29
30							30
31							31
32							32
33							33
34							34
35							35
36							36
37							37

Mini Practice Set 2 (continued)

GENERAL JOURNAL   PAGE _____

	DATE	DESCRIPTION	POST. REF.	DEBIT	CREDIT	
1						1
2						2
3						3
4						4
5						5
6						6
7						7
8						8
9						9
10						10
11						11
12						12
13						13
14						14
15						15
16						16
17						17
18						18
19						19
20						20
21						21
22						22
23						23
24						24
25						25
26						26
27						27
28						28
29						29
30						30
31						31
32						32
33						33
34						34
35						35
36						36
37						37

Mini Practice Set 2 (continued)

GENERAL LEDGER

ACCOUNT _____ ACCOUNT NO. _____

DATE	DESCRIPTION	POST. REF.	DEBIT	CREDIT	BALANCE	
					DEBIT	CREDIT

ACCOUNT _____ ACCOUNT NO. _____

DATE	DESCRIPTION	POST. REF.	DEBIT	CREDIT	BALANCE	
					DEBIT	CREDIT

Mini Practice Set 2   (continued)

ACCOUNT _____ ACCOUNT NO. _____

	DATE	DESCRIPTION	POST. REF.	DEBIT	CREDIT	BALANCE	
						DEBIT	CREDIT

ACCOUNT _____ ACCOUNT NO. _____

	DATE	DESCRIPTION	POST. REF.	DEBIT	CREDIT	BALANCE	
						DEBIT	CREDIT

ACCOUNT _____ ACCOUNT NO. _____

	DATE	DESCRIPTION	POST. REF.	DEBIT	CREDIT	BALANCE	
						DEBIT	CREDIT

ACCOUNT _____ ACCOUNT NO. _____

	DATE	DESCRIPTION	POST. REF.	DEBIT	CREDIT	BALANCE	
						DEBIT	CREDIT

ACCOUNT _____ ACCOUNT NO. _____

	DATE	DESCRIPTION	POST. REF.	DEBIT	CREDIT	BALANCE	
						DEBIT	CREDIT

ACCOUNT _____ ACCOUNT NO. _____

	DATE	DESCRIPTION	POST. REF.	DEBIT	CREDIT	BALANCE	
						DEBIT	CREDIT

● **Mini Practice Set 2**   (continued)

ACCOUNT _____ ACCOUNT NO. _____

DATE	DESCRIPTION	POST. REF.	DEBIT	CREDIT	BALANCE	
					DEBIT	CREDIT

ACCOUNT _____ ACCOUNT NO. _____

DATE	DESCRIPTION	POST. REF.	DEBIT	CREDIT	BALANCE	
					DEBIT	CREDIT

ACCOUNT _____ ACCOUNT NO. _____

DATE	DESCRIPTION	POST. REF.	DEBIT	CREDIT	BALANCE	
					DEBIT	CREDIT

ACCOUNT _____ ACCOUNT NO. _____

DATE	DESCRIPTION	POST. REF.	DEBIT	CREDIT	BALANCE	
					DEBIT	CREDIT

ACCOUNT _____ ACCOUNT NO. _____

DATE	DESCRIPTION	POST. REF.	DEBIT	CREDIT	BALANCE	
					DEBIT	CREDIT

Mini Practice Set 2 (continued)

ACCOUNT _____ ACCOUNT NO. _____

DATE	DESCRIPTION	POST. REF.	DEBIT	CREDIT	BALANCE	
					DEBIT	CREDIT

ACCOUNT _____ ACCOUNT NO. _____

DATE	DESCRIPTION	POST. REF.	DEBIT	CREDIT	BALANCE	
					DEBIT	CREDIT

ACCOUNT _____ ACCOUNT NO. _____

DATE	DESCRIPTION	POST. REF.	DEBIT	CREDIT	BALANCE	
					DEBIT	CREDIT

ACCOUNT _____ ACCOUNT NO. _____

DATE	DESCRIPTION	POST. REF.	DEBIT	CREDIT	BALANCE	
					DEBIT	CREDIT

Mini Practice Set 2   (continued)

(5)

BANK RECONCILIATION FORM

PLEASE EXAMINE YOUR STATEMENT AT ONCE. ANY DISCREPANCY SHOULD BE REPORTED TO THE BANK IMMEDIATELY.

CHECKS OUTSTANDING		
Number	Amount	
TOTAL		

1. Record any transactions appearing on this statement but not listed in your checkbook.

2. List any checks still outstanding in the space provided to the right.

3. Enter the balance shown on this statement here.

4. Enter deposits recorded in your checkbook but not shown on this statement.

5. Total Lines 3 and 4 and enter here.

6. Enter total checks outstanding here.

7. Subtract Line 6 from Line 5. This adjusted bank balance should agree with your checkbook balance.

(7)

		No. 114
$		
Date		20
To		
For		

	Dollars	Cents
Balance brought forward		
Add deposits		
Total		
Less this check		
Balance carried forward		

Fast Track Tutoring Service
75 Knoll Ridge Drive
Austin, TX 78708

114

71-627
3222

DATE _____ 20 ___

PAY TO THE
ORDER OF _____ $ _____

_____ DOLLARS

🏛 Citibank

MEMO _____ _____

⑊3222 716 27⑊ 1123 4533⑊ 0114

Mini Practice Set 2   (continued)

(8)

ACCT. NO.	ACCOUNT NAME	TRIAL BALANCE		INCOME STATEMENT		BALANCE SHEET	
		DEBIT	CREDIT	DEBIT	CREDIT	DEBIT	CREDIT
1							
2							
3							
4							
5							
6							
7							
8							
9							
10							
11							
12							
13							
14							
15							
16							
17							
18							
19							
20							
21							
22							

Mini Practice Set 2   (continued)

(9)

(10)

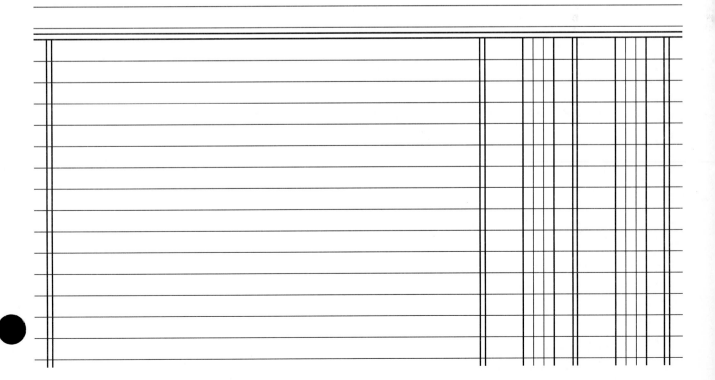

Mini Practice Set 2   (concluded)

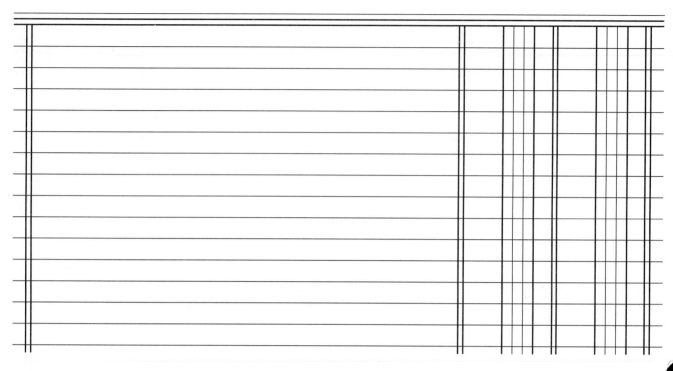

(11)

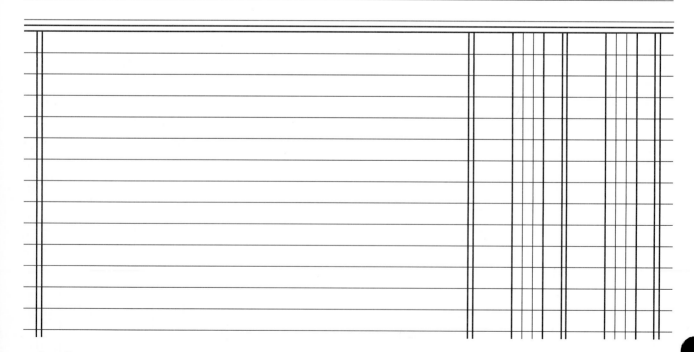

Analyze: _____

MINI PRACTICE SET

Fast Track Tutoring Service

Audit Test

Directions: *Use your completed solutions to answer the following questions. Write the answer in the space to the left of each question.*

_____ **1.** Did the transaction on December 18 increase or decrease owner's capital?

_____ **2.** What was the balance in the Private Lessons Fees account on December 23?

_____ **3.** Did the transaction on December 8 increase or decrease accounts receivable?

_____ **4.** What was the amount of office supplies purchased during the month?

_____ **5.** What was the checkbook balance after the bank service charge was recorded on the check stub?

_____ **6.** What account was debited to record the bank service charge amount?

_____ **7.** What was the total amount of outstanding checks listed on the bank reconciliation statement?

_____ **8.** To which creditor did Fast Track Tutoring Service owe the most money on December 31?

_____ **9.** What was the balance of the owner's capital account reported on the trial balance?

_____ **10.** To what section of the work sheet was the balance of the Jennifer Rachael, Withdrawals account extended?

_____ **11.** What was the total of the Income Statement Debit column of the work sheet before the net income or net loss was determined?

_____ **12.** What was the amount of net income or net loss for December?

_____ **13.** What was the amount of total revenue for the period?

_____ **14.** From what source did Fast Track Tutoring Service earn most of its revenue?

_____ **15.** What were the total expenses for the month?

_____ **16.** Did all the temporary capital accounts appear on the income statement?

_____ **17.** How many asset accounts were listed on the balance sheet?

_____ **18.** What were Fast Track Tutoring Service's total liabilities at the end of the month?

_____ **19.** How many closing entries were needed to close the temporary capital accounts?

_____ **20.** To close Rent Expense, was the account debited or credited?

_____ **21.** How many accounts in the general ledger were closed?

_____ **22.** The final closing entry closed which account?

_____ **23.** How many accounts were listed on the post-closing trial balance?

_____ **24.** What was the balance in the Jennifer Rachael, Capital account reported on the post-closing trial balance?

_____ **25.** What were the debit and credit totals of the post-closing trial balance?

CHAPTER 12 Payroll Accounting

Study Plan

Check Your Understanding

Section 1	*Read Section 1 on pages 288–291 and complete the following exercises on page 292.*
	❑ Thinking Critically
	❑ Computing in the Business World
	❑ Problem 12-1 *Calculating Gross Earnings*
Section 2	*Read Section 2 on pages 293–297 and complete the following exercises on page 298.*
	❑ Thinking Critically
	❑ Computing in the Business World
	❑ Problem 12-2 *Determining Taxes on Gross Earnings*
	❑ Problem 12-3 *Analyzing a Source Document*
Section 3	*Read Section 3 on pages 299–303 and complete the following exercises on page 304.*
	❑ Thinking Critically
	❑ Analyzing Accounting
	❑ Problem 12-4 *Preparing a Payroll Check*

Summary	*Review the Chapter 12 Summary on page 305 in your textbook.*
	❑ Key Concepts
Review and Activities	*Complete the following questions and exercises on pages 306–307 in your textbook.*
	❑ Using Key Terms
	❑ Understanding Accounting Concepts and Procedures
	❑ Case Study
	❑ Conducting an Audit with Alex
	❑ Internet Connection
	❑ Workplace Skills
Computerized Accounting	*Read the Computerized Accounting information on page 308 in your textbook.*
	❑ *Making the Transition from a Manual to a Computerized System*
	❑ *Preparing the Payroll in Peachtree*
Problems	*Complete the following end-of-chapter problems for Chapter 12.*
	❑ Problem 12-5 *Calculating Gross Pay*
	❑ Problem 12-6 *Preparing a Payroll Register*
	❑ Problem 12-7 *Preparing Payroll Checks and Earnings Records*
	❑ Problem 12-8 *Preparing the Payroll*
	❑ Problem 12-9 *Preparing the Payroll Register*
Challenge Problem	❑ Problem 12-10 *Calculating Gross Earnings*
Chapter Reviews and Working Papers	*Complete the following exercises for Chapter 12 in your Chapter Reviews and Working Papers.*
	❑ Chapter Review
	❑ Self-Test

CHAPTER 12 REVIEW Payroll Accounting

Part 1 Accounting Vocabulary (15 points)

Directions: *Using terms from the following list, complete the sentences below. Write the letter of the term you have chosen in the space provided.*

Total Points	42
Student's Score	

A. accumulated earnings	**E.** exemption	**I.** pay period	**M.** salary
B. commission	**F.** gross earnings	**J.** payroll	**N.** timecard
C. deduction	**G.** net pay	**K.** payroll clerk	**O.** wage
D. direct deposit	**H.** overtime rate	**L.** payroll register	**P.** 401(k)

_____ *I* _____ **0.** The _____ is the amount of time for which an employee is paid.

_____ **1.** An amount subtracted from an employee's gross earnings is a(n) _____.

_____ **2.** The employer's deposit of net pay in an employee's personal bank account is known as _____.

_____ **3.** A(n) _____ is a list of the employees of a business and the payments due to each employee for a specific pay period.

_____ **4.** A fixed amount of money paid to an employee for each pay period is a(n) _____.

_____ **5.** An allowance claimed by a taxpayer that reduces the amount of taxes that must be paid is a(n) _____.

_____ **6.** The year-to-date gross earnings of an employee are called _____.

_____ **7.** A type of account that allows employees to defer paying taxes until retirement is called a(n) _____.

_____ **8.** The total amount earned by an employee in a pay period is called _____.

_____ **9.** The _____ is a form that summarizes information about employees' earnings for each pay period.

_____ **10.** An amount paid to an employee based on a percentage of the employee's sales is a(n) _____.

_____ **11.** The _____ is the amount of money left after all deductions are subtracted from the gross earnings paid to an employee.

_____ **12.** The person who is responsible for preparing the payroll is called a(n) _____.

_____ **13.** The _____ is 1½ times an employee's regular hourly rate of pay and is paid for all hours worked over 40 per work week.

_____ **14.** A record of the arrival time, departure time, and total number of hours worked each day for an employee is kept on a(n) _____.

_____ **15.** A(n) _____ is an amount of money paid to an employee at a specific rate per hour worked.

Part 2 FICA Deductions (6 points)

Directions: *Using the social security rate of 6.2% and the Medicare rate of 1.45%, calculate the amounts of the deductions for each of the following employees.*

Name	Gross Earnings	Social Security Deduction	Medicare Deduction
0. Brown, Diane	$294.53	*18.26*	*4.27*
1. Erickson, Sean	385.59	_____	_____
2. Gomez, Juan	215.58	_____	_____
3. McNeil, Mary	337.77	_____	_____
4. Oller, José	184.30	_____	_____
5. Quinn, Betty	394.06	_____	_____
6. Thomas, Judy	214.44	_____	_____

Part 3 Calculating Commissions (6 points)

Directions: *The following employees are paid a salary of $195.00 per week plus a commission of 5% of all sales made. Calculate the gross earnings for each employee.*

Name	Sales	Gross Earnings
0. Robert Jacovitz	$ 823.75	*$236.19*
1. Vincent Lee	903.29	_____
2. Lorna Singhali	396.50	_____
3. Sam Throton	703.48	_____
4. Catherine Walker	803.84	_____
5. Carl Martinez	1,128.40	_____
6. Amy Prez	734.49	_____

Part 4 Calculating Overtime Pay (4 points)

Directions: *The Protech Company pays an overtime rate of 1½ for all hours worked over 40 per work week. Calculate the overtime rate for each employee.*

Name	Hourly Wage	Overtime Rate
0. Jack Lapolla	$8.80	*$13.20*
1. Mary Arcompora	7.20	_____
2. Jody Swan	6.74	_____
3. Patricia Dobson	9.45	_____
4. Joseph Wong	7.50	_____

Part 5 Preparing the Payroll (11 points)

Directions: *Read each of the following statements to determine whether the statement is true or false. Write your answer in the space provided.*

True   **0.** The employee payroll is a major expense for most companies.

_____   **1.** When a company has only a few employees, paychecks are often written on the company's regular checking account.

_____   **2.** The employer acts as a tax collection agent for the federal government.

_____   **3.** The amount of taxes withheld from each employee's paycheck is the exact amount that the employee will owe at the end of the tax year.

_____   **4.** If an employee qualifies as exempt, he or she may not be required to pay federal or state income taxes in a given year.

_____   **5.** An employee's gross earnings may be calculated by any of the four methods—salary, piece rate, hourly wage, or commission—but never by a combination of these methods.

_____   **6.** To ensure that taxpayers have the funds to pay their taxes, employers are required to withhold a certain amount of money from employees' earnings.

_____   **7.** Most factory employees are paid on a salary basis.

_____   **8.** A person has the same social security number for life.

_____   **9.** Employees' earnings records are kept on a monthly basis to make it easier to complete government reports that are required.

_____   **10.** The payroll register is the source of information for preparing the paychecks.

_____   **11.** A business may obtain a daily printout on employee work hours by using electronic badge readers.

Working Papers *for Section Problems*

Problem 12-1 Calculating Gross Earnings

Employee	Total Hours	Pay Rate	Regular Earnings	Overtime Earnings	Gross Earnings
Clune, David	33½	$6.95	$232.83	–0–	$232.83
Lang, Richard					
Longas, Jane					
Quinn, Betty					
Sullivan, John					
Talbert, Kelly					
Trimbell, Gene					
Varney, Heidi					
Wallace, Kevin					

Problem 12-2 Determining Taxes on Gross Earnings

Employee	Marital Status	Allowances	Gross Earnings	Deductions Social Security Tax	Medicare Tax	Federal Inc. Tax	State Inc. Tax	Total	Net Pay
Cleary, Kevin	S	0	155.60						
Halley, James	S	1	184.10						
Hong, Kim	S	0	204.65						
Jackson, Marvin	M	1	216.40						
Sell, Richard	M	2	196.81						
Totals									

Problem 12-3 Analyzing a Source Document

Employee Pay Statement — Detach and retain this statement.											260
Period Ending	Earnings Regular	Overtime	Total	Deductions Social Security Tax	Med. Tax	Federal Income Tax	State Income Tax	Hosp. Ins.	Other	Total	Net Pay
1/15/20--	315.00	–0–	315.00	2)	1)	3)					

Problem 12-4 Preparing a Payroll Check

PAYROLL REGISTER

PAY PERIOD ENDING _March 23_   20--

DATE OF PAYMENT _March 23, 20--_

EMPLOYEE NUMBER	NAME	MAR. STATUS	ALLOW.	TOTAL HOURS	RATE	EARNINGS REGULAR	EARNINGS OVERTIME	EARNINGS TOTAL	DEDUCTIONS SOC. SEC. TAX	DEDUCTIONS MED. TAX	DEDUCTIONS FED. INC. TAX	DEDUCTIONS STATE INC. TAX	DEDUCTIONS HOSP. INS.	DEDUCTIONS OTHER	DEDUCTIONS TOTAL	NET PAY	CK. NO.
18	Burns, Janice	S	1	42	7.80	312 00	23 40	335 40	20 79	4 86	35 00	6 71	4 10	—	71 46	263 94	79

Heather's Dance School
23 Kingdom Street
Danbury, TX 75430

79

63-947 / 670

Date _____ 20 ____

Pay to the Order of _____

$ _____

_____ Dollars

W Worster Bank
PATTON, TEXAS

⑈06700947⑈ 3939 043 4⑈7⑈

Employee Pay Statement
Detach and retain this statement.

79

Period Ending	Earnings Regular	Overtime	Total	Deductions Social Security Tax	Med. Tax	Federal Income Tax	State Income Tax	Hosp. Ins.	Other	Total	Net Pay

Notes

Computerized Accounting Using Peachtree

Software Objectives

When you have completed this chapter, you will be able to use Peachtree to:

1. Update an employee record.
2. Calculate gross earnings.
3. Print payroll checks.
4. Calculate and record payroll deductions.
5. Print a Payroll Register report.
6. Print a Current Earnings report.

Problem 12-5   Calculating Gross Pay

INSTRUCTIONS

Beginning a Session

Step 1   Select the problem set: Wilderness Rentals (Prob. 12-5).
Step 2   Rename the company by adding your initials, e.g., Wilderness (Prob. 12-5: XXX).
Step 3   Set the system date to February 1, 2004.

Completing the Accounting Problem

Step 4   Review the payroll information provided in your textbook.
Step 5   Update the employee record for John Gilmartin to include his regular and overtime hourly rate.

   All of the employee records have already been set up for you, except that John Gilmartin's record does not include the pay rates. Follow the instructions provided here to record this information.

   To update an employee's record:

   • Choose **Employees/Sales Reps** from the _**Maintain**_ menu.
   • Type **GIL** in the _Employee ID_ field.
   • Click the **Pay Info** tab.
   • Type **6.80** for the regular hourly rate and **10.20** for the overtime rate.
   • Compare the information you entered to the employee record shown in Figure 12-5A.
   • Click to save the changes and then click 🗄 Close to close the data entry window.

> **✳ Notes**
>
> _You can use the **Employee/Sales Reps** option to update any of the following employee record fields: address, social security number, hire date, and pay rate._

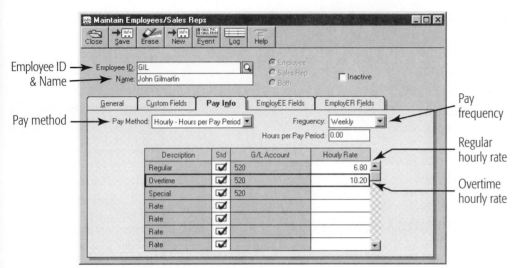

Employee ID & Name

Pay method

Pay frequency

Regular hourly rate

Overtime hourly rate

Figure 12-5A *Completed Employee Record (John Gilmartin)*

Step 6   Record the payroll for John Gilmartin (43 hours).

To record a payroll entry:

- Choose **Payroll Entry** from the *Tasks* menu to display the Payroll Entry window.
- Type **GIL** in the *Employee ID* field.

TIP: Click 🔍 or press **SHIFT+?** when the cursor is in the *Employee ID* field to display a list of employees and their IDs.

- Type **40** in the *Regular Hours* field.
- Type **3** in the *Overtime Hours* field and press **ENTER**.

     As you enter the regular and overtime hours (if any), Peachtree automatically calculates the gross pay based on the rate/salary information stored in the employee's record. As you can see, Peachtree also includes fields to record the payroll taxes and other deductions. You will learn how to record information in these fields in a later problem.

- Proof the information you just recorded. Check all of the information you entered. If you notice a mistake, move to that field and make the correction. Compare the information on your screen to the completed transaction shown in Figure 12-5B.
- Click [Post] to record the payroll entry.

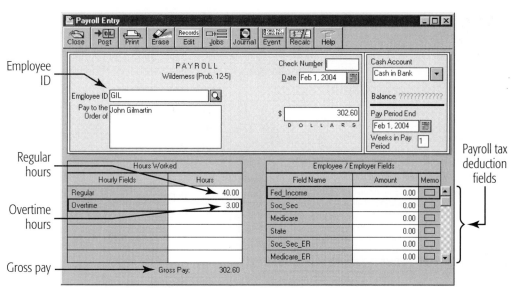

Figure 12-5B *Completed Payroll Entry (John Gilmartin)*

Step 7   Record a payroll entry for each of the following employees: Arlene Stone, Tom Driscoll, and Ann Ryan.

TIP: To record the payroll entry for an employee who earned a commission, you must calculate the commission amount and manually enter it in the *Commission* field.

Step 8   Print a Payroll Register and proof your work.

To print a Payroll Register report:

- Choose **Payroll** from the ***Reports*** menu to display the Select a Report window. (See Figure 12-5B.)

TIP: As a shortcut, you can double-click a report title to go directly to the report screen.

- Select Payroll Register in the report list.
- Click [Screen] and then click **OK** to display the report.
- Click [Print] to print the report.
- Click [Close] to close the report window.

Peachtree Guide

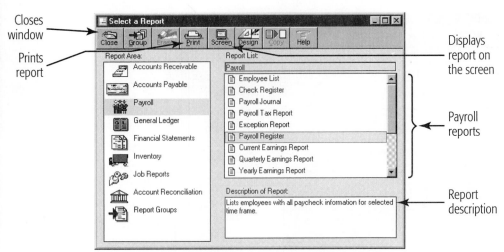

Closes window

Prints report

Displays report on the screen

Payroll reports

Report description

Figure 12-5C *Select a Report Window*

Step 9 If you notice any errors, choose the **Payroll Entry** command again, click [Records Edit], select the record you want to edit, and post the changes.

Step 10 Answer the analyze question.

Ending the Session

Step 11 Click the **Close Problem** button in the Glencoe Smart Guide window. Select the save option as directed by your teacher.

Continuing a Problem from a Previous Session

If you want to continue working on a problem that you did not complete in a previous session, follow step 1. The management system will retrieve your files from your last session.

Mastering Peachtree

Can you customize the employee record to store extra information such as position/title, review date, and benefit plan? Explain your answer.

Problem 12-7 Preparing Payroll Checks and Earnings Records

INSTRUCTIONS

Beginning a Session

Step 1 Select the problem set: Kits & Pups Grooming (Prob. 12-7).

TIP: Make sure that you set the system date before you print any payroll checks.

Step 2 Rename the company and set the system date to October 16, 2004.

DO YOU HAVE A QUESTION

Q. *Why don't the Peachtree payroll checks look like real checks?*

A. When you choose to print payroll checks, Peachtree prints only the pertinent information since it assumes that you are using pre-printed checks. A pre-printed check is a real check with the company name, routing numbers, and other information. Peachtree simply prints the date, employee name, amount, and deductions. If you are printing on plain paper, only these items appear.

Completing the Accounting Problem

Step 3   Review the payroll information provided in your textbook.

Step 4   Print a payroll check for Mildred Hurd.

The payroll information (hours and deductions) for the pay period ending October 16 has already been recorded for you. Normally, you would enter the earnings data and deductions yourself before printing payroll checks.

To print a payroll check:

- Choose **Payroll Entry** from the *Tasks* menu.
- Click [Records Edit] and choose the payroll entry for Mildred Hurd.
- Review the payroll information for Mildred Hurd. Her net pay should be $219.48.
- Click [Print] to print a payroll check.
- Choose **PR MultiP Chks 1 Stub** or an equivalent form.

> **Notes**
>
> *The payroll earnings and deductions have already been entered for the employees.*

By choosing the payroll check form, you let Peachtree know how it should organize the information it is about to print. The layout for the employee name, check amount, and deductions depend on the particular form.

- Click **Real** to print a real check and enter **92** for the first check number.

Step 5   Print payroll checks for José Montego, Amanda Pilly, and Margaret Steams.

Step 6   Print a Payroll Register for this pay period.

To print a Payroll Register report for a specific pay period:

- Choose **Payroll** from the *Reports* menu.
- Select Payroll Register in the report list.
- Click [Screen].
- Choose **This Week-to-Date** for date range on the Filter options tab and then press **OK**.

The date range should show October 10, 2004 to October 16, 2004. If the report is already on the screen, click [Options] to select a pay period.

- Click [Print] to print the report.
- Click [Close] to close the report window.

Step 7   Print a Current Earnings report for José Montego and Amanda Pilly.

TIP: Use the report filter options to select which employee you want to appear on the Current Earnings report.

Step 8   Answer the analyze question.

Ending the Session

Step 9   Click the **Close Problem** button in the Glencoe Smart Guide window. Select the save option as directed by your teacher.

Mastering Peachtree

Where can you obtain pre-printed payroll checks? Are there different styles from which to choose? Explain.

Problem 12-8   Preparing the Payroll

INSTRUCTIONS

Beginning a Session

Step 1   Select the problem set: Outback Guide Service (Prob. 12-8).

> **TIP:** Make sure that you set the system date before you print any payroll checks.

Step 2   Rename the company and set the system date to October 16, 2004.

Completing the Accounting Problem

Step 3   Review the payroll information provided in your textbook.

Step 4   Record the payroll and print a payroll check for all of the employees.

To process the payroll and print checks:

- Choose **Payroll Entry** from the *Tasks* menu.
- Manually enter the payroll information (rate, taxes, and other deductions) for an employee.
- Review the payroll information.
- Click 🖶 to print a payroll check.
- Choose **PR MultiP Chks 1 Stub** or an equivalent form.

     By choosing the payroll check form, you let Peachtree know how it should organize the information it is about to print. The layout for the employee name, check amount, and deductions depend on the particular form.

- Click **Real** to print a real check and enter **82** for the first check number.

Step 5   Print a Payroll Register for the pay period.

To print a Payroll Register report for a specific pay period:

- Choose **Payroll** from the *Reports* menu.
- Select Payroll Register in the report list.
- Click 🖵 .
- Choose **This Week-to-Date** for date range on the Filter options tab and then press **OK**.

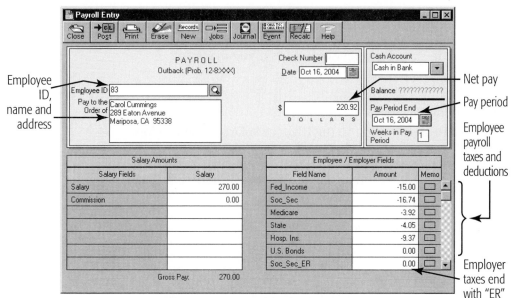

Figure 12-8A *Payroll Entry Window*

The date range should show October 10, 2004 to October 16, 2004.

If the report is already on the screen, click [Options] to select a pay period.

- Click [Print] to print the report.

- Click [Close] to close the report window.

Step 6   Print a Current Earnings report for all of the employees.

Step 7   Answer the Analyze question.

Ending the Session

Step 8   Click the **Close Problem** button in the Glencoe Smart Guide window. Select the save option as directed by your teacher.

Problem 12-9   Preparing the Payroll Register

INSTRUCTIONS

Beginning a Session

Step 1   Select the problem set: Showbiz Video (Prob. 12-9).

Step 2   Rename the company and set the system date to October 23, 2004.

Completing the Accounting Problem

Step 3   Review the payroll information provided in your textbook.

Step 4   Process the payroll information for all of the employees, but do not print payroll checks.

TIP: Remember that you must manually enter the payroll taxes and other deductions. Be sure to enter the deductions as negative amounts.

Step 5   Print a Payroll Register for the pay period.

Step 6   Proof your work. If necessary, use the **Payroll Entry** option to edit any employee pay records. Print revised reports if you make any changes.

Step 7   Answer the Analyze question.

Checking Your Work and Ending the Session

Step 8   Click the **Close Problem** button in the Glencoe Smart Guide window.

Step 9   If your teacher has asked you to check your solution, select *Check my answer to this problem.* Review, print, and close the report.

Step 10   Click the **Close Problem** button and select the save option as directed by your teacher.

Problem 12-10   Calculating Gross Earnings

INSTRUCTIONS

Beginning a Session

Step 1   Select the problem set: Job Connection (Prob. 12-10).

Step 2   Rename the company and set the system date to October 23, 2004.

Completing the Accounting Problem

Step 3   Review the payroll information provided in your textbook.

Step 4   Process the payroll information for all employees to compute gross earnings. **Note:** You do **not** have to record the payroll taxes and other deductions.

Step 5   Print a Payroll Register for the pay period.

Step 6   Proof your work.

Step 7   Answer the Analyze question.

Notes

You must manually compute and record commission earnings.

Ending the Session

Step 8   Click the **Close Problem** button in the Glencoe Smart Guide window.

Notes

Leave the check number field blank.

Mastering Peachtree

Explain the step necessary to update an employee's marital status and number of exemptions.

FAQs

Why doesn't Peachtree automatically calculate the payroll taxes?

For a real company, Peachtree will automatically calculate all of the payroll taxes. To perform these calculations, a company must have the tax tables for the current year. For the payroll problems in your text, the base year is 2004. To avoid potential software conflicts, the automatic payroll tax calculation feature was turned off.

Computerized Accounting Using Spreadsheets

Problem 12-6   Preparing a Payroll Register

Completing the Spreadsheet

Step 1 Read the instructions for Problem 12-6 in your textbook. This problem involves preparing a payroll register.

Step 2 Open the Glencoe Accounting: Electronic Learning Center software.

Step 3 From the Program Menu, click on the **Peachtree Accounting Software and Spreadsheet Applications** icon.

Step 4 Log onto the Management System by typing your user name and password.

Step 5 Under the Chapter Problems tab, select the template: PR12-6a.xls. The template should look like the one shown below.

```
PROBLEM 12-6
PREPARING A PAYROLL REGISTER


(name)
(date)


PAYROLL REGISTER
PAY PERIOD ENDING OCTOBER 9, 20--

                                                       EARNINGS       > <
EMPLOYEE         NAME          MARITAL  ALLOW.  TOTAL   HOURLY  REGULAR OVERTIME > <        NET
NUMBER                         STATUS           HOURS   RATE                     > <        PAY
   108      Dumser, James                                        0.00    0.00   > <       0.00
   112      Job, Gail                                            0.00    0.00   > <       0.00
   102      Liptak, James                                        0.00    0.00   > <       0.00
   109      Stern, Bruce                                         0.00    0.00   > <       0.00
TOTAL                                                            0.00    0.00   > <       0.00
```

Step 6 Key your name and today's date in the cells containing the *(name)* and *(date)* placeholders.

Step 7 Enter the marital status, number of allowances, total hours worked, and hourly rate for each employee in the appropriate cells of the spreadsheet template. The spreadsheet template will automatically calculate the regular earnings, overtime earnings, total earnings, Social Security tax, Medicare tax, and state income tax for each employee.

TIP: The cells for Social Security tax, Medicare tax, and state income tax are set up to round these numbers to two decimal places. When you are entering data in this spreadsheet template, always round numbers to two decimal places when rounding is necessary.

Step 8 Use the tax tables in your textbook to determine the federal income tax for each employee. Enter the federal income tax for each employee.

Step 9 Enter the hospital insurance deduction of $6.75 for the employees who have health and hospital insurance.

Chapter 12 ■ 281

Step 10 Enter the union dues of $4.50 for the employees who are union members. The spreadsheet template automatically calculates the total deductions and net pay for each employee.

Step 11 Save the spreadsheet using the **Save** option from the *File* menu. You should accept the default location for the save as this is handled by the management system.

Step 12 Print the completed spreadsheet.

TIP: If your spreadsheet is too wide to fit on an 8.5-inch wide piece of paper, you can change your print settings to print the worksheet *landscape.* Landscape means that the worksheet will be printed broadside on the page. Some spreadsheet applications also allow you to choose a "print to page" option. This function will reduce the width and/or depth of the worksheet to fit on one page.

Step 13 Exit the spreadsheet program.

Step 14 In the Close Options box, select the location where you would like to save your work.

Step 15 Answer the Analyze question from your textbook for this problem.

What-If Analysis

If James Dumser worked 43 hours, what would his net pay be?

_____

TIP: Remember to update the federal withholding tax to reflect Mr. Dumser's gross pay.

Spreadsheet Guide

Working Papers *for End-of-Chapter Problems*

Problem 12-5   Calculating Gross Pay

Name	Regular Hours	Overtime Hours	Total Hours	Hourly Rate	Salary	Commission	Gross Pay
Driscoll, Tom							
Gilmartin, John							
Ryan, Ann							
Stone, Arlene							

Analyze: _____

_____

Problem 12-6   Preparing a Payroll Register

PAYROLL REGISTER

PAY PERIOD ENDING _____ 20 _____

DATE OF PAYMENT _____

EMPLOYEE NUMBER	NAME	MAR. STATUS	ALLOW.	TOTAL HOURS	RATE	EARNINGS			SOC. SEC. TAX	MED. TAX	FED. INC. TAX	STATE INC. TAX	HOSP. INS.	OTHER	TOTAL	NET PAY	CK. NO.
						REGULAR	OVERTIME	TOTAL									
1																	
2																	
3																	
4																	
25	TOTALS																

Other Deductions: Write the appropriate code letter to the left of the amount: B—U.S. Savings Bonds; C—Credit Union; UD—Union Dues; UW—United Way.

Analyze: _____

Problem 12-7 Preparing Payroll Checks and Earnings Records

PAYROLL REGISTER

PAY PERIOD ENDING *October 16*   20 --   DATE OF PAYMENT *October 16, 20--*

EMPLOYEE NUMBER	NAME	MAR. STATUS	ALLOW.	TOTAL HOURS	RATE	EARNINGS REGULAR	EARNINGS OVERTIME	EARNINGS TOTAL	DEDUCTIONS SOC. SEC. TAX	MED. TAX	FED. INC. TAX	STATE INC. TAX	HOSP. INS.	OTHER	TOTAL	NET PAY	CK. NO.
162	Hurd, Mildred	S	0	38	7.60	288 80		288 80	17 91	4 19	35 00	7 22		B 5 00	69 32	219 48	
157	Montego, José	S	1	39	7.90	308 10		308 10	19 10	4 47	30 00	7 70	5 10		66 37	241 73	
151	Pilly, Amanda	M	2	36	8.10	291 60		291 60	18 08	4 23	10 00	7 29	7 60	B 5 00	52 20	239 40	
163	Steams, Margaret	S	0	41	7.60	304 00	11 40	315 40	19 55	4 57	40 00	7 89			72 01	243 39	
	TOTALS					1,192 50	11 40	1,203 90	74 64	17 46	115 00	30 10	12 70	10 00	259 90	944 00	

Other Deductions: Write the appropriate code letter to the left of the amount: B—U.S. Savings Bonds; C—Credit Union; UD—Union Dues; UW—United Way.

Problem 12-7   (continued)

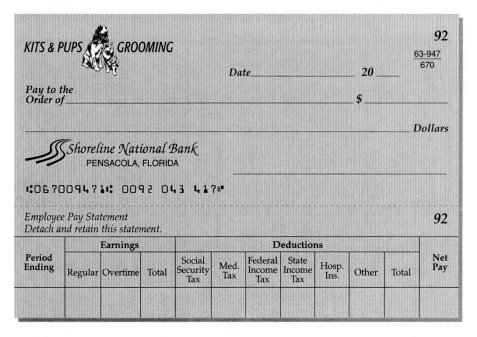

Problem 12-7   (continued)

KITS & PUPS GROOMING										94 63-947/670

Date_____ 20 _____

Pay to the
Order of_____ $ _____

_____ Dollars

Shoreline National Bank
PENSACOLA, FLORIDA

⑆067009471⑆ 0094 043 417⑈

Employee Pay Statement
Detach and retain this statement.   94

Period Ending	Earnings			Deductions							Net Pay
	Regular	Overtime	Total	Social Security Tax	Med. Tax	Federal Income Tax	State Income Tax	Hosp. Ins.	Other	Total	

KITS & PUPS GROOMING										95 63-947/670

Date_____ 20 _____

Pay to the
Order of_____ $ _____

_____ Dollars

Shoreline National Bank
PENSACOLA, FLORIDA

⑆067009471⑆ 0095 043 417⑈

Employee Pay Statement
Detach and retain this statement.   95

Period Ending	Earnings			Deductions							Net Pay
	Regular	Overtime	Total	Social Security Tax	Med. Tax	Federal Income Tax	State Income Tax	Hosp. Ins.	Other	Total	

Problem 12-7   (continued)

EMPLOYEE'S EARNINGS RECORD FOR QUARTER ENDING _October 31, 20--_

Last Name: _Montego_
First: _José_
Initial: _M._
Address: _28 Cambell Avenue_
Pensacola, FL 32526

EMPLOYEE NO. _157_
POSITION _Sales Associate_
RATE OF PAY _$7.90_
MARITAL STATUS _S_
ALLOWANCES _1_
SOC. SEC. NO. _021-54-7641_

PAY PERIOD		EARNINGS			DEDUCTIONS							NET PAY	ACCUMULATED EARNINGS
NO.	ENDED	REGULAR	OVERTIME	TOTAL	SOC. SEC. TAX	MED. TAX	FED. INC. TAX	STATE INC. TAX	HOSP. INS.	OTHER	TOTAL		
													9414 32
1	10/2	260 70		260 70	16 16	3 78	24 00	6 52	5 10	—	55 56	205 14	9675 02
2	10/9	300 20		300 20	18 61	4 35	30 00	7 51	5 10	—	65 57	234 63	9975 22
3													
4													
5													
6													
7													
8													
9													
10													
11													
12													
13													
QUARTERLY TOTALS													

Other Deductions: B—U.S. Savings Bonds; C—Credit Union; UD—Union Dues; UW—United Way.

Problem 12-7   (concluded)

EMPLOYEE'S EARNINGS RECORD FOR QUARTER ENDING *October 31, 20--*

Pilly Last Name	*Amanda* First	*G.* Initial
162 Clinton Avenue Address		
Pensacola, FL 32502		

MARITAL STATUS **M**   ALLOWANCES **2**

EMPLOYEE NO. **151**

POSITION *Assistant Manager*

RATE OF PAY *$8.10*

SOC. SEC. NO. *021-56-7302*

PAY PERIOD		EARNINGS			DEDUCTIONS							NET PAY	ACCUMULATED EARNINGS
NO.	ENDED	REGULAR	OVERTIME	TOTAL	SOC. SEC. TAX	MED. TAX	FED. INC. TAX	STATE INC. TAX	HOSP. INS.	OTHER	TOTAL		
													9655 30
1	10/2	2755 40		2755 40	1707	399	700	689	760	B 500	4755	227 85	9930 70
2	10/9	3155 90		3155 90	1959	458	1300	790	760	B 500	5767	258 23	10,246 60
3													
4													
5													
6													
7													
8													
9													
10													
11													
12													
13													
QUARTERLY TOTALS													

Other Deductions: B—U.S. Savings Bonds; C—Credit Union; UD—Union Dues; UW—United Way.

Analyze:

Problem 12-8   Preparing the Payroll

NO. __73__

NAME __Ted Dame__

SOC. SEC. NO. __093-48-7423__

WEEK ENDING __10/16/20--__

DAY	IN	OUT	IN	OUT	IN	OUT	TOTAL
M	8:58	12:03	12:55	5:09			
T	8:55	11:55	1:00	4:00			
W	9:30	12:10	1:04	3:30			
Th	8:57	12:03	12:59	6:00			
F	8:58	12:00	1:00	6:05			
S	9:00	12:00					
S							
					TOTAL HOURS		

	HOURS	RATE	AMOUNT
REGULAR			
OVERTIME			
	TOTAL EARNINGS		

SIGNATURE _____ DATE _____

NO. __92__

NAME __James Usdavin__

SOC. SEC. NO. __087-46-3875__

WEEK ENDING __10/16/20--__

DAY	IN	OUT	IN	OUT	IN	OUT	TOTAL
M	8:55	12:06	1:01	5:35			
T	7:58	11:01	12:03	6:38			
W	9:03	1:10	2:00	6:00			
Th	7:59	11:55	1:10	4:51			
F	9:01	12:06	1:05	3:47			
S	9:00	12:03					
S							
					TOTAL HOURS		

	HOURS	RATE	AMOUNT
REGULAR			
OVERTIME			
	TOTAL EARNINGS		

SIGNATURE _____ DATE _____

PAYROLL REGISTER   PAY PERIOD ENDING __20___   DATE OF PAYMENT _____

EMPLOYEE NUMBER	NAME	MAR. STATUS	ALLOW.	TOTAL HOURS	RATE	EARNINGS REGULAR	EARNINGS OVERTIME	EARNINGS TOTAL	DEDUCTIONS SOC. SEC. TAX	DEDUCTIONS MED. TAX	DEDUCTIONS FED. INC. TAX	DEDUCTIONS STATE INC. TAX	DEDUCTIONS HOSP. INS.	DEDUCTIONS OTHER	DEDUCTIONS TOTAL	NET PAY	CK. NO.
1																	
2																	
3																	
4																	
5																	
6																	
25	TOTALS																

Problem 12-8 (continued)

(3)

<table>
<tr><td colspan="2"></td><td align="right">82</td></tr>
<tr><td>Outback Guide Service</td><td></td><td>91-182
1721</td></tr>
<tr><td></td><td>Date _____ 20 ____</td><td></td></tr>
<tr><td>Pay to the
Order of _____</td><td>$ _____</td><td></td></tr>
<tr><td colspan="3">_____ Dollars</td></tr>
<tr><td>CNB Canyon National Bank
MARIPOSA, CALIFORNIA</td><td></td><td></td></tr>
<tr><td colspan="3">⑆1721091182⑆ 082 015 1189064⑈</td></tr>
</table>

Employee Pay Statement
Detach and retain this statement.   82

| Period Ending | Earnings ||| Deductions |||||||| Net Pay |
	Regular	Overtime	Total	Social Security Tax	Med. Tax	Federal Income Tax	State Income Tax	Hosp. Ins.	Other	Total	

<table>
<tr><td colspan="2"></td><td align="right">83</td></tr>
<tr><td>Outback Guide Service</td><td></td><td>91-182
1721</td></tr>
<tr><td></td><td>Date _____ 20 ____</td><td></td></tr>
<tr><td>Pay to the
Order of _____</td><td>$ _____</td><td></td></tr>
<tr><td colspan="3">_____ Dollars</td></tr>
<tr><td>CNB Canyon National Bank
MARIPOSA, CALIFORNIA</td><td></td><td></td></tr>
<tr><td colspan="3">⑆1721091182⑆ 083 015 1189064⑈</td></tr>
</table>

Employee Pay Statement
Detach and retain this statement.   83

| Period Ending | Earnings ||| Deductions |||||||| Net Pay |
	Regular	Overtime	Total	Social Security Tax	Med. Tax	Federal Income Tax	State Income Tax	Hosp. Ins.	Other	Total	

Problem 12-8   (continued)

Outback Guide Service

84

91-182
1721

Date_____ 20 _____

Pay to the
Order of_____ $ _____

_____ Dollars

CNB *Canyon National Bank*
MARIPOSA, CALIFORNIA

⑆172109118 2⑆ 084 015 1189064⑈

Employee Pay Statement
Detach and retain this statement.

84

Period Ending	Earnings			Deductions							Net Pay
	Regular	Overtime	Total	Social Security Tax	Med. Tax	Federal Income Tax	State Income Tax	Hosp. Ins.	Other	Total	

Outback Guide Service

85

91-182
1721

Date_____ 20 _____

Pay to the
Order of_____ $ _____

_____ Dollars

CNB *Canyon National Bank*
MARIPOSA, CALIFORNIA

⑆172109118 2⑆ 085 015 1189064⑈

Employee Pay Statement
Detach and retain this statement.

85

Period Ending	Earnings			Deductions							Net Pay
	Regular	Overtime	Total	Social Security Tax	Med. Tax	Federal Income Tax	State Income Tax	Hosp. Ins.	Other	Total	

Problem 12-8   (continued)

Outback Guide Service

86

91-182
1721

Date_____ 20 _____

Pay to the
Order of_____ $ _____

_____ Dollars

CNB *Canyon National Bank*
MARIPOSA, CALIFORNIA

⑆1721091182⑆ 086 015 1189064⑈

Employee Pay Statement
Detach and retain this statement.

86

Period Ending	Earnings			Deductions							Net Pay
	Regular	Overtime	Total	Social Security Tax	Med. Tax	Federal Income Tax	State Income Tax	Hosp. Ins.	Other	Total	

Outback Guide Service

87

91-182
1721

Date_____ 20 _____

Pay to the
Order of_____ $ _____

_____ Dollars

CNB *Canyon National Bank*
MARIPOSA, CALIFORNIA

⑆1721091182⑆ 087 015 1189064⑈

Employee Pay Statement
Detach and retain this statement.

87

Period Ending	Earnings			Deductions							Net Pay
	Regular	Overtime	Total	Social Security Tax	Med. Tax	Federal Income Tax	State Income Tax	Hosp. Ins.	Other	Total	

Problem 12-8 (continued)

EMPLOYEE'S EARNINGS RECORD FOR QUARTER ENDING _December 31, 20--_

Last Name	_Cummings_
First	_Carol_
Initial	_T._
Address	_289 Eaton Avenue_
	Mariposa, CA 95338

EMPLOYEE NO.	_83_
POSITION	_Director_
RATE OF PAY	_$270.00 Salary_
MARITAL STATUS	_M_
ALLOWANCES	_1_
SOC. SEC. NO.	_091-56-7024_

PAY PERIOD		EARNINGS			DEDUCTIONS							NET PAY	ACCUMULATED EARNINGS
NO.	ENDED	REGULAR	OVERTIME	TOTAL	SOC. SEC. TAX	MED. TAX	FED. INC. TAX	STATE INC. TAX	HOSP. INS.	OTHER	TOTAL		
													12,15000
1	10/9	270000		270000	1674	392	1500	405	937	—	4908	22092	12,42000
2													
3													
4													
5													
6													
7													
8													
9													
10													
11													
12													
13													
QUARTERLY TOTALS													

Other Deductions: B—U.S. Savings Bonds; C—Credit Union; UD—Union Dues; UW—United Way.

(4)

Problem 12-8   (continued)

EMPLOYEE'S EARNINGS RECORD FOR QUARTER ENDING _December 31, 20--_

Last Name	_Dame_
First	_Ted_
Initial	_K._
Address	_14 Merton Avenue_
	Mariposa, CA 95338
EMPLOYEE NO.	_73_
POSITION	_Equipment Clerk_
RATE OF PAY	_$6.95_
MARITAL STATUS	_S_
ALLOWANCES	_0_
SOC. SEC. NO.	_093-48-7423_

PAY PERIOD		EARNINGS			DEDUCTIONS							NET PAY	ACCUMULATED EARNINGS
NO.	ENDED	REGULAR	OVERTIME	TOTAL	SOC. SEC. TAX	MED. TAX	FED. INC. TAX	STATE INC. TAX	HOSP. INS.	OTHER	TOTAL		
1	10/9	26410		26410	1637	383	3200	396	543		6159	20251	4,01622
2													4,28032
3													
4													
5													
6													
7													
8													
9													
10													
11													
12													
13													
QUARTERLY TOTALS													

Other Deductions: B—U.S. Savings Bonds; C—Credit Union; UD—Union Dues; UW—United Way.

Problem 12-8   (continued)

EMPLOYEE'S EARNINGS RECORD FOR QUARTER ENDING _December 31, 20--_

Last Name: _Lengyel_
First: _Tom_
Initial: _B._
Address: _926 Amsterdam Avenue_
Mariposa, CA 95338

EMPLOYEE NO. _79_
POSITION _Guide_
RATE OF PAY _$160.00 + 5%_
MARITAL STATUS _M_
ALLOWANCES _1_
SOC. SEC. NO. _210-50-7261_

PAY PERIOD		EARNINGS			DEDUCTIONS							NET PAY	ACCUMULATED EARNINGS
NO.	ENDED	REGULAR	OVERTIME	TOTAL	SOC. SEC. TAX	MED. TAX	FED. INC. TAX	STATE INC. TAX	HOSP. INS.	OTHER	TOTAL		
													4,818 00
1	10/9	219 40		219 40	13 60	3 18	6 00	3 29	9 37	10 00 B	45 44	173 96	5,037 40
2													
3													
4													
5													
6													
7													
8													
9													
10													
11													
12													
13													
QUARTERLY TOTALS													

Other Deductions: B—U.S. Savings Bonds; C—Credit Union; UD—Union Dues; UW—United Way.

Problem 12-8 (continued)

EMPLOYEE'S EARNINGS RECORD FOR QUARTER ENDING __December 31, 20--__

Last Name: Robinson   **First:** Jean   **Initial:** A.
Address: 12 Meadow Avenue
Mariposa, CA 95338

EMPLOYEE NO. 46
POSITION Guide
RATE OF PAY $140.00 + 5%
MARITAL STATUS S   **ALLOWANCES** 1
SOC. SEC. NO. 036-59-7206

PAY PERIOD NO.	ENDED	EARNINGS REGULAR	OVERTIME	TOTAL	DEDUCTIONS SOC. SEC. TAX	MED. TAX	FED. INC. TAX	STATE INC. TAX	HOSP. INS.	OTHER	TOTAL	NET PAY	ACCUMULATED EARNINGS
													2,786 35
1	10/9	209 30		209 30	12 98	3 03	15 00	3 14	5 43		39 58	169 72	2,995 65
2													
3													
4													
5													
6													
7													
8													
9													
10													
11													
12													
13													
QUARTERLY TOTALS													

Other Deductions: B—U.S. Savings Bonds; C—Credit Union; UD—Union Dues; UW—United Way.

Problem 12-8   (continued)

EMPLOYEE'S EARNINGS RECORD FOR QUARTER ENDING _December 31, 20--_

Usdavin	James	P.
Last Name	First	Initial

Address _19 Paterson Avenue_
Mariposa, CA 95338

EMPLOYEE NO. _92_

MARITAL STATUS _S_   ALLOWANCES _0_

POSITION _Stock Clerk_

SOC. SEC. NO. _087-46-3875_

RATE OF PAY _$6.65_

PAY PERIOD		EARNINGS			DEDUCTIONS							NET PAY	ACCUMULATED EARNINGS
NO.	ENDED	REGULAR	OVERTIME	TOTAL	SOC. SEC. TAX	MED. TAX	FED. INC. TAX	STATE INC. TAX	HOSP. INS.	OTHER	TOTAL		
1	10/9	2066 15		2066 15	12 78	2 99	23 00	3 09	5 43		47 29	158 86	3,172 15
2													3,378 30
3													
4													
5													
6													
7													
8													
9													
10													
11													
12													
13													
QUARTERLY TOTALS													

Other Deductions: B—U.S. Savings Bonds; C—Credit Union; UD—Union Dues; UW—United Way.

Problem 12-8   (concluded)

EMPLOYEE'S EARNINGS RECORD FOR QUARTER ENDING *December 31, 20--*

Last Name *Wong*
First *Kim*
Initial *P.*

Address *28 Millrose Avenue*
Mariposa, CA 95338

EMPLOYEE NO. *66*
POSITION *Guide*
RATE OF PAY *$140.00 + 5%*

MARITAL STATUS *S*
ALLOWANCES *0*
SOC. SEC. NO. *019-53-7302*

| PAY PERIOD | | EARNINGS | | | DEDUCTIONS | | | | | | | NET PAY | ACCUMULATED EARNINGS |
NO.	ENDED	REGULAR	OVERTIME	TOTAL	SOC. SEC. TAX	MED. TAX	FED. INC. TAX	STATE INC. TAX	HOSP. INS.	OTHER	TOTAL		
1	10/9	21120		21120	1309	306	2300	317	543	B 1000	5775	15345	3,67245
2													3,88365
3													
4													
5													
6													
7													
8													
9													
10													
11													
12													
13													
	QUARTERLY TOTALS												

Other Deductions: B—U.S. Savings Bonds; C—Credit Union; UD—Union Dues; UW—United Way.

Analyze:

Problem 12-9 Preparing the Payroll Register

PAYROLL REGISTER

PAY PERIOD ENDING _____ **DATE OF PAYMENT** _____ **20** ___

EMPLOYEE NUMBER	NAME	MAR. STATUS	ALLOW.	TOTAL HOURS	RATE	EARNINGS			DEDUCTIONS							NET PAY	CK. NO.
						REGULAR	OVERTIME	TOTAL	SOC. SEC. TAX	MED. TAX	FED. INC. TAX	STATE INC. TAX	HOSP. INS.	OTHER	TOTAL		
1																	
2																	
3																	
4																	
5																	
6																	
7																	
8																	
9																	
10																	
11																	
12																	
13																	
14																	
15																	
16																	
17																	
18																	
25	TOTALS																

Other Deductions: Write the appropriate code letter to the left of the amount: B—U.S. Savings Bonds; C—Credit Union; UD—Union Dues; UW—United Way.

Analyze: _____

Problem 12-10   Source Documents

Instructions: *Use the following source documents to record the transactions for this problem.*

Job Connect
405 McLocklin Drive
Durham, NC 27713

INTEROFFICE MEMORANDUM

TO: *Payroll Clerk*
FROM: *Richard Tang*
DATE: *10/23/20--*
SUBJECT: *Payroll*

Please note the following information necessary for preparing payroll for the week ending October 23. Total office sales were $8,420.00, and phone sales were $1,375.00. Pam Darrah made seven (7) job placements.

NO. **15**
NAME **Doris Franco**
SOC. SEC. NO.
WEEK ENDING **10/23/20--**

DAY	IN	OUT	IN	OUT	IN	OUT	TOTAL
M	9:00	12:01	12:35	5:35			8
T	9:01	12:02	12:37	5:36			8
W	8:00	11:59	12:28	5:31			9
Th	8:58	12:01	12:29	5:46			8¼
F	9:02	11:58	12:31	5:29			8
S							
S							
					TOTAL HOURS		41¼

	HOURS	RATE	AMOUNT
REGULAR			
OVERTIME			
TOTAL EARNINGS			

SIGNATURE _____ DATE _____

NO. **14**
NAME **Susan Dilloway**
SOC. SEC. NO.
WEEK ENDING **10/23/20--**

DAY	IN	OUT	IN	OUT	IN	OUT	TOTAL
M	9:03	12:01	12:32	5:28			8
T	8:30	12:29	1:00	3:29			6½
W	9:01	12:03	12:29	5:31			8
Th	9:02	11:59	12:31	5:30			8
F	9:01	12:00	12:31	5:29			8
S							
S							
						TOTAL HOURS	38½

	HOURS	RATE	AMOUNT
REGULAR			
OVERTIME			
TOTAL EARNINGS			

SIGNATURE _____ DATE _____

NO. **17**
NAME **David Facini**
SOC. SEC. NO.
WEEK ENDING **10/23/20--**

DAY	IN	OUT	IN	OUT	IN	OUT	TOTAL
M	3:00	8:01					5
T	2:59	8:02					5
W	3:01	8:02					5
Th	3:00	8:00					5
F	3:00	6:01					3
S							
S							
						TOTAL HOURS	23

	HOURS	RATE	AMOUNT
REGULAR			
OVERTIME			
TOTAL EARNINGS			

SIGNATURE _____ DATE _____

Problem 12-10   Calculating Gross Earnings

Name	Gross Earnings
Austin, Lynn	
Darrah, Pam	
Dilloway, Susan	
Facini, David	
Franco, Doris	
Miller, Barbara	
Womack, Charlene	
Total Gross Earnings	

Analyze: _____

_____

CHAPTER  12 Payroll Accounting

Self-Test

Part A True or False

Directions: _Circle the letter_ T _in the Answer column if the statement is true; circle the letter_ F _if the statement is false._

Answer

T F **1.** A payroll register is prepared for each pay period.

T F **2.** Most businesses use computers to prepare the payroll.

T F **3.** The social security tax and Medicare tax are both part of the FICA system.

T F **4.** Form W-4 lists the marital status and the number of exemptions claimed by each employee.

T F **5.** A person can change their social security number at any time.

T F **6.** The number of hours worked multiplied by the hourly wage gives the net earnings for the pay period.

T F **7.** Most employees claim more than eight exemptions on their W-4 form.

T F **8.** Overtime is paid to most employees after 44 hours of work in a pay week.

T F **9.** The payroll register summarizes information about employees' earnings for the pay period.

T F **10.** The social security system was established by the Federal Insurance Contributions Act.

T F **11.** Payroll is not a major expense of most businesses.

T F **12.** The account Medicare Tax Payable is a liability of the business.

Part B   Fill in the Missing Term

Directions: *In the Answer column, write the letter of the word or phrase that best completes the sentence. Some answers may be used more than once.*

A. accumulated earnings	**D.** direct deposit	**H.** pay period	**K.** salary
B. commission	**E.** gross earnings	**I.** payroll	**L.** timecard
C. deduction	**F.** net pay	**J.** payroll register	**M.** wage
	G. overtime rate		

Answer

_____   **1.** An amount paid to employees at a specific rate per hour is a(n) _____.

_____   **2.** The amount of money actually received by the employee after all deductions are subtracted is called the _____.

_____   **3.** _____ are the year-to-date gross earnings of an employee.

_____   **4.** A(n) _____ is paid to the employee as a percentage of the employee's sales.

_____   **5.** The amount of time for which an employee is paid is called the _____.

_____   **6.** Most businesses use a(n) _____ to keep track of an hourly wage employee's hours.

_____   **7.** The _____ is the total amount earned by the employee in the pay period.

_____   **8.** A(n) _____ is an amount subtracted from gross earnings.

_____   **9.** A list of employees in a business and the earnings due each employee for a specific period of time is a(n) _____.

_____   **10.** A(n) _____ is the deposit by the employer of an employee's net pay into a personal bank account.

CHAPTER 13   Payroll Liabilities and Tax Records

Study Plan

Check Your Understanding

Section 1	*Read Section 1 on pages 316–320 and complete the following exercises on page 321.* ❑ Thinking Critically ❑ Computing in the Business World ❑ Problem 13-1 *Determining Payroll Amounts*
Section 2	*Read Section 2 on pages 322–325 and complete the following exercises on page 326.* ❑ Thinking Critically ❑ Communicating Accounting ❑ Problem 13-2 *Calculating Employer's Payroll Taxes* ❑ Problem 13-3 *Identifying Entries for Payroll Liabilities*
Section 3	*Read Section 3 on pages 327–336 and complete the following exercises on page 337.* ❑ Thinking Critically ❑ Analyzing Accounting ❑ Problem 13-4 *Payment of Payroll Liabilities* ❑ Problem 13-5 *Analyzing a Source Document*
Summary	*Review the Chapter 13 Summary on page 339 in your textbook.* ❑ Key Concepts
Review and Activities	*Complete the following questions and exercises on pages 340–341 in your textbook.* ❑ Using Key Terms ❑ Understanding Accounting Concepts and Procedures ❑ Case Study ❑ Conducting an Audit with Alex ❑ Internet Connection ❑ Workplace Skills
Computerized Accounting	*Read the Computerized Accounting information on page 342 in your textbook.* ❑ *Making the Transition from a Manual to a Computerized System* ❑ *Recording and Paying Payroll Tax Liabilities in Peachtree*
Problems	*Complete the following end-of-chapter problems for Chapter 13 in your textbook.* ❑ Problem 13-6 *Calculating Employer's Payroll Taxes* ❑ Problem 13-7 *Recording the Payment of the Payroll* ❑ Problem 13-8 *Journalizing Payroll Transactions* ❑ Problem 13-9 *Recording and Posting Payroll Transactions*
Challenge Problem	❑ Problem 13-10 *Recording and Posting Payroll Transactions*
Chapter Reviews and Working Papers	*Complete the following exercises for Chapter 13 in your Chapter Reviews and Working Papers.* ❑ Chapter Review ❑ Self-Test

CHAPTER 13 REVIEW — Payroll Liabilities and Tax Records

Part 1   Accounting Vocabulary (5 points)

Total Points	35
Student's Score	

Directions: *Using terms from the following list, complete the sentences below. Write the letter of the term you have chosen in the space provided.*

A. federal tax deposit coupon	**C.** Form 941	**E.** Form W-3
B. Form 940	**D.** Form W-2	**F.** unemployment taxes

____A____ **0.** The form that is prepared and sent with the employer's check to show the amount of taxes being sent to the federal government is a _____.

_____ **1.** The transmittal of income and tax statements that is filed by the employer with the Internal Revenue Service is called _____.

_____ **2.** _____ is the tax return that includes both federal and state unemployment taxes paid by the employer during the year.

_____ **3.** The document that reports the accumulated amounts of federal income taxes and FICA taxes withheld from employees' earnings for the quarter is _____.

_____ **4.** _____ are usually paid only by the employer and collected to provide funds for workers who are temporarily out of work.

_____ **5.** The wage and tax statement that summarizes an employee's earnings and tax deductions for the previous calendar year is called _____.

Part 2   Payroll Taxes and Reports (10 points)

Directions: *Read each of the following statements to determine whether the statement is true or false. Write your answer in the space provided.*

____True____ **0.** The taxes that an employer must pay are FICA taxes and unemployment taxes.

_____ **1.** The Unemployment Tax Payable account is used to record both federal and state unemployment taxes.

_____ **2.** Both the employee and the employer pay the same rate for social security and Medicare taxes.

_____ **3.** Amounts withheld from gross earnings and held by the employer until the time of payment are assets of the business.

_____ **4.** The salary expense of a business is equal to the total gross earnings.

_____ **5.** When a business transfers money from its regular checking account to the payroll checking account, the check is written for the amount of gross earnings.

_____ **6.** The employer's payroll taxes are operating expenses of the business.

_____ **7.** Employees' wages are a liability of the business.

_____ **8.** The Cash in Bank account is credited for the total amount that is paid by the employer to the employees.

_____ **9.** An employer is required to file only an annual tax report on employee earnings and on taxes paid by the employee and the employer.

_____ **10.** Form W-2 must be prepared and given to each employee by January 31 of the year following that in which the taxes were deducted.

Part 3   Payroll Transactions (14 points)

Directions: *The following list contains account titles for recording payroll transactions. Determine the account(s) to be debited and credited in the transactions below. Write your answers in the space provided.*

A. Cash in Bank	**E.** Medicare Tax Payable	**H.** U.S. Savings Bonds Payable
B. Employees' Federal Income Tax Payable	**F.** Federal Unemployment Tax Payable	**I.** Life Insurance Premiums Payable
C. Employees' State Income Tax Payable	**G.** State Unemployment Tax Payable	**J.** Payroll Tax Expense
D. Social Security Tax Payable		**K.** Salaries Expense

Debit	Credit	Transaction
I	*A*	**0.** Record the payment of life insurance premiums withheld from the employees' earnings.
_____	_____	**1.** Record the payment of the employer's federal unemployment taxes.
_____	_____	**2.** Record the employer's payroll taxes.
_____	_____	**3.** Record the purchase of savings bonds for the employees.
_____	_____	**4.** Record the payment of employees' state income taxes.
_____	_____	**5.** Record the payment of FICA taxes and employees' federal income taxes.
_____	_____	**6.** Record the payment of the employer's state unemployment taxes.
_____	_____	**7.** Record the payment of the weekly payroll less the amounts withheld for employees' federal income tax, employees' state income tax, FICA taxes, life insurance premiums, and U.S. savings bonds.

Part 4   The Debits and Credits of the Payroll Accounts (6 points)

Directions: *Answer each of the following statements by writing in the word "Debit" or "Credit" in the space provided.*

Debit	**0.** The Salaries Expense account has a normal _____ balance.
_____	**1.** The total amount of net pay of all employees is entered on the _____ side of the Cash in Bank account.
_____	**2.** An increase in the State Unemployment Tax Payable account is recorded as a _____.
_____	**3.** The Medicare Tax Payable account has a normal _____ balance.
_____	**4.** The Payroll Tax Expense account has a normal _____ balance.
_____	**5.** When a payment is made to the federal government for the employees' federal income tax, an entry is made on the _____ side of the Employees' Federal Income Tax Payable account.
_____	**6.** The total amount of gross earnings is entered on the _____ side of the Salaries Expense account.

Working Papers *for Section Problems*

Problem 13-1   Determining Payroll Amounts

1. _____
2. _____
3. _____
4. _____
5. _____

Problem 13-2   Calculating Employer's Payroll Taxes

Social Security Tax Payable	$	_____
Medicare Tax Payable	$	_____
Federal Unemployment Tax Payable	$	_____
State Unemployment Tax Payable	$	_____

Problem 13-3   Identifying Entries for Payroll Liabilities

Payroll Item	Entry to Record Payroll	Entry to Record Employer's Payroll Taxes
Employees' federal income tax		
Employer's social security tax		
U.S. savings bonds		
Employer's Medicare tax		
Federal unemployment tax		
Employees' state income tax		
Union dues		
Employees' social security tax		
State unemployment tax		
Employees' Medicare tax		

Problem 13-4   Payment of Payroll Liabilities

GENERAL JOURNAL   PAGE _____

	DATE	DESCRIPTION	POST. REF.	DEBIT	CREDIT	
1						1
2						2
3						3
4						4
5						5
6						6
7						7
8						8
9						9
10						10

Problem 13-5   Analyzing a Source Document

GENERAL JOURNAL   PAGE ___*14*___

	DATE	DESCRIPTION	POST. REF.	DEBIT	CREDIT	
1						1
2						2
3						3
4						4
5						5
6						6
7						7
8						8
9						9
10						10

Computerized Accounting Using Peachtree

Software Objectives

When you have completed this chapter, you will be able to use Peachtree to:
1. Record the employer's payroll taxes.
2. Record the payment of tax liabilities.
3. Print General Journal and General Ledger reports to verify the payroll entries.

Problem 13-7 Recording the Payment of the Payroll

INSTRUCTIONS

Beginning a Session

Step 1 Select the problem set: Kits & Pups Grooming (Prob. 13-7).

Step 2 Rename the company and set the system date to December 31, 2004.

Completing the Accounting Problem

Step 3 Review the payroll information provided in your textbook.

Step 4 Record the payroll entry using the **General Journal Entry** option.

TIP: You can use the Add and Remove buttons in the General Journal Entry window to edit a multi-part entry.

Step 5 Print a General Journal report and a General Ledger report.

Step 6 Proof your work.

Step 7 Answer the Analyze question.

Checking Your Work and Ending the Session

Step 8 Click the **Close Problem** button in the Glencoe Smart Guide window.

Step 9 If your teacher has asked you to check your solution, select *Check my answer to this problem*. Review, print, and close the report.

Step 10 Click the **Close Problem** button and select the save option as directed by your teacher.

Problem 13-8 Journalizing Payroll Transactions

INSTRUCTIONS

Beginning a Session

Step 1 Select the problem set: Outback Guide Service (Prob. 13-8).

Step 2 Rename the company and set the system date to December 31, 2004.

Completing the Accounting Problem

Step 3 Review the payroll information provided in your textbook.

Step 4 Add a new General Ledger account—**242 Union Dues Payable**. Make sure that you identify the account type as *Other Current Liabilities*.

Step 5 Record the entry for the payment of the payroll using the **General Journal Entry** option.

DO YOU HAVE A QUESTION ?

Q. *Can Peachtree automatically generate the journal entries to record the payment of the payroll and the employer's payroll tax liabilities?*

A. Yes, Peachtree will automatically record the payroll journal entries if you use the payroll features to record each employee's earnings and deductions. You must also enter the employer's tax liabilities for each employee. When you post a payroll entry, Peachtree updates the necessary general ledger accounts.

In this chapter, however, the focus is on manually recording the payroll entries. You will use the general journal to manually record the entries.

Step 6 Record the employer's payroll taxes.

Step 7 Print a General Journal report and a General Ledger report.

Step 8 Proof your work.

Step 9 Answer the Analyze question.

Ending the Session

Step 10 Click the **Close Problem** button in the Glencoe Smart Guide window and select the save option as directed by your teacher.

Problem 13-9 Recording and Posting Payroll Transactions

INSTRUCTIONS

Beginning a Session

Step 1 Select the problem set: Showbiz Video (Prob. 13-9).

Step 2 Rename the company and set the system date to December 31, 2004.

Completing the Accounting Problem

Step 3 Review the transactions provided in your textbook.

Step 4 Record the transactions.

Step 5 Print a General Journal report and a General Ledger report.

Step 6 Proof your work.

Step 7 Answer the Analyze question.

Checking Your Work and Ending the Session

Step 8 Click the **Close Problem** button in the Glencoe Smart Guide window.

Step 9 If your teacher has asked you to check your solution, select *Check my answer to this problem*. Review, print, and close the report.

Step 10 Click the **Close Problem** button and select the appropriate save option.

Problem 13-10 Recording and Posting Payroll Transactions

INSTRUCTIONS

Beginning a Session

Step 1 Select the problem set: Job Connect (Prob. 13-10).

Step 2 Rename the company and set the system date to December 31, 2004.

Completing the Accounting Problem

Step 3 Review the payroll information provided in your textbook.

Step 4 Record the transactions.

Step 5 Prepare Form 8109 for each of the two federal tax deposits. Use the forms provided in the working papers.

Step 6 Print a General Journal report and a General Ledger report.

Step 7 Proof your work.

Step 8 Answer the Analyze question.

Ending the Session

Step 9 Click the **Close Problem** button in the Glencoe Smart Guide window.

FAQs

Can you print a Form 8109 using the Peachtree software?

No, Peachtree does not include a Form 8109 report. You must manually prepare this form when you submit a payroll tax deposit.

Computerized Accounting Using Spreadsheets

Problem 13-6   Calculating Employer's Payroll Taxes

Completing the Spreadsheet

Step 1   Read the instructions for Problem 13-6 in your textbook. This problem involves calculating employer's payroll taxes.

Step 2   Open the Glencoe Accounting: Electronic Learning Center software.

Step 3   From the Program Menu, click on the **Peachtree Accounting Software and Spreadsheet Applications** icon.

Step 4   Log onto the Management System by typing your user name and password.

Step 5   Under the Chapter Problems tab, select the template: PR13-6a.xls. The template should look like the one shown below.

```
PROBLEM 13-6
CALCULATING EMPLOYER'S PAYROLL TAXES

(name)
(date)

     Total         Social Security      Medicare        Federal            State
Gross Earnings         Tax               Tax        Unemployment Tax   Unemployment Tax
                  $0.00            $0.00           $0.00              $0.00
                  $0.00            $0.00           $0.00              $0.00
                  $0.00            $0.00           $0.00              $0.00
                  $0.00            $0.00           $0.00              $0.00
                  $0.00            $0.00           $0.00              $0.00
```

Step 6   Key your name and today's date in the cells containing the *(name)* and *(date)* placeholders.

Step 7   Enter the total gross earnings for the first employee in cell A11 of the spreadsheet template: **914.80**. Remember, it is not necessary to enter a dollar sign. The spreadsheet template will automatically calculate the Social Security tax, Medicare tax, federal unemployment tax, and state unemployment tax for the first employee using the rates stated in your textbook.

**TIP:**   The cells for Social Security tax, Medicare tax, federal unemployment tax, and state unemployment tax are set up to round these numbers to two decimal places. When you are entering data in this spreadsheet template, always round numbers to two decimal places when rounding is necessary.

Step 8   Enter the total gross earnings for the remaining employees. The Social Security tax, Medicare tax, federal unemployment tax, and state unemployment tax will be automatically calculated for each employee.

TIP: To check your work, multiply the total gross earnings of each employee by the tax rates given in your textbook.

Step 9 Save the spreadsheet using the **Save** option from the *File* menu. You should accept the default location for the save as this is handled by the management system.

Step 10 Print the completed spreadsheet.

Step 11 Exit the spreadsheet program.

Step 12 In the Close Options box, select the location where you would like to save your work.

Step 13 Answer the Analyze question from your textbook for this problem.

What-If Analysis

What would the employer's payroll taxes be on total gross earnings of $1,891.02, assuming the employee had not reached the taxable earnings limit?

_____

Working Papers *for End-of-Chapter Problems*

Problem 13-6   Calculating Employer's Payroll Taxes

Total Gross Earnings	Social Security Tax	Medicare Tax	Federal Unemployment Tax	State Unemployment Tax
$ 914.80				
1,113.73				
2,201.38				
791.02				
1,245.75				

Analyze: _____

_____

_____

_____

_____

Problem 13-7   Recording the Payment of the Payroll

PAYROLL REGISTER

PAY PERIOD ENDING *December 31* _____ 20__   DATE OF PAYMENT *December 31, 20--* _____

EMPLOYEE NUMBER	NAME	MAR. STATUS	ALLOW.	TOTAL HOURS	RATE	EARNINGS			DEDUCTIONS							NET PAY	CK. NO.
						REGULAR	OVERTIME	TOTAL	SOC. SEC. TAX	MED. TAX	FED. INC. TAX	STATE INC. TAX	HOSP. INS.	OTHER	TOTAL		

25 | | | | | | TOTALS | | | | | | | | | | | | | | 25

Other Deductions: Write the appropriate code letter to the left of the amount: B—U.S. Savings Bonds; C—Credit Union; UD—Union Dues; UW—United Way.

Problem 13-7   (continued)

(1)

GENERAL JOURNAL   PAGE ___46___

DATE	DESCRIPTION	POST. REF.	DEBIT	CREDIT	
1					1
2					2
3					3
4					4
5					5
6					6
7					7
8					8
9					9
10					10

(2)

GENERAL LEDGER (PARTIAL)

ACCOUNT __Cash in Bank__   ACCOUNT NO. ___101___

DATE		DESCRIPTION	POST. REF.	DEBIT	CREDIT	BALANCE DEBIT	BALANCE CREDIT
20--							
Dec.	24	Balance	✓			17352 10	

ACCOUNT __Employees' Federal Income Tax Payable__   ACCOUNT NO. ___210___

DATE		DESCRIPTION	POST. REF.	DEBIT	CREDIT	BALANCE DEBIT	BALANCE CREDIT
20--							
Dec.	24	Balance	✓				240 00

ACCOUNT __Employees' State Income Tax Payable__   ACCOUNT NO. ___215___

DATE		DESCRIPTION	POST. REF.	DEBIT	CREDIT	BALANCE DEBIT	BALANCE CREDIT
20--							
Dec.	24	Balance	✓				180 79

Problem 13-7   (concluded)

ACCOUNT ___Social Security Tax Payable___   ACCOUNT NO. ___235___

DATE		DESCRIPTION	POST. REF.	DEBIT	CREDIT	BALANCE	
						DEBIT	CREDIT
20--							
Dec.	24	Balance	✓				1 9 1 25

ACCOUNT ___Medicare Tax Payable___   ACCOUNT NO. ___230___

DATE		DESCRIPTION	POST. REF.	DEBIT	CREDIT	BALANCE	
						DEBIT	CREDIT
20--							
Dec.	24	Balance	✓				4 5 31

ACCOUNT ___Hospital Insurance Premiums Payable___   ACCOUNT NO. ___225___

DATE		DESCRIPTION	POST. REF.	DEBIT	CREDIT	BALANCE	
						DEBIT	CREDIT
20--							
Dec.	24	Balance	✓				5 2 26

ACCOUNT ___Salaries Expense___   ACCOUNT NO. ___525___

DATE		DESCRIPTION	POST. REF.	DEBIT	CREDIT	BALANCE	
						DEBIT	CREDIT
20--							
Dec.	24	Balance	✓			4 8 4 1 7 86	

Analyze: _____

_____

_____

_____

Problem 13-8   Journalizing Payroll Transactions

GENERAL JOURNAL   PAGE ___*15*___

	DATE	DESCRIPTION	POST. REF.	DEBIT	CREDIT	
1						1
2						2
3						3
4						4
5						5
6						6
7						7
8						8
9						9
10						10
11						11
12						12
13						13
14						14
15						15
16						16
17						17
18						18
19						19
20						20

Analyze: _____

_____

Problem 13-9   Source Documents

Instructions: *Use the following source documents to record the transactions for this problem.*

PAYROLL REGISTER

PAY PERIOD ENDING *December 13*   20——   DATE OF PAYMENT *December 13, 20——*

EMPLOYEE NUMBER	NAME	MAR. STATUS	ALLOW.	TOTAL HOURS	RATE	EARNINGS			DEDUCTIONS							NET PAY	CK. NO.
						REGULAR	OVERTIME	TOTAL	SOC. SEC. TAX	MED. TAX	FED. INC. TAX	STATE INC. TAX	HOSP. INS.	OTHER	TOTAL		
105	Arcompora, M.	M	2					627 00	38 87	9 09	106 59	15 68	3 00	B 5 00	178 23	448 77	
137	Fox, B.	M	1					430 00	26 66	6 24	73 10	10 75	3 00	——	119 75	310 25	
25					TOTALS			3,840 58	238 12	55 69	639 00	96 02	21 00	B 20 00	1,069 83	2,770 75	2206

Other Deductions: Write the appropriate code letter to the left of the amount: B—U.S. Savings Bonds; C—Credit Union; UD—Union Dues; UW—United Way.

$ *2,770.75*   No. 2206
Date *December 13*   20——
To *Payroll Account*
For *Salaries Expense*

	Dollars	Cents
Balance brought forward	21,932	14
Add deposits		
Total	21,932	14
Less this check	2,770	75
Balance carried forward	19,161	39

$ *100.00*   No. 2216
Date *December 16*   20——
To *Northwest Bank*
For *U.S. Savings Bonds*

	Dollars	Cents
Balance brought forward	17,934	77
Add deposits		
Total	17,934	77
Less this check	100	00
Balance carried forward	17,834	77

SHOWBIZ VIDEO
7575 Ingram Blvd.
Spokane, WA 99204

INTEROFFICE MEMORANDUM

TO: *Payroll Clerk*
FROM: *Greg Failla*
DATE: *December 13, 20——*
SUBJECT: *Payroll tax rates*

Social security—6.2%
Medicare—1.45%
Fed. unemployment—0.8%
State unemployment—5.4%

$ *148.00*   No. 2217
Date *December 16*   20——
To *American Insurance Co.*
For *Hospital Insurance*

	Dollars	Cents
Balance brought forward	17,834	77
Add deposits		
Total	17,834	77
Less this check	148	00
Balance carried forward	17,686	77

$ *1,226.62*   No. 2215
Date *December 16*   20——
To *Internal Revenue Service*
For *Fed. income and FICA taxes*

	Dollars	Cents
Balance brought forward	19,161	39
Add deposits		
Total	19,161	39
Less this check	1,226	62
Balance carried forward	17,934	77

Problem 13-9 Recording and Posting Payroll Transactions

(1), (3)

GENERAL JOURNAL

PAGE _____

	DATE	DESCRIPTION	POST. REF.	DEBIT	CREDIT	
1						1
2						2
3						3
4						4
5						5
6						6
7						7
8						8
9						9
10						10
11						11
12						12
13						13
14						14
15						15
16						16
17						17
18						18
19						19
20						20
21						21
22						22
23						23
24						24
25						25
26						26
27						27
28						28
29						29

Problem 13-9 (continued)

(2), (3)

GENERAL LEDGER (PARTIAL)

ACCOUNT __Cash in Bank__   ACCOUNT NO. __101__

DATE		DESCRIPTION	POST. REF.	DEBIT	CREDIT	BALANCE DEBIT	BALANCE CREDIT
20--							
Dec.	6	Balance	✓			21 932 14	

ACCOUNT __Employees' Federal Income Tax Payable__   ACCOUNT NO. __210__

DATE	DESCRIPTION	POST. REF.	DEBIT	CREDIT	BALANCE DEBIT	BALANCE CREDIT

ACCOUNT __Employees' State Income Tax Payable__   ACCOUNT NO. __215__

DATE		DESCRIPTION	POST. REF.	DEBIT	CREDIT	BALANCE DEBIT	BALANCE CREDIT
20--							
Dec.	6	Balance	✓				286 08

ACCOUNT __Social Security Tax Payable__   ACCOUNT NO. __235__

DATE	DESCRIPTION	POST. REF.	DEBIT	CREDIT	BALANCE DEBIT	BALANCE CREDIT

ACCOUNT __Medicare Tax Payable__   ACCOUNT NO. __230__

DATE	DESCRIPTION	POST. REF.	DEBIT	CREDIT	BALANCE DEBIT	BALANCE CREDIT

Problem 13-9 (continued)

ACCOUNT __Hospital Insurance Premiums Payable__   ACCOUNT NO. __225__

DATE		DESCRIPTION	POST. REF.	DEBIT	CREDIT	BALANCE DEBIT	BALANCE CREDIT
20--							
Dec.	6	Balance	✓				127 00

ACCOUNT __U.S. Savings Bonds Payable__   ACCOUNT NO. __245__

DATE		DESCRIPTION	POST. REF.	DEBIT	CREDIT	BALANCE DEBIT	BALANCE CREDIT
20--							
Dec.	6	Balance	✓				80 00

ACCOUNT __Federal Unemployment Tax Payable__   ACCOUNT NO. __220__

DATE		DESCRIPTION	POST. REF.	DEBIT	CREDIT	BALANCE DEBIT	BALANCE CREDIT

ACCOUNT __State Unemployment Tax Payable__   ACCOUNT NO. __240__

DATE		DESCRIPTION	POST. REF.	DEBIT	CREDIT	BALANCE DEBIT	BALANCE CREDIT

ACCOUNT __Payroll Tax Expense__   ACCOUNT NO. __515__

DATE		DESCRIPTION	POST. REF.	DEBIT	CREDIT	BALANCE DEBIT	BALANCE CREDIT
20--							
Dec.	6	Balance	✓			4614 13	

ACCOUNT __Salaries Expense__   ACCOUNT NO. __525__

DATE		DESCRIPTION	POST. REF.	DEBIT	CREDIT	BALANCE DEBIT	BALANCE CREDIT
20--							
Dec.	6	Balance	✓			33655 22	

Problem 13-9 (concluded)

Analyze: _____

_____

_____

_____

Problem 13-10   Recording and Posting Payroll Transactions

GENERAL JOURNAL   PAGE _____

	DATE	DESCRIPTION	POST. REF.	DEBIT	CREDIT	
1						1
2						2
3						3
4						4
5						5
6						6
7						7
8						8
9						9
10						10
11						11
12						12
13						13
14						14
15						15
16						16
17						17
18						18
19						19
20						20
21						21
22						22
23						23
24						24
25						25
26						26
27						27
28						28
29						29

Problem 13-10 (continued)

GENERAL LEDGER (PARTIAL)

ACCOUNT **Cash in Bank**   ACCOUNT NO. **101**

DATE		DESCRIPTION	POST. REF.	DEBIT	CREDIT	BALANCE DEBIT	BALANCE CREDIT
20--							
Dec.	31	Balance	✓			2944161	

ACCOUNT **Employees' Federal Income Tax Payable**   ACCOUNT NO. **210**

DATE	DESCRIPTION	POST. REF.	DEBIT	CREDIT	BALANCE DEBIT	BALANCE CREDIT

ACCOUNT **Employees' State Income Tax Payable**   ACCOUNT NO. **215**

DATE	DESCRIPTION	POST. REF.	DEBIT	CREDIT	BALANCE DEBIT	BALANCE CREDIT

ACCOUNT **Federal Unemployment Tax Payable**   ACCOUNT NO. **220**

DATE		DESCRIPTION	POST. REF.	DEBIT	CREDIT	BALANCE DEBIT	BALANCE CREDIT
20--							
Dec.	15	Balance	✓				46411

ACCOUNT **Medicare Tax Payable**   ACCOUNT NO. **230**

DATE	DESCRIPTION	POST. REF.	DEBIT	CREDIT	BALANCE DEBIT	BALANCE CREDIT

Problem 13-10 (continued)

ACCOUNT __Social Security Tax Payable__   ACCOUNT NO. __235__

DATE	DESCRIPTION	POST. REF.	DEBIT	CREDIT	BALANCE DEBIT	BALANCE CREDIT

ACCOUNT __State Unemployment Tax Payable__   ACCOUNT NO. __240__

DATE	DESCRIPTION	POST. REF.	DEBIT	CREDIT	BALANCE DEBIT	BALANCE CREDIT
20--						
Dec. 15	Balance	✓				3 1 3 2 73

ACCOUNT __Payroll Tax Expense__   ACCOUNT NO. __515__

DATE	DESCRIPTION	POST. REF.	DEBIT	CREDIT	BALANCE DEBIT	BALANCE CREDIT
20--						
Dec. 15	Balance	✓			7 9 5 3 65	

ACCOUNT __Salaries Expense__   ACCOUNT NO. __525__

DATE	DESCRIPTION	POST. REF.	DEBIT	CREDIT	BALANCE DEBIT	BALANCE CREDIT
20--						
Dec. 15	Balance	✓			5 8 0 1 3 45	

Analyze: _____

_____

Problem 13-10   (continued)

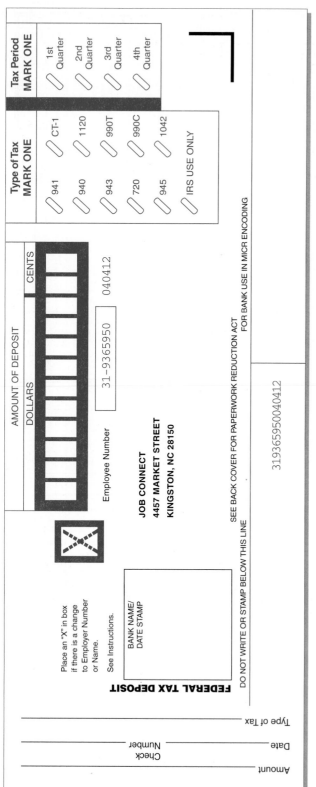

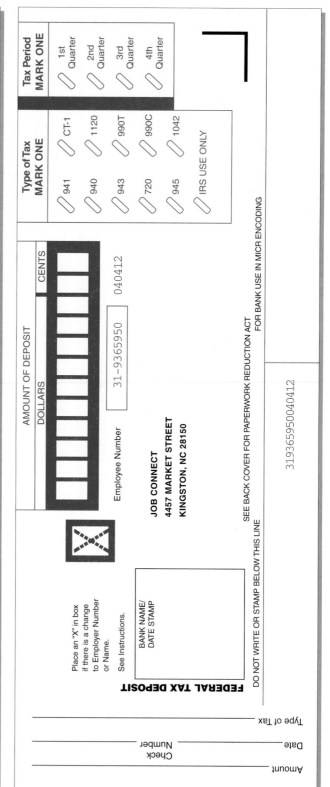

Problem 13-10   (concluded)

	No. 1602
$ _____	
Date _____ 20 ___	
To _____	
For _____	

	Dollars	Cents
Balance brought forward	29,441	61
Add deposits		
Total		
Less this check		
Balance carried forward		

Job Connect   **1602**
4457 Market Street
Kingstown, NC 28150   4-58 / 810

DATE _____ 20 ___

PAY TO THE ORDER OF _____ $ _____

_____ DOLLARS

SNB *Security National Bank*
KINGSTOWN, NC

MEMO _____

⑈0810 0058⑈ 4163 697⑈ 1602

	No. 1603
$ _____	
Date _____ 20 ___	
To _____	
For _____	

	Dollars	Cents
Balance brought forward		
Add deposits		
Total		
Less this check		
Balance carried forward		

Job Connect   **1603**
4457 Market Street
Kingstown, NC 28150   4-58 / 810

DATE _____ 20 ___

PAY TO THE ORDER OF _____ $ _____

_____ DOLLARS

SNB *Security National Bank*
KINGSTOWN, NC

MEMO _____

⑈0810 0058⑈ 4163 697⑈ 1603

	No. 1604
$ _____	
Date _____ 20 ___	
To _____	
For _____	

	Dollars	Cents
Balance brought forward		
Add deposits		
Total		
Less this check		
Balance carried forward		

Job Connect   **1604**
4457 Market Street
Kingstown, NC 28150   4-58 / 810

DATE _____ 20 ___

PAY TO THE ORDER OF _____ $ _____

_____ DOLLARS

SNB *Security National Bank*
KINGSTOWN, NC

MEMO _____

⑈0810 0058⑈ 4163 697⑈ 1604

	No. 1605
$ _____	
Date _____ 20 ___	
To _____	
For _____	

	Dollars	Cents
Balance brought forward		
Add deposits		
Total		
Less this check		
Balance carried forward		

Job Connect   **1605**
4457 Market Street
Kingstown, NC 28150   4-58 / 810

DATE _____ 20 ___

PAY TO THE ORDER OF _____ $ _____

_____ DOLLARS

SNB *Security National Bank*
KINGSTOWN, NC

MEMO _____

⑈0810 0058⑈ 4163 697⑈ 1605

CHAPTER **13** Payroll Liabilities and Tax Records

Self-Test

Part A   True or False

Directions: *Circle the letter* T *in the Answer column if the statement is true; circle the letter* F *if the statement is false.*

Answer

T   F   **1.** The Cash in Bank account is debited for the amount the employees actually earn in the pay period.

T   F   **2.** The only taxes that the employer must pay are unemployment taxes.

T   F   **3.** The amount entered for Payroll Tax Expense is the total gross earnings of the pay period.

T   F   **4.** Social security tax is paid by the employer and the employees.

T   F   **5.** Amounts deducted from employees' earnings and held for payment by the employer become liabilities to the business.

T   F   **6.** The entry for Salaries Expense is recorded each pay period but the entry for Payroll Tax Expense is recorded only at the end of the year.

T   F   **7.** Federal withholding taxes and social security taxes are normally paid once a year by the employer.

T   F   **8.** The payroll register is the source of information for preparing the journal entry for payroll.

T   F   **9.** Form W-2 must be prepared and given to each employee by January 31 of the year following that in which the taxes were deducted.

T   F   **10.** The employer's payroll taxes are operating expenses of the business.

Part B   Debit or Credit

Directions: *Each of the following statements can be completed with the word Debit or Credit. Circle the correct word in the Answer column.*

Answer

Debit   Credit   **1.** The total amount of gross earnings is entered on the _____ side of the Salaries Expense account.

Debit   Credit   **2.** The account Employees' Federal Income Tax Payable would normally have a _____ balance.

Debit   Credit   **3.** Salaries Expense would normally have a _____ balance.

Debit   Credit   **4.** The total net pay for the period is entered on the _____ side of the Cash in Bank account.

Debit   Credit   **5.** The Medicare Tax Payable account would normally have a _____ balance.

Debit   Credit   **6.** When a payment is made to the state government for the employees' state income tax, an entry is made on the _____ side of the Employees' State Income Tax Payable account.

Debit   Credit   **7.** The Payroll Tax Expense account normally has a _____ balance.

Debit   Credit   **8.** A decrease in U.S. Savings Bonds Payable would be a _____.

Debit   Credit   **9.** An increase in State Unemployment Tax Payable would be a _____.

Debit   Credit   **10.** The account Insurance Premiums Payable would normally have a _____ balance.

MINI PRACTICE SET 3

Green Thumb Plant Service

Instructions: *Complete the following time cards and use to record payroll information in the payroll register.*

(1)

NO. __019__
NAME __Michael Alter__
SOC. SEC. NO. __049-71-8436__
WEEK ENDING __7/29/20––__

DAY	IN	OUT	IN	OUT	IN	OUT	TOTAL
M			2:00	5:00			
T			2:00	6:00			
W			3:00	5:00			
Th			2:00	6:00			
F			2:00	6:00			
S			9:00	2:00			
S							
					TOTAL HOURS		

		HOURS	RATE	AMOUNT
REGULAR				
OVERTIME				
	TOTAL EARNINGS			

SIGNATURE _____ DATE _____

NO. __018__
NAME __Christine Cuddy__
SOC. SEC. NO. __223-56-0992__
WEEK ENDING __7/29/20––__

DAY	IN	OUT	IN	OUT	IN	OUT	TOTAL
M	9:00	12:00	12:30	5:00			
T	9:00	11:30	12:00	5:00			
W	9:00	1:00					
Th	9:00	12:00	12:30	4:00			
F	8:30	1:00	1:30	3:00			
S	9:00	1:30					
S							
					TOTAL HOURS		

		HOURS	RATE	AMOUNT
REGULAR				
OVERTIME				
	TOTAL EARNINGS			

SIGNATURE _____ DATE _____

NO. __013__
NAME __Joclyn Filley__
SOC. SEC. NO. __042-97-3814__
WEEK ENDING __7/29/20––__

DAY	IN	OUT	IN	OUT	IN	OUT	TOTAL
M	9:00	12:00	1:00	3:00			
T	9:00	12:00	1:00	5:00			
W	8:00	12:00	1:00	5:00			
Th	9:00	12:00	1:00	3:30			
F	9:00	12:00	1:00	4:00			
S	9:00	12:00					
S							
					TOTAL HOURS		

		HOURS	RATE	AMOUNT
REGULAR				
OVERTIME				
	TOTAL EARNINGS			

SIGNATURE _____ DATE _____

NO. __016__
NAME __Daniel Ripp__
SOC. SEC. NO. __011-79-2118__
WEEK ENDING __7/29/20––__

DAY	IN	OUT	IN	OUT	IN	OUT	TOTAL
M	9:00	12:00	12:30	5:00			
T	9:00	12:30	1:00	6:00			
W	9:00	12:00	1:00	4:30			
Th	8:30	12:30	1:00	5:00			
F	9:00	11:30	12:00	5:00			
S	9:00	1:00					
S							
					TOTAL HOURS		

		HOURS	RATE	AMOUNT
REGULAR				
OVERTIME				
	TOTAL EARNINGS			

SIGNATURE _____ DATE _____

Mini Practice Set 3

Federal Income Tax Table

SINGLE Persons—WEEKLY Payroll Period
(For Wages Paid in 1997)

If the wages are—		And the number of withholding allowances claimed is—										
At least	But less than	0	1	2	3	4	5	6	7	8	9	10
		The amount of income tax to be withheld is—										
125	130	11	4	0	0	0	0	0	0	0	0	0
130	135	12	5	0	0	0	0	0	0	0	0	0
135	140	13	5	0	0	0	0	0	0	0	0	0
140	145	14	6	0	0	0	0	0	0	0	0	0
145	150	14	7	0	0	0	0	0	0	0	0	0
150	155	15	8	0	0	0	0	0	0	0	0	0
155	160	16	8	1	0	0	0	0	0	0	0	0
160	165	17	9	1	0	0	0	0	0	0	0	0
165	170	17	10	2	0	0	0	0	0	0	0	0
170	175	18	11	3	0	0	0	0	0	0	0	0
175	180	19	11	4	0	0	0	0	0	0	0	0
180	185	20	12	4	0	0	0	0	0	0	0	0
185	190	20	13	5	0	0	0	0	0	0	0	0
190	195	21	14	6	0	0	0	0	0	0	0	0
195	200	22	14	7	0	0	0	0	0	0	0	0
200	210	23	15	8	0	0	0	0	0	0	0	0
210	220	25	17	9	2	0	0	0	0	0	0	0
220	230	26	18	11	3	0	0	0	0	0	0	0
230	240	28	20	12	5	0	0	0	0	0	0	0
240	250	29	21	14	6	0	0	0	0	0	0	0
250	260	31	23	15	8	0	0	0	0	0	0	0
260	270	32	24	17	9	2	0	0	0	0	0	0
270	280	34	26	18	11	3	0	0	0	0	0	0
280	290	35	27	20	12	5	0	0	0	0	0	0
290	300	37	29	21	14	6	0	0	0	0	0	0
300	310	38	30	23	15	8	0	0	0	0	0	0
310	320	40	32	24	17	9	1	0	0	0	0	0
320	330	41	33	26	18	11	3	0	0	0	0	0
330	340	43	35	27	20	12	4	0	0	0	0	0
340	350	44	36	29	21	14	6	0	0	0	0	0

Mini Practice Set 3 (continued)   Federal Income Tax Table

MARRIED Persons—**WEEKLY** Payroll Period

(For Wages Paid in 1997)

If the wages are—		And the number of withholding allowances claimed is—										
At least	But less than	0	1	2	3	4	5	6	7	8	9	10
		The amount of income tax to be withheld is—										
340	350	33	26	18	10	3	0	0	0	0	0	0
350	360	35	27	19	12	4	0	0	0	0	0	0
360	370	36	29	21	13	6	0	0	0	0	0	0
370	380	38	30	22	15	7	0	0	0	0	0	0
380	390	39	32	24	16	9	1	0	0	0	0	0
390	400	41	33	25	18	10	2	0	0	0	0	0
400	410	42	35	27	19	12	4	0	0	0	0	0
410	420	44	36	28	21	13	5	0	0	0	0	0
420	430	45	38	30	22	15	7	0	0	0	0	0
430	440	47	39	31	24	16	8	1	0	0	0	0
440	450	48	41	33	25	18	10	2	0	0	0	0
450	460	50	42	34	27	19	11	4	0	0	0	0
460	470	51	44	36	28	21	13	5	0	0	0	0
470	480	53	45	37	30	22	14	7	0	0	0	0
480	490	54	47	39	31	24	16	8	1	0	0	0
490	500	56	48	40	33	25	17	10	2	0	0	0
500	510	57	50	42	34	27	19	11	4	0	0	0
510	520	59	51	43	36	28	20	13	5	0	0	0
520	530	60	53	45	37	30	22	14	7	0	0	0
530	540	62	54	46	39	31	23	16	8	0	0	0
540	550	63	56	48	40	33	25	17	10	2	0	0
550	560	65	57	49	42	34	26	19	11	3	0	0
560	570	66	59	51	43	36	28	20	13	5	0	0
570	580	68	60	52	45	37	29	22	14	6	0	0
580	590	69	62	54	46	39	31	23	16	8	0	0
590	600	71	63	55	48	40	32	25	17	9	2	0
600	610	72	65	57	49	42	34	26	19	11	3	0
610	620	74	66	58	51	43	35	28	20	12	5	0
620	630	75	68	60	52	45	37	29	22	14	6	0
630	640	77	69	61	54	46	38	31	23	15	8	0
640	650	78	71	63	55	48	40	32	25	17	9	2
650	660	80	72	64	57	49	41	34	26	18	11	3
660	670	81	74	66	58	51	43	35	28	20	12	5
670	680	83	75	67	60	52	44	37	29	21	14	6
680	690	84	77	69	61	54	46	38	31	23	15	8
690	700	86	78	70	63	55	47	40	32	24	17	9
700	710	87	80	72	64	57	49	41	34	26	18	11
710	720	89	81	73	66	58	50	43	35	27	20	12
720	730	90	83	75	67	60	52	44	37	29	21	14
730	740	92	84	76	69	61	53	46	38	30	23	15

Mini Practice Set 3 (continued) (2), (3), (4), (5), (6)

PAYROLL REGISTER

PAY PERIOD ENDING _____

DATE OF PAYMENT _____ 20 ___

EMPLOYEE NUMBER	NAME	MAR. STATUS	ALLOW.	TOTAL HOURS	RATE	EARNINGS REGULAR	EARNINGS OVERTIME	EARNINGS TOTAL	SOC. SEC. TAX	MED. TAX	FED. INC. TAX	STATE INC. TAX	HOSP. INS.	OTHER	TOTAL	NET PAY	CK. NO.
1																	
2																	
3																	
4																	
5																	
6																	
7																	
8																	
9																	
10																	
11																	
12																	
13																	
14																	
15																	
16																	
17																	
18																	
19																	
20																	
21																	
22																	
23																	
24																	
25																	
TOTALS																	

Other Deductions: Write the appropriate code letter to the left of the amount: B—U.S. Savings Bonds; C—Credit Union; UD—Union Dues; UW—United Way.

Mini Practice Set 3   (continued)

(7)

	Dollars	Cents
$ _____ No. 972		
Date _____ 20 ___		
To _____		
For _____		
	Dollars	Cents
Balance brought forward	8,371	42
Add deposits		
Total		
Less this check		
Balance carried forward		

GREEN THUMB
PLANT SERVICE
456 Lindenhurst Street
Kingsbury, Michigan 03855

972

53-215
113

DATE _____ 20 ___

PAY TO THE
ORDER OF _____ $ _____

_____ DOLLARS

LB Lexington Bank
KINGSBURY, MICHIGAN

MEMO _____ _____

⑆011302153⑆ 331 234 9⑈ 0972

(12)

	Dollars	Cents
$ _____ No. 973		
Date _____ 20 ___		
To _____		
For _____		
	Dollars	Cents
Balance brought forward		
Add deposits		
Total		
Less this check		
Balance carried forward		

GREEN THUMB
PLANT SERVICE
456 Lindenhurst Street
Kingsbury, Michigan 03855

973

53-215
113

DATE _____ 20 ___

PAY TO THE
ORDER OF _____ $ _____

_____ DOLLARS

LB Lexington Bank
KINGSBURY, MICHIGAN

MEMO _____ _____

⑆011302153⑆ 331 234 9⑈ 0973

(14)

	Dollars	Cents
$ _____ No. 974		
Date _____ 20 ___		
To _____		
For _____		
	Dollars	Cents
Balance brought forward		
Add deposits		
Total		
Less this check		
Balance carried forward		

GREEN THUMB
PLANT SERVICE
456 Lindenhurst Street
Kingsbury, Michigan 03855

974

53-215
113

DATE _____ 20 ___

PAY TO THE
ORDER OF _____ $ _____

_____ DOLLARS

LB Lexington Bank
KINGSBURY, MICHIGAN

MEMO _____ _____

⑆011302153⑆ 331 234 9⑈ 0974

(7)

Patriot Bank
CONCORD, MASSACHUSETTS

Date _____ 20 ___

Checks and other items are received for deposit subject to
the terms and conditions of this bank's collection agreement.

GREEN THUMB
PLANT SERVICE
PAYROLL ACCOUNT
456 Lindenhurst Street
Kingsbury, Michigan 03855

⑆011302153⑆ 0001 290 3⑈

BE SURE EACH ITEM IS ENDORSED

	DOLLARS	CENTS
CASH		
CHECKS (List Singly)		
1		
2		
3		
4		
5		
6		
7		
8		
TOTAL		

Mini Practice Set 3   (continued)
(8), (11), (13), (14)

GENERAL JOURNAL   PAGE _____

	DATE	DESCRIPTION	POST. REF.	DEBIT	CREDIT	
1						1
2						2
3						3
4						4
5						5
6						6
7						7
8						8
9						9
10						10
11						11
12						12
13						13
14						14
15						15
16						16
17						17
18						18
19						19
20						20
21						21
22						22
23						23
24						24
25						25
26						26
27						27
28						28
29						29
30						30
31						31
32						32
33						33
34						34
35						35
36						36

Mini Practice Set 3 (continued)

GENERAL LEDGER (PARTIAL)

ACCOUNT __Cash in Bank__ ACCOUNT NO. __101__

DATE		DESCRIPTION	POST. REF.	DEBIT	CREDIT	BALANCE DEBIT	BALANCE CREDIT
20--							
July	22	Balance	✓			8 3 7 1 42	

ACCOUNT __Employees' Federal Income Tax Payable__ ACCOUNT NO. __205__

DATE		DESCRIPTION	POST. REF.	DEBIT	CREDIT	BALANCE DEBIT	BALANCE CREDIT
20--							
July	22	Balance	✓				1 8 3 00

ACCOUNT __Employees' State Income Tax Payable__ ACCOUNT NO. __210__

DATE		DESCRIPTION	POST. REF.	DEBIT	CREDIT	BALANCE DEBIT	BALANCE CREDIT
20--							
July	22	Balance	✓				2 4 5 74

ACCOUNT __Social Security Tax Payable__ ACCOUNT NO. __215__

DATE		DESCRIPTION	POST. REF.	DEBIT	CREDIT	BALANCE DEBIT	BALANCE CREDIT
20--							
July	22	Balance	✓				2 1 7 96

Mini Practice Set 3   (continued)

ACCOUNT __Medicare Tax Payable_____   ACCOUNT NO. __220__

DATE		DESCRIPTION	POST. REF.	DEBIT	CREDIT	BALANCE DEBIT	BALANCE CREDIT
20--							
July	22	Balance	✓				5 4 44

ACCOUNT __Insurance Premiums Payable_____   ACCOUNT NO. __225__

DATE		DESCRIPTION	POST. REF.	DEBIT	CREDIT	BALANCE DEBIT	BALANCE CREDIT
20--							
July	22	Balance	✓		.		1 7 1 00

ACCOUNT __Federal Unemployment Tax Payable__   ACCOUNT NO. __235__

DATE		DESCRIPTION	POST. REF.	DEBIT	CREDIT	BALANCE DEBIT	BALANCE CREDIT
20--							
July	8	Balance	✓				3 0 71
	15		G18		1 6 43		4 7 14
	22		G18		1 4 36		6 1 50

ACCOUNT __State Unemployment Tax Payable__   ACCOUNT NO. __240__

DATE		DESCRIPTION	POST. REF.	DEBIT	CREDIT	BALANCE DEBIT	BALANCE CREDIT
20--							
July	8	Balance	✓				2 0 6 20
	15		G18		1 0 4 16		3 1 0 36
	22		G18		9 6 79		4 0 7 15

Mini Practice Set 3 (continued)

ACCOUNT ___U.S. Savings Bonds Payable___ ACCOUNT NO. ___245___

DATE		DESCRIPTION	POST. REF.	DEBIT	CREDIT	BALANCE DEBIT	BALANCE CREDIT
20--							
July	8	Balance	✓				4000
	15		G18		2000		6000
	22		G18		2000		8000

ACCOUNT ___United Way Payable___ ACCOUNT NO. ___250___

DATE		DESCRIPTION	POST. REF.	DEBIT	CREDIT	BALANCE DEBIT	BALANCE CREDIT
20--							
July	8	Balance	✓				1200
	15		G18		1200		2400
	22		G18		1200		3600

ACCOUNT ___Payroll Tax Expense___ ACCOUNT NO. ___620___

DATE		DESCRIPTION	POST. REF.	DEBIT	CREDIT	BALANCE DEBIT	BALANCE CREDIT
20--							
July	8	Balance	✓			568920	
	15		G18	36941		605861	
	22		G18	36617		642478	

ACCOUNT ___Salaries Expense___ ACCOUNT NO. ___630___

DATE		DESCRIPTION	POST. REF.	DEBIT	CREDIT	BALANCE DEBIT	BALANCE CREDIT
20--							
July	15	Balance	✓			4394739	
	22		G18	296314		4691053	

Mini Practice Set 3   (continued)

(9)

GREEN THUMB PLANT SERVICE
PAYROLL ACCOUNT
456 Lindenhurst Street
Kingsbury, Michigan 03855

310

53-215
113

Date_____ 20 _____

Pay to the
Order of_____ $ _____

_____ Dollars

Patriot Bank
CONCORD, MASSACHUSETTS

⑈011302153⑈ 0001 290 3⑊ 0310

Employee Pay Statement
Detach and retain this statement.

310

Period Ending	Earnings			Deductions							Net Pay
	Regular	Overtime	Total	Social Security Tax	Med. Tax	Federal Income Tax	State Income Tax	Hosp. Ins.	Other	Total	

GREEN THUMB PLANT SERVICE
PAYROLL ACCOUNT
456 Lindenhurst Street
Kingsbury, Michigan 03855

311

53-215
113

Date_____ 20 _____

Pay to the
Order of_____ $ _____

_____ Dollars

Patriot Bank
CONCORD, MASSACHUSETTS

⑈011302153⑈ 0001 290 3⑊ 0311

Employee Pay Statement
Detach and retain this statement.

311

Period Ending	Earnings			Deductions							Net Pay
	Regular	Overtime	Total	Social Security Tax	Med. Tax	Federal Income Tax	State Income Tax	Hosp. Ins.	Other	Total	

Mini Practice Set 3   (continued)

GREEN THUMB PLANT SERVICE
PAYROLL ACCOUNT
456 Lindenhurst Street
Kingsbury, Michigan 03855

312

53-215
113

Date _____ 20 _____

Pay to the
Order of _____ $ _____

_____ Dollars

Patriot Bank
CONCORD, MASSACHUSETTS

⑆011302153⑆ 0001 290 3⑆ 0312

Employee Pay Statement
Detach and retain this statement.

312

Period Ending	Earnings			Deductions							Net Pay
	Regular	Overtime	Total	Social Security Tax	Med. Tax	Federal Income Tax	State Income Tax	Hosp. Ins.	Other	Total	

GREEN THUMB PLANT SERVICE
PAYROLL ACCOUNT
456 Lindenhurst Street
Kingsbury, Michigan 03855

313

53-215
113

Date _____ 20 _____

Pay to the
Order of _____ $ _____

_____ Dollars

Patriot Bank
CONCORD, MASSACHUSETTS

⑆011302153⑆ 0001 290 3⑆ 0313

Employee Pay Statement
Detach and retain this statement.

313

Period Ending	Earnings			Deductions							Net Pay
	Regular	Overtime	Total	Social Security Tax	Med. Tax	Federal Income Tax	State Income Tax	Hosp. Ins.	Other	Total	

Mini Practice Set 3   (continued)

GREEN THUMB
PLANT SERVICE
PAYROLL ACCOUNT
456 Lindenhurst Street
Kingsbury, Michigan 03855

314

53-215 / 113

Date_____ 20 _____

Pay to the
Order of _____ $ _____

_____ Dollars

Patriot Bank
CONCORD, MASSACHUSETTS

⑈011302153⑈ 0001 290 3⑈ 0314

Employee Pay Statement
Detach and retain this statement.

314

| Period Ending | Earnings | | | Deductions | | | | | | | Net Pay |
	Regular	Overtime	Total	Social Security Tax	Med. Tax	Federal Income Tax	State Income Tax	Hosp. Ins.	Other	Total	

GREEN THUMB
PLANT SERVICE
PAYROLL ACCOUNT
456 Lindenhurst Street
Kingsbury, Michigan 03855

315

53-215 / 113

Date_____ 20 _____

Pay to the
Order of _____ $ _____

_____ Dollars

Patriot Bank
CONCORD, MASSACHUSETTS

⑈011302153⑈ 0001 290 3⑈ 0315

Employee Pay Statement
Detach and retain this statement.

315

| Period Ending | Earnings | | | Deductions | | | | | | | Net Pay |
	Regular	Overtime	Total	Social Security Tax	Med. Tax	Federal Income Tax	State Income Tax	Hosp. Ins.	Other	Total	

Mini Practice Set 3   (continued)

GREEN THUMB PLANT SERVICE
PAYROLL ACCOUNT
456 Lindenhurst Street
Kingsbury, Michigan 03855

316

53-215
113

Date_____ 20 ____

Pay to the
Order of _____ $ _____

_____ **Dollars**

Patriot Bank
CONCORD, MASSACHUSETTS

⑆011302153⑆ 0001 290 3⑃ 0316

Employee Pay Statement
Detach and retain this statement.

316

Period Ending	Earnings			Deductions							Net Pay
	Regular	Overtime	Total	Social Security Tax	Med. Tax	Federal Income Tax	State Income Tax	Hosp. Ins.	Other	Total	

GREEN THUMB PLANT SERVICE
PAYROLL ACCOUNT
456 Lindenhurst Street
Kingsbury, Michigan 03855

317

53-215
113

Date_____ 20 ____

Pay to the
Order of _____ $ _____

_____ **Dollars**

Patriot Bank
CONCORD, MASSACHUSETTS

⑆011302153⑆ 0001 290 3⑃ 0317

Employee Pay Statement
Detach and retain this statement.

317

Period Ending	Earnings			Deductions							Net Pay
	Regular	Overtime	Total	Social Security Tax	Med. Tax	Federal Income Tax	State Income Tax	Hosp. Ins.	Other	Total	

Mini Practice Set 3   (continued)

(10)

EMPLOYEE'S EARNINGS RECORD FOR QUARTER ENDING *September 30, 20--*

Alter   *Michael*
Last Name   First   Initial

Address
479 Lindon Street
Kingsbury, Michigan

EMPLOYEE NO. **019**
POSITION *Supply Clerk*
RATE OF PAY *7.10*

MARITAL STATUS **S**
ALLOWANCES **1**
SOC. SEC. NO. **049-71-8436**

Accumulated earnings (beginning): 2,572 10

| PAY PERIOD | | EARNINGS | | | DEDUCTIONS | | | | | | | NET PAY | ACCUMULATED EARNINGS |
NO.	ENDED	REGULAR	OVERTIME	TOTAL	SOC. SEC. TAX	MED. TAX	FED. INC. TAX	STATE INC. TAX	HOSP. INS.	OTHER	TOTAL		
1	7/8	158 60		158 60	9 83	2 30	8 00	3 17	6 00	5 00	34 30	124 30	2,730 70
2	7/15	154 10		154 10	9 55	2 23	8 00	3 08	6 00	5 00	33 86	120 24	2,884 80
3	7/22	147 30		147 30	9 13	2 13	6 00	2 94	6 00	5 00	31 20	116 10	3,032 10
4													
5													
6													
7													
8													
9													
10													
11													
12													
13													
QUARTERLY TOTALS													

Other Deductions: B—U.S. Savings Bonds; C—Credit Union; UD—Union Dues; UW—United Way.

Mini Practice Set 3   (continued)

EMPLOYEE'S EARNINGS RECORD FOR QUARTER ENDING *September 30, 20--*

Last Name: *Millette*   **First:** *Greg*   Initial

Address: *86 Meadow Road*

Kingsbury, Michigan

EMPLOYEE NO. *011*

POSITION *Salesperson*

RATE OF PAY *$450/week + 10%*

MARITAL STATUS *M*

ALLOWANCES *2*

SOC. SEC. NO. *046-29-8403*

| PAY PERIOD | | EARNINGS | | | DEDUCTIONS | | | | | | | NET PAY | ACCUMULATED EARNINGS |
NO.	ENDED	REGULAR	OVERTIME	TOTAL	SOC. SEC. TAX	MED. TAX	FED. INC. TAX	STATE INC. TAX	HOSP. INS.	OTHER	TOTAL		
													9,349 20
1	7/8	526 10		526 10	32 62	7 63	44 00	10 52	9 00	5 00	108 77	417 33	9,875 30
2	7/15	519 60		519 60	32 22	7 53	42 00	10 39	9 00	5 00	106 14	413 46	10,394 90
3	7/22	584 20		584 20	36 22	8 47	51 00	11 68	9 00	5 00	121 37	462 83	10,979 10
4													
5													
6													
7													
8													
9													
10													
11													
12													
13													
QUARTERLY TOTALS													

Other Deductions: B—U.S. Savings Bonds; C—Credit Union; UD—Union Dues; UW—United Way.

Mini Practice Set 3   (concluded)

(12)

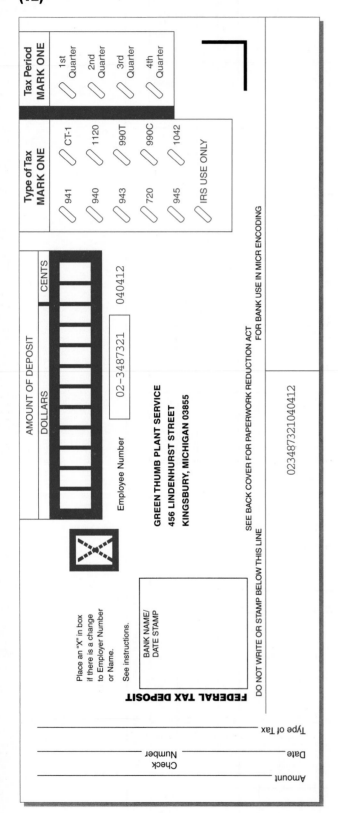

Computerized Accounting Using Peachtree

Mini Practice Set 3

INSTRUCTIONS

Beginning a Session

Step 1 Open the Glencoe Accounting: Electronic Learning Center software.

Step 2 Click on the **Peachtree Accounting Software and Spreadsheet Applications** icon.

Step 3 Log onto the Management System by typing your user name and password.

Step 4 Under the Chapter Problems tab, select the problem set: Green Thumb Plant Service (MP-3).

Step 5 Rename the company by adding your initials, e.g., Green Thumb (MP-3: XXX).

Step 6 Set the system date to July 29, 2004.

Completing the Accounting Problem

Step 7 Review the payroll information shown in your textbook for Green Thumb Plant Service.

Step 8 Change employee record 022 using the **Employees/Sales Reps** option. Enter your name in the *Name* field. Do not change any of the other employee information.

TIP: All of the employee information is already recorded in the problem set for you.

Step 9 Record the weekly payroll and print checks for all employees using the **Payroll Entry** option.

    IMPORTANT: You must manually enter each employee's payroll tax deductions and other deductions. Use the federal tax tables found in your textbook. Remember to enter the employee deductions (Fed_Income, Soc_Sec, etc.) as **negative** amounts.

TIP: Select *PR MultiP Chks 1 Stub* (or equivalent) for the payroll check format, and use 310 for the first payroll check number.

TIP: Peachtree automatically generates the entries to record the payroll, but it does not record the employer's payroll tax expense.

Step 10 Print a Payroll Register report for the current week.

Peachtree Guide

TIP: While viewing a Payroll Register report, you can double-click a report item to go directly to the Payroll Entry window.

Step 11 Proof your work. Make any corrections as needed and print a revised report, if necessary.

Step 12 Print a Payroll Journal for the current week.

Step 13 Calculate and record the employer's payroll tax expense (Social Security, Medicare, FUTA, and SUTA) using the **General Journal Entry** option. One employee, Greg Millette, is over the FUTA/SUTA limit. Remember to take this into account when you calculate the employee's payroll taxes.

Step 14 Record the deposit for the taxes owed to the federal government, and enter the monthly insurance premium ($228) using the **General Journal Entry** option. Manually complete Form 8109.

TIP: Display a General Ledger report to determine the balances in the payroll tax liability accounts.

Step 15 Print a General Journal report and proof your work.

Step 16 Print a General Ledger report.

Step 17 Print Quarterly Earnings reports for Michael Alter and Greg Millette.

Analyzing Your Work

Step 18 Answer the Analyze questions.

Checking Your Work and Ending the Session

Step 19 Click the **Close Problem** button in the Glencoe Smart Guide window.

Step 20 If your teacher has asked you to check your solution, select *Check my answer to this problem.* Review, print, and close this report.

Step 21 Click the **Close Problem** button and select the appropriate save option.

● MINI PRACTICE SET 3

Green Thumb Plant Service

Audit Test

Instructions: *Use your completed solutions to answer the following questions. Write the answer in the space to the left of each question.*

Answer

_____ **1.** What rate is used to compute employee state income tax?

_____ **2.** What rate is used to compute the employer's Federal unemployment tax?

_____ **3.** What commission amount did Greg Millette earn?

_____ **4.** How many employees reached the maximum taxable amount for the social security tax this period?

_____ **5.** What was the total net pay for the pay period ending July 29, 20--?

_____ **6.** How many payroll checks were issued for this period?

_____ **7.** What was the amount of check 972?

_____ **8.** What was the amount paid to American Insurance Company for employee hospital insurance?

_____ **9.** What accounts were debited when check 973 was recorded in the general ledger?

_____ **10.** What is the ending balance of the Employees' Federal Income Tax Payable account at July 31?

_____ **11.** What is the ending balance of the
 Cash in Bank account at month end?

_____ **12.** What is the amount of payroll
 check 312?

_____ **13.** What is the amount of accumulated
 earnings for Michael Alter after the
 July 29 paycheck?

_____ **14.** What amount was remitted with the
 941 tax deposit coupon on July 29?

_____ **15.** What total amount of federal
 income tax was withheld from the
 paycheck of Greg Millette at the
 July 29 pay period?

_____ **16.** What is the total of payroll liabilities at July 29?

_____ **17.** What amount was debited to Salaries
 Expense on July 29?

_____ **18.** What is the balance in the Green
 Thumb Plant Service regular bank
 account after check 974 is recorded?

_____ **19.** What is the next pay period date for
 this business?

CHAPTER 14   Accounting for Sales and Cash Receipts

Study Plan

Check Your Understanding

Section 1	*Read Section 1 on pages 354–356 and complete the following exercises on page 357.* ❏ Thinking Critically ❏ Communication Accounting ❏ Problem 14-1 *Recording Merchandising Transactions*
Section 2	*Read Section 2 on pages 358–365 and complete the following exercises on page 366.* ❏ Thinking Critically ❏ Analyzing Accounting ❏ Problem 14-2 *Recording Sales on Account and Sales Returns and Allowances Transactions*
Section 3	*Read Section 3 on pages 367–375 and complete the following exercises on page 376.* ❏ Thinking Critically ❏ Analyzing Accounting ❏ Problem 14-3 *Analyzing a Source Document* ❏ Problem 14-4 *Recording Cash Receipts*
Summary	*Review the Chapter 14 Summary on page 377 in your textbook.* ❏ Key Concepts
Review and Activities	*Complete the following questions and exercises on pages 378–379 in your textbook.* ❏ Using Key Terms ❏ Understanding Accounting Concepts and Procedures ❏ Case Study ❏ Conducting an Audit with Alex ❏ Internet Connection ❏ Workplace Skills
Computerized Accounting	*Read the Computerized Accounting information on page 380 in your textbook.* ❏ *Making the Transition from a Manual to a Computerized System* ❏ *Entering Sales and Cash Receipts in Peachtree*
Problems	*Complete the following end-of-chapter problems for Chapter 14.* ❏ Problem 14-5 *Recording Sales and Cash Receipts* ❏ Problem 14-6 *Posting Sales and Cash Receipts* ❏ Problem 14-7 *Recording Sales and Cash Receipts* ❏ Problem 14-8 *Recording Sales and Cash Receipts Transactions*
Challenge Problem	❏ Problem 14-9 *Recording and Posting Sales and Cash Receipts*
Chapter Reviews and Working Papers	*Complete the following exercises for Chapter 14 in your Chapter Reviews and Working Papers.* ❏ Chapter Review ❏ Self-Test

CHAPTER 14 REVIEW — Accounting for Sales and Cash Receipts

Part 1   Accounting Vocabulary (24 points)

Directions: *Using terms from the following list, complete the sentences below. Write the letter of the term you have chosen in the space provided.*

A. accounts receivable subsidiary ledger	**G.** contra account	**N.** merchandising business	**T.** sales on account
B. bankcard	**H.** controlling account	**O.** receipt	**U.** sales return
C. cash discount	**I.** credit card	**P.** retailer	**V.** sales slip
D. cash receipt	**J.** credit memorandum	**Q.** sales	**W.** sales tax
E. cash sale	**K.** credit terms	**R.** sales allowance	**X.** subsidiary ledger
F. charge customer	**L.** inventory	**S.** sales discount	**Y.** wholesaler
	M. merchandise		

___X___   **0.** A(n) _____ is a book that is summarized in a controlling account in the general ledger.

_____   **1.** The amount a customer may deduct if the payment for merchandise is made within a certain time is a(n) _____.

_____   **2.** An account whose balance decreases another account's balance is a(n) _____.

_____   **3.** A(n) _____ is a credit card issued by a bank and honored by many businesses.

_____   **4.** A(n) _____ is a form that serves as a record of cash received.

_____   **5.** A(n) _____ is a business that sells to the final user.

_____   **6.** A(n) _____ is a transaction that occurs when a business receives full payment for the merchandise sold at the time of the sale.

_____   **7.** A form that lists the details of a sale and is used as a record of the transaction is a(n) _____.

_____   **8.** The _____ maintains a list in alphabetical order of the charge customers of a business.

_____   **9.** The cash received by a business is referred to as a(n) _____.

_____   **10.** The goods a business buys for resale to customers are known as _____.

_____   **11.** A(n) _____ is a customer to whom a sale on account is made.

_____   **12.** Merchandise returned to the seller for full credit is a(n) _____.

_____   **13.** Accounts Receivable is a(n) _____ because its balance must equal the total of the accounts receivable subsidiary ledger.

_____   **14.** Many states and some cities require that a business add a(n) _____, or a percentage of the selling price of the goods, at the time of the sale.

_____   **15.** The _____ of a sale set out the time allowed for payment.

_____   **16.** A(n) _____ is a business that sells to retailers.

_____   **17.** A charge customer is entitled to charge merchandise with a(n) _____.

_____   **18.** The items of merchandise a business has in stock are referred to as _____.

_____   **19.** A(n) _____ permits a customer to pay for the merchandise at a later date.

_____   **20.** An example of a(n) _____ is Wal-Mart.

_____   **21.** A(n) _____ is a document prepared by the seller granting credit for damaged or returned merchandise.

_____   **22.** A price reduction granted by a business for damaged goods kept by the customer is called a(n) _____.

_____   **23.** The revenue account for a merchandising business is _____.

_____   **24.** A cash discount issued by the seller is a(n) _____.

Part 2   Analyzing Sales and Cash Receipts Transactions (17 points)

Directions: *Read each of the following statements to determine whether the statement is true or false. Write your answer in the space provided.*

<u>True</u>   **0.** Retailers include clothing stores, CD and tape shops, and automobile dealerships.

_____ **1.** The account Merchandise Inventory is classified in the chart of accounts as an asset.

_____ **2.** A sale on account is paid for in cash when the merchandise is sold.

_____ **3.** A sales slip is usually prepared in multiple copies with the customer receiving the original and the business keeping the remaining copies.

_____ **4.** Sales taxes are not usually charged to governmental agencies.

_____ **5.** In a merchandising business, the most frequent type of transaction is the sale of merchandise.

_____ **6.** Electrical supply companies, auto parts distributors, and food supply companies are examples of wholesalers.

_____ **7.** Two of the accounts used by merchandising businesses are Merchandise Inventory and Professional Fees.

_____ **8.** The cash register tape is the source document for the journal entry to record the day's cash sales.

_____ **9.** Sales Discounts is classified as a contra revenue account.

_____ **10.** A sales discount increases the revenue account Sales.

_____ **11.** When a cash sale occurs, the details of the sale are printed on two tapes in the cash register at the same time.

_____ **12.** A cash discount is recorded at the time the sale is made.

_____ **13.** Bank card sales are processed the same way as a store's regular charge card sales.

_____ **14.** A cash discount is calculated on the total of a sales slip, including the sales tax.

_____ **15.** The most widely used bank card in North America is American Express.

_____ **16.** A proof is usually prepared at the end of each day to show that the amount of cash in the cash register equals the amount of cash sales recorded on the cash register tape.

_____ **17.** A cash discount is an advantage only to the buyer because he or she is able to purchase the merchandise at a reduced cost.

Part 3   Rules of Debit and Credit for Sales and Cash Receipts Transactions (11 points)

Directions: *For each of the sentences given below, draw a line under the answer that completes the statement accurately.*

	Answer 1	Answer 2
0. The normal balance side of the Merchandise Inventory account is a	<u>Debit</u>	Credit
1. The normal balance side of the Sales Tax Payable account is a	Debit	Credit
2. The normal balance side of the Sales Discounts account is a	Debit	Credit
3. The normal balance side of the Sales account is a	Debit	Credit
4. The increase side of the Sales Tax Payable account is a	Debit	Credit
5. The decrease side of the Sales Discounts account is a	Debit	Credit
6. The decrease side of the Sales Tax Payable account is a	Debit	Credit
7. The decrease side of the Sales account is a	Debit	Credit
8. The decrease side of the Merchandise Inventory account is a	Debit	Credit
9. The increase side of the Sales Discounts account is a	Debit	Credit
10. The increase side of the Sales account is a	Debit	Credit
11. The increase side of the Merchandise Inventory account is a	Debit	Credit

Working Papers *for Section Problems*

Problem 14-1   Recording Merchandising Transactions

Problem 14-2   Recording Sales on Account and Sales Returns and Allowances Transactions

GENERAL JOURNAL   PAGE _____

	DATE	DESCRIPTION	POST. REF.	DEBIT	CREDIT	
1						1
2						2
3						3
4						4
5						5
6						6
7						7
8						8
9						9
10						10
11						11
12						12
13						13
14						14
15						15
16						16
17						17
18						18
19						19

Problem 14-3 Analyzing a Source Document

GENERAL JOURNAL   PAGE _____

	DATE	DESCRIPTION	POST. REF.	DEBIT	CREDIT	
1						1
2						2
3						3
4						4
5						5
6						6
7						7
8						8
9						9
10						10
11						11

Problem 14-4 Recording Cash Receipts

GENERAL JOURNAL   PAGE _____

	DATE	DESCRIPTION	POST. REF.	DEBIT	CREDIT	
1						1
2						2
3						3
4						4
5						5
6						6
7						7
8						8
9						9
10						10
11						11
12						12
13						13
14						14
15						15

⬤

Computerized Accounting Using Peachtree

Software Objectives
====

When you have completed this chapter, you will be able to use Peachtree to:

1. Record sales on account transactions using the **Sales/Invoicing** option.
2. Enter cash receipts using the **Receipts** option.
3. Record credit memorandums.
4. Print a Sales Journal report and a Cash Receipts Journal Report.
5. Print a General Ledger report.

Problem 14-5   Recording Sales and Cash Receipts

Review the transactions listed in your textbook for Sunset Surfwear, a California-based merchandising store. As you will learn, the process for recording the sales and cash receipts transactions using the Peachtree accounting software is different than the method you learned in your text. Instead of recording these transactions in a general journal, you will record sales on account using the **Sales/Invoicing** option and process cash receipts with the **Receipts** option.

INSTRUCTIONS

Beginning a Session

> **Step 1**   Select the problem set: Sunset Surfwear (Prob. 14-5).
> **Step 2**   Rename the company by adding your initials, e.g., Sunset (Prob. 14-5: XXX).
> **Step 3**   Set the system date to January 31, 2004.

Completing the Accounting Problem

The instructions in this section explain how to enter sales on account, credit memorandums, and cash receipts using the Peachtree software. To simplify the data entry process, you will batch similar transactions by type and then enter them using the appropriate software task option.

Entering Sales on Account

> **Step 4**   Review the transactions for Sunset Surfwear and identify the sales on account.
> **Step 5**   Enter the sale on account transaction for January 1.

> ***January 1, Sold $300 in merchandise plus a sales tax of $18 on account to Martha Adams, Sales Slip 777.***

> *To enter the sale on account:*

> • Choose **Sales/Invoicing** from the *Tasks* menu to display the Sales/Invoicing window.
> • Click [DUE ▸ Service] and then click **OK** when the warning message appears to display a simplified entry form. (See Figure 14-5A.) **Note:** You must perform this step only once per session.

> You can use the simplified form to enter the sales on account for Sunset Surfwear since you do not have to complete the following fields: quantity, item number, unit cost, and freight. Using a simplified form makes the data entry process easier.

- Type **ADA** (the account code for Martha Adams) in the *Customer ID* field.

  If you do not know the account code for a customer, click the 🔍 button, highlight the customer name and click the **OK** button.

TIP: As a shortcut, remember that you can press **SHIFT+?** when you are in a Lookup field to display a list of choices.

- Type **777** for the sales slip number in the *Invoice #* field.

- Type **1/1/04** to record the transaction date in the *Date* field. Make sure that Peachtree shows 2004 for the year. If not, change the system date.

- Move to the *Description* field by pressing **ENTER** or by clicking in the field.

  You can skip over the *Ship To, Customer PO, Terms,* and *Sales Rep ID* fields. Some of these fields, such as the *Ship To* field, are optional. You do not need to complete these fields when you are entering transactions from your text, but a company using Peachtree to keep its books might need to enter this information. For other fields, such as the *Terms* field, default information is already recorded in the field. You do not need to change this field unless different terms apply.

- Type **Sale on account** for the description.

- Skip the *GL Account* field. The **Sales** account number already appears in this field.

- Type **300.00** in the *Amount* field to record the amount of the sale.

  When you enter the amount, Peachtree automatically calculates the sales tax based on the default sales tax code established for the customer. For example, if the customer was setup with a tax exempt status, Peachtree would not include any sales tax. Peachtree also calculates and displays the invoice total and amount due.

✿ Notes

Peachtree uses the term "invoice" instead of "sales slip" for sales on account.

TIP: Remember to enter the decimal point when you enter an amount. If you enter 300, Peachtree will automatically format the amount to $3.00 unless the decimal entry option is set to manual.

- Proof the information you just recorded. Check all of the information you entered. If you notice a mistake, move to that field and make the correction. Compare the information on your screen to the completed transaction shown in Figure 14-5A.

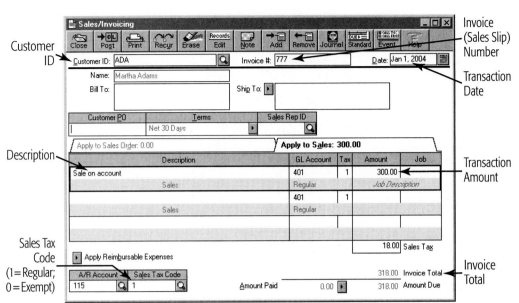

Figure 14-5A *Completed Sales/Invoicing Transaction (January 1, Sales Slip 777)*

- Click to display the Accounting Behind the Screens window. Use the information in this window to check your work again. (See Figure 14-5B.)

The Accounting Behind the Screens window shows you the accounts and the debit/credit amounts that Peachtree will record for this transaction. Although Peachtree does not show the **Accounts Receivable** subsidiary ledger information, it will automatically update the customer account balance, too. As you can see, Peachtree uses the data you entered to make a transaction "behind the scenes" that is equivalent to the transactions you learned about in your text.

For the sale on account transaction, the window should show the following: **Accounts Receivable** ($318.00 DR), **Sales** ($300.00 CR), and **Sales Tax Payable** ($18.00 CR).

- Click ⊗Cancel to close the Accounting Behind the Screens window.
- Click →GL Post to post the transaction.

If you need a printed copy of the invoice (sales slip), you could choose the **Print** option. Peachtree lets you print on plain paper or on pre-printed forms. If you choose to print an invoice, select the *Invoice Plain* form. Then, click the **Real** button to print the invoice. After Peachtree prints the invoice, the software automatically posts the transaction and is ready for the next invoice.

> ### Notes
> *Viewing the Accounting Behind the Screens window is not required each time you enter a transaction. This information, however, is useful to understand how Peachtree records a transaction such as a sale on account.*

TIP: If you notice an error after you post an entry, click [Records Edit] and choose the transaction you want to edit. Make the corrections and post the transaction again to record the changes.

Peachtree Guide

Transaction Date →

Invoice Number →

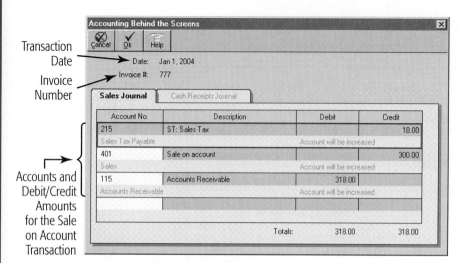

Accounts and Debit/Credit Amounts for the Sale on Account Transaction

Figure 14-5B *Accounting Behind the Screens (Sales/Invoicing)*

Step 6   Enter the remaining sales on account transactions for the month: January 5 and January 25.

TIP: If you enter a sale on account for a customer who is tax exempt, make sure that the sales tax code is set to **0** (zero).

Recording Credit Memorandums/Sales Returns

Step 7   Review the transactions shown in your textbook and identify those where the company issued a credit memorandum to a customer.

Step 8   Record the credit memorandum issued on January 10.

January 10, Issued Credit Memorandum 102 to Martha Adams for $318 covering $300 in returned merchandise plus $18 sales tax.

To enter the credit memorandum:

- Choose **Sales/Invoicing** from the *Tasks* menu to display the Sales/Invoicing window if it is not already on your screen.
- Click and then click **OK** when the warning message appears to display a simplified entry form, if necessary.
- Type **ADA** (the account code for Martha Adams) in the *Customer ID* field.
- Type **CM102** for the credit memo number in the *Invoice #* field.
- Type **1/10** to record the transaction date in the *Date* field.
- Move to the *Description* field and enter **Sales return** as the description.
- Type **410** (the **Sales Returns and Allowances** account number) in the *GL Account* field.

    For Peachtree to apply the credit to the appropriate general ledger account, you must enter the **Sales Returns and Allowances** account number in the *GL Account* field. If you do not enter this information, the program will apply the credit to sales instead of the contra-sales account.

TIP: If the *GL Account* field does not appear, choose **Global** from the *Options* menu. Change the setting to show the general ledger accounts for Accounts Receivable. You will have to close the Sales/Invoicing window and then choose this option again for the new setting to take effect.

- Type **-300.00** in the *Amount* field to record the credit amount.
- Proof the transaction. Verify that you entered the customer account code, credit memo reference, and credit amount correctly. The invoice total should show -318.00. Compare the information on your screen to the completed transaction shown in Figure 14-5C.

Notes

To record a credit memo, you must enter a negative amount in the Amount *field. The Peachtree software will also calculate the sales tax credit, if applicable.*

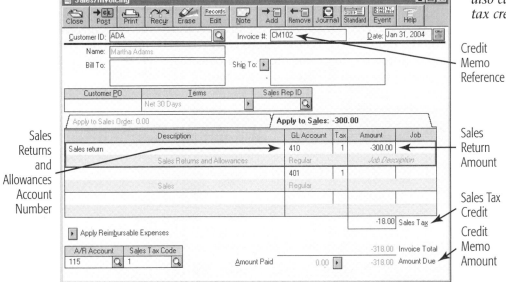

Figure 14-5C *Completed Sales Return Transaction (January 10, Credit Memo 102)*

- *Optional:* Click [Journal] to display the Accounting Behind the Screens window. Compare the information shown to the following: **Sales Tax Payable** ($18.00 DR), **Sales Returns and Allowances** ($300.00 DR), and **Accounts Receivable** ($318.00 CR). Close the Accounting Behind the Screens window when you finish.
- Click [Post] to post the credit memorandum.
- Click [Close] to close the Sales/Invoicing window.

To apply a credit memo to an invoice (sales slip):

- Choose **Receipts** from the *Tasks* menu to display the Receipts window so that you can apply the credit memo to a specific invoice.
- Click **OK** to select **Cash in Bank** as the default cash account, if prompted.
- Type **1/10/04** in the *Deposit Ticket ID* field.
- Type **ADA** as the customer ID for Martha Adams.
- Type **CM102** in the *Reference* field.

Peachtree Guide

- Record the transaction date, **1/10,** in the *Date* field.

    You do not need to change the payment method or the general ledger account in the top portion on the window. These fields do not apply to a credit memo transaction.

- Click the **Pay** box for the credit memo shown in the Apply to Invoices tab located in the lower portion of the window.

- Find the invoice to which you want to apply the credit memo— Invoice 777. Click the **Pay** box next to the invoice since the credit is for the entire amount.

TIP: If a discount amount appears when you apply a credit memo, move to the *Discount* field and delete the amount shown.

Notes

*If the credit is the same as the invoice amount, just click the **Pay** button. You do not have to change the amount. If the credit is for only a portion of the total invoice, you must specify the amount of the credit to apply to the invoice.*

After you mark both the credit memo and the invoice, the *Receipt Amount* field should show 0.00 since no cash was actually exchanged. Applying the credit memo removes the original invoice (sales slip) from the customer's record.

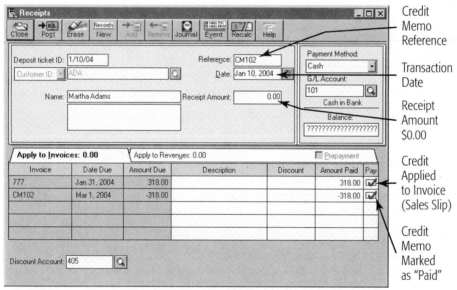

Credit Memo Reference

Transaction Date

Receipt Amount $0.00

Credit Applied to Invoice (Sales Slip)

Credit Memo Marked as "Paid"

Figure 14-5D *Receipts Window with Applied Credit Memo (January 10, Credit Memo 102)*

- *Optional:* Click [Journal] to display the Accounting Behind the Screens window. Click [Cancel] to close the Accounting Behind the Screens window.

    Check the information shown. Notice that entries show a debit and a credit to **Accounts Receivable** for the same amount. The net effect is $0.00 on **Accounts Receivable,** but the subsidiary ledger is now up-to-date.

- Click to post the transaction.

- Click [Close] to close the Receipts window.

Step 9   Record the other credit memorandums issued on January 28.

Recording Cash Receipts

Step 10   Review the transactions and identify the cash receipt transactions for Sunset Surfwear.

Step 11   Enter the January 7 cash receipt on account.

January 7, Received $400 from Alex Hamilton on account, Receipt 345.

To enter the cash receipt on account:

- Choose **Receipts** from the *Tasks* menu to display the Receipts window if it is not already on your screen.
- Type **1/7** in the *Deposit Ticket ID* field.
- Type **HAM** (the customer code for Alex Hamilton) in the *Customer ID* field, or click [Q] and select the code from the Lookup list.
- Type **345** in the *Reference* field.
- Type **1/7** for the transaction date in the *Date* field.

    Since the cash you received will go into the **Cash** account, leave the *GL Account* field as is. You do not need to change the payment method or the general ledger account in the top, right portion of the window.

- In the Apply to Invoice tab, identify the invoice to which the cash receipt should be applied. Click the **Pay** box next to that invoice to indicate that the customer paid it. After you mark the invoice, the *Receipt Amount* field should show $400.00, the amount of cash received on account.

Notes

The Deposit Ticket ID *field is useful when you reconcile the bank statement. For our purposes, however, you can use the transaction date.*

TIP: If a cash receipt on account applies to more than one invoice, you can mark several invoices to be paid in one transaction. If a customer sends only a partial payment, you can mark an invoice for payment and then change the amount to reflect the actual cash received.

- Proof the information you just recorded. If you notice a mistake, move to that field and make the correction. Compare the information on your screen to the completed transaction shown in Figure 14-5E.
- Click to post the transaction.

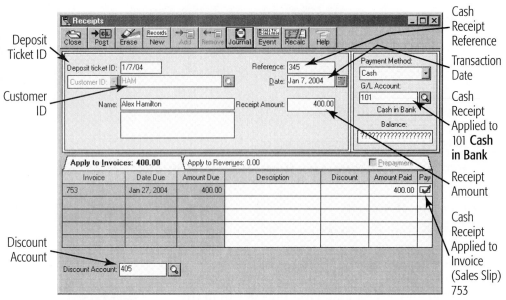

Deposit Ticket ID

Customer ID

Discount Account

Cash Receipt Reference

Transaction Date

Cash Receipt Applied to 101 **Cash in Bank**

Receipt Amount

Cash Receipt Applied to Invoice (Sales Slip) 753

Figure 14-5E *Completed Cash Receipt on Account Transaction (January 7, Receipt 345)*

Step 12 Enter the cash sale on January 15.

January 15, Recorded cash sales of $800 plus $48 in sales tax, Tape 39.

To enter the cash/bank card sales:

- Choose **Receipts** from the *Tasks* menu to display the Receipts window, if necessary.
- Type **1/15** in the *Deposit Ticket ID* field.
- Leave the *Customer ID* field empty since this is a cash sale, but enter **CASH** in the *Name* field. **Note:** Peachtree requires that you complete this field even if there is not a specific customer.
- Type **T39** in the *Reference* field.
- Type **1/15** for the transaction date in the *Date* field.
- Do not change the payment method or general ledger account. These fields should already be set to Cash and G/L Account 101 **(Cash in Bank),** respectively.

    Peachtree lets you change the general ledger account if a company has more than one cash account to which it deposits cash receipts. For the problems in your textbook, there is only one bank account and it is setup as the default cash account.

- In the Apply to Revenues tab, move to the first detail line and enter **800.00** in the *Amount* field.

    For a cash sale, you do not have to include the quantity, item, description, unit price and job information.

- If a sales tax code is not shown at the bottom of the Receipts window, enter **1** for the standard sales tax. Verify that Peachtree calculates the correct sales tax amount.

✳Notes

The steps to enter bank card sales are the same as the steps shown here to enter cash sales. Use BANKCARD instead of CASH for the customer name.

- Proof the information you just recorded. The total receipt amount should be $848.00. (See Figure 14-5F.) If you notice a mistake, move to that field and make the correction.

- Click [→GL Post] to post the transaction.

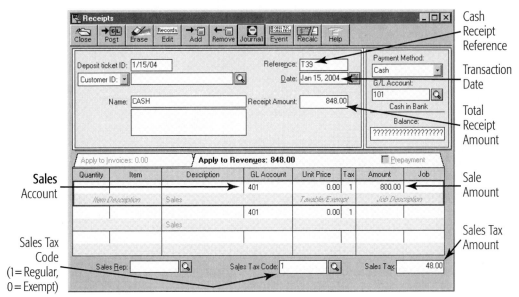

Figure 14-5F *Completed Cash Sale Transaction (January 15, Tape 39)*

Step 13   Record the remaining cash receipt transactions: January 15, January 20, and January 30.

Preparing Reports

Step 14   Print the Sales Journal report.

To print a Sales Journal report:

- Choose **Accounts Receivable** from the *Reports* menu to display the Select a Report window. (See Figure 14-5G.)

TIP: As an alternative, you can click the ▭ Sales ▭ navigation aid and then choose the Sales Journal report to go directly to the report.

- Select Sales Journal in the report list.
- Click [Screen] and then click **OK** to display the Sales Journal report.

TIP: As a shortcut, remember that you can double-click on a report in the report list to automatically display a report on the screen.

- Click [Print] to print the report.
- Click [Close] to close the report window.

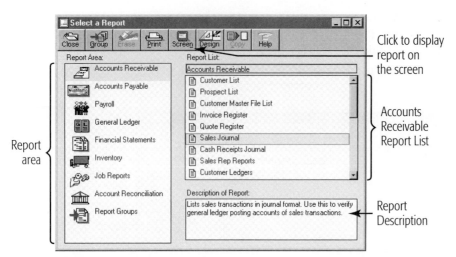

Figure 14-5G *Select a Report Window with the Accounts Receivable reports.*

Step 15 Print the Cash Receipts Journal report.

Step 16 Proof the information shown on the reports. If there are any corrections needed, choose the corresponding task option—**Sales/Invoicing** or **Receipts.** Click [Records Edit] and select the transaction to edit. Make the necessary changes and post the transaction to record your work.

Analyzing Your Work

Step 17 Choose **General Ledger** from the *Reports* menu to display the Select a Report window.

Step 18 Double-click the General Ledger report title to display the report.

Step 19 Locate the **Sales Returns and Allowances** account on the General Ledger report. What is the sum of the debits to this account during January?

Checking Your Work and Ending the Session

Step 20 Click the **Close Problem** button in the Glencoe Smart Guide window.

Step 21 If your teacher has asked you to check your solution, click *Check my answer to this problem.*

Step 22 Click **OK**.

Continuing a Problem from a Previous Session

- If you were previously directed to save your work on the network, select the problem from the scrolling menu and click **OK.** The system will retrieve your files from your last session.
- If you were previously directed to save your work on a floppy disk, insert the floppy, select the corresponding problem from the scrolling menu, and click **OK.** The system will retrieve your files from the floppy disk.

Mastering Peachtree

Why does the Sales/Invoicing form include the *Sales Rep ID* field? Although you did not need to complete this field when you entered the transactions for this problem, a company might find it useful to record this information. Explore the uses a company may have for this information. Write your findings on a separate sheet of paper.

TIP: Search the help information to learn more about the *Sales Rep ID* field.

Problem 14-6 Posting Sales and Cash Receipts

Review the General Journal entries listed in your textbook for InBeat CD Shop. Then, print the General Ledger and Customer Ledgers reports to see how Peachtree posts the transactions to the corresponding accounts.

INSTRUCTIONS

Beginning a Session

> **Step 1** Select the problem set: InBeat CD Shop (Prob. 14-6).
> **Step 2** Rename the company and set the system date to January 31, 2004.

Completing the Accounting Problem

> **Step 3** Print a General Ledger report.
> **Step 4** Print a Customer Ledgers report.

 TIP: When a report list appears, you can double-click a report title to go directly to a report, skipping the report options window.

> **Step 5** Review the reports. Compare the General Journal entries shown in your textbook to the information shown on the reports.

 TIP: Credit balances appear as negative amounts on a General Ledger report.

> **DO YOU HAVE A QUESTION**
>
> **Q.** *Why doesn't Peachtree require you to manually post transactions to the General Ledger?*
>
> **A.** Peachtree does not require you to post transactions to the General Ledger since the software automatically performs this step for you each time you record a transaction. When you record a Sales/Invoicing transaction, for example, Peachtree posts the transaction amounts to the corresponding General Ledger accounts. Automatic updates to the General Ledger is one of the advantages of using a computerized accounting system.

Analyzing Your Work

> **Step 6** Review the General Ledger report to answer the **Analyze** question shown in your textbook.

Ending the Session

> **Step 7** Click the **Close Problem** button in the Glencoe Smart Guide window and select the appropriate save option.

Mastering Peachtree

Although the General Ledger report you printed for this problem is essentially the same as a manual General Ledger report, there are a few minor differences. What are the differences between a Peachtree General Ledger report and the one that you have learned to prepare manually? Write your answer on a separate sheet of paper.

Problem 14-7   Recording Sales and Cash Receipts

INSTRUCTIONS

Beginning a Session

Step 1   Select the problem set: Shutterbug Cameras (Prob. 14-7).

Step 2   Rename the company and set the system date to January 31, 2004.

Completing the Accounting Problem

Step 3   Review the transactions listed in your textbook and group them by type—sales on account, credit memorandums, cash/bank card sales, and other cash receipts.

Step 4   Use the **Sales/Invoicing** option to record the sales on account transactions.

TIP: Refer to the instructions for Problem 14-5 if you need help entering the transactions for this problem.

When you enter the January 12 transaction for the merchandise sold on account to FastForward Productions, notice that the credit terms **2% 10, Net 30 Days** appears in the *Terms* field. The terms for FastForward Productions have already been set up for you in the problem set.

Step 5   Enter the credit memorandums issued by Shutterbug Cameras in January.

Remember that there are two steps to record a credit memorandum. First, use the **Sales/Invoicing** option to enter the credit memo. Be sure to change the general ledger account number to **410 Sales Returns and Allowances** and enter a negative invoice amount. Next, apply the credit memo to a specific invoice using the **Receipts** option. Mark both the credit memo and the invoice to which it applies as "paid." The receipt amount should be $0.00.

Step 6   Enter the cash receipts transaction for the sale of supplies to Betty's Boutique on January 3.

The process for recording a cash receipt for the sale of an asset (e.g., supplies or office equipment) is similar to the steps required to record the sale of merchandise. Use the **Cash Receipts** option, but change the *GL Account* from the default, **Sales,** account to the asset account affected by the transaction. Follow the steps listed below to record the transaction.

January 3, Received $50 in cash from the sale of supplies to Betty's Boutique, Receipt 201.

To enter the cash receipt for the sale of an asset (e.g., supplies):

- Choose **Receipts** from the *Tasks* menu to display the Receipts window, if necessary.
- Type **1/3/04** in the *Deposit Ticket ID* field.
- Enter **Betty's Boutique** in the *Name* field. **Note:** A customer account is not set up for this company, but you must still complete the *Name* field.

- Type **201** in the *Reference* field.
- Type **1/3** for the transaction date in the *Date* field.

TIP: To record the sale of an asset (e.g., supplies), you must change the *GL Account* field so that the cash receipt is applied to the appropriate general ledger account, not the default account—**Sales**.

- Do not change the payment method or general ledger account. These fields should already be set to Cash and G/L Account 101 **(Cash in Bank),** respectively.
- In the Apply to Revenues tab, move to the first detail line and enter **Sale of supplies** in the *Description* field.
- Change the general ledger account to **130** (Supplies) in the *GL Account* field.
- Enter **50.00** in the *Amount* field.
- Make sure that the sales tax amount is $0.00 since this is not a taxable transaction.
- Proof the information you just recorded. The total receipt amount should be $50.00. (See Figure 14-7A.) If you notice a mistake, move to that field and make the correction.

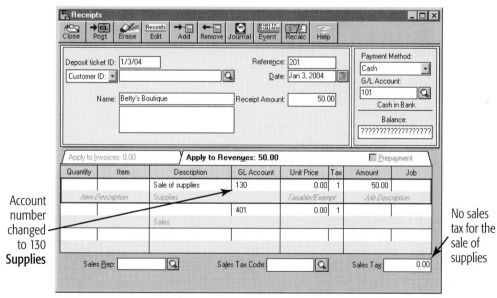

Figure 14-7A *Completed Cash Receipt for the Sale of an Asset (January 3, Receipt 201)*

- *Optional:* Click [Journal] to display the Accounting Behind the Screens window, and then review the accounts and amounts to check your work again. The entry should show the following: **Cash** ($50.00 DR) and **Supplies** ($50.00 CR). Close the window when you finish.
- Click [Post] to post the transaction.

     Chapter 14 ■ 369

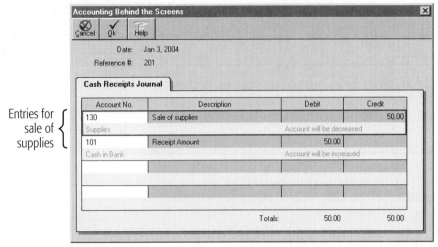

Figure 14-7B *Accounting Behind the Screens Window (January 3, Receipt 201)*

Step 7   Record the remaining cash receipts (on account, cash sales, and bank card sales).

        To record a cash receipt on account involving a discount, follow the steps you already learned to record the transaction. After you mark the invoice (sales slip) as "paid," move to the *Discount* field and enter the sales discount if Peachtree does not calculate it correctly. Verify that the *Discount* and *Amount Paid* fields are correct and then post.

Step 8   Print a Sales Journal report and a Cash Receipts Journal report.

Step 9   Proof your work. Update the transactions and print revised reports if you identify any errors.

Step 10   Answer the Analyze question shown in your textbook.

Checking Your Work and Ending the Session

Step 11   Click the **Close Problem** button in the Glencoe Smart Guide window.

Step 12   If your teacher has asked you to check your solution, click *Check my answer to this problem*. Review, print, and close the report.

Step 13   Click the **Close Problem** button and select the appropriate save option.

Mastering Peachtree

How do you set up the standard (default) customer payment terms for a company? Can you set up different payment terms for one or two customers? If so, explain how. Use a separate sheet of paper to record your answer.

Problem 14-8   Recording Sales and Cash Receipts Transactions

INSTRUCTIONS

Beginning a Session

Step 1   Select the problem set: River's Edge Canoe & Kayak (Prob. 14-8).

Step 2   Rename the company and set the system date to January 31, 2004.

Completing the Accounting Problem

Step 3   Review the transactions listed in your textbook and group them by type—sales on account, credit memorandums, cash/bank card sales, and other cash receipts.

 TIP: Refer to the instructions for Problem 14-5 if you need help entering the transactions for this problem.

Step 4   Record the sales on account transactions.
Step 5   Enter the credit memorandums.

When you apply a credit memo to a specific invoice and the customer is set up to receive a sales discount, you will most likely have to change the amounts that automatically appear. Set the discount amounts to $0.00 after you mark the credit memo and invoice as "paid." Also, if a credit is for an amount less than the original invoice (sales slip) amount, you will have to change the default amount paid to reflect the amount of the credit.

 TIP: Remember that when you apply a credit memo to an invoice using the **Receipts** options, the receipt amount must equal $0.00.

Step 6   Enter the cash receipts transactions.

 TIP: If Peachtree does not calculate a sales discount correctly, you can manually enter the discount amount in the *Discount* field in the Cash Receipts (Apply to Invoices) window.

Step 7   Print a Sales Journal report and a Cash Receipts Journal report.
Step 8   Proof your work. Update the transactions and print revised reports if you identify any errors.
Step 9   Answer the Analyze question.

Ending the Session

Step 10   Click the **Close Problem** button in the Glencoe Smart Guide window.

Mastering Peachtree

A business may have customers who are exempt from paying sales tax. Peachtree lets you set up customer accounts so that you can identify those customers who do not have to pay sales tax. When you enter a sales on account transaction, the sales tax code will automatically appear. How do you change the default sales tax code for a customer? Record your answer on a separate sheet of paper.

DO YOU HAVE A QUESTION

Q. *Why do you have to apply a credit memo to a specific invoice?*

A. Suppose a customer purchases merchandise on account for $100 and then receives a $25 credit. When you enter the $25 credit, you record it as a "negative" invoice amount. The customer's account correctly shows a balance of $75, but there are now two outstanding invoices—one for $100 and another for -$25. When you apply the credit, you mark the -$25 credit memo (invoice) as paid and then record a $25 cash receipt against the original invoice. Now there is only one outstanding invoice for $75 and the customer's account balance remains at $75 because the net cash received for this part of the transaction was $0.

Peachtree Guide

Problem 14-9   Recording and Posting Sales and Cash Receipts

INSTRUCTIONS

Beginning a Session

Step 1   Select the problem set: Buzz Newsstand (Prob. 14-9).

Step 2   Rename the company and set the system date to January 31, 2004.

Completing the Accounting Problem

Step 3   Review the transactions listed in your textbook for Buzz Newsstand.

TIP: To save time entering the transactions, group them by type— sales on account, credit memorandums, cash/bank card sales, and other cash receipts.

Step 4   Record the transactions.

Step 5   Print the following reports: Sales Journal, Cash Receipts Journal, Customer Ledgers, and General Ledger.

Step 6   Proof your work.

Step 7   Answer the Analyze question.

Ending the Session

Step 8   Click the **Close Problem** button in the Glencoe Smart Guide window and select the appropriate save option.

Mastering Peachtree

If a tax authority changes the sales tax rate, you would have to change the tax rate in the Peachtree software so that it would apply the latest rate for each sales transaction. How do you change the default sales tax? Record your answer on a separate sheet of paper.

FAQs

What steps are required to correct a sales invoice with the wrong customer ID code or sale amount?

If you enter the wrong information for a sales invoice, you can correct it even if you have already posted the transaction. Choose the **Sales/Invoicing** option and click the **Edit Records** button. Select the invoice (sales slip) you want to change. When the invoice appears in the Sales/Invoicing data entry window, make the necessary corrections and then post the updated transaction.

What steps are required to correct a cash receipt entry?

You can change any information on a cash receipt unless you have closed the current period. To make a change, choose the **Receipts** option. Click the **Edit Records** button and select the receipt you want to update. Make the changes and post the corrected transaction. Peachtree automatically applies the corrections.

Is it required to use the simplified invoice in the Sales/Invoicing window?

No. You can use the standard invoice to enter sales on account. Just leave the *Quantity* and *Item* fields empty when you complete the data entry form.

Working Papers *for End-of-Chapter Problems*

Problem 14-5   Recording Sales and Cash Receipts

GENERAL JOURNAL   PAGE _____

	DATE	DESCRIPTION	POST. REF.	DEBIT	CREDIT	
1						1
2						2
3						3
4						4
5						5
6						6
7						7
8						8
9						9
10						10
11						11
12						12
13						13
14						14
15						15
16						16
17						17
18						18
19						19
20						20
21						21
22						22
23						23
24						24
25						25
26						26
27						27
28						28
29						29
30						30
31						31
32						32
33						33
34						34
35						35

Problem 14-5   (concluded)

GENERAL JOURNAL   PAGE _____

	DATE	DESCRIPTION	POST. REF.	DEBIT	CREDIT	
1						1
2						2
3						3
4						4
5						5
6						6
7						7
8						8

Analyze: _____

_____

Problem 14-6   Posting Sales and Cash Receipts

GENERAL LEDGER

ACCOUNT __Cash in Bank_____   ACCOUNT NO. ___101___

DATE		DESCRIPTION	POST. REF.	DEBIT	CREDIT	BALANCE DEBIT	BALANCE CREDIT
20--							
Jan.	1	Balance	✓			470000	

ACCOUNT __Accounts Receivable_____   ACCOUNT NO. ___115___

DATE		DESCRIPTION	POST. REF.	DEBIT	CREDIT	BALANCE DEBIT	BALANCE CREDIT
20--							
Jan.	1	Balance	✓			387500	

Problem 14-6 (continued)

ACCOUNT _Sales Tax Payable_ ACCOUNT NO. _217_

DATE		DESCRIPTION	POST. REF.	DEBIT	CREDIT	BALANCE	
						DEBIT	CREDIT
20--							
Jan.	1	Balance	✓				20000

ACCOUNT _Sales_ ACCOUNT NO. _401_

DATE		DESCRIPTION	POST. REF.	DEBIT	CREDIT	BALANCE	
						DEBIT	CREDIT
20--							
Jan.	1	Balance	✓				888500

ACCOUNT _Sales Discounts_ ACCOUNT NO. _405_

DATE		DESCRIPTION	POST. REF.	DEBIT	CREDIT	BALANCE	
						DEBIT	CREDIT
20--							
Jan.	1	Balance	✓			15000	

ACCOUNT _Sales Returns and Allowances_ ACCOUNT NO. _410_

DATE		DESCRIPTION	POST. REF.	DEBIT	CREDIT	BALANCE	
						DEBIT	CREDIT
20--							
Jan.	1	Balance	✓			36000	

Problem 14-6 (concluded)

ACCOUNTS RECEIVABLE SUBSIDIARY LEDGER

Name *Alvarez, Alicia* _____

Address *610 Center Ave., Little Rock, AR 72201* _____

DATE		DESCRIPTION	POST. REF.	DEBIT	CREDIT	BALANCE
20--						
Jan.	1	Balance	✓			40000

Name *Greenburg, Dena* _____

Address *103 Third Ave., Pine Bluff, AR 71601* _____

DATE		DESCRIPTION	POST. REF.	DEBIT	CREDIT	BALANCE
20--						
Jan.	1	Balance	✓			50000

Name *Montoya, Joe* _____

Address *527 Madison Ave., Ft. Smith, AR 72901* _____

DATE		DESCRIPTION	POST. REF.	DEBIT	CREDIT	BALANCE
20--						
Jan.	1	Balance	✓			140000

Name *Wright, Chelsea* _____

Address *479 Cleveland St., Fayetteville, AR 72701* _____

DATE		DESCRIPTION	POST. REF.	DEBIT	CREDIT	BALANCE
20--						
Jan.	1	Balance	✓			157500

Analyze: _____

_____

Problem 14-7   Recording Sales and Cash Receipts

GENERAL JOURNAL   PAGE _____

	DATE	DESCRIPTION	POST. REF.	DEBIT	CREDIT	
1						1
2						2
3						3
4						4
5						5
6						6
7						7
8						8
9						9
10						10
11						11
12						12
13						13
14						14
15						15
16						16
17						17
18						18
19						19
20						20
21						21
22						22
23						23
24						24
25						25
26						26
27						27
28						28
29						29
30						30
31						31
32						32
33						33
34						34
35						35
36						36
37						37

Problem 14-7 (concluded)

GENERAL JOURNAL   PAGE _____

	DATE	DESCRIPTION	POST. REF.	DEBIT	CREDIT	
1						1
2						2
3						3
4						4
5						5
6						6
7						7
8						8
9						9
10						10
11						11
12						12
13						13
14						14
15						15
16						16
17						17

Analyze: _____

_____

Problem 14-8   Recording Sales and Cash Receipts Transactions

GENERAL JOURNAL   PAGE _____

	DATE		DESCRIPTION	POST. REF.	DEBIT	CREDIT	
1							1
2							2
3							3
4							4
5							5
6							6
7							7
8							8
9							9
10							10
11							11
12							12
13							13
14							14
15							15
16							16
17							17
18							18
19							19
20							20
21							21
22							22
23							23
24							24
25							25
26							26
27							27
28							28
29							29
30							30
31							31
32							32
33							33
34							34
35							35
36							36
37							37

Problem 14-8   (concluded)

GENERAL JOURNAL   PAGE _____

	DATE	DESCRIPTION	POST. REF.	DEBIT	CREDIT	
1						1
2						2
3						3
4						4
5						5
6						6
7						7
8						8
9						9
10						10
11						11
12						12
13						13
14						14
15						15
16						16
17						17

Analyze: _____

_____

Problem 14-9   Source Documents

Instructions: *Use the following source documents to record the transactions for this problem.*

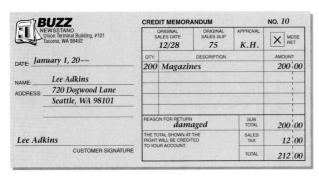

BUZZ NEWSSTAND
Union Terminal Building, #101
Tacoma, WA 98402

CREDIT MEMORANDUM   NO. 10

ORIGINAL SALES DATE	ORIGINAL SALES SLIP	APPROVAL		MDSE RET
12/28	75	K.H.	X	

DATE: January 1, 20--

QTY.	DESCRIPTION	AMOUNT
200	Magazines	200 00

NAME: Lee Adkins
ADDRESS: 720 Dogwood Lane
Seattle, WA 98101

REASON FOR RETURN damaged	SUB TOTAL	200 00
THE TOTAL SHOWN AT THE RIGHT WILL BE CREDITED TO YOUR ACCOUNT.	SALES TAX	12 00
	TOTAL	212 00

Lee Adkins
CUSTOMER SIGNATURE

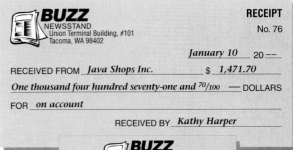

BUZZ NEWSSTAND
Union Terminal Building, #101
Tacoma, WA 98402

RECEIPT   No. 76

January 10   20 --

RECEIVED FROM   Java Shops Inc. $ 1,471.70

One thousand four hundred seventy-one and 70/100 —— DOLLARS

FOR   on account

RECEIVED BY   Kathy Harper

BUZZ NEWSSTAND
Union Terminal Building, #101
Tacoma, WA 98402

RECEIPT   No. 75

January 3   20 --

RECEIVED FROM   Rolling Hills Pharmacies $ 2,256.62

Two thousand two hundred fifty-six and 62/100 ——— DOLLARS

FOR   on account

RECEIVED BY   Kathy Harper

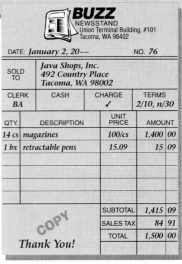

BUZZ NEWSSTAND
Union Terminal Building, #101
Tacoma, WA 98402

DATE: January 2, 20--   NO. 76

SOLD TO   Java Shops, Inc.
492 Country Place
Tacoma, WA 98002

CLERK BA	CASH	CHARGE ✓	TERMS 2/10, n/30

QTY.	DESCRIPTION	UNIT PRICE	AMOUNT
14 cs	magazines	100/cs	1,400 00
1 bx	retractable pens	15.09	15 09

	SUBTOTAL	1,415 09
	SALES TAX	84 91
Thank You!	TOTAL	1,500 00

COPY

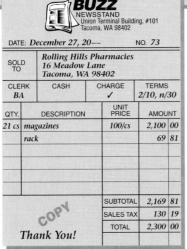

BUZZ NEWSSTAND
Union Terminal Building, #101
Tacoma, WA 98402

DATE: December 27, 20--   NO. 73

SOLD TO   Rolling Hills Pharmacies
16 Meadow Lane
Tacoma, WA 98402

CLERK BA	CASH	CHARGE ✓	TERMS 2/10, n/30

QTY.	DESCRIPTION	UNIT PRICE	AMOUNT
21 cs	magazines	100/cs	2,100 00
	rack		69 81

	SUBTOTAL	2,169 81
	SALES TAX	130 19
	TOTAL	2,300 00

COPY
Thank You!

Jan. 15
Tape 25

2,500.00   CA
150.00   ST

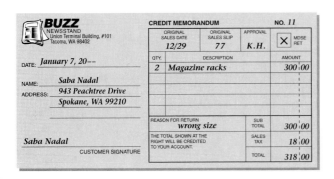

BUZZ NEWSSTAND
Union Terminal Building, #101
Tacoma, WA 98402

CREDIT MEMORANDUM   NO. 11

ORIGINAL SALES DATE	ORIGINAL SALES SLIP	APPROVAL		MDSE RET
12/29	77	K.H.	X	

DATE: January 7, 20--

QTY.	DESCRIPTION	AMOUNT
2	Magazine racks	300 00

NAME: Saba Nadal
ADDRESS: 943 Peachtree Drive
Spokane, WA 99210

REASON FOR RETURN wrong size	SUB TOTAL	300 00
THE TOTAL SHOWN AT THE RIGHT WILL BE CREDITED TO YOUR ACCOUNT.	SALES TAX	18 00
	TOTAL	318 00

Saba Nadal
CUSTOMER SIGNATURE

Jan. 15
Tape 25

2,000.00   BCS
120.00   ST

Problem 14-9   (continued)

BUZZ NEWSSTAND
Union Terminal Building, #101
Tacoma, WA 98402

RECEIPT
No. 77

January 20 20 --

RECEIVED FROM _Janson Lee_ $ _40.00_

Forty and $^{00}/_{100}$ ———————————— DOLLARS

FOR _supplies_

RECEIVED BY _Kathy Harper_

BUZZ NEWSSTAND
Union Terminal Building, #101
Tacoma, WA 98402

RECEIPT
No. 78

January 25 20 --

RECEIVED FROM _Lee Adkins_ $ _636.00_

Six hundred thirty-six and $^{00}/_{100}$ ———————————— DOLLARS

FOR _on account_

RECEIVED BY _Kathy Harper_

BUZZ NEWSSTAND
Union Terminal Building, #101
Tacoma, WA 98402

DATE: _January 31, 20--_   NO. _114_

SOLD TO	Rolling Hills Pharmacies 16 Meadow Lane Tacoma, WA 98402		
CLERK BA	CASH	CHARGE ✓	TERMS 2/10, n/30

QTY.	DESCRIPTION	UNIT PRICE	AMOUNT	
30 cs	magazines	100/cs	3,000	00
		SUBTOTAL	3,000	00
		SALES TAX	180	00
		TOTAL	3,180	00

COPY

Thank You!

Problem 14-9   Recording and Posting Sales and Cash Receipts

GENERAL JOURNAL   PAGE _____

	DATE	DESCRIPTION	POST. REF.	DEBIT	CREDIT	
1						1
2						2
3						3
4						4
5						5
6						6
7						7
8						8
9						9
10						10
11						11
12						12
13						13
14						14
15						15
16						16
17						17
18						18
19						19
20						20
21						21
22						22
23						23
24						24
25						25
26						26
27						27
28						28
29						29
30						30
31						31
32						32
33						33
34						34
35						35
36						36
37						37

Problem 14-9   (continued)

GENERAL LEDGER

ACCOUNT __Cash in Bank_____ ACCOUNT NO. __101__

DATE		DESCRIPTION	POST. REF.	DEBIT	CREDIT	BALANCE	
						DEBIT	CREDIT
20--							
Jan.	1	Balance	✓			5 0 0 0 00	

ACCOUNT __Accounts Receivable_____ ACCOUNT NO. __115__

DATE		DESCRIPTION	POST. REF.	DEBIT	CREDIT	BALANCE	
						DEBIT	CREDIT
20--							
Jan.	1	Balance	✓			6 2 4 8 00	

ACCOUNT __Supplies_____ ACCOUNT NO. __135__

DATE		DESCRIPTION	POST. REF.	DEBIT	CREDIT	BALANCE	
						DEBIT	CREDIT
20--							
Jan.	1	Balance	✓			3 0 0 00	

Problem 14-9   (continued)

ACCOUNT __Sales Tax Payable__   ACCOUNT NO. __215__

DATE		DESCRIPTION	POST. REF.	DEBIT	CREDIT	BALANCE	
						DEBIT	CREDIT
20--							
Jan.	1	Balance	✓				1 3 4 8 00

ACCOUNT __Sales__   ACCOUNT NO. __401__

DATE		DESCRIPTION	POST. REF.	DEBIT	CREDIT	BALANCE	
						DEBIT	CREDIT
20--							
Jan.	1	Balance	✓				1 0 8 0 0 00

ACCOUNT __Sales Discounts__   ACCOUNT NO. __405__

DATE		DESCRIPTION	POST. REF.	DEBIT	CREDIT	BALANCE	
						DEBIT	CREDIT
20--							
Jan.	1	Balance	✓			2 0 0 00	

ACCOUNT __Sales Returns and Allowances__   ACCOUNT NO. __410__

DATE		DESCRIPTION	POST. REF.	DEBIT	CREDIT	BALANCE	
						DEBIT	CREDIT
20--							
Jan.	1	Balance	✓			4 0 0 00	

Problem 14-9 (concluded)

ACCOUNTS RECEIVABLE SUBSIDIARY LEDGER

Name *Adkins, Lee*

Address *720 Dogwood Lane, Seattle, WA 98101*

DATE		DESCRIPTION	POST. REF.	DEBIT	CREDIT	BALANCE
20--						
Jan.	1	Balance	✓			848 00

Name *Java Shops Inc.*

Address *492 Country Place, Auburn, WA 98002*

DATE		DESCRIPTION	POST. REF.	DEBIT	CREDIT	BALANCE
20--						
Jan.	1	Balance	✓			1500 00

Name *Nadal, Saba*

Address *943 Peachtree Drive, Spokane, WA 99210*

DATE		DESCRIPTION	POST. REF.	DEBIT	CREDIT	BALANCE
20--						
Jan.	1	Balance	✓			1600 00

Name *Rolling Hills Pharmacies*

Address *16 Meadow Lane, Tacoma, WA 98402*

DATE		DESCRIPTION	POST. REF.	DEBIT	CREDIT	BALANCE
20--						
Jan.	1	Balance	✓			2300 00

Analyze: _____

_____

CHAPTER 14   Accounting for Sales and Cash Receipts

Self-Test

Part A   True or False

Directions: *Circle the letter* T *in the Answer column if the statement is true; circle the letter* F *if the statement is false.*

Answer

T   F   **1.** Merchandising businesses sell only on a cash-and-carry basis.

T   F   **2.** Businesses are required to act as agents for local and state governments in the collection of taxes.

T   F   **3.** Customer accounts are listed in alphabetical order in the accounts receivable subsidiary ledger.

T   F   **4.** Bankcard sales are recorded like cash sales because a business expects to receive its cash within a few days of the deposit.

T   F   **5.** In most states, sales made to school districts and other governmental agencies are taxable.

T   F   **6.** Prenumbered sales slips help businesses keep track of all sales made on account.

T   F   **7.** Sales discounts increases the Sales account.

T   F   **8.** A bank card holder is a charge customer of the business from whom the purchase is being made.

T   F   **9.** "2/10, n/30" means that customers may deduct 2% of the cost of the merchandise if they pay within 10 days. Otherwise they must pay the full amount within 30 days.

T   F   **10.** Cash discounts increase the amount to be received from charge customers.

Part B   Multiple Choice

Directions: *Only one of the choices given with each of the following state-*
ments is correct. Write the letter of the correct answer in the
Answer column.

Answer

_____   **1.** Sales Returns and Allowances is classified as a
(A) revenue account.
(B) owner's equity account.
(C) contra revenue account.
(D) none of the above.

_____   **2.** If merchandise is sold for $417.80 and the sales tax rate is
4%, the amount of the sales tax is
(A) $434.5l.
(B) $16.17.
(C) $20.89.
(D) none of the above.

_____   **3.** Sales Tax Payable is classified as a(n)
(A) asset account.
(B) liability account.
(C) owner's equity account.
(D) revenue account.

_____   **4.** If merchandise is sold for $325.60 and the sales tax rate is
5%, the amount to be collected from a charge customer is
(A) $309.32.
(B) $341.88.
(C) $325.60.
(D) $331.88.

_____   **5.** If the date of an invoice is May 14, the credit terms are
2/10, n/30, and the invoice was received on May 16, the
last date the discount may be taken is
(A) May 26.
(B) June 12.
(C) May 24.
(D) May 14.

CHAPTER 15
Accounting for Purchases and Cash Payments

Study Plan

Check Your Understanding

Section 1   *Read Section 1 on pages 388–391 and complete the following exercises on page 392.*
❑ Thinking Critically
❑ Computing in the Business World
❑ Problem 15-1   *Analyzing a Purchase Order*

Section 2   *Read Section 2 on pages 393–399 and complete the following exercises on page 400.*
❑ Thinking Critically
❑ Communicating Accounting
❑ Problem 15-2   *Recording Purchases Transactions*
❑ Problem 15-3   *Analyzing a Source Document*

Section 3   *Read Section 3 on pages 402–407 and complete the following exercises on page 408.*
❑ Thinking Critically
❑ Analyzing Accounting
❑ Problem 15-4   *Recording Cash Payment Transactions*

Summary   *Review the Chapter 15 Summary on page 409 in your textbook.*
❑ Key Concepts

Review and Activities   *Complete the following questions and exercises on pages 410–411 in your textbook.*
❑ Using Key Terms
❑ Understanding Accounting Concepts and Procedures
❑ Case Study
❑ Conducting an Audit with Alex
❑ Internet Connection
❑ Workplace Skills

Computerized Accounting   *Read the Computerized Accounting information on page 412 in your textbook.*
❑ *Making the Transition from a Manual to a Computerized System*
❑ *Preparing the Payroll in Peachtree*

Problems   *Complete the following end-of-chapter problems for Chapter 15.*
❑ Problem 15-5   *Determining Due Dates and Discount Amounts*
❑ Problem 15-6   *Analyzing Purchases and Cash Payments*
❑ Problem 15-7   *Recording Purchases Transactions*
❑ Problem 15-8   *Recording Cash Payment Transactions*
❑ Problem 15-9   *Recording Purchases and Cash Payment Transactions*

Challenge Problem   ❑ Problem 15-10   *Recording and Posting Purchases and Cash Payment Transactions*

Chapter Reviews and Working Papers   *Complete the following exercises for Chapter 15 in your Chapter Reviews and Working Papers.*
❑ Chapter Review
❑ Self-Test

CHAPTER 15 REVIEW

Accounting for Purchases and Cash Payments

Part 1 Accounting Vocabulary (19 points)

Total Points	41
Student's Score	

Directions: *Using terms from the following list, complete the sentences below. Write the letter of the term you have chosen in the space provided.*

A. accounts payable subsidiary ledger	**G.** FOB destination	**N.** purchase requisition
B. bankcard fee	**H.** FOB shipping point	**O.** Purchases account
C. cost of merchandise	**I.** invoice	**P.** purchases allowance
D. debit memorandum	**J.** packing slip	**Q.** purchases discount
E. discount period	**K.** premium	**R.** purchases return
F. due date	**L.** processing stamp	**S.** tickler file
	M. purchase order	**T.** Transportation In account

_____C_____ **0.** The _____ is the actual cost to the business of the merchandise to be sold to customers.

_____ **1.** A(n) _____ contains a folder for each day of the month.

_____ **2.** A(n) _____ is the period of time within which an invoice must be paid if a discount is to be taken.

_____ **3.** A(n) _____ is a written offer to a supplier to buy certain items.

_____ **4.** The _____ is a ledger that contains accounts for all creditors and the amount owed to each.

_____ **5.** A(n) _____ is a stamp placed on an invoice that outlines a set of steps to be followed in processing the invoice for payment.

_____ **6.** The _____ is the account used to record the cost of new merchandise.

_____ **7.** A written request that a certain item or items be ordered is a(n) _____.

_____ **8.** The _____ is the date by which an invoice must be paid.

_____ **9.** A bill that lists the credit terms and the quantity, description, unit price, and total cost of the items shipped to the buyer is a(n) _____.

_____ **10.** A form that lists the items included in a shipment is a(n) _____.

_____ **11.** A(n) _____ is a cash discount offered by suppliers for prompt payment.

_____ **12.** A(n) _____ is charged by a bank for handling the bankcard sales slips deposited by a business; it is usually calculated as a percentage of the total bankcard sales.

_____ **13.** _____ means that the supplier pays the shipping cost to the buyer's destination or location.

_____ **14.** The _____ is the amount paid for insurance.

_____ **15.** The cost of merchandise account that is used to record shipping charges on goods is the _____.

_____ **16.** When a business returns merchandise bought on account to the supplier for full credit, a(n) _____ occurs.

_____ **17.** _____ means that the buyer pays the shipping charge from the supplier's place of business.

_____ **18.** A price reduction received by a business for unsatisfactory merchandise kept is a(n) _____.

_____ **19.** The form a business uses to notify its supplier of a return or allowance is called a(n) _____.

Part 2   Analyzing Purchases and Cash Payment Transactions (10 points)

Directions: _Read each of the following statements to determine whether the statement is true or false. Write your answer in the space provided._

<u> True </u>   **0.** The Purchases account is a temporary equity account.

_____   **1.** The Purchases account is used to record the sale of merchandise on account.

_____   **2.** In a manual accounting system, the creditors' accounts in the accounts payable subsidiary ledger are listed in alphabetical order.

_____   **3.** Invoices are placed in a tickler file according to their invoice numbers.

_____   **4.** The discount period is calculated from the day the invoice was received.

_____   **5.** The source document for recording the purchase of merchandise on account is an invoice.

_____   **6.** Prepaid Insurance is classified as an asset account.

_____   **7.** If the invoice states FOB shipping point, it is the buyer's responsibility to pay the shipping charges from the seller's location.

_____   **8.** Bank charges and bankcard fees are paid by check.

_____   **9.** When a diagonal line is placed in the Posting Reference column, this indicates that two postings are to be made.

_____   **10.** Whether merchandise is purchased for cash or credit, the Purchases account is always debited.

Part 3   Analyzing Purchases and Cash Payment Transactions (12 points)

Directions: _Analyze the transactions below. Use the account number to identify the accounts to be debited or credited._

101 Cash in Bank	**505** Transportation In	**601** Advertising Expense
110 Prepaid Insurance	**510** Purchases Discounts	**605** Bankcard Fees Expense
215 Accounts Payable/Creditor	**515** Purchases Returns	**610** Miscellaneous Expense
501 Purchases	and Allowances	

Debit	**Credit**	
_601_	_101_	**0.** Bought an ad in the local newspaper, paying cash.
_____	_____	**1.** Purchased merchandise on account.
_____	_____	**2.** Issued a check to Tiger's Trucking Company for delivery of merchandise purchased from Gary Wholesalers.
_____	_____	**3.** Purchased merchandise for cash.
_____	_____	**4.** Issued a check to a creditor in payment of an invoice less a cash discount.
_____	_____	**5.** Wrote a check in payment of the annual insurance premium for the business.
_____	_____	**6.** Issued a debit memo to a creditor for returned merchandise.

Working Papers *for Section Problems*

Problem 15-1   Analyzing a Purchase Order

1. _____

2. _____

3. _____

4. _____

5. _____

6. _____

7. _____

8. _____

9. _____

10. _____

Problem 15-2   Recording Purchases Transactions

GENERAL JOURNAL   PAGE _____

	DATE	DESCRIPTION	POST. REF.	DEBIT	CREDIT	
1						1
2						2
3						3
4						4
5						5
6						6
7						7
8						8
9						9
10						10
11						11
12						12

Problem 15-3   Analyzing a Source Document

GENERAL JOURNAL   PAGE _____

	DATE	DESCRIPTION	POST. REF.	DEBIT	CREDIT	
1						1
2						2
3						3
4						4
5						5
6						6
7						7
8						8
9						9
10						10
11						11
12						12

Problem 15-4 Recording Cash Payment Transactions

GENERAL JOURNAL

PAGE _____

	DATE	DESCRIPTION	POST. REF.	DEBIT	CREDIT	
1						1
2						2
3						3
4						4
5						5
6						6
7						7
8						8
9						9
10						10
11						11
12						12

Computerized Accounting Using Peachtree

Software Objectives

When you have completed this chapter, you will be able to use Peachtree to:

1. Record purchases on account transactions using the **Purchases/Receive Inventory** option.
2. Enter cash payments using the **Payments** option.
3. Record debit memorandums.
4. Print a Purchase Journal report, Cash Disbursements Journal report, and a Vendor Ledgers report.
5. Print a General Ledger report.

Problem 15-6   Analyzing Purchases and Cash Payments

Review the transactions listed in your textbook for InBeat CD Shop. As you will learn, the process for recording the purchases and cash payments transactions using the Peachtree accounting software is different than the method you learned in your text. Instead of recording these transactions in a general journal, you will record purchases on account using the **Purchases/Receive Inventory** option and process cash payments with the **Payments** option.

INSTRUCTIONS

Beginning a Session

> **Step 1** Select the problem set: InBeat (Prob. 15-6).
> **Step 2** Rename the company by adding your initials, e.g., InBeat (Prob. 15-6: XXX).
> **Step 3** Set the system date to March 31, 2004.

Completing the Accounting Problem

The instructions in this section explain how to enter purchases on account, debit memorandums, and cash payments using the Peachtree software. To simplify the data entry process, you will batch similar transactions by type and then enter them using the appropriate software task option.

Entering Purchases on Account

> **Step 4** Review the transactions for InBeat CD Shop and identify the purchases on account.
> **Step 5** Enter the purchase on account transaction for March 2.
>
> > ***March 2, Purchased merchandise on account from NightVision and Company, $2,000, Invoice NV-20, terms 2/10, n/30.***
> >
> > *To enter the purchase on account:*
> >
> > - Choose **Purchases/Receive Inventory** from the *Tasks* menu to display the Purchases/Receive Inventory window.
> > - Type **NIG** (the account code for NightVision and Company) in the *Vendor ID* field.
> >
> >   If you do not know a vendor account code, click the 🔍 button, highlight the vendor name and click the **OK** button.

> **DO YOU HAVE A QUESTION**
>
> **Q.** *Why can't you use the Peachtree General Journal Entry option to record purchases on account and cash payments to vendors?*
>
> **A.** Unlike a manual general journal, the Peachtree software does not provide a way for you to identify the corresponding **Account Payable** subsidiary ledger account in the general journal. When you use the **Purchases/Receive Inventory** option, you must enter a Vendor ID. Peachtree uses this information to update both the subsidiary ledger account and the **Accounts Payable** balance.

> **TIP:** As a shortcut, remember that you can press **SHIFT+?** when you are in a Lookup field to display a list of choices.

- Type **NV-20** for the invoice number in the *Invoice #* field.
- Type **3/2/04** to record the transaction date in the *Date* field. Make sure that Peachtree shows 2004 for the year. If not, change the system date.
- Move to the *Description* field by pressing **ENTER** or by clicking in the field.

   You can skip over the *Ship To, Ship Via,* and *A/P Account* fields. Some of these fields, such as the *Ship To* field, are optional. You do not need to complete these fields when you are entering transactions from your text, but a company using Peachtree to keep its books might need to enter this information. For other fields, such as the *Terms* field, default information is already recorded in the field. You do not need to change this field unless different terms apply.

- Type **Purchased merchandise on account** for the description.
- Skip the *GL Account* field. The **Purchases** account number already appears in this field.
- Type **2000.00** in the *Amount* field to record the purchase amount.
- Proof the information you just recorded. Check all of the information you entered. If you notice a mistake, move to that field and make the correction. Compare the information on your screen to the completed transaction shown in Figure 15-6A.

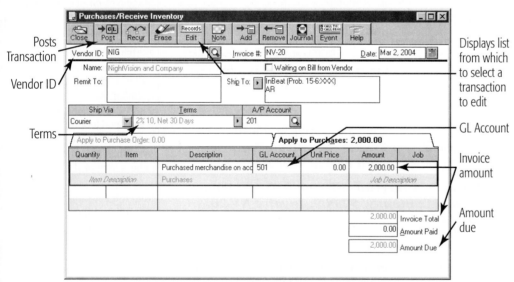

Figure 15-6A *Completed Purchases Transaction (March 2, 2004)*

- Click [Journal] to display the Accounting Behind the Screens window.

   Use the information in this window to check your work again. (See Figure 15-6B.)

The Accounting Behind the Screens window shows you the accounts and the debit/credit amounts that Peachtree will record for this transaction. Although Peachtree does not show the **Accounts Payable** subsidiary ledger information, it will automatically update the vendor account balance, too. As you can see, Peachtree uses the data you entered to make a transaction "behind the screens" that is equivalent to the transactions you learned about in your text.

For the purchase on account transaction, the window should show the following: **Purchases** ($2,000.00 DR) and **Accounts Payable** ($2,000.00 CR).

- Click ⊗ Cancel to close the Accounting Behind the Screens window.

- Click ⊕GL Post to post the transaction.

Notes

Viewing the Accounting Behind the Screens window is not required each time you enter a transaction. This information, however, is useful to understand how Peachtree records a transaction such as a purchase on account.

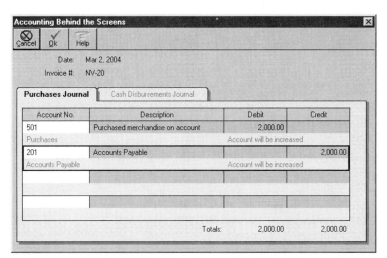

Figure 15-6B *Accounting Behind the Screens (Purchases/Receive Inventory)*

Step 6   Enter the two remaining purchases on account transactions for the month: March 7 and March 16.

Note: For the March 7 transaction, InBeat CD Shop bought supplies (not merchandise) on account. Enter **Purchased supplies on account** for the description, and make sure that the *GL Account* field shows **135 Supplies**, not **501 Purchases**. The default GL account number is set up in the vendor's record.

Recording Debit Memorandums/Purchases Returns and Allowances

Step 7   Review the transactions shown in your textbook and identify those where the company issued a debit memorandum.

Step 8   Record the debit memorandum issued on March 18.

March 18, Issued Debit Memorandum 25 for $100 to NightVision and Company for the return of merchandise.

Peachtree Guide

To enter the debit memorandum:

- Choose **Purchases/Receive Inventory** from the *Tasks* menu to display the Purchases/Receive Inventory window if it is not already on your screen.
- Type **NIG** (the account code for NightVision and Company) in the *Vendor ID* field.
- Type **DM25** for the debit memo number in the *Invoice #* field.
- Type **3/18** to record the transaction date in the *Date* field.
- Move to the *Description* field and enter **Merchandise return** as the description.
- Type **515** (the **Purchases Returns and Allowances** account number) in the *GL Account* field.

For Peachtree to apply the credit to the appropriate general ledger account, you must enter the **Purchases Returns and Allowances** account number in the *GL Account* field. If you do not enter this information, the program will apply the debit memo to purchases instead of the contra-purchases account.

Notes

Peachtree uses "credit memo" instead of "debit memo" in reference to a transaction involving a purchase return or allowance.

TIP: If the *GL Account* field does not appear, choose **Global** from the **Options** menu. Change the setting to show the general ledger accounts for Accounts Payable. You will have to close the Purchases/Receive Inventory window and then choose this option again for the new setting to take effect.

- Type **-100.00** in the *Amount* field to record the amount.

Notes

To record a debit memo, you must enter a negative amount in the Amount field.

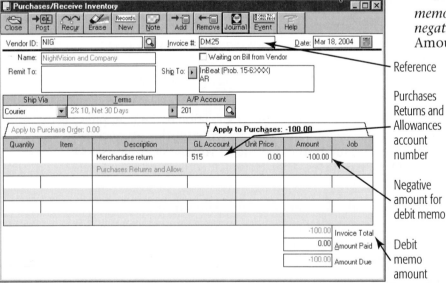

Figure 15-6C *Completed Purchases Return Transaction (March 18, Debit Memo 25)*

- Click [Post] to post the debit memorandum.
- Click [Close] to close the Purchases/Receive Inventory window.

To apply a debit memo to an invoice:
- Choose **Payments** from the *Tasks* menu.
- Click **OK** to select **Cash in Bank** as the default cash account, if prompted.
- Type **NIG** as the vendor ID for NightVision and Company.
- Enter **DM25** in the *Check Number* field.
- Type **3/18/04** in the *Date* field.
- Type **Debit Memo 25** in the *Memo* field.
- Click the **Pay** box for the debit memo shown in the Apply to Invoices tab located in the lower portion of the window. Then, if necessary, change the discount amount to **0.00**.
- Find the invoice to which you want to apply the credit memo— Invoice NV-45. Click the **Pay** box next to this invoice and then change the discount amount to **0.00** and the amount paid to **100.00**.

TIP: If a discount amount appears when you apply a debit memo, move to the *Discount* field and delete the amount shown.

Notes

*If the debit memo is the same as the invoice amount, just click the **Pay** button. You do not have to change the amount. If the debit memo is for only a portion of the total invoice, you must specify the amount to apply to the invoice.*

After you mark both the debit memo and the invoice, the *Check Amount* field should show 0.00 since no cash was actually exchanged. Applying the debit memo updates the original invoice in the vendor's record.

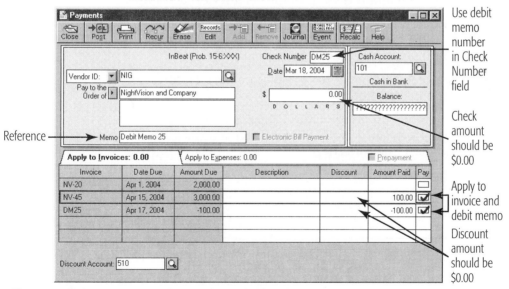

Figure 15-6D *Payments Window with Applied Debit Memo (March 18, Debit Memo 25)*

- Click [Post] to post the transaction.
- Click [Close] to close the Payments window.

      Chapter 15 ■ 399

Recording Cash Payments

Step 9 Review the transactions and identify the cash payment transactions for InBeat CD Shop. Notice that there are two types of payments—payments on account and other cash payments. You will learn how to enter both types.

Step 10 Enter the March 6 cash payment.

> ***March 6, Issued Check 250 for $85 to Penn Trucking Company for delivering merchandise from NightVision and Company.***

To enter a cash payment:

- Choose **Payments** from the *Tasks* menu.
- Skip the *Vendor ID* field and enter **Penn Trucking Company** in the *Pay to the Order of* field.

  A vendor account has not been set up for this company. Therefore, you must manually enter the payee information instead of providing a vendor ID.

- Type **250** in the *Check Number* field.
- Type **3/6** in the *Date* field.
- Type **Delivery Fee** in the *Memo* field.
- Do not change the cash account. This field should already be set to **101 Cash in Bank**.

  Peachtree lets you change the cash account if a company has more than one checking account—regular checking and payroll checking accounts, for example. For the problems in your textbook, there is only one bank account and it is setup as the default cash account.

- In the Apply to Expense tab, move to the first detail line. Type **Delivery fee** for the description, select **505 Transportation In** for the GL account, and enter **85.00** in the *Amount* field.

  For a cash payment, you do not have to include the quantity, item, unit price and job information.

- Proof the information you just recorded. The total check amount should be $85.00. (See Figure 15-6E.) If you notice a mistake, move to that field and make the correction.

- Click [→GL Post] to post the transaction.

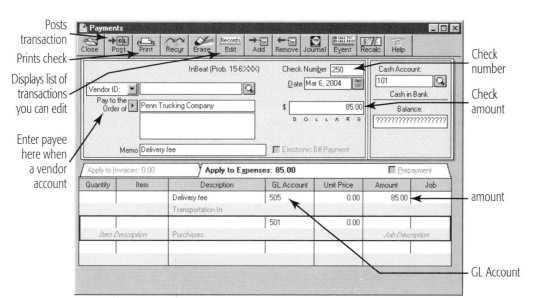

Figure 15-6E *Completed Cash Payment (March 6, Check 250)*

Step 11 Enter the cash payment on account for March 12.

***March 12, Issued Check 251 for $1,960 to NightVision and
Company in payment of invoice NV-20 for $2000 less a cash
discount of $40.***

To enter a cash payment on account:

- Choose **Payments** from the *Tasks* menu.
- Type **NIG** (the vendor code for NightVision and Company) in the
  Vendor ID field, or click 🔍 and select the code from the Lookup list.
- Type **251** in the *Check Number* field.
- Type **3/12** for the transaction date in the *Date* field.
- Type **Invoice NV-20** in the *Memo* field.
- In the Apply to Invoice tab, identify the invoice to which the cash
  payment should be applied. Click the **Pay** box next to that invoice
  to indicate that you are paying it. After you mark the invoice, the
  Check Amount field should show $1,960.00—the invoice amount
  ($2,000) less the discount ($40).
- Proof the information you just recorded. If you notice a mistake, move to that field and make the correction. Compare
  the information on your screen to the completed transaction
  shown in Figure 15-6F.
- Click [Post] to post the transaction.

🌸**Notes**

If the Discount
and Amount Paid *fields
are not correct, you can
manually change them.*

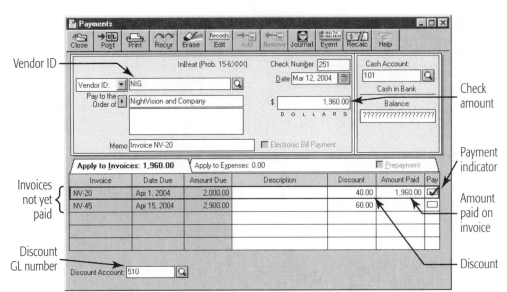

Vendor ID

Invoices not yet paid

Discount GL number

Check amount

Payment indicator

Amount paid on invoice

Discount

Figure 15-6F *Completed Cash Payment on Account Transaction (March 12, Check 251)*

Step 12   Record the remaining cash payment transactions: March 15, March 20, and March 22.

TIP: For payments not on account, be sure to record the correct GL account number.

Preparing Reports

Step 13   Print the Purchases Journal report.

To print a Purchases Journal report:

- Choose **Accounts Payable** from the **_Reports_** menu to display the Select a Report window.
- Select Purchases Journal in the report list.
- Click `Screen` and then click **OK** to display the report.
- Click `Print` to print the report.
- Click `Close` to close the report window.

Step 14   Print the Cash Disbursements Journal report.
Step 15   Print a Vendor Ledgers report.
Step 16   Proof the information shown on the reports. If there are any corrections needed, choose the corresponding task option—**Purchases/Receive Inventory** or **Payments**. Click `Records Edit` and select the transaction to edit. Make the necessary changes and post the transaction to record your work.

Analyzing Your Work

Step 17   Choose **General Ledger** from the *Reports* menu to display the Select a Report window.

Step 18   Double-click the General Ledger report title to display the report.

Step 19   Locate the **Purchases** account on the General Ledger report. What is the balance of this account?

Ending the Session

Step 20   Click the **Close Problem** button in the Glencoe Smart Guide window.

Continuing a Problem from a Previous Session

- If you were previously directed to save your work on the network, select the problem from the scrolling menu and click **OK.** The system will retrieve your files from your last session.

- If you were previously directed to save your work on a floppy disk, insert the floppy, select the corresponding problem from the scrolling menu, and click **OK.** The system will retrieve your files from the floppy disk.

Mastering Peachtree

Can you change the credit terms offered by a specific vendor? Explain your answer on a separate sheet of paper.

Problem 15-7   Recording Purchases Transactions

INSTRUCTIONS

Beginning a Session

Step 1   Select the problem set: Shutterbug Cameras (Prob. 15-7).

Step 2   Rename the company and set the system date to March 31, 2004.

Completing the Accounting Problem

Step 3   Review the transactions listed in your textbook.

TIP: Refer to the instructions for Problem 15-6 if you need help entering the transactions for this problem.

Step 4   Record the purchases on accounts.

Step 5   Enter the debit memorandums.

When you apply a credit memo to a specific invoice and the vendor offers discount, you will most likely have to change the amounts that automatically appear. Set the discount amounts to $0.00 after you mark the debit memo and invoice as "paid." Also, if a debit memo is for an amount less than the original invoice amount, you will have to change the default amount paid to reflect the amount of the debit.

TIP: Do not use the **Purchases Returns and Allowances** account when you record a debit memo for an asset account such as supplies or store equipment.

DO YOU HAVE A QUESTION

Q. *Why do you have to apply a debit memo to a specific invoice?*

A. Suppose a company purchases merchandise on account for $200 and then receives a $50 credit. When you enter the $50 credit, you record it as a "negative" invoice amount. The vendor's account correctly shows a balance of $150, but there are now two outstanding invoices—one for $200 and another for -$50. When you apply the credit, you mark the -$50 debit memo as paid and then record a $50 cash payment against the original invoice. Now there is only one outstanding invoice for $150 and the vendor's account balance remains at $150 because the net cash payment for this part of the transaction was $0.

Peachtree Guide

Step 6 Print a Purchases Journal report and a Cash Disbursements Journal report.

Step 7 Proof your work. Update the transactions and print revised reports if you identify any errors.

Step 8 Answer the Analyze question.

Checking Your Work and Ending the Session

Step 9 Click the **Close Problem** button in the Glencoe Smart Guide window.

Step 10 If your teacher has asked you to check your solution, click *Check my answer to this problem*. Review, print, and close the report.

Step 11 Click the **Close Problem** button and select the appropriate save option.

Mastering Peachtree

Peachtree displays a default General Ledger account on the Purchases/Receive Inventory data entry form when you record a new purchase. How do you set this information? Why might you want to specify a GL account other than **Purchases** for a vendor? Record your answer on a separate sheet of paper.

Problem 15-8   Recording Cash Payment Transactions

INSTRUCTIONS

Beginning a Session

Step 1 Select the problem set: Cycle Tech Bicycles (Prob. 15-8).

Step 2 Rename the company and set the system date to March 31, 2004.

Completing the Accounting Problem

Step 3 Review the transactions listed in your textbook.

TIP: Refer to the instructions for Problem 15-6 if you need help entering the transactions for this problem.

Step 4 Record the cash payments.

Use the **Payments** option to record all of the transactions except for the March 20 transaction ($275 bank card fees). Use the **General Journal** option to record this transaction because the fees are automatically withdrawn from the company's account.

For the March 28 and March 31 transactions, you must enter a multi-part transaction. For example, Cycle Tech purchased supplies and store equipment from Superior Store Equipment, Inc. on March 28. As you can see in Figure 15-8A, the purchase is applied to two different GL accounts—**140 Store Equipment** and **130 Supplies**.

TIP: If necessary, manually enter a cash discount if Peachtree does not automatically fill in the correct amount.

DO YOU HAVE A QUESTION

Q. *Does Peachtree let you change a check amount if, for example, you forget to record a discount?*

A. Yes, you can easily change a check amount for a transaction. Choose the **Payments** option and click the **Edit Records** button. Select a transaction, make the necessary changes, and post the updated transaction.

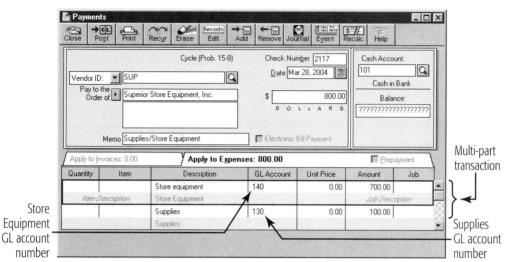

Figure 15-8A *Payment Applied to Different GL Accounts (March 28)*

Step 5   Print a Cash Disbursements Journal and a General Journal report.

Step 6   Proof your work. Update the transactions and print revised reports if you identify any errors.

Step 7   Answer the Analyze question.

Ending the Session

Step 8   Click the **Close Problem** button in the Glencoe Smart Guide window.

Problem 15-9   Recording Purchases and Cash Payment Transactions

INSTRUCTIONS

Beginning a Session

Step 1   Select the problem set: River's Edge Canoe & Kayak (Prob. 15-9).

Step 2   Rename the company and set the system date to March 31, 2004.

Completing the Accounting Problem

Step 3   Review the transactions listed in your textbook and group them by type—purchases on account, debit memorandums, and cash payments.

Step 4   Record the purchases on account.

Step 5   Record the debit memorandums.

Step 6   Record the cash payments.

Step 7   Print a Purchases Journal and a Cash Disbursements Journal report.

Step 8   Proof your work. Update the transactions and print revised reports if you identify any errors.

Step 9   Answer the Analyze question.

Checking Your Work and Ending the Session

Step 10   Click the **Close Problem** button in the Glencoe Smart Guide window.

Step 11   If your teacher has asked you to check your solution, click *Check my answer to this problem*. Review, print, and close the report.

Step 12   Click the **Close Problem** button and select the appropriate save option.

DO YOU HAVE A QUESTION

Q. *Which GL account should you use to record a debit memo transaction for damaged supplies?*

A. When you record a debit memo for damaged supplies, use the **Supplies** account, not the **Purchases Returns and Allowances** account. Only use the **Purchases Returns and Allowances** account when you record a debit memo for damaged merchandise.

Problem 15-10 Recording and Posting Purchases and Cash Payment Transactions

INSTRUCTIONS

Beginning a Session

Step 1 Select the problem set: Buzz Newsstand (Prob. 15-10).
Step 2 Rename the company and set the system date to March 31, 2004.

Completing the Accounting Problem

Step 3 Review the transactions listed in your textbook and group them by type—purchases on account, debit memorandums, and cash payments.
Step 4 Record the transactions.
Step 5 Print the following reports: Purchases Journal, Cash Disbursements Journal, Vendor Ledgers, and General Ledger.
Step 6 Proof your work. Update the transactions and print revised reports if you identify any errors.
Step 7 Answer the Analyze question.

Ending the Session

Step 8 Click the **Close Problem** button in the Glencoe Smart Guide window.

> **Notes**
>
> *Remember that Peachtree automatically posts transactions to the general ledger and subsidiary ledger accounts.*

===================== **FAQs** =====================

What steps are required to correct a purchase invoice with the wrong vendor ID code or amount?

If you enter the wrong information for a purchase invoice, you can correct it even if you have already posted the transaction. Choose the **Purchases/Receive Inventory** option and click the **Edit Records** button. Select the invoice you want to change. When the invoice appears in the data entry window, make the necessary corrections and then post the updated transaction.

What steps are required to correct a cash payment entry?

You can change any information on a cash payment unless you have closed the current period. To make a change, choose the **Payments** option. Click the **Edit Records** button and select the payment you want to update. Make the changes and post the corrected transaction. Peachtree automatically applies the corrections.

Why can't you use the Peachtree General Journal Entry option to record purchases on account and cash payments to vendors?

Unlike a manual general journal, the Peachtree software does not provide a way for you to identify the corresponding **Accounts Payable** subsidiary ledger account in the general journal. When you use the **Purchases/Receive Inventory** option, you must enter a Vendor ID. Peachtree uses this information to update both the subsidiary ledger account and the **Accounts Payable** balance.

Which GL account should you use to record a debit memo transaction for damaged supplies?

When you record a debit memo for damaged supplies, use the **Supplies** account, not the **Purchases Returns and Allowances** account (used when you record a debit memo for damaged merchandise).

Spreadsheet Guide

Computerized Accounting Using Spreadsheets

Problem 15-5   Determining Due Dates and Discount Amounts

Completing the Spreadsheet

Step 1   Read the instructions for Problem 15-5 in your textbook. This problem involves determining the due date, discount amount, and amount to be paid for six invoices.

Step 2   Open the Glencoe Accounting: Electronic Learning Center software.

Step 3   From the Program Menu, click on the **Peachtree Accounting Software and Spreadsheet Applications** icon.

Step 4   Log onto the Management System by typing your user name and password.

Step 5   Under the Chapter Problems tab, select the template: PR15-5a.xls. The template should look like the one shown below.

```
PROBLEM 15-5
DETERMINING DUE DATES AND DISCOUNT AMOUNTS

(name)
(date)

   Invoice        Invoice        Credit         Invoice        Due          Discount       Amount to
   Number         Date           Terms          Amount         Date         Amount         be Paid
                                                                            $0.00          $0.00
                                                                            $0.00          $0.00
                                                                            $0.00          $0.00
                                                                            $0.00          $0.00
                                                                            $0.00          $0.00
                                                                            $0.00          $0.00

TOTAL DISCOUNTS                                                             $0.00
```

Step 6   Key your name and today's date in the cells containing the *(name)* and *(date)* placeholders.

Step 7   Enter the invoice number, invoice date, credit terms, and invoice amount for the first invoice in the appropriate cells of the spreadsheet template. The spreadsheet template will automatically calculate the due date, discount amount, and amount to be paid for the first invoice.

TIP: Enter dates as month/day in the spreadsheet template. For example, enter March 5 as **3/5**. The spreadsheet will automatically convert this to a date format.

Step 8   Check your work by checking the due date, discount amount, and amount to be paid against your textbook, since the first invoice has been completed for you.

Step 9   Continue to enter the invoice number, invoice date, credit terms, and invoice amount for the remaining invoices. The due date, discount amount, and amount to be paid will be automatically calculated for each invoice.

TIP: Be careful when you enter the last invoice number: **00985**. Many spreadsheet programs will not recognize the two zeroes at the beginning of the number and will show it in the template as 985. To show the two zeroes at the beginning of the number, you must enter an apostrophe before the number: **'00985**. The apostrophe indicates that the number should be shown as a "label," meaning that all the digits will show including the beginning zeroes.

Step 10 Save the spreadsheet using the **Save** option from the _File_ menu. You should accept the default location for the save as this is handled by the management system.

Step 11 Print the completed spreadsheet.

Step 12 Exit the spreadsheet program.

Step 13 In the Close Options box, select the location where you would like to save your work.

Step 14 Answer the Analyze question from your textbook for this problem.

What-If Analysis

Suppose the invoice amount for Invoice #34120 were $2,001.03. What would the discount be? What would the amount to be paid be?

_____

_____

Working Papers *for End-of-Chapter Problems*

Problem 15-5   Determining Due Dates and Discount Amounts

Invoice Number	Invoice Date	Credit Terms	Invoice Amount	Due Date	Discount Amount	Amount to be Paid
24574	Mar. 5	2/10, n/30	$ 3,000.00	Mar. 15	$ 60.00	$ 2,940.00
530992	Mar. 7	3/10, n/30	$5,550.00			
211145	Mar. 12	2/15, n/60	$ 729.95			
45679	Mar. 16	n/45	$ 345.67			
34120	Mar. 23	2/10, n/30	$1,526.50			
00985	Mar. 27	n/30	$ 700.00			

Analyze: _____

_____

Problem 15-6   Analyzing Purchases and Cash Payments

Cash in Bank	*Supplies*	*Prepaid Insurance*

Accounts Payable	*Purchases*	*Transportation In*

Purchases Discounts	*Purchases Returns and Allowances*

ACCOUNTS PAYABLE SUBSIDIARY LEDGER

NightVision & Company	*Temple Store Supply*

Analyze: _____

_____

Problem 15-7 Recording Purchases Transactions

GENERAL JOURNAL   PAGE _____

	DATE		DESCRIPTION	POST. REF.	DEBIT	CREDIT	
1							1
2							2
3							3
4							4
5							5
6							6
7							7
8							8
9							9
10							10
11							11
12							12
13							13
14							14
15							15
16							16
17							17
18							18
19							19
20							20
21							21
22							22
23							23
24							24
25							25
26							26
27							27
28							28
29							29
30							30
31							31
32							32
33							33
34							34
35							35

Analyze: _____

Problem 15-8 Recording Cash Payment Transactions

GENERAL JOURNAL

PAGE _____

	DATE	DESCRIPTION	POST. REF.	DEBIT	CREDIT	
1						1
2						2
3						3
4						4
5						5
6						6
7						7
8						8
9						9
10						10
11						11
12						12
13						13
14						14
15						15
16						16
17						17
18						18
19						19
20						20
21						21
22						22
23						23
24						24
25						25
26						26
27						27
28						28
29						29
30						30
31						31
32						32
33						33
34						34
35						35

Analyze: _____

_____

Problem 15-9   Recording Purchases and Cash Payment Transactions

GENERAL JOURNAL   PAGE _____

	DATE	DESCRIPTION	POST. REF.	DEBIT	CREDIT	
1						1
2						2
3						3
4						4
5						5
6						6
7						7
8						8
9						9
10						10
11						11
12						12
13						13
14						14
15						15
16						16
17						17
18						18
19						19
20						20
21						21
22						22
23						23
24						24
25						25
26						26
27						27
28						28
29						29
30						30
31						31
32						32
33						33
34						34
35						35

Analyze: _____

_____

Problem 15-10   Source Documents

Instructions: *Use the following source documents to record the transactions for this problem.*

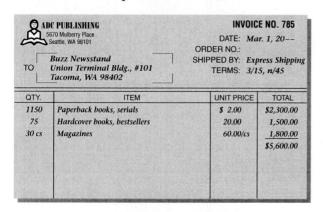

ADC PUBLISHING
5670 Mulberry Place
Seattle, WA 98101

INVOICE NO. 785

DATE: *Mar. 1, 20--*
ORDER NO.:
SHIPPED BY: *Express Shipping*
TERMS: *3/15, n/45*

TO   *Buzz Newsstand*
Union Terminal Bldg., #101
Tacoma, WA 98402

QTY.	ITEM	UNIT PRICE	TOTAL
1150	Paperback books, serials	$ 2.00	$2,300.00
75	Hardcover books, bestsellers	20.00	1,500.00
30 cs	Magazines	60.00/cs	1,800.00
			$5,600.00

$ 588.00   No. 1402
Date *March 7*   20--
To *Delta Press*
For *on account*

	Dollars	Cents
Balance brought forward	10,990	00
Add deposits		
Total	10,990	00
Less this check	588	00
Balance carried forward	10,402	00

Delta Press
One Triangle Park
Vancouver, WA 98661

INVOICE NO. DP166

DATE: *Feb. 29, 20--*
ORDER NO.:
SHIPPED BY: *Rizzo's Trucking Co.*
TERMS: *2/10, n/30*

TO   *Buzz Newsstand*
Union Terminal Bldg., #101
Tacoma, WA 98402

QTY.	ITEM	UNIT PRICE	TOTAL
30	Hardcover books	$20.00	$ 600.00

Date to be paid: 3/17
Discount: $12.00
Amount to be paid: $588.00
Check No.: 1402
REC'D FEB 29

$ 735.00   No. 1400
Date *March 3*   20--
To *Pine Forest Publications*
For *on account*

	Dollars	Cents
Balance brought forward	12,000	00
Add deposits		
Total	12,000	00
Less this check	735	00
Balance carried forward	11,265	00

Pine Forest Publications
103 Mt. Thor Road
Spokane, WA 99210

INVOICE NO. PFP98

DATE: *Feb. 25, 20--*
ORDER NO.:
SHIPPED BY: *Rizzo's Trucking Co.*
TERMS: *2/10, n/30*

TO   *Buzz Newsstand*
Union Terminal Bldg., #101
Tacoma, WA 98402

QTY.	ITEM	UNIT PRICE	TOTAL
50	Trade paperback books	$15.00	$ 750.00

Date to be paid: 3/3
Discount: $15.00
Amount to be paid: $735.00
Check No.: 1400
REC'D FEB 27

DEBIT MEMORANDUM   No. 33
Date: *Mar. 9, 20--*
Invoice No.: *ATP77*

BUZZ
NEWSSTAND
Union Terminal Building, #101
Tacoma, WA 98402

To: *American Trend Publishers*
1313 Maple Drive
Seattle, WA 98148

This day we have
debited your
account as follows:

Quantity	Item	Unit Price	Total
50	Paperback books	$2.00	$100.00

$ 275.00   No. 1401
Date *March 5*   20--
To *Rizzo's Trucking Company*
For *transportation charges*

	Dollars	Cents
Balance brought forward	11,265	00
Add deposits		
Total	11,265	00
Less this check	275	00
Balance carried forward	10,990	00

$ 3,200.00   No. 1403
Date *March 11*   20--
To *Keystone Insurance Company*
For *business insurance*

	Dollars	Cents
Balance brought forward	10,402	00
Add deposits		
Total	10,402	00
Less this check	3,200	00
Balance carried forward	7,202	00

Problem 15-10   (continued)

$ 5,432.00		No. 1404
Date March 15		20--
To ADC Publishing		
For on account—Invoice 785		

	Dollars	Cents
Balance brought forward	7,202	00
Add deposits		
Total	7,202	00
Less this check	5,432	00
Balance carried forward	1,770	00

$ 120.00		No. 1406
Date March 30		20--
To ADC Publishing		
For merchandise		

	Dollars	Cents
Balance brought forward	970	00
Add deposits		
Total	970	00
Less this check	120	00
Balance carried forward	850	00

Delta Press
One Triangle Park
Vancouver, WA 98661

INVOICE NO. DP204

DATE: *Mar. 18, 20--*
ORDER NO.:
SHIPPED BY: *Rizzo's Trucking Co.*
TERMS: *n/30*

TO   *Buzz Newsstand*
Union Terminal Bldg., #101
Tacoma, WA 98402

QTY.	ITEM	UNIT PRICE	TOTAL
20 cs	Magazines	$ 60.00/cs	$1,200.00
65	Hardcover books, bestsellers	20.00	1,300.00
2	Book racks	150.00	300.00
			$2,800.00

DEBIT MEMORANDUM   No. 34

Date: *Mar. 22, 20--*
Invoice No.: *DP204*

BUZZ NEWSSTAND
Union Terminal Building, #101
Tacoma, WA 98402

To: *Delta Press*
One Triangle Park
Vancouver, WA 98661

This day we have debited your account as follows:

Quantity	Item	Unit Price	Total
2	Book racks	$150.00	$300.00

$ 800.00		No. 1405
Date March 28		20--
To American Trend Publishers		
For on account		

	Dollars	Cents
Balance brought forward	1,770	00
Add deposits		
Total	1,770	00
Less this check	800	00
Balance carried forward	970	00

Problem 15-10 Recording and Posting Purchases and Cash Payment Transactions

GENERAL JOURNAL

PAGE _____

	DATE	DESCRIPTION	POST. REF.	DEBIT	CREDIT	
1						1
2						2
3						3
4						4
5						5
6						6
7						7
8						8
9						9
10						10
11						11
12						12
13						13
14						14
15						15
16						16
17						17
18						18
19						19
20						20
21						21
22						22
23						23
24						24
25						25
26						26
27						27
28						28
29						29
30						30
31						31
32						32
33						33
34						34
35						35
36						36
37						37
38						38

Name _____ **Date** _____ **Class** _____

Problem 15-10   (continued)

GENERAL LEDGER

ACCOUNT __Cash in Bank__ _____ ACCOUNT NO. __101__

DATE	DESCRIPTION	POST. REF.	DEBIT	CREDIT	BALANCE DEBIT	BALANCE CREDIT
20--						
Mar. 1	Balance	✓			1200000	

ACCOUNT __Prepaid Insurance__ _____ ACCOUNT NO. __140__

DATE	DESCRIPTION	POST. REF.	DEBIT	CREDIT	BALANCE DEBIT	BALANCE CREDIT

ACCOUNT __Accounts Payable__ _____ ACCOUNT NO. __201__

DATE	DESCRIPTION	POST. REF.	DEBIT	CREDIT	BALANCE DEBIT	BALANCE CREDIT
20--						
Mar. 1	Balance	✓				225000

Problem 15-10   (continued)

ACCOUNT *Purchases*   ACCOUNT NO. *501*

DATE		DESCRIPTION	POST. REF.	DEBIT	CREDIT	BALANCE DEBIT	BALANCE CREDIT
20--							
Mar.	1	Balance	✓			800000	

ACCOUNT *Transportation In*   ACCOUNT NO. *505*

DATE		DESCRIPTION	POST. REF.	DEBIT	CREDIT	BALANCE DEBIT	BALANCE CREDIT
20--							
Mar.	1	Balance	✓			150000	

ACCOUNT *Purchases Discounts*   ACCOUNT NO. *510*

DATE	DESCRIPTION	POST. REF.	DEBIT	CREDIT	BALANCE DEBIT	BALANCE CREDIT

ACCOUNT *Purchases Returns and Allowances*   ACCOUNT NO. *515*

DATE	DESCRIPTION	POST. REF.	DEBIT	CREDIT	BALANCE DEBIT	BALANCE CREDIT

Problem 15-10 (concluded)

ACCOUNTS PAYABLE SUBSIDIARY LEDGER

Name _ADC Publishing_____

Address _5670 Mulberry Place, Seattle, WA 98101_____

DATE	DESCRIPTION	POST. REF.	DEBIT	CREDIT	BALANCE

Name _American Trend Publishers_____

Address _1313 Maple Drive, Seattle, WA 98148_____

DATE	DESCRIPTION	POST. REF.	DEBIT	CREDIT	BALANCE
20--					
Mar. 1	Balance	✓			90000

Name _Delta Press_____

Address _One Triangle Park, Vancouver, WA 98661_____

DATE	DESCRIPTION	POST. REF.	DEBIT	CREDIT	BALANCE
20--					
Mar. 1	Balance	✓			60000

Name _Pine Forest Publications_____

Address _103 Mt. Thor Road, Spokane, WA 99210_____

DATE	DESCRIPTION	POST. REF.	DEBIT	CREDIT	BALANCE
20--					
Mar. 1	Balance	✓			75000

Analyze: _____

_____

CHAPTER 15 Accounting for Purchases and Cash Payments

Self-Test

Part A   True or False

Directions: *Circle the letter* T *in the Answer column if the statement is true; circle the letter* F *if the statement is false.*

Answer

T   F   **1.** A purchase order is prepared by the buyer and sent to the supplier as an *offer* to purchase merchandise or other assets.

T   F   **2.** A tickler file contains folders for each day of the month so that invoices can be placed in the folders according to their due dates.

T   F   **3.** If the date of the invoice is October 1 and terms are 2/10, n/30, a discount may be taken if the invoice is paid on or before October 31.

T   F   **4.** Creditor accounts in the accounts payable subsidiary ledger normally have debit balances.

T   F   **5.** A cash discount is an advantage to the buyer but not the seller.

T   F   **6.** One example of a good internal control procedure requires that all cash payments be authorized.

T   F   **7.** Accounts Payable is a controlling account and it is found in the general ledger.

T   F   **8.** A business must write a check to pay the bank for service charges and bank card fees charged to its checking account.

T   F   **9.** The premium paid for insurance coverage is debited to the asset account, Prepaid Insurance.

T   F   **10.** Shipping charges are always paid by the seller.

Part B   Multiple Choice

Directions: *Only one of the choices given with each of the following statements is correct. Write the letter of the correct answer in the Answer column.*

Answer

_____   **1.** If the invoice amount is $1,200.00 and the credit terms are 3/15, n/45, the amount of the discount is
(A) $36.00.
(B) $180.00.
(C) $360.00.
(D) $3.60.

_____   **2.** A box of merchandise received by a business would include a(n)
(A) invoice.
(B) purchase requisition.
(C) purchase order.
(D) packing slip.

_____   **3.** The document prepared by the seller is a(n)
(A) purchase requisition.
(B) invoice.
(C) purchase order.
(D) none of the above.

_____   **4.** Which of the following statements is *true* about the Transportation In account?
(A) It is classified as a cost of merchandise account.
(B) Its balance and increase side is a debit.
(C) Its decrease side is a credit.
(D) Its balance shows the cost of delivery charges for merchandise.
(E) All of the above.

_____   **5.** A purchases returns and allowances transaction must be posted to the
(A) Purchases and Accounts Payable accounts.
(B) Accounts Payable account.
(C) the creditor's account in the accounts payable ledger.
(D) the Accounts Payable account and the creditor's account.

_____   **6.** The Purchases account is debited when
(A) merchandise is bought for resale.
(B) merchandise is bought on account.
(C) merchandise is bought for cash.
(D) all of the above.

_____   **7.** A processing stamp is placed on the
(A) packing slip.
(B) purchase requisition.
(C) invoice.
(D) purchase order.

CHAPTER 16   Special Journals: Sales and Cash Receipts

Study Plan

Check Your Understanding

Section 1	Read Section 1 on pages 420–427 and complete the following exercises on page 428.

❏ Thinking Critically
❏ Communication Accounting
❏ Problem 16-1   *Posting Column Totals from the Sales Journal*
❏ Problem 16-2   *Analyzing a Source Document*

Section 2   Read Section 2 on pages 429–439 and complete the following exercises on page 440.

❏ Thinking Critically
❏ Computing in the Business World
❏ Problem 16-3   *Completing the Cash Receipts Journal*

Summary   Review the Chapter 16 Summary on page 441 in your textbook.

❏ Key Concepts

Review and Activities   Complete the following questions and exercises on pages 442–443 in your textbook.

❏ Using Key Terms
❏ Understanding Accounting Concepts and Procedures
❏ Case Study
❏ Conducting an Audit with Alex
❏ Internet Connection
❏ Workplace Skills

Computerized Accounting   Read the Computerized Accounting information on page 444 in your textbook.

❏ *Making the Transition from a Manual to a Computerized System*
❏ *Mastering Sales and Cash Receipts in Peachtree*

Problems   Complete the following end-of-chapter problems for Chapter 16 in your textbook.

❏ Problem 16-4   *Recording and Posting Sales and Cash Receipts*
❏ Problem 16-5   *Recording and Posting Cash Receipts*

Challenge Problem   ❏ Problem 16-6   *Recording and Posting Sales and Cash Receipts*

Chapter Reviews and Working Papers   Complete the following exercises for Chapter 16 in your Chapter Reviews and Working Papers.

❏ Chapter Review
❏ Self-Test

CHAPTER 16 REVIEW   Special Journals: Sales and Cash Receipts

Part 1   Accounting Vocabulary (4 points)

Total Points	38
Student's Score	

Directions: *Using terms from the following list, complete the sentences below. Write the letter of the term you have chosen in the space provided.*

A. cash receipts journal	**C.** sales journal	**E.** special journal
B. footing	**D.** schedule of accounts receivable	

_____**E**_____   **0.** A(n) _____, which simplifies the journalizing and posting process, has special columns that are used for recording specific types of business transactions.

_____   **1.** The sale of merchandise on account is recorded in the _____.

_____   **2.** A column total written in small pencil figures is called a(n) _____.

_____   **3.** All transactions in which cash is received are recorded in the _____.

_____   **4.** A(n) _____ is a report listing each charge customer's name and account balance and the total amount due from all charge customers.

Part 2   Recording Transactions in Special Journals (11 points)

Directions: *Record the following entries in the sales journal. Use page 6 in the sales journal.*

20--

May   3   Sold $800 in merchandise, plus $48 sales taxes, on account to Molly Brian, Sales Slip 120.

     10   Sold $1,200 in merchandise to Spring Branch School District on account, Sales Slip 121. They are a tax exempt organization.

SALES JOURNAL

PAGE _____

	DATE	SALES SLIP NO.	CUSTOMER'S ACCOUNT DEBITED	POST. REF.	SALES CREDIT	SALES TAX PAYABLE CREDIT	ACCOUNTS RECEIVABLE DEBIT	
1								1
2								2
3								3
4								4

Part 3   Posting to the Accounts Receivable Subsidiary Ledger (8 points)

Directions: *Post the first journal entry completed in Part 2 to Molly Brian's account in the accounts receivable subsidiary ledger. Indicate on the sales journal in Part 2 that the transaction has been posted.*

ACCOUNTS RECEIVABLE SUBSIDIARY LEDGER

Name _Molly Brian_

Address _865 Elmwood Place, Cincinnati, OH 45202_

DATE	DESCRIPTION	POST. REF.	DEBIT	CREDIT	BALANCE

Part 4   Analyzing Sales and Cash Receipts Transactions (15 points)

Directions: *Read each of the following statements to determine whether the statement is true or false. Write your answer in the space provided.*

True   **0.** Two advantages of special journals are that they save time in recording and posting.

_____   **1.** Only the sale of merchandise on account is recorded in the sales journal.

_____   **2.** Every transaction recorded in the cash receipts journal results in a debit to cash.

_____   **3.** The sales journal is used to record any sale of merchandise, whether on account or for cash.

_____   **4.** Sales taxes are not usually charged on sales of merchandise to government agencies.

_____   **5.** The individual amounts in the Accounts Receivable Debit column of the sales journal are to be posted on a monthly basis.

_____   **6.** The column totals from the sales journal are posted to three general ledger accounts.

_____   **7.** When posting from a special journal, post information moving from top to bottom rather than left to right.

_____   **8.** When first totaling amount columns in a special journal always use a pencil.

_____   **9.** The total of an amount column in a special journal is posted to the general ledger account named in the column heading.

_____   **10.** At the end of the month, a check mark is placed below the double ruling in the General Credit column of the cash receipts journal to indicate the column total is not posted.

_____   **11.** Amounts recorded in the General Credit column of the cash receipts journal are to be posted when the transaction is journalized.

_____   **12.** When preparing a schedule of accounts receivable, enter only accounts that have a balance.

_____   **13.** Cash discounts are computed on the total amount of merchandise sold and not the sales tax.

_____   **14.** When journalizing cash sales and bankcard sales transactions, a dash is placed in the Posting Reference column to indicate that.

_____   **15.** Most transactions recorded in the cash receipts journal result in a debit to Accounts Receivable and a credit to Cash in Bank.

Working Papers *for Section Problems*

Problem 16-1   Posting Column Totals from the Sales Journal

SALES JOURNAL

	DATE	SALES SLIP NO.	CUSTOMER'S ACCOUNT DEBITED	POST. REF.	SALES CREDIT	SALES TAX PAYABLE CREDIT	ACCOUNTS RECEIVABLE DEBIT	
1	20--							1
2	Apr. 1	47	Amy Anderson	✓	800 00	48 00	848 00	2
31	30		Totals		1200 00	720 00	1272 00	31
32								32
33								33

GENERAL LEDGER

ACCOUNT __Accounts Receivable__   ACCOUNT NO. ____115

DATE	DESCRIPTION	POST. REF.	DEBIT	CREDIT	BALANCE DEBIT	BALANCE CREDIT
20--						
Apr. 1	Balance	✓			15000 00	

ACCOUNT __Sales Tax Payable__   ACCOUNT NO. ____215

DATE	DESCRIPTION	POST. REF.	DEBIT	CREDIT	BALANCE DEBIT	BALANCE CREDIT
20--						
Apr. 1	Balance	✓				1300 00

ACCOUNT __Sales__   ACCOUNT NO. ____401

DATE	DESCRIPTION	POST. REF.	DEBIT	CREDIT	BALANCE DEBIT	BALANCE CREDIT
20--						
Apr. 1	Balance	✓				25000 00

Problem 16-2   Analyzing a Source Document

SALES JOURNAL

PAGE _____

	DATE	SALES SLIP NO.	CUSTOMER'S ACCOUNT DEBITED	POST. REF.	SALES CREDIT	SALES TAX PAYABLE CREDIT	ACCOUNTS RECEIVABLE DEBIT	
1								1
2								2
3								3
4								4
5								5
6								6
7								7

Name __M&M Consultants__

Address __2816 Mt. Odin Drive, Williamsburg, VA 23185__

DATE		DESCRIPTION	POST. REF.	DEBIT	CREDIT	BALANCE
20--						
June	1	Balance	✓			30000

Problem 16-3   Completing the Cash Receipts Journal

PAGE ___10___

CASH RECEIPTS JOURNAL

	DATE	DOC. NO.	ACCOUNT NAME	POST. REF.	GENERAL CREDIT	SALES CREDIT	SALES TAX PAYABLE CREDIT	ACCOUNTS RECEIVABLE CREDIT	SALES DISCOUNTS DEBIT	CASH IN BANK DEBIT	
1	20--										1
2	Jan. 3	R502	Jennifer Smith	✓				8000		8000	2
3	5	R503	Wilton High School	✓				310000	6200	303800	3
4	8	R504	Store Equipment	155	7500					7500	4
5	15	T42	Cash Sales	—		500000	30000			530000	5
6	15	T42	Bankcard Sales	—		120000	7200			127200	6
7	20	R505	Norwin High School	✓				240000	4800	235200	7
8	30	R506	Supplies	115	3000					3000	8
9											9
10											10
11											11
12											12
13											13
14											14
15											15
16											16
17											17
18											18
19											19
20											20
21											21
22											22
23											23
24											24
25											25
26											26

Computerized Accounting Using Peachtree

Software Objectives

When you have completed this chapter, you will be able to use Peachtree to:

1. Record sales on account using the **Sales/Invoicing** option.
2. Record cash receipts using the **Receipts** option.
3. Record partial payments by customers.

Problem 16-4   Recording and Posting Sales and Cash Receipts

INSTRUCTIONS

Beginning a Session

Step 1   Select the problem set: Shutterbug Cameras (Prob. 16-4).
Step 2   Rename the company and set the system date to May 31, 2004.

Completing the Accounting Problem

Step 3   Review the transactions in your textbook.

TIP: It is often faster to group and then enter transactions in batches. For example, enter all of the sales on account and then enter the cash sales.

Step 4   Record the sales on account using the **Sales/Invoicing** option.

TIP: Refer to Problem 14-5 if you need help entering the transactions for this problem.

Step 5   Record the cash sales using the **Receipts** option.
Step 6   Print a Sales Journal report and a Cash Receipts Journal report.
Step 7   Proof your work.
Step 8   Print a Customer Ledgers report.
Step 9   Print a General Ledger report.
Step 10   Answer the Analyze question.

Ending the Session

Step 11   Click the **Close Problem** button in the Glencoe Smart Guide window.

Mastering Peachtree

While entering a sales on account transaction, can you enter a new customer account on the fly? Explain your answer on a separate sheet of paper.

DO YOU HAVE A QUESTION

Q. *Does Peachtree include a Schedule of Accounts Receivable report?*

A. No, Peachtree does not have a report called *Schedule of Accounts Receivable*. The Customer Ledgers report is a combination of an Accounts Receivable Subsidiary Ledger report and a Schedule of Accounts Receivable. The Customer Ledgers report shows the transaction detail and a running balance. You can also print the Aged Receivables report to display the A/R balance.

Notes

Peachtree uses the term *invoice, not* sales slip, *on the sales data entry form.*

Peachtree Guide

Problem 16-5   Recording and Posting Cash Receipts

INSTRUCTIONS

Beginning a Session

Step 1   Select the problem set: River's Edge Canoe & Kayak (Prob. 16-5).

Step 2   Rename the company and set the system date to May 31, 2004.

Completing the Accounting Problem

Step 3   Review the transactions in your textbook.

Step 4   Record the cash receipts.

TIP: Remember to change the *GL Account* field for cash receipts transactions not involving the **Sales** account.

Step 5   Print a Cash Receipts Journal report.

Step 6   Proof your work.

Step 7   Print a Customer Ledgers report.

Step 8   Print a General Ledger report.

Step 9   Answer the Analyze question.

Notes

To record a partial customer payment on an invoice, enter the amount received in the Amount Paid *field.*

Checking Your Work and Ending the Session

Step 10   Click the **Close Problem** button in the Glencoe Smart Guide window.

Step 11   If your teacher has asked you to check your solution, click *Check my answer to this problem.* Review, print, and close the report.

Step 12   Click the **Close Problem** button and select the appropriate save option.

Problem 16-6   Recording and Posting Sales and Cash Receipts

INSTRUCTIONS

Beginning a Session

Step 1   Select the problem set: Buzz Newsstand (Prob. 16-6).

Step 2   Rename the company and set the system date to May 31, 2004.

Completing the Accounting Problem

Step 3   Review the transactions in your textbook.

Step 4   Record the sales on account.

Step 5   Record the cash receipts.

Step 6   Print a Sales Journal report and a Cash Receipts Journal report.

Step 7   Proof your work.

Step 8   Print a Customer Ledgers report.

Step 9   Print a General Ledger report.

Step 10   Answer the Analyze question.

Ending the Session

Step 11   Click the **Close Problem** button in the Glencoe Smart Guide window.

⬤ **Working Papers** *for End-of-Chapter Problems*

Problem 16-4   Recording and Posting Sales and Cash Receipts
(1)

SALES JOURNAL

PAGE _____

	DATE	SALES SLIP NO.	CUSTOMER'S ACCOUNT DEBITED	POST. REF.	SALES CREDIT	SALES TAX PAYABLE CREDIT	ACCOUNTS RECEIVABLE DEBIT	
1								1
2								2
3								3
4								4
5								5
6								6
7								7
8								8
9								9
10								10
11								11
12								12
13								13
14								14
15								15
16								16
17								17
18								18
19								19
20								20
21								21
22								22
23								23
24								24
25								25
26								26
27								27
28								28
29								29
30								30
31								31
32								32
33								33

Problem 16-4   (continued)

(1), (3)

PAGE ____

CASH RECEIPTS JOURNAL

	DATE	DOC. NO.	ACCOUNT NAME	POST. REF.	GENERAL CREDIT	SALES CREDIT	SALES TAX PAYABLE CREDIT	ACCOUNTS RECEIVABLE CREDIT	SALES DISCOUNTS DEBIT	CASH IN BANK DEBIT	
1											1
2											2
3											3
4											4
5											5
6											6
7											7
8											8
9											9
10											10
11											11
12											12
13											13
14											14
15											15
16											16
17											17
18											18
19											19
20											20
21											21
22											22
23											23
24											24
25											25

Problem 16-4   (continued)

(2)   ACCOUNTS RECEIVABLE SUBSIDIARY LEDGER

Name *FastForward Productions*

Address *3 Oakhill Mall, Decatur, AL 35601*

DATE	DESCRIPTION	POST. REF.	DEBIT	CREDIT	BALANCE

Name *Yoko Nakata*

Address *19 Hawthorne Street, Tuscaloosa, AL 35401*

DATE	DESCRIPTION	POST. REF.	DEBIT	CREDIT	BALANCE
20--					
May 1	Balance	✓			600 00

Name *Heather Sullivan*

Address *835 Aspen Lane, Huntsville, AL 35801*

DATE	DESCRIPTION	POST. REF.	DEBIT	CREDIT	BALANCE
20--					
May 1	Balance	✓			50 00

Problem 16-4 (concluded)

GENERAL LEDGER

ACCOUNT **Cash in Bank**   ACCOUNT NO. _101_

DATE		DESCRIPTION	POST. REF.	DEBIT	CREDIT	BALANCE DEBIT	BALANCE CREDIT
20--							
May	1	Balance	✓			500000	

ACCOUNT **Accounts Receivable**   ACCOUNT NO. _115_

DATE		DESCRIPTION	POST. REF.	DEBIT	CREDIT	BALANCE DEBIT	BALANCE CREDIT
20--							
May	1	Balance	✓			65000	

ACCOUNT **Sales Tax Payable**   ACCOUNT NO. _215_

DATE		DESCRIPTION	POST. REF.	DEBIT	CREDIT	BALANCE DEBIT	BALANCE CREDIT
20--							
May	1	Balance	✓				120000

ACCOUNT **Sales**   ACCOUNT NO. _401_

DATE		DESCRIPTION	POST. REF.	DEBIT	CREDIT	BALANCE DEBIT	BALANCE CREDIT
20--							
May	1	Balance	✓				3000000

Analyze: _____

Problem 16-5   Recording and Posting Cash Receipts

CASH RECEIPTS JOURNAL

PAGE _____

DATE	DOC. NO.	ACCOUNT NAME	POST. REF.	GENERAL CREDIT	SALES CREDIT	SALES TAX PAYABLE CREDIT	ACCOUNTS RECEIVABLE CREDIT	SALES DISCOUNTS DEBIT	CASH IN BANK DEBIT
1									
2									
3									
4									
5									
6									
7									
8									
9									
10									
11									
12									
13									
14									
15									
16									
17									
18									
19									
20									
21									
22									
23									
24									
25									
26									

Problem 16-5 (continued)

GENERAL LEDGER

ACCOUNT __Cash in Bank_____ ACCOUNT NO. __101__

DATE		DESCRIPTION	POST. REF.	DEBIT	CREDIT	BALANCE	
						DEBIT	CREDIT
20--							
May	1	Balance	✓			7 5 0 0 00	

ACCOUNT __Accounts Receivable_____ ACCOUNT NO. __115__

DATE		DESCRIPTION	POST. REF.	DEBIT	CREDIT	BALANCE	
						DEBIT	CREDIT
20--							
May	1	Balance	✓			6 9 0 0 00	

ACCOUNT __Store Equipment_____ ACCOUNT NO. __150__

DATE		DESCRIPTION	POST. REF.	DEBIT	CREDIT	BALANCE	
						DEBIT	CREDIT
20--							
May	1	Balance	✓			3 0 0 0 00	

ACCOUNT __Sales Tax Payable_____ ACCOUNT NO. __215__

DATE		DESCRIPTION	POST. REF.	DEBIT	CREDIT	BALANCE	
						DEBIT	CREDIT
20--							
May	1	Balance	✓				2 5 0 00

ACCOUNT __Sales_____ ACCOUNT NO. __401__

DATE		DESCRIPTION	POST. REF.	DEBIT	CREDIT	BALANCE	
						DEBIT	CREDIT
20--							
May	1	Balance	✓				4 0 0 0 0 00

ACCOUNT __Sales Discounts_____ ACCOUNT NO. __405__

DATE		DESCRIPTION	POST. REF.	DEBIT	CREDIT	BALANCE	
						DEBIT	CREDIT
20--							
May	1	Balance	✓			1 2 0 0 00	

Problem 16-5   (continued)

ACCOUNTS RECEIVABLE SUBSIDIARY LEDGER

Name *Adventure River Tours*

Address *Box 101, Jackson, WY 83001*

DATE		DESCRIPTION	POST. REF.	DEBIT	CREDIT	BALANCE
20--						
May	1	Balance	✓			3 0 0 0 00

Name *Paul Drake*

Address *125 Rodeo Road, Cody, WY 82414*

DATE		DESCRIPTION	POST. REF.	DEBIT	CREDIT	BALANCE
20--						
May	1	Balance	✓			8 0 0 00

Name *Celeste Everett*

Address *1824 Grays Gable, Laramie, WY 82070*

DATE		DESCRIPTION	POST. REF.	DEBIT	CREDIT	BALANCE
20--						
May	1	Balance	✓			4 0 0 00

Name *Isabel Rodriguez*

Address *626 Buffalo Road, Cheyenne, WY 82001*

DATE		DESCRIPTION	POST. REF.	DEBIT	CREDIT	BALANCE
20--						
May	1	Balance	✓			2 0 0 00

Problem 16-5   (concluded)

Name **Wildwood Resorts** _____

Address **601 Ponderosa Trail, Moose, WY 83012** _____

DATE		DESCRIPTION	POST. REF.	DEBIT	CREDIT	BALANCE
20--						
May	1	Balance	✓			250000

_____

_____

Analyze: _____

_____

Problem 16-6 Source Documents

Instructions: *Use the following source documents to record the transactions for this problem.*

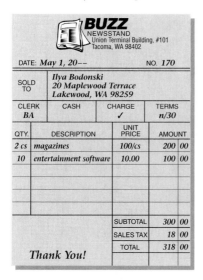

BUZZ NEWSSTAND
Union Terminal Building, #101
Tacoma, WA 98402

DATE: *May 1, 20--* NO. *170*

SOLD TO: *Ilya Bodonski*
20 Maplewood Terrace
Lakewood, WA 98259

CLERK	CASH	CHARGE	TERMS
BA		✓	n/30

QTY.	DESCRIPTION	UNIT PRICE	AMOUNT
2 cs	magazines	100/cs	200 00
10	entertainment software	10.00	100 00
		SUBTOTAL	300 00
		SALES TAX	18 00
		TOTAL	318 00

Thank You!

BUZZ NEWSSTAND
Union Terminal Building, #101
Tacoma, WA 98402

RECEIPT No. 147

May 7 20 --

RECEIVED FROM *Rothwell Management Inc.* $ *294.00*

Two hundred ninety-four and 00/100 ——————— DOLLARS

FOR *on account (300 less 2% discount)*

RECEIVED BY *Kathy Harper*

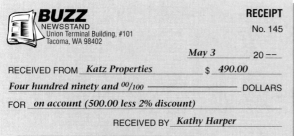

BUZZ NEWSSTAND
Union Terminal Building, #101
Tacoma, WA 98402

RECEIPT No. 145

May 3 20 --

RECEIVED FROM *Katz Properties* $ *490.00*

Four hundred ninety and 00/100 ——————— DOLLARS

FOR *on account (500.00 less 2% discount)*

RECEIVED BY *Kathy Harper*

BUZZ NEWSSTAND
Union Terminal Building, #101
Tacoma, WA 98402

DATE: *April 30, 20--* NO. *162*

SOLD TO: *Rothwell Management Inc.*
16 University Place
Vancouver, WA 98661

CLERK	CASH	CHARGE	TERMS
BA		✓	2/10, n/30

QTY.	DESCRIPTION	UNIT PRICE	AMOUNT
2 cs	Magazines	100/cs	200 00
75	Daily newspapers	1.00	75 00
1 bx	Pocket combs	8.02	8 02
		SUBTOTAL	283 02
		SALES TAX	16 98
		TOTAL	300 00

COPY

Thank You!

BUZZ NEWSSTAND
Union Terminal Building, #101
Tacoma, WA 98402

DATE: *April 26, 20--* NO. *159*

SOLD TO: *Katz Properties*
103 Prospect Point
Bellevue, WA 98009

CLERK	CASH	CHARGE	TERMS
BA		✓	2/10, n/30

QTY.	DESCRIPTION	UNIT PRICE	AMOUNT
4 cs	Magazines	100/cs	400 00
2	Desk lamps	35.85	71 70
		SUBTOTAL	471 70
		SALES TAX	28 30
		TOTAL	500 00

COPY

Thank You!

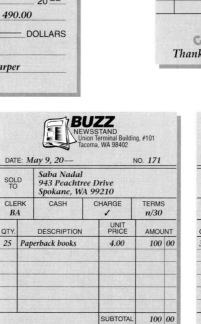

BUZZ NEWSSTAND
Union Terminal Building, #101
Tacoma, WA 98402

DATE: *May 9, 20--* NO. *171*

SOLD TO: *Saba Nadal*
943 Peachtree Drive
Spokane, WA 99210

CLERK	CASH	CHARGE	TERMS
BA		✓	n/30

QTY.	DESCRIPTION	UNIT PRICE	AMOUNT
25	Paperback books	4.00	100 00
		SUBTOTAL	100 00
		SALES TAX	6 00
		TOTAL	106 00

Thank You!

BUZZ NEWSSTAND
Union Terminal Building, #101
Tacoma, WA 98402

DATE: *May 10, 20--* NO. *172*

SOLD TO: *Java Shops, Inc.*
449 Country Place
Auburn, WA 98002

CLERK	CASH	CHARGE	TERMS
BA		✓	2/10, n/30

QTY.	DESCRIPTION	UNIT PRICE	AMOUNT
3 cs	Magazines	100/cs	300 00
12	Hardcover books	25.00	300 00
		SUBTOTAL	600 00
		SALES TAX	36 00
		TOTAL	636 00

Thank You!

BUZZ NEWSSTAND
Union Terminal Building, #101
Tacoma, WA 98402

RECEIPT No. 146

May 5 20 --

RECEIVED FROM *Straka Stores* $ *60.00*

Sixty and 00/100 ——————— DOLLARS

FOR *supplies*

RECEIVED BY *Kathy Harper*

Problem 16-6   (continued)

BUZZ
NEWSSTAND
Union Terminal Building, #101
Tacoma, WA 98402

DATE: *May 12, 20--*   NO. *173*

SOLD TO	Lee Adkins 720 Dogwood Lane Seattle, WA 98101		
CLERK *BA*	CASH	CHARGE ✓	TERMS *n/30*

QTY.	DESCRIPTION	UNIT PRICE	AMOUNT	
½ cs	magazines	100/cs	50	00
		SUBTOTAL	50	00
		SALES TAX	3	00
		TOTAL	53	00

Thank You!

BUZZ
NEWSSTAND
Union Terminal Building, #101
Tacoma, WA 98402

DATE: *May 18, 20--*   NO. *174*

SOLD TO	Katz Properties 103 Prospect Point Bellevue, WA 98009		
CLERK *BA*	CASH	CHARGE ✓	TERMS *2/10, n/30*

QTY.	DESCRIPTION	UNIT PRICE	AMOUNT	
32	Hardcover books	25.00	800	00
200	Daily newspapers	1.00	200	00
		SUBTOTAL	1,000	00
		SALES TAX	60	00
		TOTAL	1,060	00

Thank You!

BUZZ
NEWSSTAND
Union Terminal Building, #101
Tacoma, WA 98402

RECEIPT
No. 148

May 15   20 --

RECEIVED FROM *Rolling Hills Pharmacies* $ *196.00*

One hundred ninety-six and $^{00}/_{100}$ ———————— DOLLARS

FOR *on account ($200.00 less 2% discount)*

RECEIVED BY *Kathy Harper*

BUZZ
NEWSSTAND
Union Terminal Building, #101
Tacoma, WA 98402

RECEIPT
No. 149

May 20   20 --

RECEIVED FROM *Ilya Bodonski* $ *100.00*

One hundred and $^{00}/_{100}$ ———————— DOLLARS

FOR *on account*

RECEIVED BY *Kathy Harper*

```
May  15
Tape 33


           2,400.00   CA
             144.00   ST
```

```
May  15
Tape 33


           2,000.00   BCS
             120.00   ST
```

BUZZ
NEWSSTAND
Union Terminal Building, #101
Tacoma, WA 98402

DATE: *May 22, 20--*   NO. *175*

SOLD TO	Rothwell Management Inc. 16 University Place Vancouver, WA 98661		
CLERK *BA*	CASH	CHARGE ✓	TERMS *2/10, n/30*

QTY.	DESCRIPTION	UNIT PRICE	AMOUNT	
4 cs	Magazines	100/cs	400	00
200	Daily newspapers	1.00	200	00
6	Travel Planning Software	40.00	200	00
		SUBTOTAL	800	00
		SALES TAX	48	00
		TOTAL	848	00

Thank You!

Problem 16-6 (continued)

BUZZ
NEWSSTAND
Union Terminal Building, #101
Tacoma, WA 98402

RECEIPT
No. 150

May 23 20 --

RECEIVED FROM _Lee Adkins_ $ _53.00_

Fifty-three and ⁰⁰/₁₀₀ ——————————— DOLLARS

FOR _on account_

RECEIVED BY _Kathy Harper_

BUZZ
NEWSSTAND
Union Terminal Building, #101
Tacoma, WA 98402

RECEIPT
No. 153

May 28 20 --

RECEIVED FROM _Brown's Books and More_ $ _75.00_

Seventy-five and ⁰⁰/₁₀₀ ——————————— DOLLARS

FOR _used store equipment_

RECEIVED BY _Kathy Harper_

BUZZ
NEWSSTAND
Union Terminal Building, #101
Tacoma, WA 98402

RECEIPT
No. 151

May 24 20 --

RECEIVED FROM _Saba Nadal_ $ _106.00_

One hundred six and ⁰⁰/₁₀₀ ——————————— DOLLARS

FOR _on account_

RECEIVED BY _Kathy Harper_

May 30
Tape 34

2,600.00 CA
156.00 ST

BUZZ
NEWSSTAND
Union Terminal Building, #101
Tacoma, WA 98402

RECEIPT
No. 152

May 26 20 --

RECEIVED FROM _Java Shops, Inc._ $ _200.00_

Two hundred and ⁰⁰/₁₀₀ ——————————— DOLLARS

FOR _on account_

RECEIVED BY _Kathy Harper_

May 30
Tape 34

2,200.00 BCS
132.00 ST

BUZZ
NEWSSTAND
Union Terminal Building, #101
Tacoma, WA 98402

DATE: _May 27, 20--_   NO. _176_

SOLD TO	_Lee Adkins_ _720 Dogwood Lane_ _Seattle, WA 98101_		
CLERK _BA_	CASH	CHARGE ✓	TERMS _n/30_

QTY.	DESCRIPTION	UNIT PRICE	AMOUNT	
_2 cs_	_Magazines_	_100/cs_	_200_	_00_
	SUBTOTAL		_200_	_00_
	SALES TAX		_12_	_00_
	TOTAL		_212_	_00_

Thank You!

Problem 16-6   Recording and Posting Sales and Cash Receipts

SALES JOURNAL   PAGE _____

	DATE	SALES SLIP NO.	CUSTOMER'S ACCOUNT DEBITED	POST. REF.	SALES CREDIT	SALES TAX PAYABLE CREDIT	ACCOUNTS RECEIVABLE DEBIT	
1								1
2								2
3								3
4								4
5								5
6								6
7								7
8								8
9								9
10								10
11								11
12								12
13								13
14								14
15								15
16								16
17								17
18								18
19								19
20								20
21								21
22								22
23								23
24								24
25								25
26								26
27								27
28								28
29								29
30								30
31								31
32								32
33								33
34								34
35								35
36								36

Problem 16-6 (continued)

PAGE ___

CASH RECEIPTS JOURNAL

DATE	DOC. NO.	ACCOUNT NAME	POST. REF.	GENERAL CREDIT	SALES CREDIT	SALES TAX PAYABLE CREDIT	ACCOUNTS RECEIVABLE CREDIT	SALES DISCOUNTS DEBIT	CASH IN BANK DEBIT	
------	----------	--------------	------------	----------------	--------------	--------------------------	----------------------------	-----------------------	--------------------	
										1
										2
										3
										4
										5
										6
										7
										8
										9
										10
										11
										12
										13
										14
										15
										16
										17
										18
										19
										20
										21
										22
										23
										24
										25
										26

Problem 16-6   (continued)

(2)   ACCOUNTS RECEIVABLE SUBSIDIARY LEDGER

Name *Lee Adkins*

Address *720 Dogwood Lane, Seattle, WA 98101*

DATE	DESCRIPTION	POST. REF.	DEBIT	CREDIT	BALANCE

Name *Ilya Bodonski*

Address *20 Maplewood Terrace, Lakewood, WA 98259*

DATE	DESCRIPTION	POST. REF.	DEBIT	CREDIT	BALANCE

Name *Java Shops Inc.*

Address *449 Country Place, Auburn, WA 98002*

DATE	DESCRIPTION	POST. REF.	DEBIT	CREDIT	BALANCE

Name *Katz Properties*

Address *103 Prospect Point, Bellevue, WA 98009*

DATE	DESCRIPTION	POST. REF.	DEBIT	CREDIT	BALANCE
20--					
May 1	Balance	✓			50000

Problem 16-6   (continued)

Name **Saba Nadal**

Address **943 Peachtree Drive, Spokane, WA 99210**

DATE	DESCRIPTION	POST. REF.	DEBIT	CREDIT	BALANCE

Name **Rolling Hills Pharmacies**

Address **16 Meadow Lane, Tacoma, WA 98402**

DATE		DESCRIPTION	POST. REF.	DEBIT	CREDIT	BALANCE
20--						
May	5	Balance	✓			200 00

Name **Rothwell Management Inc.**

Address **16 University Place, Vancouver, WA 98661**

DATE		DESCRIPTION	POST. REF.	DEBIT	CREDIT	BALANCE
20--						
May	1	Balance	✓			300 00

Problem 16-6 (continued)

GENERAL LEDGER (PARTIAL)

ACCOUNT __Cash in Bank_____ ACCOUNT NO. ___101___

DATE		DESCRIPTION	POST. REF.	DEBIT	CREDIT	BALANCE DEBIT	BALANCE CREDIT
20--							
May	1	Balance	✓			5000 00	

ACCOUNT __Accounts Receivable_____ ACCOUNT NO. ___115___

DATE		DESCRIPTION	POST. REF.	DEBIT	CREDIT	BALANCE DEBIT	BALANCE CREDIT
20--							
May	1	Balance	✓			1000 00	

ACCOUNT __Supplies_____ ACCOUNT NO. ___135___

DATE		DESCRIPTION	POST. REF.	DEBIT	CREDIT	BALANCE DEBIT	BALANCE CREDIT
20--							
May	1	Balance	✓			300 00	

ACCOUNT __Store Equipment_____ ACCOUNT NO. ___150___

DATE		DESCRIPTION	POST. REF.	DEBIT	CREDIT	BALANCE DEBIT	BALANCE CREDIT
20--							
May	1	Balance	✓			4000 00	

ACCOUNT __Sales Tax Payable_____ ACCOUNT NO. ___215___

DATE		DESCRIPTION	POST. REF.	DEBIT	CREDIT	BALANCE DEBIT	BALANCE CREDIT
20--							
May	1	Balance	✓				400 00

Problem 16-6 (concluded)

ACCOUNT _Sales_   ACCOUNT NO. __401__

DATE		DESCRIPTION	POST. REF.	DEBIT	CREDIT	BALANCE DEBIT	BALANCE CREDIT
20--							
May	1	Balance	✓				2000000

ACCOUNT _Sales Discounts_   ACCOUNT NO. __405__

DATE		DESCRIPTION	POST. REF.	DEBIT	CREDIT	BALANCE DEBIT	BALANCE CREDIT
20--							
May	1	Balance	✓			50000	

(7)

Analyze: _____

_____

CHAPTER 16 Special Journals: Sales and Cash Receipts

Self-Test

Part A   True or False

Directions: *Circle the letter* T *in the Answer column if the statement is true; circle the letter* F *if the statement is false.*

Answer

T   F   **1.** Two major advantages of a special journal are that it saves time in recording and posting business transactions.

T   F   **2.** The cash register tape is the source document for recording cash and bank card sales.

T   F   **3.** Only customer accounts with balances are entered on the schedule of accounts receivable.

T   F   **4.** A business handles bank card sales like cash sales because it receives cash from the bank within several days after depositing its bank card sales slips.

T   F   **5.** Cash sales are recorded in the sales journal.

T   F   **6.** Footings are always completed in pencil, and column totals are written in ink.

T   F   **7.** Merchandising businesses sell strictly on the cash basis.

T   F   **8.** Customer accounts are listed in alphabetical order in the accounts receivable subsidiary ledger.

T   F   **9.** After a posting has been made from the sales or cash receipts journal to a customer's account, the customer account number is entered in the posting reference column of the journal.

T   F   **10.** Postings are made to customer accounts usually at the end of the week.

Part B   Multiple Choice

Directions: *Only one of the choices given with each of the following questions is correct. Write the letter of the correct answer in the Answer column.*

Answer

_____   **1.** The Accounts Receivable Debit column of the sales journal is used to record
(A) the amount of the sale.
(B) the amount of the sales tax.
(C) the total amount to be received from a customer.
(D) the total amount to be paid to a customer.

_____   **2.** The value of the merchandise sold is recorded in the sales journal in the
(A) Sales Tax Payable Credit column.
(B) Sales Credit column.
(C) Customer's Account Debited column.
(D) Accounts Receivable Debit column.

_____   **3.** The totals of the Sales Credit column and the Sales Tax Payable Credit column in the sales journal should be posted
(A) at the end of the month.
(B) at the end of the week.
(C) once every two weeks.
(D) on a daily basis.

_____   **4.** Special journals do the following:
(A) simplify the posting process.
(B) simplify the recording process.
(C) organize the transactions of a business.
(D) all of the above.

_____   **5.** The amounts recorded in the General Credit column of the cash receipts journal are posted
(A) on the day the transaction occurred.
(B) at the end of the week.
(C) at the end of the month.
(D) once every two weeks.

_____   **6.** The amounts recorded in the Accounts Receivable Credit column of the cash receipts journal are posted
(A) once a week.   (C) once a month.
(B) once every two weeks.   (D) on a daily basis.

_____   **7.** The following kinds of transactions are recorded in the cash receipts journal except
(A) sale of merchandise on account.
(B) cash sale of merchandise.
(C) bankcard sales.
(D) sale of other assets for cash.

 **CHAPTER 17** **Special Journals: Purchases and Cash Payments**

Study Plan

Check Your Understanding

Section 1	Read Section 1 on pages 450–456 and complete the following exercises on page 457. ❑ Thinking Critically ❑ Communication Accounting ❑ Problem 17-1 *Recording Transactions in the Purchases Journal*
Section 2	Read Section 2 on pages 458–470 and complete the following exercises on page 471. ❑ Thinking Critically ❑ Computing in the Business World ❑ Problem 17-2 *Preparing a Cash Proof* ❑ Problem 17-3 *Analyzing a Source Document*
Summary	Review the Chapter 17 Summary on page 473 in your textbook. ❑ Key Concepts
Review and Activities	Complete the following questions and exercises on pages 474–475 in your textbook. ❑ Using Key Terms ❑ Understanding Accounting Concepts and Procedures ❑ Case Study ❑ Conducting an Audit with Alex ❑ Internet Connection ❑ Workplace Skills
Computerized Accounting	Read the Computerized Accounting information on page 476 in your textbook. ❑ Mastering Purchases and Cash Payments in Peachtree ❑ Making the Transition from a Manual to a Computerized System
Problems	Complete the following end-of-chapter problems for Chapter 17 in your textbook. ❑ Problem 17-4 *Recording Payment of the Payroll* ❑ Problem 17-5 *Recording Transactions in the Purchases Journal* ❑ Problem 17-6 *Recording and Posting Purchases* ❑ Problem 17-7 *Recording and Posting Cash Payments*
Challenge Problem	❑ Problem 17-8 *Recording and Posting Purchases and Cash Payments*
Chapter Reviews and Working Papers	Complete the following exercises for Chapter 17 in your Chapter Reviews and Working Papers. ❑ Chapter Review ❑ Self-Test

CHAPTER 17 REVIEW

Special Journals: Purchases and Cash Payments

Part 1   Accounting Vocabulary (12 points)

Total Points 36

Student's Score

Directions: *Using terms from the following list, complete the sentences below. Write the letter of the term you have chosen in the space provided.*

A. Accounts Payable	**D.** accounts receivable subsidiary ledger	**G.** controlling account	**K.** purchases journal
B. accounts payable subsidiary ledger	**E.** cash payments journal	**H.** due date	**L.** sales journal
C. Accounts Receivable	**F.** cash receipts journal	**I.** general journal	**M.** schedule of accounts
		J. proving cash	payable

_____H_____   **0.** The _____ is the date by which the invoice must be paid if a discount is to be taken.

_____   **1.** A(n) _____ is a special journal used for recording the sale of merchandise on account.

_____   **2.** A(n) _____ is a separate ledger that contains accounts for all creditors.

_____   **3.** _____ is an account in the general ledger that controls the accounts receivable subsidiary ledger.

_____   **4.** The _____ is a special journal used for recording all cash received by the business.

_____   **5.** _____ is an account in the general ledger that controls the accounts payable subsidiary ledger.

_____   **6.** The _____ is an all-purpose journal used for recording transactions that do not fit into a special journal.

_____   **7.** The process of determining whether the amount of cash recorded in the accounting records of a business agrees with the amount recorded in its checkbook is called _____.

_____   **8.** A special journal used for recording all cash paid out of the business is the _____.

_____   **9.** The _____ is a separate ledger that contains all charge customer accounts.

_____   **10.** The _____ is a special journal used for recording all purchases of assets on account.

_____   **11.** The _____ is a list of all creditors in the accounts payable subsidiary ledger, the balance of each account, and the total owed to all creditors.

_____   **12.** A(n) _____ is an account in the general ledger that acts as a control on the accuracy of the accounts in the subsidiary ledger.

Part 2   Recording a Transaction in the Purchases Journal (4 points)

Directions: *The following transaction would be recorded in a purchases journal. Indicate where the transaction information would be recorded in the purchases journal below by writing the correct identifying letter in the space provided.*

Received Invoice 4208 on August 9 from Bosco Enterprises for merchandise purchased on account.

_____E_____   **0.** Amount of the credit

_____   **1.** Name of the creditor

_____   **2.** Amount of the debit

_____   **3.** The date

_____   **4.** Invoice number

PURCHASES JOURNAL   PAGE _____

	DATE	INVOICE NO.	CREDITOR'S ACCOUNT CREDITED	POST. REF.	ACCOUNTS PAYABLE CREDIT	PURCHASES DEBIT	GENERAL			
							ACCOUNT DEBITED	POST. REF.	DEBIT	
1	**(A)**	**(B)**	**(C)**	**(D)**	**(E)**	**(F)**	**(G)**	**(H)**	**(I)**	1
2										2
3										3
4										4
5										5
6										6

Part 3 Analyzing Purchases and Cash Payment Transactions (10 points)

Directions: *Read each of the following statements to determine whether the statement is true or false. Write your answer in the space provided.*

_____True_____ **0.** The account Purchases is a cost of merchandise account.

_____ **1.** Purchases of items for cash are recorded in the purchases journal.

_____ **2.** The General Debit column of the purchases journal is used to record purchases of all items other than merchandise on account.

_____ **3.** The source document for recording information in the purchases journal is an invoice.

_____ **4.** Amounts entered in the Accounts Payable Credit column of the purchases journal are posted at the end of the month.

_____ **5.** A check mark is entered in parentheses below the double rule of the General Debit column of the purchases journal to indicate the column total is not posted.

_____ **6.** The source document for recording a bank card fee is the check stub.

_____ **7.** Every transaction recorded in the cash payments journal results in a credit to cash.

_____ **8.** The schedule of accounts payable lists only creditor accounts showing a balance.

_____ **9.** The totals of the special amount columns of the cash payments journal are posted at the end of the month.

_____ **10.** Amounts entered in the Accounts Payable Debit column of the cash payments journal are posted at the end of the week.

Part 4 Recording Transactions in the Cash Payments Journal (10 points)

Directions: *The following transactions would be recorded in a cash payments journal. Indicate where the information for each transaction would be recorded in the cash payments journal below by writing the correct identifying letter(s) in the space provided.*

1. June 8, issued Check 148 for $882 to Franklin Brothers Distributors for merchandise purchased on account, Invoice 337 for $900 less a cash discount of $18

    _____A_____ **a.** Date
    _____ **b.** Check number
    _____ **c.** Name of the account to be debited
    _____ **d.** Amount of the debit
    _____ **e.** Amount of the credit

2. May 3, issued Check 601 to KM-Realty for the May rent, $500

    _____ **a.** Check number
    _____ **b.** Amount of the credit
    _____ **c.** Amount of the debit
    _____ **d.** Date
    _____ **e.** Name of the account to be debited

CASH PAYMENTS JOURNAL   PAGE _____

	DATE	DOC. NO.	ACCOUNT NAME	POST. REF.	GENERAL DEBIT	GENERAL CREDIT	ACCOUNTS PAYABLE DEBIT	PURCHASES DISCOUNTS CREDIT	CASH IN BANK CREDIT	
1	**A**	**B**	**C**	**D**	**E**	**F**	**G**	**H**	**I**	1
2										2
3										3
4										4
5										5
6										6

Working Papers _for Section Problems_

Problem 17-1 Recording Transactions in the Purchases Journal

PURCHASES JOURNAL

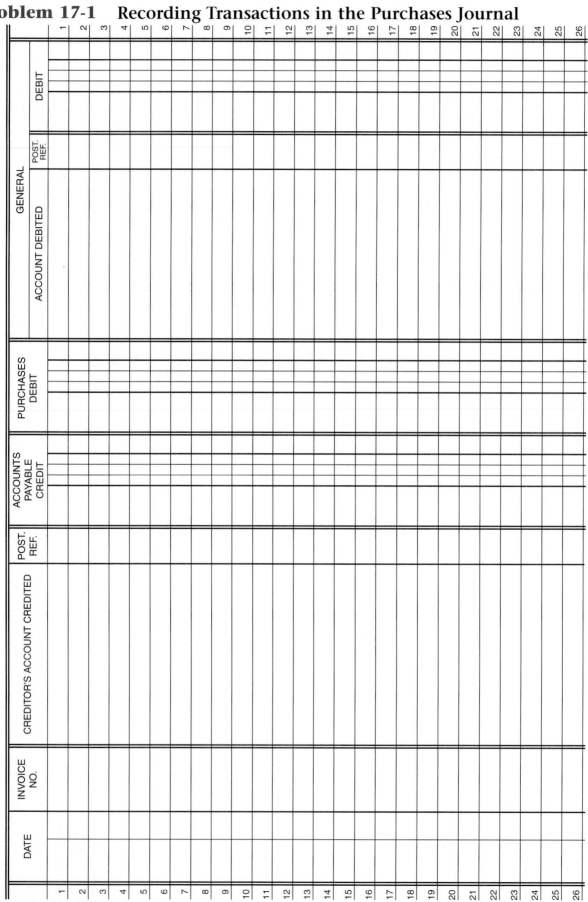

Problem 17-2   Preparing a Cash Proof

Problem 17-3 Analyzing a Source Document

Source Document (No. 104):

	No. 104
$ 873.00	20 —
Date November 2	
To Colonial Products Inc.	
For Inv. 323—$900 less 3% disc., $27.00	

	Dollars	Cents
Balance brought forward	3,486	29
Add deposits		
Total	3,486	29
Less this check	873	00
Balance carried forward	2,613	29

CASH PAYMENTS JOURNAL

PAGE _____

DATE	DOC. NO.	ACCOUNT NAME	POST. REF.	GENERAL DEBIT	GENERAL CREDIT	ACCOUNTS PAYABLE DEBIT	PURCHASES DISCOUNTS CREDIT	CASH IN BANK CREDIT	
									1
									2
									3
									4

Computerized Accounting Using Peachtree

Software Objectives

When you have completed this chapter, you will be able to use Peachtree to:

1. Record purchases on account using the **Purchase/Receive Inventory** option.
2. Record cash payments using the **Payments** option.
3. Record partial payments on account to vendors.

Problem 17-4   Recording Payment of the Payroll

INSTRUCTIONS

Beginning a Session

Step 1   Select the problem set: Denardo's Country Store (Prob. 17-4).
Step 2   Rename the company and set the system date to July 15, 2004.

Completing the Accounting Problem

Step 3   Review the payroll information in your textbook.

TIP: Refer to Problem 15-6 if you need help entering a cash payment transaction.

Step 4   Record the payment of the payroll.

TIP: Record the debit to **Salaries Expense** and enter the credits (as negative amounts) to the payroll liability accounts as a multi-part entry.

> ## DO YOU HAVE A QUESTION?
>
> **Q.** *Do you have to use the* **Payments** *option to record all payments?*
>
> **A.** For payments on account to vendors, you must use the **Payments** option so that Peachtree can update the subsidiary ledger account. Remember that the general journal does not provide a way to identify the vendor. For payments not involving vendors (e.g., payment of an insurance premium), you could use the general journal. However, the **Payments** option is designed for these kinds of transactions just like special journals are more efficient in a manual system.

Step 5   Print a Cash Disbursements Journal report.
Step 6   Proof your work.
Step 7   Answer the Analyze question.

Ending the Session

Step 8   Click the **Close Problem** button in the Glencoe Smart Guide window.

Problem 17-5   Recording Transactions in the Purchases Journal

INSTRUCTIONS

Beginning a Session

Step 1   Select the problem set: Sunset Surfwear (Prob. 17-5).
Step 2   Rename the company and set the system date to July 31, 2004.

Completing the Accounting Problem

Step 3   Review the transactions in your textbook.

TIP: Refer to Problem 15-6 if you need help entering purchases on account transactions.

Step 4   Record the purchases on account transactions using the **Purchases/Receive Inventory** option.

Step 5   Print a Purchases Journal report.

Step 6   Proof your work.

Step 7   Answer the Analyze question.

Checking Your Work and Ending the Session

Step 8   Click the **Close Problem** button in the Glencoe Smart Guide window.

Step 9   If your teacher has asked you to check your solution, click *Check my answer to this problem*. Review, print, and close the report.

Step 10   Click the **Close Problem** button and select the appropriate save option.

Problem 17-6   Recording and Posting Purchases

INSTRUCTIONS

Beginning a Session

Step 1   Select the problem set: Shutterbug Cameras (Prob. 17-6).

Step 2   Rename the company and set the system date to July 31, 2004.

Completing the Accounting Problem

Step 3   Review the transactions in your textbook.

Step 4   Record the purchases on account.

TIP: Verify the *GL Account* field each time you record an entry.

Notes

Peachtree automatically updates the general ledger accounts and subsidiary ledger accounts when you post a purchase on account entry.

Step 5   Print a Purchases Journal report.

Step 6   Proof your work.

Step 7   Print a Vendors Ledgers report and a General Ledger report.

Step 8   Answer the Analyze question.

Ending the Session

Step 9   Click the **Close Problem** button in the Glencoe Smart Guide window and select the appropriate save option.

Problem 17-7   Recording and Posting Cash Payments

INSTRUCTIONS

Beginning a Session

Step 1   Select the problem set: River's Edge Canoe & Kayak (Prob. 17-7).
Step 2   Rename the company and set the system date to July 31, 2004.

Completing the Accounting Problem

Step 3   Review the transactions in your textbook.
Step 4   Record the cash payments using the **Payments** option.

TIP: Record a payment on account using the **Apply to Invoices** tab. For cash payments other than those on account, use the **Apply to Expenses** tab. You may have to manually enter the cash discount for some payment transactions.

Step 5   Print a Cash Disbursements Journal report.
Step 6   Proof your work.
Step 7   Print a Vendors Ledgers report and a General Ledger report.
Step 8   Answer the Analyze question.

Checking Your Work and Ending the Session

Step 9   Click the **Close Problem** button in the Glencoe Smart Guide window.
Step 10   If your teacher has asked you to check your solution, click *Check my answer to this problem*. Review, print, and close the report.
Step 11   Click the **Close Problem** button and select the appropriate save option.

Problem 17-8   Recording and Posting Purchases and Cash Payments

INSTRUCTIONS

In Peachtree there are different ways to record cash disbursements. In this example, record bank services charges and bankcard fees using the **Payments** option.

Beginning a Session

Step 1   Select the problem set: Buzz Newsstand (Prob. 17-8).
Step 2   Rename the company and set the system date to July 31, 2004.

Completing the Accounting Problem

Step 3   Review the transactions in your textbook.
Step 4   Enter the purchases on account transactions.
Step 5   Record the cash payments.
Step 6   Print the following reports: Purchases Journal, Cash Disbursements Journal, and Vendors Ledgers.
Step 7   Proof your work.
Step 8   Print a General Ledger report.
Step 9   Answer the Analyze question.

Ending the Session

Step 10   Click the **Close Problem** button in the Glencoe Smart Guide window.

FAQs

What steps are required to correct a purchase invoice with the wrong vendor ID code or amount?

If you enter the wrong information for a purchase invoice, you can correct it even if you have already posted the transaction. Choose the **Purchases/Receive Inventory** option and click the **Edit Records** button. Select the invoice you want to change. When the invoice appears in the data entry window, make the necessary corrections and then post the updated transaction.

What steps are required to correct a cash payment entry?

You can change any information on a cash payment unless you have closed the current period. To make a change, choose the **Payments** option. Click the **Edit Records** button and select the payment you want to update. Make the changes and post the corrected transaction. Peachtree automatically applies the corrections.

The GL Account fields do not appear in the Purchases/Receive Inventory or Payments data entry windows.

Peachtree lets you hide the general ledger fields in the data entry windows. However, you will need to enter information in these fields to record certain kinds of transactions. To display the general ledger account fields, choose **Global** from the **Options** menu. Change the setting to show the general ledger accounts. **Note:** If the Purchases/Receive Inventory or Payments window is open, you must close the window and then choose the task option again before the new setting will take effect.

Working Papers _for End-of-Chapter Problems_
Problem 17-4   Recording Payment of the Payroll

CASH PAYMENTS JOURNAL

PAGE _____

DATE	ACCOUNT NAME	DOC. NO.	POST. REF.	GENERAL DEBIT	GENERAL CREDIT	ACCOUNTS PAYABLE DEBIT	PURCHASES DISCOUNTS CREDIT	CASH IN BANK CREDIT	
									1
									2
									3
									4
									5
									6
									7

Analyze:

Problem 17-5   Recording Transactions in the Purchases Journal

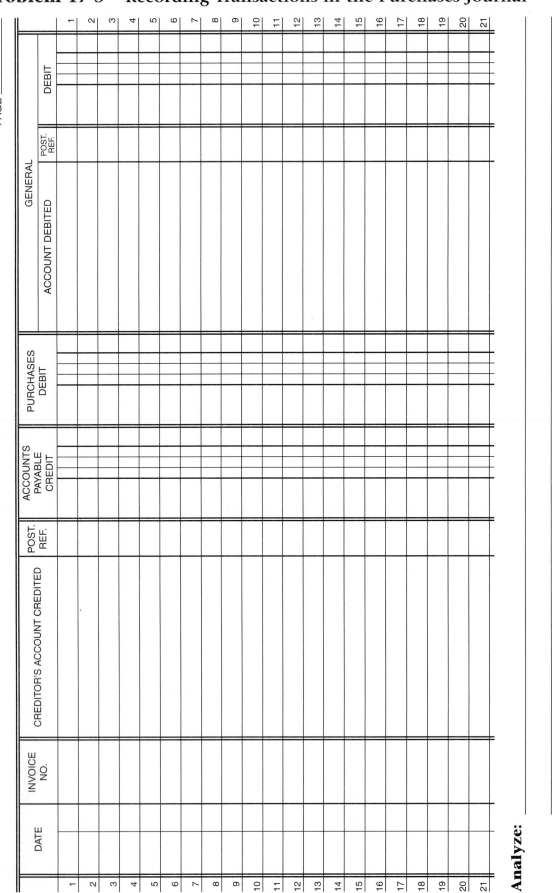

PURCHASES JOURNAL   PAGE _____

Analyze:

Problem 17-6   Recording and Posting Purchases

(1)

PURCHASES JOURNAL

PAGE _____

DATE	INVOICE NO.	CREDITOR'S ACCOUNT CREDITED	POST. REF.	ACCOUNTS PAYABLE CREDIT	PURCHASES DEBIT	GENERAL		
						ACCOUNT DEBITED	POST. REF.	DEBIT
1								
2								
3								
4								
5								
6								
7								
8								
9								
10								
11								
12								
13								
14								
15								
16								
17								
18								
19								
20								
21								
22								
23								
24								
25								

Problem 17-6   (continued)

(2), (3), (4), (5)

ACCOUNTS PAYABLE SUBSIDIARY LEDGER

Name **Allen's Repair**

Address **Two Deauville Place, Birmingham, AL 35203**

DATE	DESCRIPTION	POST. REF.	DEBIT	CREDIT	BALANCE

Name **Digital Precision Equipment**

Address **16 Military Complex, Huntsville, AL 35801**

DATE		DESCRIPTION	POST. REF.	DEBIT	CREDIT	BALANCE
20--						
July	1	Balance	✓			1 000 00

Name **Photo Emporium**

Address **Center Mall, Mobile, AL 36601**

DATE	DESCRIPTION	POST. REF.	DEBIT	CREDIT	BALANCE

Name **ProStudio Supply**

Address **Penn Center Blvd., Montgomery, AL 36104**

DATE		DESCRIPTION	POST. REF.	DEBIT	CREDIT	BALANCE
20--						
July	1	Balance	✓			2 000 00

Problem 17-6 (continued)

Name **State Street Office Supply**

Address **16 Garden Drive, Tuscaloosa, AL 35401**

DATE	DESCRIPTION	POST. REF.	DEBIT	CREDIT	BALANCE

Name **U-Tech Products**

Address **42 Ridgeway Drive, Decatur, AL 35601**

DATE		DESCRIPTION	POST. REF.	DEBIT	CREDIT	BALANCE
20--						
July	1	Balance	✓			1 50 00 0

Name **Video Optics Inc.**

Address **Three Oxford Place, Auburn, AL 36830**

DATE	DESCRIPTION	POST. REF.	DEBIT	CREDIT	BALANCE

Problem 17-6 (continued)

GENERAL LEDGER (PARTIAL)

ACCOUNT __Supplies__   ACCOUNT NO. __130__

DATE		DESCRIPTION	POST. REF.	DEBIT	CREDIT	BALANCE DEBIT	BALANCE CREDIT
20--							
July	1	Balance	✓			300 00	

ACCOUNT __Store Equipment__   ACCOUNT NO. __140__

DATE		DESCRIPTION	POST. REF.	DEBIT	CREDIT	BALANCE DEBIT	BALANCE CREDIT
20--							
July	1	Balance	✓			2500 00	

ACCOUNT __Accounts Payable__   ACCOUNT NO. __201__

DATE		DESCRIPTION	POST. REF.	DEBIT	CREDIT	BALANCE DEBIT	BALANCE CREDIT
20--							
July	1	Balance	✓				4500 00

ACCOUNT __Purchases__   ACCOUNT NO. __501__

DATE		DESCRIPTION	POST. REF.	DEBIT	CREDIT	BALANCE DEBIT	BALANCE CREDIT
20--							
July	1	Balance	✓			15000 00	

ACCOUNT __Maintenance Expense__   ACCOUNT NO. __640__

DATE		DESCRIPTION	POST. REF.	DEBIT	CREDIT	BALANCE DEBIT	BALANCE CREDIT
20--							
July	1	Balance	✓			200 00	

Problem 17-6   (concluded)

(6)

_____

_____

Analyze: _____

_____

_____

_____

Problem 17-7   Recording and Posting Cash Payments

(1), (4), (5)

PAGE _____

CASH PAYMENTS JOURNAL

DATE	DOC. NO.	ACCOUNT NAME	POST. REF.	GENERAL DEBIT	GENERAL CREDIT	ACCOUNTS PAYABLE DEBIT	PURCHASES DISCOUNTS CREDIT	CASH IN BANK CREDIT

Problem 17-7 (continued)

(2)

ACCOUNTS PAYABLE SUBSIDIARY LEDGER

Name *Mohican Falls Kayak Wholesalers*

Address *Box 17, Buffalo Road, Jackson, WY 83001*

DATE		DESCRIPTION	POST. REF.	DEBIT	CREDIT	BALANCE
20--						
July	1	Balance	✓			500 00

Name *North American Waterways Suppliers*

Address *Horse Creek Road, Casper, WY 82601*

DATE		DESCRIPTION	POST. REF.	DEBIT	CREDIT	BALANCE
20--						
July	1	Balance	✓			1400 00

Name *Office Max*

Address *142 Park Plaza, Cody, WY 82414*

DATE		DESCRIPTION	POST. REF.	DEBIT	CREDIT	BALANCE
20--						
July	1	Balance	✓			150 00

Name *Pacific Wholesalers*

Address *497 State Street, Laramie, WY 82070*

DATE		DESCRIPTION	POST. REF.	DEBIT	CREDIT	BALANCE
20--						
July	1	Balance	✓			1300 00

Problem 17-7 (continued)

Name **Rollins Plumbing Service**

Address **14 Ponderosa Road, Gillette, WY 82716**

DATE		DESCRIPTION	POST. REF.	DEBIT	CREDIT	BALANCE
20--						
July	1	Balance	✓			200 00

Name **StoreMart Supply**

Address **Box 182 Yellowstone Creek, Sheridan, WY 82801**

DATE		DESCRIPTION	POST. REF.	DEBIT	CREDIT	BALANCE
20--						
July	1	Balance	✓			900 00

Name **Trailhead Canoes**

Address **800 Trail Road, Cheyenne, WY 82001**

DATE		DESCRIPTION	POST. REF.	DEBIT	CREDIT	BALANCE
20--						
July	1	Balance	✓			700 00

Problem 17-7 (continued)

(3)

GENERAL LEDGER

ACCOUNT _Cash in Bank_   ACCOUNT NO. _101_

DATE		DESCRIPTION	POST. REF.	DEBIT	CREDIT	BALANCE DEBIT	BALANCE CREDIT
20--							
July	1	Balance	✓			8 00000	
	31		CR18	7 00000		15 00000	

ACCOUNT _Supplies_   ACCOUNT NO. _135_

DATE		DESCRIPTION	POST. REF.	DEBIT	CREDIT	BALANCE DEBIT	BALANCE CREDIT
20--							
July	1	Balance	✓			1 50000	

ACCOUNT _Prepaid Insurance_   ACCOUNT NO. _140_

DATE		DESCRIPTION	POST. REF.	DEBIT	CREDIT	BALANCE DEBIT	BALANCE CREDIT

ACCOUNT _Store Equipment_   ACCOUNT NO. _150_

DATE		DESCRIPTION	POST. REF.	DEBIT	CREDIT	BALANCE DEBIT	BALANCE CREDIT
20--							
July	1	Balance	✓			3 00000	

ACCOUNT _Accounts Payable_   ACCOUNT NO. _201_

DATE		DESCRIPTION	POST. REF.	DEBIT	CREDIT	BALANCE DEBIT	BALANCE CREDIT
20--							
July	1	Balance	✓				5 15000

Problem 17-7 (continued)

ACCOUNT __Transportation In__   ACCOUNT NO. __505__

DATE		DESCRIPTION	POST. REF.	DEBIT	CREDIT	BALANCE DEBIT	BALANCE CREDIT
20--							
July	1	Balance	✓			65000	

ACCOUNT __Purchases Discounts__   ACCOUNT NO. __510__

DATE		DESCRIPTION	POST. REF.	DEBIT	CREDIT	BALANCE DEBIT	BALANCE CREDIT
20--							
July	1	Balance	✓				150000

ACCOUNT __Advertising Expense__   ACCOUNT NO. __601__

DATE		DESCRIPTION	POST. REF.	DEBIT	CREDIT	BALANCE DEBIT	BALANCE CREDIT
20--							
July	1	Balance	✓			180000	

ACCOUNT __Miscellaneous Expense__   ACCOUNT NO. __655__

DATE		DESCRIPTION	POST. REF.	DEBIT	CREDIT	BALANCE DEBIT	BALANCE CREDIT

Problem 17-7   (concluded)

(6), (7)

Analyze: _____

_____

Problem 17-8   Source Documents

Instructions: *Use the following source documents to record the transactions for this problem.*

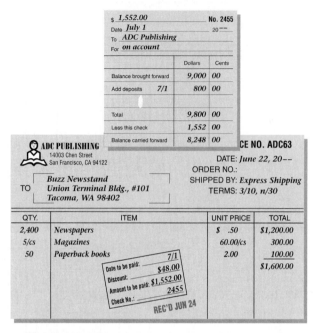

$ 1,552.00		No. 2455
Date July 1		20 --
To ADC Publishing		
For on account		
	Dollars	Cents
Balance brought forward	9,000	00
Add deposits 7/1	800	00
Total	9,800	00
Less this check	1,552	00
Balance carried forward	8,248	00

$ 1,358.00		No. 2456
Date July 2		20 --
To Candlelight Software		
For on account		
	Dollars	Cents
Balance brought forward	8,248	00
Add deposits		
Total	8,248	00
Less this check	1,358	00
Balance carried forward	6,890	00

ADC PUBLISHING
14003 Chen Street
San Francisco, CA 94122

INVOICE NO. ADC63

DATE: *June 22, 20--*
ORDER NO.:
SHIPPED BY: *Express Shipping*
TERMS: *3/10, n/30*

TO   *Buzz Newsstand*
Union Terminal Bldg., #101
Tacoma, WA 98402

QTY.	ITEM	UNIT PRICE	TOTAL
2,400	Newspapers	$ .50	$1,200.00
5/cs	Magazines	60.00/cs	300.00
50	Paperback books	2.00	100.00
			$1,600.00

Date to be paid: 7/1
Discount: $48.00
Amount to be paid: $1,552.00
Check No.:   2455
REC'D JUN 24

Candlelight Software
1466 San Diego Avenue
Tacoma, WA 98407

INVOICE NO. CS92

DATE: *June 18, 20--*
ORDER NO.:
SHIPPED BY: *Picked up*
TERMS: *3/15, n/30*

TO   *Buzz Newsstand*
Union Terminal Bldg., #101
Tacoma, WA 98402

QTY.	ITEM	UNIT PRICE	TOTAL
40	Travel planning software	$25.00	$1,000.00
80	Entertainment software	5.00	400.00
			$1,400.00

Date to be paid: 7/2
Discount: $42.00
Amount to be paid: $1,358.00
Check No.:   2456
REC'D JUN 20

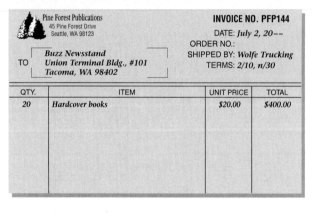

Pine Forest Publications
45 Pine Forest Drive
Seattle, WA 98123

INVOICE NO. PFP144

DATE: *July 2, 20--*
ORDER NO.:
SHIPPED BY: *Wolfe Trucking*
TERMS: *2/10, n/30*

TO   *Buzz Newsstand*
Union Terminal Bldg., #101
Tacoma, WA 98402

QTY.	ITEM	UNIT PRICE	TOTAL
20	Hardcover books	$20.00	$400.00

$ 350.00		No. 2457
Date July 4		20 --
To Nomad Computer Sales		
For on account		
	Dollars	Cents
Balance brought forward	6,890	00
Add deposits		
Total	6,890	00
Less this check	350	00
Balance carried forward	6,540	00

CorpTech Office Supply
818 McCain Street
Tacoma, WA 98402

INVOICE NO. CT67

DATE: *July 5, 20--*
ORDER NO.:
SHIPPED BY: *Picked up*
TERMS: *n/30*

TO   *Buzz Newsstand*
Union Terminal Bldg., #101
Tacoma, WA 98402

QTY.	ITEM	UNIT PRICE	TOTAL
5	Bookshelves	$300.00	$1,500.00
2	Book racks	193.00	386.00
			$1,886.00
		TX	114.00
			$2,000.00

$ 125.00		No. 2458
Date July 7		20 --
To Wolfe Trucking		
For transportation charges		
	Dollars	Cents
Balance brought forward	6,540	00
Add deposits 7/5	1,000	00
Total	7,540	00
Less this check	125	00
Balance carried forward	7,415	00

Problem 17-8   (continued)

American Trend Publishers
766 Goldrush Way
Denver, CO 80207

INVOICE NO. ATP98

DATE: *July 9, 20--*
ORDER NO.:
SHIPPED BY: *Wolfe Trucking*
TERMS: *2/10, n/30*

TO
Buzz Newsstand
Union Terminal Bldg., #101
Tacoma, WA 98402

QTY.	ITEM	UNIT PRICE	TOTAL
250	Paperback books	$2.00	$500.00
800	Newspapers	.50	400.00
			$900.00

$ 882.00   No. 2461
Date *July 16*   20--
To *American Trend Publishers*
For *on account (900 less 2% disc.)*

	Dollars	Cents
Balance brought forward	7,265	00
Add deposits		
Total	7,265	00
Less this check	882	00
Balance carried forward	6,383	00

CorpTech Office Supply
818 McCain Street
Tacoma, WA 98402

INVOICE NO. CT72

DATE: *July 12, 20--*
ORDER NO.:
SHIPPED BY: *Picked up*
TERMS: *n/30*

TO
Buzz Newsstand
Union Terminal Bldg., #101
Tacoma, WA 98402

QTY.	ITEM	UNIT PRICE	TOTAL
2 cs	Office paper	$66.50/cs	$133.00
3	Inkjet ink cartridges	50.00/ea	150.00
			$283.00
		TX	17.00
			$300.00

Candlelight Software
1466 San Diego Avenue
Tacoma, WA 98407

INVOICE NO. CS101

DATE: *July 18, 20--*
ORDER NO.:
SHIPPED BY: *Picked up*
TERMS: *n/30*

TO
Buzz Newsstand
Union Terminal Bldg., #101
Tacoma, WA 98402

QTY.	ITEM	UNIT PRICE	TOTAL
100	Entertainment software	$5.00	$500.00

$ 750.00   No. 2459
Date *July 14*   20--
To *Delta Press*
For *on account*

	Dollars	Cents
Balance brought forward	7,415	00
Add deposits		
Total	7,415	00
Less this check	750	00
Balance carried forward	6,665	00

Nomad COMPUTER SALES
1601 San Diego Avenue
Tacoma, WA 98407

INVOICE NO. NC56

DATE: *July 20, 20--*
ORDER NO.:
SHIPPED BY: *Picked up*
TERMS: *2/10, n/30*

TO
Buzz Newsstand
Union Terminal Bldg., #101
Tacoma, WA 98402

QTY.	ITEM	UNIT PRICE	TOTAL
20	Pocket electronic organizers	$10.00	$200.00

$ 1,600.00   No. 2460
Date *July 15*   20--
To *SeaTac Insurance Co.*
For *prepaid insurance*

	Dollars	Cents
Balance brought forward	6,665	00
Add deposits 7/15	2,200	00
Total	8,865	00
Less this check	1,600	00
Balance carried forward	7,265	00

$ 100.00   No. 2462
Date *July 22*   20--
To *Pine Forest Publications*
For *on account*

	Dollars	Cents
Balance brought forward	6,383	00
Add deposits 7/18	1,500	00
7/20	2,000	00
Total	9,883	00
Less this check	100	00
Balance carried forward	9,783	00

Problem 17-8   (continued)

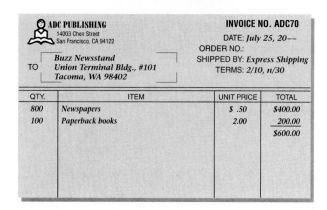

$ 2,000.00		No. 2463
Date July 23		20 --
To CorpTech Office Supply		
For on account		
	Dollars	**Cents**
Balance brought forward	9,783	00
Add deposits		
Total	9,783	00
Less this check	2,000	00
Balance carried forward	7,783	00

ADC PUBLISHING
14003 Chen Street
San Francisco, CA 94122

INVOICE NO. ADC70
DATE: *July 25, 20--*
ORDER NO.:
SHIPPED BY: *Express Shipping*
TERMS: *2/10, n/30*

TO   *Buzz Newsstand*
Union Terminal Bldg., #101
Tacoma, WA 98402

QTY.	ITEM	UNIT PRICE	TOTAL
800	Newspapers	$ .50	$400.00
100	Paperback books	2.00	200.00
			$600.00

BUZZ
NEWSSTAND
Union Terminal Building, #101
Tacoma, WA 98402

INTEROFFICE MEMORANDUM

TO: *Accounting Clerk*
FROM: *Kathy Harper, Manager*
DATE: *7/30/--*
SUBJECT: *Bank Statement Fees*

The July bank statement had the following fees:
   Bank Service Charge $ 25.00
   Bankcard Fees   130.00

$		No. 2465
Date		20
To		
For		
	Dollars	**Cents**
Balance brought forward	7,333	00
Add deposits 7/30	3,000	00
Bk. Stmt. –	155	00
Total	10,178	00
Less this check		
Balance carried forward		

$ 450.00		No. 2464
Date July 28		20 --
To Nomad Computer Sales		
For on account		
	Dollars	**Cents**
Balance brought forward	7,783	00
Add deposits		
Total	7,783	00
Less this check	450	00
Balance carried forward	7,333	00

Problem 17-8   Recording and Posting Purchases and Cash Payments

(1), (3), (4)

PAGE _____

CASH PAYMENTS JOURNAL

DATE	DOC. NO.	ACCOUNT NAME	POST. REF.	GENERAL DEBIT	GENERAL CREDIT	ACCOUNTS PAYABLE DEBIT	PURCHASES DISCOUNTS CREDIT	CASH IN BANK CREDIT
									1
									2
									3
									4
									5
									6
									7
									8
									9
									10
									11
									12
									13
									14
									15
									16
									17
									18
									19
									20
									21
									22

Problem 17-8 (continued)

(1), (3), (4)

PURCHASES JOURNAL

PAGE _____

DATE	INVOICE NO.	CREDITOR'S ACCOUNT CREDITED	POST. REF.	ACCOUNTS PAYABLE CREDIT	PURCHASES DEBIT	GENERAL		
						ACCOUNT DEBITED	POST. REF.	DEBIT

Problem 17-8 (continued)

(5), (6)

GENERAL LEDGER

ACCOUNT **Cash in Bank**   ACCOUNT NO. **101**

DATE		DESCRIPTION	POST. REF.	DEBIT	CREDIT	BALANCE DEBIT	BALANCE CREDIT
20--							
July	1	Balance	✓			900000	
	30		CR12	1050000		1950000	

ACCOUNT **Supplies**   ACCOUNT NO. **135**

DATE		DESCRIPTION	POST. REF.	DEBIT	CREDIT	BALANCE DEBIT	BALANCE CREDIT
20--							
July	1	Balance	✓			15000	

ACCOUNT **Prepaid Insurance**   ACCOUNT NO. **140**

DATE	DESCRIPTION	POST. REF.	DEBIT	CREDIT	BALANCE DEBIT	BALANCE CREDIT

ACCOUNT **Store Equipment**   ACCOUNT NO. **150**

DATE		DESCRIPTION	POST. REF.	DEBIT	CREDIT	BALANCE DEBIT	BALANCE CREDIT
20--							
July	1	Balance	✓			600000	

ACCOUNT **Accounts Payable**   ACCOUNT NO. **201**

DATE		DESCRIPTION	POST. REF.	DEBIT	CREDIT	BALANCE DEBIT	BALANCE CREDIT
20--							
July	1	Balance	✓				570000

Problem 17-8 (continued)

ACCOUNT __Purchases__   ACCOUNT NO. ___501___

DATE		DESCRIPTION	POST. REF.	DEBIT	CREDIT	BALANCE DEBIT	BALANCE CREDIT
20--							
July	1	Balance	✓			2500000	

ACCOUNT __Transportation In__   ACCOUNT NO. ___505___

DATE		DESCRIPTION	POST. REF.	DEBIT	CREDIT	BALANCE DEBIT	BALANCE CREDIT
20--							
July	1	Balance	✓			80000	

ACCOUNT __Purchases Discounts__   ACCOUNT NO. ___510___

DATE		DESCRIPTION	POST. REF.	DEBIT	CREDIT	BALANCE DEBIT	BALANCE CREDIT
20--							
July	1	Balance	✓				160000

ACCOUNT __Bankcard Fees Expense__   ACCOUNT NO. ___605___

DATE		DESCRIPTION	POST. REF.	DEBIT	CREDIT	BALANCE DEBIT	BALANCE CREDIT
20--							
July	1	Balance	✓			110000	

ACCOUNT __Miscellaneous Expense__   ACCOUNT NO. ___650___

DATE		DESCRIPTION	POST. REF.	DEBIT	CREDIT	BALANCE DEBIT	BALANCE CREDIT
20--							
July	1	Balance	✓			20000	

Problem 17-8   (continued)

(2)

ACCOUNTS PAYABLE SUBSIDIARY LEDGER

Name _ADC Publishing_

Address _5670 Mulberry Place, Seattle, WA 98101_

DATE		DESCRIPTION	POST. REF.	DEBIT	CREDIT	BALANCE
20--						
July	1	Balance	✓			1 60 0 00

Name _American Trend Publishers_

Address _1313 Maple Drive, Seattle, WA 98148_

DATE		DESCRIPTION	POST. REF.	DEBIT	CREDIT	BALANCE

Name _Candlelight Software_

Address _Six Evergreen Park, Tacoma, WA 98402_

DATE		DESCRIPTION	POST. REF.	DEBIT	CREDIT	BALANCE
20--						
July	1	Balance	✓			1 40 0 00

Name _CorpTech Office Supply_

Address _601 Cascade Park, Bellevue, WA 98009_

DATE		DESCRIPTION	POST. REF.	DEBIT	CREDIT	BALANCE

Problem 17-8 (continued)

Name *Delta Press*

Address *One Triangle Park, Vancouver, WA 98661*

DATE		DESCRIPTION	POST. REF.	DEBIT	CREDIT	BALANCE
20--						
July	1	Balance	✓			1 50 0 00

Name *Nomad Computer Sales*

Address *16 Point Drive, Ft. Lewis, WA 98433*

DATE		DESCRIPTION	POST. REF.	DEBIT	CREDIT	BALANCE
20--						
July	1	Balance	✓			1 20 0 00

Name *Pine Forest Publications*

Address *103 Mt. Thor Road, Spokane, WA 99210*

DATE		DESCRIPTION	POST. REF.	DEBIT	CREDIT	BALANCE

Problem 17-8 (concluded)

(7)

(8)

Analyze: _____

CHAPTER 17

Special Journals: Purchases and Cash Payments

Self-Test

Part A   True or False

Directions: *Circle the letter* T *in the Answer column if the statement is true; circle the letter* F *if the statement is false.*

Answer

T   F   **1.** Accounts in the accounts payable subsidiary ledger have normal debit balances.

T   F   **2.** An invoice dated June 17 with terms 2/10, n/30 must be paid by July 17 to take advantage of the cash discount.

T   F   **3.** The Accounts Payable controlling account is found in the general ledger.

T   F   **4.** Because a bank service charge is automatically deducted from the checking account of a business, it is not necessary to record an entry in the cash payments journal.

T   F   **5.** Special journals should be footed before column totals are proved.

T   F   **6.** The purchases journal is used only for recording the purchase of merchandise on account.

T   F   **7.** Transactions recorded in either the purchases or cash payments journals which affect accounts payable subsidiary ledger accounts should be posted on a daily basis, that is, as soon as the transaction is recorded.

T   F   **8.** Cash should always be proved at the end of the month.

T   F   **9.** Check stubs and the bank statement are the only two source documents used for recording transactions in the cash payments journal.

T   F   **10.** The column totals of special journals are always posted at the end of the month.

Part B   Matching

Directions: *The general journal and special journals listed below are identified by a letter. Following the list is a series of business transactions. For each transaction, indicate in which journal the transaction would be recorded by writing the identifying letter in the Answer column.*

A. cash payments journal	**C.** general journal	**E.** sales journal
B. cash receipts journal	**D.** purchases journal	

Answer

_____   **1.** Recorded bank card fees for the month.

_____   **2.** Purchased store equipment on account.

_____   **3.** Issued a debit memorandum for the return of merchandise purchased on account.

_____   **4.** Recorded bank card sales for the day.

_____   **5.** Sold merchandise on account.

_____   **6.** Purchased office supplies for cash.

_____   **7.** Issued a credit memorandum to a charge customer for the return of merchandise purchased on account.

_____   **8.** Recorded cash sales for the day.

_____   **9.** Discovered that a payment made by Port Co., a charge customer, was incorrectly credited to Porter Co.

_____   **10.** Purchased merchandise for cash.

_____   **11.** Paid the monthly utility bill.

_____   **12.** Purchased merchandise on account.

_____   **13.** Recorded the bank service charge.

CHAPTER 18 Adjustments and the Ten-Column Work Sheet

Study Plan

Check Your Understanding

Section 1	*Read Section 1 on pages 484–489 and complete the following exercises on page 490.*
	❏ Thinking Critically
	❏ Analyzing Accounting
	❏ Problem 18-1 *Analyzing the Adjustment for Merchandise Inventory*

Section 2	*Read Section 2 on pages 491–494 and complete the following exercises on page 495.*
	❏ Thinking Critically
	❏ Computing in the Business World
	❏ Problem 18-2 *Analyzing Adjustments*

Section 3	*Read Section 3 on pages 496–503 and complete the following exercises on page 504.*
	❏ Thinking Critically
	❏ Communicating Accounting
	❏ Problem 18-3 *Analyzing the Work Sheet*
	❏ Problem 18-4 *Analyzing a Source Document*

Summary	*Review the Chapter 18 Summary on page 505 in your textbook.*
	❏ Key Concepts

Review and Activities	*Complete the following questions and exercises on pages 506–507 in your textbook.*
	❏ Using Key Terms
	❏ Understanding Accounting Concepts and Procedures
	❏ Case Study
	❏ Conducting an Audit with Alex
	❏ Internet Connection
	❏ Workplace Skills

Computerized Accounting	*Read the Computerized Accounting information on page 508 in your textbook.*
	❏ *Making the Transition from a Manual to a Computerized System*
	❏ *Recording Adjusting Entries in Peachtree*

Problems	*Complete the following end-of-chapter problems for Chapter 18 in your textbook.*
	❏ Problem 18-5 *Completing a Ten-Column Work Sheet*
	❏ Problem 18-6 *Completing a Ten-Column Work Sheet*
	❏ Problem 18-7 *Completing a Ten-Column Work Sheet*
	❏ Problem 18-8 *Completing a Ten-Column Work Sheet*

Challenge Problem	❏ Problem 18-9 *Locating Errors on the Work Sheet*

Chapter Reviews and Working Papers	*Complete the following exercises for Chapter 18 in your Chapter Reviews and Working Papers.*
	❏ Chapter Review
	❏ Self-Test

CHAPTER 18 REVIEW — Adjustments and the Ten-Column Work Sheet

Part 1 Accounting Vocabulary (3 points)

Directions: *Using terms from the following list, complete the sentences below. Write the letter of the term you have chosen in the space provided.*

| Total Points | 45 |
| Student's Score | |

| **A.** adjustment | **B.** beginning inventory | **C.** ending inventory | **D.** physical inventory |

_____B_____ **0.** The merchandise a business has on hand at the beginning of a fiscal period is the _____.

_____ **1.** An amount that is added to or subtracted from an account balance to bring that balance up to date is known as a(n) _____.

_____ **2.** The merchandise on hand at the end of a fiscal period is the _____.

_____ **3.** An actual count of all the merchandise on hand and available for sale is called a(n) _____.

Part 2 Examining End-of-Period Adjustments (12 points)

Directions: *Read each of the following statements to determine whether the statement is true or false. Write your answer in the space provided.*

___True___ **0.** The amount of merchandise on hand at the end of a fiscal period is determined by a physical count.

_____ **1.** The value of the ending inventory is always less than the value of the beginning inventory.

_____ **2.** A corporation is not required to estimate in advance its federal income taxes for the year.

_____ **3.** The amount entered in the Adjustments Credit column on the line for Supplies is the amount of supplies used during the fiscal period.

_____ **4.** If the ending inventory is less than the beginning inventory, the Income Summary account is credited for the difference.

_____ **5.** The Federal Corporate Income Tax Payable account normally has a debit balance.

_____ **6.** The work sheet is the source of information for preparing the end-of-period financial statements and journal entries.

_____ **7.** Changes in account balances are not always the result of daily business transactions.

_____ **8.** Supplies used in the operation of a business are initially recorded as assets and eventually become expenses as they are consumed.

_____ **9.** A trial balance is prepared only at the end of the fiscal period.

_____ **10.** Prepaid Insurance will normally be credited in the Adjustments section of the work sheet.

_____ **11.** The Trial Balance section of the work sheet does not include general ledger accounts with zero balances.

_____ **12.** Because there are no source documents that show changes in account balances caused by internal operations, these changes must be shown through adjusting entries.

Part 3 Analyzing Adjustments (8 points)

Directions: *Using account names from the following list, determine the accounts to be debited and credited for the adjustments below. Write your answers in the space provided.*

A. Federal Corporate Income Tax Expense	**C.** Income Summary	**F.** Prepaid Insurance
B. Federal Corp. Income Tax Payable	**D.** Insurance Expense	**G.** Supplies
	E. Merchandise Inventory	**H.** Supplies Expense

Debit	Credit	
D	F	**0.** Adjustment for the insurance premiums expired.
___	___	**1.** The beginning inventory is $34,946; and the ending inventory is $36,496.
___	___	**2.** Adjustment for additional federal income taxes owed.
___	___	**3.** Adjustment for the supplies on hand.
___	___	**4.** The beginning inventory is $73,937; and the ending inventory is $72,094.

Part 4 Extending Account Balances (22 points)

Directions: *For each of the following account names, indicate whether the account will have a normal debit or credit balance in the Adjusted Trial Balance section of the work sheet. Place a check mark in the appropriate column.*

Account Name	Debit Balance	Credit Balance
0. Cash in Bank	✓	___
1. Medicare Tax Payable	___	___
2. Capital Stock	___	___
3. Sales Returns and Allowances	___	___
4. Transportation In	___	___
5. Rent Expense	___	___
6. Federal Corporate Income Tax Payable	___	___
7. Sales Discounts	___	___
8. Purchases	___	___
9. Accounts Payable	___	___
10. Supplies Expense	___	___
11. Prepaid Insurance	___	___
12. Accounts Receivable	___	___
13. Office Equipment	___	___
14. Retained Earnings	___	___
15. Payroll Tax Expense	___	___
16. Purchases Discounts	___	___
17. Sales	___	___
18. Supplies	___	___
19. Merchandise Inventory	___	___
20. Sales Tax Payable	___	___
21. Employees' State Income Tax Payable	___	___
22. Federal Unemployment Tax Payable	___	___

Working Papers *for Section Problems*

Problem 18-1   Analyzing the Adjustment for Merchandise Inventory

1. _____
2. _____
3. _____
4. _____

Problem 18-2   Analyzing Adjustments

1. Amount of Adjustment _____

   Account Debited _____

   Account Credited _____

2. Amount of Adjustment _____

   Account Debited _____

   Account Credited _____

3. Amount of Adjustment _____

   Account Debited _____

   Account Credited _____

Problem 18-3   Analyzing the Work Sheet

1. Amount? _____

2. Section? _____

3. Amount? _____

4. Amount? _____

Problem 18-4   Analyzing a Source Document

1. _____
2. _____
3. _____
4. _____
5. _____

Computerized Accounting Using Peachtree

Software Objectives

When you have completed this chapter, you will be able to use Peachtree to:

1. Print a Working Trial Balance report.
2. Record adjusting entries using the **General Journal Entry** option.
3. Print an adjusted trial balance.

Problem 18-6   Completing a Ten-Column Work Sheet

INSTRUCTIONS

Beginning a Session

Step 1   Select the problem set: Shutterbug Cameras (Prob. 18-6).
Step 2   Rename the company and set the system date to August 31, 2004.

Completing the Accounting Problem

Step 3   Review the information in your textbook.
Step 4   Print a Working Trial Balance report and use it to record the adjustments.

> **DO YOU HAVE A QUESTION**
>
> **Q.** *Does Peachtree include an option to print a ten-column work sheet?*
>
> **A.** The ten-column work sheet is a convenient way to manually prepare an adjusted trial balance, an income statement, and a balance sheet. When you use Peachtree, the program automatically prepares the financial statements so a work sheet is not needed. Peachtree does, however, include a Working Trial Balance report that you can use as an aid when recording the adjustments.

The procedures to record the adjustments using Peachtree are the same as a manual system except for the adjustment to **Merchandise Inventory**. In a manual system, you make an adjustment to the **Income Summary** and **Merchandise Inventory** accounts. For a computerized accounting system such as Peachtree you must use the **Inventory Adjustment** account instead of the **Income Summary** account. The inventory adjustment for Shutterbug Cameras is shown below.

Account	Debit	Credit
Inventory Adjustment	4,309	
Merchandise Inventory Adjusting Entry		4,309

The adjustment shown above achieves the same result as the adjustment you learned how to make in your textbook. After the adjustment, the **Merchandise Inventory** account balance reflects the value of the physical inventory at the end of the period. This change in value is posted to the **Inventory Adjustment** account. As you will see in the next chapter, this account appears in the Cost of Merchandise Sold section on an Income Statement.

Step 5   Record the adjustments using the **General Journal Entry** option.

>
> **TIP:** You can record the adjustments as one multi-part general journal entry to save time.

> **Notes**
> Use **ADJ. ENT.** for the reference and **Adjusting Entry** as the description when you record the adjustments.

Step 6   Print a General Journal and an Adjusted Trial Balance report. Set the filter options to include only the adjusting entries on the report.
Step 7   Proof your work.
Step 8   Answer the Analyze question.

Peachtree Guide

Ending the Session

> **Step 9**   Click the **Close Problem** button in the Glencoe Smart Guide window.

Mastering Peachtree

Change the report title on the General Ledger Trial balance to *Adjusted Trial Balance*. Also, widen the Account Description column so that it accommodates the longest description. Print your resulting report.

Problem 18-7   Completing a Ten-Column Work Sheet

INSTRUCTIONS

Beginning a Session

> **Step 1**   Select the problem set: Cycle Tech Bicycles (Prob. 18-7).
> **Step 2**   Rename the company and set the system date to August 31, 2004.

Completing the Accounting Problem

> **Step 3**   Review the information in your textbook.
> **Step 4**   Print a Working Trial Balance report and use it to help you prepare the adjustments.
> **Step 5**   Record the adjustments using the **General Journal Entry** option.
> **Step 6**   Print a General Journal report.
> **Step 7**   Proof your work.
> **Step 8**   Answer the Analyze question.

Checking Your Work and Ending the Session

> **Step 9**   Click the **Close Problem** button in the Glencoe Smart Guide window.
> **Step 10**   If your teacher has asked you to check your solution, click *Check my answer to this problem*. Review and print the report.
> **Step 11**   Click the **Close Problem** button and save your work.

DO YOU HAVE A QUESTION

Q. *Why do you have to use the Inventory Adjustment account instead of the Income Summary account when you adjust the Merchandise Inventory?*

A. A computerized system such as Peachtree needs to calculate the cost of merchandise sold so that it can determine the net income. The **Inventory Adjustment** account is a cost of sales account as opposed to the **Income Summary** account, which is a temporary capital account. As you will learn in the next chapter, the **Inventory Adjustment** account appears in the Cost of Merchandise Sold section on an income statement.

Problem 18-8   Completing a Ten-Column Work Sheet

INSTRUCTIONS

Beginning a Session

> **Step 1**   Select the problem set: River's Edge Canoe & Kayak (Prob. 18-8).
> **Step 2**   Rename the company and set the system date to August 31, 2004.

Completing the Accounting Problem

> **Step 3**   Review the information in your textbook.
> **Step 4**   Print a Working Trial Balance report and use it to help you prepare the adjustments.
> **Step 5**   Record the adjustments.
> **Step 6**   Print a General Journal report and a General Ledger report.
> **Step 7**   Proof your work.
> **Step 8**   Answer the Analyze question.

Ending the Session

> **Step 9**   Click the **Close Problem** button in the Glencoe Smart Guide window.

Computerized Accounting Using Spreadsheets

Problem 18-5   Completing a Ten-Column Work Sheet

Completing the Spreadsheet

Step 1   Read the instructions for Problem 18-5 in your textbook. This problem involves completing a ten-column work sheet for InBeat CD Shop.

Step 2   Open the Glencoe Accounting: Electronic Learning Center software.

Step 3   From the Program Menu, click on the **Peachtree Accounting Software and Spreadsheet Applications** icon.

Step 4   Log onto the Management System by typing your user name and password.

Step 5   Under the Chapter Problems tab, select the template: PR18-5a.xls. The template should look like the one shown below.

```
PROBLEM 18-5
COMPLETING A TEN-COLUMN WORK SHEET

(name)
(date)


INBEAT CD SHOP WORK SHEET
FOR THE YEAR ENDED AUGUST 31, 20--
```

ACCOUNT NUMBER	ACCOUNT NAME	TRIAL BALANCE DEBIT	TRIAL BALANCE CREDIT	ADJUSTMENTS DEBIT	ADJUSTMENTS CREDIT	> <	BALANCE SHEET DEBIT	BALANCE SHEET CREDIT
101	Cash in Bank	14,974.00				> <	14,974.00	
115	Accounts Receivable	3,774.00				> <	3,774.00	
130	Merchandise Inventory	86,897.00			AMOUNT	> <	86,897.00	
135	Supplies	2,940.00			AMOUNT	> <	2,940.00	
140	Prepaid Insurance	1,975.00			AMOUNT	> <	1,975.00	
150	Office Equipment	10,819.00				> <	10,819.00	
201	Accounts Payable		7,740.00			> <		7,740.00
207	Federal Corporate Income Tax Payable				AMOUNT	> <		0.00
210	Employees' Federal Income Tax Payable		291.00			> <		291.00
211	Employees' State Income Tax Payable		86.00			> <		86.00
212	Social Security Tax Payable		106.00			> <		106.00
213	Medicare Tax Payable		21.00			> <		21.00
215	Fed. Unemployment Tax Payable		32.00			> <		32.00
216	State Unemployment Tax Payable		106.00			> <		106.00
217	Sales Tax Payable		1,370.00			> <		1,370.00
301	Capital Stock		55,000.00			> <		55,000.00
305	Retained Earnings		30,928.00			> <		30,928.00
310	Income Summary	----	----	AMOUNT		> <		
401	Sales		149,136.00			> <		
501	Purchases	93,874.00				> <		
625	Federal Corporate Income Tax	2,200.00		AMOUNT		> <		
630	Insurance Expense			AMOUNT		> <		
647	Payroll Tax Expense	2,170.00				> <		
650	Miscellaneous Expense	3,662.00				> <		
655	Rent Expense	9,225.00				> <		
660	Salaries Expense	12,306.00				> <		
665	Supplies Expense			AMOUNT		> <		
		244,816.00	244,816.00	0.00	0.00	> <	121,379.00	95,680.00
	Net Income					> <		25,699.00
						> <	121,379.00	121,379.00

Spreadsheet Guide

Step 6   Key your name and today's date in the cells containing the *(name)* and *(date)* placeholders.

Step 7   The trial balance amounts are given for you. The first adjustment that must be made is to adjust beginning merchandise inventory of $86,897 to an ending balance of $77,872. To make this adjustment, you must debit Income Summary and credit Merchandise Inventory for the difference between the beginning and ending merchandise inventory amounts. Enter the Income Summary adjustment in cell E29 and the Merchandise Inventory adjustment in cell F14.

      Notice that, as you enter the adjustments, the balances for the affected accounts in the adjusted trial balance change accordingly.

Step 8   Enter the remaining adjustments into the Adjustments section of the spreadsheet template. When you have entered all of the adjustments, move the cell pointer into the Adjusted Trial Balance, Income Statement, and Balance Sheet sections of the spreadsheet template. Notice that the amounts for the Adjusted Trial Balance, Income Statement, and Balance Sheet are automatically entered. The program also calculates the column totals and the net income for InBeat CD Shop.

Step 9   Save the spreadsheet to a data disk or to the hard drive as instructed by your teacher. Use the filename *PR18-5XX* to save the spreadsheet (replace the *XX* with your initials).

Step 10   Print the completed spreadsheet.

TIP: If your spreadsheet is too wide to fit on an 8.5-inch wide piece of paper, you can change your print settings to print the worksheet *landscape.* Landscape means that the worksheet will be printed broadside on the page. Some spreadsheet applications also allow you to choose a "print to page" option. This function will reduce the width and/or depth of the worksheet to fit on one page.

Step 11   Exit the spreadsheet program.

Step 12   Answer the Analyze question from your textbook for this problem.

What-If Analysis

If Merchandise Inventory on August 31 were $80,123, what adjustments would be made? What would be the effect on net income?

_____

_____

Working Papers *for End-of-Chapter Problems*
Problem 18-5　Completing a Ten-Column Work Sheet

InBeat

Work

For the Month Ended

	ACCT. NO.	ACCOUNT NAME	TRIAL BALANCE DEBIT	TRIAL BALANCE CREDIT	ADJUSTMENTS DEBIT	ADJUSTMENTS CREDIT
1	101	Cash in Bank	14974 00			
2	115	Accounts Receivable	3774 00			
3	130	Merchandise Inventory	86897 00			
4	135	Supplies	2940 00			
5	140	Prepaid Insurance	1975 00			
6	150	Office Equipment	10819 00			
7	201	Accounts Payable		7740 00		
8	207	Fed. Corporate Income Tax Pay.				
9	210	Employees' Fed. Inc. Tax Pay.		291 00		
10	211	Employees' State Inc. Tax Pay.		86 00		
11	212	Social Security Tax Payable		106 00		
12	213	Medicare Tax Payable		21 00		
13	215	Fed. Unemployment Tax Pay.		32 00		
14	216	State Unemployment Tax Pay.		106 00		
15	217	Sales Tax Payable		1370 00		
16	301	Capital Stock		55000 00		
17	305	Retained Earnings		30928 00		
18	310	Income Summary				
19	401	Sales		149136 00		
20	501	Purchases	93874 00			
21	625	Fed. Corporate Income Tax Exp.	2200 00			
22	630	Insurance Expense				
23	647	Payroll Tax Expense	2170 00			
24	650	Miscellaneous Expense	3662 00			
25	655	Rent Expense	9225 00			
26	660	Salaries Expense	12306 00			
27	665	Supplies Expense				
28						
29			244816 00	244816 00		
30						
31						
32						
33						

CD Shop

Sheet

August 31, 20--

	ADJUSTED TRIAL BALANCE		INCOME STATEMENT		BALANCE SHEET		
	DEBIT	CREDIT	DEBIT	CREDIT	DEBIT	CREDIT	
							1
							2
							3
							4
							5
							6
							7
							8
							9
							10
							11
							12
							13
							14
							15
							16
							17
							18
							19
							20
							21
							22
							23
							24
							25
							26
							27
							28
							29
							30
							31
							32
							33

Analyze: _____

Problem 18-6 Completing a Ten-Column Work Sheet

Shutterbug

Work

For the Month Ended

	ACCT. NO.	ACCOUNT NAME	TRIAL BALANCE		ADJUSTMENTS	
			DEBIT	CREDIT	DEBIT	CREDIT
1	101	Cash in Bank				
2	115	Accounts Receivable				
3	125	Merchandise Inventory				
4	130	Supplies				
5	135	Prepaid Insurance				
6	140	Store Equipment				
7	201	Accounts Payable				
8	207	Fed. Corporate Income Tax Pay.				
9	210	Employees' Fed. Inc. Tax Pay.				
10	211	Employees' State Inc. Tax Pay.				
11	212	Social Security Tax Payable				
12	213	Medicare Tax Payable				
13	215	Sales Tax Payable				
14	216	Fed. Unemployment Tax Pay.				
15	217	State Unemployment Tax Pay				
16	301	Capital Stock				
17	305	Retained Earnings				
18	310	Income Summary				
19	401	Sales				
20	405	Sales Discounts				
21	410	Sales Returns and Allowances				
22	501	Purchases				
23	505	Transportation In				
24	510	Purchases Discounts				
25	515	Purchases Returns and Allow.				
26	601	Advertising Expense				
27	605	Bankcard Fees Expense				
28	620	Fed. Corporate Income Tax Exp.				
29		Carried Forward				
30						
31						
32						

Cameras

Sheet

August 31, 20--

	ADJUSTED TRIAL BALANCE		INCOME STATEMENT		BALANCE SHEET		
	DEBIT	CREDIT	DEBIT	CREDIT	DEBIT	CREDIT	
							1
							2
							3
							4
							5
							6
							7
							8
							9
							10
							11
							12
							13
							14
							15
							16
							17
							18
							19
							20
							21
							22
							23
							24
							25
							26
							27
							28
							29
							30
							31
							32

Problem 18-6   (concluded)

Shutterbug
Work Sheet
For the Month Ended

	ACCT. NO.	ACCOUNT NAME	TRIAL BALANCE		ADJUSTMENTS	
			DEBIT	CREDIT	DEBIT	CREDIT
1		*Brought Forward*				
2						
3	630	*Insurance Expense*				
4	640	*Maintenance Expense*				
5	645	*Miscellaneous Expense*				
6	647	*Payroll Tax Expense*				
7	650	*Rent Expense*				
8	655	*Salaries Expense*				
9	660	*Supplies Expense*				
10	670	*Utilities Expense*				

Cameras

(continued)

August 31, 20--

ADJUSTED TRIAL BALANCE		INCOME STATEMENT		BALANCE SHEET		
DEBIT	CREDIT	DEBIT	CREDIT	DEBIT	CREDIT	
						1
						2
						3
						4
						5
						6
						7
						8
						9
						10
						11
						12
						13
						14
						15
						16
						17
						18
						19
						20
						21
						22
						23
						24
						25
						26
						27
						28
						29
						30
						31
						32

Analyze: _____

_____

Problem 18-7 Completing a Ten-Column Work Sheet

Cycle Tech

Work

For the Month Ended

	ACCT. NO.	ACCOUNT NAME	TRIAL BALANCE		ADJUSTMENTS	
			DEBIT	CREDIT	DEBIT	CREDIT
1	101	Cash in Bank				
2	115	Accounts Receivable				
3	125	Merchandise Inventory				
4	130	Supplies				
5	135	Prepaid Insurance				
6	140	Store Equipment				
7	145	Office Equipment				
8	201	Accounts Payable				
9	210	Fed. Corporate Income Tax Pay.				
10	211	Employees' Fed. Inc. Tax Pay.				
11	212	Employees' State Inc. Tax Pay.				
12	213	Social Security Tax Payable				
13	214	Medicare Tax Payable				
14	215	Sales Tax Payable				
15	216	Fed. Unemployment Tax Pay.				
16	217	State Unemployment Tax Pay.				
17	301	Capital Stock				
18	305	Retained Earnings				
19	310	Income Summary				
20	401	Sales				
21	405	Sales Discounts				
22	410	Sales Returns and Allowances				
23	501	Purchases				
24	505	Transportation In				
25	510	Purchases Discounts				
26	515	Purchases Returns and Allow.				
27	601	Advertising Expense				
28	605	Bankcard Fees Expense				
29		Carried Forward				
30						
31						
32						

Bicycles

Sheet

August 31, 20--

ADJUSTED TRIAL BALANCE		INCOME STATEMENT		BALANCE SHEET		
DEBIT	CREDIT	DEBIT	CREDIT	DEBIT	CREDIT	
						1
						2
						3
						4
						5
						6
						7
						8
						9
						10
						11
						12
						13
						14
						15
						16
						17
						18
						19
						20
						21
						22
						23
						24
						25
						26
						27
						28
						29
						30
						31
						32

Problem 18-7   (concluded)

Cycle Tech
Work Sheet
For the Month Ended

	ACCT. NO.	ACCOUNT NAME	TRIAL BALANCE		ADJUSTMENTS	
			DEBIT	CREDIT	DEBIT	CREDIT
1		**Brought Forward**				
2						
3	625	*Fed. Corporate Income Tax Exp.*				
4	630	*Insurance Expense*				
5	645	*Maintenance Expense*				
6	650	*Miscellaneous Expense*				
7	655	*Payroll Tax Expense*				
8	657	*Rent Expense*				
9	660	*Salaries Expense*				
10	665	*Supplies Expense*				
11	675	*Utilities Expense*				
12						
13						
14						
15						
16						
17						
18						
19						
20						
21						
22						
23						
24						
25						
26						
27						
28						
29						
30						
31						
32						

Bicycles _____

(continued) _____

August 31, 20-- _____

	ADJUSTED TRIAL BALANCE		INCOME STATEMENT		BALANCE SHEET		
	DEBIT	CREDIT	DEBIT	CREDIT	DEBIT	CREDIT	
							1
							2
							3
							4
							5
							6
							7
							8
							9
							10
							11
							12
							13
							14
							15
							16
							17
							18
							19
							20
							21
							22
							23
							24
							25
							26
							27
							28
							29
							30
							31
							32

Analyze: _____

_____

Problem 18-8   Completing a Ten-Column Work Sheet

(1)

River's Edge

Work

For the Month Ended

	ACCT. NO.	ACCOUNT NAME	TRIAL BALANCE		ADJUSTMENTS	
			DEBIT	CREDIT	DEBIT	CREDIT
1	101	Cash in Bank				
2	115	Accounts Receivable				
3	130	Merchandise Inventory				
4	135	Supplies				
5	140	Prepaid Insurance				
6	145	Delivery Equipment				
7	150	Store Equipment				
8	201	Accounts Payable				
9	204	Fed. Corporate Income Tax Pay.				
10	210	Employees' Fed. Inc. Tax Pay.				
11	211	Employees' State Inc. Tax Pay.				
12	212	Social Security Tax Payable				
13	213	Medicare Tax Payable				
14	215	Sales Tax Payable				
15	216	Fed. Unemployment Tax Pay.				
16	217	State Unemployment Tax Pay.				
17	219	U.S. Savings Bonds Payable				
18	301	Capital Stock				
19	305	Retained Earnings				
20	310	Income Summary				
21	401	Sales				
22	405	Sales Discounts				
23	410	Sales Returns and Allowances				
24	501	Purchases				
25	505	Transportation In				
26	510	Purchases Discounts				
27	515	Purchases Returns and Allow.				
28	601	Advertising Expense				
29		Carried Forward				
30						
31						
32						

Canoe & Kayak

Sheet

August 31, 20--

	ADJUSTED TRIAL BALANCE		INCOME STATEMENT		BALANCE SHEET		
	DEBIT	CREDIT	DEBIT	CREDIT	DEBIT	CREDIT	
							1
							2
							3
							4
							5
							6
							7
							8
							9
							10
							11
							12
							13
							14
							15
							16
							17
							18
							19
							20
							21
							22
							23
							24
							25
							26
							27
							28
							29
							30
							31
							32

Problem 18-8   (continued)

River's Edge
Work Sheet
For the Month Ended

	ACCT. NO.	ACCOUNT NAME	TRIAL BALANCE		ADJUSTMENTS	
			DEBIT	CREDIT	DEBIT	CREDIT
1		*Brought Forward*				
2						
3	605	*Bankcard Fees Expense*				
4	625	*Fed. Corporate Income Tax Exp.*				
5	635	*Insurance Expense*				
6	650	*Maintenance Expense*				
7	655	*Miscellaneous Expense*				
8	658	*Payroll Tax Expense*				
9	660	*Rent Expense*				
10	665	*Salaries Expense*				
11	670	*Supplies Expense*				
12	680	*Utilities Expense*				
13						
14						
15						
16						
17						
18						
19						
20						
21						
22						
23						
24						
25						
26						
27						
28						
29						
30						
31						
32						

Canoe & Kayak

(continued)

August 31, 20--

	ADJUSTED TRIAL BALANCE			INCOME STATEMENT			BALANCE SHEET		
	DEBIT	CREDIT		DEBIT	CREDIT		DEBIT	CREDIT	
									1
									2
									3
									4
									5
									6
									7
									8
									9
									10
									11
									12
									13
									14
									15
									16
									17
									18
									19
									20
									21
									22
									23
									24
									25
									26
									27
									28
									29
									30
									31
									32

Problem 18-8   (continued)

(2)

GENERAL JOURNAL   PAGE _____

	DATE	DESCRIPTION	POST. REF.	DEBIT	CREDIT	
1						1
2						2
3						3
4						4
5						5
6						6
7						7
8						8
9						9
10						10
11						11
12						12

(3)

GENERAL LEDGER

ACCOUNT   *Merchandise Inventory*   ACCOUNT NO.   *130*

DATE	DESCRIPTION	POST. REF.	DEBIT	CREDIT	BALANCE DEBIT	BALANCE CREDIT
20--						
Aug. 1	Balance	✓			4920500	

ACCOUNT   *Supplies*   ACCOUNT NO.   *135*

DATE	DESCRIPTION	POST. REF.	DEBIT	CREDIT	BALANCE DEBIT	BALANCE CREDIT
20--						
Aug. 1	Balance	✓			302700	

ACCOUNT   *Prepaid Insurance*   ACCOUNT NO.   *140*

DATE	DESCRIPTION	POST. REF.	DEBIT	CREDIT	BALANCE DEBIT	BALANCE CREDIT
20--						
Aug. 1	Balance	✓			168000	

Problem 18-8 (concluded)

ACCOUNT __Federal Corporate Income Tax Payable__ ACCOUNT NO. __204__

DATE	DESCRIPTION	POST. REF.	DEBIT	CREDIT	BALANCE	
					DEBIT	CREDIT

ACCOUNT __Income Summary__ ACCOUNT NO. __310__

DATE	DESCRIPTION	POST. REF.	DEBIT	CREDIT	BALANCE	
					DEBIT	CREDIT

ACCOUNT __Federal Corporate Income Tax Expense__ ACCOUNT NO. __625__

DATE	DESCRIPTION	POST. REF.	DEBIT	CREDIT	BALANCE	
					DEBIT	CREDIT
20--						
Aug. 1	Balance	✓			2 4 8 0 00	

ACCOUNT __Insurance Expense__ ACCOUNT NO. __635__

DATE	DESCRIPTION	POST. REF.	DEBIT	CREDIT	BALANCE	
					DEBIT	CREDIT

ACCOUNT __Supplies Expense__ ACCOUNT NO. __670__

DATE	DESCRIPTION	POST. REF.	DEBIT	CREDIT	BALANCE	
					DEBIT	CREDIT

Analyze: _____

_____

Problem 18-9   Locating Errors on a Work Sheet

Buzz Newsstand

Work Sheet

For the Month Ended August 31, 20––

	ACCT. NO.	ACCOUNT NAME	TRIAL BALANCE DEBIT	TRIAL BALANCE CREDIT	ADJUSTMENTS DEBIT	ADJUSTMENTS CREDIT
1	101	Cash in Bank	8 1 3 1 00			
2	115	Accounts Receivable	3 6 3 00			
3	130	Merchandise Inventory	5 1 2 0 00			(a) 1 2 9 5 0 00
4	135	Supplies	9 7 4 00			(b) 4 5 4 00
5	140	Prepaid Insurance	9 8 0 00			(c) 2 4 5 00
6	145	Delivery Equipment	7 6 0 0 00			
7	150	Store Equipment	2 8 5 4 00			
8	201	Accounts Payable		4 5 1 5 00		
9	204	Fed. Corporate Income Tax Pay.		———		(d) 2 4 9 00
10	210	Employees' Fed. Inc. Tax Pay.		1 4 9 00		
11	211	Employees' State Inc. Tax Pay.	2 6 00			
12	215	Sales Tax Payable		4 2 1 00		
13	216	Social Security Tax Payable		7 9 00		
14	217	Medicare Tax Payable		1 0 00		
15	301	Capital Stock		2 5 0 0 0 00		
16	305	Retained Earnings		5 1 2 0 00		
17	310	Income Summary	———	———	(a) 1 2 9 5 0 00	
18	401	Sales		1 1 0 3 4 00		
19	410	Sales Returns and Allowances		1 2 6 00		
20	501	Purchases	1 6 8 1 9 00			
21	510	Purchases Discounts		———		
22	515	Purchases Returns and Allow.		2 4 6 00		
23	601	Advertising Expense	1 2 5 00			
24	625	Fed. Corporate Income Tax Exp.	———		(d) 2 4 9 00	
25	635	Insurance Expense	———		(c) 2 4 5 00	
26	650	Miscellaneous Expense	4 5 00			
27	655	Rent Expense	1 7 0 0 00			
28	657	Payroll Tax Expense	1 5 6 00			
29	660	Salaries Expense	1 2 6 5 00			
30	665	Supplies Expense	———			
31	675	Utilities Expense	3 4 2 00			
32			4 1 3 8 0 00	4 1 5 8 0 00		
33		Corrected TOTALS				

Analyze: _____

_____

CHAPTER 18 Adjustments and the Ten-Column Work Sheet

Self-Test

Part A True or False

Directions: *Circle the letter* T *in the Answer column if the statement is true; circle the letter* F *if the statement is false.*

Answer

T   F   **1.** The purpose of the end-of-period reports is to provide essential information about the financial position of a business organization.

T   F   **2.** The five amount sections of the ten-column work sheet are: Trial Balance, Adjustments, Adjusted Balance Sheet, Income Statement, and Ending Balance.

T   F   **3.** When preparing a work sheet, every general ledger account should be listed, even if it has a zero balance.

T   F   **4.** At the end of a period, adjustments are made to transfer the costs originally recorded in the expense accounts (temporary accounts) to the asset accounts (permanent accounts).

T   F   **5.** An account balance must be adjusted if the balance shown in the account is not up-to-date as of the last day of the fiscal period.

T   F   **6.** The ending inventory for one period is not the beginning inventory for the next period.

T   F   **7.** A physical inventory is always taken at the end of a period.

T   F   **8.** The totals of the Adjustments Debit and Credit columns do not have to be the same.

T   F   **9.** The source of information for journalizing adjusting entries at the end of a period is the Adjustments section of the work sheet.

T   F   **10.** The completed work sheet only lists the general ledger accounts and their updated balances. It does not show net income or net loss.

Part B   Fill in the Missing Term

Directions: *Using the terms in the following list, complete the sentences below.*
Write the letter of the term you have chosen in the space provided.

A. adjustment	**C.** ending inventory	**E.** ten-column work sheet
B. beginning inventory	**D.** physical inventory	

Answer

_____   **1.** The _____ has ten amount columns, including columns titled Adjustments and Adjusted Trial Balance.

_____   **2.** A(n) _____ is an amount that is added to or subtracted from an account balance to bring the balance up-to-date.

_____   **3.** A(n) _____ is an actual count of all the merchandise on hand and available for sale.

_____   **4.** The _____ is the merchandise a business has on hand and available for sale at the beginning of a period.

_____   **5.** The _____ is the merchandise a business has on hand at the end of a period.

CHAPTER 19 Financial Statements for a Corporation

Study Plan

Check Your Understanding

Section 1	*Read Section 1 on pages 516–520 and complete the following exercises on page 521.* ❏ Thinking Critically ❏ Communicating Accounting ❏ Problem 19-1 *Analyzing Stockholders' Equity Accounts* ❏ Problem 19-2 *Analyzing a Source Document*
Section 2	*Read Section 2 on pages 522–528 and complete the following exercises on page 529.* ❏ Thinking Critically ❏ Analyzing Accounting ❏ Problem 19-3 *Calculating Amounts on the Income Statement*
Section 3	*Read Section 3 on pages 531–535 and complete the following exercises on page 536.* ❏ Thinking Critically ❏ Computing in the Business World ❏ Problem 19-4 *Analyzing a Balance Sheet*
Summary	*Review the Chapter 19 Summary on page 537 in your textbook.* ❏ Key Concepts
Review and Activities	*Complete the following questions and exercises on pages 538–539 in your textbook.* ❏ Using Key Terms ❏ Understanding Accounting Concepts and Procedures ❏ Case Study ❏ Conducting an Audit with Alex ❏ Internet Connection ❏ Workplace Skills
Computerized Accounting	*Read the Computerized Accounting information on page 540 in your textbook.* ❏ *Making the Transition from a Manual to a Computerized System* ❏ *Preparing Financial Statements in Peachtree*
Problems	*Complete the following end-of-chapter problems for Chapter 19 in your textbook.* ❏ Problem 19-5 *Preparing an Income Statement* ❏ Problem 19-6 *Preparing a Statement of Retained Earnings and a Balance Sheet* ❏ Problem 19-7 *Preparing Financial Statements* ❏ Problem 19-8 *Completing a Work Sheet and Financial Statements*
Challenge Problem	❏ Problem 19-9 *Evaluating the Effect of an Error on the Income Statement*
Chapter Reviews and Working Papers	*Complete the following exercises for Chapter 19 in your Chapter Reviews and Working Papers.* ❏ Chapter Review ❏ Self-Test

CHAPTER 19 REVIEW — Financial Statements for a Corporation

Part 1   Accounting Vocabulary (19 points)

Total Points	57
Student's Score	

Directions: *Using terms from the following list, complete the sentences below. Write the letter of the term you have chosen in the space provided.*

A. administrative expenses	**H.** materiality	**O.** retained earnings
B. base year	**I.** net purchases	**P.** selling expenses
C. capital stock	**J.** net sales	**Q.** statement of retained earnings
D. comparability	**K.** operating expenses	**R.** stockholders' equity
E. full disclosure	**L.** operating income	**S.** vertical analysis
F. gross profit on sales	**M.** relevance	**T.** working capital
G. horizontal analysis	**N.** reliability	

_____**Q**_____ **0.** The changes that have taken place in the Retained Earnings account during the period are reported on the _____.

_____ **1.** _____ represents the increase in stockholders' equity from net income held by a corporation and not distributed to the stockholders as a return on their investment.

_____ **2.** _____ is the taxable income of a corporation, or the amount of income before federal income taxes.

_____ **3.** _____ is the amount of profit made during the period before expenses are deducted.

_____ **4.** The amount of sales for the period less any sales discounts, returns, or allowances is _____.

_____ **5.** The cash spent or the assets consumed to earn revenue for a business are _____.

_____ **6.** _____ represents the total investment in the corporation by its stockholders.

_____ **7.** The _____ is the amount of all costs related to merchandise purchased during the period.

_____ **8.** _____ is the value of the stockholders' claims to the assets of the corporation.

_____ **9.** _____ allows accounting information to be compared from one fiscal period to another.

_____ **10.** _____ guarantees that financial reports include enough information to be complete.

_____ **11.** _____ relates to the confidence that users have that the financial information is reasonably free from bias and error.

_____ **12.** In accounting, _____ means that the information "makes a difference" to a user in reaching a business decision.

_____ **13.** _____ in financial reporting means that information deemed relevant should be included in the reports.

_____ **14.** _____ are incurred to sell or market the merchandise sold.

_____ **15.** Costs related to the management of the business are called _____.

_____ **16.** With _____, each dollar amount reported on a financial statement is also reported as a percentage of another amount.

_____ **17.** The comparison of the same items on financial reports for two or more accounting periods is called _____.

_____ **18.** A _____ is a year or period used for comparison purposes.

_____ **19.** The amount by which current assets exceed current liabilities is known as _____.

Part 2 Listing Accounts on the Financial Statements (20 points)

Directions: *Using the following codes, indicate the financial statement(s) on which each account title would appear. Write your answer in the space provided.*

B Balance Sheet	**I** Income Statement	**S** Statement of Retained Earnings

I **0.** Rent Expense

_____ **1.** Accounts Payable

_____ **2.** Supplies Expense

_____ **3.** Merchandise Inventory

_____ **4.** Sales

_____ **5.** Supplies

_____ **6.** Capital Stock

_____ **7.** Transportation In

_____ **8.** Purchases Returns and Allowances

_____ **9.** Cash in Bank

_____ **10.** Federal Corporate Income Tax Payable

_____ **11.** Computer Equipment

_____ **12.** Prepaid Insurance

_____ **13.** Salaries Expense

_____ **14.** Insurance Expense

_____ **15.** Purchases

_____ **16.** Retained Earnings

_____ **17.** Purchases Discounts

_____ **18.** Federal Income Tax Expense

_____ **19.** Sales Returns and Allowances

_____ **20.** State Unemployment Tax Payable

Part 3 Reporting Information on Financial Statements (18 points)

Directions: *Read each of the following statements to determine whether the statement is true or false. Write your answer in the space provided.*

True **0.** The balance sheet reports the balances of all permanent accounts as of a specific date.

_____ **1.** The balance of the Capital Stock account should change every period.

_____ **2.** The total sales amount of a merchandising business includes the cost of merchandise sold and the profit made from selling that merchandise.

_____ **3.** Transportation charges increase the cost of merchandise purchased during the period.

_____ **4.** The cost of merchandise sold is obtained by subtracting the beginning inventory from the cost of merchandise available for sale.

_____ **5.** The three financial statements prepared by a merchandising corporation are the income statement, the statement of retained earnings, and the balance sheet.

_____ **6.** Federal Corporate Income Tax Expense is not an operating expense because it represents cash paid out as a result of the revenue earned rather than cash spent to earn revenue.

_____ **7.** Financial reports are prepared so that managers can evaluate past decisions and make future decisions.

_____ **8.** The stockholders' equity section of the balance sheet lists the accounts Capital Stock and Cash in Bank.

_____ **9.** The general ledger is the source of information for preparing the financial statements of a business.

_____ **10.** The federal income tax amount is listed separately on the income statement so that the operating income can be more easily seen.

_____ **11.** The statement of retained earnings is prepared before the income statement.

_____ **12.** The balance of the Retained Earnings account will always increase at the end of a period.

_____ **13.** The income statement reports the balances of the contra revenue accounts Sales Discounts and Sales Returns and Allowances.

_____ **14.** A net loss has no direct effect on the Retained Earnings account.

_____ **15.** The amount of gross profit for the period is the difference between net sales and the cost of merchandise sold.

_____ **16.** Purchases Returns and Allowances and Purchases Discounts are both contra cost of merchandise accounts.

_____ **17.** The balance sheet is prepared from the information in the Balance Sheet section of the work sheet and from the income statement.

_____ **18.** The statement of retained earnings consists of only the balance of the Retained Earnings account at the beginning of the period plus net income before taxes.

Chapter 19 ■ 517

Working Papers *for Section Problems*

Problem 19-1   Analyzing Stockholders' Equity Accounts

1. _____

2. _____

3. _____

Problem 19-2   Analyzing a Source Document

Cindy's Curtains
432 Meadowbrook Street
Wilcoxson, GA 30345-8417
404-555-2488

DATE: June 26, 20——   NO. 1441

SOLD TO: Rachel C. Washington
59 Priscilla Drive
Park Ridge, IL 60068

CLERK K.C.	CASH ✓	CHARGE	TERMS

QTY.	DESCRIPTION	UNIT PRICE	AMOUNT	
2	Curtain Rods #21847	$ 14.95	$ 29	09
4	Anchor Pieces #23104	6.75	27	00
15	Feet of ribbon/per ft.	.89	13	00
		SUBTOTAL	$ 69	09
		SALES TAX	2	76
		TOTAL	$ 71	85

Thank You!

Problem 19-3   Calculating Amounts on the Income Statement

1. Cost of merchandise available for sale _____

2. Gross profit on sales _____

3. Cost of delivered merchandise _____

4. Cost of merchandise sold _____

Problem 19-4   Analyzing a Balance Sheet

1. _____

2. _____

3. _____

4. _____

5. _____

_____

_____

_____

_____

_____

_____

6. _____

_____

Problem 19-5   Preparing an Income Statement

Sunset

Work

For the Year Ended

	ACCT. NO.	ACCOUNT NAME	TRIAL BALANCE DEBIT	TRIAL BALANCE CREDIT	ADJUSTMENTS DEBIT	ADJUSTMENTS CREDIT
1	101	Cash in Bank	15 2 7 4 00			
2	115	Accounts Receivable	4 1 2 4 00			
3	130	Merchandise Inventory	84 0 9 7 00			(a) 9 0 2 5 00
4	135	Supplies	3 7 4 0 00			(b) 2 7 2 2 00
5	140	Prepaid Insurance	1 5 8 4 00			(c) 5 2 8 00
6	145	Store Equipment	7 2 3 1 00			
7	150	Office Equipment	4 6 1 9 00			
8	201	Accounts Payable		9 3 4 0 00		
9	204	Fed. Corporate Income Tax Pay.				(d) 1 2 2 00
10	205	Employees' Fed. Inc. Tax Pay.		3 1 1 00		
11	208	Employees' State Inc. Tax Pay.		8 9 00		
12	210	Social Security Tax Payable		1 3 2 00		
13	211	Medicare Tax Payable		2 1 00		
14	212	Fed. Unemployment Tax Pay.		3 7 00		
15	213	State Unemployment Tax Pay.		1 3 4 00		
16	215	Sales Tax Payable		2 6 7 0 00		
17	301	Capital Stock		60 0 0 0 00		
18	305	Retained Earnings		14 9 2 0 00		
19	310	Income Summary			(a) 9 0 2 5 00	
20	401	Sales		137 7 1 1 00		
21	405	Sales Discounts	2 3 3 6 00			
22	410	Sales Returns and Allowances	4 1 8 8 00			
23	501	Purchases	71 0 9 7 00			
24	505	Transportation In	9 2 8 00			
25	510	Purchases Discounts		1 8 2 3 00		
26	515	Purchases Returns and Allow.		2 1 0 8 00		
27	601	Advertising Expense	8 4 0 00			
28	605	Bankcard Fees Expense	3 7 4 00			
29	630	Fed. Corporate Income Tax Exp.	2 6 0 0 00		(d) 1 2 2 00	
30		Carried Forward	203 0 3 2 00	229 2 9 6 00	9 1 4 7 00	12 3 9 7 00
31						
32						
33						

Surfwear

Sheet

December 31, 20--

	ADJUSTED TRIAL BALANCE DEBIT	ADJUSTED TRIAL BALANCE CREDIT	INCOME STATEMENT DEBIT	INCOME STATEMENT CREDIT	BALANCE SHEET DEBIT	BALANCE SHEET CREDIT	
1	15274 00				15274 00		1
2	4124 00				4124 00		2
3	75072 00				75072 00		3
4	1018 00				1018 00		4
5	1056 00				1056 00		5
6	7231 00				7231 00		6
7	4619 00				4619 00		7
8		9340 00				9340 00	8
9		122 00				122 00	9
10		311 00				311 00	10
11		89 00				89 00	11
12		132 00				132 00	12
13		21 00				21 00	13
14		37 00				37 00	14
15		134 00				134 00	15
16		2670 00				2670 00	16
17		60000 00				60000 00	17
18		14920 00				14920 00	18
19	9025 00		9025 00				19
20		137711 00		137711 00			20
21	2336 00		2336 00				21
22	4188 00		4188 00				22
23	71097 00		71097 00				23
24	928 00		928 00				24
25		1823 00		1823 00			25
26		2108 00		2108 00			26
27	840 00		840 00				27
28	374 00		374 00				28
29	2722 00		2722 00				29
30	199904 00	229418 00	91510 00	141642 00	108394 00	87776 00	30
31							31
32							32
33							33

Problem 19-5 (continued)

Sunset

Work Sheet

For the Year Ended

	ACCT. NO.	ACCOUNT NAME	TRIAL BALANCE DEBIT	TRIAL BALANCE CREDIT	ADJUSTMENTS DEBIT	ADJUSTMENTS CREDIT
1		**Brought Forward**	20 03 32 00	22 92 96 00	9 14 7 00	12 39 7 00
2						
3	635	**Insurance Expense**			(c) 52 8 00	
4	645	**Maintenance Expense**	1 23 1 00			
5	650	**Miscellaneous Expense**	2 86 0 00			
6	652	**Payroll Tax Expense**	2 17 0 00			
7	655	**Rent Expense**	9 27 0 00			
8	660	**Salaries Expense**	10 73 3 00			
9	685	**Supplies Expense**			(b) 2 72 2 00	
10			22 92 96 00	22 92 96 00	12 39 7 00	12 39 7 00
11		**Net Income**				
12						
13						
14						
15						
16						
17						
18						
19						
20						
21						
22						
23						
24						
25						
26						
27						
28						
29						
30						
31						
32						
33						

Surfwear

(continued)

December 31, 20--

	ADJUSTED TRIAL BALANCE		INCOME STATEMENT		BALANCE SHEET		
	DEBIT	CREDIT	DEBIT	CREDIT	DEBIT	CREDIT	
	19990400	22941800	9151000	14164200	10839400	8777600	1
							2
	52800		52800				3
	123100		123100				4
	286000		286000				5
	217000		217000				6
	927000		927000				7
	1073300		1073300				8
	272200		272200				9
	22941800	22941800	12102400	14164200	10839400	8777600	10
			2061800			2061800	11
			14164200	14164200	10839400	10839400	12

Computerized Accounting Using Peachtree

Software Objectives

When you have completed this chapter, you will be able to use Peachtree to:

1. Print a Balance Sheet for a corporation.
2. Print an Income Statement for a corporation.
3. Print an adjusted trial balance.

Problem 19-6   Preparing a Statement of Retained Earnings and a Balance Sheet

INSTRUCTIONS

Beginning a Session

Step 1   Select the problem set: Sunset Surfwear (Prob. 19-6).
Step 2   Rename the company and set the system date to December 31, 2004.

Completing the Accounting Problem

Step 3   Review the information in your textbook.
Step 4   Print a Balance Sheet. The Balance Sheet report is available in the Financial Statement report area.

Choose the <Predefined> Balance Sheet report whenever you are instructed to print a Balance Sheet. This report option is the default layout provided by Peachtree. As you can see, the Peachtree Balance Sheet is similar to the Balance Sheet report shown in your text. However, the Peachtree report is divided into more segments including the following parts: Current Assets, Property and Equipment, Other Assets, Current Liabilities, Long-Term Liabilities, and Capital.

Step 5   Answer the Analyze question.

Ending the Session

Step 6   Click the **Close Problem** button in the Glencoe Smart Guide window and select a save option.

Problem 19-7   Preparing Financial Statements

INSTRUCTIONS

Beginning a Session

Step 1   Select the problem set: Shutterbug Cameras (Prob. 19-7).
Step 2   Rename the company and set the system date to December 31, 2004.

Completing the Accounting Problem

Step 3   Review the information in your textbook.
Step 4   Print the following reports: Adjusted Trial Balance, Balance Sheet, and Income Statement.

Choose the Peachtree <Predefined> Income Statement report when you are instructed to print an Income Statement. As you will notice, the report includes more information than the Income Statements shown in your textbook. The default Peachtree report shows the results for the current month and the current year. For the problems in this text, these two columns will always be the same.

DO YOU HAVE A QUESTION

Q. *Where is the Statement of Retained Earnings report option located?*

A. Peachtree does not include a Statement of Retained Earnings report. However, the Balance Sheet shows you the beginning **Retained Earnings** account balance and the net income (loss). With this information you can manually prepare the report.

Notes

Peachtree does not include an option to print a Statement of Retained Earnings.

The Cost of Sales (or Cost of Merchandise Sold) on a Peachtree Income Statement is very different from the style used in the textbook. Where a manual report shows both the beginning and ending **Merchandise Inventory** account balance, the Peachtree report does not show this information. Instead, it includes the **Inventory Adjustment** account balance. The net effect is the same, in that, this account reflects the difference in the cost of the physical inventory.

Step 5   Answer the Analyze question.

Ending the Session

Step 6   Click the **Close Problem** button in the Glencoe Smart Guide window and select a save option.

Problem 19-8   Completing a Work Sheet and Financial Statements

INSTRUCTIONS

Beginning a Session

Step 1   Select the problem set: Cycle Tech Bicycles (Prob. 19-8).
Step 2   Rename the company and set the system date to December 31, 2004.

Completing the Accounting Problem

Step 3   Review the information in your textbook.
Step 4   Print a Working Trial Balance report and use it to prepare the adjustments.
Step 5   Record the adjusting entries using the **General Journal Entry** option.
Step 6   Print a General Journal report and proof your work.
Step 7   Print the following reports: Adjusted Trial Balance, Balance Sheet, and Income Statement.
Step 8   Answer the Analyze question.

Ending the Session

Step 9   Click the **Close Problem** button in the Glencoe Smart Guide window and select a save option.

DO YOU HAVE A QUESTION

Q. *Why is the Cost of Merchandise Sold section on Peachtree's predefined Income Statement different from a manual report?*

A. In Chapter 18, you learned how to make the adjusting entry for **Merchandise Inventory** using a computerized system such as the Peachtree Accounting software. The adjustment was made to an account called **Inventory Adjustment**, which is the difference between the beginning and ending inventory value. Peachtree uses the **Inventory Adjustment** account balance along with the other cost of sales accounts (**Purchases, Transportation In, Purchases Discounts,** and **Purchases Returns and Allowances**) to calculate the total cost of sales. The net effect is the same as the result obtained using the manual method.

Notes

Whenever you are instructed to print an Adjusted Trial Balance, choose the General Ledger Trial Balance report. You can change the report title if you want.

FAQs

Where is the Statement of Retained Earnings report option located?

Peachtree does not include a Statement of Retained Earnings report. However, the Balance Sheet shows you the beginning **Retained Earnings** account balance and the net income (loss). With this information you can manually prepare the report.

Computerized Accounting Using Spreadsheets

Problem 19-5   Preparing an Income Statement

Completing the Spreadsheet

Step 1   Read the instructions for Problem 19-5 in your textbook. This problem involves preparing an income statement for Sunset Surfwear.

Step 2   Open the Glencoe Accounting: Electronic Learning Center software.

Step 3   From the Program Menu, click on the **Peachtree Accounting Software and Spreadsheet Applications** icon.

Step 4   Log onto the Management System by typing your user name and password.

Step 5   Under the Chapter Problems tab, select the template: PR19-5a.xls. The template should look like the one shown below.

```
PROBLEM 19-5
PREPARING AN INCOME STATEMENT

(name)
(date)


SUNSET SURFWEAR
INCOME STATEMENT
FOR THE YEAR ENDED DECEMBER 31, 20--

Revenue:
    Sales                                                    AMOUNT
    Less: Sales Discounts                        AMOUNT
          Sales Returns & Allowances            AMOUNT      0.00
          Net Sales                                                   0.00
Cost of Merchandise Sold:
    Merchandise Inventory January 1                          AMOUNT
    Purchases                            AMOUNT
    Plus: Transportation In              AMOUNT
    Cost of Delivered Merchandise                   0.00
    Less: Purchases Discounts            AMOUNT
          Purchases Returns & Allowances AMOUNT     0.00
    Net Purchases                                            0.00
    Cost of Merchandise Available                            0.00
    Merchandise Inventory December 31                        AMOUNT
        Cost of Merchandise Sold                                      0.00
Gross Profit on Sales                                                 0.00
Operating Expenses:
    Advertising Expense                                      AMOUNT
    Bankcard Fees Expense                                    AMOUNT
    Insurance Expense                                        AMOUNT
    Maintenance Expense                                      AMOUNT
    Miscellaneous Expense                                    AMOUNT
    Payroll Tax Expense                                      AMOUNT
    Rent Expense                                             AMOUNT
    Salaries Expense                                         AMOUNT
    Supplies Expense                                         AMOUNT
    Total Operating Expenses                                          0.00
Operating Income                                                      0.00
    Less: Federal Corporate Income Tax Expense               AMOUNT
Net Income                                                            0.00
```

Step 6 Key your name and today's date in the cells containing the *(name)* and *(date)* placeholders.

Step 7 Using the data provided in the work sheet for Sunset Surfwear given in your working papers, enter the income statement data into the spreadsheet template in the cells containing the AMOUNT placeholders. The spreadsheet template will automatically calculate the net sales, cost of merchandise sold, gross profit on sales, total operating expenses, operating income, and net income. Remember, it is not necessary to enter a comma or the decimal point and ending zeroes when entering the amounts.

Step 8 Save the spreadsheet using the **Save** option from the *File* menu. You should accept the default location for the save as this is handled by the management system.

Step 9 Print the completed spreadsheet.

Step 10 Exit the spreadsheet program.

Step 11 In the Close Options box, select the location where you would like to save your work.

Step 12 Answer the Analyze question from your textbook for this problem.

What-If Analysis

If Sunset Surfwear's merchandise inventory on January 1 were $100,000, what would the cost of merchandise sold be? What would net income be?

_____

_____

Working Papers *for End-of-Chapter Problems*

Problem 19-5 (concluded)

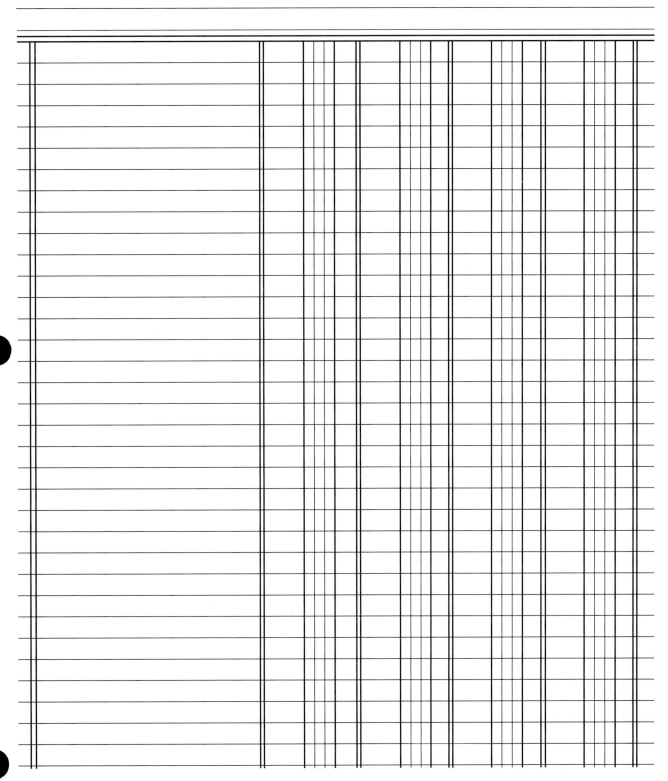

Analyze: _____

Problem 19-6 Preparing a Statement of Retained Earnings
and a Balance Sheet

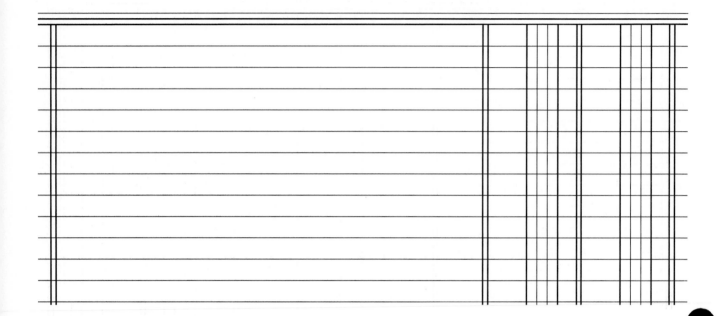

Problem 19-6   (concluded)

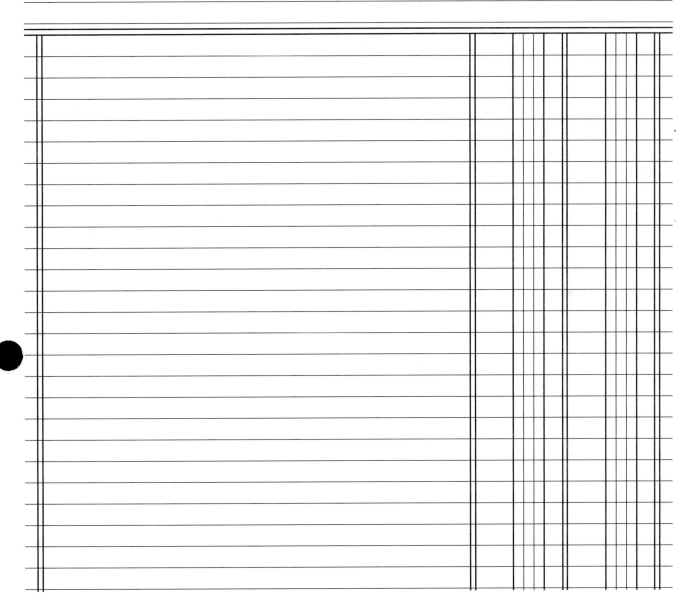

Analyze: _____

_____

Problem 19-7   Preparing Financial Statements
(1)

Shutterbug

Work

For the Year Ended

	ACCT. NO.	ACCOUNT NAME	TRIAL BALANCE DEBIT	TRIAL BALANCE CREDIT	ADJUSTMENTS DEBIT	ADJUSTMENTS CREDIT
1	101	Cash in Bank	13 603 00			
2	115	Accounts Receivable	5 418 00			
3	125	Merchandise Inventory	82 763 00			(a) 4 451 00
4	130	Supplies	2 522 00			(b) 2 039 00
5	135	Prepaid Insurance	1 350 00			(c) 475 00
6	140	Store Equipment	26 769 00			
7	201	Accounts Payable		14 481 00		
8	207	Fed. Corporate Income Tax Pay.				(d) 261 00
9	210	Employees' Fed. Inc. Tax Pay.		189 00		
10	211	Employees' State Inc. Tax Pay.		52 00		
11	212	Social Security Tax Payable		138 00		
12	213	Medicare Tax Payable		28 00		
13	215	Sales Tax Payable		891 00		
14	216	Fed. Unemployment Tax Pay.		19 00		
15	217	State Unemployment Tax Pay.		96 00		
16	301	Capital Stock		80 000 00		
17	305	Retained Earnings		19 192 00		
18	310	Income Summary			(a) 4 451 00	
19	401	Sales		92 867 00		
20	405	Sales Discounts	105 00			
21	410	Sales Returns and Allowances	885 00			
22	501	Purchases	37 491 00			
23	505	Transportation In	1 805 00			
24	510	Purchases Discounts		644 00		
25	515	Purchases Returns and Allow.		231 00		
26	601	Advertising Expense	650 00			
27	605	Bankcard Fees Expense	213 00			
28	620	Fed. Corporate Income Tax Exp.	1 720 00		(d) 261 00	
29		Carried Forward	175 294 00	208 828 00	4 712 00	7 226 00
30						
31						
32						
33						

Cameras

Sheet

December 31, 20--

ADJUSTED TRIAL BALANCE		INCOME STATEMENT		BALANCE SHEET		
DEBIT	CREDIT	DEBIT	CREDIT	DEBIT	CREDIT	
13603 00						1
5418 00						2
78312 00						3
483 00						4
875 00						5
26769 00						6
	14481 00					7
	261 00					8
	189 00					9
	52 00					10
	138 00					11
	28 00					12
	891 00					13
	19 00					14
	96 00					15
	80000 00					16
	19192 00					17
4451 00						18
	92867 00					19
105 00						20
885 00						21
37491 00						22
1805 00						23
	644 00					24
	231 00					25
650 00						26
213 00						27
1981 00						28
173041 00	209089 00					29
						30
						31
						32
						33

Problem 19-7 (continued)

Shutterbug
Work Sheet
For the Year Ended

	ACCT. NO.	ACCOUNT NAME	TRIAL BALANCE		ADJUSTMENTS	
			DEBIT	CREDIT	DEBIT	CREDIT
1		**Brought Forward**	17 5 2 9 4 00	20 8 8 2 8 00	4 7 1 2 00	7 2 2 6 00
2						
3	630	**Insurance Expense**			(c) 4 7 5 00	
4	640	**Maintenance Expense**	2 5 5 2 00			
5	645	**Miscellaneous Expense**	2 8 5 00			
6	647	**Payroll Tax Expense**	1 9 2 0 00			
7	650	**Rent Expense**	9 7 0 0 00			
8	655	**Salaries Expense**	18 7 2 0 00			
9	660	**Supplies Expense**			(b) 2 0 3 9 00	
10	670	**Utilities Expense**	3 5 7 00			
11						
12			20 8 8 2 8 00	20 8 8 2 8 00	7 2 2 6 00	7 2 2 6 00

Cameras

(continued)

December 31, 20--

ADJUSTED TRIAL BALANCE		INCOME STATEMENT		BALANCE SHEET		
DEBIT	CREDIT	DEBIT	CREDIT	DEBIT	CREDIT	
17304100	20908900					1
						2
	47500					3
255200						4
	28500					5
192000						6
970000						7
1872000						8
203900						9
35700						10
						11
20908900	20908900					12
						13
						14

Problem 19-7 (continued)

(2)

Problem 19-7 (concluded)

(3)

(4)

Analyze: _____

Problem 19-8   Completing a Work Sheet and Financial Statements

(1)

Cycle Tech

Work

For the Year Ended

	ACCT. NO.	ACCOUNT NAME	TRIAL BALANCE DEBIT	TRIAL BALANCE CREDIT	ADJUSTMENTS DEBIT	ADJUSTMENTS CREDIT
1	101	Cash in Bank	21931 00			
2	115	Accounts Receivable	1782 00			
3	125	Merchandise Inventory	24028 00			
4	130	Supplies	4159 00			
5	135	Prepaid Insurance	1800 00			
6	140	Store Equipment	24895 00			
7	145	Office Equipment	16113 00			
8	201	Accounts Payable		11224 00		
9	210	Fed. Corporate Income Tax Pay.				
10	211	Employees' Fed. Inc. Tax Pay.		522 00		
11	212	Employees' State Inc. Tax Pay.		144 00		
12	213	Social Security Tax Payable		413 00		
13	214	Medicare Tax Payable		134 00		
14	215	Sales Tax Payable		1915 00		
15	216	Fed. Unemployment Tax Pay.		54 00		
16	217	State Unemployment Tax Pay.		271 00		
17	301	Capital Stock		40000 00		
18	305	Retained Earnings		11091 00		
19	310	Income Summary				
20	401	Sales		127151 00		
21	405	Sales Discounts	246 00			
22	410	Sales Returns and Allowances	1328 00			
23	501	Purchases	66107 00			
24	505	Transportation In	983 00			
25	510	Purchases Discounts		822 00		
26	515	Purchases Returns and Allow.		376 00		
27	601	Advertising Expense	2380 00			
28	605	Bankcard Fees Expense	181 00			
29	625	Fed. Corporate Income Tax Exp.	3340 00			
30		Carried Forward	169273 00	194117 00		
31						
32						

Bicycles

Sheet

December 31, 20--

ADJUSTED TRIAL BALANCE		INCOME STATEMENT		BALANCE SHEET		
DEBIT	CREDIT	DEBIT	CREDIT	DEBIT	CREDIT	
						1
						2
						3
						4
						5
						6
						7
						8
						9
						10
						11
						12
						13
						14
						15
						16
						17
						18
						19
						20
						21
						22
						23
						24
						25
						26
						27
						28
						29
						30
						31
						32

Problem 19-8   (continued)

Cycle Tech

Work Sheet

For the Year Ended

	ACCT. NO.	ACCOUNT NAME	TRIAL BALANCE		ADJUSTMENTS	
			DEBIT	CREDIT	DEBIT	CREDIT
1		*Brought Forward*	16 9 2 7 3 00	19 4 1 1 7 00		
2						
3	630	*Insurance Expense*				
4	645	*Maintenance Expense*	1 9 5 0 00			
5	650	*Miscellaneous Expense*	1 8 3 1 00			
6	655	*Payroll Tax Expense*	8 3 4 00			
7	657	*Rent Expense*	10 8 0 0 00			
8	660	*Salaries Expense*	4 7 3 4 00			
9	665	*Supplies Expense*				
10	675	*Utilities Expense*	4 6 9 5 00			
11						
12			19 4 1 1 7 00	19 4 1 1 7 00		
13						
14						
15						
16						
17						
18						
19						
20						
21						
22						
23						
24						
25						
26						
27						
28						
29						
30						
31						
32						

Bicycles

(continued)

December 31, 20--

ADJUSTED TRIAL BALANCE		INCOME STATEMENT		BALANCE SHEET		
DEBIT	CREDIT	DEBIT	CREDIT	DEBIT	CREDIT	
						1
						2
						3
						4
						5
						6
						7
						8
						9
						10
						11
						12
						13
						14
						15
						16
						17
						18
						19
						20
						21
						22
						23
						24
						25
						26
						27
						28
						29
						30
						31
						32

Problem 19-8   (continued)
(2)

Problem 19-8   (concluded)

(3)

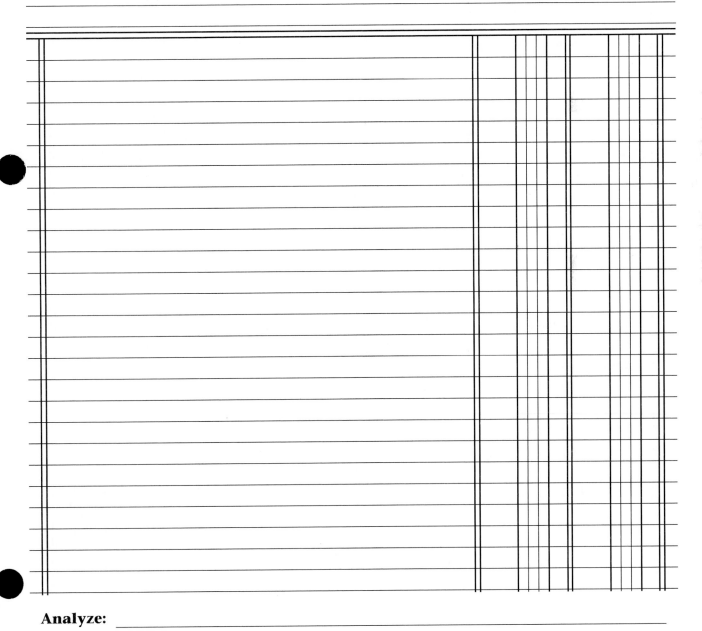

(4)

Analyze: _____

Problem 19-9   Evaluating the Effect of an Error on the Income Statement

River's Edge Canoe & Kayak

Income Statement

For the Year Ended December 31, 20--

Revenue:					
Sales				3 2 4 7 8 4 00	
Less: Sales Discounts			3 8 3 9 00		
Sales Returns and Allowances			1 2 0 9 00	5 0 4 8 00	
Net Sales					3 1 9 7 3 6 00
Cost of Merchandise Sold:					
Merchandise Inv., Jan. 1, 20--				8 4 9 2 1 00	
Purchases	2 0 8 4 1 6 00				
Cost of Delivered Merchandise		2 0 8 4 1 6 00			
Less: Purchases Discounts	9 6 2 3 00				
Purchases Returns and Allow.	4 7 2 1 00	1 4 3 4 4 00			
Net Purchases				1 9 4 0 7 2 00	
Cost of Merchandise Available				2 7 8 9 9 3 00	
Merchandise Inv., Dec. 31, 20--				8 1 3 8 5 00	
Cost of Merchandise Sold					1 9 7 6 0 8 00
Gross Profit on Sales					1 2 2 1 2 8 00
Operating Expenses:					
Advertising Expense				2 5 7 0 00	
Bankcard Fees Expense				4 1 8 2 00	
Insurance Expense				2 7 5 00	
Maintenance Expense				3 5 5 2 00	
Miscellaneous Expense				3 4 4 00	
Payroll Tax Expense				3 8 2 4 00	
Rent Expense				1 5 0 0 0 00	
Salaries Expense				2 9 3 8 1 00	
Supplies Expense				3 7 1 0 00	
Utilities Expense				2 3 7 8 00	
Total Operating Expenses					6 5 2 1 6 00
Operating Income					5 6 9 1 2 00
Less: Fed. Corporate Inc. Tax Exp.					9 4 3 6 00
Net Income					4 7 4 7 6 00

Problem 19-9   (concluded)

1. _____

2. _____ $ _____

3. _____ $ _____

4. $ _____

5. $ _____

Analyze: _____

_____

CHAPTER 19   Financial Statements for a Corporation

Self-Test

Part A   True or False

Directions: *Circle the letter* T *in the Answer column if the statement is true; circle the letter* F *if the statement is false.*

Answer

T   F   **1.** The balances of all permanent accounts as of a specific date are reported on the balance sheet.

T   F   **2.** The statement of retained earnings is prepared before the balance sheet.

T   F   **3.** Purchases Discounts is a contra account of Purchases.

T   F   **4.** The account Transportation In reduces the amount of merchandise available for sale.

T   F   **5.** The Retained Earnings account always increases at the end of the period.

T   F   **6.** The source of information for preparing the income statement is the general ledger.

T   F   **7.** Capital Stock is the only general ledger account classified as stockholders' equity.

T   F   **8.** The cost of merchandise sold is determined by subtracting the ending inventory from the cost of merchandise available for sale.

T   F   **9.** The amount of profit earned before expenses are subtracted is the gross profit on sales.

T   F   **10.** Changes in the Cash in Bank account are reported in the statement of retained earnings.

T   F   **11.** Net purchases is added to the beginning inventory to get the merchandise available for sale for the period.

T   F   **12.** Corporate Federal Income Tax Expense is not included in the total operating expenses for the period.

T   F   **13.** The income statement reports the financial position of the business as of a specific date.

T   F   **14.** The balance in the Capital Stock account never changes unless stock in the business is purchased or sold.

Part B Fill in the Missing Term

Directions: *In the Answer column, write the letter of the word or phrase that best completes the sentence. Some answers may be used more than once.*

A. Capital Stock	**C.** gross profit on sales	**F.** statement of retained
B. cost of merchandise	**D.** net purchases	earnings
available for sale	**E.** net sales	**G.** operating expenses

Answer

_____ 1. _____ is the amount of beginning inventory plus net purchases.

_____ 2. The _____ reports any changes that have taken place in the Retained Earnings account during the period.

_____ 3. _____ is the total cost of merchandise bought during the period, plus transportation charges, less returns, allowances and discounts.

_____ 4. _____ is the account used to record any investments by stockholders.

_____ 5. _____ are the assets consumed or the cash spent to earn revenue for a business.

_____ 6. On the income statement, net sales less the cost of merchandise sold is the _____.

_____ 7. The amount of sales revenue remaining after sales returns and allowances and sales discounts have been subtracted is _____.

MINI PRACTICE SET 4

In-Touch Electronics

CHART OF ACCOUNTS

ASSETS
101   Cash in Bank
105   Accounts Receivable
110   Merchandise Inventory
115   Supplies
120   Prepaid Insurance
150   Store Equipment
155   Office Equipment

LIABILITIES
201   Accounts Payable
205   Sales Tax Payable
210   Employees' Federal Income Tax Payable
211   Employees' State Income Tax Payable
212   Social Security Tax Payable
213   Medicare Tax Payable
214   Federal Unemployment Tax Payable
215   State Unemployment Tax Payable

STOCKHOLDERS' EQUITY
301   Capital Stock
302   Retained Earnings
303   Income Summary

REVENUE
401   Sales
405   Sales Discounts
410   Sales Returns and Allowances

COST OF MERCHANDISE
501   Purchases
505   Transportation In
510   Purchases Discounts
515   Purchases Returns
        and Allowances

EXPENSES
605   Advertising Expense
610   Bankcard Fees Expense
615   Miscellaneous Expense
620   Payroll Tax Expense
625   Rent Expense
630   Salaries Expense
635   Utilities Expense

Accounts Receivable Subsidiary Ledger
LOR   Sam Lorenzo
MAR   Marianne Martino
MCC   Mark McCormick
SCO   Sue Ellen Scott
TRO   Tom Trout

Accounts Payable Subsidiary Ledger
COM   Computer Systems, Inc.
DES   Desktop Wholesalers
HIT   Hi-Tech Electronics Outlet
LAS   Laser & Ink Jet Products
OFF   Office Suppliers, Inc.

Mini Practice Set 4   Source Documents

Instructions: *Use the following source documents to record the transactions for this practice set.*

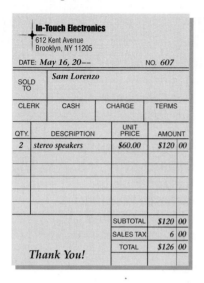

In-Touch Electronics
612 Kent Avenue
Brooklyn, NY 11205

DATE: *May 16, 20--*   NO. *607*

SOLD TO: *Sam Lorenzo*

CLERK	CASH	CHARGE	TERMS

QTY.	DESCRIPTION	UNIT PRICE	AMOUNT	
2	stereo speakers	$60.00	$120	00
		SUBTOTAL	$120	00
		SALES TAX	6	00
		TOTAL	$126	00

Thank You!

In-Touch Electronics
612 Kent Avenue
Brooklyn, NY 11205

RECEIPT
No. 356

May 17   20 --

RECEIVED FROM *Tom Trout* $ *126.00*

One hundred twenty-six and $^{00}/_{100}$ ———— DOLLARS

FOR *Payment on account*

RECEIVED BY *Tina Cordova*

In-Touch Electronics   **892**
612 Kent Avenue   74-103 / 720
Brooklyn, NY 11205

DATE *May 17*   20 --

PAY TO THE ORDER OF *Desktop Wholesalers* $ *800.00*

Eight hundred and $^{00}/_{100}$ ———— DOLLARS

UB Union Bank

MEMO _____ *Pedro Cordova*

⑈0720 0⑈033⑈ 6⑈7⑈ 5222⑈ 0892

DEBIT MEMORANDUM   No. 38

Date: *May 18, 20--*
Invoice No.: *N/A*

In-Touch Electronics
612 Kent Avenue
Brooklyn, NY 11205

To: *Laser & Ink Jet Products*
1412 Abrams Avenue
Brooklyn, NY 11205

This day we have debited your account as follows:

Quantity	Item	Unit Price	Total
1	Ink Jet Cartridge	$75.00	$75.00

In-Touch Electronics   **893**
612 Kent Avenue   74-103 / 720
Brooklyn, NY 11205

DATE *May 19*   20 --

PAY TO THE ORDER OF *Computer Systems, Inc.* $ *1,200.00*

One thousand two hundred and $^{00}/_{100}$ ———— DOLLARS

UB Union Bank

MEMO *on account*   *Pedro Cordova*

⑈0720 0⑈033⑈ 6⑈7⑈ 5222⑈ 0893

In-Touch Electronics   **894**
612 Kent Avenue   74-103 / 720
Brooklyn, NY 11205

DATE *May 19*   20 --

PAY TO THE ORDER OF *Hi-Tech Electronics Outlet* $ *1,750.00*

One thousand seven hundred fifty and $^{00}/_{100}$ ———— DOLLARS

UB Union Bank

MEMO *on account*   *Tina Cordova*

⑈0720 0⑈033⑈ 6⑈7⑈ 5222⑈ 0894

In-Touch Electronics   **895**
612 Kent Avenue   74-103 / 720
Brooklyn, NY 11205

DATE *May 19*   20 --

PAY TO THE ORDER OF *Office Suppliers, Inc.* $ *770.00*

Seven hundred seventy and $^{00}/_{100}$ ———— DOLLARS

UB Union Bank

MEMO *on account*   *Pedro Cordova*

⑈0720 0⑈033⑈ 6⑈7⑈ 5222⑈ 0895

In-Touch Electronics
612 Kent Avenue
Brooklyn, NY 11205

RECEIPT
No. 357

May 20   20 --

RECEIVED FROM *Bob Bell* $ *90.00*

Ninety and $^{00}/_{100}$ ———— DOLLARS

FOR *employee purchase of office equipment*

RECEIVED BY *Pedro Cordova*

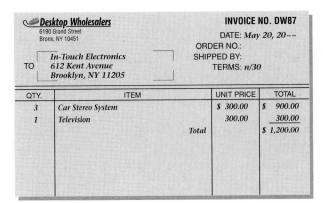

Desktop Wholesalers
6190 Grand Street
Bronx, NY 10451

INVOICE NO. DW87

DATE: *May 20, 20--*
ORDER NO.:
SHIPPED BY:
TERMS: *n/30*

TO   *In-Touch Electronics*
  612 Kent Avenue
  Brooklyn, NY 11205

QTY.	ITEM	UNIT PRICE	TOTAL
3	Car Stereo System	$ 300.00	$ 900.00
1	Television	300.00	300.00
	Total		$ 1,200.00

In-Touch Electronics
612 Kent Avenue
Brooklyn, NY 11205

RECEIPT
No. 360

May 21   20 --

RECEIVED FROM   *Marianne Martino* $ *94.50*

Ninety-four and $^{50}/_{100}$ —————————— DOLLARS

FOR   *Payment on account*

RECEIVED BY   *Pedro Cordova*

In-Touch Electronics
612 Kent Avenue
Brooklyn, NY 11205

RECEIPT
No. 358

May 20   20 --

RECEIVED FROM   *Mark McCormick* $ *210.00*

Two hundred ten and $^{00}/_{100}$ —————————— DOLLARS

FOR   *Payment on account*

RECEIVED BY   *Kelly Briggs*

In-Touch Electronics
612 Kent Avenue
Brooklyn, NY 11205

DATE: *May 21, 20--*   NO. *608*

SOLD TO   *Mark McCormick*

CLERK	CASH	CHARGE	TERMS 2/10, n/30

QTY.	DESCRIPTION	UNIT PRICE	AMOUNT
5	answering machines	$80.00	$400 00
		SUBTOTAL	$400 00
		SALES TAX	20 00
		TOTAL	$420 00

Thank You!

In-Touch Electronics
612 Kent Avenue
Brooklyn, NY 11205

RECEIPT
No. 359

May 20   20 --

RECEIVED FROM   *Sue Ellen Scott* $ *308.70*

Three hundred eight and $^{70}/_{100}$ —————————— DOLLARS

FOR   *Paid $315 less 2% on account*

RECEIVED BY   *Tina Cordova*

In-Touch Electronics
612 Kent Avenue
Brooklyn, NY 11205

896
74-103
720

DATE *May 22*   20--

PAY TO THE ORDER OF *Desktop Wholesalers* $ *1,200.00*

One thousand two hundred and $^{00}/_{100}$ —————————— DOLLARS

UB Union Bank

MEMO ——————   *Tina Cordova*

⑆0720 01033⑆ 6171 5222⑈ 0896

Hi-Tech Electronics Outlet
265 Pixie Drive
New York, NY 10006

INVOICE NO. HT99

DATE: *May 21, 20--*
ORDER NO.:
SHIPPED BY:
TERMS: *2/10, n/30*

TO   *In-Touch Electronics*
  612 Kent Avenue
  Brooklyn, NY 11205

QTY.	ITEM	UNIT PRICE	TOTAL
2	Sony VCR Systems	$ 250.00	$ 500.00
5	Intercom Systems	200.00	1,000.00
			$ 1,500.00

In-Touch Electronics
612 Kent Avenue
Brooklyn, NY 11205

DATE: *May 23, 20--*   NO. *609*

SOLD TO   *Sue Ellen Scott*

CLERK	CASH	CHARGE	TERMS 2/10, n/30

QTY.	DESCRIPTION	UNIT PRICE	AMOUNT
1	Sony DVD player	$500.00	$500 00
		SUBTOTAL	$500 00
		SALES TAX	25 00
		TOTAL	$525 00

Thank You!

In-Touch Electronics
612 Kent Avenue
Brooklyn, NY 11205

DATE: *May 24, 20--*

NAME: *Mark McCormick*
ADDRESS: *2724 S. 1st Street*
Brooklyn, NY 11205

Mark McCormick
CUSTOMER SIGNATURE

CREDIT MEMORANDUM   NO. *55*

ORIGINAL SALES DATE	ORIGINAL SALES SLIP	APPROVAL	
May 12, 20--	*605*	*TC*	☒ MDSE RET

QTY.	DESCRIPTION	AMOUNT
1	*Clarion accessory*	*$100 00*

REASON FOR RETURN *wrong model*	SUB TOTAL	*$100 00*
THE TOTAL SHOWN AT THE RIGHT WILL BE CREDITED TO YOUR ACCOUNT.	SALES TAX	*5 00*
	TOTAL	*$105 00*

In-Touch Electronics   **897**
612 Kent Avenue
Brooklyn, NY 11205   74-103 / 720

DATE *May 25*   20--

PAY TO THE ORDER OF *Surfside Insurance Co.* $ *1,600.00*

One thousand six hundred and $^{00}/_{100}$ ———— DOLLARS

UB Union Bank

MEMO *annual insurance*   *Tina Cordova*

⑆0720 01033⑆ 6171 5222⑈ 0897

In-Touch Electronics   **MEMORANDUM 26**
612 Kent Avenue
Brooklyn, NY 11205

TO: *Accounting Clerk*
FROM: *Senior Accountant*
DATE: *May 26, 20--*
SUBJECT: *Correcting entry*

Please make the entry to correct the error in debiting Purchases rather than Transportation In last month for $50.00.

Computer Systems, Inc.
351 Wood Street
New York, NY 10005

TO   *In-Touch Electronics*
612 Kent Avenue
Brooklyn, NY 11205

INVOICE NO. CS75

DATE: *May 27, 20--*
ORDER NO.:
SHIPPED BY:
TERMS: *2/10, n/30*

QTY.	ITEM	UNIT PRICE	TOTAL
20	*Various CDs*	*$ 50.00*	*$ 1,000.00*
1	*VCR*	*400.00*	*400.00*
			$ 1,400.00

In-Touch Electronics
612 Kent Avenue
Brooklyn, NY 11205

DATE: *May 28, 20--*   NO. *610*

SOLD TO   *Marianne Martino*

CLERK	CASH	CHARGE	TERMS *2/10, n/30*

QTY.	DESCRIPTION	UNIT PRICE	AMOUNT
1	*car stereo*	*$200.00*	*$200 00*
		SUBTOTAL	*$200 00*
		SALES TAX	*10 00*
		TOTAL	*$210 00*

Thank You!

Office Suppliers, Inc.
613 Cedar Grove, #75
Bronx, NY 10451

TO   *In-Touch Electronics*
612 Kent Avenue
Brooklyn, NY 11205

INVOICE NO. 9489

DATE: *May 29, 20--*
ORDER NO.:
SHIPPED BY:
TERMS:

QTY.	ITEM	UNIT PRICE	TOTAL
2 packs	*Manila Folders*	*$ 20.00*	*$ 40.00*
11 pads	*Stationery*	*10.00*	*110.00*
			$ 150.00

In-Touch Electronics   **898**
612 Kent Avenue
Brooklyn, NY 11205   74-103 / 720

DATE *May 30*   20--

PAY TO THE ORDER OF *Green Realty* $ *1,500.00*

One thousand five hundred and $^{00}/_{100}$ ———— DOLLARS

UB Union Bank

MEMO *rent*   *Tina Cordova*

⑆0720 01033⑆ 6171 5222⑈ 0898

Dec. 31
Tape 22

1,200.00	CA
60.00	ST
900.00	BCS
45.00	ST

	Dollars	Cents
$ 1,858.75 No. 899		
Date 5/31 20——		
To Payroll Account		
For Payroll—May 31		
Balance brought forward	8,093	20
less 12/31 bank svc. fee	25	00
12/31 bankcard fee	100	00
Total		
Less this check	1,858	75
Balance carried forward	6,109	45

PAYROLL REGISTER

PAY PERIOD ENDING May 31   20——   DATE OF PAYMENT May 31, 20——

EMPLOYEE NUMBER	NAME	MAR. STATUS	ALLOW.	TOTAL HOURS	RATE	EARNINGS REGULAR	OVERTIME	TOTAL	DEDUCTIONS SOC. SEC. TAX	MED. TAX	FED. INC. TAX	STATE INC. TAX	HOSP. INS.	OTHER	TOTAL	NET PAY	CK. NO.
24																	
25																	
	TOTALS					2500 00			155 00	36 25	400 00	50 00			641 25	1858 75	

Other Deductions: Write the appropriate code letter to the left of the amount: B—U.S. Savings Bonds; C—Credit Union; UD—Union Dues; UW—United Way.

In-Touch Electronics   **MEMORANDUM 27**
612 Kent Avenue
Brooklyn, NY 11205

TO: Accounting Clerk
FROM: Payroll Dept.
DATE: May 31, 20——
SUBJECT: Payroll Tax

Please record employer payroll taxes for May 31 payroll.
FICA rate = 6.2%
Medicare rate = 1.45%
Fed. unemployment tax rate = 0.8%
State unemployment tax rate = 5.4%

Notes

Computerized Accounting Using Peachtree

Mini-Practice Set 4

INSTRUCTIONS

Beginning a Session

Step 1   Select the problem set: In-Touch Electronics (MP-4).

Step 2   Rename the company and set the system date to May 31, 2004.

Completing the Accounting Problem

Step 3   Review the transactions provided in your textbook (May 16–May 31).

TIP: To save time entering transactions, group them by type and then enter the transactions in batches.

Sales and Cash Receipts

Step 4   Record the sales on account using the **Sales/Invoicing** option.

TIP: Remember that you need to change the GL Account in the Receipts window to enter a cash receipt for the sale of an asset (e.g., supplies, office equipment).

Step 5   Enter and apply any sales returns.

Step 6   Record all of the cash receipts using the **Receipts** option.

Purchases and Cash Payments

Step 7   Enter the purchases on account using the **Purchases/Receive Inventory** option.

TIP: Always verify the *GL Account* field when you enter a purchases on account transaction.

Step 8   Record and apply any purchases returns.

Step 9   Process all of the cash payments with the **Payments** option.

General Journal

Step 10 Use the **General Journal Entry** option to record the error discovered on May 26.

TIP: You can use the and buttons to edit a multi-line general journal entry.

Step 11 Record the employer's payroll taxes using the **General Journal Entry** option.

Printing Reports and Proofing Your Work

Step 12 Print the following reports: General Journal, Purchases Journal, Cash Disbursements Journal, Sales Journal, and Cash Receipts Journal.

TIP: Double-click a report title in the Select a Report window to go directly to that report.

Step 13 Proof your work. Print updated reports, if necessary.

Step 14 Print the following reports: General Ledger, Vendor Ledgers, and Customer Ledgers.

Step 15 Print a General Ledger Trial Balance.

Ending the Session

Step 16 Click the **Close Problem** button and select a save option.

Analyzing Your Work

Step 17 Answer the Analyze questions.

Peachtree Guide

Mini Practice Set 4   (continued)

SALES JOURNAL   PAGE ___18___

	DATE	SALES SLIP NO.	CUSTOMER'S ACCOUNT DEBITED	POST. REF.	SALES CREDIT	SALES TAX PAYABLE CREDIT	ACCOUNTS RECEIVABLE DEBIT	
1	20--							1
2	May 1	602	Sam Lorenzo	✓	180 00	9 00	189 00	2
3	3	603	Marianne Martino	✓	90 00	4 50	94 50	3
4	8	604	Tom Trout	✓	120 00	6 00	126 00	4
5	12	605	Mark McCormick	✓	200 00	10 00	210 00	5
6	13	606	Sue Ellen Scott	✓	300 00	15 00	315 00	6
7								7
8								8
9								9
10								10
11								11
12								12
13								13
14								14
15								15
16								16
17								17
18								18
19								19
20								20
21								21
22								22
23								23
24								24
25								25
26								26
27								27
28								28
29								29
30								30
31								31
32								32
33								33
34								34
35								35
36								36

CASH RECEIPTS JOURNAL

DATE	DOC. NO.	ACCOUNT NAME	POST. REF.	GENERAL CREDIT	SALES CREDIT	SALES TAX PAYABLE CREDIT	ACCOUNTS RECEIVABLE CREDIT	SALES DISCOUNTS DEBIT	CASH IN BANK DEBIT
20--									
May 3	R350	Sue Ellen Scott	✓				350 00	7 00	343 00
5	R351	Sam Lorenzo	✓				300 00	6 00	294 00
7	T20	Cash Sales	—		2100 00	105 00			2205 00
7	T20	Bankcard Sales				1860 00	93 00		1953 00
8	R352	Marianne Martino	✓				375 00		375 00
12	R353	Tom Trout	✓				225 00		225 00
14	R354	Sam Lorenzo	✓				189 00		189 00
15	R355	Mark McCormick	✓				250 00		250 00
15	T21	Cash Sales	—		1940 00	97 00			2037 00
15	T21	Bankcard Sales			1660 00	83 00			1743 00

Mini Practice Set 4   (continued)

PAGE _____ 12

PURCHASES JOURNAL

DATE	INVOICE NO.	CREDITOR'S ACCOUNT CREDITED	POST. REF.	ACCOUNTS PAYABLE CREDIT	PURCHASES DEBIT	GENERAL ACCOUNT DEBITED	POST. REF.	DEBIT	
20--									1
May 3	CS60	Computer Systems, Inc.	✓	60000	60000				2
4	HT88	Hi-Tech Elec. Outlet	✓	35000	35000				3
6	9451	Office Suppliers, Inc.	✓	77000		Office Equipment	155	77000	4
8	DW65	Desktop Wholesalers	✓	80000		Office Equipment	155	80000	5
10	601	Laser & Ink Jet Products	✓	100000	100000				6
									7
									8
									9
									10
									11
									12
									13
									14
									15
									16
									17
									18
									19
									20
									21
									22
									23
									24
									25
									26

Mini Practice Set 4   (continued)

CASH PAYMENTS JOURNAL

DATE		DOC. NO.	ACCOUNT NAME	POST. REF.	GENERAL DEBIT	GENERAL CREDIT	ACCOUNTS PAYABLE DEBIT	PURCHASES DISCOUNTS CREDIT	CASH IN BANK CREDIT
20-- May	1	887	Utilities Expense	635	1 2 5 00				1 2 5 00
	2	888	Desktop Wholesalers	✓			9 0 0 00		9 0 0 00
	4	889	Laser & Ink Jet Products	✓			7 5 0 00	1 5 00	7 3 5 00
	7	890	Office Suppliers, Inc.	✓			1 3 0 0 00		1 3 0 0 00
	10	891	Transportation In	505	1 7 5 00				1 7 5 00

Mini Practice Set 4   (continued)

GENERAL JOURNAL   PAGE ___7___

	DATE		DESCRIPTION	POST. REF.	DEBIT	CREDIT	
1	20--						1
2	May	5	Purchases	501	150000		2
3			Merchandise Inventory	110		150000	3
4			Memo 25				4
5							5
6							6
7							7
8							8
9							9
10							10
11							11
12							12
13							13
14							14
15							15
16							16
17							17
18							18
19							19
20							20
21							21
22							22
23							23
24							24
25							25
26							26
27							27
28							28
29							29
30							30
31							31
32							32
33							33
34							34
35							35
36							36
37							37
38							38

Mini Practice Set 4   (continued)

ACCOUNTS RECEIVABLE SUBSIDIARY LEDGER

Name *Sam Lorenzo*

Address *362 Oceanview, Miami, FL 33101*

DATE		DESCRIPTION	POST. REF.	DEBIT	CREDIT	BALANCE
20--						
May	1	Balance	✓			300 00
	1		S18	189 00		489 00
	5		CR15		300 00	189 00
	14		CR15		189 00	———

Name *Mark McCormick*

Address *14 Garden Place, Clearwater, FL 34618*

DATE		DESCRIPTION	POST. REF.	DEBIT	CREDIT	BALANCE
20--						
May	1	Balance	✓			250 00
	12		S18	210 00		460 00
	15		CR15		250 00	210 00

Name *Marianne Martino*

Address *92 Stafford Court, Fort Lauderdale, FL 33310*

DATE		DESCRIPTION	POST. REF.	DEBIT	CREDIT	BALANCE
20--						
May	1	Balance	✓			375 00
	3		S18	94 50		469 50
	8		CR15		375 00	94 50

Mini Practice Set 4   (continued)

Name **Sue Ellen Scott**

Address **302 Palm Drive, Jacksonville, FL 32203**

DATE		DESCRIPTION	POST. REF.	DEBIT	CREDIT	BALANCE
20--						
May	1	Balance	✓			3 5 0 00
	3		CR15		3 5 0 00	————
	13		S18	3 1 5 00		3 1 5 00

Name **Tom Trout**

Address **16 Del Mar, Boca Raton, FL 33431**

DATE		DESCRIPTION	POST. REF.	DEBIT	CREDIT	BALANCE
20--						
May	1	Balance	✓			2 2 5 00
	8		S18	1 2 6 00		3 5 1 00
	12		CR15		2 2 5 00	1 2 6 00

Mini Practice Set 4   (continued)

ACCOUNTS PAYABLE SUBSIDIARY LEDGER

Name **Computer Systems, Inc.**

Address **Six Gulf Place, Hialeah, FL 33010**

DATE		DESCRIPTION	POST. REF.	DEBIT	CREDIT	BALANCE
20--						
May	1	Balance	✓			1 20000
	3		P12		60000	1 80000

Name **Desktop Wholesalers**

Address **Three Surfside, Palm Springs, FL 33460**

DATE		DESCRIPTION	POST. REF.	DEBIT	CREDIT	BALANCE
20--						
May	1	Balance	✓			90000
	2		CP14	90000		————
	8		P12		80000	80000

Name **Hi-Tech Electronics Outlet**

Address **Quadrangle Complex, Orlando, FL 32802**

DATE		DESCRIPTION	POST. REF.	DEBIT	CREDIT	BALANCE
20--						
May	1	Balance	✓			1 40000
	4		P12		35000	1 75000

Mini Practice Set 4   (continued)

Name *Laser & Ink Jet Products* _____

Address *32 Cypress Blvd., Tampa, FL 33602* _____

DATE		DESCRIPTION	POST. REF.	DEBIT	CREDIT	BALANCE
20--						
May	1	Balance	✓			75000
	4		CP14	75000		———
	10		P12		100000	100000

Name *Office Suppliers, Inc.* _____

Address *56 Sunset Blvd., Panama City, FL 32401* _____

DATE		DESCRIPTION	POST. REF.	DEBIT	CREDIT	BALANCE
20--						
May	1	Balance	✓			130000
	6		P12		77000	207000
	7		CP14	130000		77000

Mini Practice Set 4   (continued)

GENERAL LEDGER

ACCOUNT __Cash in Bank_____ ACCOUNT NO. ___101___

DATE		DESCRIPTION	POST. REF.	DEBIT	CREDIT	BALANCE DEBIT	BALANCE CREDIT
20--							
May	1	Balance	✓			750000	

ACCOUNT __Accounts Receivable_____ ACCOUNT NO. ___105___

DATE		DESCRIPTION	POST. REF.	DEBIT	CREDIT	BALANCE DEBIT	BALANCE CREDIT
20--							
May	1	Balance	✓			150000	

ACCOUNT __Merchandise Inventory_____ ACCOUNT NO. ___110___

DATE		DESCRIPTION	POST. REF.	DEBIT	CREDIT	BALANCE DEBIT	BALANCE CREDIT
20--							
May	1	Balance	✓			5794900	
	5		G7		150000	5644900	

ACCOUNT __Supplies_____ ACCOUNT NO. ___115___

DATE		DESCRIPTION	POST. REF.	DEBIT	CREDIT	BALANCE DEBIT	BALANCE CREDIT
20--							
May	1	Balance	✓			50000	

ACCOUNT __Prepaid Insurance_____ ACCOUNT NO. ___120___

DATE		DESCRIPTION	POST. REF.	DEBIT	CREDIT	BALANCE DEBIT	BALANCE CREDIT
20--							
May	1	Balance	✓			30000	

Mini Practice Set 4   (continued)

ACCOUNT __Store Equipment__   ACCOUNT NO. __150__

DATE		DESCRIPTION	POST. REF.	DEBIT	CREDIT	BALANCE DEBIT	BALANCE CREDIT
20--							
May	1	Balance	✓			1300000	

ACCOUNT __Office Equipment__   ACCOUNT NO. __155__

DATE		DESCRIPTION	POST. REF.	DEBIT	CREDIT	BALANCE DEBIT	BALANCE CREDIT
20--							
May	1	Balance	✓			320000	
	6		P12	77000		397000	
	8		P12	80000		477000	

ACCOUNT __Accounts Payable__   ACCOUNT NO. __201__

DATE		DESCRIPTION	POST. REF.	DEBIT	CREDIT	BALANCE DEBIT	BALANCE CREDIT
20--							
May	1	Balance	✓				555000

ACCOUNT __Sales Tax Payable__   ACCOUNT NO. __205__

DATE		DESCRIPTION	POST. REF.	DEBIT	CREDIT	BALANCE DEBIT	BALANCE CREDIT
20--							
May	1	Balance	✓				41200

ACCOUNT __Employees' Federal Income Tax Payable__   ACCOUNT NO. __210__

DATE		DESCRIPTION	POST. REF.	DEBIT	CREDIT	BALANCE DEBIT	BALANCE CREDIT
20--							
May	1	Balance	✓				150000

Mini Practice Set 4   (continued)

ACCOUNT __Employees' State Income Tax Payable__   ACCOUNT NO. __211__

DATE		DESCRIPTION	POST. REF.	DEBIT	CREDIT	BALANCE	
						DEBIT	CREDIT
20--							
May	1	Balance	✓				2 1 5 00

ACCOUNT __Social Security Tax Payable__   ACCOUNT NO. __212__

DATE		DESCRIPTION	POST. REF.	DEBIT	CREDIT	BALANCE	
						DEBIT	CREDIT
20--							
May	1	Balance	✓				9 7 5 00

ACCOUNT __Medicare Tax Payable__   ACCOUNT NO. __213__

DATE		DESCRIPTION	POST. REF.	DEBIT	CREDIT	BALANCE	
						DEBIT	CREDIT
20--							
May	1	Balance	✓				1 8 0 00

ACCOUNT __Federal Unemployment Tax Payable__   ACCOUNT NO. __214__

DATE		DESCRIPTION	POST. REF.	DEBIT	CREDIT	BALANCE	
						DEBIT	CREDIT
20--							
May	1	Balance	✓				9 5 00

ACCOUNT __State Unemployment Tax Payable__   ACCOUNT NO. __215__

DATE		DESCRIPTION	POST. REF.	DEBIT	CREDIT	BALANCE	
						DEBIT	CREDIT
20--							
May	1	Balance	✓				1 3 0 00

Mini Practice Set 4 (continued)

ACCOUNT __Capital Stock__ ACCOUNT NO. __301__

DATE	DESCRIPTION	POST. REF.	DEBIT	CREDIT	BALANCE DEBIT	BALANCE CREDIT
20--						
May 1	Balance	✓				3500000

ACCOUNT __Retained Earnings__ ACCOUNT NO. __302__

DATE	DESCRIPTION	POST. REF.	DEBIT	CREDIT	BALANCE DEBIT	BALANCE CREDIT
20--						
May 1	Balance	✓				926000

ACCOUNT __Income Summary__ ACCOUNT NO. __303__

DATE	DESCRIPTION	POST. REF.	DEBIT	CREDIT	BALANCE DEBIT	BALANCE CREDIT

ACCOUNT __Sales__ ACCOUNT NO. __401__

DATE	DESCRIPTION	POST. REF.	DEBIT	CREDIT	BALANCE DEBIT	BALANCE CREDIT
20--						
May 1	Balance	✓				6000000

ACCOUNT __Sales Discounts__ ACCOUNT NO. __405__

DATE	DESCRIPTION	POST. REF.	DEBIT	CREDIT	BALANCE DEBIT	BALANCE CREDIT
20--						
May 1	Balance	✓			11000	

Mini Practice Set 4 (continued)

ACCOUNT __Sales Returns and Allowances__ ACCOUNT NO. __410__

DATE		DESCRIPTION	POST. REF.	DEBIT	CREDIT	BALANCE DEBIT	BALANCE CREDIT
20--							
May	1	Balance	✓			37500	

ACCOUNT __Purchases__ ACCOUNT NO. __501__

DATE		DESCRIPTION	POST. REF.	DEBIT	CREDIT	BALANCE DEBIT	BALANCE CREDIT
20--							
May	1	Balance	✓			1200000	
	5		G7	150000		1350000	

ACCOUNT __Transportation In__ ACCOUNT NO. __505__

DATE		DESCRIPTION	POST. REF.	DEBIT	CREDIT	BALANCE DEBIT	BALANCE CREDIT
20--							
May	1	Balance	✓			60000	
	10		CP14	17500		77500	

ACCOUNT __Purchases Discounts__ ACCOUNT NO. __510__

DATE		DESCRIPTION	POST. REF.	DEBIT	CREDIT	BALANCE DEBIT	BALANCE CREDIT
20--							
May	1	Balance	✓				35000

ACCOUNT __Purchases Returns and Allowances__ ACCOUNT NO. __515__

DATE		DESCRIPTION	POST. REF.	DEBIT	CREDIT	BALANCE DEBIT	BALANCE CREDIT
20--							
May	1	Balance	✓				41200

ACCOUNT __Advertising Expense__ ACCOUNT NO. __605__

DATE		DESCRIPTION	POST. REF.	DEBIT	CREDIT	BALANCE DEBIT	BALANCE CREDIT
20--							
May	1	Balance	✓			51000	

Mini Practice Set 4   (continued)

ACCOUNT ___Bankcard Fees Expense_____ ACCOUNT NO. ___610___

DATE		DESCRIPTION	POST. REF.	DEBIT	CREDIT	BALANCE	
						DEBIT	CREDIT
20--							
May	1	Balance	✓			600 00	

ACCOUNT ___Miscellaneous Expense_____ ACCOUNT NO. ___615___

DATE		DESCRIPTION	POST. REF.	DEBIT	CREDIT	BALANCE	
						DEBIT	CREDIT
20--							
May	1	Balance	✓			75 00	

ACCOUNT ___Payroll Tax Expense_____ ACCOUNT NO. ___620___

DATE		DESCRIPTION	POST. REF.	DEBIT	CREDIT	BALANCE	
						DEBIT	CREDIT
20--							
May	1	Balance	✓			1 380 00	

ACCOUNT ___Rent Expense_____ ACCOUNT NO. ___625___

DATE		DESCRIPTION	POST. REF.	DEBIT	CREDIT	BALANCE	
						DEBIT	CREDIT
20--							
May	1	Balance	✓			6 000 00	

ACCOUNT ___Salaries Expense_____ ACCOUNT NO. ___630___

DATE		DESCRIPTION	POST. REF.	DEBIT	CREDIT	BALANCE	
						DEBIT	CREDIT
20--							
May	1	Balance	✓			8 000 00	

ACCOUNT ___Utilities Expense_____ ACCOUNT NO. ___635___

DATE		DESCRIPTION	POST. REF.	DEBIT	CREDIT	BALANCE	
						DEBIT	CREDIT
20--							
May	1	Balance	✓			480 00	

Mini Practice Set 4   (continued)

In-Touch Electronics

Cash Proof

May 31, 20--

Mini Practice Set 4 (continued)

In-Touch Electronics
Schedule of Accounts Receivable
May 31, 20--

In-Touch Electronics
Schedule of Accounts Payable
May 31, 20--

Mini Practice Set 4 (concluded)

Analyze: 1. _____

2. _____

3. _____

MINI PRACTICE SET 4

In-Touch Electronics

Audit Test

Directions: *Use your completed solutions to answer the following questions. Write the answer in the space to the left of each question.*

_____ **1.** How many accounts receivable customers does the business have?

_____ **2.** How many transactions were recorded in the sales journal for this period?

_____ **3.** What total amount was posted from the Sales Tax Payable credit column of the sales journal to the Sales Tax Payable account?

_____ **4.** What were the totals for debits and credits in the sales journal?

_____ **5.** What account was credited for the May 8 transaction?

_____ **6.** What was the total of the Cash in Bank debit column for the cash receipts journal?

_____ **7.** Which account was debited for the May 21 transaction?

_____ **8.** What was the total of the Purchases Debit column in the purchases journal?

_____ **9.** How many transactions were recorded in the purchases journal?

_____ **10.** How many transactions in the cash payments journal affected the Purchases account?

_____ **11.** How many transactions were recorded in the general journal in the month of May?

_____ **12.** For the payroll entry recorded on May 31, what amount was debited to Payroll Tax Expense?

_____ **13.** What is the total of all accounts receivable subsidiary ledger accounts at month end?

_____ **14.** What is the total of all accounts payable subsidiary ledger accounts at month end?

_____ **15.** What is the balance of Cash in Bank at the end of the month?

_____ **16.** What is the total of any payroll tax liabilities at May 31?

_____ **17.** How many accounts are listed on the trial balance?

_____ **18.** Which account has the largest balance on the trial balance?

_____ **19.** Which customer owes In-Touch Electronics the most at the end of the month?

_____ **20.** What is the balance of the Sales account at month end?

CHAPTER 20
Completing the Accounting Cycle for a Merchandising Corporation

Study Plan

Check Your Understanding

Section 1	*Read Section 1 on pages 550–554 and complete the following exercises on page 555.* ❏ Thinking Critically ❏ Communicating Accounting ❏ Problem 20-1 *Identifying Accounts Affected by Closing Entries*
Section 2	*Read Section 2 on pages 556–561 and complete the following exercises on page 562.* ❏ Thinking Critically ❏ Analyzing Accounting ❏ Problem 20-2 *Analyzing a Source Document* ❏ Problem 20-3 *Organizing the Steps in the Accounting Cycle*
Summary	*Review the Chapter 20 Summary on page 563 in your textbook.* ❏ Key Concepts
Review and Activities	*Complete the following questions and exercises on pages 564–565 in your textbook.* ❏ Using Key Terms ❏ Understanding Accounting Concepts and Procedures ❏ Case Study ❏ Conducting an Audit with Alex ❏ Internet Connection ❏ Workplace Skills
Computerized Accounting	*Read the Computerized Accounting information on page 566 in your textbook.* ❏ *Making the Transition from a Manual to a Computerized System* ❏ *Closing the Accounting Period in Peachtree*
Problems	*Complete the following end-of-chapter problems for Chapter 20 in your textbook.* ❏ Problem 20-4 *Journalizing Closing Entries* ❏ Problem 20-5 *Journalizing and Posting Closing Entries* ❏ Problem 20-6 *Identifying Accounts for Closing Entries* ❏ Problem 20-7 *Completing End-of-Period Activities*
Challenge Problem	❏ Problem 20-8 *Preparing Adjusting and Closing Entries*
Chapter Reviews and Working Papers	*Complete the following exercises for Chapter 20 in your Chapter Reviews and Working Papers.* ❏ Chapter Review ❏ Self-Test

CHAPTER 20 REVIEW — Completing the Accounting Cycle for a Merchandising Corporation

Part 1   Accounting Vocabulary (6 points)

Directions: *Using the terms from the following list, complete the sentences below. Write the letter of the term you have chosen in the space provided.*

	Total Points	26
	Student's Score	

A. adjusting entries	D. post-closing trial balance	F. "Closing Entries"
B. closing entries	E. temporary accounts	G. "Adjusting Entries"
C. permanent accounts		

___G___   **0.** _____ is written in the Description column of the general journal before recording the entries that update the general ledger accounts.

_____   **1.** After the closing entries have been posted, there will be zero balances in the _____.

_____   **2.** To transfer the balances of temporary accounts to a permanent account, _____ are prepared.

_____   **3.** _____ update the general ledger accounts at the end of a period.

_____   **4.** The report prepared at the end of the period to test the equality of the general ledger after all adjusting and closing entries have been posted is the _____.

_____   **5.** Once the post-closing trial balance is prepared, the _____ should be in balance.

_____   **6.** _____ is written in the Description column of the general journal before recording the entries that bring all temporary accounts to zero balances.

Part 2   Rules for Adjusting and Closing Entries (7 points)

Directions: *Read each of the following statements to determine whether the statement is true or false. Write your answer in the space provided.*

False   **0.** The work sheet adjustments update the general ledger accounts.

_____   **1.** The sum of all the debit balances of the contra revenue, cost of merchandise, and expense accounts is the amount credited to Income Summary when recording the closing entry.

_____   **2.** The basic steps in the accounting cycle are not the same for all businesses.

_____   **3.** The account balances that appear on the post-closing trial balance are the same as those on the balance sheet.

_____   **4.** Four closing entries are required to close the temporary accounts for a merchandising business organized as a corporation.

_____   **5.** The source of information for the closing entries is the Balance Sheet section of the work sheet.

_____   **6.** After the closing entries have been posted, all of the permanent accounts will have zero balances.

_____   **7.** The temporary revenue account is closed by crediting it for its balance.

Part 3   The End-of-Period Steps in the Accounting Cycle (4 points)

Directions: *For each of the following statements, select the answer that best completes the sentence. Write your answer in the space provided.*

_____C_____   **0.** The source of information for the adjusting entries is the
   (A) Adjusted Trial Balance section of the work sheet.
   (B) Income Statement section of the work sheet.
   (C) Adjustments section of the work sheet.
   (D) Trial Balance section of the work sheet.

_____   **1.** Which of the following accounts is not a temporary account?
   (A) Rent Expense   (C) Sales Discounts
   (B) Cash in Bank   (D) Purchases Returns and Allowances

_____   **2.** Which of the following accounts would not be affected by a closing entry?
   (A) Capital Stock   (C) Retained Earnings
   (B) Sales   (D) Income Summary

_____   **3.** For a corporation, the balance of the Income Summary account is closed into
   (A) Capital Stock.   (C) Sales.
   (B) Cash in Bank.   (D) Retained Earnings.

_____   **4.** The first closing entry is made to close the
   (A) contra revenue, cost of merchandise, and expense accounts with debit balances into Income Summary.
   (B) temporary revenue and contra cost of merchandise accounts with credit balances into Income Summary.
   (C) balance of the Withdrawals account into the Retained Earnings account.
   (D) balance of the Income Summary account into the Retained Earnings account.

Part 4   Accounting Cycle for a Merchandising Business (9 points)

Directions: *In the space provided before the explanation of each step of the accounting cycle, write the letter of the step that matches the explanation.*

A. Prepare trial balance	**F.** Prepare financial statements
B. Analyze transactions	**G.** Prepare post-closing trial balance
C. Complete the work sheet	**H.** Journalize and post adjusting entries
D. Journalize business transactions	**I.** Journalize and post closing entries
E. Collect and verify data from business	**J.** Post to general and subsidiary ledgers

_____E_____   **0.** Receive and check the source documents for verification and accuracy.
_____   **1.** Examine the source documents to determine the accounts to be debited and credited.
_____   **2.** Record the information from source documents in the appropriate journals.
_____   **3.** Transfer the information in a journal entry to an individual account.
_____   **4.** Prove the equality of total debits and credits in the general ledger before making adjustments.
_____   **5.** Gather information for use in preparing the end-of-period financial statements and journal entries.
_____   **6.** Report the changes that have taken place during the period and the financial condition of the business at the end of the period.
_____   **7.** Update the general ledger accounts at the end of a period.
_____   **8.** Transfer the temporary account balances to a permanent account.
_____   **9.** Prove that the permanent general ledger accounts are in balance at the close of the accounting period.

Working Papers _for Section Problems_

Problem 20-1 Identifying Accounts Affected by Closing Entries

Account	Is the account affected by a closing entry?	During closing, is the account debited or credited?	During closing, is Income Summary debited or credited?
Accounts Receivable			
Bankcard Fees Expense			
Capital Stock			
Cash in Bank			
Equipment			
Federal Corporate Income Tax Expense			
Federal Corporate Income Tax Payable			
Income Summary			
Insurance Expense			
Merchandise Inventory			
Miscellaneous Expense			
Prepaid Insurance			
Purchases			
Purchases Discounts			
Purchases Returns and Allowances			
Retained Earnings			
Sales			
Sales Discounts			
Sales Returns and Allowances			
Sales Tax Payable			
Supplies			
Supplies Expense			
Transportation In			
Utilities Expense			

Problem 20-2   Analyzing a Source Document

CASH PAYMENTS JOURNAL

PAGE _____

DATE	DOC. NO.	ACCOUNT NAME	POST. REF.	GENERAL DEBIT	GENERAL CREDIT	ACCOUNTS PAYABLE DEBIT	PURCHASES DISCOUNTS CREDIT	CASH IN BANK CREDIT	
									1
									2
									3
									4

Your Backpack Inc.
29000 White Road
Cold Springs, TX 77282-4513

MEMORANDUM 42

TO: *Robert Chan, Chief Accountant*
FROM: *James Perkins, President*
DATE: *July 12, 20--*
SUBJECT: *New Storage Facility Rent*

Would you please make a check out to Warehouse Inc. for $750. The check is for the new storage facility we are renting. Please mail the check to:

     Mr. James Skiller, Controller
     Warehouse Inc.
     7576 County Line Highway
     Crossplains, TX 77361-8411

Problem 20-3   Organizing the Steps in the Accounting Cycle

1. _____

2. _____

3. _____

4. _____

5. _____

6. _____

7. _____

8. _____

9. _____

10. _____

Computerized Accounting Using Peachtree

Software Objectives

When you have completed this chapter, you will be able to use Peachtree to:

1. Perform the year-end closing for a corporation.
2. Print a post-closing trial balance.

Problem 20-4   Journalizing Closing Entries

INSTRUCTIONS

Beginning a Session

> **Step 1**   Select the problem set: Sunset Surfwear (Prob. 20-4).
> **Step 2**   Rename the company and set the system date to December 31, 2004.

Completing the Accounting Problem

> **Step 3**   Review the information in your textbook.
> **Step 4**   Since Peachtree records closing entries automatically, choose **System** from the *Tasks* menu and then select **Close Fiscal Year** to close the fiscal year for Sunset Surfwear.

> **TIP:** If you need help performing the closing process, refer to the instructions in Problem 10-4 (page 197). The closing process for a merchandising corporation is the same as the procedure to close a sole proprietorship.

> **Step 5**   Print a Post-Closing Trial Balance.
> **Step 6**   Answer the Analyze question.

Ending the Session

> **Step 7**   Click the **Close Problem** button in the Glencoe Smart Guide window.

Problem 20-5   Journalizing and Posting Closing Entries

INSTRUCTIONS

Beginning a Session

> **Step 1**   Select the problem set: Shutterbug Cameras (Prob. 20-5).
> **Step 2**   Rename the company and set the system date to December 31, 2004.

DO YOU HAVE A QUESTION ?

Q. *Are the steps to close a sole proprietorship any different than those to close a merchandising corporation?*

A. The steps to close a merchandising corporation are the same as those to close a sole proprietorship. Peachtree automatically closes all of the temporary accounts to a permanent account. In the case of a corporation, Peachtree closes all of the temporary accounts to the **Retained Earnings** account.

Notes

It is strongly recommended that you make a backup before performing the year-end closing if you are using Peachtree for a real company. For this problem, however, you do not have to make a backup.

Notes

Print the General Ledger Trial Balance whenever you are instructed to print a post-closing trial balance. You can change the name of the report if you want to rename it.

Completing the Accounting Problem

Step 3 Review the information in your textbook.

Step 4 Choose **System** from the *Tasks* menu and then select **Close Fiscal Year** to close the fiscal year.

Step 5 Print a Post-Closing Trial Balance.

Step 6 Answer the Analyze question.

Ending the Session

Step 7 Click the **Close Problem** button in the Glencoe Smart Guide window.

Problem 20-6   Identifying Accounts for Closing Entries

INSTRUCTIONS

Beginning a Session

Step 1 Select the problem set: Shutterbug Cameras (Prob. 20-6).

Step 2 Rename the company and set the system date to December 31, 2004.

Completing the Accounting Problem

Step 3 Review the information in your textbook.

Step 4 Print a Chart of Accounts report. (Do **not** use the General Ledger accounts in your text.) List or highlight all the accounts that will be debited when closed. Next, list all the accounts that will be credited when closed.

Step 5 Answer the Analyze question.

Ending the Session

Step 6 Click the **Close Problem** button in the Glencoe Smart Guide window.

Problem 20-8   Preparing Adjusting and Closing Entries

INSTRUCTIONS

Beginning a Session

Step 1 Select the problem set: Buzz Newsstand (Prob. 20-8).

Step 2 Rename the company and set the system date to December 31, 2004.

Completing the Accounting Problem

Step 3 Review the information in your textbook.

Step 4 Print a Working Trial Balance report and use it to prepare the adjustments.

Step 5 Record the adjusting entries.

Step 6 Print a General Journal report and proof your work.

Step 7 Answer the Analyze question.

Step 8 Click the **Save Pre-closing Balances** button in the Glencoe Smart Guide window.

Step 9 Close the fiscal year.

Step 10 Print a Post-Closing Trial Balance.

Ending the Session

Step 11 Click the **Close Problem** button in the Glencoe Smart Guide window.

Computerized Accounting Using Spreadsheets

Problem 20-7   Completing End-of-Period Activities

Completing the Spreadsheet

Step 1   Read the instructions for Problem 20-7 in your textbook. This problem involves preparing a ten-column work sheet and the end-of-period financial statements for River's Edge Canoe & Kayak.

Step 2   Open the Glencoe Accounting: Electronic Learning Center software.

Step 3   From the Program Menu, click on the **Peachtree Accounting Software and Spreadsheet Applications** icon.

Step 4   Log onto the Management System by typing your user name and password.

Step 5   Under the Chapter Problems tab, select the template: PR20-7a.xls. The template should look like the one shown below.

```
PROBLEM 20-7
COMPLETING END-OF-PERIOD ACTIVITIES

(name)
(date)


RIVER'S EDGE CANOE & KAYAK
WORK SHEET
FOR THE YEAR ENDED DECEMBER 31, 20--
```

ACCOUNT NUMBER	ACCOUNT NAME	TRIAL BALANCE DEBIT	CREDIT	ADJUSTMENTS DEBIT	CREDIT			BALANCE SHEET DEBIT	CREDIT
101	Cash in Bank	22,236.57				>	<	22,236.57	
115	Accounts Receivable	7,400.00				>	<	7,400.00	
130	Merchandise Inventory	25,000.00			AMOUNT	>	<	0.00	
135	Supplies	4,100.00			AMOUNT	>	<	0.00	
140	Prepaid Insurance	3,000.00			AMOUNT	>	<	0.00	
145	Delivery Truck	67,900.00				>	<	67,900.00	
201	Accounts Payable		13,000.00			>	<		13,000.00
210	Employers' Federal Income Tax Payable		------		AMOUNT	>	<		0.00
215	Sales Tax Payable		526.57			>	<		526.57
301	Capital Stock		40,000.00			>	<		40,000.00
305	Retained Earnings		25,400.00			>	<		25,400.00
310	Income Summary	------	------	AMOUNT		>	<		
401	Sales		175,000.00			>	<		
405	Sales Discounts	3,775.00				>	<		
410	Sales Returns & Allowances	2,500.00				>	<		
501	Purchases	75,300.00				>	<		
505	Transportation In	5,000.00				>	<		
510	Purchases Discounts		2,300.00			>	<		
515	Purchases Returns & Allowances		5,600.00			>	<		
605	Bankcard Fees Expense	3,515.00				>	<		
625	Federal Corporate Income Tax Expense	2,940.00		AMOUNT		>	<		
635	Insurance Expense	------		AMOUNT		>	<		
655	Miscellaneous Expense	5,960.00				>	<		
660	Rent Expense	9,000.00				>	<		
665	Salaries Expense	22,200.00				>	<		
670	Supplies Expense	------		AMOUNT		>	<		
680	Utilities Expense	2,000.00				>	<		
		261,826.57	261,826.57	0.00	0.00	>	<	97,536.57	78,926.57
	Net Income					>	<		53,650.00
						>	<	97,536.57	32,576.57

Step 6   Key your name and today's date in the cells containing the *(name)* and *(date)* placeholders.

Step 7   The trial balance amounts in the work sheet are given for you. The first adjustment that must be made is to adjust beginning merchandise inventory of $25,000 to an ending balance of $20,000. To make this adjustment, you must debit Income Summary and credit Merchandise Inventory for the difference between the beginning and ending merchandise inventory amounts. Enter the Income Summary adjustment in cell E25 and the Merchandise Inventory adjustment in cell F16. Remember, it is not necessary to include a comma or the decimal point and two zeroes as part of the amount. Notice that, as you enter the adjustments, the balances for the affected accounts in the adjusted trial balance change accordingly.

Step 8   Enter the remaining adjustments into the Adjustments section of the work sheet. When you have entered all of the adjustments, move the cell pointer into the Adjusted Trial Balance, Income Statement, and Balance Sheet sections of the work sheet. Notice that the amounts for the Adjusted Trial Balance, Income Statement, and Balance Sheet are automatically entered. The program also calculates the column totals and the net income for River's Edge Canoe & Kayak.

Step 9   Now scroll down below the work sheet and look at the income statement, statement of retained earnings, and balance sheet for River's Edge Canoe & Kayak. Notice the financial statements are already completed. This is because the spreadsheet template includes formulas that automatically pull information from the filled-in work sheet to complete the financial statements.

Step 10   Now scroll down below the balance sheet and complete the closing entries in the general journal. The account names and posting references are given for you.

Step 11   Scroll down below the closing entries and look at the post-closing trial balance. The amounts are automatically calculated using formulas.

Step 12   Save the spreadsheet using the **Save** option from the *File* menu. You should accept the default location for the save as this is handled by the management system.

Step 13   Print the completed spreadsheet.

TIP: If your spreadsheet is too wide to fit on an 8.5-inch wide piece of paper, you can change your print settings to print the worksheet *landscape.* Landscape means that the worksheet will be printed broadside on the page. Some spreadsheet applications also allow you to choose a "print to page" option. This function will reduce the width and/or depth of the worksheet to fit on one page.

TIP: When printing a long spreadsheet with multiple parts, you may want to insert page breaks between the sections so that each one begins printing at the top of a new page. Page breaks have already been entered into this spreadsheet template. Check your program's Help file for instructions on how to enter page breaks.

Step 14   Exit the spreadsheet program.

Step 15   In the Close Options box, select the location where you would like to save your work.

Step 16   Answer the Analyze question from your textbook for this problem.

What-If Analysis

If unexpired insurance on December 31 were $2,500, what adjustments would be made? What would net income be? How would this affect ending Retained Earnings?

⬤ **Working Papers** *for End-of-Chapter Problems*

Problem 20-4   Journalizing Closing Entries

GENERAL JOURNAL   PAGE _____

	DATE	DESCRIPTION	POST. REF.	DEBIT	CREDIT	
1						1
2						2
3						3
4						4
5						5
6						6
7						7
8						8
9						9
10						10
11						11
12						12
13						13
14						14
15						15
16						16
17						17
18						18
19						19
20						20
21						21
22						22
23						23
24						24
25						25
26						26
27						27
28						28
29						29
30						30

Analyze: _____

_____

Problem 20-5   Journalizing and Posting Closing Entries

(1)

GENERAL JOURNAL   PAGE _____

	DATE	DESCRIPTION	POST. REF.	DEBIT	CREDIT	
1						1
2						2
3						3
4						4
5						5
6						6
7						7
8						8
9						9
10						10
11						11
12						12
13						13
14						14
15						15
16						16
17						17

(2)

GENERAL LEDGER (PARTIAL)

ACCOUNT __Retained Earnings__   ACCOUNT NO. ___305___

DATE		DESCRIPTION	POST. REF.	DEBIT	CREDIT	BALANCE DEBIT	BALANCE CREDIT
20--							
Dec.	1	Balance	✓				20 41 00 00

ACCOUNT __Income Summary__   ACCOUNT NO. ___310___

DATE		DESCRIPTION	POST. REF.	DEBIT	CREDIT	BALANCE DEBIT	BALANCE CREDIT
20--							
Dec.	31	Adjusting Entry	G13	4 00 00 00		4 00 00 00	

Problem 20-5 (continued)

ACCOUNT _Sales_ ACCOUNT NO. _401_

DATE		DESCRIPTION	POST. REF.	DEBIT	CREDIT	BALANCE	
						DEBIT	CREDIT
20--							
Dec.	1	Balance	✓				15 0 0 0 0 0

ACCOUNT _Sales Returns and Allowances_ ACCOUNT NO. _410_

DATE		DESCRIPTION	POST. REF.	DEBIT	CREDIT	BALANCE	
						DEBIT	CREDIT
20--							
Dec.	1	Balance	✓			5 0 0 0 0 0	

ACCOUNT _Purchases_ ACCOUNT NO. _501_

DATE		DESCRIPTION	POST. REF.	DEBIT	CREDIT	BALANCE	
						DEBIT	CREDIT
20--							
Dec.	1	Balance	✓			9 0 0 0 0 0 0	

ACCOUNT _Transportation In_ ACCOUNT NO. _505_

DATE		DESCRIPTION	POST. REF.	DEBIT	CREDIT	BALANCE	
						DEBIT	CREDIT
20--							
Dec.	1	Balance	✓			5 0 0 0 0 0	

ACCOUNT _Purchases Discounts_ ACCOUNT NO. _510_

DATE		DESCRIPTION	POST. REF.	DEBIT	CREDIT	BALANCE	
						DEBIT	CREDIT
20--							
Dec.	1	Balance	✓				1 0 0 0 0 0

Problem 20-5 (concluded)

ACCOUNT __Purchases Returns and Allowances__   ACCOUNT NO. __515__

DATE		DESCRIPTION	POST. REF.	DEBIT	CREDIT	BALANCE DEBIT	BALANCE CREDIT
20--							
Dec.	1	Balance	✓				150000

ACCOUNT __Federal Corporate Income Tax Expense__   ACCOUNT NO. __620__

DATE		DESCRIPTION	POST. REF.	DEBIT	CREDIT	BALANCE DEBIT	BALANCE CREDIT
20--							
Dec.	1	Balance	✓			390000	
	31	Adjusting Entry	G13	80000		470000	

ACCOUNT __Miscellaneous Expense__   ACCOUNT NO. __645__

DATE		DESCRIPTION	POST. REF.	DEBIT	CREDIT	BALANCE DEBIT	BALANCE CREDIT
20--							
Dec.	1	Balance	✓			30000	

ACCOUNT __Rent Expense__   ACCOUNT NO. __650__

DATE		DESCRIPTION	POST. REF.	DEBIT	CREDIT	BALANCE DEBIT	BALANCE CREDIT
20--							
Dec.	1	Balance	✓			600000	

ACCOUNT __Supplies Expense__   ACCOUNT NO. __660__

DATE		DESCRIPTION	POST. REF.	DEBIT	CREDIT	BALANCE DEBIT	BALANCE CREDIT
20--							
Dec.	31	Adjusting Entry	G13	163000		163000	

ACCOUNT __Utilities Expense__   ACCOUNT NO. __670__

DATE		DESCRIPTION	POST. REF.	DEBIT	CREDIT	BALANCE DEBIT	BALANCE CREDIT
20--							
Dec.	1	Balance	✓			300000	

Analyze: _____

_____

Problem 20-6   Identifying Accounts for Closing Entries

Accounts Debited	**Accounts Credited**
_____	_____
_____	_____
_____	_____
_____	_____
_____	_____
_____	_____
_____	_____
_____	_____
_____	_____
_____	_____

Analyze: _____

_____

Problem 20-7   Completing End-of-Period Activities
(1), (2)

River's Edge

Work

For the Year Ended

	ACCT. NO.	ACCOUNT NAME	TRIAL BALANCE		ADJUSTMENTS	
			DEBIT	CREDIT	DEBIT	CREDIT
1	101	Cash in Bank	22 236 57			
2	115	Accounts Receivable	7 400 00			
3	130	Merchandise Inventory	25 000 00			
4	135	Supplies	4 100 00			
5	140	Prepaid Insurance	3 000 00			
6	145	Delivery Truck	67 900 00			
7	201	Accounts Payable		13 000 00		
8	204	Fed. Corporate Income Tax Pay.		——		
9	215	Sales Tax Payable		526 57		
10	301	Capital Stock		40 000 00		
11	305	Retained Earnings		25 400 00		
12	310	Income Summary	——	——		
13	401	Sales		175 000 00		
14	405	Sales Discounts	3 775 00			
15	410	Sales Returns and Allowances	2 500 00			
16	501	Purchases	75 300 00			
17	505	Transportation In	5 000 00			
18	510	Purchases Discounts		2 300 00		
19	515	Purchases Returns and Allow.		5 600 00		
20	605	Bankcard Fees Expense	3 515 00			
21	625	Fed. Corporate Income Tax Exp.	2 940 00			
22	635	Insurance Expense	——			
23	655	Miscellaneous Expense	5 960 00			
24	660	Rent Expense	9 000 00			
25	665	Salaries Expense	22 200 00			
26	670	Supplies Expense	——			
27	680	Utilities Expense	2 000 00			
28						
29						
30						
31						
32						

Canoe & Kayak

Sheet

December 31, 20--

ADJUSTED TRIAL BALANCE		INCOME STATEMENT		BALANCE SHEET		
DEBIT	CREDIT	DEBIT	CREDIT	DEBIT	CREDIT	
						1
						2
						3
						4
						5
						6
						7
						8
						9
						10
						11
						12
						13
						14
						15
						16
						17
						18
						19
						20
						21
						22
						23
						24
						25
						26
						27
						28
						29
						30
						31
						32

Problem 20-7   (continued)

(3)

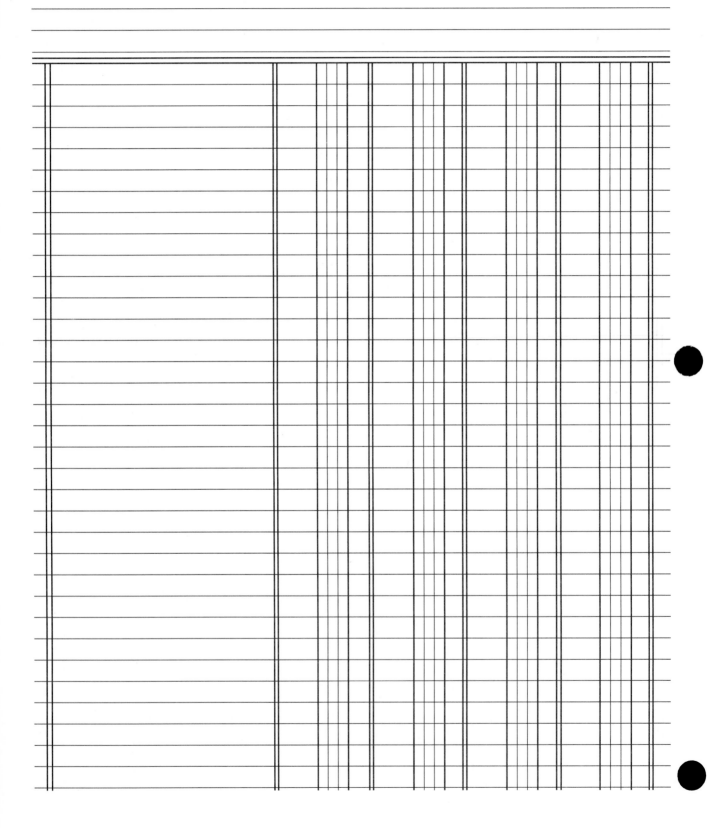

Problem 20-7   (continued)

(4)

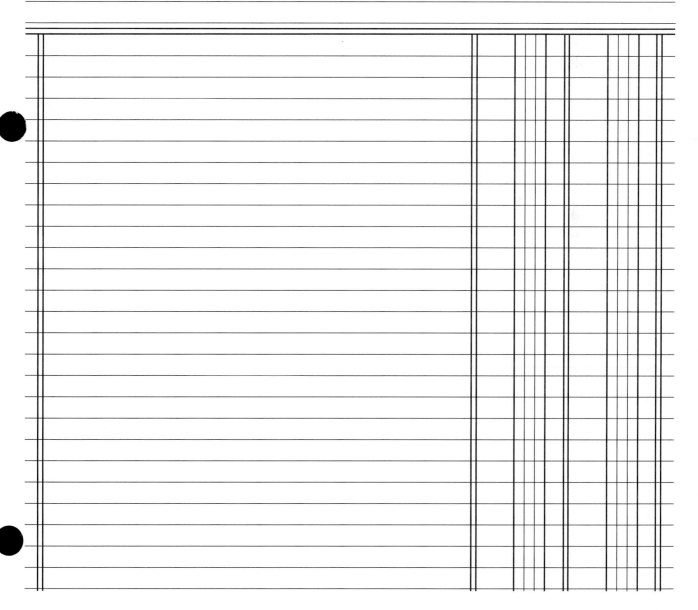

(5)

Problem 20-7   (continued)
(6), (7)

GENERAL JOURNAL   PAGE _____

	DATE		DESCRIPTION	POST. REF.	DEBIT	CREDIT	
1							1
2							2
3							3
4							4
5							5
6							6
7							7
8							8
9							9
10							10
11							11
12							12
13							13
14							14
15							15
16							16
17							17
18							18
19							19
20							20
21							21
22							22
23							23
24							24
25							25
26							26
27							27
28							28
29							29
30							30
31							31
32							32
33							33
34							34
35							35
36							36

Problem 20-7 (continued)

(7)

GENERAL LEDGER

ACCOUNT _Cash in Bank_   ACCOUNT NO. ___101___

DATE		DESCRIPTION	POST. REF.	DEBIT	CREDIT	BALANCE DEBIT	BALANCE CREDIT
20--							
Dec.	1	Balance	✓			2048297	
	31		CR19	1715170		3763467	
	31		CP22		1539810	2223657	

ACCOUNT _Accounts Receivable_   ACCOUNT NO. ___115___

DATE		DESCRIPTION	POST. REF.	DEBIT	CREDIT	BALANCE DEBIT	BALANCE CREDIT
20--							
Dec.	1	Balance	✓			1119438	
	7		G12		17500	1101938	
	31		S17	695162		1797100	
	31		CR19		1057100	740000	

ACCOUNT _Merchandise Inventory_   ACCOUNT NO. ___130___

DATE		DESCRIPTION	POST. REF.	DEBIT	CREDIT	BALANCE DEBIT	BALANCE CREDIT
20--							
Dec.	1	Balance	✓			2500000	

ACCOUNT _Supplies_   ACCOUNT NO. ___135___

DATE		DESCRIPTION	POST. REF.	DEBIT	CREDIT	BALANCE DEBIT	BALANCE CREDIT
20--							
Dec.	1	Balance	✓			396650	
	10		P16	10600		407250	
	21		P16	2750		410000	

ACCOUNT _Prepaid Insurance_   ACCOUNT NO. ___140___

DATE		DESCRIPTION	POST. REF.	DEBIT	CREDIT	BALANCE DEBIT	BALANCE CREDIT
20--							
Dec.	1	Balance	✓			300000	

Problem 20-7 (continued)

ACCOUNT ___Delivery Truck_____ ACCOUNT NO. ____145___

DATE		DESCRIPTION	POST. REF.	DEBIT	CREDIT	BALANCE DEBIT	BALANCE CREDIT
20--							
Dec.	1	Balance	✓			6 7 9 0 00	

ACCOUNT ___Accounts Payable_____ ACCOUNT NO. ____201___

DATE		DESCRIPTION	POST. REF.	DEBIT	CREDIT	BALANCE DEBIT	BALANCE CREDIT
20--							
Dec.	1	Balance	✓				1 3 0 3 0 50
	19		G12	2 5 6 00			1 2 7 7 4 50
	31		P16		9 4 3 3 50		2 2 2 0 8 00
	31		CP22	9 2 0 8 00			1 3 0 0 0 00

ACCOUNT ___Federal Corporate Income Tax Payable___ ACCOUNT NO. ____210___

DATE		DESCRIPTION	POST. REF.	DEBIT	CREDIT	BALANCE DEBIT	BALANCE CREDIT

ACCOUNT ___Sales Tax Payable_____ ACCOUNT NO. ____215___

DATE		DESCRIPTION	POST. REF.	DEBIT	CREDIT	BALANCE DEBIT	BALANCE CREDIT
20--							
Dec.	1	Balance	✓				4 6 3 00
	14		CP22	4 6 3 00			—
	31		S17		2 6 7 37		2 6 7 37
	31		CR19		2 5 9 20		5 2 6 57

ACCOUNT ___Capital Stock_____ ACCOUNT NO. ____301___

DATE		DESCRIPTION	POST. REF.	DEBIT	CREDIT	BALANCE DEBIT	BALANCE CREDIT
20--							
Dec.	1	Balance	✓				4 0 0 0 0 00

Problem 20-7 (continued)

ACCOUNT _Retained Earnings_   ACCOUNT NO. __305__

DATE		DESCRIPTION	POST. REF.	DEBIT	CREDIT	BALANCE DEBIT	BALANCE CREDIT
20--							
Dec.	1	Balance	✓				25 400 00

ACCOUNT _Income Summary_   ACCOUNT NO. __310__

DATE		DESCRIPTION	POST. REF.	DEBIT	CREDIT	BALANCE DEBIT	BALANCE CREDIT

ACCOUNT _Sales_   ACCOUNT NO. __401__

DATE		DESCRIPTION	POST. REF.	DEBIT	CREDIT	BALANCE DEBIT	BALANCE CREDIT
20--							
Dec.	1	Balance	✓				161 835 75
	31		S17		6 684 25		168 520 00
	31		CR19		6 480 00		175 000 00

ACCOUNT _Sales Discounts_   ACCOUNT NO. __405__

DATE		DESCRIPTION	POST. REF.	DEBIT	CREDIT	BALANCE DEBIT	BALANCE CREDIT
20--							
Dec.	1	Balance	✓			3 616 50	
	31		CR19	158 50		3 775 00	

ACCOUNT _Sales Returns and Allowances_   ACCOUNT NO. __410__

DATE		DESCRIPTION	POST. REF.	DEBIT	CREDIT	BALANCE DEBIT	BALANCE CREDIT
20--							
Dec.	1	Balance	✓			2 325 00	
	7		G12	175 00		2 500 00	

Problem 20-7   (continued)

ACCOUNT   *Purchases*   ACCOUNT NO.   *501*

DATE		DESCRIPTION	POST. REF.	DEBIT	CREDIT	BALANCE DEBIT	BALANCE CREDIT
20--							
Dec.	1	Balance	✓			6438500	
	11		CP22	161500		6600000	
	31		P16	930000		7530000	

ACCOUNT   *Transportation In*   ACCOUNT NO.   *505*

DATE		DESCRIPTION	POST. REF.	DEBIT	CREDIT	BALANCE DEBIT	BALANCE CREDIT
20--							
Dec.	1	Balance	✓			494900	
	21		CP22	5100		500000	

ACCOUNT   *Purchases Discounts*   ACCOUNT NO.   *510*

DATE		DESCRIPTION	POST. REF.	DEBIT	CREDIT	BALANCE DEBIT	BALANCE CREDIT
20--							
Dec.	1	Balance	✓				216200
	31		CP22		13800		230000

ACCOUNT   *Purchases Returns and Allowances*   ACCOUNT NO.   *515*

DATE		DESCRIPTION	POST. REF.	DEBIT	CREDIT	BALANCE DEBIT	BALANCE CREDIT
20--							
Dec.	1	Balance	✓				534400
	19		G12		25600		560000

ACCOUNT   *Bankcard Fees Expense*   ACCOUNT NO.   *605*

DATE		DESCRIPTION	POST. REF.	DEBIT	CREDIT	BALANCE DEBIT	BALANCE CREDIT
20--							
Dec.	1	Balance	✓			325300	
	27		CP22	26200		351500	

Problem 20-7 (continued)

ACCOUNT __Federal Corporate Income Tax Expense__   ACCOUNT NO. __625__

DATE		DESCRIPTION	POST. REF.	DEBIT	CREDIT	BALANCE DEBIT	BALANCE CREDIT
20--							
Dec.	1	Balance	✓			2 2 0 5 00	
	15		CP22	7 3 5 00		2 9 4 0 00	

ACCOUNT __Insurance Expense__   ACCOUNT NO. __635__

DATE		DESCRIPTION	POST. REF.	DEBIT	CREDIT	BALANCE DEBIT	BALANCE CREDIT

ACCOUNT __Miscellaneous Expense__   ACCOUNT NO. __655__

DATE		DESCRIPTION	POST. REF.	DEBIT	CREDIT	BALANCE DEBIT	BALANCE CREDIT
20--							
Dec.	1	Balance	✓			5 5 2 0 00	
	6		CP22	4 2 5 00		5 9 4 5 00	
	27		CP22	1 5 00		5 9 6 0 00	

ACCOUNT __Rent Expense__   ACCOUNT NO. __660__

DATE		DESCRIPTION	POST. REF.	DEBIT	CREDIT	BALANCE DEBIT	BALANCE CREDIT
20--							
Dec.	1	Balance	✓			8 2 5 0 00	
	1		CP22	7 5 0 00		9 0 0 0 00	

ACCOUNT __Salaries Expense__   ACCOUNT NO. __665__

DATE		DESCRIPTION	POST. REF.	DEBIT	CREDIT	BALANCE DEBIT	BALANCE CREDIT
20--							
Dec.	1	Balance	✓			2 0 3 5 0 00	
	12		CP22	1 8 5 0 00		2 2 2 0 0 00	

Problem 20-7   (concluded)

ACCOUNT   *Supplies Expense*   ACCOUNT NO.   *670*

DATE	DESCRIPTION	POST. REF.	DEBIT	CREDIT	BALANCE DEBIT	BALANCE CREDIT

ACCOUNT   *Utilities Expense*   ACCOUNT NO.   *680*

DATE		DESCRIPTION	POST. REF.	DEBIT	CREDIT	BALANCE DEBIT	BALANCE CREDIT
20--							
Dec.	1	Balance	✓			1837 90	
	9		CP22	57 50		1895 40	
	23		CP22	104 60		2000 00	

(8)

Analyze: _____

_____

Problem 20-8   Preparing Adjusting and Closing Entries
(1)

GENERAL JOURNAL   PAGE _____

	DATE	DESCRIPTION	POST. REF.	DEBIT	CREDIT	
1						1
2						2
3						3
4						4
5						5
6						6
7						7
8						8
9						9
10						10
11						11
12						12
13						13
14						14
15						15
16						16
17						17
18						18
19						19
20						20
21						21
22						22
23						23
24						24
25						25
26						26
27						27
28						28
29						29
30						30
31						31
32						32
33						33
34						34
35						35
36						36

Problem 20-8   (concluded)

(2)

Analyze: _____

_____

CHAPTER 20 Completing the Accounting Cycle for a Merchandising Corporation

Self-Test

Part A   True or False

Directions: *Circle the letter* T *in the Answer column if the statement is true; circle the letter* F *if the statement is false.*

Answer

T   F   **1.** The information for closing entries can be found on the Income Statement columns of the work sheet.

T   F   **2.** Revenue accounts are closed when they are credited.

T   F   **3.** All temporary accounts are closed into Income Summary.

T   F   **4.** The Retained Earnings account is closed into the Capital account.

T   F   **5.** Adjustments are prepared and posted before closing the books.

T   F   **6.** After closing the books, the Income Summary account has a credit balance.

T   F   **7.** Expense accounts are closed by crediting them.

T   F   **8.** To close Purchases Returns and Allowances and Sales Discounts will require a debit.

T   F   **9.** After closing the ledger, only the permanent accounts have balances.

T   F   **10.** The post-closing trial balance is a list of temporary accounts.

Part B   Matching

Directions: *The steps in the accounting cycle are listed below. Put the list in proper order by placing the correct letter next to the numbers 1–10.*

Answer

1. _____   **A.** Prepare the Trial Balance

2. _____   **B.** Analyze source documents

3. _____   **C.** Complete the work sheet

4. _____   **D.** Journalize transactions for source documents

5. _____   **E.** Collect and verify source documents

6. _____   **F.** Prepare financial statements

7. _____   **G.** Prepare post-closing trial balance

8. _____   **H.** Journalize and post closing entries

9. _____   **I.** Journalize and post adjusting entries

10. _____   **J.** Post to the general and subsidiary ledgers

 **CHAPTER 21**   **Accounting for Publicly Held Corporations**

Study Plan

Check Your Understanding

Section 1	Read Section 1 on pages 574–577 and complete the following exercises on page 578.
	❑ Thinking Critically
	❑ Communicating Accounting
	❑ Problem 21-1 *Examining Capital Stock Transactions*
Section 2	Read Section 2 on pages 579–582 and complete the following exercises on page 583.
	❑ Thinking Critically
	❑ Computing in the Business World
	❑ Problem 21-2 *Distributing Corporate Earnings*
	❑ Problem 21-3 *Analyzing a Source Document*
Section 3	Read Section 3 on pages 585–587 and complete the following exercises on page 588.
	❑ Thinking Critically
	❑ Analyzing Accounting
	❑ Problem 21-4 *Examining the Statement of Stockholders' Equity*
Summary	Review the Chapter 21 Summary on page 589 in your textbook.
	❑ Key Concepts
Review and Activities	Complete the following questions and exercises on pages 590–591 in your textbook.
	❑ Using Key Terms
	❑ Understanding Accounting Concepts and Procedures
	❑ Case Study
	❑ Conducting an Audit with Alex
	❑ Internet Connection
	❑ Workplace Skills
Computerized Accounting	Read the Computerized Accounting information on page 592 in your textbook.
	❑ *Making the Transition from a Manual to a Computerized System*
	❑ *Customizing Financial Reports in Peachtree*
Problems	Complete the following end-of-chapter problems for Chapter 21 in your textbook.
	❑ Problem 21-5 *Distributing Corporate Earnings*
	❑ Problem 21-6 *Journalizing the Issue of Stock*
	❑ Problem 21-7 *Journalizing Common and Preferred Stock Dividend Transactions*
	❑ Problem 21-8 *Preparing Corporate Financial Statements*
Challenge Problem	❑ Problem 21-9 *Recording Stockholders' Equity Transactions*
Chapter Reviews and Working Papers	Complete the following exercises for Chapter 21 in your Chapter Reviews and Working Papers.
	❑ Chapter Review
	❑ Self-Test

CHAPTER 21 REVIEW — Accounting for Publicly Held Corporations

Part 1   Accounting Vocabulary (10 points)

Total Points	43
Student's Score	

Directions: *Using terms from the following list, complete the sentences below. Write the letter of the term you have chosen in the space provided.*

A. authorized capital stock	**E.** dividend	**I.** proxy
B. board of directors	**F.** paid-in capital in excess of par	**J.** publicly held corporation
C. closely held corporation	**G.** par value	**K.** statement of stockholders' equity
D. common stock	**H.** preferred stock	

   K   **0.** The financial statement that reports the changes that have taken place in all of the stockholders' equity accounts during the period is the _____.

_____ **1.** The maximum number of shares of stock that a corporation may issue is called its _____.

_____ **2.** The stock that has certain privileges over common stock is called _____.

_____ **3.** When a corporation issues only one type of stock, the stock is called _____.

_____ **4.** The stockholders' equity account that is used to record the sale of stock at higher than par value is the _____ account.

_____ **5.** A corporation owned by a few persons or by a family and whose stock is not sold to the general public is called a(n) _____.

_____ **6.** A group who governs and is responsible for the affairs of the corporation is called a(n) _____.

_____ **7.** A(n) _____ is one whose stock is widely held, has a large market, and is traded on a stock exchange.

_____ **8.** _____ is the amount assigned to each share of stock and printed as a dollar amount on the stock certificates.

_____ **9.** A(n) _____ is a return on the money invested by the stockholder.

_____ **10.** A document that gives the stockholder's voting rights to someone else when the stockholder cannot attend a stockholders' meeting is called a(n) _____.

Part 2   Analyzing Transactions for a Corporation (10 points)

Directions: *Using the following account titles, analyze the transactions below. Determine the account(s) to be debited and credited. Write your answers in the space provided.*

A. Cash in Bank	**D.** Dividends—Preferred	**G.** $5 Preferred Stock
B. Common Stock	**E.** Dividends Payable—Common	**H.** Paid-in Capital in Excess of Par
C. Dividends—Common	**F.** Dividends Payable—Preferred	

Debit	Credit	
A	*B*	**0.** Issued 10,000 shares of common stock at $6 per share.
_____	_____	**1.** Issued 2,000 shares of $6 par common stock at $7.50 per share.
_____	_____	**2.** Declared a cash dividend of 85¢ per share on the 12,000 shares.
_____	_____	**3.** Issued a check for the payment of the dividend declared.
_____	_____	**4.** Issued 500 shares of $5 preferred stock, $100 par, at $100 per share.
_____	_____	**5.** Declared a cash dividend on the 500 shares of $5 preferred stock issued.

Part 3 Corporations (15 points)

Directions: *Read each of the following statements to determine whether the statement is true or false. Write your answer in the space provided.*

__True__   **0.** The Dividends account is increased on the debit side.

_____   **1.** An ownership certificate is proof of ownership in a corporation and lists the name of the stockholder, the number of shares issued, and the date they were issued.

_____   **2.** When a dividend is declared, the method used by all corporations is to debit the amount of the dividend directly into the Retained Earnings account.

_____   **3.** The stated dividend rate for preferred stock is an annual rate.

_____   **4.** Publicly held corporations cannot prepare a statement of retained earnings and must therefore prepare a statement of stockholders' equity.

_____   **5.** The usual preference that preferred stockholders have is the right to receive dividends before they are paid to common stockholders.

_____   **6.** Even though a corporation is authorized to issue two types of stock, only one account is set up to record the two types of stock.

_____   **7.** Forming a corporation is less costly than forming a sole proprietorship or a partnership.

_____   **8.** Amounts that decrease account balances are enclosed in parentheses on the statement of stockholders' equity.

_____   **9.** The board of directors has the duty to hire professional managers to operate the corporation.

_____ **10.** Both the net income earned and the dividends declared by a corporation increase the Retained Earnings account.

_____ **11.** A privately held corporation is usually owned by a small family, and a publicly held corporation is usually owned by a very large family.

_____ **12.** There are more corporations than there are sole proprietorships and partnerships in the United States.

_____ **13.** A corporation may enter into contracts, borrow money, acquire property, and sue in the courts in the same manner as a person.

_____ **14.** The only types of information reported on a statement of stockholders' equity are the number of any shares of stock issued and the total amount received for those shares.

_____ **15.** The various organization costs incurred by a corporation when getting started include attorneys' fees for legal services and payments to promoters to sell stock.

Part 4 Advantages and Disadvantages of Corporations (8 points)

Directions: *In the space provided below, indicate whether the statement expresses an advantage or a disadvantage of a corporation. Place an "A" in the space for an advantage or a "D" for a disadvantage.*

__D__   **0.** Filing of numerous reports

_____ **1.** Limited liability of the owners

_____ **2.** Close regulation by state and federal governments

_____ **3.** Risk limited to individual investment

_____ **4.** Full disclosure to the public

_____ **5.** Sale of stock between stockholders without approval of other stockholders

_____ **6.** Double taxation of the corporation and the stockholders

_____ **7.** Continuous existence of the corporation

_____ **8.** Separate legal entity

Working Papers *for Section Problems*

Problem 21-1   Examining Capital Stock Transactions

1. _____

   _____

   _____

   _____

   _____

2. _____

   _____

   _____

   _____

   _____

3. _____

   _____

   _____

   _____

   _____

   _____

Problem 21-2   Distributing Corporate Earnings

1. _____

   _____

2. _____

   _____

Problem 21-3 Analyzing a Source Document

GENERAL JOURNAL   PAGE _____

	DATE	DESCRIPTION	POST. REF.	DEBIT	CREDIT	
1						1
2						2
3						3
4						4
5						5
6						6
7						7
8						8
9						9
10						10
11						11
12						12
13						13
14						14
15						15
16						16
17						17
18						18
19						19
20						20
21						21
22						22

Problem 21-4   Examining the Statement of Stockholders' Equity

Transaction	Reported on Statement of Stockholders' Equity? (Yes/No)
1	
2	
3	
4	
5	
6	
7	
8	

Computerized Accounting Using Peachtree

Software Objectives

When you have completed this chapter, you will be able to use Peachtree to:

1. Record journal entries to record the issue of stock.
2. Record journal entries to record the distribution of earnings to owners.
3. Print a balance sheet for a publicly held corporation.

Problem 21-6   Journalizing the Issue of Stock

INSTRUCTIONS

Beginning a Session

> **Step 1**   Select the problem set: InBeat CD Shop (Prob. 21-6).
> **Step 2**   Rename the company and set the system date to June 30, 2004.

Completing the Accounting Problem

> **Step 3**   Review the information in your textbook.
> **Step 4**   Record all of the transactions using the **General Journal Entry** option.

 TIP: To save time, just enter the day of the month when you record the date for a general journal entry.

> **Step 5**   Print a General Journal report and proof your work.

 TIP: You can use the report design features to widen the *Transaction Description* column on a General Journal report.

> **Step 6**   Answer the Analyze question.

Ending the Session

> **Step 7**   Click the **Close Problem** button in the Glencoe Smart Guide window.

Mastering Peachtree

Print a Chart of Accounts report. What account types are assigned to the capital accounts? On a separate sheet of paper, discuss the significance of each account type.

DO YOU HAVE A QUESTION

Q. *Do you have to use the General Journal to record the issue of stock?*

A. Although your textbook demonstrates how to use the General Journal to record the issue of stock, you could use the **Receipts** option instead of the **General Journal Entry** option. You can record any transaction involving a cash receipt using the **Receipt** option. For consistency, however, the instructions provided below explain how to use the **General Journal Entry** option.

Peachtree Guide

Problem 21-7   Journalizing Common and Preferred Stock
Dividend Transactions

INSTRUCTIONS

Beginning a Session

Step 1   Select the problem set: Shutterbug Cameras (Prob. 21-7).

Step 2   Rename the company and set the system date to
December 31, 2004.

Completing the Accounting Problem

Step 3   Review the information in your textbook.

Step 4   Record all of the transactions using the **General Journal
Entry** option. Make sure each transaction is entered in the
correct accounting period. When entering the October transaction, verify the accounting period in the lower right hand
corner is 10/1/04 to 10/31/04. When entering the November
transaction, change the accounting period to Nov. 1, 2004 to
Nov. 30, 2004.

Step 5   Print a General Journal report and proof your work.

TIP: If you need to edit a general journal entry, click the [Records Edit] button. If you don't see the entry, click the **Show** pop-up to select the correct period.

NOTE: You must set the date filter option to **This Quarter** to print a
General Journal report that includes the entries for the
entire quarter.

Step 6   Print a General Ledger report.

NOTE: Set the General Ledger report options to *Summary by Transaction*
and choose *Period 10* through *Period 12* for the time frame. You must
set the time frame because you entered transactions across multiple
accounting periods.

Step 7   Answer the Analyze question.

Checking Your Work and Ending the Session

Step 8   Verify that the accounting period displayed in the lower right hand
corner is 12/1/04 to 12/31/04. Click the **Close Problem** button in the
Glencoe Smart Guide window.

Step 9   If your teacher has asked you to check your solution, select *Check my
answer to this problem*. Review, print, and close the report.

Step 10   Click the **Close Problem** button and select a save option.

DO YOU HAVE A QUESTION

Q. *Does Peachtree automatically generate the closing entries for a publicly held corporation?*

A. When you choose to close a fiscal year, Peachtree will close any account designated as **Equity—gets closed.** Peachtree will not, however, close any account designated as **Equity—doesn't close.** The following are accounts typically identified as this account type: **Preferred Stock, Common Stock,** and **Paid-in Capital in Excess of Par.**

Problem 21-9   Recording Stockholders' Equity Transactions

INSTRUCTIONS

Beginning a Session

Step 1   Select the problem set: Buzz Newsstand (Prob. 21-9).

Step 2   Rename the company and set the system date to December 31, 2004.

Completing the Accounting Problem

Step 3   Review the information in your textbook.

Step 4   Record all of the transactions using the **General Journal Entry** option. When entering the March transaction, set the accounting period to Mar. 1, 2004 to Mar. 31, 2004. When entering the April transaction, set the accounting period to Apr. 1, 2004 to Apr. 30, 2004, and so forth.

Step 5   Print a General Journal report and proof your work.

 TIP: Set the date filter option to print a General Journal report for the period March 1, 2004 to December 31, 2004.

Step 6   Print a Balance Sheet report.

 TIP: Choose *Range* for the time frame and select *Period 1* through *Period 12* to print a Balance Sheet for the entire year.

Step 7   Answer the Analyze question.

 TIP: Add net income to **Retained Earnings** and subtract the dividends to determine the ending **Retained Earnings** account balance.

Checking Your Work and Ending the Session

Step 8   Verify that the accounting period displayed in the lower right hand corner is 11/1/04 to 11/30/04. Click the **Close Problem** button in the Glencoe Smart Guide window.

Step 9   If your teacher has asked you to check your solution, select *Check my answer to this problem*. Review, print, and close the report.

Step 10   Click the **Close Problem** button and select a save option.

Mastering Peachtree

Change capital section title on the Balance Sheet to *Stockholders' Equity*. Save the customized report layout and print the revised Balance Sheet.

Peachtree Guide

FAQs

Why doesn't Peachtree show all of the transactions when you click the Edit Records button?

Peachtree shows only the transactions entered in the current period. Suppose the current period is *10—October 2004* and you enter a transaction dated November 15. If you chose to edit a record, this transaction would not appear in the list. Click the **Show** button in the Select General Journal Entry window and choose *All Transactions* or select the desired period to display the transactions.

The reports (e.g., General Journal, General Ledger, Balance Sheet, etc.) do not reflect all of the transactions recorded.

Peachtree allows you to enter transactions that occur over multiple accounting periods. Although this does not cause any difficulties when you enter transactions, you could encounter some anomalies when printing reports.

By default, Peachtree uses the default accounting period for most reports. Suppose the accounting period is set to *10—October 2004* and you enter transactions on Oct. 15, Nov. 1, and Dec. 15. When you print the General Journal report using the default options, only the October 15 transaction will appear because it is the only transaction for period 10. You must set the date range to include all of the periods in which you entered transactions.

Peachtree displays the error, "00/00/00 is not a valid date in the period."

If the current period is set to *10—October 2000,* Peachtree will allow you to enter transactions for October, November, and December. However, Peachtree will not permit you to enter a transaction with a date earlier than the current period (e.g., August or September).

If you receive this (or a similar) error message, choose **System** from the *Tasks* menu and then select **Change Accounting Period**. Select the accounting period in which you want to enter a transaction.

Computerized Accounting Using Spreadsheets

Problem 21-8   Preparing Corporate Financial Statements

Completing the Spreadsheet

Step 1   Read the instructions for Problem 21-8 in your textbook. This problem involves preparing a statement of stockholders' equity and a balance sheet.

Step 2   Open the Glencoe Accounting: Electronic Learning Center software.

Step 3   From the Program Menu, click on the **Peachtree Accounting Software and Spreadsheet Applications** icon.

Step 4   Log onto the Management System by typing your user name and password.

Step 5   Under the Chapter Problems tab, select the template: PR21-8a.xls. The template should look like the one shown below.

```
PROBLEM 21-8
PREPARING CORPORATE FINANCIAL STATEMENTS

(name)
(date)


RIVER'S EDGE CANOE & KAYAK
STATEMENT OF STOCKHOLDERS' EQUITY
FOR THE YEAR ENDED DECEMBER 31, 20--

                                    $100 PAR      $5 PAR      PAID-IN
                                    9% PREFERRED  COMMON      CAPITAL IN    RETAINED
                                    STOCK         STOCK       EXCESS OF PAR EARNINGS     TOTAL
Balance, January 1, 20--            AMOUNT        AMOUNT      AMOUNT        AMOUNT         0.00
Stock Issued:
  500 Shares of 9% Preferred at Par AMOUNT                                                0.00
  25,000 Shares of Common at $9                   AMOUNT      AMOUNT                       0.00
Net Income                                                                  AMOUNT         0.00
Cash Dividends:
  Preferred Stock                                                           AMOUNT         0.00
  Common Stock                                                              AMOUNT         0.00
Balance, December 31, 20--          AMOUNT        AMOUNT      AMOUNT          0.00         0.00
```

Step 6   Key your name and today's date in the cells containing the *(name)* and *(date)* placeholders.

Step 7   Enter the missing amounts in the statement of stockholders' equity in the cells containing the AMOUNT placeholders. Remember, it is not necessary to add a comma or the decimal point and ending zeroes. The total for each line will be automatically computed.

TIP: To enter a negative number, precede the amount entered by a minus sign. The spreadsheet will automatically format the number as negative using parentheses.

Step 8   Now scroll down below the statement of stockholders' equity and look at the balance sheet. Note the amounts have already been computed. The spreadsheet automatically pulls information from the statement of stockholders' equity to complete the balance sheet.

Step 9   Save the spreadsheet using the **Save** option from the *File* menu. You should accept the default location for the save as this is handled by the management system.

Step 10   Print the completed spreadsheet.

> **TIP:** If your spreadsheet is too wide to fit on an 8.5-inch wide piece of paper, you can change your print settings to print the worksheet *landscape.* Landscape means that the worksheet will be printed broadside on the page. Some spreadsheet applications also allow you to choose a "print to page" option. This function will reduce the width and/or depth of the worksheet to fit on one page.

Step 11   Exit the spreadsheet program.

Step 12   In the Close Options box, select the location where you would like to save your work.

Step 13   Answer the Analyze question from your textbook for this problem.

What-If Analysis

If net income were $511,000, how would this affect retained earnings?

Working Papers *for End-of-Chapter Problems*

Problem 21-5 Distributing Corporate Earnings

1. _____

2. _____

Analyze: _____

_____

_____

Problem 21-6 Journalizing the Issue of Stock

GENERAL JOURNAL   PAGE _____

	DATE	DESCRIPTION	POST. REF.	DEBIT	CREDIT	
1						1
2						2
3						3
4						4
5						5
6						6
7						7
8						8
9						9
10						10
11						11
12						12
13						13
14						14
15						15
16						16
17						17
18						18
19						19
20						20
21						21
22						22

Analyze: _____

_____

_____

Problem 21-7   Journalizing Common and Preferred Stock Dividend Transactions

(1)

GENERAL JOURNAL   PAGE _____

	DATE	DESCRIPTION	POST. REF.	DEBIT	CREDIT	
1						1
2						2
3						3
4						4
5						5
6						6
7						7
8						8
9						9
10						10
11						11
12						12
13						13
14						14
15						15
16						16
17						17
18						18
19						19
20						20
21						21

Problem 21-7   (concluded)

(2)

GENERAL LEDGER (PARTIAL)

ACCOUNT *Cash in Bank*   ACCOUNT NO. _101_

DATE	DESCRIPTION	POST. REF.	DEBIT	CREDIT	BALANCE DEBIT	BALANCE CREDIT
20--						
Dec. 1	Balance	✓			9865000	

ACCOUNT *Dividends Payable—Preferred*   ACCOUNT NO. _203_

DATE	DESCRIPTION	POST. REF.	DEBIT	CREDIT	BALANCE DEBIT	BALANCE CREDIT

ACCOUNT *Dividends Payable—Common*   ACCOUNT NO. _204_

DATE	DESCRIPTION	POST. REF.	DEBIT	CREDIT	BALANCE DEBIT	BALANCE CREDIT

Analyze: _____

_____

_____

Problem 21-8   Preparing Corporate Financial Statements

(1)

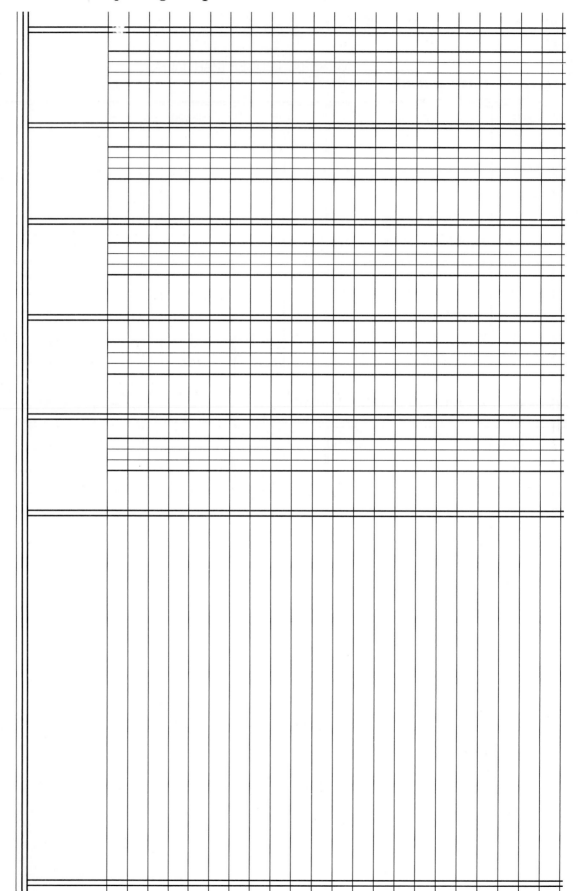

Problem 21-8   (concluded)

(2)

Analyze: _____

Problem 21-9   Source Documents

Instructions: *Use the following source documents to record the transactions for this problem.*

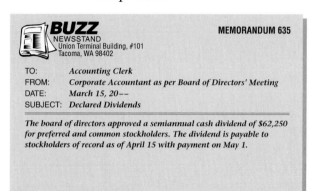

BUZZ NEWSSTAND
Union Terminal Building, #101
Tacoma, WA 98402

MEMORANDUM 635

TO: *Accounting Clerk*
FROM: *Corporate Accountant as per Board of Directors' Meeting*
DATE: *March 15, 20--*
SUBJECT: *Declared Dividends*

The board of directors approved a semiannual cash dividend of $62,250 for preferred and common stockholders. The dividend is payable to stockholders of record as of April 15 with payment on May 1.

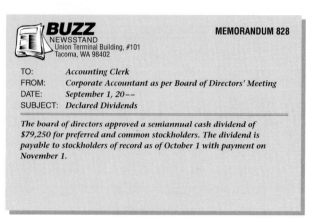

BUZZ NEWSSTAND
Union Terminal Building, #101
Tacoma, WA 98402

MEMORANDUM 828

TO: *Accounting Clerk*
FROM: *Corporate Accountant as per Board of Directors' Meeting*
DATE: *September 1, 20--*
SUBJECT: *Declared Dividends*

The board of directors approved a semiannual cash dividend of $79,250 for preferred and common stockholders. The dividend is payable to stockholders of record as of October 1 with payment on November 1.

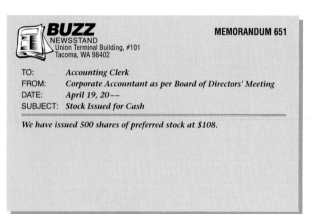

BUZZ NEWSSTAND
Union Terminal Building, #101
Tacoma, WA 98402

MEMORANDUM 651

TO: *Accounting Clerk*
FROM: *Corporate Accountant as per Board of Directors' Meeting*
DATE: *April 19, 20--*
SUBJECT: *Stock Issued for Cash*

We have issued 500 shares of preferred stock at $108.

$ *79,250.00*   No. 2451
Date *November 1*   20--
To *Dividends Checking Account*
For *Dividends Payable*

	Dollars	Cents
Balance brought forward	323,908	00
Add deposits		
Total	323,908	00
Less this check	79,250	00
Balance carried forward	244,658	00

$ *62,250.00*   No. 1256
Date *May 1*   20--
To *Dividends Checking Account*
For *Dividends Payable*

	Dollars	Cents
Balance brought forward	357,225	00
Add deposits		
Total	357,225	00
Less this check	62,250	00
Balance carried forward	294,975	00

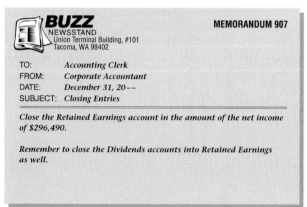

BUZZ NEWSSTAND
Union Terminal Building, #101
Tacoma, WA 98402

MEMORANDUM 907

TO: *Accounting Clerk*
FROM: *Corporate Accountant*
DATE: *December 31, 20--*
SUBJECT: *Closing Entries*

Close the Retained Earnings account in the amount of the net income of $296,490.

Remember to close the Dividends accounts into Retained Earnings as well.

Problem 21-9   Recording Stockholders' Equity Transactions

(1)

GENERAL JOURNAL   PAGE _____

	DATE	DESCRIPTION	POST. REF.	DEBIT	CREDIT	
1						1
2						2
3						3
4						4
5						5
6						6
7						7
8						8
9						9
10						10
11						11
12						12
13						13
14						14
15						15
16						16
17						17
18						18
19						19
20						20
21						21
22						22
23						23
24						24
25						25
26						26
27						27
28						28
29						29
30						30
31						31
32						32
33						33
34						34
35						35
36						36

Problem 21-9   (concluded)

(2)

Analyze:

CHAPTER 21   Accounting for Publicly Held Corporations

Self-Test

Part A   Fill in the Missing Term

Directions: *Using terms from the following list, complete the sentences below.*
Write the letter of the term you have selected in the space provided.

A. authorized capital stock	**F.** paid-in capital in excess	**I.** proxy
B. board of directors	of par	**J.** publicly held corporation
C. closely held corporation	**G.** par value	**K.** statement of stockholders'
D. common stock	**H.** preferred stock	equity
E. dividend		

Answer

_____   **1.** A document that gives the stockholder's voting rights to someone else when the stockholder does not want to attend the stockholders' meeting is called a(n) _____.

_____   **2.** The stock that has certain privileges over common stock is called _____.

_____   **3.** The financial report that shows changes that have taken place in all of the stockholders' equity accounts is called the _____.

_____   **4.** The maximum number of shares of stock that a corporation may issue is called its _____.

_____   **5.** A(n) _____ is one whose stock is widely held, has a large market, and is traded on a stock exchange.

_____   **6.** A corporation owned by a few persons or by a family and whose stock is not sold to the general public is called a(n) _____.

_____   **7.** _____ is the amount assigned to each share of stock and printed as a dollar amount on the stock certificates.

_____   **8.** A group who governs and is responsible for the affairs of the corporation is called a(n) _____.

_____   **9.** The stockholders' equity account that is used to record the sale of stock at higher than par value is the _____ account.

_____   **10.** When a corporation issues only one type of stock, the stock is called _____.

_____   **11.** A(n) _____ is a cash return on the money invested by the stockholder.

Part B True or False

Directions: *Read each of the following statements to determine whether the statement is true or false. Write your answer in the space provided.*

Answer

_____ **1.** The stockholders of a corporation have unlimited liability.

_____ **2.** Changes in stockholders' ownership end the life of a corporation.

_____ **3.** A corporation may own property in the name of the corporation.

_____ **4.** The Dividend account in a corporation is similar to the Withdrawals account in a sole proprietorship.

_____ **5.** Declaring a cash dividend requires formal action by the board of directors.

_____ **6.** The Paid-in Capital in Excess of Par account has a debit balance.

_____ **7.** Preferred stockholders have the right to vote for the board of directors.

_____ **8.** Stockholders who own stock at the date of record will receive a dividend if declared.

_____ **9.** The earnings of a corporation are taxed twice.

_____ **10.** Paid-in Capital in Excess of Par is a current asset.

Part C Analyzing Transactions

Directions: *Record each of the following unrelated transactions in the general journal forms provided.*

1. May 1. Issued 500 shares of $5 par value common stock for $5.00 per share.

	DATE	DESCRIPTION	POST. REF.	DEBIT	CREDIT	
1						1
2						2
3						3
4						4

2. May 15. Declared a cash dividend of $3.15 per share on 2,000 shares of common stock.

	DATE	DESCRIPTION	POST. REF.	DEBIT	CREDIT	
1						1
2						2
3						3
4						4

CHAPTER 22 Cash Funds

Study Plan

Check Your Understanding

Section 1	*Read Section 1 on pages 600–603 and complete the following exercises on page 604.* ❏ Thinking Critically ❏ Communicating Accounting ❏ Problem 22-1 *Preparing a Cash Proof* ❏ Problem 22-2 *Recording a Cash Overage*
Section 2	*Read Section 2 on pages 605–613 and complete the following exercises on page 614.* ❏ Thinking Critically ❏ Computing in the Business World ❏ Problem 22-3 *Analyzing a Source Document*
Summary	*Review the Chapter 22 Summary on page 615 in your textbook.* ❏ Key Concepts
Review and Activities	*Complete the following questions and exercises on pages 616–617 in your textbook.* ❏ Using Key Terms ❏ Understanding Accounting Concepts and Procedures ❏ Case Study ❏ Conducting an Audit with Alex ❏ Internet Connection ❏ Workplace Skills
Computerized Accounting	*Read the Computerized Accounting information on page 618 in your textbook.* ❏ *Making the Transition from a Manual to a Computerized System* ❏ *Maintaining Cash Funds in Peachtree*
Problems	*Complete the following end-of-chapter problems for Chapter 22 in your textbook.* ❏ Problem 22-4 *Establishing a Change Fund* ❏ Problem 22-5 *Establishing and Replenishing a Petty Cash Fund* ❏ Problem 22-6 *Establishing and Replenishing a Petty Cash Fund* ❏ Problem 22-7 *Using a Petty Cash Register* ❏ Problem 22-8 *Handling a Petty Cash Fund*
Challenge Problem	❏ Problem 22-9 *Locating Errors in a Petty Cash Register*
Chapter Reviews and Working Papers	*Complete the following exercises for Chapter 22 in your Chapter Reviews and Working Papers.* ❏ Chapter Review ❏ Self-Test

CHAPTER 22 REVIEW   Cash Funds

Part 1   Accounting Vocabulary (6 points)

Total Points	41
Student's Score	

Directions: *Using terms from the following list, complete the sentences below. Write the letter of the term you have chosen in the space provided.*

A. change fund	**D.** petty cashier	**F.** petty cash requisition
B. petty cash disbursement	**E.** petty cash register	**G.** petty cash voucher
C. petty cash fund		

_____F_____   **0.** The form used for requesting money to replenish the petty cash fund is a _____.

_____   **1.** A _____ consists of varying denominations of bills and coins and is used to make change in cash transactions.

_____   **2.** Cash that is kept on hand by a business for making small, incidental cash payments is called a _____.

_____   **3.** A _____ is a proof of payment from the petty cash fund.

_____   **4.** The person responsible for handling the petty cash fund is the _____.

_____   **5.** Any payment from the petty cash fund is called a _____.

_____   **6.** A _____ is a record of all disbursements made from the petty cash fund.

Part 2   Examining Cash Funds (8 points)

Directions: *For each of the following, select the choice that is the most suitable. Write your answer in the space provided.*

_____A_____   **0.** The Change Fund account is listed on the chart of accounts as a(n)
- (A) asset.
- (B) liability.
- (C) revenue account.
- (D) expense.

_____   **1.** Which of the following businesses would probably **not** have a change fund?
- (A) drugstore.
- (B) supermarket.
- (C) lawyer's office.
- (D) newsstand.

_____   **2.** A cash proof for the change fund should be prepared at the end of the
- (A) accounting period.
- (B) month.
- (C) day.
- (D) week.

_____   **3.** Cash Short & Over is classified as a(n)
- (A) liability.
- (B) temporary owner's equity account.
- (C) expense.
- (D) revenue account.

_____   **4.** The Petty Cash Fund account is debited
- (A) every time the fund is replenished.
- (B) when the fund is established.
- (C) when the amount of money in the fund is increased.
- (D) B and C.

_____   **5.** The petty cash fund is replenished
- (A) when its balance reaches the minimum amount.
- (B) at the end of each day.
- (C) at the end of the fiscal period.
- (D) A and C.

_____   **6.** The Petty Cash Fund account is a(n)
- (A) expense account.
- (B) revenue account.
- (C) asset account.
- (D) owner's equity account.

_____   **7.** In business, cash overages are
- (A) revenue.
- (B) expenses.
- (C) assets.
- (D) liabilities.

_____ 8. Cash shortages or overages are recorded in the
   (A) cash payments journal.   (C) general journal.
   (B) cash receipts journal.   (D) A and B.

Part 3   Accounting for Cash Funds (15 points)

Directions: _Read each of the following statements to determine whether the statement is true or false. Write your answer in the space provided._

True   **0.** The size of the petty cash fund is determined by the needs of the business.

_____ **1.** The amount of cash sales for the day is taken from the cash register tape and entered on the cash proof form.

_____ **2.** At the end of the fiscal period, the balance of the Cash Short & Over account is closed directly into Retained Earnings.

_____ **3.** Replenishing the petty cash fund increases the fund's original balance.

_____ **4.** The salesclerk usually counts the cash in the drawer, verifies its accuracy, and signs the cash proof form.

_____ **5.** Cash shortages are liabilities and are debited to the Cash Short & Over account.

_____ **6.** The size of the petty cash fund will not change unless the business finds that it needs more or less than its original estimate.

_____ **7.** The Change Fund account is debited each time the fund is replenished.

_____ **8.** Some businesses that have a petty cash fund do not use a petty cash register.

_____ **9.** A cash proof is prepared to verify that the amount of cash in the cash register drawer is equal to the total cash sales for the day.

_____ **10.** Cash overages are revenue and are recorded as credits to the Sales account.

_____ **11.** Businesses that use a petty cash envelope for recording petty cash disbursements use a new petty cash envelope for each period's disbursements.

_____ **12.** The amounts paid out of the petty cash fund must be journalized and recorded in the appropriate general ledger accounts when the petty cash fund is replenished.

_____ **13.** The petty cash register is considered an accounting journal because all amounts are posted from this register to general ledger accounts.

_____ **14.** The balance of the cash from the cash register drawer is deposited in the business's checking account after the cash in the cash register drawer is counted and the change fund is set aside.

_____ **15.** The entry to establish the petty cash fund is recorded in the cash payments journal.

Part 4   Analyzing Cash Funds Transactions (12 points)

Directions: _Using the following list of account titles, determine the account titles to be debited and credited for the transactions below._

A. Cash in Bank	**D.** Supplies	**F.** Delivery Expense
B. Change Fund	**E.** Cash Short & Over	**G.** Miscellaneous Expense
C. Petty Cash Fund		

Debit	Credit	
_B_	_A_	**0.** Established a change fund.
_____	_____	**1.** Recorded a cash overage in the change fund.
_____	_____	**2.** Established the petty cash fund.
_____	_____	**3.** Replenished the petty cash fund; petty cash vouchers were for supplies, delivery expenses, and miscellaneous expenses.
_____	_____	**4.** Increased the petty cash fund.
_____	_____	**5.** Recorded a cash shortage in the petty cash fund.
_____	_____	**6.** Decreased the change fund.

Working Papers *for Section Problems*

Problem 22-1   Preparing a Cash Proof

(1)

CASH PROOF

Date _____

Cash Register No. _____

Total cash sales (from cash register tape)		$ _____
Cash in drawer	$ _____	
Less change fund	_____	
Net cash received		$ _____
Cash short		_____
Cash over		_____

Salesclerk _____

Supervisor _____

(2)

GENERAL JOURNAL   PAGE _____

	DATE	DESCRIPTION	POST. REF.	DEBIT	CREDIT	
1						1
2						2
3						3
4						4
5						5
6						6
7						7
8						8
9						9
10						10
11						11
12						12

Problem 22-2   Recording a Cash Overage

(1)

CASH PROOF

Date _____

Cash Register No. _____

Total cash sales (from cash register tape)		$ _____
Cash in drawer	$ _____	
Less change fund	_____	
Net cash received		$ _____
Cash short		_____
Cash over		_____

Salesclerk _____

Supervisor _____

(2)

GENERAL JOURNAL   PAGE _____

	DATE	DESCRIPTION	POST. REF.	DEBIT	CREDIT	
1						1
2						2
3						3
4						4
5						5
6						6
7						7
8						8
9						9
10						10
11						11
12						12

Problem 22-3   Analyzing a Source Document

$ 39.51		No. 941
Date _December 31_		20 – –
To _Petty Cash_		
For _Replenish Fund_		

	Dollars	Cents
Balance brought forward	77,432	86
Add deposits		
Total		
Less this check	39	51
Balance carried forward	77,393	35

Riddle's Card Shop
1500 Main Street
Concord, MA 01742

941

53-215
113

DATE _December 31_   20 – –

PAY TO THE
ORDER OF _Petty Cash_ $ _39.51_

Thirty-nine and $^{51}/_{100}$ _____ DOLLARS

Patriot Bank
CONCORD, MASSACHUSETTS

MEMO _____

⑈0⑈⑈3021530 331 234 9⑈ 0941

Computerized Accounting Using Peachtree

Software Objectives

When you have completed this chapter, you will be able to use Peachtree to:
1. Record the entry to establish a change fund.
2. Record the entries to establish and replenish a petty cash fund.

Problem 22-4   Establishing a Change Fund

INSTRUCTIONS

Beginning a Session

Step 1   Select the problem set: Sunset Surfwear (Prob. 22-4).
Step 2   Rename the company by adding your initials, e.g., Sunset (Prob. 22-4: XXX).
Step 3   Set the system date to February 29, 2004.

TIP: The year 2004 is a leap year. Therefore, the end of the month is February 29.

Completing the Accounting Problem

Step 4   Review the information provided in your textbook.
Step 5   Record the entry to establish the change fund using the **General Journal Entry** option.

TIP: As a shortcut, you can type only the day of the month when you enter a transaction date.

Step 6   Manually prepare a cash proof.
Step 7   Record the cash sales using the **General Journal Entry** option.
Step 8   Print a General Journal report and proof your work.
Step 9   Answer the Analyze question.

Ending the Session

Step 10   Click the **Close Problem** button in the Glencoe Smart Guide window to save your work.

Mastering Peachtree

Explore how to export data from Peachtree into another application such as a spreadsheet program. Demonstrate your understanding of this feature by exporting the chart of accounts. Include only the general ledger ID and account description. Import the file into a spreadsheet or word processor, and then print the data.

DO YOU HAVE A QUESTION

Q. *Can you use the General Journal Entry option for transactions involving cash?*

A. You have learned how to use the **Payments** and **Receipts** options to record cash payments and cash receipts, respectively. However, you can always use the **General Ledger Entry** option to record transactions involving cash. The only disadvantage to using the **General Journal Entry** option is that Peachtree will not print checks for any cash payments transactions you record. However, this is not an issue if you manually write checks and use Peachtree only to record the transactions.

The Peachtree instructions for this chapter suggest that you record the various cash funds transactions using the **General Journal Entry** option since your textbook also uses general journal transactions. You can, however, use the **Payments** and **Receipts** options if you are more comfortable using these options.

Peachtree Guide

Problem 22-5   Establishing and Replenishing a Petty Cash Fund

INSTRUCTIONS

Beginning a Session

Step 1   Select the problem set: InBeat CD Shop (Prob. 22-5).

Step 2   Rename the company, and set the system date to February 29, 2004.

Completing the Accounting Problem

Step 3   Review the information provided in your textbook.

Step 4   Record the entry to establish the petty cash fund using the **General Journal Entry** option.

TIP: Click the [Records Edit] button if you need to edit a general journal entry you already posted.

> **DO YOU HAVE A QUESTION**
>
> **Q.** *Does Peachtree include any features to prepare a petty cash register?*
>
> **A.** Peachtree does not provide any features to prepare a petty cash register. Although you must manually prepare this document, you can use the **General Journal Entry** option to record the transactions to establish and replenish a petty cash fund.

Step 5   Record the entry to replenish the petty cash fund using the **General Journal Entry** option.

Step 6   Print a General Journal report and proof your work.

Step 7   Answer the Analyze question.

Checking Your Work and Ending the Session

Step 8   Click the **Close Problem** button in the Glencoe Smart Guide window.

Step 9   If your teacher has asked you to check your solution, select *Check my answer to this problem*. Review, print, and close the report.

Step 10   Click the **Close Problem** button and select a save option.

Problem 22-6   Establishing and Replenishing a Petty Cash Fund

INSTRUCTIONS

Beginning a Session

Step 1   Select the problem set: Shutterbug Cameras (Prob. 22-6).

Step 2   Rename the company, and set the system date to February 29, 2004.

Completing the Accounting Problem

Step 3   Review the information provided in your textbook.

Step 4   Record the entry to establish the petty cash fund.

TIP: Use the [Add] and [Remove] buttons if you need to edit a multi-part general journal entry.

Step 5   Make a list of the petty cash vouchers and manually prepare a petty cash requisition.

Step 6   Record the entry to replenish the petty cash fund.

Step 7 Print a General Journal report and proof your work.

Step 8 Answer the Analyze question.

Ending the Session

Step 9 Click the **Close Problem** button in the Glencoe Smart Guide window to save your work.

Problem 22-7   Using a Petty Cash Register

INSTRUCTIONS

Beginning a Session

Step 1 Select the problem set: Cycle Tech Bicycles (Prob. 22-7).

Step 2 Rename the company, and set the system date to February 29, 2004.

Completing the Accounting Problem

Step 3 Review the information provided in your textbook.

Step 4 Record the entry to establish the petty cash fund.

 TIP: Use the **General Journal Entry** option to record the cash fund transactions.

Step 5 Manually record the petty cash disbursements.

Step 6 Prepare a petty cash requisition.

Step 7 Record the entry to replenish the petty cash fund.

Step 8 Print a General Journal report and proof your work.

 TIP: Double-click a report title to go directly to the report, skipping the report options.

Step 9 Answer the Analyze question.

Checking Your Work and Ending the Session

Step 10 Click the **Close Problem** button in the Glencoe Smart Guide window.

Step 11 If your teacher has asked you to check your solution, select *Check my answer to this problem*. Review, print, and close the report.

Step 12 Click the **Close Problem** button and select a save option.

Peachtree Guide

Problem 22-8   Handling a Petty Cash Fund

INSTRUCTIONS

Beginning a Session

Step 1   Select the problem set: River's Edge Canoe & Kayak (Prob. 22-8).
Step 2   Rename the company, and set the system date to February 29, 2004.

Completing the Accounting Problem

Step 3   Review the information provided in your textbook.
Step 4   Record the entry to establish the petty cash fund.

> **TIP:** Use the **General Journal Entry** option to record the cash fund transactions.

Step 5   Manually record the petty cash disbursements.
Step 6   Reconcile the petty cash register and prepare a petty cash requisition. Update the petty cash register to record the replenishment information.
Step 7   Record the entry to replenish the petty cash fund.
Step 8   Record the entry to increase the petty cash fund.
Step 9   Print a General Journal report and proof your work.
Step 10   Answer the Analyze question.

Ending the Session

Step 11   Click the **Close Problem** button in the Glencoe Smart Guide window to save your work.

FAQs

Can you use the General Journal Entry option for cash fund transactions?

You have learned how to use the **Payments** and **Receipts** options to record cash payments and cash receipts, respectively. However, you can always use the **General Ledger Entry** option to record transactions involving cash. The only disadvantage to using the **General Journal Entry** option is that Peachtree will not print checks for any cash payments transactions you record. However, this is not an issue if you manually write checks and use Peachtree only to record the transactions.

You can record various cash funds transactions using the **General Journal Entry** option, but you can always work with the **Payments** and **Receipts** options if you are more comfortable using these options.

Does Peachtree include any features to prepare a petty cash register?

Peachtree does not provide any features to prepare a petty cash register. Although you must manually prepare this document, you can use the **General Journal Entry** option to record the transactions to establish and replenish a petty cash fund.

Working Papers _for End-of-Chapter Problems_

Problem 22-4 Establishing a Change Fund

(1), (3)

GENERAL JOURNAL

PAGE _____

	DATE	DESCRIPTION	POST. REF.	DEBIT	CREDIT	
1						1
2						2
3						3
4						4
5						5
6						6
7						7
8						8
9						9
10						10

Analyze: _____

_____

(2)

CASH PROOF

Date _____

Cash Register No. _____

Total cash sales
(from cash register tape) $ _____

Cash in drawer $ _____

Less change fund   _____

Net cash received $ _____

Cash short   _____

Cash over   _____

Salesclerk _____

Supervisor _____

Problem 22-5   Establishing and Replenishing a Petty Cash Fund

(1)

GENERAL JOURNAL   PAGE _____

	DATE	DESCRIPTION	POST. REF.	DEBIT	CREDIT	
1						1
2						2
3						3
4						4
5						5
6						6
7						7
8						8
9						9
10						10

(2)

GENERAL JOURNAL   PAGE _____

	DATE	DESCRIPTION	POST. REF.	DEBIT	CREDIT	
1						1
2						2
3						3
4						4
5						5
6						6
7						7
8						8
9						9
10						10

Analyze: _____

_____

Problem 22-6   Establishing and Replenishing a Petty Cash Fund
(1)

GENERAL JOURNAL   PAGE _____

	DATE	DESCRIPTION	POST. REF.	DEBIT	CREDIT	
1						1
2						2
3						3
4						4
5						5
6						6
7						7
8						8
9						9
10						10

(5)

GENERAL JOURNAL   PAGE _____

	DATE	DESCRIPTION	POST. REF.	DEBIT	CREDIT	
1						1
2						2
3						3
4						4
5						5
6						6
7						7
8						8
9						9
10						10

Analyze: _____

_____

Problem 22-6 (concluded)

(2)

Voucher No.	Account Name	Amount
101	Supplies	$ _____
102	Advertising Expense	_____
103	Miscellaneous Expense	_____
104	Delivery Expense	_____
105	Supplies	_____
106	Miscellaneous Expense	_____
107	Delivery Expense	_____
108	Miscellaneous Expense	_____
109	Supplies	_____
110	Delivery Expense	_____
111	Advertising Expense	_____
112	Miscellaneous Expense	_____
113	Advertising Expense	_____
	TOTAL	$ _____

(3)

Supplies	$ _____
Advertising Expense	_____
Delivery Expense	_____
Miscellaneous Expense	_____

(4)

PETTY CASH REQUISITION

Accounts for which
payments were made: Amount

_____ $ _____

_____   _____

_____   _____

_____   _____

_____   _____

_____   _____

TOTAL CASH NEEDED TO REPLENISH FUND: $ _____

Requested by: _____ Date _____
                  PETTY CASHIER
Approved by: _____ Date _____
                  ACCOUNTANT
                              Check No. _____

Analyze: _____

_____

_____

_____

Problem 22-7   Source Documents

Instructions: *Use the following source documents to record the transactions for this problem.*

PETTY CASH VOUCHER	No. 0001
DATE *February 2* 20 – –	
PAID TO *Silver City Star*	$ *9.25*
FOR *Newspaper ad*	
ACCOUNT *Advertising Expense*	
APPROVED BY	PAYMENT RECEIVED BY
_____	*Dudley Hartel*

PETTY CASH VOUCHER	No. 0005
DATE *February 19* 20 – –	
PAID TO *National Express*	$ *15.00*
FOR *Parts delivered*	
ACCOUNT *Delivery Expense*	
APPROVED BY	PAYMENT RECEIVED BY
_____	*Jessica Kirby*

PETTY CASH VOUCHER	No. 0002
DATE *February 5* 20 – –	
PAID TO *Maxwell Office Supplies*	$ *5.00*
FOR *Pens and pencils*	
ACCOUNT *Supplies*	
APPROVED BY	PAYMENT RECEIVED BY
_____	*Joshua Maxwell*

PETTY CASH VOUCHER	No. 0006
DATE *February 20* 20 – –	
PAID TO *Postmaster*	$ *3.90*
FOR *Postage stamps*	
ACCOUNT *Miscellaneous Expense*	
APPROVED BY	PAYMENT RECEIVED BY
_____	*Sam Haygood*

PETTY CASH VOUCHER	No. 0003
DATE *February 9* 20 – –	
PAID TO *Tumbleweed Florist*	$ *12.50*
FOR *Flowers for employee's birthday*	
ACCOUNT *Miscellaneous Expense*	
APPROVED BY	PAYMENT RECEIVED BY
_____	*Louise Wicker*

PETTY CASH VOUCHER	No. 0007
DATE *February 22* 20 – –	
PAID TO *Krystal Clean*	$ *16.00*
FOR *Show window cleaned*	
ACCOUNT *Miscellaneous Expense*	
APPROVED BY	PAYMENT RECEIVED BY
_____	*Krystal Adams*

PETTY CASH VOUCHER	No. 0004
DATE *February 12* 20 – –	
PAID TO *Maxwell Office Supplies*	$ *3.95*
FOR *Cash register tape*	
ACCOUNT *Supplies*	
APPROVED BY	PAYMENT RECEIVED BY
_____	*Joshua Maxwell*

PETTY CASH VOUCHER	No. 0008
DATE *February 24* 20 – –	
PAID TO *Silver City Star*	$ *11.00*
FOR *Newspaper ad*	
ACCOUNT *Advertising Expense*	
APPROVED BY	PAYMENT RECEIVED BY
_____	*Dudley Hartel*

Problem 22-7 (continued)

PETTY CASH VOUCHER	No. 0009
	DATE _February 25_ 20 --
PAID TO _Maxwell Office Supplies_	$ _10.00_
FOR _Stationery_	
ACCOUNT _Supplies_	
APPROVED BY _____	PAYMENT RECEIVED BY _Joshua Maxwell_

PETTY CASH VOUCHER	No. 0013
	DATE _February 28_ 20 --
PAID TO _Lara Allen_	$ _4.00_
FOR _Tip for daily newspaper delivery_	
ACCOUNT _Miscellaneous Expense_	
APPROVED BY _____	PAYMENT RECEIVED BY _Lara Allen_

PETTY CASH VOUCHER	No. 0010
	DATE _February 26_ 20 --
PAID TO _National Express_	$ _8.25_
FOR _Packages delivered_	
ACCOUNT _Delivery Expense_	
APPROVED BY _____	PAYMENT RECEIVED BY _Jessica Kirby_

PETTY CASH VOUCHER	No. 0014
	DATE _February 28_ 20 --
PAID TO _Postmaster_	$ _6.80_
FOR _Postage stamps_	
ACCOUNT _Miscellaneous Expense_	
APPROVED BY _____	PAYMENT RECEIVED BY _Sam Haygood_

PETTY CASH VOUCHER	No. 0011
	DATE _February 27_ 20 --
PAID TO _Maxwell Office Supplies_	$ _8.00_
FOR _Supplies_	
ACCOUNT	
APPROVED BY	PAYMENT RECEIVED BY

VOID

PETTY CASH VOUCHER	No. 0015
	DATE _February 28_ 20 --
PAID TO _Silver City Star_	$ _10.00_
FOR _Newspaper ad_	
ACCOUNT _Advertising Expense_	
APPROVED BY _____	PAYMENT RECEIVED BY _Dudley Hartel_

PETTY CASH VOUCHER	No. 0012
	DATE _February 27_ 20 --
PAID TO _Maxwell Office Supplies_	$ _3.00_
FOR _Memo pads_	
ACCOUNT _Supplies_	
APPROVED BY _____	PAYMENT RECEIVED BY _Joshua Maxwell_

Problem 22-7   Using a Petty Cash Register

(1)

GENERAL JOURNAL   PAGE _____

	DATE	DESCRIPTION	POST. REF.	DEBIT	CREDIT	
1						1
2						2
3						3
4						4
5						5
6						6
7						7
8						8
9						9
10						10

(7)

GENERAL JOURNAL   PAGE _____

	DATE	DESCRIPTION	POST. REF.	DEBIT	CREDIT	
1						1
2						2
3						3
4						4
5						5
6						6
7						7
8						8
9						9
10						10

Problem 22-7   (continued)   **(2), (3), (4), (5)**

PAGE _____

PETTY CASH REGISTER

DATE	VOU. NO.	DESCRIPTION	PAYMENTS	SUPPLIES	DELIVERY EXPENSE	MISC. EXPENSE	DISTRIBUTION OF PAYMENTS — GENERAL ACCOUNT NAME	GENERAL AMOUNT	
									1
									2
									3
									4
									5
									6
									7
									8
									9
									10
									11
									12
									13
									14
									15
									16
									17
									18
									19
									20
									21
									22
									23
									24
									25

Problem 22-7   (concluded)

(6)

PETTY CASH REQUISITION

Accounts for which
payments were made: Amount

          \$ _____

_____   _____

_____   _____

_____   _____

_____   _____

_____   _____

TOTAL CASH NEEDED TO REPLENISH FUND: \$ _____

Requested by: _____ Date _____
               PETTY CASHIER

Approved by: _____ Date _____
             ACCOUNTANT

                Check No. _____

Analyze: _____

_____

Problem 22-8   Handling a Petty Cash Fund

(1)

GENERAL JOURNAL   PAGE _____

	DATE	DESCRIPTION	POST. REF.	DEBIT	CREDIT	
1						1
2						2
3						3
4						4
5						5
6						6
7						7

(7)

GENERAL JOURNAL   PAGE _____

	DATE	DESCRIPTION	POST. REF.	DEBIT	CREDIT	
1						1
2						2
3						3
4						4
5						5
6						6
7						7
8						8
9						9
10						10

(9)

GENERAL JOURNAL   PAGE _____

	DATE	DESCRIPTION	POST. REF.	DEBIT	CREDIT	
1						1
2						2
3						3
4						4
5						5
6						6
7						7

Problem 22-8 (continued)   **(2), (3), (4), (5), (8)**

PAGE _____

PETTY CASH REGISTER

DATE	VOU. NO.	DESCRIPTION	PAYMENTS	DISTRIBUTION OF PAYMENTS			GENERAL	
				SUPPLIES	DELIVERY EXPENSE	MISC. EXPENSE	ACCOUNT NAME	AMOUNT
1								
2								
3								
4								
5								
6								
7								
8								
9								
10								
11								
12								
13								
14								
15								
16								
17								
18								
19								
20								
21								
22								
23								
24								

Problem 22-8 (concluded)

(6)

PETTY CASH REQUISITION

Accounts for which
payments were made: Amount

_____ $ _____

_____   _____

_____   _____

_____   _____

_____   _____

_____

TOTAL CASH NEEDED TO REPLENISH FUND: $ _____

Requested by: _____ Date _____
                PETTY CASHIER

Approved by: _____ Date _____
                ACCOUNTANT

                          Check No. _____

Analyze: _____

_____

Problem 22-9   Locating Errors in a Petty Cash Register

Petty Cash Disbursements

Item	Date	Amt.	Item	Date	Amt.
Delivery charge	Feb. 4	$ 7.60	Order forms	Feb. 5	$ 9.45
Delivery charge	14	9.65	Memo pads	6	12.14
Delivery charge	27	8.75	Writing tablets	9	9.43
			Wrapping paper	9	8.49
Newspaper ad	Feb. 7	$10.00	Pens/pencils	20	7.24
Newspaper ad	10	8.50	Coffee filters	25	3.14
			Fax paper	28	9.30
Stamps	Feb. 2	$ 8.25	Gasoline	28	11.42
Stamps	11	9.00	Gasket	28	6.28
			Telephone directory	28	4.30

Analyze: _____

_____

_____

Problem 22-9 (concluded) (1), (2), (3), (4)

PETTY CASH REGISTER

PAGE ___

DATE	VOU. NO.	DESCRIPTION	PAYMENTS	SUPPLIES	DELIVERY EXPENSE	MISC. EXPENSE	GENERAL ACCOUNT NAME	GENERAL AMOUNT
20--								
Feb. 1	—	Est. fund $150 Ck. 948						
2	101	Postage stamps	825			825		
4	102	Delivery charge	670			670		
5	103	Order forms	945			945		
6	104	Memo pads	1214	1214				
7	105	Newspaper ad	1000				Advertising Expense	1000
9	106	Writing tablets	943	934				
9	107	Wrapping paper	849	849				
10	108	Newspaper ad	852			850		
11	109	Stamps	900				Postage	900
14	110	VOID						
14	111	Delivery charge	965		965			
20	112	Pens/pencils	724	724				
25	113	Coffee filters	314			314		
27	114	Delivery charge	875		675			
28	115	Fax paper	930	930				
28	116	Gasoline	1142				Gasoline Expense	1142
28	117	Gasket	628				Maintenance Expense	628
28	118	Telephone directory	430			430		
28		Totals	13890	4651	1646	3834		3670
		Reconciled Balance	706					
		Cash Over	104					
		Replenishment Check	14190					
		Total	15000					

CHAPTER 22   Cash Funds

Self-Test

Part A   Fill in the Missing Term

Directions: *In the Answer column, write the letter of the word or phrase that best completes the sentence.*

A. cash proof	**E.** petty cash fund	**H.** petty cash voucher
B. change fund	**F** petty cash register	**I.** petty cashier
C. over	**G.** petty cash requisition	**J.** short
D. petty cash disbursement		

Answer

_____   **1.** A(n) _____ is any payment made from the petty cash fund.

_____   **2.** A(n) _____ is a form prepared by the petty cashier to request cash for replenishing the petty cash fund.

_____   **3.** If the change fund was established for $100 and there are $296 in cash receipts and the cash balance is $400, cash for the day is said to be _____.

_____   **4.** Every payment made from the petty cash fund must be supported by a(n) _____.

_____   **5.** A(n) _____ is usually used in retail stores such as supermarkets for making change for cash customers.

_____   **6.** The _____ is responsible for making payments from the petty cash fund.

_____   **7.** Many businesses use a(n) _____ for paying small cash payments.

_____   **8.** If the petty cash fund was established for $50.00 and there is $4.00 in cash with $45.00 in vouchers, cash is said to be _____.

_____   **9.** All payments made from the petty cash fund are recorded in the _____.

_____   **10.** A(n) _____ is prepared to verify that the amount of cash in the drawer is equal to the total cash sales for the day plus the change fund cash.

Part B   True or False

Directions: *Circle the letter* T *in the Answer column if the statement is true; circle the letter* F *if the statement is false.*

Answer

T   F   **1.** The size of the change fund does not change unless the business finds it needs more or less than its original estimate.

T   F   **2.** Change funds are classified as assets and are listed directly below Cash in Bank in the chart of accounts.

T   F   **3.** Once a business establishes a petty cash fund for a set amount, the Internal Revenue Service does not permit the size of the fund to be changed.

T   F   **4.** The purpose of a change fund is to enable the cashier using the cash register to have enough coins and currency to conduct business for the day.

T   F   **5.** Salesclerks are usually required to sign the cash proof to indicate they have counted the cash in the drawer and verified its accuracy.

T   F   **6.** If there is a cash shortage at the end of the day, the amount of cash recorded on the cash register tape for the day's cash sales will be less than the amount of cash in the drawer.

T   F   **7.** The account Cash Short & Over is a temporary equity account.

T   F   **8.** The normal balance of the Cash Short & Over account is a credit balance.

T   F   **9.** Cash shortages are losses to the business; cash overages are gains or revenues.

T   F   **10.** If cash shortages occur more frequently than cash overages, the account Cash Short & Over will have a credit balance.

T   F   **11.** Businesses use a petty cash fund because writing checks for small amounts is costly, time consuming, and impractical.

T   F   **12.** For internal control reasons, at least two people should be responsible for the petty cash fund, and the petty cash box should be kept in a locked desk drawer or safe.

T   F   **13.** The petty cash fund is debited each time the fund is replenished.

T   F   **14.** Each time a payment is made from the petty cash fund, a prenumbered voucher must be prepared to verify proof of payment.

T   F   **15.** Replenishing the petty cash fund restores the fund to its original balance.

CHAPTER 23   Plant Assets and Depreciation

Study Plan

Check Your Understanding

Section 1	*Read Section 1 on pages 626–628 and complete the exercises on page 629.*
	❏ Thinking Critically
	❏ Communicating Accounting
	❏ Problem 23-1 *Classifying Asset Accounts*
Section 2	*Read Section 2 on pages 630–631 and complete the exercises on page 632.*
	❏ Thinking Critically
	❏ Computing in the Business World
	❏ Problem 23-2 *Calculating Depreciation Expense*
	❏ Problem 23-3 *Completing a Plant Asset Record*
Section 3	*Read Section 3 on pages 633–640 and complete the exercises on page 641.*
	❏ Thinking Critically
	❏ Communicating Accounting
	❏ Problem 23-4 *Analyzing a Source Document*
	❏ Problem 23-5 *Preparing a Depreciation Schedule and Journalizing the Depreciation Adjusting Entry*

Summary	*Review the Chapter 23 Summary on page 643 in your textbook.*
	❏ Key Concepts
Review and Activities	*Complete the following questions and exercises on pages 644–645.*
	❏ Using Key Terms
	❏ Understanding Accounting Concepts and Procedures
	❏ Case Study
	❏ Conducting an Audit with Alex
	❏ Internet Connection
	❏ Workplace Skills
Computerized Accounting	*Read the Computerized Accounting information on page 646.*
	❏ *Making the Transition from a Manual to a Computerized System*
	❏ *Recording Depreciation in Peachtree*
Problems	*Complete the following end-of-chapter problems for Chapter 23.*
	❏ Problem 23-6 *Opening a Plant Asset Record*
	❏ Problem 23-7 *Recording Adjusting Entries for Depreciation*
	❏ Problem 23-8 *Reporting Depreciation Expense on the Work Sheet and Financial Statements*
	❏ Problem 23-9 *Calculating and Recording Depreciation Expense*
	❏ Problem 23-10 *Calculating and Recording Adjustments*
Challenge Problem	❏ Problem 23-11 *Examining Depreciation Adjustments*
Chapter Reviews and Working Papers	*Complete the following exercises for Chapter 23 in your Chapter Reviews and Working Papers.*
	❏ Chapter Review
	❏ Self-Test

CHAPTER 23 REVIEW   Plant Assets and Depreciation

Part 1   Accounting Vocabulary (6 points)

Directions: *Using terms from the following list, complete the sentences below. Write the letter of the term you have chosen in the space provided.*

Total Points	26
Student's Score	

A. accumulated depreciation	**D.** depreciation	**F.** plant assets
B. book value	**E.** disposal value	**G.** straight-line depreciation
C. current assets		

_____E_____ **0.** The estimated value of a plant asset at its replacement time is called _____.

_____ **1.** _____ are long-lived assets that are used in the production or sale of other assets or services over several accounting periods.

_____ **2.** _____ is a method of equally distributing the depreciation expense on a plant asset over its estimated useful life.

_____ **3.** Allocating the cost of a plant asset over the asset's useful life is called _____.

_____ **4.** The original cost of a plant asset less its accumulated depreciation is the _____.

_____ **5.** _____ is the total amount of depreciation for a plant asset that has been recorded up to a specific point in time.

_____ **6.** _____ are either used up or converted to cash during a one-year accounting period.

Part 2   Accounting for Depreciation (11 points)

Directions: *Read each of the following statements to determine whether the statement is true or false. Write your answer in the space provided.*

___False___ **0.** Depreciation Expense is reported on the income statement in the cost of goods sold section.

_____ **1.** The amount of depreciation taken for a plant asset is usually recorded in the accounting records at the beginning of the fiscal period.

_____ **2.** All plant assets, including land, depreciate in value.

_____ **3.** The cost of a plant asset is the price paid for the asset plus taxes, installation charges, and delivery charges.

_____ **4.** Depreciation amounts are estimates of the decrease in value or usefulness of a plant asset over a period of time.

_____ **5.** Accumulated Depreciation is reported on the balance sheet as a liability.

_____ **6.** Depreciation Expense is recorded by an adjusting entry made in the general journal.

_____ **7.** The adjusting entry for depreciation affects two accounts for each type of plant asset: Depreciation Expense and Delivery Equipment.

_____ **8.** Delivery equipment, office equipment, buildings, and land are long-lived assets because they are expected to produce benefits for the business for more than one year.

_____ **9.** The plant asset record does not list the accumulated depreciation of an asset or its book value at the end of each year.

_____ **10.** Accumulated Depreciation is classified as a contra plant asset account.

_____ **11.** Current assets include cash, merchandise, equipment, and accounts receivable.

Part 3   Analyzing the Depreciation of Equipment (9 points)

Directions: *On January 3, Washington Delivery Service purchased a new delivery truck for $20,000. The delivery truck has an estimated disposal value of $3,200 and an estimated useful life of seven years. Using this information, select the answer that best completes each of the following statements. Write your answer in the space provided.*

_____**B**_____   **0.** The amount that will be debited to Delivery Equipment is
  (A) $16,800.   (C) $3,200.
  (B) $20,000.   (D) $23,200.

_____   **1.** The estimated annual depreciation amount using the straight-line method is
  (A) $3,200.   (C) $2,857.
  (B) $16,800.   (D) $2,400.

_____   **2.** The estimated depreciation amount will be recorded as a debit to
  (A) Accumulated Depreciation—Delivery Equipment.
  (B) Delivery Expense.
  (C) Depreciation Expense—Delivery Equipment.
  (D) Delivery Equipment.

_____   **3.** At the end of the fiscal period, the adjusting entry for the depreciation is a
  (A) debit to Depreciation Expense—Delivery Equipment and a credit to Delivery Equipment.
  (B) debit to Depreciation Expense—Delivery Equipment and a credit to Accumulated Depreciation—Delivery Equipment.
  (C) debit to Accumulated Depreciation—Delivery Equipment and a credit to Depreciation Expense—Delivery Equipment.
  (D) debit to Delivery Equipment and a credit to Accumulated Depreciation—Delivery Equipment.

_____   **4.** After the adjusting entries are posted to the general ledger, Depreciation Expense—Delivery Equipment will have
  (A) a zero balance.   (C) a debit balance.
  (B) either a debit or credit balance.   (D) a credit balance.

_____   **5.** After the adjusting entries are posted, the Delivery Equipment account will have a
  (A) debit balance equal to the original purchase price less the amount of the accumulated depreciation.
  (B) debit balance for the amount of the depreciation.
  (C) debit balance equal to the original purchase price.
  (D) credit balance for the amount of the accumulated depreciation.

_____   **6.** After the closing entry is posted, the Depreciation Expense—Delivery Equipment account will have
  (A) a zero balance.   (C) a credit balance.
  (B) a debit balance.   (D) either a debit or credit balance.

_____   **7.** At the beginning of the next fiscal period, Accumulated Depreciation—Delivery Equipment will have
  (A) a debit balance.   (C) either a debit or credit balance.
  (B) a credit balance.   (D) a zero balance.

_____   **8.** The book value of the delivery truck at the end of four years is
  (A) $9,600.   (C) $10,400.
  (B) $12,800.   (D) $7,200.

_____   **9.** If the Delivery Equipment had been purchased on October 1 instead of January 3, the estimated depreciation for the first year would be
  (A) $400.   (C) $200.
  (B) $1,200.   (D) $600.

Working Papers *for Section Problems*

Problem 23-1   Classifying Asset Accounts

Asset	Current Asset	Plant Asset
Accounts Receivable	✓	
Building		
Cash in Bank		
Change Fund		
Delivery Equipment		
Land		
Merchandise Inventory		
Office Equipment		
Office Furniture		
Petty Cash Fund		
Prepaid Insurance		
Store Equipment		
Supplies		

Problem 23-2   Calculating Depreciation Expense

	Asset	(1) Amount to be Depreciated	Depreciation Rate	(2) Annual Depreciation	Months Owned	(3) First Year Depreciation
1	Cash register	$		$		$
2	Computer	$		$		$
3	Conference table	$		$		$
4	Delivery truck	$		$		$
5	Desk	$		$		$

Problem 23-3 Completing a Plant Asset Record

PLANT ASSET RECORD

ITEM _____   GENERAL LEDGER ACCOUNT _____

SERIAL NUMBER _____   MANUFACTURER _____

PURCHASED FROM _____   EST. DISPOSAL VALUE _____

ESTIMATED LIFE _____   LOCATION _____

DEPRECIATION
METHOD _____   DEPRECIATION
PER YEAR _____

DATE	EXPLANATION	ASSET			ACCUMULATED DEPRECIATION			BOOK VALUE
		DEBIT	CREDIT	BALANCE	DEBIT	CREDIT	BALANCE	

Problem 23-4 Analyzing a Source Document

(1)   GENERAL JOURNAL   PAGE _____

	DATE	DESCRIPTION	POST. REF.	DEBIT	CREDIT	
1						1
2						2
3						3

(2)   GENERAL JOURNAL   PAGE _____

	DATE	DESCRIPTION	POST. REF.	DEBIT	CREDIT	
1						1
2						2
3						3

(3)   GENERAL JOURNAL   PAGE _____

	DATE	DESCRIPTION	POST. REF.	DEBIT	CREDIT	
1						1
2						2
3						3

Problem 23-5 Preparing a Depreciation Schedule and Journalizing the Depreciation Adjusting Entry

(1)

Date	Cost	Annual Depreciation	Accumulated Depreciation	Book Value
January 7	$2,360	———	———	$2,360
First year				
Second year				
Third year				
Fourth year				
Fifth year				

(2), (3)

GENERAL JOURNAL   PAGE _____40_____

	DATE	DESCRIPTION	POST. REF.	DEBIT	CREDIT	
1						1
2						2
3						3
4						4
5						5
6						6
7						7
8						8
9						9
10						10
11						11
12						12

(4)

_____

_____

Computerized Accounting Using Peachtree

Software Objectives

When you have completed this chapter, you will be able to use Peachtree to:

1. Record adjusting entries for depreciation.
2. Prepare financial statements that include accumulated depreciation and depreciation expenses.

Problem 23-7   Recording Adjusting Entries for Depreciation

INSTRUCTIONS

Beginning a Session

Step 1   Select the problem set: InBeat CD Shop (Prob. 23-7).
Step 2   Rename the company by adding your initials, e.g., InBeat (Prob. 23-7: XXX).
Step 3   Set the system date to December 31, 2004.

Completing the Accounting Problem

Step 4   Review the information provided in your textbook.
Step 5   Record the adjusting entries for depreciation using the **General Journal Entry** option.

TIP: As a shortcut, you can use the General Ledger navigation aid shown at the bottom of the Peachtree window to access the General Journal Entry window.

Step 6   Print a General Journal report and proof your work.
Step 7   Answer the Analyze question.

Checking Your Work and Ending the Session

Step 8   Click the **Close Problem** button in the Glencoe Smart Guide window.
Step 9   If your teacher has asked you to check your solution, select *Check my answer to this problem.* Review, print, and close the report.
Step 10 Click the **Close Problem** button and select a save option.

Mastering Peachtree

On a separate sheet of paper, list the account types assigned to each of the following general ledger accounts: **Store Equipment, Accum. Depr.—Store Equipment,** and **Depr. Exp.—Store Equipment**.

DO YOU HAVE A QUESTION

Q. *Does Peachtree include any options to track plant assets?*

A. No, Peachtree does not include any options to track plant assets. However, there are specialized programs designed to help a company keep track of its assets and prepare depreciation schedules. As another alternative, you could use a spreadsheet program for this task.

Notes

Peachtree automatically posts general journal entries to the corresponding general ledger accounts.

Peachtree Guide

Problem 23-8 Reporting Depreciation Expense on the Work Sheet and Financial Statements

INSTRUCTIONS

Beginning a Session

Step 1 Select the problem set: Shutterbug Cameras (Prob. 23-8).

Step 2 Rename the company by adding your initials.

Step 3 Set the system date to December 31, 2004.

Completing the Accounting Problem

Step 4 Review the information provided in your textbook.

Step 5 Record the adjusting entries for depreciation using the **General Journal Entry** option.

Notes

Peachtree does not include an option to complete a work sheet.

TIP: Set the date range from 12/31/04 to 12/31/04 to print only the adjusting entries.

Step 6 Print a General Journal report and proof your work.

Step 7 Print an Income Statement and a Balance Sheet.

TIP: Use the predefined financial statements when instructed to print an Income Statement or Balance Sheet.

Step 8 Manually prepare a Statement of Retained Earnings.

Step 9 Answer the Analyze question.

Ending the Session

Step 10 Click the **Close Problem** button in the Glencoe Smart Guide window to save your work.

Problem 23-9   Calculating and Recording Depreciation Expense

INSTRUCTIONS

Beginning a Session

Step 1   Select the problem set: Cycle Tech Bicycles (Prob. 23-9).
Step 2   Rename the company by adding your initials.
Step 3   Set the system date to December 31, 2004.

Completing the Accounting Problem

Step 4   Review the information provided in your textbook.
Step 5   Calculate the depreciation for the first two years.
Step 6   Record the depreciation adjustment for the first year using the **General Journal Entry** option.
Step 7   Print a General Journal report and proof your work.
Step 8   Print a General Ledger report for the manufacturing equipment (accumulated depreciation and depreciation expense) general ledger accounts.

 TIP: Set the report filter options to control which accounts appear on the General Ledger report.

Step 9   Answer the Analyze question.

Checking Your Work and Ending the Session

Step 10   Click the **Close Problem** button in the Glencoe Smart Guide window.
Step 11   If your teacher has asked you to check your solution, select *Check my answer to this problem*. Review, print, and close the report.
Step 12   Click the **Close Problem** button and select a save option.

Problem 23-10 Calculating and Recording Adjustments

INSTRUCTIONS

Beginning a Session

Step 1 Select the problem set: River's Edge Canoe & Kayak (Prob. 23-10).
Step 2 Rename the company by adding your initials.
Step 3 Set the system date to December 31, 2004.

Completing the Accounting Problem

Step 4 Review the information provided in your textbook.
Step 5 Record all of the adjusting entries.

TIP: Remember to use the **Inventory Adjustment** account to record the merchandise inventory adjustment.

Step 6 Print a General Journal report and proof your work.
Step 7 Print an Income Statement and a Balance Sheet.
Step 8 Click the **Save Pre-closing Balances** button in the Glencoe Smart Guide window.
Step 9 Close the fiscal year.

TIP: To close the fiscal year, choose **System** from the *Tasks* menu and then select **Close Fiscal Year.** Do not purge the transactions when prompted.

Step 10 Print a Post-Closing Trial Balance.
Step 11 Answer the Analyze question.

Ending the Session

Step 12 Click the **Close Problem** button in the Glencoe Smart Guide window.

FAQs

Can you edit a general journal entry from an earlier period after you close the fiscal year?

No, you cannot edit a general journal entry after you close the fiscal year. You must make a correcting entry, or restore a backup and then make the correction.

Working Papers *for End-of-Chapter Problems*

Problem 23-6   Opening a Plant Asset Record

PLANT ASSET RECORD

ITEM _____   GENERAL LEDGER ACCOUNT _____

SERIAL NUMBER _____   MANUFACTURER _____

PURCHASED FROM _____   EST. DISPOSAL VALUE _____

ESTIMATED LIFE _____   LOCATION _____

DEPRECIATION METHOD _____   DEPRECIATION PER YEAR _____

DATE	EXPLANATION	ASSET			ACCUMULATED DEPRECIATION			BOOK VALUE
		DEBIT	CREDIT	BALANCE	DEBIT	CREDIT	BALANCE	

Analyze: _____

_____

Problem 23-7   Recording Adjusting Entries for Depreciation

GENERAL JOURNAL   PAGE _____

	DATE	DESCRIPTION	POST. REF.	DEBIT	CREDIT	
1						1
2						2
3						3
4						4
5						5
6						6
7						7

Analyze: _____

_____

Problem 23-8   Reporting Depreciation Expense on the Work Sheet and Financial Statements

(1), (2)

Shutterbug

Work

For the Year Ended

	ACCT. NO.	ACCOUNT NAME	TRIAL BALANCE DEBIT	TRIAL BALANCE CREDIT	ADJUSTMENTS DEBIT	ADJUSTMENTS CREDIT
1	101	Cash in Bank	9 30000			
2	105	Change Fund	50000			
3	110	Petty Cash Fund	20000			
4	115	Accounts Receivable	1 20000			
5	125	Merchandise Inventory	50 00000			(a) 3 69000
6	130	Supplies	4 00000			(c) 2 96000
7	135	Prepaid Insurance	2 40000			(b) 1 20000
8	140	Office Equipment	26 00000			
9	142	Accum. Depr.—Office Equip.		7 50000		
10	145	Store Equipment	19 20000			
11	147	Accum. Depr.—Store Equip.		3 60000		
12	201	Accounts Payable		1 51000		
13	207	Fed. Corporate Income Tax Pay.	—	—		(d) 60000
14	215	Sales Tax Payable		1 32000		
15	301	Capital Stock		51 36500		
16	305	Retained Earnings		24 00000		
17	310	Income Summary	—	—	(a) 3 69000	
18	401	Sales		66 94000		
19	410	Sales Returns and Allowances	87500			
20	501	Purchases	21 00000			
21	505	Transportation In	3 10000			
22	510	Purchases Discounts		21500		
23	515	Purchases Returns and Allow.		1 60000		
24	601	Advertising Expense	3 00000			
25	610	Cash Short & Over	5000			
26	615	Depr. Exp.—Office Equip.	—			
27	617	Depr. Exp.—Store Equip.	—			
28	620	Fed. Corporate Income Tax Exp.	5 00000		(d) 60000	
29		Carry Forward	143 03500	158 05000		
30						
31						
32						
33						

Cameras

Sheet

December 31, 20--

	ADJUSTED TRIAL BALANCE		INCOME STATEMENT		BALANCE SHEET		
	DEBIT	CREDIT	DEBIT	CREDIT	DEBIT	CREDIT	
							1
							2
							3
							4
							5
							6
							7
							8
							9
							10
							11
							12
							13
							14
							15
							16
							17
							18
							19
							20
							21
							22
							23
							24
							25
							26
							27
							28
							29
							30
							31
							32
							33

Problem 23-8 (continued)

	ACCT. NO.	ACCOUNT NAME	TRIAL BALANCE		ADJUSTMENTS	
			DEBIT	CREDIT	DEBIT	CREDIT
1		*Brought Forward*	14303500	15805000		
2						
3	630	*Insurance Expense*	—		(b) 120000	
4	640	*Maintenance Expense*	140000			
5	645	*Miscellaneous Expense*	42500			
6	650	*Rent Expense*	600000			
7	655	*Salaries Expense*	604000			
8	660	*Supplies Expense*	—		(c) 296000	
9	670	*Utilities Expense*	115000			
10			15805000	15805000		
11		*Net Income*				
12						
13						
14						
15						
16						
17						
18						
19						
20						
21						
22						
23						
24						
25						
26						
27						
28						
29						
30						
31						
32						

Cameras

(continued)

December 31, 20--

ADJUSTED TRIAL BALANCE		INCOME STATEMENT		BALANCE SHEET		
DEBIT	CREDIT	DEBIT	CREDIT	DEBIT	CREDIT	
						1
						2
						3
						4
						5
						6
						7
						8
						9
						10
						11
						12
						13
						14
						15
						16
						17
						18
						19
						20
						21
						22
						23
						24
						25
						26
						27
						28
						29
						30
						31
						32

Problem 23-8   (continued)

(3)

Problem 23-8 (concluded)

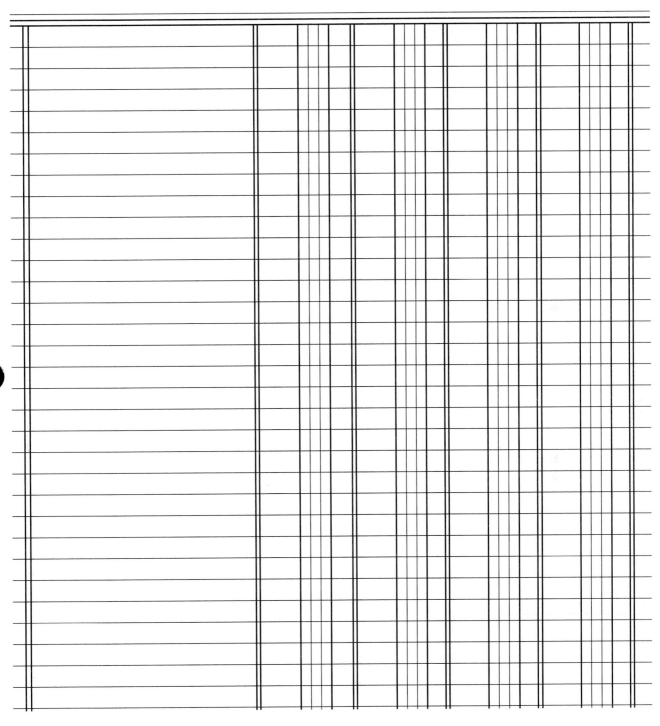

Analyze: _____ _____

_____ _____

_____ _____

Problem 23-9 Calculating and Recording Depreciation Expense

(1)

Date	Cost	Annual Depreciation	Accumulated Depreciation	Book Value
Purchased Aug. 1	$410,000	————	————	$410,000
First year				
Second year				

(2)

Depreciation Expense— Manufacturing Equipment

Accumulated Depreciation— Manufacturing Equipment

(3)

GENERAL JOURNAL   PAGE _____

	DATE	DESCRIPTION	POST. REF.	DEBIT	CREDIT	
1						1
2						2
3						3
4						4
5						5
6						6
7						7

Problem 23-9 (concluded)

(4)

GENERAL LEDGER

ACCOUNT _____ ACCOUNT NO. _____

DATE	DESCRIPTION	POST. REF.	DEBIT	CREDIT	BALANCE	
					DEBIT	CREDIT

ACCOUNT _____ ACCOUNT NO. _____

DATE	DESCRIPTION	POST. REF.	DEBIT	CREDIT	BALANCE	
					DEBIT	CREDIT

Analyze: _____

_____

Problem 23-10 Calculating and Recording Adjustments
(1), (2)

River's Edge

Work

For the Year Ended

	ACCT. NO.	ACCOUNT NAME	TRIAL BALANCE DEBIT	TRIAL BALANCE CREDIT	ADJUSTMENTS DEBIT	ADJUSTMENTS CREDIT
1	101	Cash in Bank	6 69000			
2	105	Change Fund	20000			
3	115	Accounts Receivable	12 40000			
4	130	Merchandise Inventory	16 30000			
5	135	Supplies	4 85000			
6	140	Prepaid Insurance	6 00000			
7	145	Delivery Truck	32 00000			
8	147	Accum. Depr.—Delivery Truck		16 00000		
9	150	Store Equipment	13 00000			
10	152	Accum. Depr.—Store Equip.		6 00000		
11	155	Building	160 00000			
12	157	Accum. Depr.—Building		60 00000		
13	160	Land	55 00000			
14	201	Accounts Payable		2 30000		
15	204	Fed. Corporate Income Tax Pay.	—	—		
16	215	Sales Tax Payable		1 62000		
17	301	Capital Stock		140 00000		
18	305	Retained Earnings		20 52000		
19	310	Income Summary	—	—		
20	401	Sales		180 00000		
21	501	Purchases	96 00000			
22	505	Transportation In	5 00000			
23	601	Advertising Expense	3 50000			
24	615	Depr. Exp.—Store Equip.	—			
25	620	Depr. Exp.—Delivery Truck	—			
26	622	Depr. Exp.—Building	—			
27	625	Fed. Corporate Income Tax Exp.	2 40000			
28		Carry Forward	413 34000	426 44000		
29						
30						
31						
32						
33						

Canoe & Kayak

Sheet

December 31, 20--

ADJUSTED TRIAL BALANCE		INCOME STATEMENT		BALANCE SHEET		
DEBIT	CREDIT	DEBIT	CREDIT	DEBIT	CREDIT	
						1
						2
						3
						4
						5
						6
						7
						8
						9
						10
						11
						12
						13
						14
						15
						16
						17
						18
						19
						20
						21
						22
						23
						24
						25
						26
						27
						28
						29
						30
						31
						32
						33

Problem 23-10   (continued)

River's Edge
Work Sheet
For the Year Ended

	ACCT. NO.	ACCOUNT NAME	TRIAL BALANCE		ADJUSTMENTS	
			DEBIT	CREDIT	DEBIT	CREDIT
1		*Brought Forward*	4 13 34 0 00	4 26 44 0 00		
2						
3	630	Gas Expense	1 40 0 00			
4	635	Insurance Expense	—			
5	655	Miscellaneous Expense	5 40 0 00			
6	670	Supplies Expense	—			
7	680	Utilities Expense	6 30 0 00			
8			4 26 44 0 00	4 26 44 0 00		
9		*Net Income*				
10						
11						
12						
13						
14						
15						
16						
17						
18						
19						
20						
21						
22						
23						
24						
25						
26						
27						
28						
29						
30						
31						
32						

Canoe & Kayak

(continued)

December 31, 20--

	ADJUSTED TRIAL BALANCE		INCOME STATEMENT		BALANCE SHEET		
	DEBIT	CREDIT	DEBIT	CREDIT	DEBIT	CREDIT	
							1
							2
							3
							4
							5
							6
							7
							8
							9
							10
							11
							12
							13
							14
							15
							16
							17
							18
							19
							20
							21
							22
							23
							24
							25
							26
							27
							28
							29
							30
							31
							32

Problem 23-10 (continued)
(3), (4)

GENERAL JOURNAL   PAGE _____

	DATE	DESCRIPTION	POST. REF.	DEBIT	CREDIT	
1						1
2						2
3						3
4						4
5						5
6						6
7						7
8						8
9						9
10						10
11						11
12						12
13						13
14						14
15						15
16						16
17						17
18						18
19						19
20						20
21						21
22						22
23						23
24						24
25						25
26						26
27						27
28						28
29						29
30						30
31						31
32						32
33						33
34						34
35						35
36						36

Problem 23-10   (continued)

GENERAL LEDGER

ACCOUNT __Merchandise Inventory__   ACCOUNT NO. ___130___

DATE		DESCRIPTION	POST. REF.	DEBIT	CREDIT	BALANCE DEBIT	BALANCE CREDIT
20--							
Dec.	31	Balance	✓			1630000	

ACCOUNT __Supplies__   ACCOUNT NO. ___135___

DATE		DESCRIPTION	POST. REF.	DEBIT	CREDIT	BALANCE DEBIT	BALANCE CREDIT
20--							
Dec.	31	Balance	✓			485000	

ACCOUNT __Prepaid Insurance__   ACCOUNT NO. ___140___

DATE		DESCRIPTION	POST. REF.	DEBIT	CREDIT	BALANCE DEBIT	BALANCE CREDIT
20--							
Dec.	31	Balance	✓			600000	

ACCOUNT __Accumulated Depreciation—Delivery Truck__   ACCOUNT NO. ___147___

DATE		DESCRIPTION	POST. REF.	DEBIT	CREDIT	BALANCE DEBIT	BALANCE CREDIT
20--							
Dec.	31	Balance	✓				1600000

Problem 23-10   (continued)

ACCOUNT   *Accumulated Depreciation—Store Equipment*   ACCOUNT NO.   *152*

DATE	DESCRIPTION	POST. REF.	DEBIT	CREDIT	BALANCE DEBIT	BALANCE CREDIT
20--						
Dec. 31	Balance	✓				600000

ACCOUNT   *Accumulated Depreciation—Building*   ACCOUNT NO.   *157*

DATE	DESCRIPTION	POST. REF.	DEBIT	CREDIT	BALANCE DEBIT	BALANCE CREDIT
20--						
Dec. 31	Balance	✓				6000000

ACCOUNT   *Federal Corporate Income Tax Payable*   ACCOUNT NO.   *204*

DATE	DESCRIPTION	POST. REF.	DEBIT	CREDIT	BALANCE DEBIT	BALANCE CREDIT

ACCOUNT   *Retained Earnings*   ACCOUNT NO.   *305*

DATE	DESCRIPTION	POST. REF.	DEBIT	CREDIT	BALANCE DEBIT	BALANCE CREDIT
20--						
Dec. 31	Balance	✓				2052000

Problem 23-10 (continued)

ACCOUNT _Income Summary_   ACCOUNT NO. ___310___

DATE	DESCRIPTION	POST. REF.	DEBIT	CREDIT	BALANCE DEBIT	BALANCE CREDIT

ACCOUNT _Sales_   ACCOUNT NO. ___401___

DATE	DESCRIPTION	POST. REF.	DEBIT	CREDIT	BALANCE DEBIT	BALANCE CREDIT
20--						
Dec. 31	Balance	✓				18 000 00

ACCOUNT _Purchases_   ACCOUNT NO. ___501___

DATE	DESCRIPTION	POST. REF.	DEBIT	CREDIT	BALANCE DEBIT	BALANCE CREDIT
20--						
Dec. 31	Balance	✓			9 600 00	

ACCOUNT _Transportation In_   ACCOUNT NO. ___505___

DATE	DESCRIPTION	POST. REF.	DEBIT	CREDIT	BALANCE DEBIT	BALANCE CREDIT
20--						
Dec. 31	Balance	✓			500 00	

Problem 23-10   (continued)

ACCOUNT ___*Advertising Expense*___   ACCOUNT NO. ___*601*___

DATE		DESCRIPTION	POST. REF.	DEBIT	CREDIT	BALANCE	
						DEBIT	CREDIT
20--							
Dec.	31	Balance	✓			350000	

ACCOUNT ___*Depreciation Expense—Store Equipment*___   ACCOUNT NO. ___*615*___

DATE		DESCRIPTION	POST. REF.	DEBIT	CREDIT	BALANCE	
						DEBIT	CREDIT

ACCOUNT ___*Depreciation Expense—Delivery Truck*___   ACCOUNT NO. ___*620*___

DATE		DESCRIPTION	POST. REF.	DEBIT	CREDIT	BALANCE	
						DEBIT	CREDIT

ACCOUNT ___*Depreciation Expense—Building*___   ACCOUNT NO. ___*622*___

DATE		DESCRIPTION	POST. REF.	DEBIT	CREDIT	BALANCE	
						DEBIT	CREDIT

Problem 23-10   (continued)

ACCOUNT __*Federal Corporate Income Tax Expense*_____   ACCOUNT NO. ___*625*___

DATE		DESCRIPTION	POST. REF.	DEBIT	CREDIT	BALANCE	
						DEBIT	CREDIT
20--							
Dec.	*31*	*Balance*	✓			2 40 0 00	

ACCOUNT __*Gas Expense*_____   ACCOUNT NO. ___*630*___

DATE		DESCRIPTION	POST. REF.	DEBIT	CREDIT	BALANCE	
						DEBIT	CREDIT
20--							
Dec.	*31*	*Balance*	✓			1 40 0 00	

ACCOUNT __*Insurance Expense*_____   ACCOUNT NO. ___*635*___

DATE		DESCRIPTION	POST. REF.	DEBIT	CREDIT	BALANCE	
						DEBIT	CREDIT

ACCOUNT __*Miscellaneous Expense*_____   ACCOUNT NO. ___*655*___

DATE		DESCRIPTION	POST. REF.	DEBIT	CREDIT	BALANCE	
						DEBIT	CREDIT
20--							
Dec.	*31*	*Balance*	✓			5 40 0 00	

Problem 23-10 (concluded)

ACCOUNT _Supplies Expense_ ACCOUNT NO. _670_

DATE	DESCRIPTION	POST. REF.	DEBIT	CREDIT	BALANCE DEBIT	CREDIT

ACCOUNT _Utilities Expense_ ACCOUNT NO. _680_

DATE	DESCRIPTION	POST. REF.	DEBIT	CREDIT	BALANCE DEBIT	CREDIT
20--						
Dec. 31	Balance	✓			6300 00	

Analyze: _____

Problem 23-11 Examining Depreciation Adjustments

1. _____

2. _____

Analyze: _____

CHAPTER 23   Plant Assets and Depreciation

Self-Test

Part A   True or False

Directions: *Circle the letter* T *in the Answer column if the statement is true; circle the letter* F *if the statement is false.*

Answer

T   F   **1.** If estimated annual depreciation is $3,600, a plant asset that was owned only four months during the year would have a depreciation expense of $1,200.

T   F   **2.** For accounting purposes, the cost of land is not depreciated.

T   F   **3.** The normal balance of Accumulated Depreciation— Computer Equipment is a debit.

T   F   **4.** Depreciation Expense is classified as an expense, has a normal credit balance, and is reported on the income statement.

T   F   **5.** The cost of a plant asset is the price paid for the asset when it is purchased, plus any installation and delivery charges.

T   F   **6.** The book value of a plant asset is determined by subtracting the accumulated depreciation to date from the initial cost of the asset.

T   F   **7.** Accumulated Depreciation—Store Equipment is a contra asset account and is reported on the income statement.

T   F   **8.** A company will often decide to replace, sell, or discard a plant asset while the asset still has some monetary value.

T   F   **9.** The straight-line method of depreciation allocates the same amount of depreciation expense each year over the estimated useful life of the asset.

T   F   **10.** The estimated disposal value of a plant asset is the part of the asset's cost that the business expects to get back at the end of the asset's useful life.

Part B   Multiple Choice

Directions: *Only one of the choices given with each of the following statements is correct. Write the letter of the correct answer in the Answer column.*

Answer

_____   **1.** Among the following accounts, the only non-plant asset is
(A) Supplies.
(B) Computer Equipment.
(C) Land.
(D) Accumulated Depreciation—Office Equipment.

_____   **2.** The cost of a plant asset is determined by the purchase price for the asset and all of the following *except*
(A) sales taxes.
(B) delivery charges.
(C) estimated disposal value of the asset.
(D) installation charges.

_____   **3.** Each of the following is one of the four factors that affect the depreciation estimate *except*
(A) the cost of the plant asset.
(B) the estimated useful life of the asset.
(C) the depreciation method used.
(D) the location of the asset.

Directions: *Using the information below, choose the correct answers for questions 4 though 6.*

A computer was purchased on January 4 at a cost of $3,800. The computer has an estimated disposal value of $200 and an estimated useful life of six years.

Answer

_____   **4.** The estimated amount to be depreciated on this computer is
(A) $3,800.   (C) $600.
(B) $3,600.   (D) $200.

_____   **5.** The estimated annual depreciation expense is
(A) $633.33.   (C) $600.
(B) $3,600.   (D) $200.

_____   **6.** If the computer had been purchased on August 4 instead of in January, the estimated depreciation expense for the partial year would be
(A) $200.   (C) $600.
(B) $3,600.   (D) $250.

CHAPTER 24   Uncollectible Accounts Receivable

Study Plan

Check Your Understanding

Section 1	Read Section 1 on pages 652–656 and complete the following exercises on page 657. ❑ Thinking Critically ❑ Communicating Accounting ❑ Problem 24-1 *Using the Direct Write-Off Method*
Section 2	Read Section 2 on pages 658–665 and complete the following exercises on page 666. ❑ Thinking Critically ❑ Analyzing Accounting ❑ Problem 24-2 *Writing Off Accounts Under the Allowance Method*
Section 3	Read Section 3 on pages 667–669 and complete the following exercises on page 670. ❑ Thinking Critically ❑ Computing in the Business World ❑ Problem 24-3 *Estimating Uncollectible Accounts Expense Using the Percentage of Net Sales Method*

Summary	Review the Chapter 24 Summary on page 671 in your textbook. ❑ Key Concepts
Review and Activities	Complete the following questions and exercises on pages 672–673. ❑ Using Key Terms ❑ Understanding Accounting Concepts and Procedures ❑ Case Study ❑ Conducting an Audit with Alex ❑ Internet Connection ❑ Workplace Skills
Computerized Accounting	Read the Computerized Accounting information on page 674. ❑ *Making the Transition from a Manual to a Computerized System* ❑ *Accounts Receivable in Peachtree*
Problems	Complete the following end-of-chapter problems for Chapter 24. ❑ Problem 24-4 *Using the Direct Write-Off Method* ❑ Problem 24-5 *Calculating and Recording Estimated Uncollectible Accounts Expense* ❑ Problem 24-6 *Writing Off Accounts Under the Allowance Method* ❑ Problem 24-7 *Estimating Uncollectible Accounts Expense* ❑ Problem 24-8 *Reporting Uncollectible Amounts on the Financial Statements*
Challenge Problem	❑ Problem 24-9 *Using the Allowance Method for Write-Offs*
Chapter Reviews and Working Papers	Complete the following exercises for Chapter 24 in your Chapter Reviews and Working Papers. ❑ Chapter Review ❑ Self-Test

CHAPTER 24 REVIEW — Uncollectible Accounts Receivable

Part 1 Accounting Vocabulary (5 points)

Directions: *Using terms from the following list, complete the sentences below. Write the letter of the term you have chosen in the space provided.*

A. aging of accounts receivable method	**C.** book value of accounts receivable	**E.** percentage of net sales method
B. allowance method	**D.** direct write-off method	**F.** uncollectible accounts

Total Points 39

Student's Score

    _F_   **0.** Accounts receivable accounts that cannot be collected are called _____.

_____ **1.** The amount a business can reasonably expect to receive from all its charge customers is called the _____.

_____ **2.** When a business determines that an actual amount is uncollectible, the _____ is used to remove the uncollectible amount from the accounts receivable subsidiary ledger and the controlling account in the general ledger.

_____ **3.** When the _____ is used to estimate the uncollectible amount, each customer's account is examined and classified according to its due date.

_____ **4.** When using the _____ of estimating uncollectible accounts expense, a business assumes that a certain percentage of each year's net sales will be uncollectible.

_____ **5.** The _____ of accounting for uncollectible accounts matches potential bad debts expenses with sales made during the same fiscal period.

Part 2 Accounting for Uncollectible Accounts Receivable (16 points)

Directions: *Using the following list, analyze the transactions below. Determine the account(s) to be debited and credited. Write your answers in the space provided.*

General Ledger Accounts		Subsidiary Ledger Accounts
A. Cash in Bank	**D.** Sales Tax Payable	**G.** Jim Wright
B. Accounts Receivable	**E.** Sales	**H.** Ti Yong
C. Allowance for Uncollectible Accounts	**F.** Uncollectible Accounts Expense	

Debit	Credit	
_B,H_	_D,E_	**0.** Sold merchandise on account, plus sales tax, to Ti Yong.
_____	_____	**1.** Wrote off the account of Ti Yong as uncollectible using the allowance method.
_____	_____	**2.** Sold merchandise on account, plus sales tax, to Jim Wright.
_____	_____	**3.** Reinstated Ti Yong's account.
_____	_____	**4.** Received a check for payment on account from Ti Yong.
_____	_____	**5.** Wrote off Jim Wright's account as uncollectible using the direct write-off method.
_____	_____	**6.** Reinstated the account of Jim Wright.
_____	_____	**7.** Received a check from Jim Wright for payment of his account.
_____	_____	**8.** Estimated that 3% of the net sales would be uncollectible.

Part 3 Extending Credit (10 points)

Directions: *Read each of the following statements to determine whether the statement is true or false. Write your answer in the space provided.*

True **0.** Two common methods used to estimate bad debts expense are the percentage of net sales method and the aging of accounts receivable method.

_____ **1.** When the direct write-off method is used for writing off an uncollectible account, Uncollectible Accounts Expense is the account debited for the amount of the loss.

_____ **2.** The two accounts affected by the adjusting entry for the allowance method of accounting for uncollectible accounts are Uncollectible Accounts Expense and Accounts Receivable.

_____ **3.** Before reinstating a charge customer's account, the receipt of cash to pay off the amount owed must be journalized.

_____ **4.** The book value of accounts receivable is the difference between the balance of Accounts Receivable and the balance of Allowance for Uncollectible Accounts.

_____ **5.** Businesses that sell on credit usually expect to sell more than if they accepted only cash.

_____ **6.** Allowance for Uncollectible Accounts is classified as a contra asset account and appears on the balance sheet as a deduction from Cash in Bank.

_____ **7.** Charge customers' accounts that are declared uncollectible become a liability to the business.

_____ **8.** Allowance for Uncollectible Accounts usually has a zero balance at the end of a fiscal period.

_____ **9.** Uncollectible accounts are sometimes paid at a later date by the customer whose account was written off.

_____ **10.** The two general ledger accounts affected by the direct write-off method of accounting for uncollectible accounts are Uncollectible Accounts Expense and Allowance for Uncollectible Accounts.

Part 4 Estimating Uncollectible Accounts Expense (8 points)

Directions: *The Ramona Estevez Company uses the allowance method of handling uncollectible accounts. Before any adjustments, the ledger contains the following balances:*

Sales	$400,000
Accounts Receivable	120,000
Sales Discounts	20,000
Allowance for Uncollectible Accounts	500
Sales Returns and Allowances	10,000
Uncollectible Accounts Expense	0

The Ramona Estevez Company estimates that the uncollectible accounts for the year will be 2% of the net sales. Using this information, answer the following questions.

$370,000 **0.** The net sales for the fiscal year are _____.

_____ **1.** The estimated percentage of net sales that will be uncollectible is _____.

_____ **2.** The estimated uncollectible account expense for the fiscal year is _____.

_____ **3.** The account to be debited for the estimated uncollectible amount is _____.

_____ **4.** After the adjusting entry is posted, the balance of the Allowance for Uncollectible Accounts account is _____.

_____ **5.** The account to be credited for the estimated uncollectible amount is _____.

_____ **6.** After posting the adjusting entry, the balance of the Uncollectible Accounts Expense account is _____.

_____ **7.** The book value of accounts receivable after the adjusting entry is posted is _____.

_____ **8.** The financial statement on which Uncollectible Accounts Expense is reported is the _____.

Working Papers *for Section Problems*

Problem 24-1   Using the Direct Write-Off Method

(1)

GENERAL JOURNAL   PAGE _____

	DATE	DESCRIPTION	POST. REF.	DEBIT	CREDIT	
1						1
2						2
3						3
4						4
5						5
6						6
7						7
8						8
9						9
10						10
11						11
12						12
13						13
14						14
15						15
16						16
17						17
18						18
19						19
20						20
21						21
22						22
23						23
24						24
25						25
26						26
27						27
28						28
29						29
30						30

Problem 24-1   (continued)

(2)

GENERAL LEDGER

ACCOUNT _Cash in Bank_____ ACCOUNT NO. ___101___

	DATE		DESCRIPTION	POST. REF.	DEBIT	CREDIT	BALANCE	
							DEBIT	CREDIT
	20--							
	Apr.	1	Balance	✓			9 4 2 8 00	

ACCOUNT _Accounts Receivable_____ ACCOUNT NO. ___115___

	DATE		DESCRIPTION	POST. REF.	DEBIT	CREDIT	BALANCE	
							DEBIT	CREDIT
	20--							
	Apr.	1	Balance	✓			7 2 9 0 00	

ACCOUNT _Sales Tax Payable_____ ACCOUNT NO. ___215___

	DATE		DESCRIPTION	POST. REF.	DEBIT	CREDIT	BALANCE	
							DEBIT	CREDIT
	20--							
	Apr.	1	Balance	✓				2 4 8 00

ACCOUNT _Sales_____ ACCOUNT NO. ___401___

	DATE		DESCRIPTION	POST. REF.	DEBIT	CREDIT	BALANCE	
							DEBIT	CREDIT
	20--							
	Apr.	1	Balance	✓				24 1 6 0 00

ACCOUNT _Uncollectible Accounts Expense_____ ACCOUNT NO. ___680___

	DATE		DESCRIPTION	POST. REF.	DEBIT	CREDIT	BALANCE	
							DEBIT	CREDIT
	20--							
	Apr.	1	Balance	✓			9 2 8 00	

Problem 24-1 (concluded)

(2)

ACCOUNTS RECEIVABLE SUBSIDIARY LEDGER

Name **Sonya Dickson** _____

Address _____

DATE		DESCRIPTION	POST. REF.	DEBIT	CREDIT	BALANCE

Problem 24-2   Writing Off Accounts Under the Allowance Method
(1)

GENERAL JOURNAL   PAGE _____

	DATE	DESCRIPTION	POST. REF.	DEBIT	CREDIT	
1						1
2						2
3						3
4						4
5						5
6						6
7						7
8						8
9						9
10						10
11						11
12						12
13						13
14						14
15						15
16						16
17						17
18						18
19						19
20						20
21						21
22						22
23						23
24						24
25						25
26						26
27						27
28						28
29						29
30						30

Problem 24-2   (continued)
(2)

ACCOUNTS RECEIVABLE SUBSIDIARY LEDGER

Name *Jack Bowers* _____

Address _____

DATE		DESCRIPTION	POST. REF.	DEBIT	CREDIT	BALANCE
20--						
May	1	Balance	✓			1050 00

GENERAL LEDGER (PARTIAL)

ACCOUNT *Cash in Bank* _____ ACCOUNT NO. ___101___

DATE		DESCRIPTION	POST. REF.	DEBIT	CREDIT	BALANCE DEBIT	BALANCE CREDIT
20--							
Nov.	1	Balance	✓			9420 00	

ACCOUNT *Accounts Receivable* _____ ACCOUNT NO. ___115___

DATE		DESCRIPTION	POST. REF.	DEBIT	CREDIT	BALANCE DEBIT	BALANCE CREDIT
20--							
May	1	Balance	✓			2040 00	

Problem 24-2 (concluded)

ACCOUNT _Allowance for Uncollectible Accounts_ ACCOUNT NO. _117_

DATE	DESCRIPTION	POST. REF.	DEBIT	CREDIT	BALANCE DEBIT	BALANCE CREDIT
20--						
May 1	Balance	✓				1 20 0 00

ACCOUNT _Uncollectible Accounts Expense_ ACCOUNT NO. _675_

DATE	DESCRIPTION	POST. REF.	DEBIT	CREDIT	BALANCE DEBIT	BALANCE CREDIT

(3)

Problem 24-3   Estimating Uncollectible Accounts Expense Using the Percentage of Net Sales Method

(1)

Company	Net Sales	Percentage of Net Sales	Uncollectible Accounts Expense
Andrews Co.		2%	
The Book Nook		1%	
Cable, Inc.		$1\frac{1}{2}\%$	
Davis, Inc.		2%	
Ever-Sharp Co.		$1\frac{1}{4}\%$	

(2)

GENERAL JOURNAL   PAGE ___21___

	DATE	DESCRIPTION	POST. REF.	DEBIT	CREDIT	
1						1
2						2
3						3
4						4
5						5
6						6
7						7
8						8
9						9
10						10
11						11
12						12

Computerized Accounting Using Peachtree

Software Objectives

When you have completed this chapter, you will be able to use Peachtree to:

1. Record a transaction to write off an account using the direct write-off method.
2. Record estimated uncollectible accounts expense.
3. Record a transaction to write off an account using the allowance method.
4. Print financial statements that include uncollectible amounts.

Problem 24-4   Using the Direct Write-Off Method

INSTRUCTIONS

Beginning a Session

Step 1   Select the problem set: Sunset Surfwear (Prob. 24-4).
Step 2   Rename the company by adding your initials.
Step 3   Set the system date to June 30, 2004.

Completing the Accounting Problem

Step 4   Review the information provided in your textbook.
Step 5   Record the June 1 transaction using the **Receipts** option.

> ***June 1 Wrote off the $288.75 account of Alex Hamilton as uncollectible, Memo 223.***

To record a transaction to write off an account:

- Choose **Receipts** from the *Tasks* menu.
- Type **6/1/04** in the *Deposit Ticket ID* field.
- Enter **HAM** in the *Customer ID* field to select the record for Alex Hamilton.
- Type **Memo 223** in the *Reference* field.
- Enter **6/1/04** in the *Date* field.
- Move to the *GL Account* field shown below the *Payment Method* field.

TIP: You must identify the **Uncollectible Accounts Expense** as the Cash account to record a transaction to write off an invoice.

- Enter **670** (Uncollectible Accounts Expense) in the *GL Account* field.

  Changing the **Cash** account to **Uncollectible Accounts Expense** is required to write off an account. When you mark an invoice as "paid," Peachtree will debit **Uncollectible Accounts Expense** instead of **Cash.** Peachtree will also credit **Accounts Receivable.**

- Click the **Pay** button next to the outstanding invoice.
- Compare the information on your screen to the completed **Receipts** windows shown in Figure 24-4A. If necessary, make any changes before you continue.

DO YOU HAVE A QUESTION

Q. *Can you use the **General Journal Entry** task option to record a transaction to write off an uncollectible account?*

A. No, you cannot use the **General Journal Entry** option to record a transaction to write off an uncollectible account. As you may remember, Peachtree does not provide a way to identify an accounts receivable subsidiary ledger account. Therefore, you must use the **Receipts** task option.

Notes

*You must use the **Receipts** task option to record a transaction to write off an account as uncollectible.*

Enter date of the deposit

Identify the customer

Enter the GL account for Uncollectible Accounts Expense

Select the item to be written off

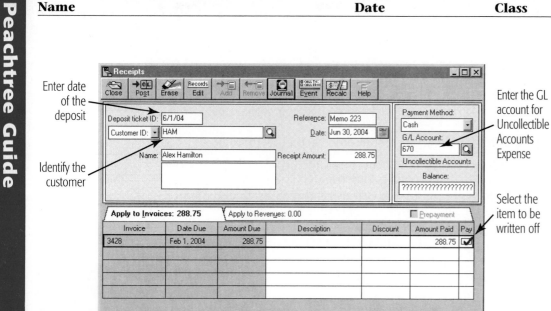

Figure 24-4A *Accounts Write-Off Transaction (June 1)*

- Click the ![Journal] button to display the Accounting Behind the Screens window. (See Figure 24-4B.)

  As you can see, **Uncollectible Accounts Expense** is debited $288.75 and **Accounts Receivable** is credited $288.75.

- Close the Accounting Behind the Screens window.
- Click ![Post] to post the transaction.

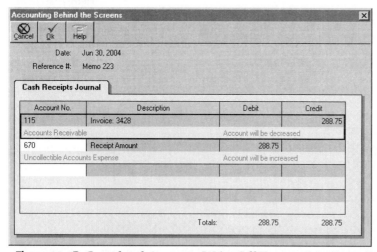

Figure 24-4B *Completed Accounts Write-Off Transaction (June 1)*

Step 6   Enter the remaining transactions to write off the other uncollectible accounts. (June 4, June 14, and June 29).

Step 7   Enter the June 22 transaction to record the cash receipt from a customer whose account was previously written off.

June 22, Received $288.75 from Alex Hamilton in full payment of his account, which was written off previously, Memorandum 298 and Receipt 944.

To reinstate an account and record the cash receipt:

- Use the **Sales/Invoicing** task option to enter a new sales invoice for $288.75.

  Enter **Memo 298** for the invoice number. In the Apply to Sales tab, make sure that you enter **670** (Uncollectible Accounts Expense) in the *GL Accounts* field. Also, remember to change the sales tax to $0.00. (See Figure 24-4C.)

- Choose the **Receipts** option to record the cash receipt.

  Record the receipt just as you would record any other receipt on account. **IMPORTANT:** Be sure to change the Cash *GL Account* field back to the **Cash in Bank** (101) account when you enter a cash receipt.

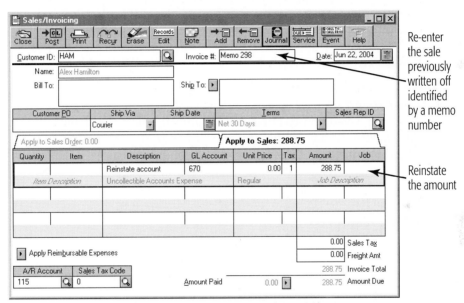

Figure 24-4C *Reinstated Account (June 22)*

Step 8   Print the following reports: Cash Receipts Journal, Sales Journal, Customer Ledgers, and General Ledger.

Step 9   Proof your work.

Step 10   Answer the Analyze question.

Ending the Session

Step 11   Click the **Close Problem** button in the Glencoe Smart Guide window to save your work.

Mastering Peachtree

Does Peachtree include any reports that show you which accounts are overdue and by how long? On a separate sheet of paper, describe the information provided on the report.

Problem 24-5 Calculating and Recording Estimated Uncollectible Accounts Expense

INSTRUCTIONS

Beginning a Session

Step 1 Select the problem set: InBeat CD Shop (Prob. 24-5).

Step 2 Rename the company, and set the system date to June 30, 2004.

Completing the Accounting Problem

Step 3 Review the information provided in your textbook.

Step 4 Record the uncollectible accounts adjustment using the **General Ledger Entry** option.

Step 5 Print a General Journal report and a General Ledger report to proof your work.

Notes

Peachtree automatically posts entries to the general ledger.

TIP: You can access the reports using the General Ledger navigation aid.

Step 6 Answer the Analyze question.

Checking Your Work and Ending the Session

Step 7 Click the **Close Problem** button in the Glencoe Smart Guide window.

Step 8 If your teacher has asked you to check your solution, select *Check my answer to this problem*. Review, print, and close the report.

Step 9 Click the **Close Problem** button and select a save option.

Problem 24-6   Writing Off Accounts Under the Allowance Method

INSTRUCTIONS

Beginning a Session

Step 1   Select the problem set: Shutterbug Cameras (Prob. 24-6).

Step 2   Rename the company, and set the system date to June 30, 2004.

Completing the Accounting Problem

Step 3   Review the information provided in your textbook.

Step 4   Record the transactions to write off the bad debts using the **Receipts** option.

TIP: Remember to change the Cash GL Account to **Allowance for Uncollectible Accounts** when you write off an account using the allowance method. Also, check the Accounting Behind the Screens window to verify your work.

Step 5   Enter the transactions to reinstate Jimmy Thompson's account and record the receipt on account.

> **IMPORTANT:** Use the **Sales/Invoicing** option to reinstate an account that was previously written off. For the allowance method, record the **Allowance for Uncollectible Accounts** general ledger on the Apply to Sales tab. Also, make sure the sales tax is $0.00.

Step 6   Record the adjustment for estimated uncollectible accounts.

Step 7   Record the closing entry for **Uncollectible Accounts Expense** using the **General Journal Entry**. (**Note:** Don't use the **Close Fiscal Year** option. Manually enter the closing entry.)

Step 8   Print the following reports to proof your work: Cash Receipts Journal, Sales Journal, Customer Ledgers, General Journal, and General Ledger.

Step 9   Print a Balance Sheet.

Step 10   Answer the Analyze question.

Ending the Session

Step 11   Click the **Close Problem** button in the Glencoe Smart Guide window to save your work.

Peachtree Guide

Problem 24-7   Estimating Uncollectible Accounts Expense

INSTRUCTIONS

Beginning a Session

Step 1   Select the problem set: Cycle Tech Bicycles (Prob. 24-7).

Step 2   Rename the company, and set the system date to June 30, 2004.

Completing the Accounting Problem

Step 3   Review the information provided in your textbook.

Step 4   Complete the analysis of the accounts receivable provided in your working papers.

Step 5   Based on your analysis, record the uncollectible accounts adjustment using the **General Ledger Entry** option.

Step 6   Print a General Journal report and a General Ledger report to proof your work.

TIP: Use the Windows calculator accessory to help you perform the analysis of the accounts receivable.

Step 7   Answer the Analyze question.

Checking Your Work and Ending the Session

Step 8   Click the **Close Problem** button in the Glencoe Smart Guide window.

Step 9   If your teacher has asked you to check your solution, select *Check my answer to this problem*. Review, print, and close the report.

Step 10   Click the **Close Problem** button and select a save option.

Problem 24-8   Reporting Uncollectible Amounts on the Financial Statements

INSTRUCTIONS

Beginning a Session

Step 1 Select the problem set: River's Edge Canoe & Kayak (Prob. 24-8).
Step 2 Rename the company, and set the system date to December 31, 2004.

Completing the Accounting Problem

Step 3 Review the information provided in your textbook.
Step 4 Record the adjustment for the uncollectible accounts expense.
Step 5 Print a General Journal report and proof your work.
Step 6 Print a Balance Sheet and an Income Statement.
Step 7 Click the **Save Pre-closing Balances** button in the Glencoe Smart Guide window.
Step 8 Close the fiscal year.

Notes

Peachtree does not include an option to print a ten-column work sheet or a Statement of Retained Earnings.

TIP: To close the fiscal year, choose **System** from the *Tasks* menu and choose **Close Fiscal Year.** You do not have to make a backup. When you are asked whether you want to purge the transactions, select **No.**

Step 9 Print a Post-Closing Trial Balance.
Step 10 Answer the Analyze question.

Ending the Session

Step 11 Click the **Close Problem** button in the Glencoe Smart Guide window to save your work.

Problem 24-9   Using the Allowance Method for Write-Offs

INSTRUCTIONS

Beginning a Session

Step 1   Select the problem set: Buzz Newsstand (Prob. 24-9).

Step 2   Rename the company, and set the system date to December 31, 2004.

Completing the Accounting Problem

Step 3   Review the information provided in your textbook.

Step 4   Record the transactions. Remember to enter each transaction in the proper accounting period. Use the **System** option from the **Tasks** menu to change the accounting period before entering each transaction.

Step 5   Print the following reports to proof your work: Cash Receipts Journal, Sales Journal, and Customer Ledgers.

TIP: When you print the reports, change the date range options to include the transactions for the entire year, not just the current period.

Step 6   Answer the Analyze question.

Checking Your Work and Ending the Session

Step 7   Verify that the accounting period displayed is 12/1/04 to 12/31/04. Click the **Close Problem** button in the Glencoe Smart Guide window.

Step 8   If your teacher has asked you to check your solution, select *Check my answer to this problem*. Review, print, and close the report.

Step 9   Click the **Close Problem** button and select a save option.

FAQs

Why don't some Peachtree reports show all of the transactions?

By default, most Peachtree reports show only those transactions entered in the current period. If you entered transactions over multiple periods, you must change the report date option. For example, change the date range to include the entire year.

Working Papers *for End-of-Chapter Problems*

Problem 24-4   Using the Direct Write-Off Method

(1)

GENERAL JOURNAL   PAGE _____

	DATE	DESCRIPTION	POST. REF.	DEBIT	CREDIT	
1						1
2						2
3						3
4						4
5						5
6						6
7						7
8						8
9						9
10						10
11						11
12						12
13						13
14						14
15						15
16						16
17						17
18						18
19						19
20						20
21						21
22						22
23						23
24						24
25						25
26						26
27						27
28						28
29						29
30						30
31						31
32						32
33						33
34						34

Problem 24-4 (continued)

(2)

ACCOUNTS RECEIVABLE SUBSIDIARY LEDGER

Name **Martha Adams**

Address _____

DATE		DESCRIPTION	POST. REF.	DEBIT	CREDIT	BALANCE
20--						
June	1	Balance	✓			100 80

Name **Alex Hamilton**

Address _____

DATE		DESCRIPTION	POST. REF.	DEBIT	CREDIT	BALANCE
20--						
June	1	Balance	✓			288 75

Name **Helen Jun**

Address _____

DATE		DESCRIPTION	POST. REF.	DEBIT	CREDIT	BALANCE
20--						
June	1	Balance	✓			243 60

Name **Nate Moulder**

Address _____

DATE		DESCRIPTION	POST. REF.	DEBIT	CREDIT	BALANCE
20--						
June	1	Balance	✓			57 75

Problem 24-4   (concluded)

GENERAL LEDGER

ACCOUNT *Cash in Bank*   ACCOUNT NO. ___101___

DATE	DESCRIPTION	POST. REF.	DEBIT	CREDIT	BALANCE DEBIT	BALANCE CREDIT
20--						
June 1	Balance	✓			10650 16	

ACCOUNT *Accounts Receivable*   ACCOUNT NO. ___115___

DATE	DESCRIPTION	POST. REF.	DEBIT	CREDIT	BALANCE DEBIT	BALANCE CREDIT
20--						
June 1	Balance	✓			8016 50	

ACCOUNT *Uncollectible Accounts Expense*   ACCOUNT NO. ___675___

DATE	DESCRIPTION	POST. REF.	DEBIT	CREDIT	BALANCE DEBIT	BALANCE CREDIT

Analyze: _____

_____

Problem 24-5 Calculating and Recording Estimated Uncollectible Accounts Expense

(1) _____

(2)

GENERAL JOURNAL   PAGE _____

	DATE	DESCRIPTION	POST. REF.	DEBIT	CREDIT	
1						1
2						2
3						3
4						4
5						5
6						6

(3)

GENERAL LEDGER (PARTIAL)

ACCOUNT _Allowance for Uncollectible Accounts_   ACCOUNT NO. ___117___

DATE	DESCRIPTION	POST. REF.	DEBIT	CREDIT	BALANCE DEBIT	BALANCE CREDIT
20--						
June 1	Balance	✓				4 0 0 0 00

ACCOUNT _Uncollectible Accounts Expense_   ACCOUNT NO. ___670___

DATE	DESCRIPTION	POST. REF.	DEBIT	CREDIT	BALANCE DEBIT	BALANCE CREDIT

Analyze: _____

_____

_____

Problem 24-6   Source Documents

Instructions: *Use the following source documents to record the transactions for this problem.*

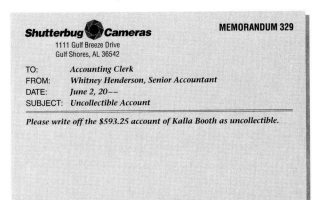

Shutterbug Cameras
1111 Gulf Breeze Drive
Gulf Shores, AL 36542

MEMORANDUM 329

TO: *Accounting Clerk*
FROM: *Whitney Henderson, Senior Accountant*
DATE: *June 2, 20--*
SUBJECT: *Uncollectible Account*

Please write off the $593.25 account of Kalla Booth as uncollectible.

Shutterbug Cameras
1111 Gulf Breeze Drive
Gulf Shores, AL 36542

MEMORANDUM 474

TO: *Accounting Clerk*
FROM: *Whitney Henderson, Senior Accountant*
DATE: *June 12, 20--*
SUBJECT: *Uncollectible Account*

Please write off the account of FastForward Productions ($945.00) as uncollectible.

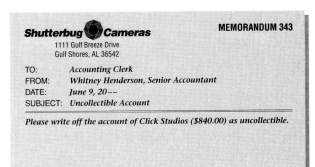

Shutterbug Cameras
1111 Gulf Breeze Drive
Gulf Shores, AL 36542

MEMORANDUM 343

TO: *Accounting Clerk*
FROM: *Whitney Henderson, Senior Accountant*
DATE: *June 9, 20--*
SUBJECT: *Uncollectible Account*

Please write off the account of Click Studios ($840.00) as uncollectible.

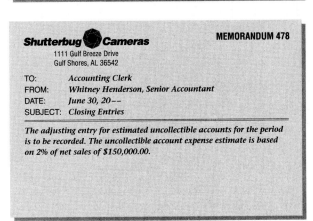

Shutterbug Cameras
1111 Gulf Breeze Drive
Gulf Shores, AL 36542

MEMORANDUM 478

TO: *Accounting Clerk*
FROM: *Whitney Henderson, Senior Accountant*
DATE: *June 30, 20--*
SUBJECT: *Closing Entries*

The adjusting entry for estimated uncollectible accounts for the period is to be recorded. The uncollectible account expense estimate is based on 2% of net sales of $150,000.00.

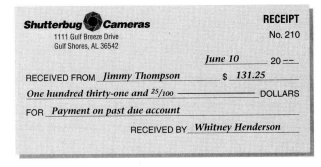

Shutterbug Cameras
1111 Gulf Breeze Drive
Gulf Shores, AL 36542

RECEIPT
No. 210

           June 10   20 --

RECEIVED FROM *Jimmy Thompson* $ *131.25*

One hundred thirty-one and $^{25}/100$ ————— DOLLARS

FOR *Payment on past due account*

         RECEIVED BY *Whitney Henderson*

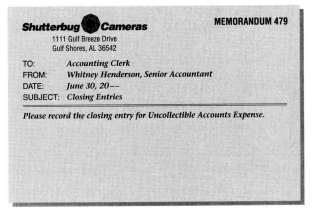

Shutterbug Cameras
1111 Gulf Breeze Drive
Gulf Shores, AL 36542

MEMORANDUM 479

TO: *Accounting Clerk*
FROM: *Whitney Henderson, Senior Accountant*
DATE: *June 30, 20--*
SUBJECT: *Closing Entries*

Please record the closing entry for Uncollectible Accounts Expense.

Problem 24-6 Writing Off Accounts Under the Allowance Method

(1)

GENERAL JOURNAL   PAGE _____

	DATE	DESCRIPTION	POST. REF.	DEBIT	CREDIT	
1						1
2						2
3						3
4						4
5						5
6						6
7						7
8						8
9						9
10						10
11						11
12						12
13						13
14						14
15						15
16						16
17						17
18						18
19						19
20						20
21						21
22						22
23						23
24						24
25						25
26						26
27						27
28						28
29						29
30						30
31						31
32						32
33						33
34						34

Problem 24-6 (continued)

(2)

GENERAL LEDGER

ACCOUNT _Cash in Bank_ ACCOUNT NO. _101_

DATE		DESCRIPTION	POST. REF.	DEBIT	CREDIT	BALANCE DEBIT	BALANCE CREDIT
20--							
June	1	Balance	✓			9306 54	

ACCOUNT _Accounts Receivable_ ACCOUNT NO. _115_

DATE		DESCRIPTION	POST. REF.	DEBIT	CREDIT	BALANCE DEBIT	BALANCE CREDIT
20--							
June	1	Balance	✓			23102 00	

ACCOUNT _Allowance for Uncollectible Accounts_ ACCOUNT NO. _117_

DATE		DESCRIPTION	POST. REF.	DEBIT	CREDIT	BALANCE DEBIT	BALANCE CREDIT
20--							
June	1	Balance	✓				3164 00

ACCOUNT _Income Summary_ ACCOUNT NO. _310_

DATE	DESCRIPTION	POST. REF.	DEBIT	CREDIT	BALANCE DEBIT	BALANCE CREDIT

ACCOUNT _Uncollectible Accounts Expense_ ACCOUNT NO. _665_

DATE	DESCRIPTION	POST. REF.	DEBIT	CREDIT	BALANCE DEBIT	BALANCE CREDIT

Problem 24-6   (continued)
(2)

ACCOUNTS RECEIVABLE SUBSIDIARY LEDGER

Name *Kalla Booth*

Address *1416 Halprin Avenue, Mobile, AL 36604*

DATE		DESCRIPTION	POST. REF.	DEBIT	CREDIT	BALANCE
20--						
June	1	Balance	✓			593 25

Name *Click Studios*

Address *1300 Nice Avenue, Mobile, AL 36610*

DATE		DESCRIPTION	POST. REF.	DEBIT	CREDIT	BALANCE
20--						
June	1	Balance	✓			840 00

Name *FastForward Productions*

Address *3937 Channel Drive, Mobile, AL 36617*

DATE		DESCRIPTION	POST. REF.	DEBIT	CREDIT	BALANCE
20--						
June	1	Balance	✓			945 00

Name *Jimmy Thompson*

Address *1616 Parkway Drive, Mobile, AL 36609*

DATE		DESCRIPTION	POST. REF.	DEBIT	CREDIT	BALANCE
20--						
June	1	Balance	✓			—

Problem 24-6   (concluded)

(3)

Analyze: _____

_____

Problem 24-7   Estimating Uncollectible Accounts Expense

(1)

Customer Name	Total Amount Owed	Not Yet Due	Days Past Due				
			1–30 Days	31–60 Days	61–90 Days	91–180 Days	Over 180
N. Bellis	$ 722	$ 722					
G. Buresh	1,362		$ 761		$ 601		
Rachel D'Souza	209	209					
S. Garfield	449		132	$ 317			
Greg Kellogg	271					$ 271	
Rishi Nadal	1,066	640		426			
Megan O'Hara	48					48	
ProTeam Sponsors Inc.	1,998	1,998					
Heidi Spencer	790	428	362				
Ed Young	296						$ 296
Totals							

(2)

Age Group	Amount	Estimated Percentage Uncollectible	Estimated Uncollectible Amount
Not yet due		2%	
1–30 days past due		4%	
31–60 days past due		20%	
61–90 days past due		30%	
91–180 days past due		45%	
Over 180 days past due		60%	
Totals			

Problem 24-7 (concluded)

(3)

GENERAL JOURNAL   PAGE _____

	DATE	DESCRIPTION	POST. REF.	DEBIT	CREDIT	
1						1
2						2
3						3
4						4
5						5
6						6

(4)

GENERAL LEDGER (PARTIAL)

ACCOUNT _Accounts Receivable_   ACCOUNT NO. __115__

DATE		DESCRIPTION	POST. REF.	DEBIT	CREDIT	BALANCE DEBIT	BALANCE CREDIT
20--							
June	30	Balance	✓			7 2 1 1 00	

ACCOUNT _Allowance for Uncollectible Accounts_   ACCOUNT NO. __117__

DATE		DESCRIPTION	POST. REF.	DEBIT	CREDIT	BALANCE DEBIT	BALANCE CREDIT
20--							
June	30	Balance	✓				1 4 2 00

ACCOUNT _Uncollectible Accounts Expense_   ACCOUNT NO. __670__

DATE	DESCRIPTION	POST. REF.	DEBIT	CREDIT	BALANCE DEBIT	BALANCE CREDIT

Analyze: Book value of accounts receivable: _____

Problem 24-8   Reporting Uncollectible Amounts on the Financial Statements

(1), (2)

River's Edge

Work

For the Year Ended

	ACCT. NO.	ACCOUNT NAME	TRIAL BALANCE		ADJUSTMENTS	
			DEBIT	CREDIT	DEBIT	CREDIT
1	101	Cash in Bank	21 633 50			
2	115	Accounts Receivable	10 168 45			
3	117	Allow. for Uncollectible Accounts		400 00		
4	130	Merchandise Inventory	39 391 75			(b) 3 630 25
5	135	Supplies	2 875 00			(c) 1 900 00
6	140	Prepaid Insurance	3 100 00			(d) 2 000 00
7	150	Store Equipment	30 000 00			
8	152	Accum. Depr.—Store Equip.		3 610 00		(e) 500 00
9	201	Accounts Payable		3 960 00		
10	204	Fed. Corporate Income Tax Pay.	—	—		(f) 1 806 00
11	215	Sales Tax Payable		613 10		
12	301	Capital Stock		40 000 00		
13	305	Retained Earnings		9 764 15		
14	310	Income Summary	—	—	(b) 3 630 25	
15	401	Sales		152 875 20		
16	410	Sales Returns and Allowances	3 585 00			
17	501	Purchases	81 860 00			
18	505	Transportation In	3 956 00			
19	510	Purchases Discounts		740 00		
20	515	Purchases Returns and Allow.		1 221 00		
21	605	Bankcard Fees Expense	452 75			
22	620	Depr. Exp.—Store Equip.	—	—	(e) 500 00	
23	625	Fed. Corporate Income Tax Exp.	3 750 00		(f) 1 806 00	
24	635	Insurance Expense	—	—	(d) 2 000 00	
25	655	Miscellaneous Expense	730 00			
26	660	Rent Expense	9 600 00			
27	670	Supplies Expense	—	—	(c) 1 900 00	
28	675	Uncollectible Accounts Expense	—	—		
29	680	Utilities Expense	2 081 00			
30			213 183 45	213 183 45		
31						
32						
33						

Canoe & Kayak

Sheet

June 30, 20--

ADJUSTED TRIAL BALANCE		INCOME STATEMENT		BALANCE SHEET		
DEBIT	CREDIT	DEBIT	CREDIT	DEBIT	CREDIT	
						1
						2
						3
						4
						5
						6
						7
						8
						9
						10
						11
						12
						13
						14
						15
						16
						17
						18
						19
						20
						21
						22
						23
						24
						25
						26
						27
						28
						29
						30
						31
						32
						33

Problem 24-8   (continued)

(3)

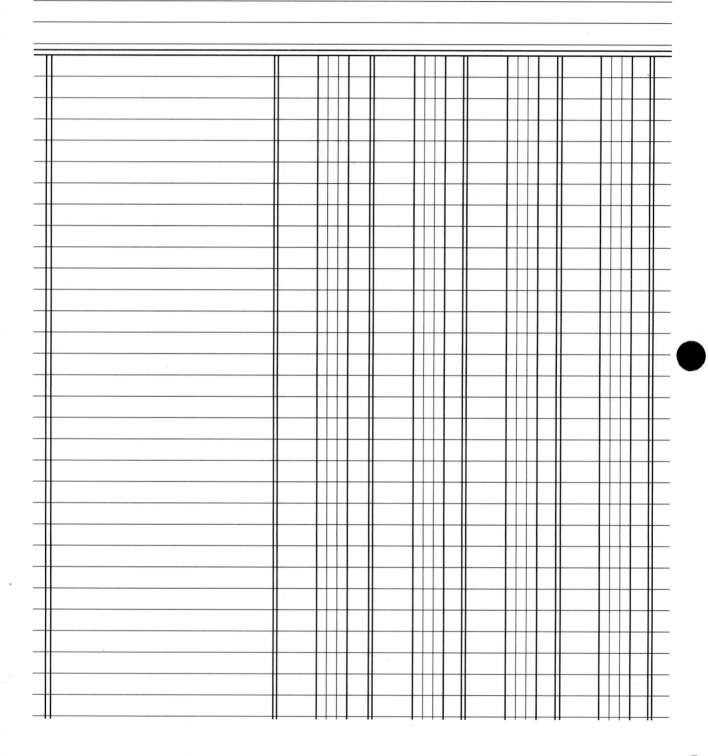

Problem 24-8   (continued)

(3)

(3)

Problem 24-8   (continued)
(4), (5)

GENERAL JOURNAL   PAGE _____

	DATE	DESCRIPTION	POST. REF.	DEBIT	CREDIT	
1						1
2						2
3						3
4						4
5						5
6						6
7						7
8						8
9						9
10						10
11						11
12						12
13						13
14						14
15						15
16						16
17						17
18						18
19						19
20						20
21						21
22						22
23						23
24						24
25						25
26						26
27						27
28						28
29						29
30						30
31						31
32						32
33						33
34						34
35						35
36						36

Problem 24-8   (continued)

(5)

GENERAL LEDGER

ACCOUNT _Cash in Bank_ _____ ACCOUNT NO. __101__

DATE	DESCRIPTION	POST. REF.	DEBIT	CREDIT	BALANCE DEBIT	BALANCE CREDIT
20--						
June 30	Balance	✓			21633 50	

ACCOUNT _Accounts Receivable_ _____ ACCOUNT NO. __115__

DATE	DESCRIPTION	POST. REF.	DEBIT	CREDIT	BALANCE DEBIT	BALANCE CREDIT
20--						
June 30	Balance	✓			10168 45	

ACCOUNT _Allowance for Uncollectible Accounts_ _____ ACCOUNT NO. __117__

DATE	DESCRIPTION	POST. REF.	DEBIT	CREDIT	BALANCE DEBIT	BALANCE CREDIT
20--						
June 30	Balance	✓				400 00

ACCOUNT _Merchandise Inventory_ _____ ACCOUNT NO. __130__

DATE	DESCRIPTION	POST. REF.	DEBIT	CREDIT	BALANCE DEBIT	BALANCE CREDIT
20--						
June 30	Balance	✓			39391 75	

ACCOUNT _Supplies_ _____ ACCOUNT NO. __135__

DATE	DESCRIPTION	POST. REF.	DEBIT	CREDIT	BALANCE DEBIT	BALANCE CREDIT
20--						
June 30	Balance	✓			2875 00	

ACCOUNT _Prepaid Insurance_ _____ ACCOUNT NO. __140__

DATE	DESCRIPTION	POST. REF.	DEBIT	CREDIT	BALANCE DEBIT	BALANCE CREDIT
20--						
June 30	Balance	✓			3100 00	

Problem 24-8 (continued)

ACCOUNT _Store Equipment_ _____ ACCOUNT NO. ___150___

DATE		DESCRIPTION	POST. REF.	DEBIT	CREDIT	BALANCE	
						DEBIT	CREDIT
20--							
June	30	Balance	✓			3000000	

ACCOUNT _Accumulated Depreciation—Store Equipment_ _____ ACCOUNT NO. ___152___

DATE		DESCRIPTION	POST. REF.	DEBIT	CREDIT	BALANCE	
						DEBIT	CREDIT
20--							
June	30	Balance	✓				361000

ACCOUNT _Accounts Payable_ _____ ACCOUNT NO. ___201___

DATE		DESCRIPTION	POST. REF.	DEBIT	CREDIT	BALANCE	
						DEBIT	CREDIT
20--							
June	30	Balance	✓				396000

ACCOUNT _Federal Corporate Income Tax Payable_ _____ ACCOUNT NO. ___204___

DATE		DESCRIPTION	POST. REF.	DEBIT	CREDIT	BALANCE	
						DEBIT	CREDIT

ACCOUNT _Sales Tax Payable_ _____ ACCOUNT NO. ___215___

DATE		DESCRIPTION	POST. REF.	DEBIT	CREDIT	BALANCE	
						DEBIT	CREDIT
20--							
June	30	Balance	✓				61310

ACCOUNT _Capital Stock_ _____ ACCOUNT NO. ___301___

DATE		DESCRIPTION	POST. REF.	DEBIT	CREDIT	BALANCE	
						DEBIT	CREDIT
20--							
June	30	Balance	✓				4000000

Problem 24-8   (continued)

ACCOUNT __*Retained Earnings*_____   ACCOUNT NO. ___305___

DATE		DESCRIPTION	POST. REF.	DEBIT	CREDIT	BALANCE DEBIT	BALANCE CREDIT
20--							
June	30	Balance	✓				9 7 6 4 15

ACCOUNT __*Income Summary*_____   ACCOUNT NO. ___310___

DATE		DESCRIPTION	POST. REF.	DEBIT	CREDIT	BALANCE DEBIT	BALANCE CREDIT

ACCOUNT __*Sales*_____   ACCOUNT NO. ___401___

DATE		DESCRIPTION	POST. REF.	DEBIT	CREDIT	BALANCE DEBIT	BALANCE CREDIT
20--							
June	30	Balance	✓				1 5 2 8 7 5 20

ACCOUNT __*Sales Returns and Allowances*_____   ACCOUNT NO. ___410___

DATE		DESCRIPTION	POST. REF.	DEBIT	CREDIT	BALANCE DEBIT	BALANCE CREDIT
20--							
June	30	Balance	✓			3 5 8 5 00	

ACCOUNT __*Purchases*_____   ACCOUNT NO. ___501___

DATE		DESCRIPTION	POST. REF.	DEBIT	CREDIT	BALANCE DEBIT	BALANCE CREDIT
20--							
June	30	Balance	✓			8 1 8 6 0 00	

ACCOUNT __*Transportation In*_____   ACCOUNT NO. ___505___

DATE		DESCRIPTION	POST. REF.	DEBIT	CREDIT	BALANCE DEBIT	BALANCE CREDIT
20--							
June	30	Balance	✓			3 9 5 6 00	

Problem 24-8   (continued)

ACCOUNT ___Purchases Discounts___   ACCOUNT NO. ___510___

DATE		DESCRIPTION	POST. REF.	DEBIT	CREDIT	BALANCE DEBIT	BALANCE CREDIT
20--							
June	30	Balance	✓				740 00

ACCOUNT ___Purchases Returns and Allowances___   ACCOUNT NO. ___515___

DATE		DESCRIPTION	POST. REF.	DEBIT	CREDIT	BALANCE DEBIT	BALANCE CREDIT
20--							
June	30	Balance	✓				1221 00

ACCOUNT ___Bankcard Fees Expense___   ACCOUNT NO. ___605___

DATE		DESCRIPTION	POST. REF.	DEBIT	CREDIT	BALANCE DEBIT	BALANCE CREDIT
20--							
June	30	Balance	✓			452 75	

ACCOUNT ___Depreciation Expense—Store Equipment___   ACCOUNT NO. ___620___

DATE		DESCRIPTION	POST. REF.	DEBIT	CREDIT	BALANCE DEBIT	BALANCE CREDIT

ACCOUNT ___Federal Corporate Income Tax Expense___   ACCOUNT NO. ___625___

DATE		DESCRIPTION	POST. REF.	DEBIT	CREDIT	BALANCE DEBIT	BALANCE CREDIT
20--							
June	30	Balance	✓			3750 00	

ACCOUNT ___Insurance Expense___   ACCOUNT NO. ___635___

DATE		DESCRIPTION	POST. REF.	DEBIT	CREDIT	BALANCE DEBIT	BALANCE CREDIT

Problem 24-8 (concluded)

ACCOUNT _Miscellaneous Expense_ ACCOUNT NO. _655_

DATE		DESCRIPTION	POST. REF.	DEBIT	CREDIT	BALANCE	
						DEBIT	CREDIT
20--							
June	30	Balance	✓			730 00	

ACCOUNT _Rent Expense_ ACCOUNT NO. _660_

DATE		DESCRIPTION	POST. REF.	DEBIT	CREDIT	BALANCE	
						DEBIT	CREDIT
20--							
June	30	Balance	✓			9600 00	

ACCOUNT _Supplies Expense_ ACCOUNT NO. _670_

DATE		DESCRIPTION	POST. REF.	DEBIT	CREDIT	BALANCE	
						DEBIT	CREDIT

ACCOUNT _Uncollectible Accounts Expense_ ACCOUNT NO. _675_

DATE		DESCRIPTION	POST. REF.	DEBIT	CREDIT	BALANCE	
						DEBIT	CREDIT

ACCOUNT _Utilities Expense_ ACCOUNT NO. _680_

DATE		DESCRIPTION	POST. REF.	DEBIT	CREDIT	BALANCE	
						DEBIT	CREDIT
20--							
June	30	Balance	✓			2081 00	

Analyze: _____

_____

Problem 24-9 Using the Allowance Method for Write-Offs

GENERAL JOURNAL

PAGE _____

	DATE		DESCRIPTION	POST. REF.	DEBIT	CREDIT	
1							1
2							2
3							3
4							4
5							5
6							6
7							7
8							8
9							9
10							10
11							11
12							12
13							13
14							14
15							15
16							16
17							17
18							18
19							19

ACCOUNTS RECEIVABLE SUBSIDIARY LEDGER

Name _Lee Adkins_ _____

Address _____

DATE		DESCRIPTION	POST. REF.	DEBIT	CREDIT	BALANCE
_20--_						
Jan.	_1_	_Balance_	✓			_1 9 4 50_

Analyze: _____

_____

CHAPTER  Uncollectible Accounts Receivable

Self-Test

Part A   True or False

Directions: *Circle the letter* T *in the Answer column if the statement is true; circle the letter* F *if the statement is false.*

Answer

T   F   **1.** When a business uses the allowance method, an adjusting entry must be made.

T   F   **2.** The two general ledger accounts affected by the direct write-off method of accounting for uncollectible accounts are Uncollectible Accounts Expense and Accounts Payable.

T   F   **3.** Another term for uncollectible accounts is bad debts.

T   F   **4.** The Allowance for Uncollectible Accounts account is classified as a contra asset account.

T   F   **5.** When a business sells goods or services on account, it knows which charge customers' accounts will be uncollectible.

T   F   **6.** When an account is written off as uncollectible, an explanation should be written on the account.

T   F   **7.** Large businesses with many charge customers normally use the direct write-off method of accounting for uncollectible accounts.

T   F   **8.** The normal balance of Allowance for Uncollectible Accounts is a credit.

T   F   **9.** Under the allowance method, Allowance for Uncollectible Accounts is debited when a charge customer's account is written off as a bad debt.

T   F   **10.** Businesses that sell on credit usually expect to sell more than if they accepted only cash.

T   F   **11.** When the direct write-off method of accounting is used, Accounts Receivable and the customer's account in the subsidiary ledger are credited when it is determined that the charge customer is not going to pay.

Part B   Multiple Choice

Directions: *Only one of the choices given with each of the following statements is correct. Write the letter of the correct answer in the Answer column.*

Answer

_____   **1.** Allowance for Uncollectible Accounts is all of the following except
(A) a contra asset account.
(B) listed on the balance sheet just below Accounts Receivable.
(C) increased on the debit side.
(D) a valuation account.

_____   **2.** If a company had net sales of $900,000 and estimates that its uncollectible accounts will be 3% of net sales, what is the amount of the adjustment?
(A) $900,000
(B) $27,000
(C) $2,700
(D) $270

_____   **3.** Under the direct write-off method, the journal entry used to write off the account as uncollectible affects which two general ledger accounts?
(A) Uncollectible Accounts Expense/Allowance for Uncollectible Accounts
(B) Uncollectible Accounts Expense/Cash in Bank
(C) Allowance for Uncollectible Accounts/Accounts Receivable
(D) Uncollectible Accounts Expense/Accounts Receivable

_____   **4.** With an Accounts Receivable account balance of $15,000 and an Allowance for Uncollectible Accounts balance of $2,500, what is the book value of accounts receivable?
(A) $15,000
(B) $2,500
(C) $17,500
(D) $12,500

CHAPTER 25 Inventories

Study Plan

Check Your Understanding

Section 1
Read Section 1 on pages 680–682 and complete the following exercises on page 683.
- ❏ Thinking Critically
- ❏ Communicating Accounting
- ❏ Problem 25-1 *Preparing Inventory Reports*

Section 2
Read Section 2 on pages 684–687 and complete the following exercises on page 688.
- ❏ Thinking Critically
- ❏ Computing in the Business World
- ❏ Problem 25-2 *Determining Inventory Costs*

Section 3
Read Section 3 on pages 690–691 and complete the following exercises on page 692.
- ❏ Thinking Critically
- ❏ Analyzing Accounting
- ❏ Problem 25-3 *Analyzing a Source Document*

Summary
Review the Chapter 25 Summary on page 693 in your textbook.
- ❏ Key Concepts

Review and Activities
Complete the following questions and exercises on pages 694–695 in your textbook.
- ❏ Using Key Terms
- ❏ Understanding Accounting Concepts and Procedures
- ❏ Case Study
- ❏ Conducting an Audit with Alex
- ❏ Internet Connection
- ❏ Workplace Skills

Computerized Accounting
Read the Computerized Accounting information on page 696 in your textbook.
- ❏ *Making the Transition from a Manual to a Computerized System*
- ❏ *Maintaining and Closing Inventories in Peachtree*

Problems
Complete the following end-of-chapter problems for Chapter 25 in your textbook.
- ❏ Problem 25-4 *Calculating the Cost of Ending Inventory*
- ❏ Problem 25-5 *Completing an Inventory Sheet*
- ❏ Problem 25-6 *Calculating Gross Profit on Sales*
- ❏ Problem 25-7 *Reporting Ending Inventory on the Income Statement*

Challenge Problem
- ❏ Problem 25-8 *Calculating Cost of Merchandise Sold and Gross Profit on Sales*

Chapter Reviews and Working Papers
Complete the following exercises for Chapter 25 in your Chapter Reviews and Working Papers.
- ❏ Chapter Review
- ❏ Self-Test

CHAPTER 25 REVIEW   Inventories

Part 1   Accounting Vocabulary (9 points)

Directions: *Using terms from the following list, complete the sentences below. Write the letter of the term you have chosen in the space provided.*

Total Points	33
Student's Score	

A. conservatism principle	**E.** market value	**H.** point-of-sale terminal
B. consistency principle	**F.** periodic inventory system	**I.** specific identification method
C. first-in, first-out method	**G.** perpetual inventory system	**J.** weighted average cost method
D. last-in, first-out method		

    E   **0.** _____ is the current price that is being charged for similar items of merchandise in the market.

         1. The inventory costing method under which the cost of the items on hand is determined by the average cost of all identical items purchased during the period is the _____.

         2. The _____ is the inventory costing method that assumes the last items purchased are the first items sold.

         3. The _____ is the accounting guideline that states a business should report its financial position in amounts that are least likely to result in an overstatement of income or property values.

         4. The inventory costing method that assumes the first items purchased were the first items sold is the _____.

         5. The inventory costing method under which the exact cost of each item on the inventory sheet must be determined and assigned to that item is the _____.

         6. The _____ requires a constant, up-to-date record of merchandise on hand.

         7. The _____ requires a physical count of all merchandise on hand to determine the quantity of merchandise on hand.

         8. A _____ reads bar codes and enters the information into a computer.

         9. The _____ requires that businesses not normally change their chosen method of inventory costing.

Part 2   Comparing Inventory Costing Methods (6 points)

Directions: *Read each of the statements below and determine the inventory method that completes the statement. Write the identifying letter of your choice in the space provided.*

A. first-in, first-out method	**C.** specific identification method
B. last-in, first-out method	**D.** weighted average cost method

    C   **0.** The _____ is a time-consuming process.

         1. The _____ is used by businesses that have a low unit volume of merchandise with high unit prices.

         2. According to the _____, the items still on hand at the end of the fiscal period are assumed to be the last items purchased.

         3. The _____ assumes that the items still on hand at the end of the period are the first ones purchased.

         4. The _____ takes into account the costs of all the merchandise available for sale during the period.

         5. The _____ is the most realistic costing method.

         6. The last-in, first-out method and the _____ are based on certain assumptions about the items remaining in inventory.

Part 3   Calculating Inventory Costs (6 points)

Directions: *The Lindborg Craft Shop has the following record of crewel kits for the month of April:*

Beginning inventory	13 units @ $3.48	=	$ 45.24
Purchased April 4	15 units @ $3.51	=	52.65
Purchased April 9	20 units @ $3.67	=	73.40
Purchased April 14	10 units @ $3.71	=	37.10
Purchased April 26	15 units @ $3.74	=	56.10
	73		$264.49

At the end of April, there were 22 units on hand. Based on the above information, complete the following statements.

$82.07   **0.** The value of the ending inventory using the FIFO method is _____.

_____   **1.** The value of the ending inventory using the LIFO method is _____.

_____   **2.** The value of the ending inventory using the weighted average cost method is _____.

_____   **3.** The purchase that will have the greatest impact on the weighted average cost method was made on _____.

_____   **4.** If the LIFO method is used and if the current market value of its inventory is $80.37, the Lindborg Craft Shop would report the value of its inventory at _____.

_____   **5.** The _____ method produces the highest value for the ending inventory.

_____   **6.** The _____ method produces the lowest value for the ending inventory.

Part 4   Choosing an Inventory Costing Method (12 points)

Directions: *Read each of the following statements to determine whether the statement is true or false. Write your answer in the space provided.*

True   **0.** A perpetual inventory system can be established without a computer.

_____   **1.** When a cash register is linked to a computer, it is said to be online.

_____   **2.** The costing method used to determine the value of the ending inventory will not affect a company's gross profit on sales or net income.

_____   **3.** A business may change inventory costing methods without obtaining permission from the Internal Revenue Service.

_____   **4.** The market value of the merchandise on hand is always lower than the original cost.

_____   **5.** The most commonly used method of determining the quantity of merchandise on hand is the perpetual inventory system.

_____   **6.** A physical inventory should be conducted at least once a year.

_____   **7.** The weighted average cost method is the most accurate inventory costing method.

_____   **8.** A periodic inventory system provides management with continuous merchandise inventory information.

_____   **9.** The specific identification method can often be used by businesses that sell large items such as automobiles.

_____   **10.** When choosing an inventory costing method, a business's owner or manager should consider only the present economic conditions.

_____   **11.** An inventory control system includes the quantity of merchandise on hand at a given time and the selling price of that merchandise.

_____   **12.** The lower-of-cost-or-market rule for reporting inventory value allows a business to follow a conservative approach.

Working Papers *for Section Problems*

Problem 25-1   Preparing Inventory Reports

INVENTORY SHEET

Date _____ Clerk _____ Page _____

STOCK NO.	ITEM	UNIT	QUANTITY	UNIT COST	TOTAL VALUE
					TOTAL

Problem 25-2   Determining Inventory Costs

(a) Specific Identification Method _____

(b) First-In, First-Out Method _____

(c) Last-In, First-Out Method _____

(d) Weighted Average Cost Method _____

Problem 25-3   Analyzing a Source Document

1. _____

_____

_____

2. _____

_____

_____

_____

_____

Computerized Accounting Using Peachtree

Software Objectives

When you have completed this chapter, you will be able to use Peachtree to:

1. Update an inventory record.
2. Print an Inventory Valuation Report, a Cost of Goods Sold Journal, and an Item Costing Report.
3. Record the purchase of inventory.
4. Record the sale of merchandise.
5. Print an Income Statement and Balance Sheet that shows the cost of goods sold.

Problem 25-4   Calculating the Cost of Ending Inventory

INSTRUCTIONS

Beginning a Session

Step 1   Select the problem set: Sunset Surfwear (Prob. 25-4).

Step 2   Rename the company, and set the system date to December 31, 2004.

Completing the Accounting Problem

Step 3   Review the information provided in your textbook.

Step 4   Update the inventory record for the wet suit (Item 231WS). Change the cost to $244.

To update an inventory item:

- Choose **Inventory Items** from the **Maintain** menu.
- Type **231WS** in the *Item ID* field.
- Move to the *Cost* field and enter **244.00** for the item cost.

Compare your screen to the inventory item shown in Figure 25-4A.

- Click ![Save] to record the changes.
- Close the Maintain Inventory Items window.

DO YOU HAVE A QUESTION

Q. *What inventory valuation methods does Peachtree support?*

A. Peachtree supports the following inventory valuation methods: FIFO, LIFO, and average cost. However, once you set up an item and specify the valuation method, you cannot change this information. For that reason, you can print an Inventory Valuation Report based on only one valuation method.

Notes

When you record purchases and sales, Peachtree automatically updates the merchandise inventory account.

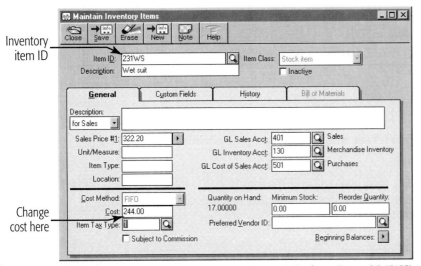

Inventory item ID

Change cost here

Figure 25-4A *Maintain Inventory Items Window (Item 231WS)*

Step 5 Print an Inventory Valuation Report.

  The Inventory Valuation Report shows costing method, quantity on hand, and item value for each inventory item. Peachtree automatically calculates the inventory valuation based on the method set up for each item.

 TIP: Choose **Inventory** from the *Reports* menu to access the inventory reports.

Step 6 Print a Cost of Goods Sold Journal.

  By default, Peachtree uses the current period. To view the Cost of Goods Sold Journal, you must change the report options date to "This Year." The report shows the cost of the items at the time they are sold.

Step 7 Print an Item Costing Report.

  The Item Costing Report gives a detailed listing of all transactions that involved inventory items and their effect on inventory valuation. Compare the information shown on the report to the purchases shown in your textbook.

 TIP: When you choose to print this report, change the printer setup to print in landscape mode.

Ending the Session

Step 8 Click the **Close Problem** button in the Glencoe Smart Guide window to save your work.

Mastering Peachtree

On a separate sheet of paper, explain how you can record minimum quantity and reorder quantity values for an inventory item. How would a company use this information?

Problem 25-7 Reporting Ending Inventory on the Income Statement

INSTRUCTIONS

Beginning a Session

Step 1 Select the problem set: Cycle Tech Bicycles (Prob. 25-7).
Step 2 Rename the company, and set the system date to December 31, 2004.

Completing the Accounting Problem

Step 3 Review the information provided in your textbook.
Step 4 Print the following reports: Inventory Valuation Report, Cost of Goods Sold Journal, and Item Costing Report.

TIP: Remember to change the date range for the Cost of Goods Sold Journal to "This Year."

Step 5   Print an Income Statement and a Balance Sheet.

Ending the Session

Step 6   Click the **Close Problem** button in the Glencoe Smart Guide window.

Mastering Peachtree

On a separate sheet of paper, record what inventory valuation method is set for the Model #8274 ten-speed bicycle? How do you set the inventory valuation method?

Problem 25-8   Calculating Cost of Merchandise Sold and Gross Profit on Sales

INSTRUCTIONS

Beginning a Session

Step 1   Select the problem set: Buzz Newsstand (Prob. 25-8).
Step 2   Rename the company, and set the system date to May 31, 2004.

Completing the Accounting Problem

Step 3   Review the information provided in your textbook.
Step 4   Record the merchandise purchases transactions using the **Purchases/ Receive Inventory** option.

> **IMPORTANT:** The invoices are provided in your working papers. Be sure to complete the *Quantity, Item,* and *Unit Price* fields on the Apply to Purchases tab when you record the purchases using the **Purchases/ Receive Inventory** option. See the completed Purchases/Receive Inventory transaction shown in Figure 25-8.

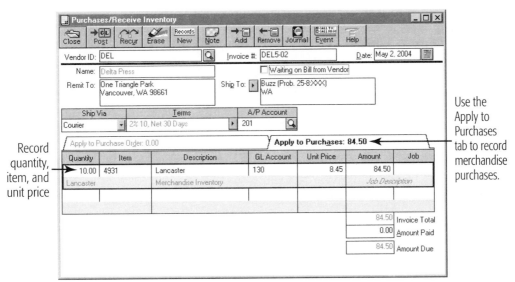

Figure 25-8A *Completed Merchandise Purchase Transaction (May 2)*

Step 5   Record the transportation charges using the **Payments** option. All of the transportation charges are paid in cash to Wolfe Trucking.

Step 6   Record the camera sales using the **Receipts** option.

To record the camera sales:

- Determine the number of cameras sold.
- Choose the **Receipts** option.
- Enter **5/31** for the date, type **Cash Sales** in the *Name* field, and input **T290** for the reference.
- Enter **5/31/04** in the *Date* field.
- On the Apply to Revenues tab enter the information (quantity sold, item ID, and price) for each camera brand as a separate line item.
- Select **1** for the sales tax code.
- Verify the total receipt amount ($857.37) and post.

Step 7   Print a Purchases Journal, Cash Disbursements Journal, and a Cash Receipts Journal to proof your work.

Step 8   Print the following reports: Inventory Valuation Report, Cost of Goods Sold Journal and Item Costing Report.

Step 9   Print an Income Statement.

Step 10 Answer the Analyze question.

Ending the Session

Step 11 Click the **Close Problem** button in the Glencoe Smart Guide window to save your work.

FAQs

Can you change the inventory valuation method for an inventory item?

No, once you set up an inventory item, you cannot change the inventory valuation method. You could delete the item and re-enter it if you have not entered any transactions that affect the item.

Computerized Accounting Using Spreadsheets

Problem 25-6   Calculating Gross Profit on Sales

Completing the Spreadsheet

Step 1 Read the instructions for Problem 25-6 in your textbook. This problem involves calculating gross profit on sales using each of the four inventory costing methods.

Step 2 Open the Glencoe Accounting: Electronic Learning Center software.

Step 3 From the Program Menu, click on the **Peachtree Accounting Software and Spreadsheet Applications** icon.

Step 4 Log onto the Management System by typing your user name and password.

Step 5 Under the Chapter Problems tab, select the template: PR25-6a.xls. The template should look like the one shown below.

```
PROBLEM 25-6
CALCULATING GROSS PROFIT ON SALES

(name)
(date)

                              SPECIFIC                                    WEIGHTED
                              IDENTIFICATION    FIFO          LIFO        AVERAGE COST
                              METHOD            METHOD        METHOD      METHOD

Net Sales
  Purchases Available for Sale
  Cost of Ending Inventory
Cost of Merchandise Sold          $0.00          $0.00         $0.00         $0.00
Gross Profit on Sales             $0.00          $0.00         $0.00         $0.00
```

Step 6 Key your name and today's date in the cells containing the *(name)* and *(date)* placeholders.

Step 7 For each of the four inventory costing methods, enter the following data in the appropriate cells of the spreadsheet template: net sales, purchases available for sale, and cost of ending inventory. The spreadsheet will automatically calculate the cost of merchandise sold and the gross profit on sales for each inventory costing method.

Step 8 Save the spreadsheet using the **Save** option from the *File* menu. You should accept the default location for the save as this is handled by the management system.

Step 9 Print the completed spreadsheet.

Step 10 Exit the spreadsheet program.

Step 11 In the Close Options box, select the location where you would like to save your work.

Step 12 Answer the Analyze question from your textbook for this problem.

Spreadsheet Guide

What-If Analysis

If the cost of ending inventory using the last-in, first-out method were $21,399.13, what would gross profit on sales be?

_____

● **Working Papers** *for End-of-Chapter Problems*

Problem 25-4   Calculating the Cost of Ending Inventory

a. Specific Identification Method   _____

b. FIFO   _____

c. LIFO   _____

d. Weighted Average Method   _____

Analyze: _____

Problem 25-5   Completing an Inventory Sheet

INVENTORY RECORD						
ITEM NO.	ITEM	ENDING INVENTORY	COST PER UNIT	CURRENT MARKET VALUE	PRICE TO BE USED	TOTAL COST
0247	Blank CDs	24	2.67	2.88	2.67	64.08
0391	Blank CDs	36	2.80	2.74		
0388	Cable #4	21	2.91	3.05		
0379	CD Cleaner	6	6.36	8.33		
0380	CD Cleaner	19	7.49	7.51		
0274	Audio Plug	23	6.90	6.95		
0276	Dust Cover	12	8.13	7.95		
0277	Headset	14	9.25	9.57		
0181	Cable #9	18	2.06	2.52		
0193	Cable #5	9	2.29	2.74		
0419	Headset	8	8.42	8.73		
0420	Headset	14	8.98	9.19		
					TOTAL COST	

Analyze: _____

Problem 25-6   Calculating Gross Profit on Sales

	Specific Identification Method	First-In, First-Out Method	Last-In, First-Out Method	Weighted Average Cost Method
Net Sales	$	$	$	$
Cost of Merchandise Sold	$	$	$	$
Gross Profit on Sales	$	$	$	$

Analyze: _____

Problem 25-7   Reporting Ending Inventory on the Income Statement

	FIFO Method	LIFO Method	Weighted Average Cost Method
Ending Inventory	$	$	$
Cost of Merchandise Sold			

FIFO Method

Problem 25-7 (concluded)
LIFO Method

Weighted Average Cost Method

Analyze: _____

Problem 25-8 Source Documents

Instructions: *Use the following source documents to record the transactions for this problem.*

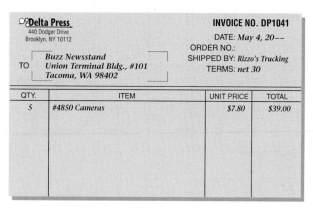

Delta Press
440 Dodger Drive
Brooklyn, NY 10112

INVOICE NO. DP1033
DATE: *May 2, 20--*
ORDER NO.:
SHIPPED BY: *Rizzo's Trucking*
TERMS: *net 30*

TO
Buzz Newsstand
Union Terminal Bldg., #101
Tacoma, WA 98402

QTY.	ITEM	UNIT PRICE	TOTAL
10	#4931 Cameras	$8.45	$84.50

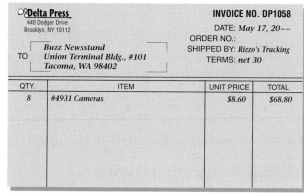

Delta Press
440 Dodger Drive
Brooklyn, NY 10112

INVOICE NO. DP1052
DATE: *May 14, 20--*
ORDER NO.:
SHIPPED BY: *Rizzo's Trucking*
TERMS: *net 30*

TO
Buzz Newsstand
Union Terminal Bldg., #101
Tacoma, WA 98402

QTY.	ITEM	UNIT PRICE	TOTAL
5	#9265 Cameras	$8.25	$41.25

Delta Press
440 Dodger Drive
Brooklyn, NY 10112

INVOICE NO. DP1041
DATE: *May 4, 20--*
ORDER NO.:
SHIPPED BY: *Rizzo's Trucking*
TERMS: *net 30*

TO
Buzz Newsstand
Union Terminal Bldg., #101
Tacoma, WA 98402

QTY.	ITEM	UNIT PRICE	TOTAL
5	#4850 Cameras	$7.80	$39.00

Delta Press
440 Dodger Drive
Brooklyn, NY 10112

INVOICE NO. DP1058
DATE: *May 17, 20--*
ORDER NO.:
SHIPPED BY: *Rizzo's Trucking*
TERMS: *net 30*

TO
Buzz Newsstand
Union Terminal Bldg., #101
Tacoma, WA 98402

QTY.	ITEM	UNIT PRICE	TOTAL
8	#4931 Cameras	$8.60	$68.80

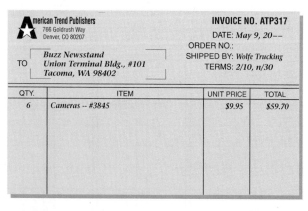

American Trend Publishers
766 Goldrush Way
Denver, CO 80207

INVOICE NO. ATP317
DATE: *May 9, 20--*
ORDER NO.:
SHIPPED BY: *Wolfe Trucking*
TERMS: *2/10, n/30*

TO
Buzz Newsstand
Union Terminal Bldg., #101
Tacoma, WA 98402

QTY.	ITEM	UNIT PRICE	TOTAL
6	Cameras -- #3845	$9.95	$59.70

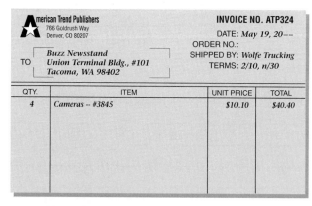

American Trend Publishers
766 Goldrush Way
Denver, CO 80207

INVOICE NO. ATP324
DATE: *May 19, 20--*
ORDER NO.:
SHIPPED BY: *Wolfe Trucking*
TERMS: *2/10, n/30*

TO
Buzz Newsstand
Union Terminal Bldg., #101
Tacoma, WA 98402

QTY.	ITEM	UNIT PRICE	TOTAL
4	Cameras -- #3845	$10.10	$40.40

WOLFE TRUCKING
515 Main Street
Denver, CO 80208

INVOICE NO. WT50557
DATE: *May 9, 20--*
ORDER NO.:
SHIPPED BY:
TERMS: *Due upon receipt*

TO
Buzz Newsstand
Union Terminal Bldg., #101
Tacoma, WA 98402

DATE	SERVICE	AMOUNT
5/9	Delivered Cameras	$4.00

WOLFE TRUCKING
515 Main Street
Denver, CO 80208

INVOICE NO. WT50603
DATE: *May 19, 20--*
ORDER NO.:
SHIPPED BY:
TERMS: *Due upon receipt*

TO
Buzz Newsstand
Union Terminal Bldg., #101
Tacoma, WA 98402

DATE	SERVICE	AMOUNT
5/19	Delivered Cameras	$5.00

Problem 25-8   (continued)

Delta Press		INVOICE NO. DP1067	
440 Dodger Drive		DATE: *May 27, 20--*	
Brooklyn, NY 10112		ORDER NO.:	
		SHIPPED BY: *Rizzo's Trucking*	
TO	*Buzz Newsstand*	TERMS: *net 30*	
	Union Terminal Bldg., #101		
	Tacoma, WA 98402		

QTY.	ITEM	UNIT PRICE	TOTAL
8	*#9265 Cameras*	*$8.30*	*$66.40*

Delta Press		INVOICE NO. DP1071	
440 Dodger Drive		DATE: *May 29, 20--*	
Brooklyn, NY 10112		ORDER NO.:	
		SHIPPED BY: *Rizzo's Trucking*	
TO	*Buzz Newsstand*	TERMS: *net 30*	
	Union Terminal Bldg., #101		
	Tacoma, WA 98402		

QTY.	ITEM	UNIT PRICE	TOTAL
4	*#4931 Cameras*	*$8.85*	*$35.40*

Problem 25-8 Calculating Cost of Merchandise Sold and Gross Profit on Sales

(1)

#3845 _____   #4931 _____

#9265 _____   #4850 _____

(2)

	Item			
	3845	**4931**	**9265**	**4850**
Sales for Month				
Value of Beginning Inventory				
Purchases for May				
Transportation Costs				
Net Purchases for May				
Goods Available for Sale				
Value of Ending Inventory				
Cost of Merchandise Sold				
Gross Profit on Sales				

Analyze: _____

CHAPTER 25   Inventories

Self-Test

Part A   True or False

Directions: *Circle the letter* T *in the Answer column if the statement is true; circle the letter* F *if the statement is false.*

Answer

T   F   **1.** The specific identification method is used by most businesses.

T   F   **2.** The LIFO method assumes that the first items purchased are the ones still remaining.

T   F   **3.** A perpetual inventory system can be established without using a computer.

T   F   **4.** When the inventory is valued using the weighted average cost method, the value is usually between the values determined by the LIFO and FIFO methods.

T   F   **5.** The market value of the merchandise on hand is always higher than the original cost.

T   F   **6.** The consistency principle does not permit businesses to change inventory costing methods so the financial statements can be compared.

T   F   **7.** The weighted average cost method is the most accurate of the inventory costing methods.

T   F   **8.** The costing method used to determine the value of the ending inventory will affect the gross profit on sales.

T   F   **9.** An automobile dealership could use the specific identification costing method without much difficulty.

T   F   **10.** If a business uses a perpetual inventory system, a periodic inventory is never needed.

T   F   **11.** The FIFO method assumes that the items still in inventory were the last ones purchased.

T   F   **12.** A business must take the higher of the determined cost of the existing inventory or the current market replacement value.

Part B Fill in the Missing Term

Directions: _In the Answer column, write the letter of the word or phrase that best completes the sentence. Some answers may be used more than once._

A. conservatism principle	**F.** periodic inventory system
B. consistency principle	**G.** perpetual inventory system
C. FIFO method	**H.** point-of-sale terminal
D. LIFO method	**I.** specific identification method
E. market value	**J.** weighted average cost method

Answer

_____ **1.** A cash register that inputs data into a computer is called a _____.

_____ **2.** The current price being charged for an item of merchandise in the market is called _____.

_____ **3.** The _____ is usually used by businesses that input all purchases and sales into a computer system when the transactions occur.

_____ **4.** _____ is an inventory method that assumes that the items purchased at the beginning of the period are the first items sold.

_____ **5.** The _____ presents amounts that are least likely to result in an overstatement of income or property values when reporting a business's financial position.

_____ **6.** An inventory method in which the actual cost of each item must be determined is the _____.

_____ **7.** A _____ is used when items on hand are counted to update the inventory records.

_____ **8.** _____ is an inventory method in which the cost of items on hand is determined by averaging the costs of all similar items purchased during the period.

_____ **9.** Businesses do not normally change inventory costing methods because of the _____.

_____ **10.** _____ is an inventory method that assumes that the items purchased at the end of the period are the first items sold.

CHAPTER 26 Notes Payable and Receivable

Study Plan

Check Your Understanding

Section 1	*Read Section 1 on pages 702–706 and complete the exercises on page 707.* ❑ Thinking Critically ❑ Computing in the Business World ❑ Problem 26-1 *Calculating Interest and Finding Maturity Values* ❑ Problem 26-2 *Calculating Interest*
Section 2	*Read Section 2 on pages 708–714 and complete the exercises on page 715.* ❑ Thinking Critically ❑ Communicating Accounting ❑ Problem 26-3 *Recording the Issuance of an Interest-Bearing Note Payable* ❑ Problem 26-4 *Recording the Issuance of a Noninterest-Bearing Note Payable*
Section 3	*Read Section 3 on pages 716–717 and complete the exercises on page 718.* ❑ Thinking Critically ❑ Analyzing Accounting ❑ Problem 26-5 *Analyzing a Source Document*
Summary	*Review the Chapter 26 Summary on page 719 in your textbook.* ❑ Key Concepts
Review and Activities	*Complete the following questions and exercises on pages 720–721.* ❑ Using Key Terms ❑ Understanding Accounting Concepts and Procedures ❑ Case Study ❑ Conducting an Audit with Alex ❑ Internet Connection ❑ Workplace Skills
Computerized Accounting	*Read the Computerized Accounting information on page 722.* ❑ *Making the Transition from a Manual to a Computerized System* ❑ *Recording Notes Receivable and Payable in Peachtree*
Problems	*Complete the following end-of-chapter problems for Chapter 26.* ❑ Problem 26-6 *Recording Transactions for Interest-Bearing Notes Payable* ❑ Problem 26-7 *Recording Transactions for Noninterest-Bearing Notes Payable* ❑ Problem 26-8 *Recording Notes Payable and Notes Receivable* ❑ Problem 26-9 *Recording Notes Payable and Notes Receivable*
Challenge Problem	❑ Problem 26-10 *Renewing a Note Receivable*
Chapter Reviews and Working Papers	*Complete the following exercises for Chapter 26 in your Chapter Reviews and Working Papers.* ❑ Chapter Review ❑ Self-Test

CHAPTER 26 REVIEW Notes Payable and Receivable

Part 1 Accounting Vocabulary (18 points)

Directions: *Using terms from the following list, complete the sentences below. Write the letter of the term you have chosen in the space provided.*

Total Points	47	
Student's Score		

A. bank discount	**F.** issue date	**K.** note payable	**P.** principal
B. face value	**G.** maker	**L.** note receivable	**Q.** proceeds
C. interest	**H.** maturity date	**M.** other expense	**R.** promissory note
D. interest-bearing note payable	**I.** maturity value	**N.** other revenue	**S.** term
E. interest rate	**J.** noninterest-bearing note payable	**O.** payee	

_____*B*_____ **0.** The _____ of a promissory note is the amount of money written on the face of the note.

_____ **1.** The date on which a note is written is called its _____.

_____ **2.** The _____ of the note is the person or business promising to repay the principal and interest.

_____ **3.** A(n) _____ is a promissory note issued to a creditor or by a business to borrow money from a bank.

_____ **4.** The _____ is the date on which the note must be paid.

_____ **5.** The amount of interest to be charged stated as a percentage of the principal is called the _____.

_____ **6.** The amount being borrowed is the _____ of the note.

_____ **7.** A promissory note that a business accepts from a customer who needs additional time to pay a debt is called a(n) _____.

_____ **8.** _____ is the fee charged for the use of money.

_____ **9.** A note that requires the face value plus interest be paid on the maturity date is called a(n) _____.

_____ **10.** The _____ is the amount of time that the borrower has to repay a promissory note.

_____ **11.** The person or business to whom a promissory note is made payable is the _____.

_____ **12.** A(n) _____ is a written promise to pay a business or a person a certain amount of money at a specific time.

_____ **13.** The interest deducted in advance from a non-interest-bearing note payable is called the _____.

_____ **14.** An expense that does not result from the normal operations of the business is called a(n) _____.

_____ **15.** A promissory note from which the interest has been deducted in advance and which therefore has no interest rate stated on the note itself is called a(n) _____.

_____ **16.** The amount of cash actually received by the borrower of a non-interest-bearing note payable is called the _____.

_____ **17.** The _____ of a note is the principal plus the interest.

_____ **18.** _____ is revenue that a business receives or earns from activities outside the normal operations of the business.

Part 2 Examining Notes Payable and Receivable (15 points)

Directions: *Read each of the following statements to determine whether the statement is true or false. Write your answer in the space provided.*

___*True*___ **0.** Promissory notes are formal documents that provide evidence that credit was granted or received.

_____ **1.** When a noninterest-bearing note payable is paid, the interest charge is transferred from the Notes Payable account to the Interest Expense account.

_____ **2.** Interest = Principal × Interest Rate × Time is the equation for calculating interest on a promissory note.

_____ **3.** A note receivable is an asset to the business receiving the note.
_____ **4.** Discount on Notes Payable is a liability account.
_____ **5.** Interest rates are usually stated on an annual basis.
_____ **6.** The maturity value of a noninterest-bearing note payable is the same as its face value.
_____ **7.** Notes Receivable is classified as a contra asset account, and its normal balance is a credit.
_____ **8.** Both the term and the issue date are needed to determine the maturity date of a note.
_____ **9.** Borrowing periods of less than one year cannot be used in calculating interest.
_____ **10.** The interest on a 12.5%, $3,500 promissory note for two years is $437.50.
_____ **11.** On interest-bearing notes, the face value and the principal are the same.
_____ **12.** A business may not issue a note payable to borrow money from a bank.
_____ **13.** A noninterest-bearing note payable is the same as an interest-free note.
_____ **14.** Interest income is an example of other revenue and is reported separately on the income statement.
_____ **15.** The payment of a noninterest-bearing note payable and the recognition of the interest expense are always recorded with two separate journal entries in the cash payments journal and in the general journal.

Part 3 Analyzing Transactions Affecting Notes Payable and Receivable
(14 points)

Directions: _Using the following account names, analyze the transactions below. Determine the account(s) to be debited and credited. Write your answers in the space provided._

A. Cash in Bank	**D.** Notes Payable	**G.** Sales
B. Accounts Receivable	**E.** Discount on Notes Payable	**H.** Interest Expense
C. Notes Receivable	**F.** Interest Income	

Debit	Credit	
_B_	_G_	**0.** Sold merchandise on account to a customer.
_____	_____	**1.** Received an interest-bearing note from a customer for payment on account.
_____	_____	**2.** Issued an interest-bearing note payable to the bank for cash.
_____	_____	**3.** Received a check for the payment of the interest-bearing note from the customer.
_____	_____	**4.** Issued a noninterest-bearing note to the bank for cash.
_____	_____	**5.** Wrote a check to the bank for payment of the interest-bearing note.
_____	_____	**6.** Wrote a check to the bank for payment on the noninterest-bearing note.
_____	_____	**7.** Received the interest due on a note receivable and renewed the note for 90 days.

Working Papers *for Section Problems*

Problem 26-1   Calculating Interest and Finding Maturity Values

	Principal	Interest Rate	Term (in days)	Interest	Maturity Value
1	$ 4,000.00	11.50%	60	$	$
2	10,000.00	11.75%	90		
3	6,500.00	12.75%	60		
4	900.00	12.25%	120		
5	2,400.00	12.00%	180		

Problem 26-2   Calculating Interest

	Principal	Interest Rate	Term	Interest
1	$ 600.00	15.00%	90 days	$
2	3,500.00	12.00%	60 days	
3	9,600.00	9.00%	4 months	
4	2,500.00	10.00%	180 days	
5	1,500.00	11.50%	6 months	

Problem 26-3   Recording the Issuance of an Interest-Bearing Note Payable

1. _____

2. _____

3. _____

4. _____

Problem 26-4   Recording the Issuance of a Noninterest-Bearing Note Payable

1. _____

_____

2. _____

_____

Problem 26-5   Analyzing a Source Document

GENERAL JOURNAL   PAGE _____

	DATE	DESCRIPTION	POST. REF.	DEBIT	CREDIT	
1						1
2						2
3						3
4						4
5						5
6						6
7						7
8						8
9						9
10						10

Computerized Accounting Using Peachtree

Software Objectives

When you have completed this chapter, you will be able to use Peachtree to:

1. Record transactions involving notes payable.
2. Record notes receivable transactions.

Problem 26-6   Recording Transactions for Interest-Bearing Notes Payable

INSTRUCTIONS

Beginning a Session

Step 1   Select the problem set: Sunset Surfwear (Prob. 26-6).

Step 2   Rename the company, and set the system date to December 31, 2004.

Completing the Accounting Problem

Step 3   Review the information provided in your textbook.

Step 4   Record the transactions using the **Receipts** and **Payments** options. Remember to enter each transaction in the appropriate accounting period. Use the **System** option from the **Tasks** menu to change the accounting period before entering each transaction.

> **DO YOU HAVE A QUESTION**
>
> **Q.** *Can you use Peachtree to record a multi-part cash payment entry?*
>
> **A.** Using Peachtree you can record a multi-part cash payment entry. For example, you can record the payment of a notes payable with interest using the **Payments** option. Simply record each part of the entry in the space provided on the Apply to Expenses tab. Be sure to change the *GL Account* field for each part.

 TIP: You can enter a multi-part transaction using the **Payments** option to record the payment of a note and interest. (See Figure 26-6A.)

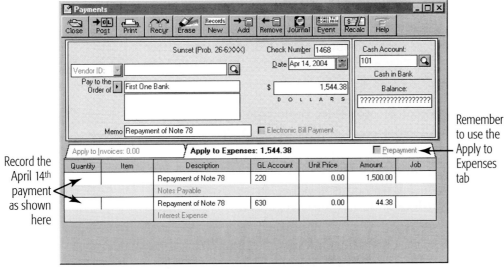

Record the April 14th payment as shown here

Remember to use the Apply to Expenses tab

Figure 26-6A *Multi-Part Cash Payment Entry (April 14)*

Step 5 Print a Cash Receipts Journal and a Cash Disbursements Journal to proof your work.

TIP: Be sure to set the date range on the journal reports to print the transactions for the entire year.

Step 6 Answer the Analyze question.

Ending the Session

Step 7 Verify that the accounting period of 8/1/04 to 8/31/04 is displayed in the lower right hand corner. Click the **Close Problem** button in the Glencoe Smart Guide window.

Mastering Peachtree

Answer the following on a separate sheet of paper. Does Peachtree provide any features that allow you to set up a reminder to pay a note? Explain your answer.

Problem 26-7   Recording Transactions for Noninterest-Bearing Notes Payable

INSTRUCTIONS

Beginning a Session

Step 1 Select the problem set: InBeat CD Shop (Prob. 26-7).
Step 2 Rename the company, and set the system date to December 31, 2004.

Completing the Accounting Problem

Step 3 Review the information provided in your textbook.
Step 4 Record the notes payable transactions. Remember to enter each transaction in the appropriate accounting period. Use the **System** option from the *Tasks* menu to change the accounting period.

TIP: When you record the cash receipt for a discounted note, enter the discount as a negative amount on the Apply to Revenues tab.

Step 5 Print a Cash Receipts Journal and a Cash Disbursements Journal to proof your work. Set the date range to include the entire year.
Step 6 Answer the Analyze question.

Checking Your Work and Ending the Session

Step 7 Verify that the accounting period displayed is 12/1/04 to 12/31/04. Click the **Close Problem** button in the Glencoe Smart Guide window.
Step 8 If your teacher has asked you to check your solution, select *Check my answer to this problem*. Review, print, and close the report.
Step 9 Click the **Close Problem** button and select a save option.

Peachtree Guide

Problem 26-8   Recording Notes Payable and Notes Receivable

INSTRUCTIONS

Beginning a Session

Step 1   Select the problem set: Cycle Tech Bicycles (Prob. 26-8).

Step 2   Rename the company, and set the system date to December 31, 2004.

Completing the Accounting Problem

Step 3   Review the information provided in your textbook.

Step 4   Record the transactions. Be sure to enter each transaction in the proper accounting period (month). Use the **System** option from the *Tasks* menu to set the accounting period before entering each transaction.

> **IMPORTANT:** Use the **Receipts** option to record a transaction where a customer replaces an accounts receivable balance with a promissory note. Change the Cash (GL Account) to **Notes Receivable**. Mark the invoice(s) as "paid" and post the transaction. Be sure to reset the Cash account before you record any other cash receipts.

Step 5   Print a Cash Receipts Journal and a Cash Disbursements Journal to proof your work.

Step 6   Answer the Analyze question.

Ending the Session

Step 7   Verify that the accounting period displayed in the lower right hand corner of your screen is 12/1/04 to 12/31/04. Click the **Close Problem** button in the Glencoe Smart Guide window to save your work.

Problem 26-9   Recording Notes Payable and Notes Receivable

INSTRUCTIONS

Beginning a Session

Step 1   Select the problem set: River's Edge Canoe & Kayak (Prob. 26-9).

Step 2   Rename the company, and set the system date to September 30, 2004.

Completing the Accounting Problem

Step 3   Review the information provided in your textbook.

Step 4   Record the transactions. Be sure to enter each transaction in the proper accounting period. Use the **System** option from the *Tasks* menu to set the accounting period before entering each transaction.

> **IMPORTANT:** Use the **Receipts** option to record a transaction where a customer replaces an accounts receivable balance with a promissory note. Change the Cash (GL Account) to **Notes Receivable**. Mark the invoice(s) as "paid" and post the transaction. Be sure to reset the Cash account before you record any other cash receipts.
>
> Use the **Payments** option to record a transaction when a company issues a note to a vendor in place of an amount owed on account. Change the Cash (GL Account) to **Notes Payable**. Mark the invoice(s) as "paid" and post the transaction. Be sure to reset the Cash account before you record any other cash payments.

Name Date Class

Step 5 Print a Cash Receipts Journal and a Cash Disbursements Journal to proof your work.

TIP: Be sure to set the date range on the journal reports to print the transactions for the entire year.

Step 6 Answer the Analyze question.

Checking Your Work and Ending the Session

Step 7 Verify that the accounting period displayed in the lower right hand corner of your screen is 9/1/04 to 9/30/04. Click the **Close Problem** button in the Glencoe Smart Guide window.

Step 8 If your teacher has asked you to check your solution, select *Check my answer to this problem.* Review, print, and close the report.

Step 9 Click the **Close Problem** button and select a save option.

Problem 26-10 Renewing a Note Receivable

INSTRUCTIONS

Beginning a Session

Step 1 Select the problem set: Buzz Newsstand (Prob. 26-10).

Step 2 Rename the company, and set the system date to September 30, 2004.

Completing the Accounting Problem

Step 3 Review the information provided in your textbook.

Step 4 Record the transactions. Be sure to record each transaction in the proper accounting period.

Step 5 Print a Sales Journal, Cash Receipts Journal and a General Journal to proof your work.

Step 6 Answer the Analyze question.

Ending the Session

Step 7 Verify that the accounting period displayed on your screen is 9/1/04 to 9/30/04. Click the **Close Problem** button in the Glencoe Smart Guide window to save your work.

FAQs

Why don't some Peachtree reports show all of the transactions?

By default, most Peachtree reports show only those transactions entered in the current period. If you entered transactions over multiple periods, you must change the report date option. For example, change the date range to include the entire year.

Problem 26-6   Recording Transactions for Interest-Bearing Notes Payable

CASH RECEIPTS JOURNAL

PAGE _____

	DATE	DOC. NO.	ACCOUNT NAME	POST. REF.	GENERAL DEBIT	GENERAL CREDIT	SALES CREDIT	SALES TAX PAYABLE CREDIT	ACCOUNTS RECEIVABLE CREDIT	CASH IN BANK DEBIT	
1											1
2											2
3											3
4											4
5											5
6											6
7											7
8											8
9											9
10											10

CASH PAYMENTS JOURNAL

PAGE _____

	DATE	DOC. NO.	ACCOUNT NAME	POST. REF.	GENERAL DEBIT	GENERAL CREDIT	ACCOUNTS PAYABLE DEBIT	PURCHASES DISCOUNTS CREDIT	CASH IN BANK CREDIT	
1										1
2										2
3										3
4										4
5										5
6										6
7										7
8										8
9										9
10										10

Analyze: _____

Problem 26-7 Recording Transactions for Noninterest-Bearing Notes Payable

CASH RECEIPTS JOURNAL

PAGE _____

DATE	DOC. NO.	ACCOUNT NAME	POST. REF.	GENERAL DEBIT	GENERAL CREDIT	SALES CREDIT	SALES TAX PAYABLE CREDIT	ACCOUNTS RECEIVABLE CREDIT	CASH IN BANK DEBIT

CASH PAYMENTS JOURNAL

PAGE _____

DATE	DOC. NO.	ACCOUNT NAME	POST. REF.	GENERAL DEBIT	GENERAL CREDIT	ACCOUNTS PAYABLE DEBIT	PURCHASES DISCOUNTS CREDIT	CASH IN BANK CREDIT

Analyze:

Problem 26-8   Recording Notes Payable and Notes Receivable

CASH RECEIPTS JOURNAL

PAGE _____

| DATE | DOC. NO. | ACCOUNT NAME | POST. REF. | GENERAL | | SALES CREDIT | SALES TAX PAYABLE CREDIT | ACCOUNTS RECEIVABLE CREDIT | CASH IN BANK DEBIT |
				DEBIT	CREDIT				

CASH PAYMENTS JOURNAL

PAGE _____

| DATE | DOC. NO. | ACCOUNT NAME | POST. REF. | GENERAL | | ACCOUNTS PAYABLE DEBIT | PURCHASES DISCOUNTS CREDIT | CASH IN BANK CREDIT |
				DEBIT	CREDIT			

Problem 26-8   (concluded)

GENERAL JOURNAL   PAGE _____

DATE	DESCRIPTION	POST. REF.	DEBIT	CREDIT
1				
2				
3				
4				
5				
6				
7				
8				
9				
10				
11				
12				
13				
14				
15				
16				
17				
18				
19				
20				
21				
22				
23				
24				
25				
26				

Analyze: _____

Problem 26-9   Recording Notes Payable and Notes Receivable

CASH RECEIPTS JOURNAL   PAGE _____

DATE	DOC. NO.	ACCOUNT NAME	POST. REF.	GENERAL DEBIT	GENERAL CREDIT	SALES CREDIT	SALES TAX PAYABLE CREDIT	ACCOUNTS RECEIVABLE CREDIT	CASH IN BANK DEBIT
1									
2									
3									
4									
5									
6									
7									
8									
9									
10									

CASH PAYMENTS JOURNAL   PAGE _____

DATE	DOC. NO.	ACCOUNT NAME	POST. REF.	GENERAL DEBIT	GENERAL CREDIT	ACCOUNTS PAYABLE DEBIT	PURCHASES DISCOUNTS CREDIT	CASH IN BANK CREDIT
1								
2								
3								
4								
5								
6								
7								
8								
9								
10								

Analyze: _____

Problem 26-9 (concluded)

GENERAL JOURNAL

PAGE _____

	DATE	DESCRIPTION	POST. REF.	DEBIT	CREDIT	
1						1
2						2
3						3
4						4
5						5
6						6
7						7
8						8
9						9
10						10
11						11
12						12
13						13
14						14
15						15
16						16
17						17
18						18
19						19
20						20
21						21
22						22
23						23
24						24
25						25
26						26

Analyze: _____

Problem 26-10 Source Documents

Instructions: *Use the following source documents to record the transactions for this business.*

BUZZ NEWSSTAND
Union Terminal Building, #101
Tacoma, WA 98402

DATE: *March 14, 20--*   NO. *388*

SOLD TO	*Saba Nadal* *1306 Hampstead Ct.* *Seattle, WA 98134*		
CLERK *B.A.*	CASH	CHARGE ✓	TERMS *n/30*

QTY.	DESCRIPTION	UNIT PRICE	AMOUNT	
30	*Travel planning software*	*$40.00*	*$1,200*	*00*
6 cs	*Magazines*	*100/cs*	*600*	*00*
		SUBTOTAL	*$1,800*	*00*
		SALES TAX	*108*	*00*
		TOTAL	*$1,908*	*00*

Thank You!

NOTE NO. 417

$ ___1,908.00___   Date *June 12* ___ 20 --

Ninety days _____ after date I promise to pay to

Buzz Newsstand _____ the sum of

One thousand nine hundred eight dollars ___ with interest at the

rate of ___10%___ per year.

Due date *September 10* 20 --

Saba Nadal

NOTE NO. 416

$ ___1,908.00___   Date *April 13* ___ 20 --

Sixty days _____ after date I promise to pay to

Buzz Newsstand _____ the sum of

One thousand nine hundred eight dollars ___ with interest at the

rate of ___9%___ per year.

Due date *June 12* ___ 20 --

Saba Nadal

BUZZ NEWSSTAND
Union Terminal Building, #101
Tacoma, WA 98402

RECEIPT
No. 1555

September 10 20 --

RECEIVED FROM *Saba Nadal* $ *1,955.05*

One thousand nine hundred fifty-five and [05]/100 ___ DOLLARS

FOR *Payment for note issued June 12, 20 --*

RECEIVED BY *Kathy Harper*

BUZZ NEWSSTAND
Union Terminal Building, #101
Tacoma, WA 98402

RECEIPT
No. 1387

June 12 20 --

RECEIVED FROM *Saba Nadal* $ *28.23*

Twenty-eight and [23]/100 ___ DOLLARS

FOR *Interest on note*

RECEIVED BY *Kathy Harper*

Problem 26-10   Renewing a Note Receivable

GENERAL JOURNAL   PAGE _____

	DATE		DESCRIPTION	POST. REF.	DEBIT	CREDIT	
1							1
2							2
3							3
4							4
5							5
6							6
7							7
8							8
9							9
10							10
11							11
12							12
13							13
14							14
15							15
16							16
17							17
18							18
19							19
20							20
21							21
22							22
23							23
24							24
25							25
26							26

Analyze: _____

CHAPTER 26 — Notes Payable and Receivable

Self-Test

Part A Fill in the Missing Term

Directions: *In the Answer column, write the letter of the word or phrase that best completes the sentence. Not all of the terms will be used.*

A. bank discount	**G.** issue date	**M.** note receivable
B. Discount on Notes Payable	**H.** maker	**N.** payee
	I. maturity date	**O.** principal
C. face value	**J.** maturity value	**P.** proceeds
D. interest	**K.** noninterest-bearing note payable	**Q.** promissory note
E. interest-bearing note		**R.** term
F. interest rate	**L.** note payable	

Answer

_____ 1. The _____ is the percentage of the principal that is charged for the use of the money.

_____ 2. The amount being borrowed when a promissory note is issued or received is called the _____.

_____ 3. A contra liability account representing future interest charges that have already been paid is the _____ account.

_____ 4. The _____ is the due date of a note or the date on which the principal and interest must be paid.

_____ 5. The _____ of a promissory note is the amount of time the borrower has to repay it.

_____ 6. _____ is the principal plus the interest on a promissory note.

_____ 7. The _____ is the date on which a note is written.

_____ 8. The _____ on a promissory note is the person or business that promises to repay the principal and the interest.

_____ 9. A(n) _____ is a note from which the interest has been deducted in advance.

_____ 10. The amount of cash actually received by the borrower when a noninterest-bearing note payable is issued is the _____.

_____ 11. The charge for the use of the principal borrowed on a promissory note is the _____.

_____ 12. A(n) _____ is a note that requires the face value plus interest to be paid at maturity.

Part B   True or False

Directions: *Circle the letter* T *in the answer column if the statement is true; circle the letter* F *if the statement is false.*

Answer

T   F   **1.** The due date for a 30-day note dated April 10 is May 9.

T   F   **2.** When a note is signed, the maker agrees to repay the note within a certain period of time.

T   F   **3.** The Interest Expense account is increased by a credit.

T   F   **4.** The account Discount on Notes Payable has a normal debit balance.

T   F   **5.** Notes Payable is credited when a company issues a promise to repay a debt.

T   F   **6.** A person or business may issue a promissory note to obtain a loan from a bank.

T   F   **7.** Interest expense for a noninterest-bearing note is recorded on the maturity date.

MINI PRACTICE SET 5

Kite Loft Inc.

CHART OF ACCOUNTS

ASSETS
101   Cash in Bank
105   Accounts Receivable
110   Merchandise Inventory
115   Supplies
120   Prepaid Insurance
125   Office Equipment
130   Store Equipment

LIABILITIES
201   Accounts Payable
205   Employees' Federal Income
          Tax Payable
210   Sales Tax Payable

STOCKHOLDERS' EQUITY
301   Capital Stock
305   Retained Earnings
310   Income Summary

REVENUE
401   Sales
405   Sales Discounts
410   Sales Returns and Allowances

COST OF MERCHANDISE
501   Purchases
505   Transportation In
510   Purchases Discounts
515   Purchases Returns and Allowances

EXPENSES
605   Advertising Expense
610   Bankcard Fees Expense
615   Insurance Expense
620   Miscellaneous Expense
625   Rent Expense
630   Salaries Expense
635   Supplies Expense
640   Utilities Expense
650   Federal Income Tax Expense

Accounts Receivable Subsidiary Ledger
BES   Best Toys
LAR   Lars' Specialties
SER   Serendipity Shop
SMA   Small Town Toys
TOY   The Toy Store

Accounts Payable Subsidiary Ledger
BRA   Brad Kites, Ltd.
CRE   Creative Kites, Inc.
EAS   Easy Glide Co.
RED   Reddi-Bright Manufacturing
STA   Stars Kites Outlet
TAY   Taylor Office Supplies

Mini Practice Set 5   Source Documents

Instructions: *Use the following source documents to record the transactions for this practice set.*

Reddi & Bright
MANUFACTURING
127 Hill Street, #5000
Druid Hills, GA 30333

INVOICE NO. 410

DATE: *Dec. 16, 20--*
ORDER NO.:
SHIPPED BY:
TERMS:

TO Kite Loft Inc.
112 Ashby Drive
Atlanta, GA 30308

QTY.	ITEM	UNIT PRICE	TOTAL
	General merchandise		$1,475.00

Taylor Office Supplies
212 Morningside Drive
Atlanta, GA 30305

INVOICE NO. 830

DATE: *December 17, 20--*
ORDER NO.:
SHIPPED BY:
TERMS:

TO Kite Loft Inc.
112 Ashby Drive
Atlanta, GA 30308

QTY.	ITEM	UNIT PRICE	TOTAL
2	Calendar/Planner	$40.00	$80.00

Kite Loft Inc.
112 Ashby Drive
Atlanta, GA 30308

610
4-571
6212

DATE *December 16* 20--

PAY TO THE ORDER OF *Internal Revenue Service* $ *1,050.00*

One thousand fifty and 00/100 ———————— DOLLARS

S *Sanwa Bank*

MEMO *Qtrly. fed. inc. tax*   *Michael Ramspart*

⑆621245?⑆ 2323 1112⑈ 0610

Kite Loft Inc.
112 Ashby Drive
Atlanta, GA 30308

RECEIPT
No. 358

December 17 20--

RECEIVED FROM *Best Toys* $ *1,965.60*

One thousand nine hundred sixty-five and 60/100 —— DOLLARS

FOR *Sales slip #479 for $2,003.40, less $37.80 discount*

RECEIVED BY *Michael Ramspart*

Kite Loft Inc.
112 Ashby Drive
Atlanta, GA 30308

611
4-571
6212

DATE *December 16* 20--

PAY TO THE ORDER OF *Brad Kites, Ltd.* $ *2,548.00*

Two thousand five hundred forty-eight and 00/100 ——— DOLLARS

S *Sanwa Bank*

MEMO *#112 $2600 less disc.*   *Michael Ramspart*

⑆621245?⑆ 2323 1112⑈ 0611

Kite Loft Inc.
112 Ashby Drive
Atlanta, GA 30308

DATE: *December 19, 20--*   NO. *484*

SOLD TO *Best Toys*

CLERK	CASH	CHARGE	TERMS

QTY.	DESCRIPTION	UNIT PRICE	AMOUNT	
26	Kites	$100.00	$2,600	00
		SUBTOTAL	$2,600	00
		SALES TAX	156	00
		TOTAL	$2,756	00

Thank You!

Kite Loft Inc.
112 Ashby Drive
Atlanta, GA 30308

612
4-571
6212

DATE *December 17* 20--

PAY TO THE ORDER OF *Payroll Account* $ *4,750.00*

Four thousand seven hundred fifty and 00/100 ——— DOLLARS

S *Sanwa Bank*

MEMO *Monthly payroll*   *Michael Ramspart*

⑆621245?⑆ 2323 1112⑈ 0612

Mini Practice Set 5   (continued)

Kite Loft Inc.
112 Ashby Drive
Atlanta, GA 30308

RECEIPT
No. 359

December 19 20 --

RECEIVED FROM _Lars' Specialties_ $ _1,716.00_

One thousand seven hundred sixteen and $^{00}/_{100}$ —— DOLLARS

FOR _Payment of sales slip #480 for $1,749, less $33 discount_

RECEIVED BY _Michael Ramspart_

Brad Kites, Ltd.
633 Louise Street
Atlanta, GA 30303

INVOICE NO. 215
DATE: _Dec. 20, 20--_
ORDER NO.:
SHIPPED BY:
TERMS:

TO   _Kite Loft Inc._
112 Ashby Drive
Atlanta, GA 30308

QTY.	ITEM	UNIT PRICE	TOTAL
50	Kites	$31.20	$1,560.00

Kite Loft Inc.
112 Ashby Drive
Atlanta, GA 30308

613
4-571
6212

DATE _December 20_ 20--

PAY TO THE ORDER OF _Creative Kites, Inc._ $ _375.00_

Three hundred seventy-five and $^{00}/_{100}$ —— DOLLARS

S _Sanwa Bank_

MEMO _on account_   _Michael Ramspart_

⑆621245710⑆ 2323 1112'' 0613

Kite Loft Inc.
112 Ashby Drive
Atlanta, GA 30308

CREDIT MEMORANDUM   NO. _44_

ORIGINAL SALES DATE	ORIGINAL SALES SLIP	APPROVAL	
Dec. 19, 20--	484	M.R.	☒ MDSE RET

DATE: _December 21, 20--_

NAME: _Best Toys_

ADDRESS:

QTY.	DESCRIPTION	AMOUNT
1	Kite	$ 100 00

REASON FOR RETURN _damaged_   SUB TOTAL $ 100 00

THE TOTAL SHOWN AT THE RIGHT WILL BE CREDITED TO YOUR ACCOUNT.   SALES TAX 6 00

Katie Sims   TOTAL $ 106 00

CUSTOMER SIGNATURE

Kite Loft Inc.
112 Ashby Drive
Atlanta, GA 30308

DATE: _December 23, 20--_   NO. _485_

SOLD TO	_Lars' Specialties_		
CLERK	CASH	CHARGE	TERMS

QTY.	DESCRIPTION	UNIT PRICE	AMOUNT
100	Kites	$15.80	$1,580 00
		SUBTOTAL	$1,580 00
		SALES TAX	94 80
		TOTAL	$1,674 80

Thank You!

Kite Loft Inc.
112 Ashby Drive
Atlanta, GA 30308

RECEIPT
No. 360

December 23 20 --

RECEIVED FROM _Serendipity Shop_ $ _300.00_

Three hundred and $^{00}/_{100}$ —— DOLLARS

FOR _Payment on account_

RECEIVED BY _Michael Ramspart_

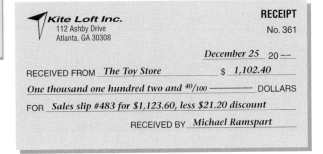

Kite Loft Inc.
112 Ashby Drive
Atlanta, GA 30308

614
4-571
6212

DATE _December 23_ 20--

PAY TO THE ORDER OF _Easy Glide Co._ $ _1,852.20_

One thousand eight hundred fifty-two and $^{20}/_{100}$ —— DOLLARS

S _Sanwa Bank_

MEMO _#326 $1890 less disc._   _Michael Ramspart_

⑆621245710⑆ 2323 1112'' 0614

Kite Loft Inc.
112 Ashby Drive
Atlanta, GA 30308

RECEIPT
No. 361

December 25 20 --

RECEIVED FROM _The Toy Store_ $ _1,102.40_

One thousand one hundred two and $^{40}/_{100}$ —— DOLLARS

FOR _Sales slip #483 for $1,123.60, less $21.20 discount_

RECEIVED BY _Michael Ramspart_

Mini Practice Set 5   (continued)

DEBIT MEMORANDUM   No. *28*

Kite Loft Inc.
112 Ashby Drive
Atlanta, GA 30308

Date: *December 26, 20--*
Invoice No.: *215*

To: *Brad Kites, Ltd.*
633 Louise Street
Atlanta, GA 30303

This day we have debited your account as follows:

Quantity	Item	Unit Price	Total
1	misc. merchandise	$150.00	$150.00

Kite Loft Inc.   **616**
112 Ashby Drive
Atlanta, GA 30308   4-571 / 6212

DATE *December 29* 20--

PAY TO THE ORDER OF *Stars Kites Outlet* $ *1,625.00*

One thousand six hundred twenty-five and 00/100 ———— DOLLARS

S *Sanwa Bank*

MEMO *on account*   *Michael Ramspart*

⑆621245711⑆ 2323 1112⑈ 0616

EASY GLIDE CO.   **INVOICE NO. 335**
124 Merric Blvd., #2A
Atlanta, GA 30301   DATE: *Dec. 26, 20--*

ORDER NO.:
SHIPPED BY:
TERMS:

TO   *Kite Loft Inc.*
112 Ashby Drive
Atlanta, GA 30308

QTY.	ITEM	UNIT PRICE	TOTAL
	Specialty kites		$1,630.00

Kite Loft Inc.
112 Ashby Drive
Atlanta, GA 30308

DATE: *December 29, 20--*   NO. *486*

SOLD TO | *The Toy Store*

CLERK	CASH	CHARGE	TERMS

QTY.	DESCRIPTION	UNIT PRICE	AMOUNT	
50	Kites Variety Pack	$39.80	$1,990	00
		SUBTOTAL	$1,990	00
		SALES TAX	119	40
		TOTAL	$2,109	40

Thank You!

Kite Loft Inc.   **615**
112 Ashby Drive
Atlanta, GA 30308   4-571 / 6212

DATE *December 28* 20--

PAY TO THE ORDER OF *Daily Examiner* $ *120.00*

One hundred twenty and 00/100 ———— DOLLARS

S *Sanwa Bank*

MEMO *monthly advertising*   *Michael Ramspart*

⑆621245711⑆ 2323 1112⑈ 0615

Kite Loft Inc.   **617**
112 Ashby Drive
Atlanta, GA 30308   4-571 / 6212

DATE *December 30* 20--

PAY TO THE ORDER OF *Reddi-Bright Manufacturing* $ *700.00*

Seven hundred and 00/100 ———— DOLLARS

S *Sanwa Bank*

MEMO *on account*   *Michael Ramspart*

⑆621245711⑆ 2323 1112⑈ 0617

Kite Loft Inc.   **RECEIPT**
112 Ashby Drive
Atlanta, GA 30308   No. *362*

December 28 20 --

RECEIVED FROM *Small Town Toys* $ *450.00*

Four hundred fifty and 00/100 ———— DOLLARS

FOR *Payment on account*

RECEIVED BY *Michael Ramspart*

Kite Loft Inc.
112 Ashby Drive
Atlanta, GA 30308

DATE: *December 30, 20--*   NO. *487*

SOLD TO | *Serendipity Shop*

CLERK	CASH	CHARGE	TERMS

QTY.	DESCRIPTION	UNIT PRICE	AMOUNT	
28	Kites	$20.00	$560	00
		SUBTOTAL	$560	00
		SALES TAX	33	60
		TOTAL	$593	60

Thank You!

---

770 ■ **Mini Practice Set 5**

Mini Practice Set 5 (continued)

	No. 618
$ _____	
Date *December 31* 20 __	
To _____	
For _____	

	Dollars	Cents
Balance brought forward		
Less Bank Svc. Chg.	*10*	*00*
Less Bankcard fee	*150*	*00*
Total		
Less this check		
Balance carried forward		

Kite Loft Inc.
112 Ashby Drive
Atlanta, GA 30308

618
4-571
6212

DATE *December 31* 20 __

PAY TO THE ORDER OF *Remote Trucking Co.* $ *51.60*

Fifty-one and 60/100 ——————————— DOLLARS

S *Sanwa Bank*

MEMO *transport. charges* *Michael Ramspart*

⑈621245711⑈ 2323 11112⑈ 0618

	No. 619
$ _____	
Date *December 31* 20 __	
To _____	
For _____	

	Dollars	Cents
Balance brought forward		
Add deposits *12/31/-- (T41)*	*4,234*	*81*
12/31/-- (T41)	*1,840*	*45*
Total		
Less this check		
Balance carried forward		

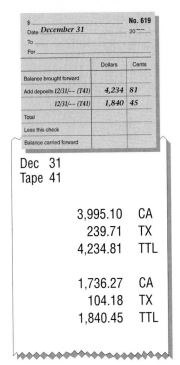

```
Dec  31
Tape 41


    3,995.10   CA
      239.71   TX
    4,234.81   TTL

    1,736.27   CA
      104.18   TX
    1,840.45   TTL
```

Notes

Computerized Accounting Using Peachtree

Mini Practice Set 5

INSTRUCTIONS

Beginning a Session

Step 1   Select the problem set: Kite Loft Inc. (MP-5).

Step 2   Rename the company, and set the system date to December 31, 2004.

Completing the Accounting Problem

Step 3   Review the transactions provided in your textbook (December 16–December 31).

TIP: To save time entering transactions, group them by type and then enter the transactions in batches.

Sales and Cash Receipts

Step 4   Record the sales on account using the **Sales/Invoicing** option.

TIP: Remember that you need to change the GL Account in the Receipts window to enter a cash receipt for the sale of an asset (e.g., supplies, office equipment).

Step 5   Enter and apply any sales returns.

Step 6   Record all of the cash receipts using the **Receipts** option.

TIP: Always verify the sales discount amount when you record a Cash Receipt. Peachtree may not always compute the discount correctly.

Purchases and Cash Payments

Step 7   Enter the purchases on account using the **Purchases/Receive Inventory** option.

TIP: Always verify the *GL Account* field when you enter a purchases on account transaction.

Step 8   Record and apply any purchases returns.

Step 9   Process all of the cash payments with the **Payments** option.

General Journal

Step 10 Use the **General Journal Entry** option to record the adjusting entries.

Peachtree Guide

TIP: You can use the Add and Remove buttons to edit a multi-line general journal entry.

Printing Reports and Proofing Your Work

Step 11 Print the following reports: General Journal, Purchases Journal, Cash Disbursements Journal, Sales Journal, and Cash Receipts Journal.

TIP: Double-click a report title in the Select a Report window to go directly to that report.

Step 12 Proof your work. Print updated reports, if necessary.
Step 13 Print the following reports: General Ledger, Vendor Ledgers, and Customer Ledgers.
Step 14 Print a General Ledger Trial Balance.
Step 15 Print an Income Statement and a Balance Sheet.
Step 16 Manually prepare a Statement of Retained Earnings.

Saving Your Work

Step 17 Click the **Save the Pre-closing Balances** button in the Glencoe Smart Guide window.

Closing the Fiscal Year

Step 18 Use the **Close Fiscal Year** option in the *Tasks* menu to perform the year-end closing.
Step 19 Print a Post-Closing Trial Balance.

Analyzing Your Work

Step 20 Answer the Analyze questions.

Ending the Session

Step 21 Click the **Close Problem** button in the Glencoe Smart Guide window.

Mini Practice Set 5 (continued)
(1), (4)

SALES JOURNAL

PAGE ___22___

	DATE		SALES SLIP NO.	CUSTOMER'S ACCOUNT DEBITED	POST. REF.	SALES CREDIT	SALES TAX PAYABLE CREDIT	ACCOUNTS RECEIVABLE DEBIT	
1	20--								1
2	Dec.	7	479	Best Toys	✓	1 8 9 0 00	1 1 3 40	2 0 0 3 40	2
3		9	480	Lars' Specialties	✓	1 6 5 0 00	9 9 00	1 7 4 9 00	3
4		9	481	Serendipity Shop	✓	1 2 1 9 00	7 3 14	1 2 9 2 14	4
5		12	482	Small Town Toys	✓	8 7 5 00	5 2 50	9 2 7 50	5
6		15	483	The Toy Store	✓	1 0 6 0 00	6 3 60	1 1 2 3 60	6
7									7
8									8
9									9
10									10
11									11
12									12
13									13
14									14
15									15
16									16
17									17
18									18
19									19
20									20
21									21
22									22
23									23
24									24
25									25
26									26
27									27
28									28
29									29
30									30
31									31
32									32
33									33

Mini Practice Set 5   (continued)

CASH RECEIPTS JOURNAL

DATE	DOC. NO.	ACCOUNT NAME	POST. REF.	GENERAL CREDIT	SALES CREDIT	SALES TAX PAYABLE CREDIT	ACCOUNTS RECEIVABLE CREDIT	SALES DISCOUNTS DEBIT	CASH IN BANK DEBIT
20-- Dec. 2	R351	Best Toys	✓				3195 90	60 30	3135 60
3	R352	Store Equipment	130	200 00					200 00
6	R353	Lars' Specialties	✓				1897 40	35 80	1861 60
8	R354	Serendipity Shop	✓				763 60	14 40	749 20
10	R355	Small Town Toys	✓				1284 80		1284 80
12	R356	The Toy Store	✓				1240 20	23 40	1216 80
13	R357	Supplies	115	30 00					30 00
15	T40	Cash Sales	—		3650 70	219 04			3869 74
15	T40	Bankcard Sales	—		1812 40	108 74			1921 14

Mini Practice Set 5   (continued)

PAGE __21__

PURCHASES JOURNAL

DATE	INVOICE NO.	CREDITOR'S ACCOUNT CREDITED	POST. REF.	ACCOUNTS PAYABLE CREDIT	PURCHASES DEBIT	GENERAL ACCOUNT DEBITED	POST. REF.	DEBIT
20--								
Dec. 3	CL213	Creative Kites, Inc.	✓	1 5 0 0 00	1 5 0 0 00			
4	803	Taylor Office Supplies	✓	1 2 5 00		Office Equipment	125	1 2 5 00
7	112	Brad Kites, Ltd.	✓	2 6 0 0 00	2 6 0 0 00			
11	514	Stars Kites Outlet	✓	3 2 5 0 00	3 2 5 0 00			
14	326	Easy Glide Co.	✓	1 8 9 0 00	1 8 9 0 00			

Mini Practice Set 5   (continued)

CASH PAYMENTS JOURNAL

DATE		DOC. NO.	ACCOUNT NAME	POST. REF.	GENERAL DEBIT	ACCOUNTS PAYABLE DEBIT	PURCHASES DISCOUNTS CREDIT	CASH IN BANK CREDIT	
20--									1
Dec.	2	601	Rent Expense	625	70000			70000	2
	5	602	Brad Kites, Ltd.	✓		137500	2750	134750	3
	6	603	Stars Kites Outlet	✓		147000	2940	144060	4
	7	604	Transportation In	505	3720			3720	5
	9	605	Creative Kites, Inc.	✓		109000	2180	106820	6
	11	606	Easy Glide Co.	✓		123500	2470	121030	7
	14	607	Reddi-Bright Mfg.	✓		228000		228000	8
	15	608	Utilities Expense	640	16500			16500	9
	15	609	Taylor Office Supplies	✓		12500		12500	10
									11
									12
									13
									14
									15
									16
									17
									18
									19
									20
									21
									22
									23
									24
									25
									26
									27
									28

Mini Practice Set 5   (continued)
(1), (13), (14)

GENERAL JOURNAL   PAGE ___12___

	DATE		DESCRIPTION	POST. REF.	DEBIT	CREDIT	
1	20--						1
2	Dec.	3	Purchases	501	1 50 00 0		2
3			Merchandise Inventory	110		1 50 00 0	3
4			Memo 30				4
5		5	Sales Returns and Allowances	410	1 20 00		5
6			Sales Tax Payable	210	7 20		6
7			Accts. Rec./Small Town Toys	105 ✓		1 27 20	7
8			Credit Memo 43				8
9		12	Accts. Pay./Reddi-Bright Mfg.	201 ✓	8 0 00		9
10			Purchases Returns and Allowances	515		8 0 00	10
11			Debit Memo 27				11
12							12
13							13
14							14
15							15
16							16
17							17
18							18
19							19
20							20
21							21
22							22
23							23
24							24
25							25
26							26
27							27
28							28
29							29
30							30
31							31
32							32
33							33
34							34
35							35
36							36

Mini Practice Set 5   (continued)
(1)

GENERAL JOURNAL   PAGE _____

	DATE	DESCRIPTION	POST. REF.	DEBIT	CREDIT	
1						1
2						2
3						3
4						4
5						5
6						6
7						7
8						8
9						9
10						10
11						11
12						12
13						13
14						14
15						15
16						16
17						17
18						18
19						19
20						20

(2)

ACCOUNTS RECEIVABLE SUBSIDIARY LEDGER

Name **Best Toys** _____

Address **13400 Midway Road, Dallas, TX 75244** _____

DATE		DESCRIPTION	POST. REF.	DEBIT	CREDIT	BALANCE
20--						
Dec.	1	Balance	✓			3 1 9 5 90
	2		CR23		3 1 9 5 90	————
	7		S22	2 0 0 3 40		2 0 0 3 40

Mini Practice Set 5 (continued)

ACCOUNTS RECEIVABLE SUBSIDIARY LEDGER

Name *Lars' Specialties*

Address *601 O'Hara Road, Arlington, TX 76010*

DATE		DESCRIPTION	POST. REF.	DEBIT	CREDIT	BALANCE
20--						
Dec.	1	Balance	✓			1 8 9 7 40
	6		CR23		1 8 9 7 40	———
	9		S22	1 7 4 9 00		1 7 4 9 00

Name *Serendipity Shop*

Address *835 Coronado Drive, Corpus Christi, TX 78403*

DATE		DESCRIPTION	POST. REF.	DEBIT	CREDIT	BALANCE
20--						
Dec.	1	Balance	✓			7 63 60
	8		CR23		7 63 60	———
	9		S22	1 2 9 2 14		1 2 9 2 14

Name *Small Town Toys*

Address *103 Cedar Park, Dallas, TX 75244*

DATE		DESCRIPTION	POST. REF.	DEBIT	CREDIT	BALANCE
20--						
Dec.	1	Balance	✓			1 4 1 2 00
	5		G12		1 2 7 20	1 2 8 4 80
	10		CR23		1 2 8 4 80	———
	12		S22	9 2 7 50		9 2 7 50

Mini Practice Set 5   (continued)

ACCOUNTS RECEIVABLE SUBSIDIARY LEDGER

Name *The Toy Store*

Address *70 South Washington Street, Fort Worth, TX 76101*

DATE		DESCRIPTION	POST. REF.	DEBIT	CREDIT	BALANCE
20--						
Dec.	1	Balance	✓			1 2 4 0 20
	12		CR23		1 2 4 0 20	—
	15		S22	1 1 2 3 60		1 1 2 3 60

ACCOUNTS PAYABLE SUBSIDIARY LEDGER

Name *Brad Kites, Ltd.*

Address *633 Louise Street NW, Atlanta, GA 30303*

DATE		DESCRIPTION	POST. REF.	DEBIT	CREDIT	BALANCE
20--						
Dec.	1	Balance	✓			1 3 7 5 00
	5		CP24	1 3 7 5 00		—
	7		P21		2 6 0 0 00	2 6 0 0 00

Name *Creative Kites, Inc.*

Address *1900 Talman Avenue North, Chicago, IL 60647*

DATE		DESCRIPTION	POST. REF.	DEBIT	CREDIT	BALANCE
20--						
Dec.	1	Balance	✓			1 0 9 0 00
	3		P21		1 5 0 0 00	2 5 9 0 00
	9		CP24	1 0 9 0 00		1 5 0 0 00

Mini Practice Set 5 (continued)

ACCOUNTS PAYABLE SUBSIDIARY LEDGER

Name *Easy Glide Co.*

Address *124 Merric Blvd. #2A, Atlanta, GA 30301*

DATE		DESCRIPTION	POST. REF.	DEBIT	CREDIT	BALANCE
20--						
Dec.	1	Balance	✓			1 23500
	11		CP24	1 23500		——
	14		P21		1 89000	1 89000

Name *Reddi-Bright Manufacturing*

Address *127 Hill Street #5000, Druid Hills, GA 30333*

DATE		DESCRIPTION	POST. REF.	DEBIT	CREDIT	BALANCE
20--						
Dec.	1	Balance	✓			2 36000
	12		G12	8000		2 28000
	14		CP24	2 28000		——

Name *Stars Kites Outlet*

Address *150 Vista Avenue, St. Louis, MO 63110*

DATE		DESCRIPTION	POST. REF.	DEBIT	CREDIT	BALANCE
20--						
Dec.	1	Balance	✓			1 47000
	6		CP24	1 47000		——
	11		P21		3 25000	3 25000

Mini Practice Set 5   (continued)

ACCOUNTS PAYABLE SUBSIDIARY LEDGER

Name *Taylor Office Supplies*

Address *212 Morningside Drive, Atlanta, GA 30305*

DATE		DESCRIPTION	POST. REF.	DEBIT	CREDIT	BALANCE
20--						
Dec.	4		P21		12500	12500
	15		CP24	12500		—

(3)

GENERAL LEDGER

ACCOUNT   *Cash in Bank*   ACCOUNT NO.   *101*

DATE		DESCRIPTION	POST. REF.	DEBIT	CREDIT	BALANCE DEBIT	BALANCE CREDIT
20--							
Dec.	1	Balance	✓			1848029	

ACCOUNT   *Accounts Receivable*   ACCOUNT NO.   *105*

DATE		DESCRIPTION	POST. REF.	DEBIT	CREDIT	BALANCE DEBIT	BALANCE CREDIT
20--							
Dec.	1	Balance	✓			850910	
	5		G12		12720	838190	

ACCOUNT   *Merchandise Inventory*   ACCOUNT NO.   *110*

DATE		DESCRIPTION	POST. REF.	DEBIT	CREDIT	BALANCE DEBIT	BALANCE CREDIT
20--							
Dec.	1	Balance	✓			3176698	
	3		G12		150000	3026698	

Name   Date   Class

Mini Practice Set 5   (continued)

ACCOUNT _Supplies_   ACCOUNT NO. _115_

DATE	DESCRIPTION	POST. REF.	DEBIT	CREDIT	BALANCE DEBIT	BALANCE CREDIT
20--						
Dec. 1	Balance	✓			1251 46	
13		CR23		30 00	1221 46	

ACCOUNT _Prepaid Insurance_   ACCOUNT NO. _120_

DATE	DESCRIPTION	POST. REF.	DEBIT	CREDIT	BALANCE DEBIT	BALANCE CREDIT
20--						
Dec. 1	Balance	✓			2460 00	

ACCOUNT _Office Equipment_   ACCOUNT NO. _125_

DATE	DESCRIPTION	POST. REF.	DEBIT	CREDIT	BALANCE DEBIT	BALANCE CREDIT
20--						
Dec. 1	Balance	✓			6600 00	
4		P21	125 00		6725 00	

ACCOUNT _Store Equipment_   ACCOUNT NO. _130_

DATE	DESCRIPTION	POST. REF.	DEBIT	CREDIT	BALANCE DEBIT	BALANCE CREDIT
20--						
Dec. 1	Balance	✓			10800 00	
3		CR23		200 00	10600 00	

ACCOUNT _Accounts Payable_   ACCOUNT NO. _201_

DATE	DESCRIPTION	POST. REF.	DEBIT	CREDIT	BALANCE DEBIT	BALANCE CREDIT
20--						
Dec. 1	Balance	✓				7530 00
12		G12	80 00			7450 00

Mini Practice Set 5   (continued)

ACCOUNT __Federal Corporate Income Tax Payable_____ ACCOUNT NO. ___205___

DATE	DESCRIPTION	POST. REF.	DEBIT	CREDIT	BALANCE DEBIT	BALANCE CREDIT

ACCOUNT __Sales Tax Payable_____ ACCOUNT NO. ___210___

DATE		DESCRIPTION	POST. REF.	DEBIT	CREDIT	BALANCE DEBIT	BALANCE CREDIT
20--							
Dec.	1	Balance	✓				895 80
	5		G12	7 20			888 60

ACCOUNT __Capital Stock_____ ACCOUNT NO. ___301___

DATE		DESCRIPTION	POST. REF.	DEBIT	CREDIT	BALANCE DEBIT	BALANCE CREDIT
20--							
Dec.	1	Balance	✓				25000 00

ACCOUNT __Retained Earnings_____ ACCOUNT NO. ___305___

DATE		DESCRIPTION	POST. REF.	DEBIT	CREDIT	BALANCE DEBIT	BALANCE CREDIT
20--							
Dec.	1	Balance	✓				13000 00

ACCOUNT __Income Summary_____ ACCOUNT NO. ___310___

DATE	DESCRIPTION	POST. REF.	DEBIT	CREDIT	BALANCE DEBIT	BALANCE CREDIT

Mini Practice Set 5 (continued)

ACCOUNT ___Sales_____ ACCOUNT NO. ___401___

DATE		DESCRIPTION	POST. REF.	DEBIT	CREDIT	BALANCE	
						DEBIT	CREDIT
20--							
Dec.	1	Balance	✓				10815139

ACCOUNT ___Sales Discounts_____ ACCOUNT NO. ___405___

DATE		DESCRIPTION	POST. REF.	DEBIT	CREDIT	BALANCE	
						DEBIT	CREDIT
20--							
Dec.	1	Balance	✓			21000	

ACCOUNT ___Sales Returns and Allowances_____ ACCOUNT NO. ___410___

DATE		DESCRIPTION	POST. REF.	DEBIT	CREDIT	BALANCE	
						DEBIT	CREDIT
20--							
Dec.	1	Balance	✓			17540	
	5		G12	12000		29540	

ACCOUNT ___Purchases_____ ACCOUNT NO. ___501___

DATE		DESCRIPTION	POST. REF.	DEBIT	CREDIT	BALANCE	
						DEBIT	CREDIT
20--							
Dec.	1	Balance	✓			2376113	
	3		G12	150000		2526113	

Mini Practice Set 5   (continued)

ACCOUNT _Transportation In_ _____ ACCOUNT NO. ___505___

DATE		DESCRIPTION	POST. REF.	DEBIT	CREDIT	BALANCE	
						DEBIT	CREDIT
20--							
Dec.	1	Balance	✓			1 2 7 5 80	
	7		CP24	3 7 20		1 3 1 3 00	

ACCOUNT _Purchases Discounts_ _____ ACCOUNT NO. ___510___

DATE		DESCRIPTION	POST. REF.	DEBIT	CREDIT	BALANCE	
						DEBIT	CREDIT
20--							
Dec.	1	Balance	✓				4 1 5 75

ACCOUNT _Purchases Returns and Allowances_ _____ ACCOUNT NO. ___515___

DATE		DESCRIPTION	POST. REF.	DEBIT	CREDIT	BALANCE	
						DEBIT	CREDIT
20--							
Dec.	1	Balance	✓				3 9 0 85
	12		G12		8 0 00		4 7 0 85

ACCOUNT _Advertising Expense_ _____ ACCOUNT NO. ___605___

DATE		DESCRIPTION	POST. REF.	DEBIT	CREDIT	BALANCE	
						DEBIT	CREDIT
20--							
Dec.	1	Balance	✓			4 3 0 00	

ACCOUNT _Bankcard Fees Expense_ _____ ACCOUNT NO. ___610___

DATE		DESCRIPTION	POST. REF.	DEBIT	CREDIT	BALANCE	
						DEBIT	CREDIT
20--							
Dec.	1	Balance	✓			1 4 2 0 57	

Mini Practice Set 5 (continued)

ACCOUNT _Insurance Expense_ .... ACCOUNT NO. ___615___

DATE	DESCRIPTION	POST. REF.	DEBIT	CREDIT	BALANCE DEBIT	BALANCE CREDIT

ACCOUNT _Miscellaneous Expense_ .... ACCOUNT NO. ___620___

DATE	DESCRIPTION	POST. REF.	DEBIT	CREDIT	BALANCE DEBIT	BALANCE CREDIT
20--						
Dec. 1	Balance	✓			247 52	

ACCOUNT _Rent Expense_ .... ACCOUNT NO. ___625___

DATE	DESCRIPTION	POST. REF.	DEBIT	CREDIT	BALANCE DEBIT	BALANCE CREDIT
20--						
Dec. 1	Balance	✓			7700 00	
2		CP24	700 00		8400 00	

ACCOUNT _Salaries Expense_ .... ACCOUNT NO. ___630___

DATE	DESCRIPTION	POST. REF.	DEBIT	CREDIT	BALANCE DEBIT	BALANCE CREDIT
20--						
Dec. 1	Balance	✓			34871 18	

ACCOUNT _Supplies Expense_ .... ACCOUNT NO. ___635___

DATE	DESCRIPTION	POST. REF.	DEBIT	CREDIT	BALANCE DEBIT	BALANCE CREDIT

Mini Practice Set 5   (continued)

ACCOUNT _Utilities Expense_   ACCOUNT NO. ___640___

DATE		DESCRIPTION	POST. REF.	DEBIT	CREDIT	BALANCE DEBIT	BALANCE CREDIT
20--							
Dec.	1	Balance	✓			2 2 7 4 36	
	15		CP24	1 6 5 00		2 4 3 9 36	

ACCOUNT _Federal Corporate Income Tax Expense_   ACCOUNT NO. ___650___

DATE		DESCRIPTION	POST. REF.	DEBIT	CREDIT	BALANCE DEBIT	BALANCE CREDIT
20--							
Dec.	1	Balance	✓			3 1 5 0 00	

(6)

Mini Practice Set 5 (continued)

(7)

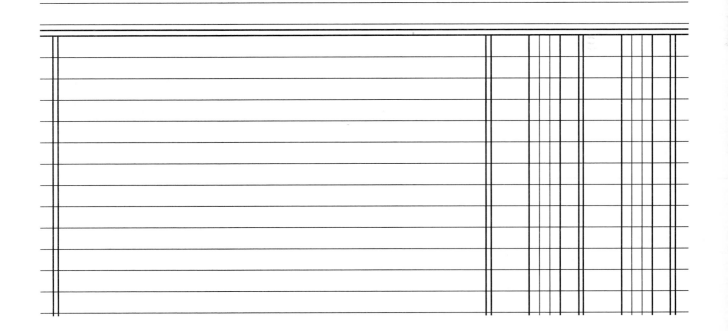

(7)

Mini Practice Set 5 (continued)
(8), (9)

	ACCT. NO.	ACCOUNT NAME	TRIAL BALANCE		ADJUSTMENTS	
			DEBIT	CREDIT	DEBIT	CREDIT
1						
2						
3						
4						
5						
6						
7						
8						
9						
10						
11						
12						
13						
14						
15						
16						
17						
18						
19						
20						
21						
22						
23						
24						
25						
26						
27						
28						
29						
30						
31						
32						
33						

ADJUSTED TRIAL BALANCE		INCOME STATEMENT		BALANCE SHEET		
DEBIT	CREDIT	DEBIT	CREDIT	DEBIT	CREDIT	
						1
						2
						3
						4
						5
						6
						7
						8
						9
						10
						11
						12
						13
						14
						15
						16
						17
						18
						19
						20
						21
						22
						23
						24
						25
						26
						27
						28
						29
						30
						31
						32
						33

Mini Practice Set 5   (continued)
(10)

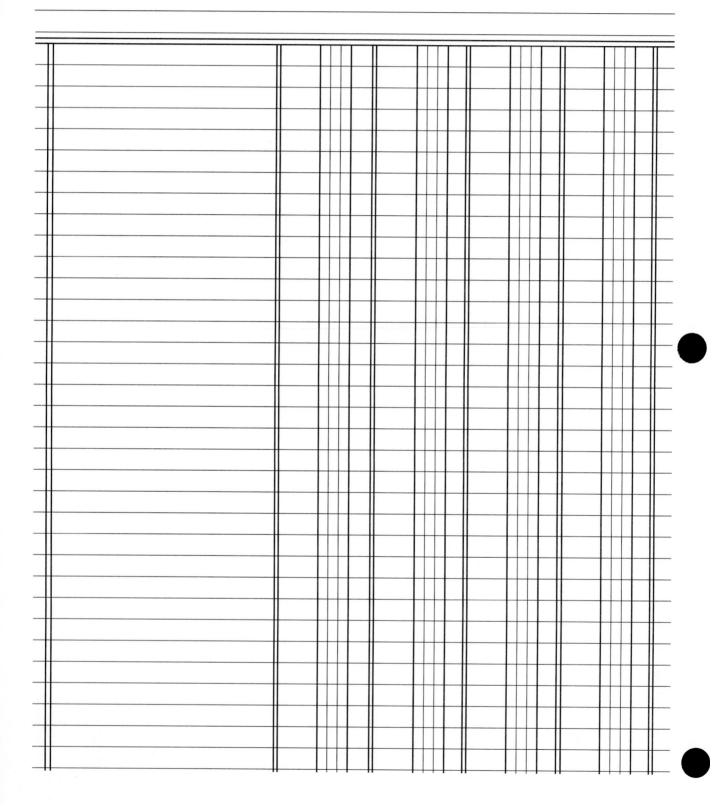

Mini Practice Set 5 (continued)

(11)

(12)

Mini Practice Set 5   (concluded)
(15)

Analyze:

1. _____

2. _____

3. _____

MINI PRACTICE SET **5**

Kite Loft Inc.

Audit Test

Directions: *Use your completed solutions to answer the following questions. Write the answer in the space to the left of each question.*

Answer

_____ **1.** What is the total of debits and credits in the Sales journal at the end of December?

_____ **2.** What is the total of debits and credits in the Cash Receipts journal at the end of December?

_____ **3.** What is the total of debits and credits in the Purchases journal at the end of December?

_____ **4.** What is the total of debits and credits in the Cash Payments journal at the end of December?

_____ **5.** For the transaction on December 26, which account was credited?

_____ **6.** What amount was credited to the Merchandise Inventory account as an adjustment to inventory?

_____ **7.** What amount was debited to the Income Summary account to close the expense accounts for the month?

_____ **8.** What is the ending balance of the Best Toys accounts receivable subsidiary ledger account?

_____ **9.** What is the ending balance for the Accounts Receivable general ledger account? Does the balance agree with the total of the subsidiary ledger accounts?

_____ **10.** What is the ending balance for the Reddi-Bright Manufacturing accounts payable subsidiary ledger account?

11. What is the ending balance for the Accounts Payable general ledger account? Does the balance agree with the total of the subsidiary ledger accounts?

12. How many transactions during the month of December affected the Cash in Bank account?

13. Has the amount owed to Stars Kites Outlet been paid off by the end of December?

14. How many checks were issued by the business in December?

15. What was the total amount credited to Sales for the month?

16. What was the date of the trial balance?

17. How many accounts were affected by adjusting entries?

18. What was the total of operating expenses for the period?

19. What is the ending balance for Retained Earnings for the period?

20. What is the amount of total assets for the business at December 31?

21. How many accounts are listed on the trial balance?

22. How many accounts on the trial balance have debit balances?

23. Which account on the trial balance has the largest balance?

24. What is the amount of total liabilities for the business at December 31?

25. How many accounts are listed on the post-closing trial balance?

CHAPTER 27   Partnership Equity

Study Plan

Check Your Understanding

Section 1	*Read Section 1 on pages 734–737 and complete the following exercises on page 738.* ❏ Thinking Critically ❏ Communicating Accounting ❏ Problem 27-1 *Recording Partners' Investments*
Section 2	*Read Section 2 on pages 739–743 and complete the following exercises on page 744.* ❏ Thinking Critically ❏ Computing in the Business World ❏ Problem 27-2 *Determining Partners' Fractional Shares* ❏ Problem 27-3 *Analyzing a Source Document*
Summary	*Review the Chapter 27 Summary on page 745 in your textbook.* ❏ Key Concepts
Review and Activities	*Complete the following questions and exercises on pages 746–747 in your textbook.* ❏ Using Key Terms ❏ Understanding Accounting Concepts and Procedures ❏ Case Study ❏ Conducting an Audit with Alex ❏ Internet Connection ❏ Workplace Skills
Computerized Accounting	*Read the Computerized Accounting information on page 748 in your textbook.* ❏ *Making the Transition from a Manual to a Computerized System* ❏ *Setting Up a New Company in Peachtree*
Problems	*Complete the following end-of-chapter problems for Chapter 27 in your textbook.* ❏ Problem 27-4 *Dividing Partnership Earnings* ❏ Problem 27-5 *Calculating the Percentage of Each Partner's Capital Investment* ❏ Problem 27-6 *Recording Investments of Partners* ❏ Problem 27-7 *Sharing Losses Based on Capital Balances* ❏ Problem 27-8 *Partners' Withdrawals* ❏ Problem 27-9 *Preparing Closing Entries for a Partnership*
Challenge Problem	❏ Problem 27-10 *Evaluating Methods of Dividing Partnership Earnings*
Chapter Reviews and Working Papers	*Complete the following exercises for Chapter 27 in your Chapter Reviews and Working Papers.* ❏ Chapter Review ❏ Self-Test

CHAPTER 27 REVIEW   Partnership Equity

Part 1   Accounting Vocabulary (2 points)

Directions: *Using terms from the following list, complete the sentences below. Write the letter of the term you have chosen in the space provided.*

Total Points	35
Student's Score	

A. mutual agency	**B.** partnership agreement

_____ **1.** Within a partnership, the relationship that allows any partner to enter into agreements that are binding on all other partners is called _____.

_____ **2.** A _____ is a written document that sets out the terms under which a partnership will operate.

Part 2   Partnerships (10 points)

Directions: *Read each of the following statements to determine whether the statement is true or false. Write your answer in the space provided.*

__True__ **0.** Withdrawals within a partnership are recorded the same way as are the withdrawals of the owner of a sole proprietorship.

_____ **1.** When a partner invests assets in the partnership, he or she retains personal rights of ownership.

_____ **2.** A partnership may be formed through an oral agreement between two or more individuals.

_____ **3.** The amount of the withdrawals by each of the partners must always be equal.

_____ **4.** The partnership agreement should include the procedures for sharing profits and losses but should not include the investment of each partner.

_____ **5.** Noncash assets that are invested in the business are recorded at their current market value.

_____ **6.** Separate capital accounts are set up for each partner, but only one withdrawal account is used by all of the partners.

_____ **7.** Partners are not required to pay federal, state, or personal income taxes on their share of the business's net income.

_____ **8.** If a specific method for dividing net income or net loss among the partners is not set out in the partnership agreement, then the law provides that the division shall be equal among the partners.

_____ **9.** The division of partnership profits and losses is usually based on the partners' contributions of services and capital.

_____ **10.** When using the fractional-share basis, a partnership's net income or loss is divided equally among the partners.

Part 3 Analyzing Transactions for a Partnership (15 points)

Directions: *Teresa Hardee and Gail Taylor, two high school seniors, have formed a partnership to operate a baby-sitting service. Analyze the transactions below to determine the accounts to be debited and credited. Use the following account names.*

A. Cash in Bank	**D.** Teresa Hardee, Capital	**G.** Gail Taylor, Withdrawals
B. Baby Care Supplies	**E.** Gail Taylor, Capital	**H.** Income Summary
C. Play Equipment	**F.** Teresa Hardee, Withdrawals	

Debit	Credit	
A,B,C	*D*	**0.** Teresa Hardee invested cash, baby care supplies, and play equipment in the business.
_____	_____	**1.** Gail Taylor invested a slide in the business.
_____	_____	**2.** Recorded an additional cash investment by each partner.
_____	_____	**3.** Recorded a cash withdrawal by Teresa Hardee.
_____	_____	**4.** Gail Taylor withdrew baby care supplies.
_____	_____	**5.** Recorded the closing entry for the equal distribution of net income for each partner.
_____	_____	**6.** Recorded the closing entry for closing the withdrawals account for Gail Taylor.
_____	_____	**7.** Recorded the closing entry for closing the withdrawals account for Teresa Hardee.

Part 4 Advantages and Disadvantages of Partnerships (8 points)

Directions: *In the space provided below, indicate whether the statement expresses an advantage or a disadvantage of a partnership. Place an "A" in the space for an advantage or a "D" for a disadvantage.*

_*A*_ **0.** Opportunity to bring together abilities, experiences, and resources
_____ **1.** Ease of formation
_____ **2.** Limited life of the partnership
_____ **3.** Decision making without formal meetings
_____ **4.** Shared responsibility for the decision of one of the partners
_____ **5.** Inability to transfer one partner's interest in the partnership without the consent of the other partners
_____ **6.** No levying of federal and state income taxes against the partnership
_____ **7.** Personal liability for the debts of the partnership
_____ **8.** Few legal restrictions

Working Papers *for Section Problems*

Problem 27-1   Recording Partners' Investments

GENERAL JOURNAL   PAGE _____

	DATE	DESCRIPTION	POST. REF.	DEBIT	CREDIT	
1						1
2						2
3						3
4						4
5						5
6						6
7						7
8						8
9						9
10						10
11						11
12						12
13						13
14						14
15						15
16						16
17						17

Problem 27-2   Determining Partners' Fractional Shares

Ratio	Fractions
1. 3:1	_____
2. 5:3:1	_____
3. 3:2:2:1	_____
4. 2:1:1	_____
5. 2:1	_____

Problem 27-3   Analyzing a Source Document

GENERAL JOURNAL   PAGE ___*42*___

	DATE	DESCRIPTION	POST. REF.	DEBIT	CREDIT	
1						1
2						2
3						3
4						4
5						5

Computerized Accounting Using Peachtree

Software Objectives

When you have completed this chapter, you will be able to use Peachtree to:

1. Record investments in a partnership.
2. Record partner withdrawals.
3. Allocate profits and losses to the partners by different methods.

Problem 27-6   Recording Investments of Partners

INSTRUCTIONS

Beginning a Session

Step 1   Select the problem set: JR Landscaping (Prob. 27-6).
Step 2   Rename the company, and set the system date to May 31, 2004.

Completing the Accounting Problem

Step 3   Review the information provided in your textbook.
Step 4   Enter the transactions to record the investment by each partner.

> **TIP:** Use the **General Journal Entry** option to record the entry for the partners' investment.

Step 5   Print a General Journal report and proof your work.
Step 6   Answer the Analyze question.

Ending the Session

Step 7   Click the **Close Problem** button in the Glencoe Smart Guide window to save your work.

DO YOU HAVE A QUESTION

Q. *Does Peachtree support partnerships?*

A. Yes, Peachtree does support the partnership form of business. When you create a new company Peachtree provides four choices for the form of business: corporation, S corporation, partnership, and sole proprietorship. Peachtree creates unique equity accounts depending on the type of business. For example, Peachtree includes an equity account called **Partners' Contributions** if you choose to let the program create the chart of accounts for you.

Problem 27-7   Sharing Losses Based on Capital Balances

INSTRUCTIONS

Beginning a Session

Step 1   Select the problem set: In Shape Fitness (Prob. 27-7).
Step 2   Rename the company, and set the system date to December 31, 2004.

Completing the Accounting Problem

Step 3   Review the information provided in your textbook.
Step 4   Record the entry to divide the loss between the two partners using the **General Journal Entry** option.
Step 5   Print a General Journal report and proof your work.
Step 6   Answer the Analyze question.

Checking Your Work and Ending the Session

Step 7   Click the **Close Problem** button in the Glencoe Smart Guide window.
Step 8   If your teacher has asked you to check your solution, select *Check my answer to this problem.*
Step 9   Click the **Close Problem** button and select a save option.

Notes

Peachtree does not automatically divide net profit (loss) between partners when you close the fiscal year. You must manually perform this step.

Problem 27-8   Partners' Withdrawals

INSTRUCTIONS

Beginning a Session

Step 1   Select the problem set: Travel Essentials (Prob. 27-8).

Step 2   Rename the company, and set the system date to December 31, 2004.

Completing the Accounting Problem

Step 3   Review the information provided in your textbook.

Step 4   Enter the transaction to record the partners' withdrawals using the **General Journal Entry** option.

Step 5   Print a General Journal report and proof your work.

TIP: You can use the report options to print only the entries you recorded. Set the date range from 12/31/04 to 12/31/04.

Step 6   Answer the Analyze question.

Ending the Session

Step 7   Click the **Close Problem** button in the Glencoe Smart Guide window to save your work.

Problem 27-9   Preparing Closing Entries for a Partnership

INSTRUCTIONS

Beginning a Session

Step 1   Select the problem set: Travel Essentials (Prob. 27-9).

Step 2   Rename the company, and set the system date to December 31, 2004.

Completing the Accounting Problem

Step 3   Review the information provided in your textbook.

Step 4   Using the **General Journal Entry** form, manually record the closing entries to divide the net loss between the partners and to close the withdrawal accounts.

Step 5   Print a General Journal report and proof your work.

Step 6   Answer the Analyze question.

Ending the Session

Step 7   Click the **Close Problem** button in the Glencoe Smart Guide window to save your work.

Peachtree Guide

Computerized Accounting Using Spreadsheets

Problem 27-5   Calculating the Percentage of Each Partner's Capital Investment

Completing the Spreadsheet

Step 1   Read the instructions for Problem 27-5 in your textbook. This problem involves calculating a partner's percentage ownership in a partnership.

Step 2   Open the Glencoe Accounting: Electronic Learning Center software.

Step 3   From the Program Menu, click on the **Peachtree Accounting Software and Spreadsheet Applications** icon.

Step 4   Log onto the Management System by typing your user name and password.

Step 5   Under the Chapter Problems tab, select the template: PR27-5a.xls. The template should look like the one shown below.

```
PROBLEM 27-5
CALCULATING THE PERCENTAGE OF
EACH PARTNER'S CAPITAL INVESTMENT

(name)
(date)

                  INDIVIDUAL              TOTAL              PARTNER'S
              PARTNER'S INVESTMENT  PARTNERSHIP INVESTMENT  PERCENTAGE OWNERSHIP
                                                                0.00%
        1                                                       0.00%
        2                                                       0.00%
        3                                                       0.00%
        4
```

Step 6   Key your name and today's date in the cells containing the *(name)* and *(date)* placeholders.

Step 7   Enter each partner's individual investment and total partnership investment in the appropriate cells of the spreadsheet template. The spreadsheet template will automatically calculate the partner's percentage ownership.

Step 8   Save the spreadsheet using the **Save** option from the *File* menu. You should accept the default location for the save as this is handled by the management system.

Step 9   Print the completed spreadsheet.

Step 10   Exit the spreadsheet program.

Step 11   In the Close Options box, select the location where you would like to save your work.

Step 12   Answer the Analyze question from your textbook for this problem.

What-If Analysis

If Partner 1's individual investment were $50,000 and the total partnership investment were $200,000, what would the partner's percentage of the total ownership be?

_____

_____

● **Working Papers** *for End-of-Chapter Problems*

Problem 27-4   Dividing Partnership Earnings

	Share of Net Income		
Net Income	**Partner 1**	**Partner 2**	**Partner 3**
1. $45,000			
2. $89,700			
3. $22,000			
4. $32,000			
5. $92,700			

Analyze: _____
_____
_____
_____

Problem 27-5   Calculating the Percentage of Each Partner's Capital Investment

●

1. _____
2. _____
3. _____
4. _____

Analyze: _____
_____
_____
_____

Problem 27-6 Recording Investments of Partners

GENERAL JOURNAL   PAGE _____

	DATE	DESCRIPTION	POST. REF.	DEBIT	CREDIT	
1						1
2						2
3						3
4						4
5						5
6						6
7						7
8						8
9						9
10						10
11						11
12						12

Analyze: _____

_____

Problem 27-7 Sharing Losses Based on Capital Balances

Share percentages:
M. DeJesus = 35,000/80,000 = .4375
N. Faircloth = 45,000/80,000 = .5625

GENERAL JOURNAL   PAGE __*14*__

	DATE	DESCRIPTION	POST. REF.	DEBIT	CREDIT	
1						1
2						2
3						3
4						4
5						5
6						6
7						7
8						8
9						9
10						10
11						11
12						12

Analyze: _____

_____

Problem 27-8 Partners' Withdrawals

GENERAL JOURNAL   PAGE __42__

	DATE	DESCRIPTION	POST. REF.	DEBIT	CREDIT	
1						1
2						2
3						3
4						4
5						5
6						6
7						7
8						8
9						9
10						10
11						11
12						12

Analyze: _____

_____

_____

_____

Problem 27-9 Preparing Closing Entries for a Partnership

GENERAL JOURNAL   PAGE _____

	DATE	DESCRIPTION	POST. REF.	DEBIT	CREDIT	
1						1
2						2
3						3
4						4
5						5
6						6
7						7
8						8
9						9
10						10
11						11
12						12

Problem 27-9 (concluded)

GENERAL LEDGER (PARTIAL)

ACCOUNT __Barbara Scott, Capital__ ACCOUNT NO. __301__

DATE		DESCRIPTION	POST. REF.	DEBIT	CREDIT	BALANCE	
						DEBIT	CREDIT
20--							
Dec.	31	Balance	✓				6731200

ACCOUNT __Barbara Scott, Withdrawals__ ACCOUNT NO. __305__

DATE		DESCRIPTION	POST. REF.	DEBIT	CREDIT	BALANCE	
						DEBIT	CREDIT
20--							
Dec.	31	Balance	✓			660000	

ACCOUNT __Martin Towers, Capital__ ACCOUNT NO. __310__

DATE		DESCRIPTION	POST. REF.	DEBIT	CREDIT	BALANCE	
						DEBIT	CREDIT
20--							
Dec.	31	Balance	✓				4960100

ACCOUNT __Martin Towers, Withdrawals__ ACCOUNT NO. __315__

DATE		DESCRIPTION	POST. REF.	DEBIT	CREDIT	BALANCE	
						DEBIT	CREDIT
20--							
Dec.	31	Balance	✓			540000	

ACCOUNT __Income Summary__ ACCOUNT NO. __320__

DATE	DESCRIPTION	POST. REF.	DEBIT	CREDIT	BALANCE	
					DEBIT	CREDIT

Analyze: _____

_____

_____

Problem 27-10 **Evaluating Methods of Dividing Partnership Earnings**

1. Garrity: _____

O'Riley: _____

White: _____

2. Garrity: _____

O'Riley: _____

White: _____

3. Garrity: _____

O'Riley: _____

White: _____

Analyze: _____

_____

_____

Notes

CHAPTER 27 — Partnership Equity

Self-Test

Part A   Fill in the Missing Term

Directions: *Using the terms from the following list, complete the sentences below. Write the letter of the term you select in the space provided.*

A. mutual agency	**B.** partnership agreement

Answer

_____ 1. Within the partnership, the relationship that allows any partner to act on behalf of other partners is called _____.

_____ 2. A _____ is a written document that sets out the terms under which the partnership will operate.

Part B   True or False

Directions: *For each of the statements that follow, indicate in the space provided whether you agree or disagree with the statement by writing* True *if you agree or* False *if you disagree.*

Answer

_____ 1. In a partnership, each partner can act as an agent and enter into contracts for the partnership.

_____ 2. Regardless of how partnership net income is shared, net loss is always shared equally by the partners.

_____ 3. A partnership has to pay federal income taxes.

_____ 4. In a partnership, each individual partner is liable to creditors for debts of the partnership.

_____ 5. A partnership must have a written agreement as to how the partners will share income and losses.

_____ 6. A partnership agreement must be in writing to be valid.

_____ 7. An association of two or more persons to carry on a business for a profit as co-owners is called a partnership.

_____ 8. One of the major advantages of a partnership is the unlimited liability of the partners.

_____ 9. One of the major advantages of a partnership is its ease of formation.

_____ 10. The amount that a partner withdraws affects the division of net income.

Part C   Analyze the Transactions

Directions: *Alice James and Ruth Simpson formed a partnership called Best Deal School Supplies. Analyze the transactions that follow to determine the accounts to be debited and credited. Use the account numbers listed below.*

101	Cash in Bank	**302**	Alice James, Withdrawals
103	Merchandise Inventory	**303**	Ruth Simpson, Capital
104	Store Equipment	**304**	Ruth Simpson, Withdrawals
301	Alice James, Capital	**310**	Income Summary

Debit   **Credit**

_____   _____   **1.** Ruth Simpson invested cash in the partnership.

_____   _____   **2.** The partnership purchased store equipment for cash.

_____   _____   **3.** Alice James withdrew cash from the business.

_____   _____   **4.** Ruth Simpson withdrew merchandise from the business.

_____   _____   **5.** Record the closing entry for sharing the profits equally.

_____   _____   **6.** Record the closing entry for the withdrawals accounts.

_____   _____   **7.** Record the closing entry for sharing a loss.

CHAPTER 28 — Financial Statements and Liquidation of a Partnership

Study Plan

Check Your Understanding

Section 1	*Read Section 1 on pages 754–755 and complete the following exercises on page 756.*
	❏ Thinking Critically
	❏ Communicating Accounting
	❏ Problem 28-1 *Preparing the Income Statement and Balance Sheet for a Partnership*
	❏ Problem 28-2 *Analyzing a Source Document*
Section 2	*Read Section 2 on pages 757–761 and complete the following exercises on page 762.*
	❏ Thinking Critically
	❏ Computing in the Business World
	❏ Problem 28-3 *Recording a Loss and Gain on the Sale of Noncash Assets by a Partnership*
Summary	*Review the Chapter 28 Summary on page 763 in your textbook.*
	❏ Key Concepts
Review and Activities	*Complete the following questions and exercises on pages 764–765 in your textbook.*
	❏ Using Key Terms
	❏ Understanding Accounting Concepts and Procedures
	❏ Case Study
	❏ Conducting an Audit with Alex
	❏ Internet Connection
	❏ Workplace Skills
Computerized Accounting	*Read the Computerized Accounting information on page 766 in your textbook.*
	❏ Making the Transition from a Manual to a Computerized System
	❏ Setting Up General Ledger in Peachtree
Problems	*Complete the following end-of-chapter problems for Chapter 28 in your textbook.*
	❏ Problem 28-4 *Preparing an Income Statement and Balance Sheet for a Partnership*
	❏ Problem 28-5 *Liquidating the Partnership with Losses on the Sale of Noncash Assets*
	❏ Problem 28-6 *Recording a Gain or Loss on the Sale of Noncash Assets by a Partnership*
	❏ Problem 28-7 *Preparing a Statement of Changes in Partners' Equity*
	❏ Problem 28-8 *Liquidating the Partnership*
Challenge Problem	❏ Problem 28-9 *Completing End-of-Period Activities for a Partnership*
Chapter Reviews and Working Papers	*Complete the following exercises for Chapter 28 in your Chapter Reviews and Working Papers.*
	❏ Chapter Review
	❏ Self-Test

CHAPTER 28 REVIEW — Financial Statements and Liquidation of a Partnership

Total Points	25
Student's Score	

Part 1   Understanding Financial Statements of a Partnership
(5 points)

Directions: *Read each of the following statements to determine whether the statement is true or false. Write your answer in the space provided.*

    True   **0.** Partnerships involve more than one owner.

          1. The income statement for a partnership shows each partner's share of income or loss.

          2. Withdrawals by partners are shown on the income statement.

          3. The statement of changes in partners' equity is similar to the statement of stockholders' equity.

          4. The beginning capital balance for each partner in a partnership is reported in the Partners' Equity section of the balance sheet.

          5. Withdrawals and division of profits or loss are reported on the statement of changes in partners' equity.

Part 2   Analyzing Partnership Liquidation Transactions (10 points)

Directions: *Read each of the following statements to determine whether the statement is true or false. Write your answer in the space provided.*

    True   **0.** Partners must agree to liquidate the business.

          1. In liquidation the debts of a partnership must be paid before any cash is distributed to the partners.

          2. In liquidation of a partnership the cash is distributed to partners based on the profit and loss sharing agreement.

          3. When noncash assets are sold at a gain the partners' capital accounts are increased.

          4. When noncash assets are sold at a loss the cash on hand is reduced.

          5. Each partner receives the same amount of cash as the final step in the partnership liquidation process.

          6. When noncash assets are sold for cash the partnership may suffer a loss or a gain.

          7. When a partnership stops operations and ends the partnership the partnership is liquidated.

          8. Losses from partnership liquidation are added to the partners' withdrawal accounts.

          9. The cash remaining in the partnership after the debts are paid is distributed to each partner based on the final balance in their capital accounts.

          10. If a noncash asset is sold at a gain, the assets of the partnership increase.

Part 3   Recording Liquidation Transactions (10 points)

Directions: *Using the following list of account names, determine the accounts to be debited and credited for the liquidating entries below.*

A. Cash in Bank	**C.** Equipment	**E.** Roger Vogel, Capital
B. Inventory	**D.** Notes Payable	**F.** Lydia Parry, Capital

Debit	**Credit**	
A	*B*	**0.** Sold some of the inventory at carrying value.
_____	_____	**1.** Record a loss from the sale of equipment.
_____	_____	**2.** Record a gain from the sale of inventory.
_____	_____	**3.** Paid the note payable.
_____	_____	**4.** Paid cash to Roger Vogel.
_____	_____	**5.** Paid cash to Lydia Parry.

Working Papers *for Section Problems*

Problem 28-1   Preparing the Income Statement and Balance Sheet for a Partnership

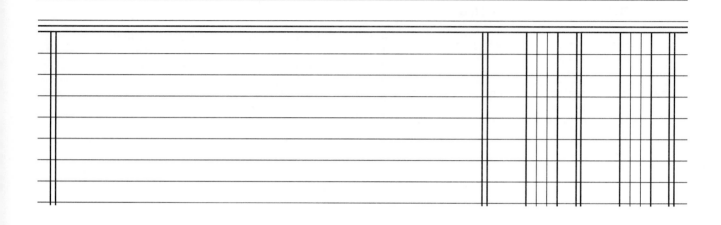

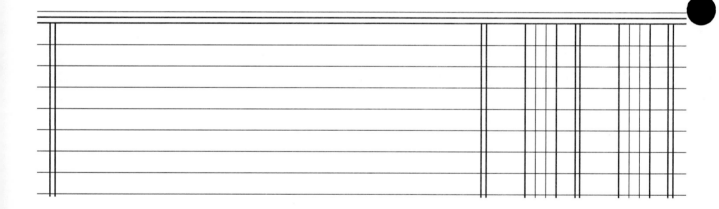

Problem 28-2   Analyzing a Source Document

Gain = $26,400
Shares of gain:

Larry Bass = _____

John Buie = _____

Teri Anderson = _____

Robert Norman = _____

Paula Dunham = _____

John Ruppe = _____

Problem 28-3 Recording a Loss and Gain on the Sale of Noncash Assets by a Partnership

GENERAL JOURNAL

PAGE _____

	DATE	DESCRIPTION	POST. REF.	DEBIT	CREDIT	
1						1
2						2
3						3
4						4
5						5
6						6
7						7
8						8
9						9
10						10
11						11
12						12
13						13
14						14
15						15
16						16
17						17
18						18
19						19
20						20

Computerized Accounting Using Peachtree

Software Objectives

When you have completed this chapter, you will be able to use Peachtree to:

1. Record transactions to account for partnership liquidation losses.
2. Record transactions to account for partnership liquidation gains.

Problem 28-5   Liquidating the Partnership with Losses on the Sale of Noncash Assets

INSTRUCTIONS

Beginning a Session

Step 1   Select the problem set: Pasta Mia Restaurant Supply (Prob. 28-5).
Step 2   Rename the company, and set the system date to September 21, 2004.

Completing the Accounting Problem

Step 3   Review the information provided in your textbook.
Step 4   Enter the transactions to liquidate the partnership.

> **TIP:** Use the **General Journal Entry** option to record the entries to liquidate the partnership.

DO YOU HAVE A QUESTION

Q. *Can you print a Statement of Changes in Partners' Equity report using the Peachtree software?*

A. No, Peachtree does not include an option to print a Statement of Changes in Partners' Equity report. You have to manually prepare this report using the information found on the Balance Sheet for a partnership.

Step 5   Print a General Journal report and proof your work.
Step 6   Answer the Analyze question.

Checking Your Work and Ending the Session

Step 7   Click the **Close Problem** button in the Glencoe Smart Guide window.
Step 8   If your teacher has asked you to check your solution, select *Check my answer to this problem.* Review, print, and close the report.
Step 9   Click the **Close Problem** button and select a save option.

Problem 28-6   Recording a Gain or Loss on the Sale of Noncash Assets by a Partnership

INSTRUCTIONS

Beginning a Session

Step 1   Select the problem set: Industrial Tool & Machine (Prob. 28-6).

Step 2   Rename the company, and set the system date to June 4, 2004.

Completing the Accounting Problem

Step 3   Review the information provided in your textbook. Be sure to enter the transactions in the proper accounting period. Use the **System** option from the ***Tasks*** menu to change the accounting period before entering each transaction.

Step 4   Enter the transactions to liquidate the partnership.

Step 5   Print a General Journal report and proof your work.

TIP: Set the General Journal report date range to include the entries from May 1 to June 30.

Step 6   Anwer the Analyze question.

Ending the Session

Step 7   Verify that the accounting period displayed on your screen is 6/1/04 to 6/30/04. Click the **Close Problem** button in the Glencoe Smart Guide window to save your work.

Problem 28-8   Liquidating the Partnership

INSTRUCTIONS

Beginning a Session

Step 1   Select the problem set: Alpine Gifts & Flowers (Prob. 28-8).

Step 2   Rename the company, and set the system date to October 15, 2004.

Completing the Accounting Problem

Step 3   Review the information provided in your textbook.

Step 4   Enter the transactions to liquidate the partnership.

Step 5   Print a General Journal report and proof your work.

Step 6   Anwer the Analyze question.

Ending the Session

Step 7   Click the **Close Problem** button in the Glencoe Smart Guide window to save your work.

Computerized Accounting Using Spreadsheets

Problem 28-4 Preparing an Income Statement and Balance Sheet for a Partnership

Completing the Spreadsheet

Step 1 Read the instructions for Problem 28-4 in your textbook. This problem involves preparing an income statement and a balance sheet for a partnership.

Step 2 Open the Glencoe Accounting: Electronic Learning Center software.

Step 3 From the Program Menu, click on the **Peachtree Accounting Software and Spreadsheet Applications** icon.

Step 4 Log onto the Management System by typing your user name and password.

Step 5 Under the Chapter Problems tab, select the template: PR28-4a.xls. The template should look like the one shown below.

```
PROBLEM 28-4
PREPARING AN INCOME STATEMENT AND
BALANCE SHEET FOR A PARTNERSHIP

(name)
(date)


Joy Webster %                         AMOUNT
Diana Ruiz %                          AMOUNT


Net Income                                              AMOUNT
Division of Net Income:
  Webster                             0.00
  Ruiz                                0.00


       Partners' Equity          Webster          Ruiz         Total Equity
Beginning Capital, January 1        0.00            0.00              0.00
Add: Net Income                     0.00            0.00              0.00
     Investments                 6,000.00        5,500.00         11,500.00
Subtotal                         6,000.00        5,500.00         11,500.00
Less: Withdrawals                1,800.00        1,200.00          3,000.00
Ending Capital, December 31      4,200.00        4,300.00          8,500.00
```

Step 6 Key your name and today's date in the cells containing the *(name)* and *(date)* placeholders.

Step 7 Joy Webster and Diana Ruiz share in the partnership equally. Therefore, each has a 50% share of the profits. Enter Webster's and Ruiz's partnership percentage in cells B10 and B11: **50**.

TIP: Cells B10 and B11 are formatted for percentages. Therefore, it is not necessary to enter a percent sign after the number, nor is it necessary to enter the number as a decimal.

Step 8   Now enter net income in cell C13: **5780**. Remember, it is not necessary to enter a comma or the decimal point and ending zeroes. The division of net income for Webster and Ruiz will be automatically calculated.

Step 9   Now scroll down below the division of net income and look at the balance sheet. The partners' equity section has been completed.

Step 10   Save the spreadsheet using the **Save** option from the *File* menu. You should accept the default location for the save as this is handled by the management system.

Step 11   Print the completed spreadsheet.

Step 12   Exit the spreadsheet program.

Step 13   In the Close Options box, select the location where you would like to save your work.

Step 14   Answer the Analyze question from your textbook for this problem.

What-If Analysis

If Webster's partnership percentage were 60% and Ruiz's partnership percentage were 40%, what would the division of net income be? How would this affect each partner's ending capital?

_____

_____

Problem 28-9   Completing End-of-Period Activities for a Partnership

Completing the Spreadsheet

Step 1   Read the instructions for Problem 28-9 in your textbook. This problem involves preparing the end-of-period financial statements for a partnership.

Step 2   Open the Glencoe Accounting: Electronic Learning Center software.

Step 3   From the Program Menu, click on the **Peachtree Accounting Software and Spreadsheet Applications** icon.

Step 4   Log onto the Management System by typing your user name and password.

Step 5   Under the Chapter Problems tab, select the template: PR28-9a.xls. The template should look like the one shown below.

```
PROBLEM 28-9
COMPLETING END-OF-PERIOD ACTIVITIES FOR A PARTNERSHIP


(name)
(date)


Smooth %                                              AMOUNT
Overhill %                                            AMOUNT


R & C ROOFING
INCOME STATEMENT
FOR THE YEAR ENDED DECEMBER 31, 20--

Revenue:
  Consulting Fees                      15,900.00
  Roofing Fees                         62,750.00
Total Revenue                                         78,650.00
Expenses:
  Advertising Expense                   2,400.00
  Depreciation Expense - Office Equipment  185.00
  Depreciation Expense - Truck          3,900.00
  Depreciation Expense - Building       1,200.00
  Insurance Expense                     1,200.00
  Office Supplies Expense                 335.00
  Roofing Supplies Expense             11,470.00
  Salaries Expense                     28,109.00
  Truck Expense                         1,400.00
  Utilities Expense                     2,095.00
Total Expense                                         52,294.00
Net Income                                            26,356.00
Division of Net Income:
  Richard Smooth                            0.00
  Carrie Overhill                           0.00
Net Income                                                 0.00
```

Spreadsheet Guide

Step 6   Key your name and today's date in the cells containing the *(name)* and *(date)* placeholders.

Step 7   Richard Smooth and Carrie Overhill agree to divide R & C Roofing's net income or loss on the following basis: Smooth, ¾; Overhill, ¼. Therefore, Smooth has a 75% partnership percentage, and Overhill has a 25% partnership percentage. Enter Smooth's and Overhill's partnership percentages in cells B9 and B10.

TIP: Cells B9 and B10 are formatted for percentages. Therefore, it is not necessary to enter a percent sign after the number, nor is it necessary to enter the number as a decimal.

Step 8   Now scroll down below the partnership percentages and look at the income statement, statement of changes in partners' equity, and balance sheet for R & C Roofing. Notice the financial statements are already completed, using information from the work sheet in your working papers and from the partnership percentages you entered in cells B9 and B10.

Step 9   Save the spreadsheet using the **Save** option from the *File* menu. You should accept the default location for the save as this is handled by the management system.

Step 10   Print the completed spreadsheet.

TIP: When printing a long spreadsheet with multiple parts, you may want to insert page breaks between the sections so that each one begins printing at the top of a new page. Page breaks have already been entered into this spreadsheet template. Check your program's Help file for instructions on how to enter page breaks.

Step 11   Exit the spreadsheet program.

Step 12   In the Close Options box, select the location where you would like to save your work.

Step 13   Answer the Analyze question from your textbook for this problem.

What-If Analysis

If Smooth and Overhill shared in the partnership equally, what would the division of net income be? How would this affect each partner's ending capital?

● Working Papers *for End-of-Chapter Problems*

Problem 28-4   Preparing an Income Statement and
Balance Sheet for a Partnership

Webster and Ruiz

Income Statement (partial)

For the Period Ending December 31, 20--

Webster and Ruiz

Balance Sheet (partial)

December 31, 20--

Analyze: _____

_____

_____

Problem 28-5 Liquidating the Partnership with Losses on the Sale of Noncash Assets

GENERAL JOURNAL

PAGE _____

	DATE	DESCRIPTION	POST. REF.	DEBIT	CREDIT	
1						1
2						2
3						3
4						4
5						5
6						6
7						7
8						8
9						9
10						10
11						11
12						12
13						13
14						14
15						15
16						16
17						17
18						18
19						19
20						20
21						21
22						22
23						23
24						24
25						25
26						26
27						27
28						28
29						29
30						30

Analyze: _____

_____

_____

Problem 28-6   Recording a Gain or Loss on the Sale of Noncash Assets by a Partnership

GENERAL JOURNAL   PAGE _____

	DATE		DESCRIPTION	POST. REF.	DEBIT	CREDIT	
1							1
2							2
3							3
4							4
5							5
6							6
7							7
8							8
9							9
10							10
11							11
12							12
13							13
14							14
15							15
16							16
17							17
18							18
19							19
20							20
21							21
22							22
23							23
24							24
25							25
26							26
27							27
28							28
29							29
30							30

Analyze: _____

_____

_____

Problem 28-7 Preparing a Statement of Changes in Partners' Equity

Analyze: _____

_____

Problem 28-8 Liquidating the Partnership

GENERAL JOURNAL

	DATE	DESCRIPTION	POST. REF.	DEBIT	CREDIT	
1						1
2						2
3						3
4						4
5						5
6						6
7						7
8						8
9						9
10						10
11						11
12						12
13						13
14						14
15						15
16						16
17						17
18						18
19						19
20						20
21						21
22						22
23						23
24						24
25						25
26						26
27						27
28						28
29						29
30						30

Analyze: _____

_____

_____

Problem 28-9   Completing End-of-Period Activities for a Partnership

R&C

Work

For the Year Ended

	ACCT. NO.	ACCOUNT NAME	TRIAL BALANCE DEBIT	TRIAL BALANCE CREDIT	ADJUSTMENTS DEBIT	ADJUSTMENTS CREDIT
1	101	Cash in Bank	17928 00			
2	105	Accounts Receivable	4310 00			
3	110	Office Supplies	495 00			(a) 335 00
4	115	Roofing Supplies	15610 00			(b) 11470 00
5	120	Prepaid Insurance	2400 00			(c) 1200 00
6	150	Office Equipment	2650 00			
7	155	Accum. Depr.—Office Equip.		1016 00		(d) 185 00
8	160	Truck	19890 00			
9	165	Accum. Depr.—Truck		3100 00		(e) 3900 00
10	170	Building	30000 00			
11	175	Accum. Depr.—Building		3600 00		(f) 1200 00
12	180	Land	10000 00			
13	201	Accounts Payable		7945 00		
14	301	R. Smooth, Capital		42238 00		
15	305	R. Smooth, Withdrawals	8700 00			
16	310	C. Overhill, Capital		17538 00		
17	315	C. Overhill, Withdrawals	8100 00			
18	320	Income Summary	—	—		
19	401	Consulting Fees		15900 00		
20	405	Roofing Fees		62750 00		
21	501	Advertising Expense	2400 00			
22	505	Depr. Exp.—Office Equip.	—		(d) 185 00	
23	510	Depr. Expense—Truck	—		(e) 3900 00	
24	515	Depr. Expense—Building	—		(f) 1200 00	
25	520	Insurance Expense	—		(c) 1200 00	
26	525	Office Supplies Expense	—		(a) 335 00	
27	530	Roofing Supplies Expense	—		(b) 11470 00	
28	535	Salaries Expense	28109 00			
29	540	Truck Expense	1400 00			
30	545	Utilities Expense	2095 00			
31			154087 00	154087 00	18290 00	18290 00
32		Net Income				
33						
34						

Roofing

Sheet

December 31, 20--

| ADJUSTED TRIAL BALANCE | | INCOME STATEMENT | | BALANCE SHEET | | |
DEBIT	CREDIT	DEBIT	CREDIT	DEBIT	CREDIT	
1792800				1792800		1
431000				431000		2
16000				16000		3
414000				414000		4
120000				120000		5
265000				265000		6
	120100				120100	7
1989000				1989000		8
	700000				700000	9
3000000				3000000		10
	480000				480000	11
1000000				1000000		12
	794500				794500	13
	4223800				4223800	14
870000				870000		15
	1753800				1753800	16
810000				810000		17
——	——	——		——		18
	1590000		1590000			19
	6275000		6275000			20
240000		240000				21
18500		18500				22
390000		390000				23
120000		120000				24
120000		120000				25
33500		33500				26
1147000		1147000				27
2810900		2810900				28
140000		140000				29
209500		209500				30
15937200	15937200	5229400	7865000	10707800	8072200	31
		2635600			2635600	32
		7865000	7865000	10707800	10707800	33
						34

Problem 28-9   (continued)

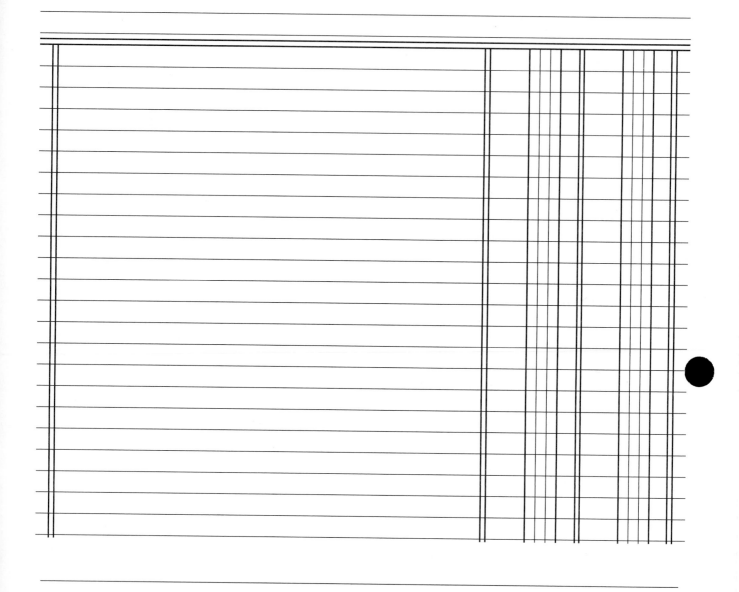

Problem 28-9   (continued)

Problem 28-9 (concluded)

GENERAL JOURNAL

PAGE _____

	DATE	DESCRIPTION	POST. REF.	DEBIT	CREDIT	
1						1
2						2
3						3
4						4
5						5
6						6
7						7
8						8
9						9
10						10
11						11
12						12
13						13
14						14
15						15
16						16
17						17
18						18
19						19
20						20
21						21
22						22
23						23
24						24
25						25
26						26
27						27
28						28
29						29
30						30
31						31
32						32
33						33
34						34
35						35
36						36
37						37

Analyze: _____

CHAPTER 28 Financial Statements and Liquidation of a Partnership

Self-Test

Part A   Steps in Liquidating a Partnership

Directions: *Shown below are the four steps in liquidating a partnership. Rearrange these activities in the order in which they would be completed during the liquidation process.*

Answer

_____ **1.** All cash remaining after the creditors are paid is distributed to the partners based on the final balance in the partners' accounts.

_____ **2.** All gains and losses from the sale of noncash assets are added to or deducted from the capital accounts of the partners based on the partnership agreement.

_____ **3.** All noncash assets are sold for cash.

_____ **4.** All partnership creditors are paid.

Part B   True or False

Directions: *Read each of the following statements to determine whether the statement is true or false. Write your answer in the space provided.*

Answer

_____ **1.** Partnerships involve more than one owner.

_____ **2.** The balance sheet for a partnership shows each partner's share of income or loss.

_____ **3.** Withdrawals by partners are shown on the balance sheet.

_____ **4.** The statement of changes in partners' equity is similar to the statement of owner's equity.

_____ **5.** The ending capital balance for each partner in a partnership is reported in the Partners' Equity section of the balance sheet.

_____ **6.** Withdrawals and division of profits or loss are reported on the statement of changes in partners' equity.

_____ **7.** Partners must agree to liquidate the business.

_____ **8.** In liquidation the debts of a partnership are paid after cash is distributed to the partners.

_____ **9.** In liquidation of a partnership the cash is distributed to partners based upon the profit and loss sharing agreement.

_____ **10.** When noncash assets are sold at a loss the partners' capital accounts are decreased.

_____ **11.** When noncash assets are sold at a gain the cash on hand is increased.

_____ **12.** Each partner receives the same amount of cash as the final step in the partnership liquidation process.

_____ **13.** When noncash assets are sold for cash the partnership may suffer a loss or a gain.

_____ **14.** When a partnership stops operations and ends the partnership the partnership is liquidated.

_____ **15.** Gains from partnership liquidation are added to the partners' withdrawal accounts.

_____ **16.** The cash remaining in the partnership after the debts are paid is distributed to each partner based on the final balance in their capital accounts.

_____ **17.** If a noncash asset is sold at a loss, the assets of the partnership decrease.

MINI PRACTICE SET 6

Fine Finishes

CHART OF ACCOUNTS

ASSETS
101   Cash in Bank
105   Accounts Receivable—Mountain View City School District
120   Computer Equipment
130   Office Supplies
135   Office Equipment
140   Painting Supplies
145   Painting Equipment

LIABILITIES
205   Accounts Payable—Custom Color
210   Accounts Payable—J & J Hardware and Lumber
215   Accounts Payable—Paint Palace

PARTNERS' EQUITY
301   Laura Andersen, Capital
302   Laura Andersen, Withdrawals
303   David Ingram, Capital
304   David Ingram, Withdrawals
305   Sean Woo, Capital
306   Sean Woo, Withdrawals
310   Income Summary

REVENUE
401   Painting Fees
405   Consultation Fees

EXPENSES
505   Advertising Expense
510   Miscellaneous Expense
515   Rent Expense
520   Utilities Expense

    Mini Practice Set 6 ■ **839**

Mini Practice Set 6   Source Documents

Instructions: *Use the following source documents to record the transactions for this practice set.*

---

fine finishes
755 Brewton Street
Forest Hills, AL 36105

MEMORANDUM 1

TO: Accounting Clerk
FROM: Senior Accountant
DATE: February 1, 20--
SUBJECT: Partner Investment

Record partners' investments with following amounts:

	Andersen	Ingram	Woo
Cash	$1,500.00	$1,000.00	$1,200.00
Computer Equip.	–	2,800.00	–
Office Equip.	100.00	–	–
Painting Supplies	150.00	–	225.00
Painting Equip.	1,375.00	–	1,675.00
Total	$3,125.00	$3,800.00	$3,100.00

---

fine finishes   **1101**
755 Brewton Street   71-821
Forest Hills, AL 36105   3321

                          DATE February 1   20--

PAY TO THE
ORDER OF Taft Leasing Co. $ 1,500.00

One thousand five hundred and 00/100 ———————— DOLLARS

    ❀ Barclays Bank

MEMO Rent   Laura Andersen

⑈332171821⑈ 4516 2133⑈ 1101

---

fine finishes   **1102**
755 Brewton Street   71-821
Forest Hills, AL 36105   3321

                          DATE February 1   20--

PAY TO THE
ORDER OF Call an Expert $ 25.00

Twenty-five and 00/100 ————————————— DOLLARS

    ❀ Barclays Bank

MEMO Newspaper ad   Laura Andersen

⑈332171821⑈ 4516 2133⑈ 1102

---

fine finishes   **1103**
755 Brewton Street   71-821
Forest Hills, AL 36105   3321

                          DATE February 1   20--

PAY TO THE
ORDER OF City of Mountain View $ 55.00

Fifty-five and 00/100 ————————————— DOLLARS

    ❀ Barclays Bank

MEMO Business license   Laura Andersen

⑈332171821⑈ 4516 2133⑈ 1103

---

fine finishes   **1104**
755 Brewton Street   71-821
Forest Hills, AL 36105   3321

                          DATE February 1   20--

PAY TO THE
ORDER OF Western Utilities $ 100.00

One hundred and 00/100 ————————————— DOLLARS

    ❀ Barclays Bank

MEMO Utilities deposit   Laura Andersen

⑈332171821⑈ 4516 2133⑈ 1104

---

fine finishes   **1105**
755 Brewton Street   71-821
Forest Hills, AL 36105   3321

                          DATE February 1   20--

PAY TO THE
ORDER OF GTE $ 175.00

One hundred seventy-five and 00/100 ———————— DOLLARS

    ❀ Barclays Bank

MEMO Telephone svc   Laura Andersen

⑈332171821⑈ 4516 2133⑈ 1105

---

fine finishes   **RECEIPT**
755 Brewton Street   No. 01
Forest Hills, AL 36105

                              February 2   20--

RECEIVED FROM McGuires $ 250.00

Two hundred fifty and 00/100 ———————————— DOLLARS

FOR $250 deposit for McGuires contract

                    RECEIVED BY Laura Andersen

Custom Color   **INVOICE NO. 742**
3167 Turner Place, #1A
Wildwood, AL 36120   DATE: Feb. 2, 20--

                                          ORDER NO.:
      Fine Finishes   SHIPPED BY:
TO   755 Brewton Street   TERMS:
      Forest Hills, AL 36105

QTY.	ITEM	UNIT PRICE	TOTAL
5	Paint & Border Stencils	$40.00	$200.00

Mini Practice Set 6 (continued)

fine finishes
755 Brewton Street
Forest Hills, AL 36105

1106
71-821
3321

DATE *February 4* 20—

PAY TO THE ORDER OF *Office Max* $ *115.00*

One hundred fifteen and 00/100 ——————————— DOLLARS

✹ *Barclays Bank*

MEMO *Office supplies* *Laura Andersen*

⑊3321718 21⑊ 4516 2133⑊ 1106

Paint Palace
612 James Avenue
Montgomery, AL 36105

INVOICE NO. 1162

DATE: Feb. 8, 20—
ORDER NO.:
SHIPPED BY:
TERMS:

TO *Fine Finishes*
755 Brewton Street
Forest Hills, AL 36105

QTY.	ITEM	UNIT PRICE	TOTAL
2	Painting equipment	$187.50	$375.00

---

fine finishes
755 Brewton Street
Forest Hills, AL 36105

RECEIPT
No. 02

February 5 20—

RECEIVED FROM *McGuires* $ *450.00*

Four hundred fifty and 00/100 ——————— DOLLARS

FOR *Balance on McGuires contract*

RECEIVED BY *Laura Andersen*

---

fine finishes
755 Brewton Street
Forest Hills, AL 36105

RECEIPT
No. 03

February 10 20—

RECEIVED FROM *Prospective Client* $ *60.00*

Sixty and 00/100 ——————————————— DOLLARS

FOR *Color and painting consultation*

RECEIVED BY *Laura Andersen*

---

fine finishes
755 Brewton Street
Forest Hills, AL 36105

1107
71-821
3321

DATE *February 6* 20—

PAY TO THE ORDER OF *Mountain View Chamber of Commerce* $ *45.00*

Forty-five and 00/100 ——————————— DOLLARS

✹ *Barclays Bank*

MEMO *Permit* *Laura Andersen*

⑊3321718 21⑊ 4516 2133⑊ 1107

---

fine finishes
755 Brewton Street
Forest Hills, AL 36105

INVOICE NO. 101

DATE: Feb. 12, 20—
ORDER NO.:
TERMS:

TO *Mountain View*
City School District

DATE	SERVICE	AMOUNT
	Cafeteria Painting at elementary school	$835.00

---

fine finishes
755 Brewton Street
Forest Hills, AL 36105

1108
71-821
3321

DATE *February 14* 20—

PAY TO THE ORDER OF *Custom Color* $ *200.00*

Two hundred and 00/100 ——————————— DOLLARS

✹ *Barclays Bank*

MEMO *On account* *Laura Andersen*

⑊3321718 21⑊ 4516 2133⑊ 1108

Mini Practice Set 6   (continued)

fine finishes		1109
755 Brewton Street		71-821
Forest Hills, AL 36105		3321

DATE *February 15* 20--

PAY TO THE ORDER OF *Laura Andersen* $ *650.00*

Six hundred fifty and ⁰⁰/₁₀₀ _____ DOLLARS

✦ *Barclays Bank*

MEMO *Personal withdrawal* *Laura Andersen*

⑆332171821⑆ 4516 2133ıı 1109

---

fine finishes		1110
755 Brewton Street		71-821
Forest Hills, AL 36105		3321

DATE *February 15* 20--

PAY TO THE ORDER OF *David Ingram* $ *650.00*

Six hundred fifty and ⁰⁰/₁₀₀ _____ DOLLARS

✦ *Barclays Bank*

MEMO *Personal withdrawal* *Laura Andersen*

⑆332171821⑆ 4516 2133ıı 1110

---

fine finishes		1111
755 Brewton Street		71-821
Forest Hills, AL 36105		3321

DATE *February 15* 20--

PAY TO THE ORDER OF *Sean Woo* $ *650.00*

Six hundred fifty and ⁰⁰/₁₀₀ _____ DOLLARS

✦ *Barclays Bank*

MEMO *Personal withdrawal* *Laura Andersen*

⑆332171821⑆ 4516 2133ıı 1111

---

fine finishes	**RECEIPT**
755 Brewton Street	No. 04
Forest Hills, AL 36105	

February 15 20--

RECEIVED FROM *Wicker & Hartel Law Office* $ *1,000.00*

One thousand and ⁰⁰/₁₀₀ _____ DOLLARS

FOR *Deposit on contract*

RECEIVED BY *Laura Andersen*

---

fine finishes		1112
755 Brewton Street		71-821
Forest Hills, AL 36105		3321

DATE *February 16* 20--

PAY TO THE ORDER OF *Odds & Ends (Painting Supplies)* $ *135.00*

One hundred thirty-five and ⁰⁰/₁₀₀ _____ DOLLARS

✦ *Barclays Bank*

MEMO *Painting supplies* *Laura Andersen*

⑆332171821⑆ 4516 2133ıı 1112

Custom Color		**INVOICE NO. 750**
3167 Turner Place, #1A		DATE: *Feb. 16, 20--*
Wildwood, AL 36120		ORDER NO.:
		SHIPPED BY:
TO *Fine Finishes*		TERMS:
755 Brewton Street		
Forest Hills, AL 36105		

QTY.	ITEM	UNIT PRICE	TOTAL
5	*Paint gallons*	$79.00	$395.00

---

fine finishes		1113
755 Brewton Street		71-821
Forest Hills, AL 36105		3321

DATE *February 16* 20--

PAY TO THE ORDER OF *Mountain View Realtors* $ *77.00*

Seventy-seven and ⁰⁰/₁₀₀ _____ DOLLARS

✦ *Barclays Bank*

MEMO *Advertisement* *Laura Andersen*

⑆332171821⑆ 4516 2133ıı 1113

---

fine finishes	**RECEIPT**
755 Brewton Street	No. 05
Forest Hills, AL 36105	

February 18 20--

RECEIVED FROM *Prospective Client* $ *125.00*

One hundred twenty-five and ⁰⁰/₁₀₀ _____ DOLLARS

FOR *Painting consultation*

RECEIVED BY *Laura Andersen*

Mini Practice Set 6   (continued)

fine finishes   **1114**
755 Brewton Street   71-821 / 3321
Forest Hills, AL 36105

DATE *February 19*   20 —

PAY TO THE ORDER OF *A-1 Repair Services* $ *85.00*

Eighty-five and 00/100 ——————————— DOLLARS

⚓ *Barclays Bank*

MEMO *Computer repair*   *Laura Andersen*

⑊3321?1821⑊ 451b 2133‴ 1114

---

fine finishes   **RECEIPT**
755 Brewton Street   No. 07
Forest Hills, AL 36105

February 25   20 —

RECEIVED FROM *Maintenance Service* $ *575.00*

Five hundred seventy-five and 00/100 ——————— DOLLARS

FOR *Minor repairs to garage*

RECEIVED BY *Laura Andersen*

---

fine finishes   **1115**
755 Brewton Street   71-821 / 3321
Forest Hills, AL 36105

DATE *February 21*   20 —

PAY TO THE ORDER OF *Paint Palace* $ *375.00*

Three hundred seventy-five and 00/100 ——————— DOLLARS

⚓ *Barclays Bank*

MEMO *On account*   *Laura Andersen*

⑊3321?1821⑊ 451b 2133‴ 1115

---

fine finishes   **1116**
755 Brewton Street   71-821 / 3321
Forest Hills, AL 36105

DATE *February 28*   20 —

PAY TO THE ORDER OF *Laura Andersen* $ *650.00*

Six hundred fifty and 00/100 ——————————— DOLLARS

⚓ *Barclays Bank*

MEMO *Personal withdrawal*   *David Ingram*

⑊3321?1821⑊ 451b 2133‴ 111b

---

fine finishes   **RECEIPT**
755 Brewton Street   No. 06
Forest Hills, AL 36105

February 22   20 —

RECEIVED FROM *Wicker & Hartel Law Office* $ *2,000.00*

Two thousand and 00/100 ——————————— DOLLARS

FOR *Final payment*

RECEIVED BY *Laura Andersen*

---

fine finishes   **1117**
755 Brewton Street   71-821 / 3321
Forest Hills, AL 36105

DATE *February 28*   20 —

PAY TO THE ORDER OF *David Ingram* $ *650.00*

Six hundred fifty and 00/100 ——————————— DOLLARS

⚓ *Barclays Bank*

MEMO *Personal withdrawal*   *Laura Andersen*

⑊3321?1821⑊ 451b 2133‴ 111?

Hardware & Lumber   **INVOICE NO. 207**
J&J   315 Rooster Lane
Wildwood, AL 36121   DATE: *Feb. 24, 20 —*

ORDER NO.:
SHIPPED BY:
TO   *Fine Finishes*   TERMS:
    755 Brewton Street
    Forest Hills, AL 36105

QTY.	ITEM	UNIT PRICE	TOTAL
10	Paint brushes	$9.00	$90.00

---

fine finishes   **1118**
755 Brewton Street   71-821 / 3321
Forest Hills, AL 36105

DATE *February 28*   20 —

PAY TO THE ORDER OF *Sean Woo* $ *650.00*

Six hundred fifty and 00/100 ——————————— DOLLARS

⚓ *Barclays Bank*

MEMO *Personal withdrawal*   *David Ingram*

⑊3321?1821⑊ 451b 2133‴ 111b

Computerized Accounting Using Peachtree

Mini Practice Set 6

INSTRUCTIONS

Beginning a Session

Step 1 Select the problem set: Fine Finishes (MP-6).
Step 2 Rename the company, and set the system date to February 29, 2004.

Completing the Accounting Problem

Step 3 Review the transactions provided in your textbook.
Step 4 Record all of the business transactions using the **General Journal Entry** option.

> **TIP:** As a shortcut, you can type just the day of the month when you enter a general journal entry.

> **TIP:** You can use the ⊞Add and ⊟Remove buttons to edit a multi-line general journal entry.

Step 5 Print a General Journal report and proof your work.

> **TIP:** Double-click a report title in the Select a Report window to go directly to that report.

Step 6 Print a General Ledger report.

> **TIP:** Set the General Ledger report format option to "Summary by Transaction" to save paper when you print this report.

Step 7 Print a General Ledger Trial Balance.
Step 8 Print an Income Statement and a Balance Sheet.

> **TIP:** Choose the custom Income Statement report option, not the <Predefined> Income Statement.

Step 9   Manually prepare a Statement of Partners' Equity.

Step 10   Click the **Save Pre-closing Balances** button in the Glencoe Smart Guide window. It is important that you save your work before the closing process.

Closing the Period

Step 11   Close the current period. Use the **General Journal Entry** form to enter the closing entries manually.

                 IMPORTANT: Fine Finishes operates on a monthly fiscal period. Therefore, you must manually close the current period by entering the closing entries. Peachtree can close only a fiscal year.

Step 12   Print a General Journal report and proof your work.

Step 13   Print a Post-Closing Trial Balance.

> **TIP:** Using the report options you can change the title of a report.

Step 14   Answer the Analyze questions.

Ending the Session

Step 15   Click the **Close Problem** button in the Glencoe Smart Guide window.

Mini Practice Set 6 (continued)

(1), (4), (9)

GENERAL LEDGER

ACCOUNT _____ ACCOUNT NO. _____

DATE	DESCRIPTION	POST. REF.	DEBIT	CREDIT	BALANCE DEBIT	BALANCE CREDIT

ACCOUNT _____ ACCOUNT NO. _____

DATE	DESCRIPTION	POST. REF.	DEBIT	CREDIT	BALANCE DEBIT	BALANCE CREDIT

Mini Practice Set 6 (continued)

ACCOUNT _____ ACCOUNT NO. _____

DATE	DESCRIPTION	POST. REF.	DEBIT	CREDIT	BALANCE	
					DEBIT	CREDIT

ACCOUNT _____ ACCOUNT NO. _____

DATE	DESCRIPTION	POST. REF.	DEBIT	CREDIT	BALANCE	
					DEBIT	CREDIT

ACCOUNT _____ ACCOUNT NO. _____

DATE	DESCRIPTION	POST. REF.	DEBIT	CREDIT	BALANCE	
					DEBIT	CREDIT

ACCOUNT _____ ACCOUNT NO. _____

DATE	DESCRIPTION	POST. REF.	DEBIT	CREDIT	BALANCE	
					DEBIT	CREDIT

ACCOUNT _____ ACCOUNT NO. _____

DATE	DESCRIPTION	POST. REF.	DEBIT	CREDIT	BALANCE	
					DEBIT	CREDIT

Mini Practice Set 6 (continued)

ACCOUNT _____ ACCOUNT NO. _____

DATE	DESCRIPTION	POST. REF.	DEBIT	CREDIT	BALANCE	
					DEBIT	CREDIT

ACCOUNT _____ ACCOUNT NO. _____

DATE	DESCRIPTION	POST. REF.	DEBIT	CREDIT	BALANCE	
					DEBIT	CREDIT

ACCOUNT _____ ACCOUNT NO. _____

DATE	DESCRIPTION	POST. REF.	DEBIT	CREDIT	BALANCE	
					DEBIT	CREDIT

ACCOUNT _____ ACCOUNT NO. _____

DATE	DESCRIPTION	POST. REF.	DEBIT	CREDIT	BALANCE	
					DEBIT	CREDIT

ACCOUNT _____ ACCOUNT NO. _____

DATE	DESCRIPTION	POST. REF.	DEBIT	CREDIT	BALANCE	
					DEBIT	CREDIT

Mini Practice Set 6   (continued)

ACCOUNT _____ ACCOUNT NO. _____

DATE	DESCRIPTION	POST. REF.	DEBIT	CREDIT	BALANCE	
					DEBIT	CREDIT

ACCOUNT _____ ACCOUNT NO. _____

DATE	DESCRIPTION	POST. REF.	DEBIT	CREDIT	BALANCE	
					DEBIT	CREDIT

ACCOUNT _____ ACCOUNT NO. _____

DATE	DESCRIPTION	POST. REF.	DEBIT	CREDIT	BALANCE	
					DEBIT	CREDIT

ACCOUNT _____ ACCOUNT NO. _____

DATE	DESCRIPTION	POST. REF.	DEBIT	CREDIT	BALANCE	
					DEBIT	CREDIT

Mini Practice Set 6   (continued)

ACCOUNT _____ ACCOUNT NO. _____

DATE	DESCRIPTION	POST. REF.	DEBIT	CREDIT	BALANCE DEBIT	BALANCE CREDIT

ACCOUNT _____ ACCOUNT NO. _____

DATE	DESCRIPTION	POST. REF.	DEBIT	CREDIT	BALANCE DEBIT	BALANCE CREDIT

ACCOUNT _____ ACCOUNT NO. _____

DATE	DESCRIPTION	POST. REF.	DEBIT	CREDIT	BALANCE DEBIT	BALANCE CREDIT

Mini Practice Set 6   (continued)

ACCOUNT _____ ACCOUNT NO. _____

DATE		DESCRIPTION	POST. REF.	DEBIT	CREDIT	BALANCE	
						DEBIT	CREDIT

ACCOUNT _____ ACCOUNT NO. _____

DATE		DESCRIPTION	POST. REF.	DEBIT	CREDIT	BALANCE	
						DEBIT	CREDIT

ACCOUNT _____ ACCOUNT NO. _____

DATE		DESCRIPTION	POST. REF.	DEBIT	CREDIT	BALANCE	
						DEBIT	CREDIT

ACCOUNT _____ ACCOUNT NO. _____

DATE		DESCRIPTION	POST. REF.	DEBIT	CREDIT	BALANCE	
						DEBIT	CREDIT

Mini Practice Set 6 (continued)

(2), (3), (9)

GENERAL JOURNAL

PAGE _____

	DATE	DESCRIPTION	POST. REF.	DEBIT	CREDIT	
1						1
2						2
3						3
4						4
5						5
6						6
7						7
8						8
9						9
10						10
11						11
12						12
13						13
14						14
15						15
16						16
17						17
18						18
19						19
20						20
21						21
22						22
23						23
24						24
25						25
26						26
27						27
28						28
29						29
30						30
31						31
32						32
33						33
34						34
35						35
36						36
37						37

GENERAL JOURNAL   PAGE _____

	DATE	DESCRIPTION	POST. REF.	DEBIT	CREDIT	
1						1
2						2
3						3
4						4
5						5
6						6
7						7
8						8
9						9
10						10
11						11
12						12
13						13
14						14
15						15
16						16
17						17
18						18
19						19
20						20
21						21
22						22
23						23
24						24
25						25
26						26
27						27
28						28
29						29
30						30
31						31
32						32
33						33
34						34
35						35
36						36
37						37
38						38

Mini Practice Set 6   (continued)

GENERAL JOURNAL   PAGE _____

	DATE		DESCRIPTION	POST. REF.	DEBIT	CREDIT	
1							1
2							2
3							3
4							4
5							5
6							6
7							7
8							8
9							9
10							10
11							11
12							12
13							13
14							14
15							15
16							16
17							17
18							18
19							19
20							20
21							21
22							22
23							23
24							24
25							25
26							26
27							27
28							28
29							29
30							30
31							31
32							32
33							33
34							34
35							35
36							36
37							37
38							38

Mini Practice Set 6   (continued)

GENERAL JOURNAL   PAGE _____

	DATE		DESCRIPTION	POST. REF.	DEBIT	CREDIT	
1							1
2							2
3							3
4							4
5							5
6							6
7							7
8							8
9							9
10							10
11							11
12							12
13							13
14							14
15							15
16							16
17							17
18							18
19							19
20							20
21							21
22							22
23							23
24							24
25							25
26							26
27							27
28							28
29							29
30							30
31							31
32							32
33							33
34							34
35							35
36							36
37							37
38							38

Mini Practice Set 6 (continued) **(5)**

ACCT. NO.	ACCOUNT NAME	TRIAL BALANCE		INCOME STATEMENT		BALANCE SHEET	
		DEBIT	CREDIT	DEBIT	CREDIT	DEBIT	CREDIT
1							
2							
3							
4							
5							
6							
7							
8							
9							
10							
11							
12							
13							
14							
15							
16							
17							
18							
19							
20							
21							
22							
23							
24							
25							
26							

Mini Practice Set 6   (continued)

(6)

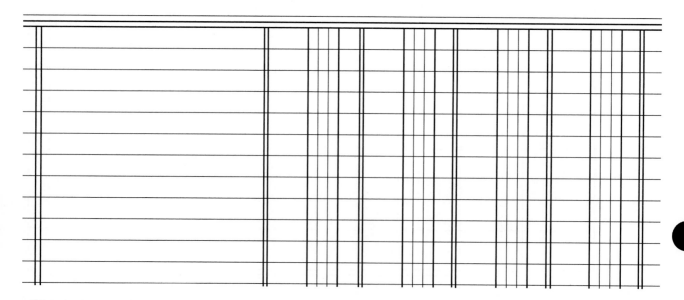

(7)

Mini Practice Set 6   (continued)

(8)

Mini Practice Set 6 (concluded)
(10)

Analyze: 1. _____

2. _____

3. _____

4. _____

MINI PRACTICE SET **6**

Fine Finishes

Audit Test

Directions: *Use your completed solutions to answer the following questions. Write the answer in the space to the left of each question.*

Answer

_____ **1.** How many checks were issued by Fine Finishes in the month of February?

_____ **2.** What is the total ending balance of the Accounts Payable accounts at February 28?

_____ **3.** What is the ending balance of the Accounts Receivable account at February 28?

_____ **4.** What total amount was credited to the Painting Fees revenue account for the month?

_____ **5.** What were the total expenses for the month?

_____ **6.** What amount was debited to the Income Summary account to close the expense accounts for the period?

_____ **7.** How many accounts were listed on the trial balance dated February 28, 20--?

_____ **8.** What was the net income for the period?

_____ **9.** When net income was divided between the partners, how much was allocated to Laura Andersen?

_____ **10.** What total withdrawals were made by all three partners for the period?

_____   **11.** What was the ending balance for the David Ingram, Capital account?

_____   **12.** What was the amount of total assets for the business at February 28?

_____   **13.** What was the amount of total liabilities for the business at February 28?

_____   **14.** How many accounts were listed on the post-closing trial balance?

_____   **15.** At month end, what debts remain unpaid by Fine Finishes?

_____   **16.** What was the total amount of debits to the Cash in Bank account for the period?

Recording Transactions in the Combination Journal

Problem A-1   Analyzing Transactions for Combination Journal Entries

Date	Transaction	General Dr.	General Cr.	Accounts Receivable Dr.	Accounts Receivable Cr.	Sales Cr.	Sales Tax Payable Cr.	Accounts Payable Dr.	Accounts Payable Cr.	Purchases Dr.	Cash in Bank Dr.	Cash in Bank Cr.
Dec. 1	Debit	✓										
	Credit								✓			
2	Debit											
	Credit											
5	Debit											
	Credit											
10	Debit											
	Credit											
13	Debit											
	Credit											
15	Debit											
	Credit											
18	Debit											
	Credit											
22	Debit											
	Credit											
25	Debit											
	Credit											
25	Debit											
	Credit											
30	Debit											
	Credit											
31	Debit											
	Credit											

Problem A-2 Recording Transactions
Totaling, Proving, and Ruling the Combination Journal

COMBINATION

	DATE	ACCOUNT NAME	DOC. NO.	POST. REF.	GENERAL		ACCOUNTS RECEIVABLE	
					DEBIT	CREDIT	DEBIT	CREDIT
1								
2								
3								
4								
5								
6								
7								
8								
9								
10								
11								
12								
13								
14								
15								
16								
17								
18								
19								
20								
21								
22								
23								
24								
25								
26								
27								
28								
29								
30								
31								
32								
33								

JOURNAL

MEDICAL FEES CREDIT	LABORATORY FEES CREDIT	ACCOUNTS PAYABLE		MEDICAL SUPPLIES DEBIT	CASH IN BANK		
		DEBIT	CREDIT		DEBIT	CREDIT	
							1
							2
							3
							4
							5
							6
							7
							8
							9
							10
							11
							12
							13
							14
							15
							16
							17
							18
							19
							20
							21
							22
							23
							24
							25
							26
							27
							28
							29
							30
							31
							32
							33

Problem A-3   Recording Transactions
Totaling, Proving, and Ruling the Combination Journal

COMBINATION

	DATE		ACCOUNT NAME	DOC. NO.	POST. REF.	GENERAL DEBIT	GENERAL CREDIT	ACCOUNTS RECEIVABLE DEBIT	ACCOUNTS RECEIVABLE CREDIT
1									
2									
3									
4									
5									
6									
7									
8									
9									
10									
11									
12									
13									
14									
15									
16									
17									
18									
19									
20									
21									
22									
23									
24									
25									
26									
27									
28									
29									
30									
31									
32									
33									
34									
35									
36									

JOURNAL

PAGE_____

SALES CREDIT	SALES TAX PAYABLE CREDIT	ACCOUNTS PAYABLE		PURCHASES DEBIT	CASH IN BANK		
		DEBIT	CREDIT		DEBIT	CREDIT	
							1
							2
							3
							4
							5
							6
							7
							8
							9
							10
							11
							12
							13
							14
							15
							16
							17
							18
							19
							20
							21
							22
							23
							24
							25
							26
							27
							28
							29
							30
							31
							32
							33
							34
							35
							36

Problem A-4   Recording Adjusting and Closing Entries in a Combination Journal

In Beat CD Shop
Work Sheet
For Period Ended December 31, 20--

Line	ACCT. NO.	ACCOUNT NAME	ADJUSTMENTS DEBIT	ADJUSTMENTS CREDIT	INCOME STATEMENT DEBIT	INCOME STATEMENT CREDIT	BALANCE SHEET DEBIT	BALANCE SHEET CREDIT
1	120	Merchandise Inventory	(a) 2000000				2600000	
2	125	Supplies		(b) 27000			9500	
3	130	Prepaid Insurance		(c) 70000			10000	
4								
5								
6	137	Accum. Depr.—Store Equip.		(d) 180000				540000
7								
8								
9	205	Federal Income Tax Payable		(e) 60000				60000
10								
11								
12	301	Capital Stock						2840000
13	305	Retained Earnings						840000
14	310	Income Summary		(a) 2000000		200000		
15	401	Sales				4600000		
16	405	Sales Returns and Allowances			40500			
17	501	Purchases			1800000			
18	505	Transportation In			120000			
19	510	Purchases Discounts				22500		
20	515	Purchases Returns and Allow.				15000		
21	620	Depr. Expense—Store Equip.	(d) 180000		180000			
22	625	Federal Income Tax Expense	(e) 60000		140000			
23	630	Insurance Expense	(c) 70000		70000			
24	650	Miscellaneous Expense			50000			
25	655	Rent Expense			600000			
26	665	Supplies Expense	(b) 27000		27000			

Problem A-4 (concluded)

(1), (2)

COMBINATION JOURNAL (PARTIAL)

	DATE	ACCOUNT NAME	DOC. NO.	POST. REF.	GENERAL DEBIT	GENERAL CREDIT	ACCOUNTS RECEIVABLE DEBIT	ACCOUNTS RECEIVABLE CREDIT
1								
2								
3								
4								
5								
6								
7								
8								
9								
10								
11								
12								
13								
14								
15								
16								
17								
18								
19								
20								
21								
22								
23								
24								
25								
26								
27								
28								
29								
30								
31								
32								
33								

APPENDIX  The Accrual Basis of Accounting

Problem B-1   Identifying Accruals and Deferrals

Item	Prepaid Expense	Unearned Revenue	Accrued Expense	Accrued Revenue
1				
2				
3				
4				
5				
6				
7				
8				
9				
10				
11				

Problem B-2   Recording Adjusting Entries

GENERAL JOURNAL   PAGE _____

	DATE	DESCRIPTION	POST. REF.	DEBIT	CREDIT	
1						1
2						2
3						3
4						4
5						5
6						6
7						7
8						8
9						9
10						10
11						11
12						12
13						13
14						14
15						15
16						16
17						17
18						18
19						19
20						20

Problem B-3   Recording Transactions for Notes Payable

GENERAL JOURNAL   PAGE _____

	DATE	DESCRIPTION	POST. REF.	DEBIT	CREDIT	
1						1
2						2
3						3
4						4
5						5
6						6
7						7
8						8
9						9
10						10
11						11
12						12
13						13
14						14
15						15
16						16
17						17
18						18
19						19
20						20

Problem B-4   Recording Accrued Expenses

GENERAL JOURNAL   PAGE _____

	DATE	DESCRIPTION	POST. REF.	DEBIT	CREDIT	
1						1
2						2
3						3
4						4
5						5
6						6
7						7
8						8
9						9
10						10
11						11
12						12
13						13
14						14
15						15
16						16
17						17
18						18
19						19
20						20

APPENDIX C Federal Personal Income Tax

1997 Tax Table

If line 38 (taxable income) is—		And you are—			
At least	But less than	Single	Married filing jointly *	Married filing separately	Head of a house-hold
		Your tax is—			
$0	$5	$0	$0	$0	$0
5	15	2	2	2	2
15	25	3	3	3	3
25	50	6	6	6	6
50	75	9	9	9	9
75	100	13	13	13	13
100	125	17	17	17	17
125	150	21	21	21	21
150	175	24	24	24	24
175	200	28	28	28	28
200	225	32	32	32	32
225	250	36	36	36	36
250	275	39	39	39	39
275	300	43	43	43	43
300	325	47	47	47	47
325	350	51	51	51	51
350	375	54	54	54	54
375	400	58	58	58	58
400	425	62	62	62	62
425	450	66	66	66	66
450	475	69	69	69	69
475	500	73	73	73	73
500	525	77	77	77	77
525	550	81	81	81	81
550	575	84	84	84	84
575	600	88	88	88	88
600	625	92	92	92	92
625	650	96	96	96	96
650	675	99	99	99	99
675	700	103	103	103	103
700	725	107	107	107	107
725	750	111	111	111	111
750	775	114	114	114	114
775	800	118	118	118	118
800	825	122	122	122	122
825	850	126	126	126	126
850	875	129	129	129	129
875	900	133	133	133	133
900	925	137	137	137	137
925	950	141	141	141	141
950	975	144	144	144	144
975	1,000	148	148	148	148
1,000					
1,000	1,025	152	152	152	152
1,025	1,050	156	156	156	156
1,050	1,075	159	159	159	159
1,075	1,100	163	163	163	163
1,100	1,125	167	167	167	167
1,125	1,150	171	171	171	171
1,150	1,175	174	174	174	174
1,175	1,200	178	178	178	178
1,200	1,225	182	182	182	182
1,225	1,250	186	186	186	186
1,250	1,275	189	189	189	189
1,275	1,300	193	193	193	193

If line 38 (taxable income) is—		And you are—			
At least	But less than	Single	Married filing jointly *	Married filing separately	Head of a house-hold
		Your tax is—			
1,300	1,325	197	197	197	197
1,325	1,350	201	201	201	201
1,350	1,375	204	204	204	204
1,375	1,400	208	208	208	208
1,400	1,425	212	212	212	212
1,425	1,450	216	216	216	216
1,450	1,475	219	219	219	219
1,475	1,500	223	223	223	223
1,500	1,525	227	227	227	227
1,525	1,550	231	231	231	231
1,550	1,575	234	234	234	234
1,575	1,600	238	238	238	238
1,600	1,625	242	242	242	242
1,625	1,650	246	246	246	246
1,650	1,675	249	249	249	249
1,675	1,700	253	253	253	253
1,700	1,725	257	257	257	257
1,725	1,750	261	261	261	261
1,750	1,775	264	264	264	264
1,775	1,800	268	268	268	268
1,800	1,825	272	272	272	272
1,825	1,850	276	276	276	276
1,850	1,875	279	279	279	279
1,875	1,900	283	283	283	283
1,900	1,925	287	287	287	287
1,925	1,950	291	291	291	291
1,950	1,975	294	294	294	294
1,975	2,000	298	298	298	298
2,000					
2,000	2,025	302	302	302	302
2,025	2,050	306	306	306	306
2,050	2,075	309	309	309	309
2,075	2,100	313	313	313	313
2,100	2,125	317	317	317	317
2,125	2,150	321	321	321	321
2,150	2,175	324	324	324	324
2,175	2,200	328	328	328	328
2,200	2,225	332	332	332	332
2,225	2,250	336	336	336	336
2,250	2,275	339	339	339	339
2,275	2,300	343	343	343	343
2,300	2,325	347	347	347	347
2,325	2,350	351	351	351	351
2,350	2,375	354	354	354	354
2,375	2,400	358	358	358	358
2,400	2,425	362	362	362	362
2,425	2,450	366	366	366	366
2,450	2,475	369	369	369	369
2,475	2,500	373	373	373	373
2,500	2,525	377	377	377	377
2,525	2,550	381	381	381	381
2,550	2,575	384	384	384	384
2,575	2,600	388	388	388	388
2,600	2,625	392	392	392	392
2,625	2,650	396	396	396	396
2,650	2,675	399	399	399	399
2,675	2,700	403	403	403	403

If line 38 (taxable income) is—		And you are—			
At least	But less than	Single	Married filing jointly *	Married filing separately	Head of a house-hold
		Your tax is—			
2,700	2,725	407	407	407	407
2,725	2,750	411	411	411	411
2,750	2,775	414	414	414	414
2,775	2,800	418	418	418	418
2,800	2,825	422	422	422	422
2,825	2,850	426	426	426	426
2,850	2,875	429	429	429	429
2,875	2,900	433	433	433	433
2,900	2,925	437	437	437	437
2,925	2,950	441	441	441	441
2,950	2,975	444	444	444	444
2,975	3,000	448	448	448	448
3,000					
3,000	3,050	454	454	454	454
3,050	3,100	461	461	461	461
3,100	3,150	469	469	469	469
3,150	3,200	476	476	476	476
3,200	3,250	484	484	484	484
3,250	3,300	491	491	491	491
3,300	3,350	499	499	499	499
3,350	3,400	506	506	506	506
3,400	3,450	514	514	514	514
3,450	3,500	521	521	521	521
3,500	3,550	529	529	529	529
3,550	3,600	536	536	536	536
3,600	3,650	544	544	544	544
3,650	3,700	551	551	551	551
3,700	3,750	559	559	559	559
3,750	3,800	566	566	566	566
3,800	3,850	574	574	574	574
3,850	3,900	581	581	581	581
3,900	3,950	589	589	589	589
3,950	4,000	596	596	596	596
4,000					
4,000	4,050	604	604	604	604
4,050	4,100	611	611	611	611
4,100	4,150	619	619	619	619
4,150	4,200	626	626	626	626
4,200	4,250	634	634	634	634
4,250	4,300	641	641	641	641
4,300	4,350	649	649	649	649
4,350	4,400	656	656	656	656
4,400	4,450	664	664	664	664
4,450	4,500	671	671	671	671
4,500	4,550	679	679	679	679
4,550	4,600	686	686	686	686
4,600	4,650	694	694	694	694
4,650	4,700	701	701	701	701
4,700	4,750	709	709	709	709
4,750	4,800	716	716	716	716
4,800	4,850	724	724	724	724
4,850	4,900	731	731	731	731
4,900	4,950	739	739	739	739
4,950	5,000	746	746	746	746

Continued on next page

* This column must also be used by a qualifying widow(er).

Problem C-1   Preparing Form 1040EZ

Form **1040EZ**

Department of the Treasury—Internal Revenue Service
Income Tax Return for Single and Joint Filers With No Dependents (99) **1997**

OMB No. 1545-0675

Use the IRS label here

Your first name and initial   Last name

If a joint return, spouse's first name and initial   Last name

Home address (number and street). If you have a P.O. box, see page 7.   Apt. no.

City, town or post office, state, and ZIP code. If you have a foreign address, see page 7.

Your social security number

Spouse's social security number

Presidential Election Campaign (See page 7.)

Note: *Checking "Yes" will not change your tax or reduce your refund.*
Do you want $3 to go to this fund? ▶   Yes ☐ No ☐
If a joint return, does your spouse want $3 to go to this fund? ▶   Yes ☐ No ☐

Dollars   **Cents**

Income

Attach Copy B of Form(s) W-2 here. Enclose but do not attach any payment with your return.

1 Total wages, salaries, and tips. This should be shown in box 1 of your W-2 form(s). Attach your W-2 form(s).   1

2 Taxable interest income. If the total is over $400, you cannot use Form 1040EZ.   2

3 Unemployment compensation (see page 9).   3

4 Add lines 1, 2, and 3. This is your **adjusted gross income.** If under $9,770, see page 9 to find out if you can claim the earned income credit on line 8a.   4

Note: *You* **must** *check Yes or No.*

5 Can your parents (or someone else) claim you on their return?
Yes. Enter amount from worksheet on back. ☐
No. If **single,** enter 6,800.00. If **married,** enter 12,200.00. See back for explanation.   5

6 Subtract line 5 from line 4. If line 5 is larger than line 4, enter 0. This is your **taxable income.** ▶ 6

Payments and tax

7 Enter your Federal income tax withheld from box 2 of your W-2 form(s).   7

8a Earned income credit (see page 9).
b Nontaxable earned income: enter type and amount below.
Type ___ $ ___   8a

9 Add lines 7 and 8a. These are your **total payments.**   9

10 Tax. Use the amount on **line 6** to find your tax in the tax table on pages 20—24 of the booklet. Then, enter the tax from the table on this line.   10

Refund

Have it directly deposited! See page 13 and fill in 11b, 11c, and 11d.

11a If line 9 is larger than line 10, subtract line 10 from line 9. This is your **refund.**   11a

b Routing number
c Type: Checking ☐ Savings ☐   **d** Account number

Amount you owe

12 If line 10 is larger than line 9, subtract line 9 from line 10. This is the **amount you owe.** See page 13 for details on how to pay.   12

I have read this return. Under penalties of perjury, I declare that to the best of my knowledge and belief, the return is true, correct, and accurately lists all amounts and sources of income I received during the tax year.

Sign here ▶
Keep copy for your records.

Your signature | Spouse's signature if joint return
Date | Your occupation | Date | Spouse's occupation

For Official Use Only

1 2 3 4 5
6 7 8 9 10

For Privacy Act and Paperwork Reduction Act Notice, see page 18.   Cat. No. 11329W   1997 Form 1040EZ

Problem C-1   (concluded)

1997 Form 1040EZ page 2

Use this form if

- Your filing status is single or married filing jointly.
- You do not claim any dependents.
- You (and your spouse if married) were under 65 on January 1, 1998, and not blind at the end of 1997.
- Your taxable income (line 6) is less than $50,000.
- You had **only** wages, salaries, tips, taxable scholarship or fellowship grants, unemployment compensation, or Alaska Permanent Fund dividends, and your taxable interest income was not over $400. **But** if you earned tips, including allocated tips, that are not included in box 5 and box 7 of your W-2, you may not be able to use Form 1040EZ. See page 8.
- You did not receive any advance earned income credit payments.

If you are not sure about your filing status, see page 6. If you have questions about dependents, use TeleTax topic 354 (see page 18). If you **cannot use this form,** use TeleTax topic 352 (see page 18).

Filling in your return

For tips on how to avoid common mistakes, see page 3.

Because this form is read by a machine, please print your numbers inside the boxes like this:

9 8 7 6 5 4 3 2 1 0   Do not type your numbers. Do not use dollar signs.

If you received a scholarship or fellowship grant or tax-exempt interest income, such as on municipal bonds, see the booklet before filling in the form. Also, see the booklet if you received a Form 1099-INT showing Federal income tax withheld or if Federal income tax was withheld from your unemployment compensation or Alaska Permanent Fund dividends.

Remember, you must report all wages, salaries, and tips even if you do not get a W-2 form from your employer. You must also report all your taxable interest income, including interest from banks, savings and loans, credit unions, etc., even if you do not get a Form 1099-INT.

Worksheet for dependents who checked "Yes" on line 5

Use this worksheet to figure the amount to enter on line 5 if someone can claim you (or your spouse if married) as a dependent, even if that person chooses not to do so. To find out if someone can claim you as a dependent, use TeleTax topic 354 (see page 18).

A. Enter the amount from line 1 on the front.	**A.** _____
B. Minimum standard deduction.	**B.** _____ 650.00
C. Enter the LARGER of line A or line B here.	**C.** _____
D. Maximum standard deduction. If single, enter 4,150.00; if married, enter 6,900.00.	**D.** _____
E. Enter the SMALLER of line C or line D here. This is your standard deduction.	**E.** _____

F. Exemption amount.
  • If single, enter 0.
  • If married and—
    —both you and your spouse can be claimed as dependents, enter 0.
    —only one of you can be claimed as a dependent, enter 2,650.00.
	F. _____

G. Add lines E and F. Enter the total here and on line 5 on the front.	**G.** _____

If you checked "No" on line 5 because no one can claim you (or your spouse if married) as a dependent, enter on line 5 the amount shown below that applies to you.

- Single, enter 6,800.00. This is the total of your standard deduction (4,150.00) and your exemption (2,650.00).
- Married, enter 12,200.00. This is the total of your standard deduction (6,900.00), your exemption (2,650.00), and your spouse's exemption (2,650.00).

Mailing your return

Mail your return by **April 15, 1998.** Use the envelope that came with your booklet. If you do not have that envelope, see page 28 for the address to use.

Paid preparer's use only

See page 14.

Under penalties of perjury, I declare that I have examined this return, and to the best of my knowledge and belief, it is true, correct, and accurately lists all amounts and sources of income received during the tax year. This declaration is based on all information of which I have any knowledge.

Preparer's signature ▶	Date	Check if self-employed ☐	Preparer's SSN
Firm's name (or yours if self-employed) and address ▶		EIN	
		ZIP code	

Problem C-2   Preparing Form 1040EZ

Form 1040EZ

Department of the Treasury—Internal Revenue Service

Income Tax Return for Single and Joint Filers With No Dependents (99) **1997**   OMB No. 1545-0675

Use the IRS label here

Your first name and initial   Last name

If a joint return, spouse's first name and initial   Last name

Home address (number and street). If you have a P.O. box, see page 7.   Apt. no.

City, town or post office, state, and ZIP code. If you have a foreign address, see page 7.

Your social security number

Spouse's social security number

Presidential Election Campaign
(See page 7.)

Note: *Checking "Yes" will not change your tax or reduce your refund.*

Do you want $3 to go to this fund? ▶   Yes ☐ No ☐

If a joint return, does your spouse want $3 to go to this fund? ▶   Yes ☐ No ☐

Dollars   **Cents**

Income

Attach Copy B of Form(s) W-2 here. Enclose but do not attach any payment with your return.

1 Total wages, salaries, and tips. This should be shown in box 1 of your W-2 form(s). Attach your W-2 form(s).   1

2 Taxable interest income. If the total is over $400, you cannot use Form 1040EZ.   2

3 Unemployment compensation (see page 9).   3

4 Add lines 1, 2, and 3. This is your **adjusted gross income.** If under $9,770, see page 9 to find out if you can claim the earned income credit on line 8a.   4

Note: *You **must** check Yes or No.*

5 Can your parents (or someone else) claim you on their return?

Yes. Enter amount from worksheet on back. ☐

No. If **single,** enter 6,800.00. If **married,** enter 12,200.00. See back for explanation. ☐   5

6 Subtract line 5 from line 4. If line 5 is larger than line 4, enter 0. This is your **taxable income.** ▶   6

Payments and tax

7 Enter your Federal income tax withheld from box 2 of your W-2 form(s).   7

8a **Earned income credit** (see page 9).
  b Nontaxable earned income: enter type and amount below.

Type $ 8a

9 Add lines 7 and 8a. These are your **total payments.**   9

10 **Tax.** Use the amount on **line 6** to find your tax in the tax table on pages 20—24 of the booklet. Then, enter the tax from the table on this line.   10

Refund

Have it directly deposited! See page 13 and fill in 11b, 11c, and 11d.

11a If line 9 is larger than line 10, subtract line 10 from line 9. This is your **refund.**   11a

  b Routing number

  c Type: Checking ☐ Savings ☐

  d Account number

Amount you owe

12 If line 10 is larger than line 9, subtract line 9 from line 10. This is the **amount you owe.** See page 13 for details on how to pay.   12

I have read this return. Under penalties of perjury, I declare that to the best of my knowledge and belief, the return is true, correct, and accurately lists all amounts and sources of income I received during the tax year.

Sign here

Keep copy for your records.

Your signature   Spouse's signature if joint return

Date   Your occupation   Date   Spouse's occupation

For Official Use Only

1 2 3 4 5

6 7 8 9 10

For Privacy Act and Paperwork Reduction Act Notice, see page 18.   Cat. No. 11329W   1997 Form 1040EZ

Problem C-2   (concluded)

1997 Form 1040EZ page 2

Use this form if

- Your filing status is single or married filing jointly.
- You do not claim any dependents.
- You had **only** wages, salaries, tips, taxable scholarship or fellowship grants, unemployment compensation, or Alaska Permanent Fund dividends, and your taxable interest income was not over $400. **But** if you earned tips, including allocated tips, that are not included in box 5 and box 7 of your W-2, you may not be able to use Form 1040EZ. See page 8.
- You did not receive any advance earned income credit payments.

- You (and your spouse if married) were under 65 on January 1, 1998, and not blind at the end of 1997.
- Your taxable income (line 6) is less than $50,000.

If you are not sure about your filing status, see page 6. If you have questions about dependents, use TeleTax topic 354 (see page 18). If you **cannot use this form,** use TeleTax topic 352 (see page 18).

Filling in your return

For tips on how to avoid common mistakes, see page 3.

Because this form is read by a machine, please print your numbers inside the boxes like this:

$\boxed{9\ 8\ 7\ 6\ 5\ 4\ 3\ 2\ 1\ 0}$

Do not type your numbers. Do not use dollar signs.

If you received a scholarship or fellowship grant or tax-exempt interest income, such as on municipal bonds, see the booklet before filling in the form. Also, see the booklet if you received a Form 1099-INT showing Federal income tax withheld or if Federal income tax was withheld from your unemployment compensation or Alaska Permanent Fund dividends.

Remember, you must report all wages, salaries, and tips even if you do not get a W-2 form from your employer. You must also report all your taxable interest income, including interest from banks, savings and loans, credit unions, etc., even if you do not get a Form 1099-INT.

Worksheet for dependents who checked "Yes" on line 5

Use this worksheet to figure the amount to enter on line 5 if someone can claim you (or your spouse if married) as a dependent, even if that person chooses not to do so. To find out if someone can claim you as a dependent, use TeleTax topic 354 (see page 18).

A. Enter the amount from line 1 on the front.	**A.** _____
B. Minimum standard deduction.	**B.** _____ 650.00
C. Enter the LARGER of line A or line B here.	**C.** _____
D. Maximum standard deduction. If single, enter 4,150.00; if married, enter 6,900.00.	**D.** _____
E. Enter the SMALLER of line C or line D here. This is your standard deduction.	**E.** _____

F. Exemption amount.
  • If single, enter 0.
  • If married and—
    —both you and your spouse can be claimed as dependents, enter 0.
    —only one of you can be claimed as a dependent, enter 2,650.00.
	F. _____

G. Add lines E and F. Enter the total here and on line 5 on the front.	**G.** _____

If you checked "No" on line 5 because no one can claim you (or your spouse if married) as a dependent, enter on line 5 the amount shown below that applies to you.

- Single, enter 6,800.00. This is the total of your standard deduction (4,150.00) and your exemption (2,650.00).
- Married, enter 12,200.00. This is the total of your standard deduction (6,900.00), your exemption (2,650.00), and your spouse's exemption (2,650.00).

Mailing your return

Mail your return by **April 15, 1998.** Use the envelope that came with your booklet. If you do not have that envelope, see page 28 for the address to use.

Paid preparer's use only

See page 14.

Under penalties of perjury, I declare that I have examined this return, and to the best of my knowledge and belief, it is true, correct, and accurately lists all amounts and sources of income received during the tax year. This declaration is based on all information of which I have any knowledge.

Preparer's signature ▶		Date	Check if self-employed ☐	Preparer's SSN
Firm's name (or yours if self-employed) and address ▶			EIN	
			ZIP code	

APPENDIX  E   Additional Reinforcement Problems

Reinforcement Problem 3A   Determining the Effects of Business Transactions on the Accounting Equation

| Transaction | Assets | | | | | = | Liabilities | + | Owner's Equity |
	Cash in Bank	Accounts Receivable	Office Furniture	Computer Equipment	Office Equipment	=	Accounts Payable	+	Pamela Wong, Capital
1									
Balance						=		+	
2									
Balance						=		+	
3									
Balance						=		+	
4									
Balance						=		+	
5									
Balance						=		+	
6									
Balance						=		+	
7									
Balance						=		+	
8									
Balance						=		+	
9									
Balance						=		+	
10									
Balance						=		+	
11									
Balance						=		+	

Reinforcement Problem 3A   (continued)

Analyze: **a.** _____

           b. _____

           c. _____

           d. _____

Computerized Accounting Using Spreadsheets

Problem 3A   Determining the Effects of Business Transactions on the Accounting Equation

Completing the Spreadsheet

Step 1   Read the instructions for Additional Reinforcement Problem 3A in your textbook. This problem involves entering transactions in the accounting equation.

Step 2   Open the Glencoe Accounting: Electronic Learning Center software.

Step 3   From the Program Menu, click on the **Peachtree Accounting Software and Spreadsheet Applications** icon.

Step 4   Log onto the Management System by typing your user name and password.

Step 5   Under the Chapter Problems tab, select the template: PRO3Aa.xls. The template should look like the one shown below.

```
PROBLEM 3A
DETERMINING THE EFFECTS OF BUSINESS
TRANSACTIONS ON THE ACCOUNTING EQUATION

(name)
(date)
```

			ASSETS			LIABILITIES	OWNER'S EQUITY
Transaction	Cash in Bank	Accounts Receivable	Office Furniture	Computer Equipment	Office Equipment =	Accounts Payable +	Pamela Wong, Capital
1							
2							
3							
4							
5							
6							
7							
8							
9							
10							
11							
BALANCE	$0	$0	$0	$0	$0	$0	$0

```
TOTAL ASSETS                            $0

TOTAL LIABILITIES                       $0
TOTAL OWNER'S EQUITY                    $0
TOTAL LIABILITIES + OWNER'S EQUITY      $0
```

Step 6   Key your name and today's date in the cells containing the *(name)* and *(date)* placeholders.

Step 7   In the first transaction, Ms. Wong, the owner of the business, opened a checking account for the business. Remember from Chapter 2 that two parts of the accounting equation are affected by this transaction: Cash in Bank and Pamela Wong, Capital. Cash in Bank is increasing, and Pamela Wong, Capital, is increasing. To record this transaction in the spreadsheet template, move the cell pointer to cell B12 and enter **48000**.

Spreadsheet Guide

TIP: Remember, to enter data into the cell, you must first key the data and then press **Enter**. Do *not* enter a dollar sign or a comma when you enter the data.

Step 8 Next, move the cell pointer to cell J12. Enter **48000** in cell J12 to record the increase in Pamela Wong, Capital. Do *not* include a dollar sign or a comma as part of the cell entry—the spreadsheet template will automatically format the data when it is entered. Move the cell pointer to cell J24. Notice that the spreadsheet automatically calculates the balance in each account as you enter the data.

Step 9 To check your work, look at rows 27 through 31 in column D. Total assets equal $48,000. Total liabilities plus owner's equity also equal $48,000. The accounting equation is in balance.

Step 10 Analyze the remaining transactions in Problem 3A and enter the appropriate data into the spreadsheet template.

TIP: To decrease an account balance, precede the amount entered by a minus sign. For example, to decrease Cash in Bank by $1,500, enter **–1500** in the Cash in Bank column.

Check the totals at the bottom of the spreadsheet after each transaction has been entered. Remember, total assets should always equal total liabilities plus owner's equity.

Step 11 Save the spreadsheet using the **Save** option from the *File* menu. You should accept the default location for the save as this is handled by the management system.

Step 12 Print the completed spreadsheet.

TIP: If your spreadsheet is too wide to fit on an 8.5-inch wide piece of paper, you can change your print settings to print the worksheet *landscape*. Landscape means that the worksheet will be printed broadside on the page.

Step 13 Exit the spreadsheet program.

Step 14 In the Close Options box, select the location where you would like to save your work.

Step 15 Answer the Analyze question from your textbook.

What-If Analysis

TIP: Always save your work before performing What-If Analysis. It is not necessary to save your work after performing What-If Analysis unless your teacher instructs you to do so.

If Ms. Wong paid $550 cash for a new printer for the business, what would the Cash in Bank balance be?

Reinforcement Problem 4A   Analyzing Transactions Affecting Assets, Liabilities, and Owner's Equity

(1), (2), (3)

(4) Sum of debit balances: _____

(5) Sum of credit balances: _____

Analyze: _____

Reinforcement Problem 5A   Analyzing Transactions Affecting Revenue, Expenses, and Withdrawals

Chart of Accounts (partial)

Cash in Bank
Accounts Receivable—
   Adams, Bell, and Cox, Inc.
Office Equipment
Computer Equipment

Accounts Payable—
   Computer Warehouse, Inc.
Pamela Wong, Capital
Pamela Wong, Withdrawals

Design Revenue
Maintenance Expense
Rent Expense
Utilities Expense

Reinforcement Problem 5A (concluded)

(4)

Account Name	Debit Balances	Credit Balances

Analyze: _____

Reinforcement Problem 6A Recording General Journal Transactions

GENERAL JOURNAL   PAGE _____

	DATE	DESCRIPTION	POST. REF.	DEBIT	CREDIT	
1						1
2						2
3						3
4						4
5						5
6						6
7						7
8						8
9						9
10						10
11						11
12						12
13						13
14						14
15						15
16						16
17						17
18						18
19						19
20						20
21						21
22						22
23						23
24						24
25						25
26						26
27						27
28						28
29						29
30						30
31						31
32						32
33						33
34						34
35						35

Analyze: _____

Reinforcement Problem 7A Journalizing and Posting Transactions
(1), (3)

GENERAL LEDGER

ACCOUNT _____ ACCOUNT NO. _____

DATE	DESCRIPTION	POST. REF.	DEBIT	CREDIT	BALANCE DEBIT	BALANCE CREDIT

ACCOUNT _____ ACCOUNT NO. _____

DATE	DESCRIPTION	POST. REF.	DEBIT	CREDIT	BALANCE DEBIT	BALANCE CREDIT

ACCOUNT _____ ACCOUNT NO. _____

DATE	DESCRIPTION	POST. REF.	DEBIT	CREDIT	BALANCE DEBIT	BALANCE CREDIT

ACCOUNT _____ ACCOUNT NO. _____

DATE	DESCRIPTION	POST. REF.	DEBIT	CREDIT	BALANCE DEBIT	BALANCE CREDIT

ACCOUNT _____ ACCOUNT NO. _____

DATE	DESCRIPTION	POST. REF.	DEBIT	CREDIT	BALANCE DEBIT	BALANCE CREDIT

Reinforcement Problem 7A (continued)

ACCOUNT _____ ACCOUNT NO. _____

DATE	DESCRIPTION	POST. REF.	DEBIT	CREDIT	BALANCE	
					DEBIT	CREDIT

ACCOUNT _____ ACCOUNT NO. _____

DATE	DESCRIPTION	POST. REF.	DEBIT	CREDIT	BALANCE	
					DEBIT	CREDIT

ACCOUNT _____ ACCOUNT NO. _____

DATE	DESCRIPTION	POST. REF.	DEBIT	CREDIT	BALANCE	
					DEBIT	CREDIT

ACCOUNT _____ ACCOUNT NO. _____

DATE	DESCRIPTION	POST. REF.	DEBIT	CREDIT	BALANCE	
					DEBIT	CREDIT

ACCOUNT _____ ACCOUNT NO. _____

DATE	DESCRIPTION	POST. REF.	DEBIT	CREDIT	BALANCE	
					DEBIT	CREDIT

ACCOUNT _____ ACCOUNT NO. _____

DATE	DESCRIPTION	POST. REF.	DEBIT	CREDIT	BALANCE	
					DEBIT	CREDIT

Name _____ Date _____ Class _____

Reinforcement Problem 7A (continued)

(2)

GENERAL JOURNAL   PAGE _____

	DATE	DESCRIPTION	POST. REF.	DEBIT	CREDIT	
1						1
2						2
3						3
4						4
5						5
6						6
7						7
8						8
9						9
10						10
11						11
12						12
13						13
14						14
15						15
16						16
17						17
18						18
19						19
20						20
21						21
22						22
23						23
24						24
25						25
26						26
27						27
28						28
29						29
30						30
31						31
32						32
33						33
34						34
35						35

Reinforcement Problem 7A   (concluded)
(4)

Analyze: _____

Reinforcement Problem 8A   Preparing a Six-Column Work Sheet

ACCT. NO.	ACCOUNT NAME	TRIAL BALANCE DEBIT	TRIAL BALANCE CREDIT	INCOME STATEMENT DEBIT	INCOME STATEMENT CREDIT	BALANCE SHEET DEBIT	BALANCE SHEET CREDIT
1							
2							
3							
4							
5							
6							
7							
8							
9							
10							
11							
12							
13							
14							
15							
16							
17							
18							
19							
20							
21							
22							
23							
24							
25							
26							

Reinforcement Problem 8A (concluded)

Analyze: _____

_____

Reinforcement Problem 9A Interpreting Financial Information

_____

_____

_____

_____

_____

_____

_____

_____

_____

_____

_____

_____

_____

_____

Reinforcement Problem 10A   Preparing Closing Entries

Thunder Graphics Desktop Publishing
Work Sheet
For the Year Ended December 31, 20—

ACCT. NO.	ACCOUNT NAME	TRIAL BALANCE DEBIT	TRIAL BALANCE CREDIT	INCOME STATEMENT DEBIT	INCOME STATEMENT CREDIT	BALANCE SHEET DEBIT	BALANCE SHEET CREDIT
101	Cash in Liberty State Bank	340000				340000	
105	Accts. Rec.—Adams, Bell, and Cox	140000				140000	
110	Accts. Rec.—Roger McFall	40000				40000	
113	Accts. Rec.—Designers Boutique	120000				120000	
115	Accts. Rec.—Pat Cooper	60000				60000	
120	Office Equipment	300000				300000	
125	Office Furniture	930000				930000	
130	Computer Equipment	2100000				2100000	
201	Accts. Pay.—Solutions Software		210000				210000
205	Accts. Pay.—Pro Internet Service		120000				120000
207	Accts. Pay.—Computer Warehouse		1700000				1700000
301	Pamela Wong, Capital		1430000				1430000
305	Pamela Wong, Withdrawals	800000				800000	
310	Income Summary						
401	Design Revenue		2400000		2400000		
405	Print Production Revenue		1500000		1500000		
501	Rent Expense	1200000		1200000			
515	Maintenance Expense	320000		320000			
520	Advertising Expense	200000		200000			
525	Utilities Expense	480000		480000			
540	Office Supplies Expense	180000		180000			
545	Miscellaneous Expense	150000		150000			
		7360000	7360000	2530000	3900000	4830000	3460000
	Net Income			1370000			1370000
				3900000	3900000	4830000	4830000

Reinforcement Problem 10A   (concluded)

GENERAL JOURNAL

PAGE _____

	DATE	DESCRIPTION	POST. REF.	DEBIT	CREDIT	
1						1
2						2
3						3
4						4
5						5
6						6
7						7
8						8
9						9
10						10
11						11
12						12
13						13
14						14
15						15
16						16
17						17
18						18
19						19
20						20
21						21
22						22
23						23
24						24
25						25
26						26
27						27
28						28
29						29
30						30

Analyze: _____

_____

_____

Reinforcement Problem 11A   Recording Deposits in the Checkbook

(1)

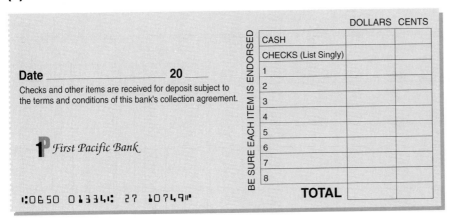

(2), (3)

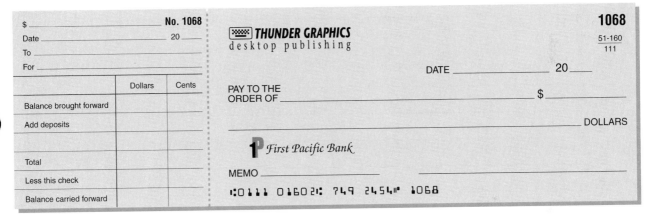

(4)

	Dollars	Cents
$ _____ **No. 1069**		
Date _____ 20 ___		
To _____		
For _____		
Balance brought forward		
Add deposits		
Total		
Less this check		
Balance carried forward		

Reinforcement Problem 11A (concluded)

(5)

GENERAL JOURNAL   PAGE _____ *21*

	DATE	DESCRIPTION	POST. REF.	DEBIT	CREDIT	
1						1
2						2
3						3
4						4
5						5
6						6
7						7
8						8
9						9
10						10

(6)

a. _____

b. _____

c. _____

d. _____

e. _____

Analyze: _____

_____

Reinforcement Problem 12A   Preparing a Payroll Register

PAYROLL REGISTER

PAY PERIOD ENDING _____ 20 _____   DATE OF PAYMENT _____

EMPLOYEE NUMBER	NAME	MAR. STATUS	ALLOW.	TOTAL HOURS	RATE	EARNINGS			DEDUCTIONS							NET PAY	CK. NO.
						REGULAR	OVERTIME	TOTAL	SOC. SEC. TAX	MED. TAX	FED. INC. TAX	STATE INC. TAX	HOSP. INS.	OTHER	TOTAL		
1																	
2																	
3																	
4																	
25	TOTALS																

Other Deductions: Write the appropriate code letter to the left of the amount: B—U.S. Savings Bonds; C—Credit Union; UD—Union Dues; UW—United Way.

Analyze:

Reinforcement Problem 13A　Recording Payroll Transactions

PAYROLL REGISTER

PAY PERIOD ENDING December 17　　20 -- 　　DATE OF PAYMENT December 17, 20--

EMPLOYEE NUMBER	NAME	MAR. STATUS	ALLOW.	TOTAL HOURS	RATE	EARNINGS			DEDUCTIONS							NET PAY	CK. NO.
						REGULAR	OVERTIME	TOTAL	SOC. SEC. TAX	MED. TAX	FED. INC. TAX	STATE INC. TAX	HOSP. INS.	OTHER	TOTAL		
173	Don Hoffman	M	1	22	6.95	152 90		152 90	9 48	2 22	24 00	2 29	7 85		45 84	107 06	
168	Manual Gongas	S	0	36	7.10	255 60		255 60	15 85	3 71	39 00	3 83	4 75	3 25	70 39	185 21	
167	Riley Sullivan	M	2	40	7.40	296 00		296 00	18 35	4 29	43 00	4 44	7 85	3 25	81 18	214 82	
175	Marcy Jackson	S	1	38	6.95	264 10		264 10	16 37	3 83	39 00	3 96	4 75	3 25	71 16	192 94	
TOTALS						968 60		968 60	60 05	14 05	145 00	14 52	25 20	9 75	268 57	700 03	

Other Deductions: Write the appropriate code letter to the left of the amount: B—U.S. Savings Bonds; C—Credit Union; UD—Union Dues; UW—United Way.

Reinforcement Problem 13A   (concluded)

GENERAL JOURNAL

PAGE _____

	DATE	DESCRIPTION	POST. REF.	DEBIT	CREDIT	
1						1
2						2
3						3
4						4
5						5
6						6
7						7
8						8
9						9
10						10
11						11
12						12
13						13
14						14
15						15
16						16
17						17
18						18
19						19
20						20
21						21
22						22
23						23
24						24
25						25
26						26
27						27
28						28
29						29
30						30

Analyze: _____

_____

Reinforcement Problem 14A   Recording and Posting Sales and Cash Receipt Transactions

(1), (4)

GENERAL LEDGER

ACCOUNT _____ ACCOUNT NO. _____

DATE	DESCRIPTION	POST. REF.	DEBIT	CREDIT	BALANCE	
					DEBIT	CREDIT

ACCOUNT _____ ACCOUNT NO. _____

DATE	DESCRIPTION	POST. REF.	DEBIT	CREDIT	BALANCE	
					DEBIT	CREDIT

ACCOUNT _____ ACCOUNT NO. _____

DATE	DESCRIPTION	POST. REF.	DEBIT	CREDIT	BALANCE	
					DEBIT	CREDIT

Reinforcement Problem 14A   (continued)

ACCOUNT _____   ACCOUNT NO. _____

DATE	DESCRIPTION	POST. REF.	DEBIT	CREDIT	BALANCE	
					DEBIT	CREDIT

ACCOUNT _____   ACCOUNT NO. _____

DATE	DESCRIPTION	POST. REF.	DEBIT	CREDIT	BALANCE	
					DEBIT	CREDIT

ACCOUNT _____   ACCOUNT NO. _____

DATE	DESCRIPTION	POST. REF.	DEBIT	CREDIT	BALANCE	
					DEBIT	CREDIT

Reinforcement Problem 14A   (continued)

(2)

ACCOUNTS RECEIVABLE SUBSIDIARY LEDGER

Name _____

Address _____

DATE		DESCRIPTION	POST. REF.	DEBIT	CREDIT	BALANCE

Name _____

Address _____

DATE		DESCRIPTION	POST. REF.	DEBIT	CREDIT	BALANCE

Name _____

Address _____

DATE		DESCRIPTION	POST. REF.	DEBIT	CREDIT	BALANCE

Name _____

Address _____

DATE		DESCRIPTION	POST. REF.	DEBIT	CREDIT	BALANCE

Analyze: _____

Reinforcement Problem 14A (concluded)

(3)

GENERAL JOURNAL

PAGE _____

	DATE	DESCRIPTION	POST. REF.	DEBIT	CREDIT	
1						1
2						2
3						3
4						4
5						5
6						6
7						7
8						8
9						9
10						10
11						11
12						12
13						13
14						14
15						15
16						16
17						17
18						18
19						19
20						20
21						21
22						22
23						23
24						24
25						25
26						26
27						27
28						28
29						29
30						30
31						31
32						32
33						33
34						34
35						35
36						36

Reinforcement Problem 15A   Recording Purchases and Cash Payment Transactions

General Ledger (partial)		Accounts Payable Subsidiary Ledger (partial)
Cash in Bank	Purchases	Carter Office Supply
Accounts Receivable	Purchases Discounts	Dancing Wind
Prepaid Insurance	Transportation In	Clothing Manufacturing
Supplies	Purchases Returns	Wilmington Shirt
Accounts Payable	and Allowances	Manufacturing
Sales Tax Payable		

GENERAL JOURNAL

PAGE _____

	DATE	DESCRIPTION	POST. REF.	DEBIT	CREDIT	
1						1
2						2
3						3
4						4
5						5
6						6
7						7
8						8
9						9
10						10
11						11
12						12
13						13
14						14
15						15
16						16
17						17
18						18
19						19
20						20
21						21
22						22
23						23
24						24
25						25
26						26
27						27
28						28

Reinforcement Problem 15A (concluded)

GENERAL JOURNAL

PAGE _____

	DATE	DESCRIPTION	POST. REF.	DEBIT	CREDIT	
1						1
2						2
3						3
4						4
5						5
6						6
7						7
8						8
9						9
10						10
11						11
12						12
13						13
14						14
15						15

Analyze: _____

_____

Reinforcement Problem 16A   Recording and Posting Sales, Cash Receipts, and General Journal Transactions

(1)

GENERAL LEDGER

ACCOUNT _____ ACCOUNT NO. _____

DATE	DESCRIPTION	POST. REF.	DEBIT	CREDIT	BALANCE DEBIT	BALANCE CREDIT

ACCOUNT _____ ACCOUNT NO. _____

DATE	DESCRIPTION	POST. REF.	DEBIT	CREDIT	BALANCE DEBIT	BALANCE CREDIT

ACCOUNT _____ ACCOUNT NO. _____

DATE	DESCRIPTION	POST. REF.	DEBIT	CREDIT	BALANCE DEBIT	BALANCE CREDIT

ACCOUNT _____ ACCOUNT NO. _____

DATE	DESCRIPTION	POST. REF.	DEBIT	CREDIT	BALANCE DEBIT	BALANCE CREDIT

Reinforcement Problem 16A   (continued)

ACCOUNT _____ ACCOUNT NO. _____

DATE	DESCRIPTION	POST. REF.	DEBIT	CREDIT	BALANCE	
					DEBIT	CREDIT

ACCOUNT _____ ACCOUNT NO. _____

DATE	DESCRIPTION	POST. REF.	DEBIT	CREDIT	BALANCE	
					DEBIT	CREDIT

ACCOUNT _____ ACCOUNT NO. _____

DATE	DESCRIPTION	POST. REF.	DEBIT	CREDIT	BALANCE	
					DEBIT	CREDIT

(9)

Reinforcement Problem 16A (continued)

(2)

ACCOUNTS RECEIVABLE SUBSIDIARY LEDGER

Name _____

Address _____

DATE	DESCRIPTION	POST. REF.	DEBIT	CREDIT	BALANCE

Name _____

Address _____

DATE	DESCRIPTION	POST. REF.	DEBIT	CREDIT	BALANCE

Name _____

Address _____

DATE	DESCRIPTION	POST. REF.	DEBIT	CREDIT	BALANCE

Name _____

Address _____

DATE	DESCRIPTION	POST. REF.	DEBIT	CREDIT	BALANCE

Reinforcement Problem 16A   (continued)

Name _____

Address _____

	DATE	DESCRIPTION	POST. REF.	DEBIT	CREDIT	BALANCE

Name _____

Address _____

	DATE	DESCRIPTION	POST. REF.	DEBIT	CREDIT	BALANCE

Name _____

Address _____

	DATE	DESCRIPTION	POST. REF.	DEBIT	CREDIT	BALANCE

Reinforcement Problem 16A   (continued)

SALES JOURNAL

PAGE _____

	DATE	SALES SLIP NO.	CUSTOMER'S ACCOUNT DEBITED	POST. REF.	SALES CREDIT	SALES TAX PAYABLE CREDIT	ACCOUNTS RECEIVABLE DEBIT	
1								1
2								2
3								3
4								4
5								5
6								6
7								7
8								8
9								9
10								10
11								11
12								12
13								13
14								14
15								15
16								16
17								17
18								18
19								19
20								20
21								21
22								22
23								23
24								24
25								25
26								26
27								27
28								28
29								29
30								30
31								31
32								32
33								33
34								34

Reinforcement Problem 16A (continued)

CASH RECEIPTS JOURNAL

PAGE _____

DATE	DOC. NO.	ACCOUNT NAME	POST. REF.	GENERAL CREDIT	SALES CREDIT	SALES TAX PAYABLE CREDIT	ACCOUNTS RECEIVABLE CREDIT	SALES DISCOUNTS DEBIT	CASH IN BANK DEBIT
1									
2									
3									
4									
5									
6									
7									
8									
9									
10									
11									
12									
13									
14									
15									
16									
17									
18									
19									
20									
21									
22									
23									
24									
25									

Reinforcement Problem 16A   (concluded)

GENERAL JOURNAL   PAGE _____

	DATE	DESCRIPTION	POST. REF.	DEBIT	CREDIT	
1						1
2						2
3						3
4						4
5						5
6						6
7						7
8						8
9						9
10						10
11						11
12						12
13						13
14						14
15						15
16						16
17						17
18						18
19						19
20						20
21						21
22						22
23						23
24						24
25						25
26						26
27						27
28						28
29						29
30						30
31						31
32						32
33						33

Analyze: _____

_____

_____

Reinforcement Problem 17A   Recording Special Journal and
General Journal Transactions

SALES JOURNAL

PAGE _____

	DATE	SALES SLIP NO.	CUSTOMER'S ACCOUNT DEBITED	POST. REF.	SALES CREDIT	SALES TAX PAYABLE CREDIT	ACCOUNTS RECEIVABLE DEBIT	
1								1
2								2
3								3
4								4
5								5
6								6
7								7
8								8
9								9
10								10
11								11
12								12
13								13
14								14
15								15
16								16
17								17
18								18
19								19
20								20
21								21
22								22
23								23
24								24
25								25
26								26
27								27
28								28
29								29
30								30
31								31
32								32
33								33
34								34

Reinforcement Problem 17A   (continued)

PAGE ____

CASH RECEIPTS JOURNAL

DATE	DOC. NO.	ACCOUNT NAME	POST. REF.	GENERAL CREDIT	SALES CREDIT	SALES TAX PAYABLE CREDIT	ACCOUNTS RECEIVABLE CREDIT	SALES DISCOUNTS DEBIT	CASH IN BANK DEBIT
1									
2									
3									
4									
5									
6									
7									
8									
9									
10									
11									
12									
13									
14									
15									
16									
17									
18									
19									
20									
21									
22									
23									
24									
25									

Reinforcement Problem 17A   (continued)

PURCHASES JOURNAL

PAGE _____

DATE	INVOICE NO.	CREDITOR'S ACCOUNT CREDITED	POST. REF.	ACCOUNTS PAYABLE CREDIT	PURCHASES DEBIT	GENERAL ACCOUNT DEBITED	POST. REF.	DEBIT
1								
2								
3								
4								
5								
6								
7								
8								
9								
10								
11								
12								
13								
14								
15								
16								
17								
18								
19								
20								
21								
22								
23								
24								
25								
26								

Reinforcement Problem 17A   (continued)

CASH PAYMENTS JOURNAL

PAGE _____

DATE	DOC. NO.	ACCOUNT NAME	POST. REF.	GENERAL DEBIT	GENERAL CREDIT	ACCOUNTS PAYABLE DEBIT	PURCHASES DISCOUNTS CREDIT	CASH IN BANK CREDIT
1								
2								
3								
4								
5								
6								
7								
8								
9								
10								
11								
12								
13								
14								
15								
16								
17								
18								
19								
20								
21								
22								
23								
24								
25								
26								

Reinforcement Problem 17A (continued)

GENERAL JOURNAL   PAGE _____

	DATE	DESCRIPTION	POST. REF.	DEBIT	CREDIT	
1						1
2						2
3						3
4						4
5						5
6						6
7						7
8						8
9						9
10						10
11						11
12						12
13						13
14						14
15						15
16						16
17						17
18						18
19						19
20						20
21						21
22						22
23						23
24						24
25						25
26						26
27						27
28						28
29						29
30						30
31						31
32						32
33						33
34						34
35						35

Reinforcement Problem 17A   (concluded)

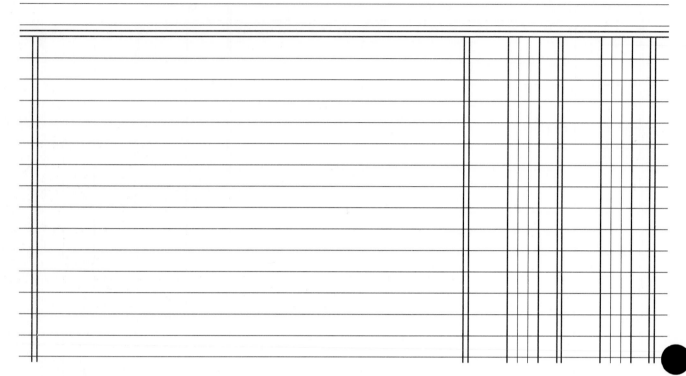

Analyze: _____

_____

Notes

Reinforcement Problem 18A — Calculating Adjustments and Preparing the Ten-Column Work Sheet

T-Shirt

Work

For the Year Ended

	ACCT. NO.	ACCOUNT NAME	TRIAL BALANCE		ADJUSTMENTS	
			DEBIT	CREDIT	DEBIT	CREDIT
1	101	Cash in Bank	14 729 00			
2	115	Accounts Receivable	5 702 00			
3	130	Merchandise Inventory	51 215 00			
4	135	Supplies	3 197 00			
5	140	Prepaid Insurance	1 800 00			
6	145	Office Equipment	7 837 00			
7	150	Store Equipment	18 504 00			
8	155	Delivery Equipment	11 754 00			
9	201	Accounts Payable		13 039 00		
10	204	Fed. Corporate Income Tax Pay.				
11	210	Employees' Fed. Inc. Tax Pay.		636 00		
12	211	Employees' State Inc. Tax Pay.		117 00		
13	212	Social Security Tax Payable		479 00		
14	213	Medicare Tax Payable		113 00		
15	215	Sales Tax Payable		3 931 00		
16	216	Fed. Unemployment Tax Pay.		79 00		
17	217	State Unemployment Tax Pay.		315 00		
18	301	Capital Stock		50 000 00		
19	305	Retained Earnings		25 425 00		
20	310	Income Summary				
21	401	Sales		133 123 00		
22	405	Sales Discounts	258 00			
23	410	Sales Returns and Allow.	1 342 00			
24	501	Purchases	72 510 00			
25	505	Transportation In	1 141 00			
26	510	Purchases Discounts		1 292 00		
27	515	Purchases Returns and Allow.		571 00		
28	601	Advertising Expense	4 205 00			
29		Carried Forward	194 194 00	229 120 00		
30						
31						
32						

Trends

Sheet

December 31, 20– –

	ADJUSTED TRIAL BALANCE		INCOME STATEMENT		BALANCE SHEET		
	DEBIT	CREDIT	DEBIT	CREDIT	DEBIT	CREDIT	
							1
							2
							3
							4
							5
							6
							7
							8
							9
							10
							11
							12
							13
							14
							15
							16
							17
							18
							19
							20
							21
							22
							23
							24
							25
							26
							27
							28
							29
							30
							31
							32

Reinforcement Problem 18A   (concluded)

T-Shirt

Work Sheet

For the Year Ended

	ACCT. NO.	ACCOUNT NAME	TRIAL BALANCE		ADJUSTMENTS	
			DEBIT	CREDIT	DEBIT	CREDIT
1		**Brought Forward**	194 194 00	229 120 00		
2						
3	605	**Bankcard Fees Expense**	6 19 00			
4	630	**Fed. Corporate Income Tax Exp.**	2 480 00			
5	640	**Insurance Expense**				
6	655	**Maintenance Expense**	1 322 00			
7	660	**Miscellaneous Expense**	3 772 00			
8	663	**Payroll Tax Expense**	1 251 00			
9	665	**Rent Expense**	10 900 00			
10	670	**Salaries Expense**	11 989 00			
11	675	**Supplies Expense**				
12	685	**Utilities Expense**	2 593 00			
13			229 120 00	229 120 00		
14						
15						
16						
17						
18						
19						
20						
21						
22						
23						
24						
25						
26						
27						
28						
29						
30						
31						
32						

Trends

(continued)

December 31, 20--

	ADJUSTED TRIAL BALANCE		INCOME STATEMENT		BALANCE SHEET		
	DEBIT	CREDIT	DEBIT	CREDIT	DEBIT	CREDIT	
							1
							2
							3
							4
							5
							6
							7
							8
							9
							10
							11
							12
							13
							14
							15
							16
							17
							18
							19
							20
							21
							22
							23
							24
							25
							26
							27
							28
							29
							30
							31
							32

Analyze:

Reinforcement Problem 19A   Preparing Financial Statements

T-Shirt

Work

For the Year Ended

	ACCT. NO.	ACCOUNT NAME	TRIAL BALANCE		ADJUSTMENTS	
			DEBIT	CREDIT	DEBIT	CREDIT
1	101	Cash in Bank	19731 00			
2	115	Accounts Receivable	6462 00			
3	130	Merchandise Inventory	25192 00		(a) 1228 00	
4	135	Supplies	4669 00			(b) 2938 00
5	140	Prepaid Insurance	2400 00			(c) 625 00
6	145	Office Equipment	14895 00			
7	150	Store Equipment	25223 00			
8	155	Delivery Truck	12750 00			
9	201	Accounts Payable		15824 00		
10	210	Fed. Corporate Income Tax Pay.				(d) 142 00
11	211	Employees' Fed. Inc. Tax Pay.		534 00		
12	212	Employees' State Inc. Tax Pay.		151 00		
13	213	Social Security Tax Payable		451 00		
14	214	Medicare Tax Payable		180 00		
15	215	Sales Tax Payable		2413 00		
16	216	Fed. Unemployment Tax Pay.		54 00		
17	217	State Unemployment Tax Pay.		282 00		
18	301	Capital Stock		50000 00		
19	305	Retained Earnings		10811 00		
20	310	Income Summary				(a) 1228 00
21	401	Sales		131551 00		
22	405	Sales Discounts	196 00			
23	410	Sales Returns and Allow.	1668 00			
24	501	Purchases	65819 00			
25	505	Transportation In	1321 00			
26	510	Purchases Discounts		789 00		
27	515	Purchases Returns and Allow.		967 00		
28	601	Advertising Expense	2117 00			
29		Carried Forward	182443 00	214007 00	1228 00	4933 00
30						
31						
32						

Trends _____

Sheet _____

December 31, 20--

ADJUSTED TRIAL BALANCE		INCOME STATEMENT		BALANCE SHEET		
DEBIT	CREDIT	DEBIT	CREDIT	DEBIT	CREDIT	
19731 00				19731 00		1
6462 00				6462 00		2
26420 00				26420 00		3
1731 00				1731 00		4
1775 00				1775 00		5
14895 00				14895 00		6
25223 00				25223 00		7
12750 00				12750 00		8
	15824 00				15824 00	9
	142 00				142 00	10
	534 00				534 00	11
	151 00				151 00	12
	451 00				451 00	13
	180 00				180 00	14
	2413 00				2413 00	15
	54 00				54 00	16
	282 00				282 00	17
	50000 00				50000 00	18
	10811 00				10811 00	19
	1228 00		1228 00			20
	131551 00		131551 00			21
196 00		196 00				22
1668 00		1668 00				23
65819 00		65819 00				24
1321 00		1321 00				25
	789 00		789 00			26
	967 00		967 00			27
2117 00		2117 00				28
180108 00	215377 00	71121 00	134535 00	108987 00	80842 00	29
						30
						31
						32

Reinforcement Problem 19A   (continued)

T-Shirt

Work Sheet

For the Year Ended

	ACCT. NO.	ACCOUNT NAME	TRIAL BALANCE				ADJUSTMENTS			
			DEBIT		CREDIT		DEBIT		CREDIT	
1		**Brought Forward**	18 244 00		21 400 700		1 228 00		4 933 00	
2										
3	605	**Bankcard Fees Expense**	328 00							
4	630	**Fed. Corporate Income Tax Exp.**	3 510 00				(d) 142 00			
5	640	**Insurance Expense**					(c) 625 00			
6	655	**Maintenance Expense**	1 350 00							
7	660	**Miscellaneous Expense**	931 00							
8	663	**Payroll Tax Expense**	834 00							
9	665	**Rent Expense**	12 700 00							
10	670	**Salaries Expense**	7 234 00							
11	675	**Supplies Expense**					(b) 2 938 00			
12	685	**Utilities Expense**	4 677 00							
13			21 400 700		21 400 700		4 933 00		4 933 00	
14		**Net Income**								
15										
16										
17										
18										
19										
20										
21										
22										
23										
24										
25										
26										
27										
28										
29										
30										
31										
32										

Trends
(continued)
December 31, 20--

	ADJUSTED TRIAL BALANCE		INCOME STATEMENT		BALANCE SHEET		
	DEBIT	CREDIT	DEBIT	CREDIT	DEBIT	CREDIT	
	18010800	21537700	7112100	13453500	10898700	8084200	1
							2
		32800	32800				3
		365200	365200				4
		62500	62500				5
		135000	135000				6
		93100	93100				7
		83400	83400				8
		1270000	1270000				9
		723400	723400				10
		293800	293800				11
		467700	467700				12
	21537700	21537700	10639000	13453500	10898700	8084200	13
			2814500			2814500	14
			13453500	13453500	10898700	10898700	15
							16
							17
							18
							19
							20
							21
							22
							23
							24
							25
							26
							27
							28
							29
							30
							31
							32

Reinforcement Problem 19A (continued)
(1)

Reinforcement Problem 19A   (continued)

(2)

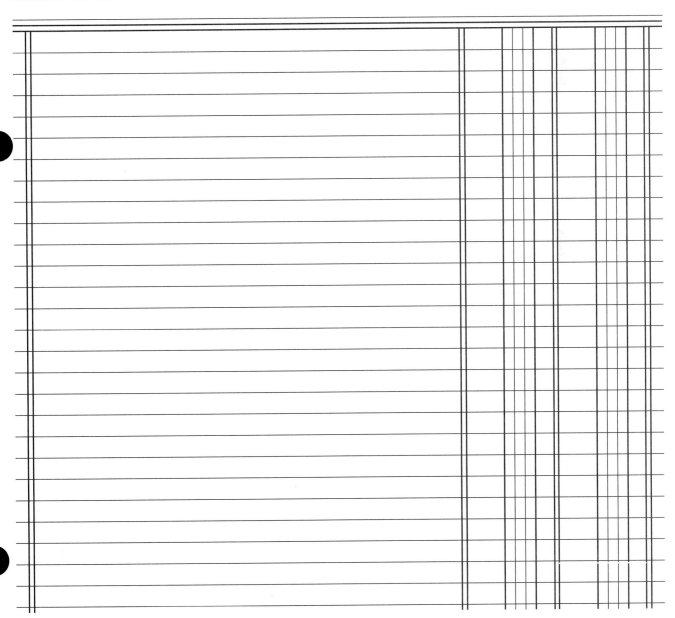

(3)

Reinforcement Problem 19A   (concluded)

Analyze: _____

_____

Reinforcement Problem 20A   Journalizing Closing Entries

Account Names and Balances as of December 31, 20 – – :

Sales	$94,412.00
Purchases Discounts	750.00
Purchases Returns and Allowances	455.00
Sales Discounts	867.00
Purchases	35,000.00
Transportation In	1,700.00
Advertising Expense	900.00
Bankcard Fees Expense	647.00
Federal Income Tax Expense	5,343.00
Insurance Expense	1,200.00
Miscellaneous Expense	369.00
Rent Expense	18,000.00
Supplies Expense	2,612.00
Utilities Expense	4,200.00
Sales Returns and Allowances	1,735.00

Reinforcement Problem 20A   (concluded)

GENERAL JOURNAL   PAGE _____

	DATE	DESCRIPTION	POST. REF.	DEBIT	CREDIT	
1						1
2						2
3						3
4						4
5						5
6						6
7						7
8						8
9						9
10						10
11						11
12						12
13						13
14						14
15						15
16						16
17						17
18						18
19						19
20						20
21						21
22						22
23						23
24						24
25						25
26						26
27						27
28						28
29						29
30						30
31						31
32						32
33						33

Analyze: _____

_____

Reinforcement Problem 21A   Recording Stockholders' Equity Transactions

GENERAL JOURNAL

PAGE _____

	DATE		DESCRIPTION	POST. REF.	DEBIT	CREDIT	
1							1
2							2
3							3
4							4
5							5
6							6
7							7
8							8
9							9
10							10
11							11
12							12
13							13
14							14
15							15
16							16
17							17
18							18
19							19
20							20
21							21
22							22
23							23
24							24
25							25
26							26
27							27
28							28
29							29
30							30
31							31
32							32
33							33
34							34
35							35
36							36
37							37

Reinforcement Problem 21A   (concluded)

GENERAL JOURNAL   PAGE _____

	DATE	DESCRIPTION	POST. REF.	DEBIT	CREDIT	
1						1
2						2
3						3
4						4
5						5
6						6
7						7
8						8
9						9
10						10
11						11
12						12
13						13
14						14
15						15

Analyze: _____

_____

_____

Reinforcement Problem 22A   Maintaining a Petty Cash Register

PAGE _____

PETTY CASH REGISTER

DATE	VOU. NO.	DESCRIPTION	PAYMENTS	DISTRIBUTION OF PAYMENTS				
				OFFICE SUPPLIES	DELIVERY EXPENSE	MISC. EXPENSE	GENERAL	
							ACCOUNT NAME	AMOUNT
1								1
2								2
3								3
4								4
5								5
6								6
7								7
8								8
9								9
10								10
11								11
12								12
13								13
14								14
15								15
16								16
17								17
18								18
19								19
20								20
21								21
22								22
23								23
24								24

Analyze:

Reinforcement Problem 23A Calculating and Recording Depreciation Expense

(1)

Date	Cost	Annual Depreciation	Accumulated Depreciation	Book Value

(2)

GENERAL JOURNAL   PAGE _____

	DATE	DESCRIPTION	POST. REF.	DEBIT	CREDIT	
1						1
2						2
3						3
4						4
5						5
6						6
7						7
8						8
9						9
10						10
11						11
12						12
13						13

Reinforcement Problem 23A   (concluded)

GENERAL LEDGER (PARTIAL)

ACCOUNT   *Delivery Truck*   ACCOUNT NO.   *150*

DATE		DESCRIPTION	POST. REF.	DEBIT	CREDIT	BALANCE	
						DEBIT	CREDIT
2004							
Oct.	12		G41	7890000		7890000	

ACCOUNT   *Accumulated Depreciation—Delivery Truck*   ACCOUNT NO.   *155*

DATE		DESCRIPTION	POST. REF.	DEBIT	CREDIT	BALANCE	
						DEBIT	CREDIT

(3) a. _____

_____

_____

b. _____

c. _____

d. _____

Analyze: _____

_____

_____

_____

Computerized Accounting Using Spreadsheets

Problem 23A   Calculating and Recording Depreciation Expense

Completing the Spreadsheet

Step 1   Read the instructions for Problem 23A in your textbook. This problem involves preparing a depreciation schedule.

Step 2   Open the Glencoe Accounting: Electronic Learning Center software.

Step 3   From the Program Menu, click on the **Peachtree Accounting Software and Spreadsheet Applications** icon.

Step 4   Log onto the Management System by typing your user name and password.

Step 5   Under the Chapter Problems tab, select the template: PR23Aa.xls. The template should look like the one shown below.

```
PROBLEM 23A
CALCULATING AND RECORDING
DEPRECIATION EXPENSE

(name)
(date)

                                        Annual        Accumulated        Book
      Date              Cost         Depreciation     Depreciation       Value
Oct. 12, 2000          AMOUNT                                           AMOUNT
Dec. 31, 2000                            $0              $0               $0
Dec. 31, 2001                            $0              $0               $0
Dec. 31, 2002                            $0              $0               $0
Dec. 31, 2003                            $0              $0             AMOUNT
```

Step 6   Key your name and today's date in the cells containing the *(name)* and *(date)* placeholders.

Step 7   Enter the cost, original book value, and salvage value of the delivery truck in the cells containing the AMOUNT placeholders. The annual depreciation, accumulated depreciation, and book value for each year will be automatically computed.

Step 8   Save the spreadsheet using the **Save** option from the *File* menu. You should accept the default location for the save as this is handled by the management system.

Step 9   Print the completed spreadsheet.

Step 10   Exit the spreadsheet program.

Step 11   In the Close Options box, select the location where you would like to save your work.

Step 12   Answer the Analyze question from your textbook for this problem.

TIP: If your spreadsheet is too wide to fit on an 8.5-inch wide piece of paper, you can change your print settings to print the work sheet *landscape*. Landscape means the work sheet will be printed broadside on the page.

Appendix E ■ **939**

TIP: Always save your work before performing What-If Analysis. It is not necessary to save your work after performing What-If Analysis unless your teacher instructs you to do so.

What-If Analysis

If the salvage value were $1,500, what would the annual depreciation for each year be?

_____

_____

Reinforcement Problem 24A   Calculating and Recording Uncollectible Accounts Expense

(1)

Estimate of uncollectible accounts: _____

(2)

GENERAL JOURNAL   PAGE _____

	DATE	DESCRIPTION	POST. REF.	DEBIT	CREDIT	
1						1
2						2
3						3
4						4
5						5
6						6

(3)

GENERAL LEDGER (PARTIAL)

ACCOUNT _____   ACCOUNT NO. _____

DATE	DESCRIPTION	POST. REF.	DEBIT	CREDIT	BALANCE DEBIT	BALANCE CREDIT

ACCOUNT _____   ACCOUNT NO. _____

DATE	DESCRIPTION	POST. REF.	DEBIT	CREDIT	BALANCE DEBIT	BALANCE CREDIT

(4)

Book value of accounts receivable: _____

Analyze: _____

_____

_____

Reinforcement Problem 25A   Accounting for Inventories

Cost of Ending Inventory:

Specific Identification _____

_____

_____

_____

_____

FIFO _____

_____

_____

_____

_____

LIFO _____

_____

_____

_____

_____

Weighted Average Cost _____

_____

_____

_____

_____

Analyze: _____

_____

_____

Reinforcement Problem 26A   Calculating Current and Future Interest

	Interest	
Maturity Date	**Current Year**	**Following Year**

1. _____

2. _____

3. _____

4. _____

5. _____

6. _____

7. _____

8. _____

9. _____

10. _____

Analyze: _____

_____

_____

_____

Reinforcement Problem 26B   Recording Noninterest-Bearing Notes Payable

GENERAL JOURNAL   PAGE _____

	DATE	DESCRIPTION	POST. REF.	DEBIT	CREDIT	
1						1
2						2
3						3
4						4
5						5
6						6
7						7
8						8
9						9
10						10
11						11
12						12
13						13
14						14
15						15
16						16
17						17
18						18
19						19
20						20
21						21
22						22
23						23
24						24
25						25
26						26

Analyze: _____

Computerized Accounting Using Spreadsheets

Problem 26A   Calculating Current and Future Interest

Completing the Spreadsheet

Step 1   Read the instructions for Problem 26A in your textbook. This problem involves determining the maturity date and interest expense to be paid in the current and following year for ten notes.

Step 2   Open the Glencoe Accounting: Electronic Learning Center software.

Step 3   From the Program Menu, click on the **Peachtree Accounting Software and Spreadsheet Applications** icon.

Step 4   Log onto the Management System by typing your user name and password.

Step 5   Under the Chapter Problems tab, select the template: PR26Aa.xls. The template should look like the one shown below.

```
PROBLEM 26A
CALCULATING CURRENT AND
FUTURE INTEREST

(name)
(date)
```

	Amount	Issue Date	Interest Rate	Term	Maturity Date	Interest Current Year	Interest Following Year
1		10-Dec		30 days	9-Jan	$0.00	$0.00
2		21-Nov		60 days	20-Jan	$0.00	$0.00
3		10-Oct		90 days	8-Jan	$0.00	$0.00
4		5-Dec		60 days	3-Feb	$0.00	$0.00
5		10-Nov		120 days	10-Mar	$0.00	$0.00
6		8-Sep		180 days	7-Mar	$0.00	$0.00
7		17-Nov		70 days	26-Jan	$0.00	$0.00
8		1-Oct		6 months	1-Apr	$0.00	$0.00
9		1-Dec		3 months	1-Mar	$0.00	$0.00
10		1-Aug		9 months	1-May	$0.00	$0.00

Step 6   Key your name and today's date in the cells containing the *(name)* and *(date)* placeholders.

Step 7   Enter the amount and interest rate for the first note in the appropriate cells of the spreadsheet template. The spreadsheet template will automatically calculate the interest for the current year and following year for the first note.

TIP: When entering the interest rates, it is not necessary to enter a percent sign after the number, nor is it necessary to enter the number as a decimal. For example, enter 9% as **9** in cell D11. The spreadsheet will automatically format this as a percent.

Step 8 Continue to enter the amount and interest rate for the remaining notes. The current year interest and following year interest will be automatically calculated for each note.

Step 9 Save the spreadsheet to a data disk or to the hard drive as instructed by your teacher. Use the filename *PR26-AXX* to save the spreadsheet (replace the *XX* with your initials).

Step 10 Print the completed spreadsheet.

Step 11 Exit the spreadsheet program.

Step 12 Answer the Analyze question from your textbook for this problem.

TIP: Always save your work before performing What-If Analysis. It is not necessary to save your work after performing What-If Analysis unless your teacher instructs you to do so.

What-If Analysis

Suppose the note amount for Note #10 were $3,333. What would the current year interest be? What would the following year interest be?

_____

_____

Reinforcement Problem 27A   Recording Partners' Investments

GENERAL JOURNAL   PAGE _____

	DATE		DESCRIPTION	POST. REF.	DEBIT	CREDIT	
1							1
2							2
3							3
4							4
5							5
6							6
7							7
8							8
9							9
10							10
11							11
12							12
13							13
14							14
15							15
16							16
17							17
18							18
19							19
20							20
21							21
22							22
23							23
24							24
25							25
26							26

Analyze: _____

_____

Reinforcement Problem 28A   Financial Statements for a Partnership

GENERAL JOURNAL

PAGE _____

	DATE	DESCRIPTION	POST. REF.	DEBIT	CREDIT	
1						1
2						2
3						3
4						4
5						5
6						6
7						7
8						8
9						9
10						10
11						11
12						12
13						13
14						14
15						15
16						16
17						17
18						18
19						19
20						20
21						21
22						22
23						23
24						24
25						25
26						26
27						27
28						28
29						29
30						30
31						31
32						32

Analyze: _____

_____

PEACHTREE APPENDIX

Computerized Accounting Using Peachtree
Setting Up a New Company

Software Objectives

When you have completed this appendix, you will be able to use Peachtree to:

1. Create a new company.
2. Enter or edit a chart of accounts.
3. Record customer and vendor data.
4. Enter beginning balances.
5. Set the accounting options.

OVERVIEW

Peachtree Accounting guides you step-by-step through the process of creating a new company. Follow the steps below to create a new company, enter a chart of accounts, prepare customer/vendor records, and enter account balances.

Before you start the Peachtree software, gather all of the information you will need to set up your new company. Depending on the type of business you plan to create, you will need some or all of the following:

- Chart of Accounts
- Customer List
- Vendor List
- General Ledger, Customer, and Vendor Account Balances
- Accounting Periods (number periods/year, first accounting period, and fiscal year range)

Note: You should be familiar with the *Peachtree Accounting* software before attempting to create a new company. For example, you should be able to create a chart of accounts and enter customer/vendor records.

GETTING STARTED

Step 1   Start the *Peachtree Accounting* software and choose **New Company** from the **File** menu. The New Company Setup window (as shown in Figure A1) will appear on your screen.

      If you were working with another company, the program will display a message telling you that creating a new company will close the current company. Press **OK** to continue.

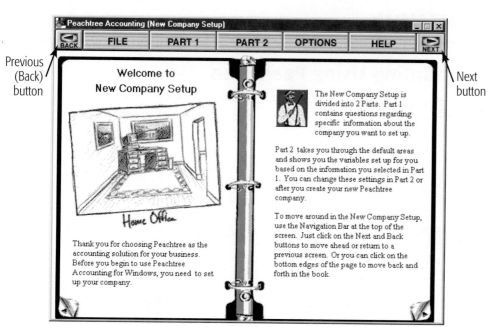

Previous (Back) button

Next button

Figure A1 *New Company Setup Window*

Step 2   Read the information provided on the welcome screen.

Step 3   Click the **Next** button in the upper, right corner to move to the next screen and then review the information presented.

SETTING UP A NEW COMPANY: PART ONE

Step 4   Click the **Next** button to enter the company information and tax ID numbers. (See Figure A2.)

Note: Don't worry if you can't complete the new company setup in one session. Once you enter the company name, you can quit the setup program at any time. The next time you choose to create a new company, the Peachtree setup program will allow you to continue where you left off.

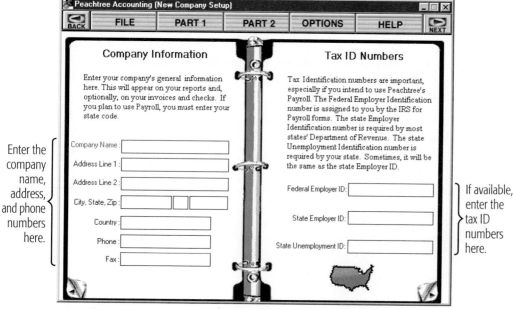

Enter the company name, address, and phone numbers here.

If available, enter the tax ID numbers here.

Figure A2 *Company Information/Tax ID Numbers Window*

Step 5 Enter the company name, street address, city, state, and ZIP code.

Unless you have the telephone number, fax number, and tax ID numbers, you can skip these fields. If you were setting up a real company, you would most likely have this information available.

Step 6 Review the information you entered. Click the **Next** button when you are ready to move to the next screen.

Step 7 As shown in Figure A3, identify the business type (corporation, S corporation, partnership, or sole proprietorship).

Note: The steps given in this appendix assume that you are setting up a corporation. Some of the steps may vary slightly from those shown here if you are creating a company of a different business type.

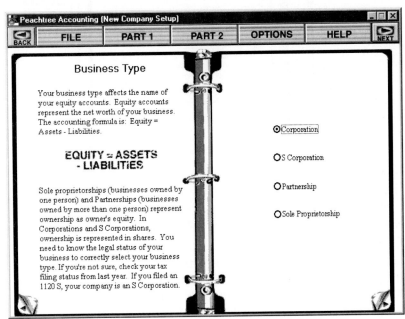

Figure A3 *Business Type Window*

Step 8 Click the **Next** button after you select the business type.

Step 9 Review the Chart of Accounts information and then click the **Next** button.

Step 10 Choose the *Build your own chart of accounts* option and click the **Next** button. (See Figure A4.)

You can choose from five different options to create a chart of accounts. If you were setting up a real business and did not have an existing chart of accounts, Peachtree provides many sample companies from which to choose a chart of accounts. Choose the first option, *Setup new company from the sample description list?*, if you are setting up a new company and you don't have a chart of accounts.

Sometimes it's easier to copy a chart of accounts from an existing company and then update the chart of accounts. For example, you could copy a chart of accounts from one of the companies in the *Glencoe Accounting* text. In these instances, choose the *Copy existing Peachtree company* option. The setup program lets you copy the chart of accounts from any of the companies already installed on your computer.

If you were using a different accounting program, such as Quicken, the setup program helps you convert those files to a Peachtree format. These options can be real time savers if you are switching from another program to Peachtree.

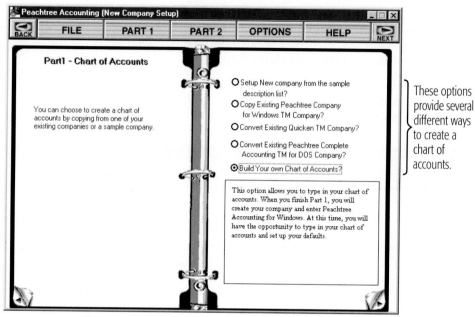

Figure A4 *Chart of Accounts Window*

Step 11 Review the cash and accrual information, and then click the **Next** button.

Peachtree lets you set up a business using either the cash or the accrual accounting method. All of the concepts presented in your text-book are based on the accrual accounting method. Therefore, the steps presented here assume that you will be using the accrual method for your new business.

Step 12 Set the accounting method to accrual, and then click the **Next** button.

Step 13 Read the information that explains the two different processing methods—batch and real-time. Choose the *Real-Time* option to have Peachtree automatically update your accounting records each time you enter a transaction. (See Figure A5.) Click **Next** to continue.

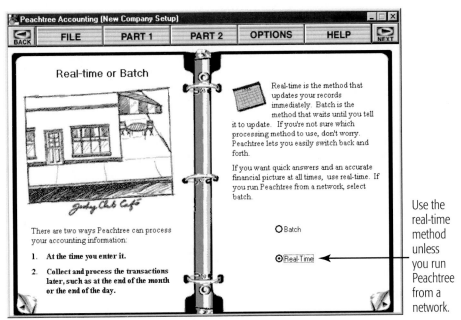

Figure A5 *Processing Method Window*

Step 14 Review the information that describes how Peachtree uses the accounting periods to process transactions and generate reports. Click **Next** to proceed to the window shown in Figure A6.

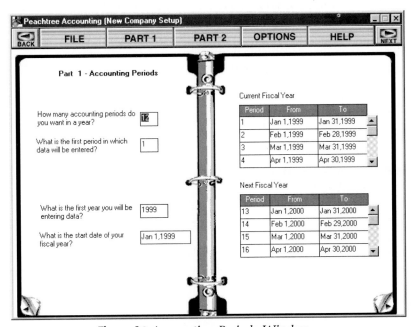

Figure A6 *Accounting Periods Window*

Step 15 Provide the information to set up the accounting periods, and then click the **Next** button to continue.

- Enter the number of accounting periods per year.

 For most businesses, you should enter **12** for the number of periods—one period for each month. However, you could enter 4 periods if the business you are creating operates on a quarterly basis.

- Specify the first period in which data will be entered.

   The value entered in this field should correspond to the period in which you will first enter data. If you specified 12 periods and you will be entering data in July, enter 7 for the first period.

- Enter the first year in which you will enter data.

- Enter the start of your fiscal year.

   Most businesses start the fiscal year in January, but the fiscal year can vary from business to business. Enter the date for the beginning of the fiscal year for your new company.

Step 16 You have just finished Part 1. Read the information provided and click **Next** twice to continue.

Step 17 When prompted, click the **Create** button to create your new company.

   The setup program will create the data files for your new company. Be patient as this process may take a few moments.

SETTING UP A NEW COMPANY: PART TWO

General Ledger

Step 18 Review the items on the setup checklist that Peachtree displays after it creates the company data files. (See Figure A7.)

   As you can see, there are quite a few items on the setup checklist. The items that you must complete depends on the company you are creating. For every new company, you **must** complete the first two items on the General Ledger checklist. If you plan on using subsidiary ledger accounts for customers and vendors, you must also complete the Accounts Payable and Accounts Receivable items. Unless you are beginning a new company from scratch, you will have to enter beginning balances too.

   Note: Refer to the Peachtree user's guide if you need to set up the payroll, inventory, or jobs modules. This information is not provided here.

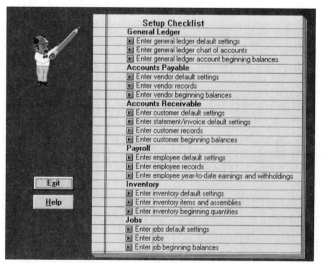

Figure A7 *Setup Checklist*

Step 19 Click the button next to the *Enter general ledger default settings* checklist item.

Step 20 Enter the rounding accounting and click the **OK** button. Use the general ledger account you plan to assign to the *Retained Earnings* account. (Use the *Capital* account if you are setting up a sole proprietorship.)

Note: Click the **Help** button if you want to learn more about a particular option such as the rounding account.

Step 21 Click **Yes** whenever Peachtree asks if you want to mark a task as completed. Click the **No** button only if you did not complete the task. Peachtree updates the checklist to show you which items you have completed.

Step 22 Choose the *Enter general ledger chart of accounts* option to begin entering the chart of accounts for your new company.

When you choose any of the checklist options, such as the option to enter a chart of accounts, the Peachtree program automatically chooses the appropriate option for you. For example, you could have selected the **Chart of Accounts** option from the *Maintain* menu.

Note: If you need to interrupt the second part of the setup process, click the **Exit** button shown in the Checklist Setup window. A message will show you how to display the checklist when you begin the next session.

Step 23 Enter the chart of accounts for your new company. (See the Maintain Chart of Accounts window in Figure A8.)

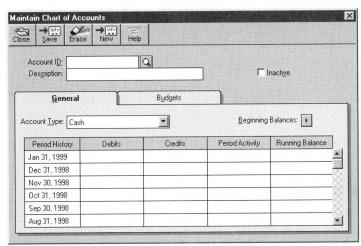

Figure A8 *Maintain Chart of Accounts Window*

Step 24 Click the **Close** button when you finish entering the chart of accounts.

Step 25 If your company is a new business, you do not have to enter beginning balances. Skip to Step 28 if you need to set up customer and vendor accounts. If you do not plan to have Accounts Receivable and Accounts Payable subsidiary ledger accounts, you are now finished with the setup process. Click the **Exit** button in the Setup Checklist window and go to Step 47.

Step 26   Choose the *Enter general ledger account beginning balances* option and follow these instructions to enter the beginning balances.

- Select the period to enter beginning balances.

    Choose the first period in which you will be entering transactions. For example, if you will be entering transactions starting in July, choose 7/1/XX to 7/31/XX. Make sure that you choose a period for the current year. You will probably have to scroll down past several other periods to get to the current year.

- Enter the beginning balances. (See Figure A9.) Click the **OK** button when you finish.

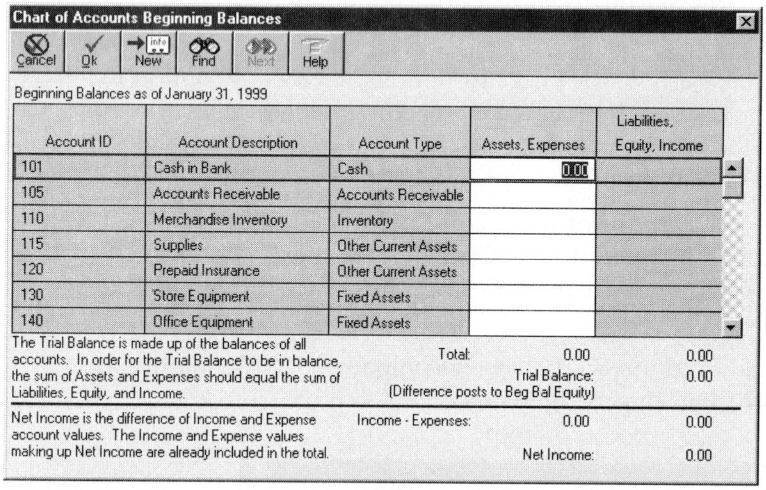

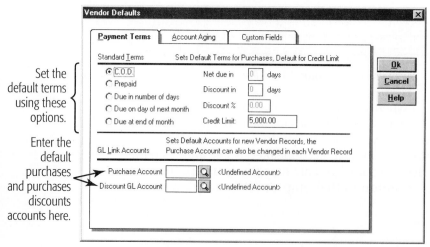

Figure A9 *Chart of Accounts Beginning Balances Window*

Step 27   Continue with Step 28 if you need to set up the Accounts Payable and Accounts Receivable modules. Otherwise, click the **Exit** button and then go to Step 48. You are now finished setting up the new company.

Accounts Payable

Step 28   Choose the *Enter vendor default settings* option. Review the information shown in the Vendor Defaults window shown in Figure A10.

Figure A10 *Vendor Defaults Window*

Peachtree Appendix *(side tab)*

Step 29   Enter the standard payment terms that are offered by most of the company's vendors.

        For example, choose *Due in number of days* if most vendors offer a discount. You will also need to enter the number of days (net and discount days), discount percent (e.g., 2%), and the credit limit. You can always change the terms offered by a particular vendor. The settings you enter here are the default settings.

Step 30   Enter the **Purchases** and **Purchases Discounts** general ledger account numbers. Peachtree needs these account numbers to integrate the Accounts Payable module with the General Ledger.

Step 31   You should not have to enter any account aging or custom fields. Click the **OK** button to accept the payment terms and choose to mark this item as completed.

Step 32   Choose the *Enter vendor records* checklist item. Peachtree displays the Maintain Vendors window.

Step 33   Enter the vendor records. Complete as many of the fields as possible on the *General* tab. (See Figure A11.) Then, click the *Purchases Defaults* tab. Enter the default purchases account and change the terms if this vendor offers terms different from the default terms you already set up.

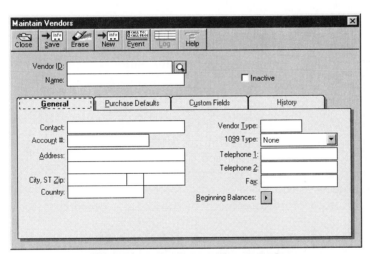

Figure A11 *Maintain Vendors Window*

Step 34   Click the **Close** button when you finish entering the vendor records. Indicate that you want to mark this item as completed.

Step 35   Choose the *Enter vendor beginning balances* option if you need to enter outstanding invoices. Otherwise, skip to Step 37.

Step 36 Select each vendor (shown in the Vendor Beginning Balance window) that has outstanding invoices. (See Figure A12.) Enter the beginning balance information. When you finish, close the window.

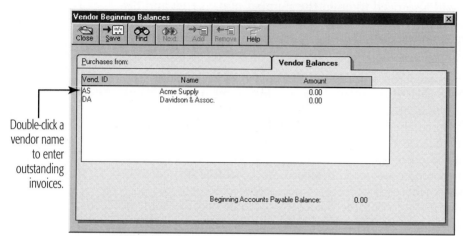

Double-click a vendor name to enter outstanding invoices.

Figure A12 *Vendor Beginning Balances Window*

Accounts Receivable

Step 37 Choose the *Enter customer default settings* option.

Step 38 Enter the default payment terms, **Sales** account, and **Sales Discounts** account. Then, click the **OK** button to record the information.

Note: If necessary, enter the account aging, custom fields, finance charges, and pay methods information.

Step 39 Select the *Enter statement/invoice default settings* option. Review the information in the Statement/Invoice Defaults window and then click **OK**. You should not have to change any of these settings.

Step 40 Choose the *Enter customer records* option. Peachtree displays the Maintain Customers/Prospects window.

Step 41 Enter the customer records. Complete as many of the fields as possible on the *General* tab. (See Figure A13.) Then, click the *Sales Defaults* tab. Verify the default sales account. Change the terms if the customer receives terms different from the default terms you already set up.

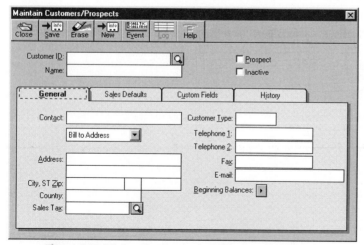

Figure A13 *Maintain Customers/Prospects Window*

Peachtree Appendix

Step 42 Click the **Close** button when you finish entering the customer records. Indicate that you want to mark this item as completed.

Step 43 Choose the *Enter customer beginning balances* option if you need to enter outstanding invoices. Otherwise, skip to Step 45.

Step 44 Select each customer (shown in the Customer Beginning Balance window) that has outstanding invoices. Enter the beginning balance information. When you finish, close the window.

Step 45 Click the **Exit** button on the Setup Checklist. You have completed all of the steps on the checklist. Just a few more steps to go.

Step 46 If you are setting up a service business, you have completed the entire setup process and you can begin entering transactions. Go to Step 48.

Step 47 If you are creating a merchandising business, you need to set up the sales tax settings.

- Click the ***Maintain*** menu, choose **Sales Taxes**, and then select **Sales Tax Authorities**.
- Enter a state sales tax authority and an exempt authority. You must enter an ID, description, tax rate, and sales tax payable GL account for both tax authorities. (See Figure A14 for an example tax authority.)
- Close the Maintain Sales Tax Authorities window when you finish.
- Click the ***Maintain*** menu, choose **Sales Taxes**, and then select **Sales Tax Codes**.
- Enter a sales tax code and an exempt code. You must enter a code and a description for each one. Then, complete the process by identifying the tax authority for each code. (See Figure A15 for an example sales tax code.)
- Close the Maintain Sales Tax Codes window when you finish.

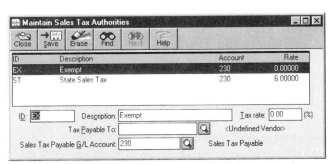

Figure A14 *Maintain Sales Tax Authorities Window*

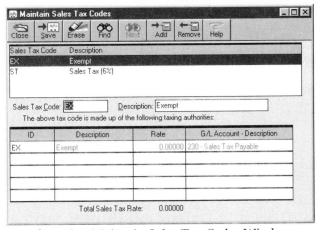

Figure A15 *Maintain Sales Tax Codes Window*

Step 48 Backup your work to a floppy disk before you process any transactions. Once you enter any transactions you cannot change the beginning balances.

Step 49 Congratulations! You can now begin working with and using the company data files you just set up.

Using a Ten-Key Numeric Keypad Appendix

Ten-key numeric keypads are found on electronic calculators and microcomputer keyboards. When you are keying quantities of numerical data, your ability to input numbers by touch will make your task easier and faster.

Key Locations

The ten-key numeric keypad is usually arranged into four rows of three keys. The locations of the 1 to 9 keys are the same on all equipment. The locations of the 0 (zero), decimal, and enter keys—as well as other function keys—vary depending on the equipment. The following illustrations show some typical arrangements.

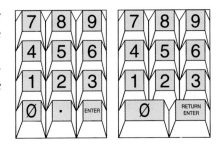

Home Position

On the ten-key numeric keypad, the 4-5-6 keys are called the **home keys.** These keys are the "starting point" from which you will operate the other number keys. The index finger of your right hand should rest on the 4 key, your middle finger on the 5 key, and your ring finger on the 6 key. Most keypads have a special "help" on the home keys so you can easily locate them: there may be a raised dot on the 5 key or the surfaces of the 4-5-6 keys may be concave (indented).

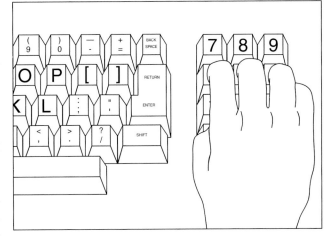

From the home keys, you reach up or down to tap other keys. The index finger is also used for the 7 and 1 keys. The middle finger is used for the 8 and 2 keys. The ring finger is used for the 9 and 3 keys.

The fingers used for the 0 (zero), decimal, and enter keys depend on the arrangement of the keypad. On some keypads, the thumb is used to tap the 0 (zero) key and the ring finger for the decimal key. The enter key on a microcomputer may be operated by the little finger or the thumb, depending on its location. On an electronic calculator, numbers are entered by using function keys: plus (+), minus (–), multiply (×), divide (÷), and so on. The fingers used to operate these keys depend on the keys' location on the keyboard. Locate these keys on your keypad and determine the correct fingers to use to operate them.

Entering Numbers by Touch

Throughout the remaining pages of this appendix, you will learn to locate and operate the ten-key numeric keypad by touch. That is, you will enter numbers on the keypad without looking at your fingers.

Your practice materials consist of columns of numbers. If you are using an electronic calculator, tap the plus (+) key after you have entered a number in a column. After entering all the numbers in a column, tap the equals (=) key. If you are using a microcomputer, tap the enter key after you have entered a number in a column. This will force a line break; each time you strike the enter key, the cursor will move to the next line. After entering all the numbers in a column, tap the enter key *twice* to leave extra space between the columns of numbers.

You will not be totaling these columns of numbers. You are learning now to enter numbers by touch, not how to add a column of figures. Also, if you are using a microcomputer, a special software program must be used if the numbers are to be added.

Using the 4-5-6 Keys

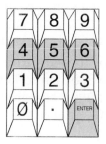

1. Locate the 4-5-6 keys (the home keys) on your keypad. Also locate the enter key if you're using a microcomputer or the plus key if you're using a calculator.
2. Place your index finger on the 4 key, your middle finger on the 5 key, and your ring finger on the 6 key.
3. To enter a number, tap the number keys, one at a time, in the same order as you read the digits from left to right. Always keep your fingers on the home keys.
4. When you have entered the last digit, tap the enter key (microcomputer) or the plus key (calculator).
5. Using the following problems, practice entering columns of numbers. Practice at a comfortable pace until you feel confident about each key's location.
6. After entering all of the numbers in a column, tap the enter key twice (microcomputer) or tap the equals key once (calculator).

1.	2.	3.	4.	5.	6.
444	555	666	456	554	664
555	666	454	654	445	445
666	444	545	465	564	566
456	654	446	556	664	645
564	546	646	656	565	465
646	465	546	465	655	654

7.	8.	9.	10.	11.	12.
456	564	646	555	666	444
654	546	465	666	454	545
446	646	546	456	654	465
556	656	465	554	445	564
664	565	655	664	466	566
645	465	654	444	555	666

13.	14.	15.	16.	17.	18.
654	666	464	666	456	555
546	546	656	654	454	545
456	546	656	654	454	545
465	646	546	555	446	454
444	654	654	556	445	456
555	564	546	554	444	654

19.	20.	21.	22.	23.	24.
5,655	4,556	456	55	445	6,656
45	645	4,564	4	56	4,655
6	54	655	54	6,664	566
456	46	4,545	5,554	465	465
664	564	5,664	564	5,644	64
56	5	65	445	56	544

Using the 1, 7 and 0 Keys

1. Locate the 1, 7 and 0 (zero) keys on your keypad.

2. Place your fingers on the home keys.

3. Practice the reach from the home keys to each new key. Reach down to the 1 key and up to the 7 key with your index finger. Be sure to return your finger to the home keys after tapping the 1 and 7 keys. Strike the 0 (zero) key with your thumb.

4. Using the following problems, practice entering columns of numbers containing the new keys. Practice at a comfortable pace until you feel confident about each key's location. Be sure to keep your fingers in home-key position.

1.	**2.**	**3.**	**4.**	**5.**	**6.**
444	014	140	107	011	141
471	107	701	074	170	117
174	740	701	104	710	417
741	101	704	007	004	047
710	114	471	411	471	104
407	441	117	047	174	114

7.	**8.**	**9.**	**10.**	**11.**	**12.**
741	710	407	014	147	740
101	114	441	140	701	701
704	471	117	107	074	104
007	411	017	011	170	710
004	471	174	141	117	417
047	104	114	444	471	174

13.	**14.**	**15.**	**16.**	**17.**	**18.**
170	140	104	111	777	410
701	147	107	147	111	140
107	014	401	174	444	014
741	041	701	741	714	741
147	074	101	710	741	471
410	047	010	410	704	147

19.	**20.**	**21.**	**22.**	**23.**	**24.**
1,044	456	145	17	101	1,404
540	4,540	6,147	7,100	47	40
7,055	74	567	1,105	1,075	140
607	415	10	574	157	1,714
4,441	510	106	177	7,775	1,570
17	1,750	1,045	50	147	1,104

Using the 3 and 9 Keys

1. Locate the 3 and 9 keys on your keypad.
2. Place your fingers on the home keys.
3. Practice the reach from the home keys to each new key. Reach down to the 3 key and up to the 9 key with your ring finger. Be sure to return your finger to the home keys after tapping the 3 and 9 keys.
4. Using the following problems, practice entering columns of numbers containing the new keys. Practice at a comfortable pace until you feel confident about each key's location. Be sure to keep your fingers in home-key position.

1.	**2.**	**3.**	**4.**	**5.**	**6.**
666	669	339	966	939	699
999	663	363	393	363	936
333	936	336	966	393	939
963	396	936	633	639	336
639	936	636	393	369	696
399	363	996	993	369	939

7.	**8.**	**9.**	**10.**	**11.**	**12.**
963	639	399	669	663	936
396	936	363	339	363	336
936	636	993	966	393	966
633	393	993	939	363	393
639	369	369	699	936	939
336	696	939	666	999	333

13.	**14.**	**15.**	**16.**	**17.**	**18.**
369	333	963	639	669	339
396	666	369	963	663	336
393	999	639	936	636	933
696	369	396	966	363	699
693	963	393	939	939	633
639	639	693	333	393	399

19.	**20.**	**21.**	**22.**	**23.**	**24.**
416	19	165	1,497	1,975	6,914
6,069	7,035	1,913	313	961	351
976	1,346	6	7,643	93	177
1,515	507	19	491	4,149	6,543
109	1,397	1,016	16	4,973	46
3,419	737	409	3,499	549	347

Using the 2 and 8 Keys

1. Locate the 2 and 8 keys on your keypad.
2. Place your fingers on the home keys.
3. Practice the reach from the home keys to each new key. Reach down to the 2 key and up to the 8 key with your middle finger. Be sure to return your finger to the home keys after tapping the 2 and 8 keys.
4. Using the following problems, practice entering columns of numbers containing the new keys. Practice at a comfortable pace until you feel confident about each key's location. Be sure to keep your fingers in home-key position.

1.	2.	3.	4.	5.	6.
555	228	885	285	582	828
888	852	285	258	558	825
222	522	825	525	582	852
582	252	588	858	825	258
822	528	258	582	525	885
522	855	852	825	582	282

7.	8.	9.	10.	11.	12.
582	822	522	228	852	522
252	528	855	885	285	825
588	258	258	285	825	525
858	582	825	582	558	582
825	525	582	828	528	852
852	885	282	555	888	222

13.	14.	15.	16.	17.	18.
888	585	222	828	522	228
222	522	555	825	852	822
852	555	888	852	285	825
258	582	258	258	852	828
582	258	852	885	825	258
528	282	528	282	558	522

19.	20.	21.	22.	23.	24.
498	8,650	3,907	670	4,323	83
2,889	61	778	7,494	3,362	4,428
5,268	201	9,165	9,726	565	733
102	1,750	319	50	975	10
2,500	850	90	586	64	4,953
20	796	9,594	13	1,456	684

Using the Decimal Key

1. Locate the decimal key on your keypad.
2. Place your fingers on the home keys.
3. Depending on the arrangement of keys on your numeric keypad, you may use your thumb, your middle finger, or your ring finger to tap the decimal key. Practice the reach from the home keys to the decimal key. Be sure to return your finger to the home keys after tapping the decimal key.
4. Using the following problems, practice entering columns of numbers containing the decimal key. Practice at a comfortable pace until you feel confident about the key's location. Be sure to keep your fingers in home-key position.

1.	2.	3.	4.	5.	6.
.777	.978	.998	8.78	7.88	8.79
.888	.987	.879	8.89	7.87	7.98
.999	.878	.787	8.87	8.97	9.89
.789	.987	.878	7.88	9.77	9.87
.897	.789	.797	9.87	7.97	7.89
.978	.797	.899	7.98	8.79	9.78

7.	8.	9.	10.	11.	12.
.456	.564	.654	6.54	6.45	4.66
.546	.645	.666	4.56	4.56	6.45
.546	.456	.654	5.46	6.45	4.65
.546	.555	.546	5.64	6.54	6.45
.655	.456	.465	4.46	5.64	5.56
.465	.656	.545	5.66	5.44	6.54

13.	14.	15.	16.	17.	18.
.111	.132	.231	2.21	3.31	2.23
.222	.213	.211	3.22	2.32	3.21
.333	.123	.223	3.12	1.33	1.22
.123	.213	.233	3.22	3.12	1.13
.321	.231	.321	2.12	1.23	3.12
.113	.111	.222	2.22	1.22	2.11

19.	20.	21.	22.	23.	24.
146.53	544.00	654.87	91.07	112.39	48.11
214.98	734.08	101.06	37.79	216.49	13.87
734.56	408.96	141.69	84.13	479.17	46.51
273.16	456.00	454.00	17.50	146.32	19.30
105.14	349.98	913.54	72.37	557.34	68.34
607.40	366.08	204.67	72.20	126.67	92.73

Practice entering the following columns of numbers by touch.

1.	2.	3.	4.	5.	6.
654	321	980	213	798	927
984	302	957	316	980	945
870	651	867	620	981	254
907	543	697	531	972	842
987	503	314	631	874	964
870	324	426	264	803	973

7.	8.	9.	10.	11.	12.
4,792	2,489	2,940	4,892	4,209	9,842
7,306	3,491	6,783	1,246	9,812	7,956
8,217	5,397	7,617	6,036	1,567	1,154
6,783	1,569	1,215	7,263	1,465	1,450
2,769	7,056	6,578	8,754	6,056	4,718
1,190	2,356	8,754	1,270	4,998	2,531

13.	14.	15.	16.	17.	18.
990	2,574	972	4,123	928	456
72	5	9,547	60	8,619	61
69	4,626	747	19	50	5,741
474	103	621	21	1	5,787
7,674	7	304	1,584	198	53
903	55	73	9,569	3	2,209

19.	20.	21.	22.	23.	24.
4.50	7.87	17.28	1.75	42.69	98.42
1.47	5.25	23.75	6.72	73.50	30.91
2.89	2.40	66.61	8.10	12.46	53.97
6.01	9.81	17.00	8.46	12.49	88.60
9.58	4.04	54.06	2.79	10.82	29.03
7.14	1.69	55.08	1.90	23.77	62.20

25.	26.	27.	28.	29.	30.
468.	48.2	.8	284.0	41.87	154.88
.489	2,537.	5,827.	100.	4,057.4	888.
214.2	852.	.024	8.45	89.45	.0082
7.12	3.978	18.73	56.0	2.25	200.08
6,394.4	257.0	85.00	23.00	20.0	632.48
.58	.2684	1.045	.89	36.248	64.1

31.	32.	33.	34.	35.	36.
6,880.62	97.41	43.75	6.60	41.15	68.02
3,507.05	600.92	42.67	.39	9.02	48.76
1,921.13	925.15	91.93	31.00	20.09	86.78
5,983.04	315.92	35.40	2.43	30.17	65.90
3,674.24	105.84	54.23	5.99	10.48	26.63
4,586.39	308.15	24.21	11.48	7.43	88.33

37.	38.	39.	40.	41.	42.
$ 267.14	$ 9.38	$ 162.50	$147.50	$ 38.95	$ 19.80
2,175.10	8,631.40	397.00	74.16	1,313.56	681.12
4,012.87	78.15	66.34	915.64	1,745.73	6,320.79
214.54	125.54	1,126.97	400.38	2,674.13	575.95
94.69	804.93	1,278.20	940.77	813.56	100.47
1,637.00	544.60	127.90	7.18	2.14	0.65

43.	44.	45.	46.	47.	48.
$ 9.95	$127.60	$ 5.45	$ 47.60	$ 92.60	$ 75.45
249.95	644.73	25.00	137.80	943.80	428.20
145.95	29.50	8.27	0.50	16.59	0.38
10.47	7.03	16.23	109.46	430.34	117.55
158.47	27.25	545.91	181.65	60.00	76.80
37.13	5.07	112.77	9.79	26.85	18.23

49.	50.	51.	52.	53.	54.
$ 655.20	$ 37.30	$ 250.30	$ 412.95	$ 740.65	$ 68.49
1,469.98	397.67	43.98	964.95	2,110.75	121.68
3,754.17	380.04	287.02	1,818.56	3,571.34	61.12
834.79	1,428.62	1,909.41	243.50	2,904.91	243.50
41.41	2,233.38	58.99	74.68	1,271.49	314.17
273.07	914.00	758.38	1,003.16	2,675.54	388.93

55.	56.	57.	58.	59.	60.
$ 61.93	$ 446.00	$ 20.67	$ 78.30	$ 519.02	$ 8.68
1,296.13	4,466.73	216.37	14.39	3,113.56	62.36
200.00	61.45	445.39	14.60	102.55	43.12
157.43	258.16	5,650.00	352.49	39.95	611.18
14.97	900.62	1,426.15	617.32	1,874.05	21.67
869.42	25.15	109.15	803.70	3,130.78	1,972.32

61.	62.	63.	64.	65.	66.
$ 267.50	$ 425.21	$ 1.25	$ 467.54	$ 65.27	$ 9.78
4.19	414.50	0.18	95.14	102.38	5.94
87.64	1,684.84	585.56	6,926.95	8,216.58	652.25
654.84	49.95	7.50	35.00	1,852.84	3,782.70
1,750.67	720.65	11.60	7.13	4.60	39.25
141.82	77.61	23.55	154.95	79.15	36.87